The Bottom Line Book of
Everyday
SOLUTIONS

How to Fix, Solve, Protect OR Prevent Practically ANYTHING

HOME • TRAVEL • FAMILY • MONEY

Bottom Line® Books publishes the advice of expert authorities in many fields. But the use of a book is not a substitute
for health, legal, accounting, or other professional services.
Consult a competent professional for answers to your
specific questions.

The Bottom Line Book of Everyday Solutions
How to Fix, Solve, Protect or Prevent Practically Anything

Includes index
ISBN 0-88723-254-X

Bottom Line® Books is a registered trademark of
Boardroom® Inc.
281 Tresser Blvd., Stamford, CT 06901

Concept and Creation:
Information Resources Management Associates, LLC, Weston, CT

Graphics coordination and Production:
Visual Connection, Fairfield, CT

Printed in the United States of America

The Bottom Line Book of Everyday SOLUTIONS

How to Fix, Solve, Protect OR Prevent Practically ANYTHING

INFORMATION RESOURCES MANAGEMENT ASSOCIATES:

Editor-in-Chief	Graeme G. Keeping	Design	Christina R. Williams
Managing Editor	Kimberly M. Restivo	Design Consultant	Peter B. Kinseley Mary Treschitta
Senior Staff Editors	Atessa Helm Brad Ketchum, Jr. II Richard M. Marshall	Art Direction & Layout Art Associate	Esmee J. Snyder Terry Laug
Senior Editors	Kristin Freeley Vera Gibbons Lillian F. Ketchum Julie Moline Heather Rogalski Neil Shister Judith Jorden Whyte	Illustrators Charts & Tables	David Brown Daniel P. Guidera Charles W. Mackey Maureen Kehoe Sharon O'Brien
Associate Editors	Tracey Ann Dean Darius Helm Esther Miller Deborah Tall	Advisory Experts Legal Accounting Law Enforcement Security	 Kate Clarke Shister, PhD David Michael, CPA Chief Anthony P. Land Brian Weidman, Investigator
Chief of Research	Edwige Landwerlin		Officer Patrick Daubert

About This Book

In these pages we present expert solutions for day-to-day problems in a clear, easy-to-follow format. This is a think and do book…where you'll find tips and secrets, shortcuts and smart solutions to hundreds of common dilemmas: what to do when you lose a button and there's no needle and thread (p. 84); how to hang a picture straight—the first time (p. 84); what to do about leftovers (p. 82), an aching back (p. 160), lost airline tickets (p. 241), and how to lose two pounds a week (p. 213).

We want to help you live better, healthier, safer, and wealthier. So we provide tips on money management, credit restoration, safe flying, and safe tax loopholes.

You'll learn how not to get ripped off by a plumber (p. 42), the IRS (p. 327), a broker (p. 336), a banker (p. 272), or a car dealer (p. 290). You'll be reminded to look over your home, your life, your family and ascertain the warning signs of things that might go wrong. And you'll find how to solve real problems, survive real crises, be smart (p. 216), and perform in an emergency (p. 21).

We hope you'll turn to **The Bottom Line Book of Everyday Solutions** for time-saving, money-saving, and face-saving scenarios that will get you through the day, the night, and the rest of your life. Every effort is made to keep our information fresh and up-to-date, but note that some information, especially Web addresses, change frequently.

THE EDITORS

Shortcuts, Tips & Traps

Throughout this book you will see icons perched on top of "information boxes." Each icon designates a ready reference to helpful information that you can put to use immediately or tuck away in your memory for when the time is right.

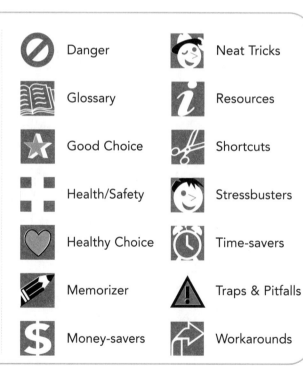

Danger

Glossary

Good Choice

Health/Safety

Healthy Choice

Memorizer

Money-savers

Neat Tricks

Resources

Shortcuts

Stressbusters

Time-savers

Traps & Pitfalls

Workarounds

House & Home

Personal & Family

contents

Travel Tips & Skills

223

The Business of Living

271

PART 1

Safe Home

**Security &
Maintenance**

**Basic
Housekeeping**

House & Home

Safe Home

Safe Home, Secure Home

Safety at home. Most of us take it for granted, but ensuring a safe home means reducing the risks of burglary, fire, killer gases, such as carbon monoxide and radon, polluted drinking water, plus scores of other lurking threats to home and hearth.

BETTER HOME SAFETY

What is your home's safety rating?

Compare each area of your home against the checklists to the right and on the following page. If the major items are covered, check off the appropriate box. If you cannot check off more than half the boxes, your family is living dangerously! You can learn what steps to take on the following pages.

SMART HOME SAFETY AUDIT

Attic
- ❑ Smoke detector near chimney
- ❑ Chimney cleaned within past year
- ❑ Combustible materials stored away from wiring and heating
- ❑ No frayed or damaged wiring
- ❑ Safe access ladder or steps

Basement
- ❑ Smoke and carbon monoxide detectors near furnace
- ❑ Fire extinguisher, charged
- ❑ Combustible and corrosive materials stored away from heat sources

Bathrooms
- ❑ Slip-resistant flooring and carpeting fixed with anti-slip tape
- ❑ Shatterproof shower doors
- ❑ Secure towel racks and grab-handles able to withstand a fall
- ❑ Anti-slip bathtub and shower protection
- ❑ Shower and tub faucets with scald-protection devices
- ❑ Safety latches on cabinets to prevent children from getting to medications and cleansers
- ❑ Electrical outlets with "ground-fault" circuit interrupters
- ❑ Light switches located well away from water sources

Bedrooms
- ❑ Smoke and carbon monoxide detectors in each bedroom
- ❑ Fire extinguisher, charged
- ❑ Low-voltage nightlights in children's bedrooms
- ❑ Fire escape ladders and smoke masks

Master Bedroom
- ❑ Telephone
- ❑ List of emergency numbers
- ❑ Central controls for alarm system
- ❑ Central controls for home and outdoor lighting
- ❑ Flashlight
- ❑ If you have toddlers, intercom or baby monitor

Garage
- ❑ Smoke detector, fresh battery
- ❑ Fire extinguisher, charged
- ❑ Carbon monoxide detector
- ❑ Double security locks and dead-bolts on access doors
- ❑ Fire-retardant door between garage and house

Kitchen
- ❑ Smoke detector, fresh battery
- ❑ Fire extinguisher designed for grease fires, charged
- ❑ Shutoff valves for gas appliances and water—clearly tagged
- ❑ "Ground-fault" circuit interrupter on kitchen outlets

If you have an automatic door opener on your garage door, regularly test the reversing mechanism that sends the door up if it were to close on an object, animal or small child. A roll of paper towels works perfectly. Open the garage door, then close it on the roll of paper towels. The door should reverse immediately when the bottom hits the roll.

- ❑ Minimum of appliances plugged into a single outlet
- ❑ Appliances away from sink
- ❑ Safe storage for sharp knives
- ❑ Safety latches on cabinets containing cleaning chemicals
- ❑ Range hood regularly checked for grease buildup
- ❑ Telephone cords far from stove
- ❑ List of emergency telephone numbers near the phone and evident to baby-sitters
- ❑ Scatter rugs and carpets secured with skid-resistant tape

Laundry Room
- ❑ Smoke detector, fresh battery
- ❑ Fire extinguisher, charged
- ❑ Carbon monoxide detector (if dryer is gas fired)
- ❑ Log page to track last time dryer vent was cleaned

Living Areas
- ❑ Smoke detectors in hallways and stairwells, fresh batteries
- ❑ Fire extinguisher in one centralized closet on each floor, charged
- ❑ Limit of one or two lamps or appliances per electrical outlet
- ❑ TV, audio and computer equipment protected by surge protector
- ❑ If you have children, no furniture near windows
- ❑ If you live in an apartment, grates or bars on windows to prevent mishaps
- ❑ Scatter rugs and carpeting secured by skid-resistant tape
- ❑ No electrical wires running under carpet

IS YOUR HOME SAFE FROM INTRUDERS?

Doors & Windows

- Dead bolts that operate with keys on all external doors
- Doors always locked, even when you are home
- Main entry doors equipped with "peephole" viewers
- Windows kept closed and locked, with keyed locks
- Window locks with multiple positions so that even slightly open windows can be secured
- Keys handy for inside locks and dead bolts in case of fire
- Patio doors and sliders equipped with safety locking bars
- Large glass sliders marked or curtained to stop people from walking into them

Lighting

- Home brightened with outdoor lighting system connected to two or three central switches in house, including central switch in master bedroom
- Outdoor lights that switch on automatically
- Indoor lights connected to timers that will switch on lights automatically

Alarms

If you do not have an alarm system, consider one now. Prices for simple do-it-yourself installations start as low as $60. More complex systems can protect your home from intruders and fire with remote monitoring for a monthly fee. Alarm-equipped homes should be checked regularly to determine if all functions are working properly. (See page 39.)

"MUST HAVE" EMERGENCY NUMBERS

Every household needs a list of emergency numbers posted in two locations: one by the central phone (usually in the kitchen) and one by the phone in the master bedroom. Here is the information you need on your list:

1. **Emergency numbers for fire, police and ambulance** — Is 911 the emergency number for your community? If so, you do not need to post separate numbers for fire, police and ambulance.
2. **Your family name, address and phone number** — Does your community have "enhanced 911"? Enhanced 911 allows the 911 dispatcher to immediately see the phone number and address of the caller's location on a computer screen. If your town does NOT have enhanced 911, put your address and telephone number on the list. Anybody's mind can go blank in an emergency—even yours!
3. **Phone number for your local poison control center**
4. **Phone number for gas company**
5. **Phone number for electric company**
6. **Names and numbers of two friends or relatives**
7. **Names and numbers of two neighbors**

Make sure you check the information every few months to keep your list up-to-date. Teach children how to use 911 or how to get help in an emergency before a *real* emergency strikes!

SMART & SAFE UTILITY MANAGEMENT

Electric

- All electrical cords neatly harnessed
- As few appliances or lamps per outlet as possible
- No multiple extension cords
- No appliance cords running under carpets or sofas (may overheat and cause fire)
- Protective childproof covers on unused outlets
- If circuit breakers "pop" frequently, there are too many appliances on circuit

Gas

- All primary gas shutoff valves tagged
- Gas appliances cleaned and checked yearly

Oil

- Oil-fired heaters cleaned at least once a year
- Tanks and supply lines checked for leakage
- Oil spills around heating unit absorbed with sand or kitty litter

Water

- Tested for lead content and other contaminants
- Water-heater temperature no higher than 120° to prevent scalding
- Anti-scalding faucets installed where children bathe
- No standing water on the property where toddlers can get into it or mosquito larvae can mature.

CORDLESS PHONE ALERT

Cordless telephones are convenient, but not if you have a power outage because they require electricity to operate. Make sure you have at least one conventional phone; in certain emergencies it may be the only one that works.

Cell phones can be excellent safety investments for your home and your car. Plus monthly service fees are dropping.

SAFETY CHECKLIST FOR YOUR BABY-SITTER

You wouldn't leave your children in an unsafe environment. Yet that's what happens when they're in the care of a baby-sitter who is not prepared for an emergency. Here's what to do when you can't be there:

➤ **Post emergency numbers** (see Emergency Phone Number List, on previous page). Leave the number where you can be reached, but assume that you won't be able to get home in time to do anything. A call to you should be the *last* emergency call, not the first.

➤ **Warn baby-sitters** to check around the home for dangers—matches, sharp objects, cleaning chemicals, electrical dangers, heaters. Children will often go for the forbidden things the minute their parents aren't there to stop them.

➤ **Arrange meals** that your baby-sitter does not have to cook. If she absolutely needs to use the stove, tell her to use only the back burners and to turn all pot handles toward the inside.

➤ **If you have a microwave,** make sure your sitter knows how to use it safely and that the children are kept away from it. Remind the sitter that metals, such as aluminum foil and flatware, cannot go in the microwave and that food must not be covered while it is cooking. Paper, glass and ceramics are safe.

➤ **When children go to bed,** the sitter must check to be sure there are no small "choking" objects near the bed and close the door on the way out. If there is a fire, this will help keep smoke from spreading.

➤ **Fire extinguisher locations** should be known to the baby-sitters. They should also know how to use them. Familiarize the sitter with the **family fire-escape plan**—especially if older children know how to evacuate.

➤ **If there is smoke, fire or gas odor**, the baby-sitter must get everyone out of the house. Tell her to take the children to a neighbor's house, call 911 or the fire department, then call you.

Remind baby-sitters to lock all doors and windows and to be security conscious if strangers come to the door. Also, they should not provide any information to anyone they do not recognize on the telephone.

Finally, if you have a regular sitter, consider paying for him or her to take a Red Cross course in first aid and CPR. Many communities also offer certification classes for baby-sitters age 12 and up. Contact your local Red Cross chapter for details. These classes are inexpensive and worth every penny.

FIRE SAFETY

A fire can happen in the best of homes, old or new. *The National Safety Council* reports that more than 500,000 residential fires occur annually in the United States. Most fatal home fires occur between 10 p.m. and 6 a.m. Smoke inhalation is the major killer, not flames.

Do not make the mistake of thinking a fire can't happen in your home. Plan for a fire. Know what you and your family will do. Ensure personal and family safety with a few simple, inexpensive defense measures, such as smoke detectors and fire extinguishers. Most importantly, practice an escape plan.

Prevention Is Your Best Protection

The absolute first line of defense for a fire is to prevent one from happening.

Perform a fire audit. Check your home for obvious fire hazards— frayed electrical wires or too many extension cords on a single plug. Are flammable materials— gasoline, gas grill propane and kerosene—all stored in safe areas, such as basements, garages or in outside sheds, away from heat?

In most communities, the fire department will perform a fire safety inspection if requested. At the very least, they will furnish free literature on fire safety and show family members how to use fire extinguishers and how to plan an escape route.

Stoves & Chimneys

Chimneys are leading fire starters, particularly when they are used to exhaust wood stoves, fireplaces, coal stoves or kerosene heaters. Creosote and other flammable waste builds up in chimneys, especially near the top and at curved joints. This residue can burst into flames when sparked by a hot fire.

Heat generated by a chimney fire is sufficient to ignite the house structure, frequently in the attic or at the roof line. Eliminate this danger by cleaning chimneys at least once a year, especially if a wood stove or fireplace is used frequently. If you have not had a chimney cleaned during the prior heating season, avoid prolonged wood-burning and highly volatile fires. Never use a fireplace to burn trash.

Cooking & Heating

Oil and gas heating systems are safe and dependable, but require periodic checking—at the very least, once a year. Gas lines and appliances should be checked by a plumber or gas technician for possible leaks. If you live in an earthquake region, gas lines should be checked for leaks immediately following any major tremor.

Oil-fired furnaces and water heaters should be checked and

cleaned annually. Burner and fuel injectors require maintenance to keep them operating safely and efficiently. Be sure your burner is checked at least once a year, ideally before the beginning of the heating season.

Safety & Savings

Oil and gas service companies offer heating system contracts that include regular maintenance schedules. Most contracts also include insurance and warranties on major heating unit parts.

Most importantly, with a contract, you save significantly on the cost of service calls, and you are assured that a service person will show up in an emergency.

SAVE YOUR FAMILY WITH SMOKE DETECTORS

The best fire-warning strategy is to place smoke detectors in hallways immediately outside sleeping areas. A detector in each bedroom is the safest strategy.

Detectors should also be installed in kitchens and basements. When fire breaks out, on average you have less than four minutes to react and leave the dwelling safely.

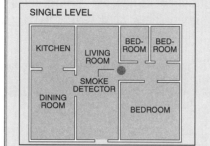

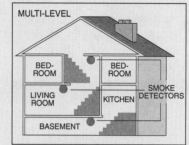

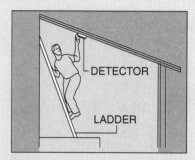

Single-floor homes: At least one detector in a hallway outside of bedrooms. A kitchen smoke detector is recommended.

Multiple-floor dwellings: At least one detector on each floor outside bedrooms. Basement detector at the top of the stairwell.

Sloped ceilings: At the highest point of the ceiling. Choose long-life lithium batteries or consider wired installations.

BE SURE SMOKE DETECTORS WORK

Make smoke-detector testing part of your household cleaning routine. Test batteries by pressing the "push-to-test" button. Some models can be tested by rapidly moving a flashlight across the test button. Vacuum the detectors' sensors, and test responsiveness by holding an extinguished, smoldering candle or match beneath them. You should hear the alarm signal within 20 seconds. The signal should cease when the smoke clears. Manufacturers recommend weekly testing.

BE SAVVY ABOUT SMOKE DETECTORS

Smoke detectors save lives, save property and provide peace of mind. Studies show that because of smoke-detector awareness, home fire deaths have declined by 4% a year. In a majority of communities, it's a violation of zoning laws not to have them. But according to the *Federal Emergency Management Agency* (FEMA), smoke detectors may fail to warn fire victims in as many as one-third of all fires!

Why Smoke Detectors Fail

Smoke detector failure is most frequently due to dead or depleted batteries. Fire authorities estimate that as many as one in three home smoke detectors has improperly installed batteries or dead batteries, or the batteries have been removed. Some smoke detectors now come with six-year lithium batteries.

Even the best-quality smoke detectors wear out. Fire authorities recommend that smoke detectors be replaced every 10 years. This will also enable you to keep up with the latest available technology.

Watch out for improperly placed detectors, which won't warn people in time for them to escape. The detector will not go off if it is located where smoke can't reach it. Fires in chimneys, between walls or on the roof may not trigger a detector. Also, smoke from a basement or first-floor fire may not trigger a detector on the second floor in enough time for everyone to get out safely.

What You Must Know About Smoke Detectors

There are two kinds of smoke detectors—each one specialized to detect different kinds of fire. *Ionization detectors* are best for intensely hot, blazing fires that don't produce a lot of smoke. *Example*: a pan of burning fat or cooking oil. *Photoelectric detectors* are superior at alerting you to slow-burning fires that produce a lot of smoke. *Example*: smoldering wood or upholstery. Both types of detectors should be installed in appropriate locations.

FIRE DRILLS AT HOME

Plan for a fire. Work out an escape route for every family member. Tell children what to do in case of fire or smoke. Have them practice the "fireman's crawl," nose and belly close to the floor for maximum oxygen.

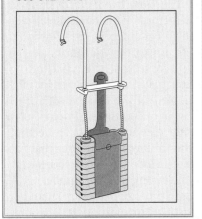

LIFE-SAVING LADDER

When the only way to safety is out the window, a foldaway fire ladder could save lives.

Models come in 15-foot lengths. They can support up to 1,000 pounds and cost approximately $50. Choose a model with spacers that keep the treads away from the walls, and practice using it with family members. *Contact First Alert, 800-392-1395.*

Teach kids the buddy system, making older children responsible in an emergency for a younger sibling. Wake them up, then escape together. Teach family members to get out without stopping for belongings. And never go back inside a burning building.

Establish an outdoor emergency location where all family members meet immediately following an emergency exit. Have regular fire drills. Practice with your children and make sure they know what they are supposed to do. Quiz youngsters periodically on escape routes and procedures.

Escaping from Upper Stories

If bedrooms are on the upper floors of your home, ensure your lives with escape ladders.

If you do get a ladder, practice using it. Teach young children how to install the ladder and use it. Build their confidence prior to an emergency.

Another effective safety device is a smoke helmet, a fire-resistant hat and face mask that protects against smoke and flames.

FIRE KNOW-HOW

Is your home equipped with a fire extinguisher? Where is it and how do you use it? If your answers are vague, you're not as safe as you could be.

If you buy only one fire extinguisher, it should be classified "A-B-C," indicating it is effective against all three kinds of fires. Type A-B-C is recommended for general home use.

- *Type A* fires involve wood, paper and fabric.
- *Type B* fires are caused by flammable liquids (grease, gasoline).
- *Type C* fires are electrical fires (TVs, computers, VCRs).

You should have an extinguisher on each level of your house that is capable of protecting the entire level. Keep the extinguishers fully charged, and make sure that family members know how to use them.

Best Size Extinguisher

Generally, bigger is better, but only if family members likely to use it can lift it and aim the spray. The average floor-size extinguisher weighs about 30 pounds. You should be able to manage a 14- to 15-inch model. A 17-inch extinguisher is heavier, but has more spraying power. Protect your kitchen with a smaller *sodium bicarbonate* extinguisher for maximum effect on grease fires. Some even come in white!

Cheap at *Any* Price

Expect to pay between $40 and $60 for a high-quality extinguisher in the full-floor model range. Any extinguisher you buy should carry the *Underwriters Laboratories'* (UL) labels, which also indicate the letters A-B-C for different fire types.

FIRE IN THE DRYER? NOT UNCOMMON...

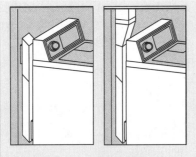

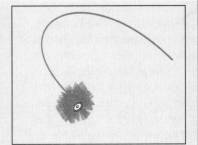

Dryer Beware — A common cause of fire alarms is clothes dryer vents, where accumulations of lint can ignite in the large vent pipe exhausting dryer heat. Change round plastic vent ducts for adjustable aluminum units that handle the same air volume. Clean dryer lint trays after every load to help keep the vent pipes clear.

Dryer Vent Brush — The easy way to clean dryer vents is to buy a dryer vent brush. The nylon bristles fit conveniently into the 4-inch dryer vent tube and the 10-foot handle extends into the vent pipe. Regular use ensures maximum dryer efficiency. They're available through the *Improvements* catalog. Call 800-642-2112 to order one.

Toxic Self-Defense

Be aware of the toxic substances that are often used in construction, household and personal products, and cleaning agents and pesticides that find their way into our lungs via dust and drinking water. The Environmental Protection Agency (EPA) estimates that radon gas alone causes about 15,000 deaths each year. Your home, sweet home will be safer if you know about the lurking dangers and how to combat them.

ASBESTOS MENACE

If your house was built prior to the 1970s, chances are there is asbestos in your home. If so, you probably will want to have it removed. Asbestos was once used for ceilings, floors and plumbing and heating systems. It has also been linked to lung and stomach cancer.

If you suspect there is asbestos in your home, call your local health department for help and advice in diagnosing and removing asbestos—both jobs should only be undertaken by qualified experts. Asbestos removal is not a do-it-yourself project.

CARBON MONOXIDE DANGERS

Carbon monoxide (CO) is a colorless, odorless, tasteless gas produced by the combustion of wood, coal, oil or natural gas in furnaces, stoves or even fireplaces. CO is lethal, silently poisoning between 3,000 and 4,000 people every year in the U.S., killing about 1,000.

Know What to Do

No home with heating appliances should be without a carbon monoxide detector. These detectors monitor the levels of CO gas in the immediate vicinity of their sensors. An alarm sounds if CO achieves dangerous levels.

Like smoke detectors, CO detectors should be placed in strategic locations, such as bedrooms and in the basement, at least 25 feet away from the furnace. Detectors should not be installed within one foot of the ceiling or at wall intersections where there is little or no air movement.

CO poisoning can be prevented by proper maintenance of heating equipment. Annual cleaning of burners, flues and chimneys will ensure that conditions for CO buildup are not present.

If you suspect CO in your home:
- Immediately open windows and doors.
- Evacuate the house. Get medical attention.
- Call the fire department to report the problem and request an inspection.
- Call your fuel company for an immediate repair of furnaces, heaters and chimneys.

Prevent CO Poisoning

1. Turn on the kitchen exhaust fan when using a gas oven.
2. Open the garage door *before* starting the car.
3. Back the car out of the garage to let it warm up.
4. Have a heating technician check gas furnace, boiler and water heater for proper venting of combustion gases.
5. *Never* close the fireplace damper while live coals are still burning.
6. Install CO detectors in strategic locations and observe any alarm.

FIGHT FORMALDEHYDE

Formaldehyde is used in thousands of products, ranging from cosmetics and disinfectants to wrinkle-proof fabrics, pressed wood and home-insulation. All of these are apt to release harmful formaldehyde vapors.

The gas is an eye and respiratory irritant and, in high concen-

---

⚠️

CO POISONING OR FLU?

The symptoms of carbon monoxide poisoning are so similar to influenza that many CO victims misdiagnose the problem.

The highest incidence of CO poisoning actually occurs during flu season, which is also the heating season.

If several family members seem to have come down with the flu within a couple of hours of each other, be suspicious. Young children are affected more than adults. If you experience the symptoms, and they disappear once you leave the house, suspect CO.

Here are the more common symptoms of CO poisoning:

➤ Headache
➤ Dizziness or weakness
➤ Bright cherry-red lips
➤ Shortness of breath
➤ Flushed skin
➤ Nausea or vomiting

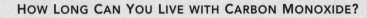

HOW LONG CAN YOU LIVE WITH CARBON MONOXIDE?

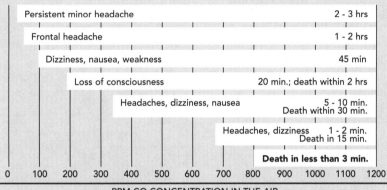

Persistent minor headache	2 - 3 hrs
Frontal headache	1 - 2 hrs
Dizziness, nausea, weakness	45 min
Loss of consciousness	20 min.; death within 2 hrs
Headaches, dizziness, nausea	5 - 10 min. Death within 30 min.
Headaches, dizziness	1 - 2 min. Death in 15 min.
	Death in less than 3 min.

0   100   200   300   400   500   600   700   800   900   1000   1100   1200

PPM CO CONCENTRATION IN THE AIR

Carbon monoxide is measured in air samples as parts per million (PPM). CO levels vary depending on your home's insulation quality, ventilation and the natural seepage of fresh air into the house. It is possible to suffer low-level CO poisoning over days or weeks from low-level CO leakage from a furnace or water heater. Musty air, moisture on windows, a mostly yellow burner flame, instead of blue, are telltale signs of CO danger.

trations, damages the body's DNA and the ability of cells to repair themselves. It may also combine with other chemicals to form cancer-causing agents.

The most dangerous formaldehyde product you are likely to find in your home is "blown-in" urea-formaldehyde insulation, which is no longer used, but is present in many older homes. Home testing kits for measuring formaldehyde concentrations are available at hardware stores.

Formaldehyde in Fabrics

Many fabrics, especially wrinkle-free products, contain formaldehyde.

You can minimize the risk by:

- Washing new clothes and bedding many times before first use.
- Selecting silk, natural wool or wholly synthetic fibers over permanent-press, wrinkle-proof, moth-proof and wash-and-wear fabrics.

GET THE LEAD OUT

Lead is one of the most toxic of the heavy metals, often affecting children. It can be inhaled as dust, ingested in paint chips or water, or can leach from lead pipes in older buildings.

Lead Poisoning

Lead accumulates in the kidneys, bone marrow and nerves.

Young children are especially susceptible. Symptoms of lead poisoning—which are not always present—may include stomach pains, vomiting, constipation and weight loss.

Lead poisoning can cause birth defects, learning disabilities, damage to the central nervous system, mental retardation and serious kidney defects.

Where's the Lead?

If your house or apartment was built prior to 1978, it's likely that there's lead where you live. Lead is often found in the water pipes, particularly old lead pipes, but also in copper pipes where lead-based solder may have been used in the joints. According to the *Environmental Protection Agency* (EPA), more than 57 million U.S. homes fall into the lead-affected category.

LEAD CRYSTAL & LEAD GLAZING

The lead in lead crystal decanters and in the glaze used on some older earthenware can leach into drinks kept in them. Don't store wine in crystal decanters. Keep it in its original bottle, then pour it into the decanter before you serve it. Pour leftover wine back into the wine bottle.

Test-It-Yourself Kits

Inexpensive lead test kits can be purchased in hardware stores. Kits for testing water include a mail-in test tube that is sent to a lab. The fee is around $15 to $25, and the lab results are back to you in about 10 days.

You can also buy test pads that are dampened and placed on surfaces in the home. A color change in the pad indicates the presence of lead.

Eliminate Lead Sources

Lead paint was used extensively up until the mid-1970s in interior and exterior oil paints.

Loose or peeling lead paint should be removed. Then paint over tightly adhered paint to make the rooms safe. If you decide to remove lead paint, use a qualified contractor, and while the paint is being removed, evacuate your house, seal off the affected rooms and don't return until the rooms have been cleaned and tested for safety.

Is Your Water Lead-Free?

If your water supply is acidic—a pH lower than 6—or if you have soft water, it can corrode pipes. Stagnant water in the pipes dissolves lead particles, contaminating drinking water. If your home fits the danger criteria, test your water supply for lead. The EPA has established 15 parts of lead per billion as safe for drinking water.

MERCURY PAINT?

Most of us have heard of the dangers of lead paint, but did you know that mercury can be a hazard too? Although mercury is no longer added to latex paint, there has been no recall of existing paints that contain it, and some cans may still be on shelves at knock-down prices. *The National Pesticide Telecommunications Network (800-858-7378)* lists the mercury content of 1,600 paints. Check to make sure that any paint you intend to use is mercury free.

RADON TESTING

Radon is an odorless gas created by the natural breakdown of uranium in rocks and soil. Outdoors, atmospheric dilution virtually eliminates radon danger. In your home, however, radon gas particles remain suspended in the air and can get into your lungs. Breathe enough radon gas particles over time and lung cancer can result.

Not in My House

The EPA estimates that 1 out of 15 U.S. homes has unhealthy levels of radon. The particles can enter your home via well water or as a gas seeping through cracks and openings in basement foundations. Sump-pump openings and basement drains are major entry points. Radon hovers in basement air and gets circulated throughout the house by natural airflow, aided by heating and air conditioning systems that pump the particles into the rest of the house.

How Much Is Too Much?

Radon gas is measured in picocuries per liter. According to the EPA, one to two picocuries per liter of air is average for most homes. If the level rises to four picocuries per liter in your home's living area, the EPA compares that level of exposure to smoking 10 cigarettes a day.

As the picocurie level rises, so does the danger. At 40 picocuries, for instance, each family member is at the same risk as smoking two packs of cigarettes a day.

Radon Reduction

Reducing radon to safe levels can be as simple as patching cracks, covering sump pits and ventilating the basement, but tools and training beyond those of the average homeowner are usually required for more extensive mitigation. Contact the local or state EPA authorities for advice.

EVERYDAY PRODUCTS ALERT

Many seemingly ordinary household items, such as apple seeds, lanolin and a shampoo you might use on your children, can hurt you and your family. Take stock and decide whether the items on the list

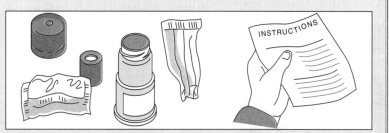

FIND YOUR OWN RADON LEVEL

Radon testing kits are readily available at hardware stores and home outlets for a nominal charge. The kits contain testing materials that are sent to an EPA-approved lab. The testing costs about $15 to $25, and the results come back within two weeks. There are separate kits for air and water. If tests indicate dangerously high radon levels, you should contact local and state EPA authorities for more help and recommendations on what to do. Generally, curing a radon problem is not a major expense.

below are worth the risk. At the very least, use them with caution. And if you can live without them—do.

■ *Appliance alert.* Medical science knows little about the long-term effects of energy pollution—harmful electromagnetic fields or radiation given off by home appliances. Some believe that such fields disrupt the immune system, making us more susceptible to damaging diseases, though this theory is controversial.

■ *Computer monitors.* Older video display terminals generate electromagnetic pollution, particularly from the rear of the tube. Newer monitors are shielded to reduce this pollution. Nevertheless, the further you position yourself from the monitor, the safer you are.

■ *Electric heating pads.* Electric blankets and heating pads give off high electromagnetic energy fields. Because they rest right next to your body for extended periods, these items may be particularly hazardous.

■ *Clock radios.* Battery powered models are okay, but plug-in clock radios should be stationed at least a foot from your head.

■ *Hair dryers.* These radiate high-energy pollution and are used close to the brain. Keep a good arm's-length distance when using a hair dryer, and try to reduce usage. Consider a model where the motor is wall-mounted and the air flows through a hose assembly.

■ *Microwave ovens.* Older models are susceptible to microwave leakage. Any model will leak over time, so stand clear while they're operating. Microwave oven leakage has been linked to skin cancer, birth defects, blood disorders and other serious ailments.

Avoid microwaving food for longer than 30 minutes, since lengthy cooking times can transform food chemistry, which some believe is dangerous. Never microwave in plastic containers or wrapping, which forces plastic molecules into the food. Children should be discouraged from peeking into a microwave to watch the cooking action (popcorn popping fascinates youngsters).

To avoid microwave oven leaks, don't slam the door and clean the door seal regularly with warm water and dishwashing liquid. Test the unit often (see box below), especially if it is an older model.

■ *Cleaning products.* As a general rule, the tougher the cleaning job, the more dangerous the cleaner. Bathroom cleaners that kill mildew and bacteria and lift soap scum contain potent chemicals that can burn your eyes, hands and even your lungs. Read the warnings, and err on the side of caution. Cleansers containing *ammonia, potassium hydroxide, sodium xylene sulfonate, acids* or *bleaches* should be handled with extreme care and stored beyond the reach of children.

Fumes from commercial cleaners containing the above ingredients can cause eye inflammation, dizziness and headaches. Using such cleaners in conjunction with one another in a confined area can seriously damage your respiratory system.

■ *Drain cleaners.* Most drain cleaners contain acids and lye, a potent caustic that burns skin, can cause blindness and may be fatal if swallowed. Store the sealed bottles in childproof locations. Use all of the product and wash and dispose of the container immediately.

■ *Oven cleaners.* These products are dangerous to the person using them and those who are within range of the fumes. They contain lye, ammonia and other harmful chemicals.

■ *Furniture polish.* Some of these products contain *phenol* and *nitrobenzene.* These chemicals are most dangerous if they are inhaled, but polish containing these and other damaging chemicals can continue to give off harmful vapors even after they have been applied.

■ *Metal cleaners.* These cleaners often contain ammonia and harmful petroleum distillates. Make sure you protect your hands with rubber gloves when applying these products.

■ *Carpet and upholstery shampoo.* Avoid shampoos that contain *perchloroethylene*

or *naphthalene,* both of which are highly toxic. Keep the area where you are using the shampoos well ventilated during the application process and drying period.

■ *Spot removers.* Alcohol, toluene, dry-cleaning fluid, degreasing and spot-removing substances are all air pollutants. Some are highly toxic. Use them as sparingly as possible. If at all feasible, store them away from the house.

■ *Drugs.* Both prescription and nonprescription drugs should be stored safely. If you have children in the home, a locked cabinet is the safest option. Never remove labels from bottles. Dispose of prescription drugs when you no longer need them. The humidity of a bathroom medicine cabinet may cause drugs to lose potency.

If you have young or teen-aged children, be aware that glues and solvents are sometimes used as inhalants, with potentially lethal results. Even when they don't kill, they can cause irreversible brain damage.

■ *Fuels and paints.* Gasoline is an air pollutant and a fire hazard, and is sometimes used as an inhalant by children. Kerosene, lighter fluid, barbecue starter and all paint products are similarly hazardous. These are products essential to most homes, but they should

BEWARE LEAKY MICROWAVE

Test for microwave energy leaks regularly with an inexpensive radiation leakage card. Moving the card around the door seal while the oven is operating registers leaks on a sensor that signals safe and dangerous radiation levels. Cards are available in most hardware stores.

HAZARDOUS PLANTS

There are about 80 plants you might have in or about your home that can be hazardous if ingested or even touched. Children and pets are often victims, experiencing symptoms ranging from rashes and mouth burns to dangerous poisoning. Here are the more common ones you'll want to avoid:

➤ Apple seeds
➤ Apricot pits
➤ Avocado leaves
➤ Azalea bushes
➤ Castor bean seeds
➤ Cherry pits
➤ Daffodil bulbs
➤ Eggplant leaves
➤ Foxglove
➤ Holly berries
➤ Iris flowers
➤ Jonquil bulbs
➤ Lillies of the valley
➤ Mistletoe berries
➤ Narcissus bulbs
➤ Peach pits
➤ Philodendron leaves
➤ Poinsettia leaves
➤ Potato greens
➤ Prune pits
➤ Rhododendron bushes
➤ Rhubarb leaves
➤ Sweet pea seeds
➤ Tomato leaves

be stored in tightly sealed containers away from living areas and heat sources. Sheds or outdoor bins are best. Garage storage is safer than the basement, and any fuel storage should be in *Underwriters Laboratory*–approved containers.

■ *Pesticides.* Most pesticides are potentially more harmful than the pests they kill. Buy only as much as you need for the job at hand, store them in a locked cabinet and dispose of any leftover pesticide at a hazardous waste facility. Don't let children or pets play near areas where you have recently applied a pesticide. And avoid using these chemicals on plants that bear fruit or vegetables that you are planning to eat.

Consider pesticide alternatives such as *diatomaceous earth*, sold as silicon dioxide (see p. 24). It kills most insects by clogging their joints. Also, you can test various home-brew pesticides made from natural ingredients (see p. 26).

DRINKING WATER HAZARDS

There are hundreds of pollutants in U.S. drinking water which can make you ill or which may create health problems

over time. These toxins fall into two categories: *inorganic*, such as lead, radon gas and pesticides, and *microbial*, such as protozoa, bacteria and viruses. Microbial pollutants are effectively reduced by chemical water treatment, such as chlorination, used by municipal water systems.

To Filter or Not to Filter

The public water supply is considered safe to drink. But if you are worried about the taste, odor, clarity and potential health

NOT-SO-HELPFUL PERSONAL-CARE PRODUCTS

Toothpaste
Many whitening and tartar-control pastes contain ingredients that can irritate lips and skin near the mouth. And swirl-style toothpastes contain certain dyes that can trigger allergic reactions.

Try a sensitive-formula toothpaste if you have a reaction to a stronger one. Nontoxic shampoos and toothpastes are available at health food stores.

Lindane Shampoo
Lindane, a chlorinated hydrocarbon pesticide, is found in a shampoo often used to get rid of head lice in children. It is toxic to the nervous system, and questions have been raised about its safety when used to treat children.

Lanolin
This skin care product commonly used by nursing mothers, is derived from the wool of sheep—which more often than not has been dipped in pesticides. A 1988 study found traces of 16 pesticides in lanolin samples, including diazinon and chloropyrifos. Consider not using lanolin on or near babies. There are plenty of soft-skin alternatives.

DEET
N,N-Diethyl-m-toluamide, aka DEET, is a popular insect repellent. DEET can affect the central nervous system and is particularly dangerous to children. It has been implicated in seizures and even coma. As much as 56% of the DEET applied to the skin surface is absorbed, with about 17% making it to the bloodstream.

If you must use a product containing DEET, only spray it onto clothing. Avoid direct skin contact, bathe as soon as possible after use and launder clothes.

hazards of your water, a purification system may be the answer. Filters can attach to your faucet, sit on the counter or be installed beneath the sink. *Cost:* $50 to $1,000, plus the cost for periodic filter replacement.

What About Bottled Water?

The "pure water" alternative to filtering is bottled water, but over time it's more expensive and you're not necessarily getting better water. What really matters is the source being used by the

CHOOSE THE BEST WAY TO PURIFY WATER

No single filter removes all contaminants. The first step is to have your water tested by a laboratory certified by the *Water Quality Association* or recommended by your local health department or EPA office. The water test prescribed in most real-estate transactions is for coliform only. *Recommended:* a full-spectrum test for trace minerals and organic pollutants done by a lab. *Cost:* $100–$160. Once you know what you want to filter, you can choose the right system.

If you trust your municipal water supply system, a simple filtration system will offer better tasting and odor-free water. If your home runs on well water and there's a question of purity, consider combining an ultraviolet (UV) light system with a filter system to cover all the bases.

Carbon Filters
These filters improve taste and eliminate odors. The tap water flows into a canister of activated carbon, which effectively removes chlorine and some minerals, but leaves behind microbes, metallic impurities and inorganic chemicals.

Ultraviolet Light
This is the best purifier for eliminating bacteria, viruses, algae, fungi and protozoa. Water passes through a canister where it's bombarded by UV light which kills the microbes but has little effect on chemical pollution.

Distillation Process
These units boil water, and the condensed residue is then filtered through activated carbon. This system produces the purest filtered water, but distillation still does not remove all harmful bacteria.

Reverse Osmosis Filters
Usually installed under the sink, these filters hold a semi-porous membrane which is effective on bacteria, lead, mercury, iron and most other contaminants. They tend to waste water in the filtering process and reduce the water pressure.

PURE WATER & YOUR HEART

Purifying water eliminates some good along with the bad, especially minerals, such as magnesium, which are essential to good health.

According to the *U.S. Academy of Sciences*, more than 50 studies in nine countries link reduced magnesium intake to heart disease.

Adding magnesium and calcium to soft water could potentially reduce the annual death rate from cardiovascular disease by 150,000 in the U.S.

vendor. In some cases, you're simply buying filtered tap water.

The best sources are natural springs that are rich in minerals—high in magnesium and calcium and low in sodium.

Before selecting a vendor, determine the source of the water. Request the results of laboratory tests which will tell you what the water contains and in what amounts.

Buy bottled water in clear containers, like glass and transparent, not translucent, plastic.

ALLERGEN ATTACK

Molds, mildew, bacteria, viruses and dust mites suspended in your home's air supply can cause severe health problems. Asthma, hay fever, other allergic reactions and even lung infections can result.

Harmful airborne organisms, called "bioaerosols," are everywhere you live and sleep. The most evil-sounding are dust mites, which consume human (and pet) skin and live in our bedding, furniture and carpets. Up to 15% of us are estimated to be allergic to dust mites.

If you keep your home's relative humidity below 50%, molds and dust mites do not grow.

Air Shampoo
- Buy a HEPA (high-efficiency particulate absolute) air purifier for the bedroom
- Use a dehumidifier
- Eliminate moisture resulting from leaks and damp areas
- Clean or change forced-air furnace filters regularly
- Vent the house with fresh air using fans frequently
- Launder all bedding regularly
- Use vinyl covers on mattresses and pillows for family members with allergies

Natural Disaster Self-Defense

Natural disasters—floods, hurricanes, tornadoes and earthquakes—are not everyday threats. While there's nothing we can do to prevent them, there are lots of steps we can take to survive them.

Most disaster injuries and fatalities can be linked to not knowing what to do and not being prepared. In most cases, panic is a bigger cause of injury and death than the event itself.

Here are some survival rules.

BE READY FOR SURVIVAL

A re there hidden natural disasters lurking in your neighborhood? Dams, for example. There are more than 74,000 of them in the U.S., of which 27,000 are listed by the *Federal Emergency Management Agency* (FEMA) as significant flash-flood hazards if they were to collapse.

If you live in an area susceptible to earthquakes, flooding, hurricanes or tornadoes, be aware of the dangers. Develop a family survival plan that includes communication between family members during a natural disaster emergency. Learn the history of natural disasters in your region from your local municipal authorities or the local chapter of the *American Red Cross*.

Survival Materials
The first step is shopping. When disaster strikes, supplies sell fast, so be sure you have the tools and goods needed to fight an emergency.

- *In flood zones*, investments in pumps and power generators can more than pay for themselves. Plywood, plastic tarps, nails and sandbags are essential. Some former flood victims even keep boats, inflatable rafts and life jackets available.
- *In hurricane country*, plywood and duct tape for windows is crucial. Basic tools for digging, chopping and sawing should be part of your survival gear.

Experienced victims in disaster-prone areas have learned to maintain a collection of critical tools and supplies. Check the Emergency Kit Necessities list on the next page to see what the experts keep on hand.

FAMILY PLAN DURING DISASTER

D isaster does not necessarily strike when everyone is home. Every member of the family should know exactly which hazards are most likely to occur and how to react and reunite in an emergency.

- Discuss disasters that are likely to happen. Tell children what to expect if they're in school during a disaster.
- Choose an out-of-area friend or relative as a contact in case of separation. Write the number in a child's lunch bag. Give everyone the number with instructions to call as soon as possible after an emergency.

⚠ DISASTER TYPES

Here are the ones you know...
- ➤ Earthquakes
- ➤ Floods
- ➤ Hurricanes
- ➤ Tornadoes
- ➤ Severe thunderstorms
- ➤ Winter storms

And some you may not have thought of...
- ➤ Extreme heat
- ➤ Landslides and mudflows
- ➤ Tidal surge or tsunamis
- ➤ Volcanoes
- ➤ Wildfires

- Teach family members how to switch off the main power and gas supplies—and when to do it or not to do it (such as in a flooded basement).
- Familiarize everyone with the emergency gear.
- Drill and quiz regularly.

PET PLAN DURING DISASTER

Y ou're evacuating, but what about the cat and dog? For health reasons they can't go to the shelter, the motel or most places. So, in advance:

- Find out from local authorities what plans are available for pets. Ask your own vet about alternatives.
- Be sure your pets' shots are current. Most kennels need proof of vaccination.
- Check distant friends or relatives for possible lodging.
- Make sure your pets are used to getting into pet carriers.
- Make sure your pets have collars with your name, address and telephone number. You could become separated.

The Last Resort
If you have to abandon your pets, leave a good supply of dried food and water. Cats should be separated from dogs even if they normally get along. Pets can behave unpredictably during the stress and trauma of an emergency.

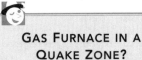

EMERGENCY KIT NECESSITIES

Have a safety plan and emergency supplies on hand. Pick a garage or basement area to store your survival gear all in one location. Leave the gear intact so that it's there when you need it.

- Basic tool kit
- Camping knife
- Can opener (manual)
- Candles
- Canned food
- Cellular phone & battery pack
- Charcoal
- Cooking grill
- Cooking utensils
- Cooler for food storage
- First aid kit
- Flashlights & extra batteries
- Fuel
- Matches
- Pet food
- Radio & extra batteries
- Sleeping gear
- Toiletries & toilet paper
- Trash bags
- Water containers
- Work boots
- Work gloves

And don't forget these personal basics:
- Cash and credit cards
- Prescription medications
- Vital records and papers
- Eyeglasses
- Insurance information

EARTHQUAKE SURVIVAL

If you're in a danger zone, be prepared. Store heavy objects on low shelves. Fasten shelving to the walls. Store glassware and breakables in latched cabinets, the closer to the floor, the better. Don't hang heavy pictures, mirrors and other objects over beds and couches. Store flammable liquids and pesticides in low, latched cabinets. If you have gas heat, the gas line should be checked for leaks annually. Gas lines should always be checked after a tremor or quake.

During the Quake

Stand in a doorway, or protect yourself under a sturdy desk or table placed near an inside wall—away from windows. You're in more danger from falling furniture and glass than from your house collapsing.

After It's Over

Shut off gas and electricity immediately. Check for damage

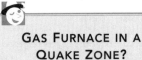

GAS FURNACE IN A QUAKE ZONE?

Following a quake, check your gas pipes and joints for leaks. A solution of water and liquid detergent wiped on joints will bubble rapidly if there's a leak.

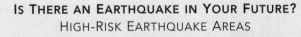

IS THERE AN EARTHQUAKE IN YOUR FUTURE?
HIGH-RISK EARTHQUAKE AREAS

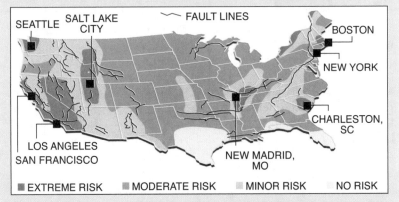

SEATTLE · SALT LAKE CITY · FAULT LINES · BOSTON · NEW YORK · LOS ANGELES · SAN FRANCISCO · NEW MADRID, MO · CHARLESTON, SC

■ EXTREME RISK ■ MODERATE RISK ■ MINOR RISK NO RISK

More than 40 of the 50 states are at risk for earthquakes. Although quakes occur mostly in California and Alaska, the three greatest earthquakes, according to FEMA, occurred not on the West Coast, but in the East and Midwest.

using a flashlight. Listen for gas and water leaks. When you're sure it's safe, turn the power back on and check the circuit breakers. Leave the gas for the utility company to reactivate.

FIGHTING FLOOD

Battle minor flooding by being prepared and following a few procedures:

- Have plywood, nails and sandbags on hand and ready to block and board up basement doors and windows.
- Have waders or at least knee-high rubber boots. Flood water is ice cold, and without protection, you won't be able to work.
- Have adequate basement pumps, including a gasoline-powered backup. Vent your pumps away from the house, so the water you've pumped doesn't flow back into the basement. Put screening around pump intakes to keep them clear of floating debris.
- Move perishable goods to an upper level, or even outdoors under tarpaulins.
- Build sandbag dikes around furnace and other appliances.
- Block lower-level sink and shower drains, and block toilets to prevent sewer lines from backing up into the house.
- Store fresh water in upper-story bathtubs in case the water supply becomes contaminated.

- Don't hurt yourself hefting sandbags, moving furniture or trying to beat off the inevitable. Keep tuned to a battery-operated radio, and when the water is winning, leave for high ground.

Major Flood Zones

Know the warning signs and community alert signals. Have an evacuation route and escape plan organized. Experienced flood victims pack vehicles days in advance and take them to temporary storage. When it's time to leave, shut off power and utilities, leave doors and windows open to give water an exit. Follow recommended evacuation routes.

SURVIVING THE BIG WINDS

Hurricanes and tornadoes have "killer" winds in common, but of the two, tornadoes are more dangerous because of their unpredictability and violent wind velocity.

About 800 tornadoes are reported in the United States each year, resulting in around 80 deaths and more than 1,500 injuries. In comparison, only about six hurricanes will hit the U.S. coastline every five years and only two will measure category 3 or higher with winds exceeding 111 miles per hour.

Watches & Warnings

Hurricane *watches* are issued by the *National Weather Service*

when winds exceed 74 miles per hour, and the storm will strike within 24 to 36 hours. Hurricane *warnings* are issued when the above storm conditions are likely to hit in less than 24 hours.

Tornado *watches* are broadcast when weather conditions are likely to produce a tornado. Tornado *warnings* are issued when a tornado is sighted.

The Best Place to Be

The safest place during a tornado is under a table in a basement, in the corner closest to the direction from which the storm is approaching. Your second choice would be a ground-level, windowless room or a bathtub, which could save your life in a tornado.

If you're outside and can't get into a building, the best place to be is face down in a ditch.

The Worst Place to Be

The worst place to be in a tornado or hurricane is in a car or a mobile home. If storm warnings are imminent, head for a

public shelter, usually a school or municipal building. The worst place to be *outside* during a hurricane is on a beach. If running for cover is not an option, throw yourself face down in a depression area as far from the water as possible.

THUNDERSTORM SAFETY

Thunder won't hurt you, but lightning can kill—the average bolt is charged with about 30 million volts of electricity. More than 90 deaths a year are attributed to lightning strikes, according to the *National Weather Service*.

Large thunderstorms are often accompanied by high winds gusting up to 60 miles per hour and hailstones that range from pea size to as large as a softball.

Where Are You Safe?

Take shelter in the house away from appliances, plumbing, the telephone—anything that can conduct

electricity (portable phones are safe indoors). Another choice is a car with the windows up, but away from trees, downed power lines or utility poles that might tumble.

Where Aren't You Safe?

Don't head for any open area, such as a golf course or a field. Also avoid standing under or near a single tree, utility pole, metal fencing or any body of water.

Avoid bicycles, metal bats, fishing poles, golf clubs and camping gear. Above all, don't be the tallest thing around!

LIGHTNING ALERT

If you're in an open field and feel your hair tingle, lightning is about to strike! Bend forward, hands on knees, feet together in a crouch position. Do not lie flat on the ground.

HOW CLOSE IS THAT LIGHTNING?

To estimate your distance in miles from a storm, count the seconds between a lightning flash and the thunder clap. Divide by five. Ten seconds between flash and clap...the storm is about 2 miles away.

Pests & Pest Control

Pests are attracted to a home by food, water and shelter. So the first line of defense is deprivation. Inside, clean counters and stove tops and empty kitchen trash frequently. Outside, keep garbage cans sealed. Wash garbage containers regularly with a strong ammonia solution.

Still, pests will come, so when they do, here's how to get rid of them.

AWAY WITH ANTS

Ants come inside for food from their outdoor nests, although some will nest indoors between walls and floors. Ants follow trails leading back to their nests. You can do battle by blotting every ant in sight with a damp paper towel. This destroys the ant trail and confuses scout ants that follow. If you can find the entry areas, caulk the access cracks.

Quick Kill

Commercial ant and roach sprays slow an invasion only temporarily. Ultimately, you must eliminate the ant colonies. Nests will be close to the house foundation, although some ants travel as far as 100 feet to an invasion site. Begin with a gallon or two of boiling water. Soak the nest entry, then stir up the soil and add more boiling water. Complete the extermination with ant killer.

Another quick remedy for ants is boric acid powder (roach powder) sprayed into entry crevices and into the ant colony itself. If you must go to the hardware store for roach powder, also buy six or more commercial ant traps and place them wherever you see ant activity. Within days, even hours, you should see a drop in numbers. The primary objective is to spread lots of traps.

⚠ ANT BAIT TRAPS: DEATH TO THE QUEEN

If ants come every season, be ready before the warm weather with a collection of ant bait traps. The bait is laced with viral diseases that the workers carry back to the nest. Once the queen eats it, she dies; then they all die. Place multiple traps where the ants wander. Change them every few weeks until ants are seen no more.

⭐ SAFE BREWS FOR ANT CONTROL

Concerned about pesticides? Try "diatomaceous earth," called *silicon dioxide*. It is a natural insect killer. Its microscopic dust particles clog insects' joints and absorb body fluids. It's effective on most insects.

The mint wall: Ants hate mint. Plant it around your foundation outside the kitchen (and anywhere else). They'll feed elsewhere.

Spicy restraint: Red chili peppers or paprika powdered at ant entry points turns them back to the nest. Borax and dried peppermint work the same. Oil of cloves seems to work, too. Talcum powder can also be effective at deterring ants.

Carpenter Ants

These one-quarter of an inch black ants burrow into damp wood, making furrowed nests. At certain stages, carpenter ants have wings which drop off after they swarm. A mature colony can number 100,000, then they swarm to form satellite colonies of about 5,000 ants. If you see them on the outside of the house, they are readying a new nest. If you see them inside your home, there probably already is a nest in the house. Carpenter ants don't eat wood, but they destroy wood fibers, leaving small sawdust piles near entrance holes. The best long-term control is to place bait traps near the colonies. The immediate remedy is to drill holes into the infested structural area and spray commercial insecticides directly into the nests. Any damp or rotting wood structure needs to be replaced. Look for multiple nest sites; seldom is there just one.

YOU NEED AN ANT EXTERMINATOR IF:

➤ The house is old and ants reappear despite repeated use of bait traps and sprays. You may have established colonies of indoor ants in the house structure (colonies can grow to 300,000 or more).

➤ Carpenter ants are found in several areas of the house and there are signs of swarming inside the house.

➤ Ant infestation occurs in several areas of the house other than the kitchen, including attics, basements and bathrooms.

➤ You don't have time to do a thorough job of tracing ant trails, caulking entry points and uprooting nests to destroy ants at their source.

Any rotting wood, such as tree stumps, firewood and old timber should be removed from around the house foundation to prevent recurrence of carpenter ants.

BENEFICIAL BATS

You don't want bats in your house, but having them somewhere nearby has its advantages. For every bat, there are 600 fewer mosquitoes every hour. A single bat digests as many as 3,000 insects each night. According to *Florida Game and Fresh Water Fish Commission*, the 39 species of bats in the United States eat hundreds of thousands of tons of insects each year!

IS THERE A BAT IN THE HOUSE?

In spring, when mature bats shift from winter roosts or maternity roosts, they'll sometimes fly into a house. Such accidents occur in late summer also, when young bats are learning to fly. If this happens, do this:

➤ Send panicky children (and adults) to another room.
➤ Close all doors leading to the rest of the house.
➤ Open all windows and doors to the outside.
➤ Let the bat find its way out.
➤ If it stops flying, let it settle quietly while you get some gloves.
➤ Cover the bat with a coffee can or plastic container.
➤ Slide a piece of cardboard between the container and the wall or ceiling, trapping the bat inside.
➤ Release the bat outdoors or open the container against a tree.
Alert: Never, ever touch a bat with your bare hands. Bats often carry rabies.

Still, we don't want bats nesting in the attic, under the eaves and shutters or even in the belfry.

Are You Living with Bats?

If there are bats present, you will see them at dusk departing from their roost. Generally, you can confirm their presence from early morning squeaking you may hear coming from the walls or attic ceiling. Bat droppings in the location also will confirm their presence. Droppings are brown or black, similar to mouse feces, crumble easily and contain mostly insect parts.

A bat's entry portal may be as small as one-quarter of an inch. A dirty stain below the opening from feces and body oils marks the spot.

BAT FACTS

➤ Bats do not get caught in human hair.
➤ Bats are not blind.
➤ Bats will bite in self-defense, so don't pick them up with bare hands.
➤ Bats are seldom aggressive.
➤ Bats will not live in well-ventilated spaces. They prefer dark, damp dwellings.
➤ Bats are so beneficial for controlling insects that many people encourage them to their property with bat houses.

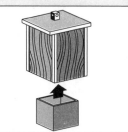

Smaller redwood bat houses, tree-mounted, can accommodate up to 30 bats. For about $40 you can keep mosquitoes down and bats from roosting in your house.

Source: Extension Wildlife Department, Auburn University, Alabama.

Bat-Proofing Solutions

Once you know where the bats live, plan a night attack while they are out feeding. Make sure all vent holes are sealed with aluminum screening. Caulk and seal all gaps and joints. Listen for the bats' return later in the night. There should be considerable confusion when they can't reenter. If, on the other hand, you don't hear any fuss, chances are you didn't plug all the gaps—they're back!

BEES, WASPS, HORNETS

Bees in buildings are a menace if they've established a colony or hive in an attic or between the walls. Nesting bees get defensive and are very likely to sting. Stings are unpleasant at best, terrifying

to young children and even lethal to people who are allergic to bee venom.

Hives in your home or near family activity should be either removed by a beekeeper or destroyed by a professional exterminator. This is not a do-it-yourself project, especially if the colony is large. Not only should the colony be destroyed, but the hive itself should be removed from the home structure so remaining honey won't attract more bees or carpet beetles from other colonies.

After removal of the hive, be sure that all potential access sources are plugged or screened. The scent of an older bee colony lasts a long time and can attract other bees.

Swarming Bees

When bee colonies mature, the bees divide, swarm and leave the

BREW-IT-YOURSELF PESTICIDES

If you are spraying your garden, especially a vegetable garden, you may be concerned about using chemical pesticides. Here are some solutions that keep bugs away without poisoning you in the process. What you will need are some empty spray bottles, a good supply of onions, hot peppers, dishwashing detergents, cooking oils, rubbing alcohol, hair spray and, for tougher bugs, like roaches, some Borax from the hardware or drug store. **Caution: Even home-brewed, natural pesticides can be dangerous to children. Mark all containers appropriately and store them out of reach.**

Pest Problem	Home-Brew Solution
Bugs	**Hot Pepper** Fill a spray bottle ¾ full of water. Add 5-10 drops of Ivory liquid, 1 teaspoon of ground hot pepper (pepper sauce will do), ½ teaspoon of garlic. For gardens, respray after a heavy rainfall or following each watering cycle. **Cooking Oil Special** Mix 3 tablespoons of dishwashing detergent and 3 tablespoons of vegetable oil into a gallon of water. Shake briskly, and pour into a spray bottle for application. **Alcohol Delight** (not recommended for vegetables) Mix 1 cup of rubbing alcohol with 1 quart of water. Test spray on plants to make sure it doesn't damage them. Double the alcohol for tougher bugs.
Ants	Mix ½ cup of lemon juice with ½ cup of water. Spray ant trails. Or, concoct a mixture of ground mint leaves, pure lemon juice and water and spray on ant trails.
Mosquitoes	Citronella candles ward off mosquitoes. Also, basil and tansy in patio planters keep them down.
Roaches	Place quarters or halves of Osage oranges in cabinets. Or, sprinkle diatomaceous earth in visiting spots. Jar lids topped with Borax and flour kills them.
Snails	Beer set in a cookie tray or saucer will lure snails and drown them.
Spiders, Mites & Worms	Mix 1 ounce of table salt in a gallon of water and spray.

or a child accidentally disturbs a nest, they will attack and sting.

Numerous aerosol wasp pesticides are available in hardware stores. These spray up to 20 feet so you can stand well back and soak the nest. Plan a night attack when all the insects are clustered on or in the nest. Light the nest with a flashlight, and spray it liberally several times. Afterward, knock the nest down (or dig up the soil) to be sure you have destroyed the nest.

If you must spray the nest during the day, be sure children and pets are indoors, wear a cap, gloves, protective goggles and a long-sleeved shirt. Spray the nest thoroughly, then leave the area so insects returning to the nest don't turn on you.

BEETLES BE GONE

A beetle visit is inevitable with warm weather and, for the most part, a vacuum cleaning will cure the problem. Generally, beetles are carried into a house on pets or under the bark of firewood. Some beetles fly, mostly at night, and they are attracted by white light. Garden lightbulbs (yellow) and screen doors are the best protection. If they do get into the house, they will feed on fabrics such as wool, silk, leather and fur (carpet beetles). Beetles multiply rapidly, so it's crucial to clear

hive. Usually the swarm will gather as a mass on trees or shrubs near the old hive. Scout bees find a new home and the swarm migrates to the new location in a day or so. Swarming bees are not especially aggressive, but they should be left alone. The biggest danger is that they might relocate in your house, so if possible, contact a beekeeper before the exterminator.

Carpenter Bees

Like all bees, these are vital to the pollination process for crops and flowers. It's preferable to avoid exterminating them, but if they're burrowing into your windowsills, treat the holes they "drill" with wasp spray or rubbing alcohol in a handspray bottle. If the bee is home, the spray will kill it. If it's away from the nest, the spray will kill any young bees in the nest.

Plug the holes with steel wool and seal them with wood filler. Heavily painted or stained wood surfaces discourage the bees, which prefer soft woods such as pine, redwood, cedar and Douglas fir.

Wasps & Hornets

They build their nests in attics, under eaves of the roof, in outdoor lighting fixtures and in the ground around the garden. Left alone, they are simply a nuisance, but if you

BEETLE BARRIER

Beetles thrive in garden areas. If your garden is far from the house, beetles are less likely to be bothersome in the house.

➤ Clear any old wood away from the house or foundation.

➤ Spray the "barrier area" with a commercial beetle insecticide, or make up your own home recipe from the "Brew-It-Yourself" chart.

➤ Plant mint around your foundation. Beetles (and ants) hate it.

➤ Dust plants and the general area with diatomaceous earth from the hardware store (see p. 24).

➤ Cover garden plants susceptible to beetle attacks with cheesecloth or pantyhose tied off at the ends.

them out as soon as you see them. Thoroughly clean potential nesting places, such as floor cracks and under moldings. After clean-up, most household insecticides will eliminate the problem.

Wood-Boring Beetles

Some beetle species infest wood that has high moisture levels. The larvae become trapped in the wood that becomes timber for new homes, although they rarely cause structural damage. Eventually, adult beetles exit the wood when it dries, leaving small holes up to $1/8$ to $1/4$ inch in diameter. Common names for these beetles are *Powder-Post Beetle*, *Anobiid Beetle* and *Old House Borer*.

CONQUERING COCKROACHES

Typically, the first sign of roaches are their eggs, which look like seeds, in the bottom of kitchen cabinets or beneath a refrigerator or dishwasher. The most common variety are small, brown *German Roaches*.

If you actually see a roach, especially during the day, you likely have a serious infestation. Roaches can be transported into your home from outside sources, such as grocery bags, or may migrate in from a neighboring unit.

There is no better treatment to get rid of roaches than the modern bait stations and growth inhibitors: *MaxForce Gel*, *Siege*, *Blue Diamond* and *Niban FG*. They pose no hazards to children and pets. The baits contain attractants that cause roaches to eat more and stop roaches from maturing. Even if roaches don't feed on the bait, they can't reproduce.

If You Need to Spray

New chemicals are safer and more effective. If the infestation is high, spray with a family of chemicals containing pyrethroids: *Conquer, Cynoff, Demand CS, Demon WP, Saga, Suspend* and *Tempo* are immediately effective, have low odor and have a long residual effect. *Baygon, Orthene, Dursban* and *Diazinon* are equally effective, but have a stronger odor. Experts claim these older products are less effective than the pyrethroids.

Roach Prevention

Treat for roaches as if you had them. Tuck bait stations underneath kitchen appliances and in cabinets under the sink. Vacuum under appliances and wipe cabinets regularly.

Large, Brown Roaches

Found outdoors, these are called *Smokey Brown* or *Pennsylvania Wood Roaches*. They aren't as hardy as German Roaches, but will make their way indoors from gutters into the attic, or from air conditioners when systems are shut down and moisture dries up. Spray outdoor areas where roaches nest with a product such as *Ficam W*, which also kills ants and centipedes. Or use a wettable powder that maintains residual strength even after rain.

FIGHTING FLEAS

Fleas lay thousands of eggs that hatch into microscopic larvae that feed off flea feces and pet hair. The larvae spin cocoons or *pupae*. In this stage, they are untouchable by sprays and chemical powders.

Pet collars were once a relatively effective means of flea control, but also required regular brushing of the pet, shampooing with flea shampoos and application of other flea products. Today there are better remedies.

- *Dogs and cats.* Today's best products, such as *Advantage*, kill fleas before they lay eggs. These topical solutions are available only from a veterinarian, and are well worth it. Once a month, apply the solution under the fur on the animal's neck. These products kill fleas within 12 hours and prevent reinfestation for at least four weeks.

- *Inside.* Should you have an infestation, it can be treated with powders brushed into carpets and wherever the pet sleeps. After vacuuming, brush the powder into the areas. Wash pet bedding in hot water.

- *Outdoors.* Use *Millennium*. It contains micro-organisms that eat flea eggs, larvae and pupae. Apply it with a garden hose sprayer. It contains no chemicals and thrives in moisture, so rain doesn't dampen its effect.

HOUSEFLIES

Houseflies transmit bacteria from wherever they've been. More annoying than dangerous, occasional flies are best combated one at a time with a common fly swatter. Spraying a room periodically with just a small amount of household pesticide, such as *Raid*, can keep flies under control. If there's no pesticide handy, a spritz of rubbing alcohol will kill a fly instantly. Even hair spray will slow a fly down to make it an easier target.

Cluster flies, the large greenish black ones, generally come from attic nests and tend to swarm in numbers. Flies are attracted to light, so if it's possible to darken a room and open doors or windows, they'll buzz off on their own. A daily swarm of flies indicates a nest nearby, or possibly a breeding source such as a dead squirrel in a chimney. You will need to eliminate the source. This is usually a good time to call in a professional.

Serious fly infestations can be controlled with fly traps or a plastic and metal device containing an attractant—flies enter and can't get out. One such device, *Fly Relief*, sells for about $38 and can hold up to 10,000 flies. This is a good solution for fly-prone attics. For about $40 you can buy a battery-operated automatic aerosol sprayer that releases fly-killer mist every 7.5, 15, and 30 minutes. Or for about $4 you can buy *Fly Scoop*, a glue-board that sits on a windowsill to trap flies.

LIQUIDATE LICE

Head lice are gray in color and about ⅛-inch long. Lice live in head hairs, are not really preventable and in most instances occur in elementary school children. Lice are spread through head-to-head contact, sharing the same floor mat, caps, combs or brushes and during sleepovers at the home of an infested friend.

An itching head is the most obvious symptom.

Control Method

Doctors prescribe a lindane-based shampoo for children over 5 years old. Lindane is a dangerous product that must be used with extreme caution. Pregnant women should avoid lindane. Among prescription brands is *Kwell*, which can be applied once, and if left for about 10 minutes can kill the eggs as well as the live lice.

Numerous over-the-counter shampoos are also effective, among them *Rid*. These are usually two-step solutions: one to kill the lice, with a subsequent treatment to kill the eggs.

Household Treatment

When lice strike a family member, assume the entire family is at risk and should be treated.

- Have everyone use the shampoo treatment prescribed by doctors.
- Wash all bedding, towels, and woolen caps in extremely hot water.
- Wash or dry clean any clothing, especially woolen sweaters and stuffed toys that may have come in contact with the lice.
- Thoroughly vacuum carpeting, couches and pillows where children may have been playing.
- Quarantine any object in question that can't be thoroughly cleaned for at least 10 days—the life cycle of the lice and eggs.
- Clean combs and brushes by soaking in a strong disinfectant or immersing in boiling water for at least 15 minutes.

VINEGAR CONDITIONER FOR LICE

Mix equal parts of white vinegar and water as an after-shampoo conditioner. The vinegar helps dissolve dead eggs that may still be clinging to hair.

MICE, RATS, OTHER RODENTS

Rodents carry threatening diseases, including the fatal hantavirus. If you have to clean up an area that has been heavily infested with mice or rats, wear a surgical mask, use a vacuum and stir as little dust as possible.

The best protection is to keep rodents out. A mouse can fit through very small holes or openings. A thin metal sheet, such as used for roof flashing, can be cut and tacked over openings. Or, stuff smaller holes tightly with steel wool or copper mesh.

Mouse droppings are the first sign of infestation. A single mouse leaves about 70 droppings a day. Mice do not go more than 30 feet from their nest, so if they're feeding in your kitchen, they are likely living in walls or between the floors nearby. Mice produce as many as 10 litters a year, with five offspring in each litter. Seldom does a house have just one mouse.

Get the Mice Out

Traps, glue-boards and feed poisons all work well. Mice will investigate anything new in their territory.

Spring traps are effective in mouse control. Professional exterminators will set multiple spring traps baited with bacon or peanut butter (cheese is not popular with mice). Continue resetting the traps for several days to ensure you get all the mice in the brood. Use gloves when handling the bodies, caution when setting the traps and do not place traps where curious children might access them.

Multiple catch traps, for about $14, can trap up to 15 mice at a time using a winding mechanism that scoops mice into a container. They'll die there in a day or two, but the humane thing is to monitor the traps and release the mice into the open—well away from your house. For larger infestations, try the *Tin Cat*, a multiple catch trap that can gobble up to 30 mice at a time.

Glue-boards, flat panels coated with thick glue to which mice adhere, are very effective traps. They're not dangerous to fingers like spring traps, but you will have to kill the trapped mice. Also, you

will need to place as many as a half-dozen glue-boards to ensure capturing the mouse colony. Place boards flush against the walls where the mice normally feed. Bait them with peanut butter or a cotton ball (nest material) placed in the center of the board.

Food baits, also called *rodenticides*, are simple to deal with, can be left unattended year-round and aren't dangerous to pets. They are particularly effective in attics and basements, where mice enter a home. The one disadvantage is that mice can die inside the walls, leaving a "dead mouse" odor.

If there's evidence of a lot of mice, use traps to eliminate the population and poisons to ensure they don't come back.

Is There a Rat in the House?

Droppings signify rats in residence. Obviously larger than mouse droppings, rat droppings number about 50 a day and

measure about ½ inch to ¾ inch in length, depending on the type of rat.

The two most common types are the *Norway* rat, with larger droppings, and the *Roof* rat. The type of rat will determine the best method of control.

Rats are more wary than mice, and avoid anything new in their territory, such as traps or bait stations. Some experts will set out traps without setting the spring mechanism for several days. Then, when rats begin to feed, set the springs.

Rats also avoid poison baits, then they will eventually nibble them. If the ingested bait only makes the rat sick, it avoids such bait traps in the future.

The Best-Laid Rat Traps

Rats will feed as far as 100 feet from their nests or dens. Roof rats nest in trees, while Norway rats burrow below ground or nest inside walls.

Eliminate rats with the basic tools, such as multiple spring traps baited with fruit for Roof rats or peanut butter and hot dog slices for Norway rats.

Set unbaited traps near openings that rats must squeeze through, and multiple traps in a line along rafters so rats jumping over one trap will hit another.

It's a good idea to tie the traps to a rafter or beam so that injured rats can't drag them into areas you can't reach.

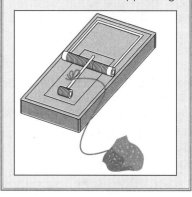

RAT TRAP BAIT SECRET

Tie bait to the spring trigger with dental floss or thread so rats can't just snatch the bait. Set at least a dozen traps in feeding areas and along rafters that serve as "ratways." Sprinkle oatmeal around traps to make them more appetizing.

Bait Boxes & Glue-Boards

There are plenty of choices at the hardware retailer for both. If children or pets are a factor, be sure to buy a tamper-proof bait station that will survive prying hands and paws. These poison centers can usually be fastened to the floor or wall.

Glue-boards can be effective, but you are forced to confront a sometimes live trapped rat— which is not the least bit fun. As with mice, the drawback with bait boxes is that rats die where they nest, and if it's in your walls, they will smell.

RAT PACKS

Norway rats, also called brown rat, sewer rat, house rat, are common to every state. They have tails shorter than the length of their head and body combined. They have small, round ears and a blunt snout. Norway rats prefer meat, fish, insects, nuts and grain foods found in garbage. Their black droppings measure about ¾ inch.

Roof rats, also called black rats or ship rats, are normally found in coastal areas. They have tails longer than head and body combined. The ears are large enough to cover their eyes and the snout is pointed. Food preference is plants, fruits, seeds and vegetables. Droppings are black and measure about ½ inch.

MANAGING MOLES

These are garden pests and will rarely enter a dwelling. They live alone, not in colonies, but a single mole can create enough lawn damage to make it appear as though multitudes are present. In fact, mole populations rarely exceed three moles per acre. Moles seldom eat roots, bulbs or plant materials. They do eat grubs and other garden insects, but not in sufficient quantities to control them. The best way to eliminate moles is with one of several commercial traps available at the hardware store. In particular, the *Harpoon Trap* from a company called *Victor* is a simple and safe solution.

MOLE CONTROL

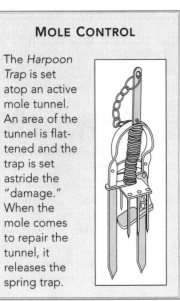

The *Harpoon Trap* is set atop an active mole tunnel. An area of the tunnel is flattened and the trap is set astride the "damage." When the mole comes to repair the tunnel, it releases the spring trap.

OFF WITH MOSQUITOES

Eliminate breeding places such as puddles that seldom dry up, old tires, birdbaths and even rain gutters.

Stagnant Water Cure

For standing water in a pond, buy *Mosquito Dunks*, which are disks that float on the water surface. They release a mosquito larvicide that settles to the bottom of the pond and kills mosquito larvae. One disk covers about 100 square feet of pond water and lasts up to 30 days.

Deck & Patio Solutions

Automatic misters for about $30, mounted above doors and around patio areas, can be very effective in mosquito control. The sprays release insecticide at regular intervals keeping mosquito activity to a minimum. Misters last up to 30 days.

One-Night Stand

If it's party time on the patio and mosquitoes aren't invited:

- Decorate the perimeter with citronella candles, in handy mini-buckets. The more, the better. They ward off not only mosquitoes, but most other night flyers as well.
- If you are not adverse to pesticides, spray surrounding bushes with a popular insect fogger before guest arrival. Be certain that food, beverages and ice cubes are inside when you spray.

WARD OFF MOSQUITOES — NATURALLY

If repellents repel you, then try using vinegar to keep mosquitoes off. Dampen tissue with white vinegar and wipe it on skin surfaces not protected by clothing. Or:

➤ Dab yourself with an ounce of citronella oil (from a health food shop), diluted by a few drops of vegetable oil or even vodka. Avoid the eye area because the mixture can sting.

➤ Plant basil around the patio, deck area, in window boxes and even in house plants near windows where mosquitoes may enter. They don't care for basil.

CLOSET MOTHS

If you're protecting clothing in closets, the most common practice is to use mothballs. These, however, contain a powerful chemical called *paradichlorobenzene* that is known to cause headaches and nausea, as well as eye, nose and throat irritation at prolonged exposure levels. Toddlers who have eaten just a single mothball suffer from seizures in about 40 minutes.

Alternate Solution

Natural products from health food stores can do the same job as mothballs. Cedar oil chips or lavender herbs packed into a child's cotton sock work fine. Fill the sock and tie the end. The following natural products are also effective:

- Dried rosemary and mint
- Dried tobacco
- Peppercorns

MOTHS IN THE PANTRY?

Kitchen moths, Indian meal-moths and Mediterranean flour moths contaminate food such as flour, cereal, pet food and birdseed. Discard infected food by placing it in a sealed plastic bag. Vacuum cabinets thoroughly with a crevice tool and spray with a low-odor pesticide with a crevice applicator. Hang moth traps, and position glue-boards with an attractant called *pheromone*, to capture any new moths that hatch.

RACCOONS & OPOSSUMS

Raccoons and opossums ravage your garbage and pilfer garden vegetables, but they will usually remain outdoors. In cold weather, however, both can climb easily enough to inhabit attics. Once in, they destroy wiring and insulation, and their excrement smells foul.

Even if confined outdoors, raccoons, in particular, need to be removed because they are prone to carrying rabies.

Harmless Opossums

As yard guests, opossums help control mice, rats and cockroaches. They aren't aggressive and have not been reported to attack cats and dogs. Opossums resist rabies, with fewer cases than any other wild animal.

Danger to Horses

Opossums can transmit a deadly disease called *equine protozoa myeloencephalitis* to horses, so if you have a stable and horse feed on your property, beware of opossums. Otherwise, you can ignore them unless they lodge in your attic.

Live Traps Work Best

The poison it takes to kill a raccoon or opossum will invariably kill pets or even children who might get hold of it. Moreover, you don't want the animal dying between the walls. Professionals recommend humane live traps to capture raccoons and opossums. Such traps cost about $50 to $75, depending on the size of the animal you need to trap. However, the problems of confronting a live trapped animal and the logistics of transporting it to some other location might warrant professional disposal.

SNAKES & LIZARDS

Not so much pests as unwanted visitors, both snakes and lizards basically go wherever there's food. If your crawl space, basement or attic is rodent infested or supporting insect colonies, then snakes (or lizards if you live in the southwest) will show up eventually. Strict rodent and insect control should keep them away. If you have a pool or pond supporting frog colonies, it too will encourage snakes into your domain.

A Snake in the House

More than likely you'll see snakes in a basement, especially if there's an old stone foundation. You can set a live trap, like the one pictured, purchased through *U-Spray Inc.* (770-985-9388) *www.bugspray.net*. The same company sells snake repellent granules, *Dr. T's Snake-Away*, which is to be spread around the outside of the foundation. Snakes can't stand the odor.

In attics, set the trap for several days, spread snake repellent in

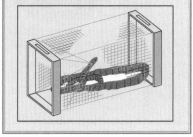

areas away from the trap or determine where a snake might be entering and block the passage. Try the trap and repellent first. Better to seal the creature outside than inside. Glue-boards work well for trapping snakes, but disposal is a problem.

SKUNKS & THEIR ODORS

Apart from pets getting sprayed, the most common skunk problem is having them move in under your deck or porch. The good news is that skunks are nomads and tend to move on once their young are ready to leave the den. Usually, offspring are born in late April or May, and the family shifts territory by late August. The best solution is to wait until night once the skunks have gone in search of food. Seal off all possible entry points to nest areas with strong wire mesh. If you think there's more than one skunk, make a flipper door hinged at the top, so the animals can't return once they exit.

Skunk Repellents

Believe it or not, there are smells that skunks don't like. Try these remedies to "offend" skunks off your property:

- Mix 1 cup lemon dishwashing detergent with 1 cup castor oil and a gallon of water. Use a garden sprayer to cover the yard area. Spray at night when the skunk family is away.
- Liberally spread mothballs in nesting places, or leave open pans of ammonia in the area (do not do this if pets or toddlers are liable to gain access).
- Some experts recommend setting up bright lamps near den entrances, or even leaving on a radio tuned to talk shows.

SKUNK TRICKS & TRAPS

Skunk in a window well: Nail cross-boards to a length of wood making a ramp. Lower into place with a fishing line to avoid being sprayed (as best you can).

Skunk in a trash bin: Loop a rope around the bin giving yourself a 20-foot length. Gently tug the bin to an open location before tipping the bin.

Skunk trap: Live traps for skunks are completely sealed to reduce the risk of skunk spray. Call professionals for this mission. They have the traps.

SIX CURES FOR SKUNK SPRAY

If a pet gets sprayed, there's plenty of "down home" advice for eliminating the stench. More likely, however, a pet-store skunk spray remedy will be your final choice. But since skunks and pets mostly encounter each other at night, when stores aren't open, here's a list of bathing solutions others have tried on their pets. First, thoroughly wet down the animal with warm water or a hose spray, then use:

Tomato juice or even tomato paste. It offers some odor relief, but the smell still lingers and gets worse on damp days. Better than nothing, but definitely a temporary fix.

Orange juice. It may be no more effective than tomato juice but is an alternative that you might have in the refrigerator.

Vinegar. You'll need two or three bottles, depending on pet size. Pour it on liberally and rinse.

Scope mouthwash. For some reason, only Scope is said to work.

Massengil douche powder. Unusual, but possible.

Special recipe. Published by *Chemical Engineering News*, mix 1 quart of hydrogen peroxide (from a drugstore), ¼ cup of baking soda, 1 teaspoon of liquid soap. Apply this mixture while it's still bubbling and rinse the pet with clean water. (This mixture was for a cat, so adjust accordingly.)

SQUIRRELS IN THE ATTIC

If there are squirrels in the neighborhood and noise in your attic, chances are the squirrels have moved in. They will do serious damage to insulation, rafters and wiring, to the extent of creating a potential fire hazard. Noise during the day indicates *gray squirrels*. Noise at night may indicate *flying squirrels* (although mice or rats can also be noisy).

Removal Procedure

Live trapping is the best method. Spring traps and glue-boards do not seduce squirrels as readily as mice or rats. Poison baits may cause death inside the attic, resulting in a smell lasting several weeks.

- *Gray squirrels:* Traps should be set near the route of entry as squirrels avoid traps near their nest. Also, you don't want to confront a squirrel in the attic because they're very protective of territory. Bait the trap with birdseed, nuts, shelled peanuts or sunflower seeds.
- *Flying squirrels:* These are extremely shy creatures and nonconfrontational. You will have to trap them in the attic close to their point of entry, or in the area where they leave droppings. (Gray squirrel droppings are scattered. Flying squirrel droppings are concentrated in a single location.) Bait traps with sunflower seeds, irresistible to flying squirrels.
- Traps should be solid or of sturdy mesh as squirrels can gnaw through almost anything.

Prevention: The Best Cure

- Cut away all tree branches overhanging your roof and eliminate all possible roof access.
- Block downspouts with wire mesh. Squirrels easily climb inside the downspouts to access a roof.
- Avoid hanging feeders from the eaves or placing them too close to the house. Otherwise, squirrels will eventually find an entry to the attic.
- Block all possible attic entry points with metal screening. Replace damaged fascia boards. Squirrels will chew their way in from even the smallest crevice.

SPIDERS & CENTIPEDES

There are about 3,000 species of spiders in the U.S., most types preferring to live outdoors. Although spiders eat thousands of insect pests, few spiders bite humans. For the most part, they can be controlled by frequent indoor vacuuming of webs and crevices where they hide. Heavy spider activity can be controlled with residual pesticides that are specified for spiders.

Spiders to Avoid

Two species are dangerous—the *black widow* and the *brown recluse* (also see p. 146). Female black widows are found in the eastern and southern U.S. About an inch long with double red triangles on a rounded black belly, their backs are sometimes spotted with dull red dots. Males are smaller, white and streaked with red and yellow coloring. The males are not dangerous, but the females are aggressive if their webs are disturbed. Be on the watch for these spiders in garages, under decks, in crawl spaces and log piles, around stacked plant pots and shrubbery near foundations.

Brown recluse spiders are less than an inch, have an oval body colored tan to brown. They are likely to appear indoors, but hide from human activity. Most bites occur when an unused room or attic is suddenly occupied, or when stored clothing, sheets or towels are disturbed.

- *A black widow bite* is very painful, leaves two distinct fang marks and can result in dizziness, headache and nausea within 30 minutes. Immediate hospitalization is essential for any such bite, with young children and older people being more susceptible to death than a healthy, nonelderly adult.
- *Brown recluse spider bites* aren't as dangerous, but

SAFE, INEXPENSIVE PLANT SPRAY

Made with botanical pyrethrums from chrysanthemum flowers, this spray effectively kills on contact red spiders, thrips, moths, gnats, leaf-eaters, spider mites, fern scales, beetles, stink bugs, mosquitoes and other insects. It is even safe to use on edibles up to the day of harvest. McArdle's Florist and Garden Center, 203-661-5600, *www.mcardles.com.*

the wound swells to about the size of a quarter and blisters quickly. The bite is surrounded by a red welt ring. Generally the spider is found stunned near its victim and should be killed and taken to a doctor along with the patient.

- If you have children who play around woodpiles, or under decks and porches, be certain such areas are free of spider activity.
- If you visit summer dwellings, attics or even guest rooms that have been unused for lengthy periods, watch out for spider activity, particularly the brown recluse variety.
- Remove woodpiles, dense shrubbery and other spider

habitats from around the house or in play areas.

- Spray with residual pesticides on a seasonal basis to discourage spider infestations.

Centipedes & Millipedes

These pests are usually found outdoors, although there is one class of centipede that lives inside the house. Found mostly in damp basements and unoccupied rooms, they feed on insects and spiders. They are, in fact, considered helpful for insect control in the garden.

Centipedes grow to about 1 inch in length and do not usually build into large numbers.

Millipedes thrive outside the home in gardens and foundation areas. In dry weather they can enter basements in large numbers.

Both of these pests are readily controlled by residual pesticide sprays or powders.

TERMINATE TERMITES

Termites cause extensive damage to wood structures and need to be eliminated from your home and immediate property.

You should never buy a home without having it pass a professional termite inspection. Also, ask for an inspection guarantee.

Call a Professional

If you have termites, treatment involves digging a trench around footings or the foundation and applying potent (and expensive) chemicals (termiticides) to form a ground barrier. Exposed rafters and wood areas in the house also need to be treated with residual pesticides. Furthermore, subsequent periodic inspections are necessary. Contact several

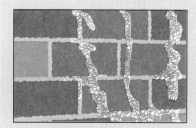

TERMITE TELLTALES

Termite | Carpenter Ant

Termites build mud tubes on foundation and wood surfaces. Tubes are usually ¼ inch to 1 inch wide. If you see them, you have termite activity that should be treated immediately. There are do-it-yourself solutions available, but the most reliable approach is to hire a professional.

Termite swarm indicating a serious infestation of termites and calling for a professional exterminator. Carpenter ants (p. 24) and termites look very similar. If it's ants, the situation may not be as critical, but you will still need to eliminate the colony.

companies for estimates, read their contracts carefully and be sure that the extermination process is guaranteed.

If you are building a new structure in an area of high termite activity, it makes good sense to treat all unpainted surfaces with a low toxicity pesticide that will penetrate the wood. Your local hardware store will recommend the best pesticide for new construction.

TICK DEFENSE

All ticks are parasites that feed on the blood of animals. They affect dogs more than cats, and although humans are not a preferred host, ticks will latch on. Their bites can lead to serious disease, the best known of which is Lyme disease.

Tick Control

Ticks hover in shrubs and bushes waiting for a victim to walk by, then they drop on to feast. Keeping a trim lawn and pruned shrubbery is essential in tick territory. If there's a heavy infestation, you may want to consider spraying your yard, particularly bushes close to the house as well as beneath decks and porches.

What Kills Ticks?

Sprays containing the following:

- *Bendiocarb* (professionals)
- *Carbaryl*
- *Diazinon*
- *Malathion*

TICK DEFENSE TACTICS

Clothing: Go into infested areas wearing long-sleeved clothing, tucked-in shirts, socks and a cap. If such attire is impractical, at least wear light-colored clothing to reveal ticks and apply repellents designed specifically for ticks.

Repellent: DEET. It's effective, and hard to find a repellent without it. Over time, DEET can be absorbed through the skin resulting in kidney problems (see p. 19). Repellents with low DEET concentrations are ineffective against ticks. Instead, use a high-concentration DEET sprayed on clothing.

Campers: Spray tents, backpacks, sleeping bags, caps (but absolutely not skin) with *Duranon Tick Repellent*. Allow several hours drying time before using the gear.

Tick kit: Make your own and keep it handy. A cosmetic purse, fine-point tweezers, packs of alcohol swabs, needle and a pack of matches.

⚠️ TICK BITE SYMPTOMS YOU NEED TO KNOW

If you or a family member has been exposed to tick territory and begin to experience the flu-like symptoms described below within a week to 10 days following your visit, there's a good possibility that it's a tick bite reaction, even though you may not have noticed a tick on the skin surface. A deer tick, for example, can be as small as the period at the end of this sentence.

- ➤ Recurring fever, chills
- ➤ Headaches, severe
- ➤ Muscle pain, stiffness
- ➤ Neck pain
- ➤ Swollen joints
- ➤ Partial paralysis
- ➤ Facial paralysis
- ➤ Nausea and vomiting

Symptoms may be accompanied by a rash, but not always. In some cases it is circular or bruise-like, surrounding the area of a bite. Almost all tick diseases are treated effectively with antibiotics if caught early enough. Early detection is crucial, so if conditions indicate a tick bite, see your doctor immediately.

Tick Species	Associated Diseases	Found In...
Deer Tick (a.k.a. Black-Legged Tick)	Lyme Disease HME Disease HGE Disease	CT, RI, NY, NJ, PA, MD, NC, WI and MN
American Dog Tick	Rocky Mountain Spotted Fever	NC, SC, GA, MO and OK
Lone Star Tick	HME Disease HGE Disease	OK, MO, GA, WI, MN, CT and NY
Rocky Mountain Wood Tick	Colorado Tick Fever Rabbit Fever (Talaremia)	CO, UT, WY, CA, OR, WA, ID, and MT
Pacific Coast Tick	Rabbit Fever (Talaremia)	TN, AR, MO, OK and KS
Relapsing Fever Tick	Relapsing Fever	TX, NM, CO, AZ, NV, CA, OR, UT, ID and MT

House & Home

Security & Maintenance

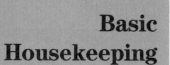

Safe Home

Security &
Maintenance

**Basic
Housekeeping**

Protecting Your Home

Don't let your home be one of the five million that will be invaded by burglars this year! An insecure home is an open invitation to thieves. A few simple actions can be the difference between keeping or losing your most precious possessions. And it can also be the difference that spells life or death for you and your loved ones. Lock up, light up and arm yourself with these common-sense protectors against intruders.

BURGLAR'S NIGHTMARE

Crooks aren't stopped by locks, latches and dead bolts. According to the FBI, most burglars enter through front doors by breaking glass panes and unlocking the door.

Almost half of illegal entries take place through ground-floor windows or rear doors, with only a minority of break-ins occurring via the second story. Being at home is your best defense. The next best defense is to make a burglar believe the house is occupied when it isn't.

- Put lights on timers set to go on at dusk and off in the late evening. For larger homes, stagger the on-off times among several timers throughout the house.
- Leave on a radio tuned to an all-talk station when you're away (TV will work, too). Burglars don't take unnecessary chances. They'll move on to a house that sounds empty.
- Keep a dog, preferably one that barks loudly at strange noises. If you can't have a dog, there are alarm devices that emit ferocious barking when triggered by sound, such as breaking glass.
- Install an alarm system. If you can't afford one, buy the next best thing—alarm stickers, which you can get through popular home improvement catalogs. Paste them on entry doors and first-floor windows.
- Similar to the "stickers only" approach, install a video camera replica aimed at main entrances. These too can be purchased through catalogs. Even though many thieves know the tricks people use to make it look as if they are home, they're more likely to pass up a house that appears occupied or seems to be protected by security devices.

When You're Away
- Consider a house-sitter who will live in your home while you're gone.
- Stop newspaper and mail deliveries, so they don't pile up and advertise your absence.
- Leave curtains and shades in their normal positions.
- Have a neighbor park a car in your driveway from time to time.
- Let the local police (and neighbors) know you're away.
- Arrange for lawn mowing if you're going to be away for an extended period.

Be Inhospitable to Burglars
No security system helps when an intruder can lie in wait and threaten you with a weapon.

Eliminate hiding places such as tall shrubbery and trellises near doors. Cut back overgrown bushes that obstruct views to doors and windows. A tree, trellis or telephone pole next to your home may give an intruder all the help needed to gain access to the upper stories. Be sure that upstairs windows are securely locked.

Security Lighting
Security lighting illuminates walkways and entrances to discourage lurkers and reduces the risk of tripping in the dark. Believe it or not, even a crook can sue you if he gets hurt on your property! Mount the fixtures as high as possible to discourage tampering. Lights activated by a motion sensor are economical since they work only when you need them and can alarm potential intruders.

TWO GREAT PLUG-INS TO FOOL A THIEF

Take advantage of technology for affordable security units that simply plug into wall sockets. Available in most hardware and home stores.

Photo cell activated timer also switches on at dusk, but you can select the time that it switches off.

Simplest (and cheapest) of these photo cell units switches on automatically at dusk and remains on until daylight.

GET THE RIGHT LOCK

Your home is most likely equipped with a good cylindrical-style or mortise-type lock at main entries. But not all houses have dead bolts. If your home doesn't, a good dead bolt or a drop bolt is your best line of defense against intruders.

Double-Sided Dead Bolts

Doors with glass or adjacent glass viewer panes are best protected with double-sided dead bolt locks, which are worked by keys on both sides of the door. They offer superior security and prevent a burglar who has broken into the house through a window from using the door to carry out large items.

But remember—the same lock that keeps burglars out also keeps you stuck inside if you happen to misplace the key. This represents a danger in case of fire. Ask your hardware dealer about safety dead bolt locks. These are locks in which the key cannot be removed from the interior side of the cylinder when the lock is activated.

Double Your Locking

In apartments and high-risk areas you can increase security with a drop bolt lock. These fasten to the surface of the door and lock into an interlocking latch assembly mounted flush with the door frame.

CHOOSE THE BEST DEAD BOLT

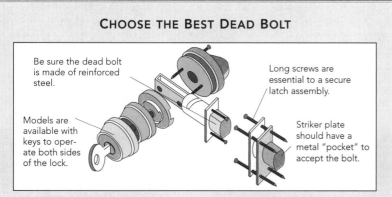

Be sure the dead bolt is made of reinforced steel.

Long screws are essential to a secure latch assembly.

Models are available with keys to operate both sides of the lock.

Striker plate should have a metal "pocket" to accept the bolt.

Dead bolt locks should have a steel-reinforced bolt to reject a hacksaw blade, and the bolt should be 1 inch to penetrate well into the door frame. Mounting screws for the strike plate should be at least 3 inches to enter the studs behind the frame. Models with double cylinders are the most secure. The more cylinder pins, the greater resistance to picking.

DEFENSIVE DOORS

Entry doors should be secure first, efficient weather blockers second, and decorative third. Depending on your neighborhood, you may not want to risk a door surrounded by glass panes or a door with glass panels. Bear in mind that the majority of break-ins occur through the front door with the burglar breaking the glass and unlatching the door. This can be prevented by using double-sided dead bolts.

Doors should be solid or metal. Hollow-core doors can be easily kicked in, so if you have one as an entry door, it should be replaced. Similarly, doors with wood-panel inserts are weaker than solid doors. In an apartment, they also reduce your protection from fire in the hallways.

NO KEYS NEEDED!

With this lock, simple digital codes provide safe and secure keyless entry for any door—home or office. Keyless electronic locks and dead bolts eliminate lost keys, hidden keys and lockouts with a simple digital code. *Intelock, 800-562-5875, www.intelock.com.*

IS YOUR DOOR A GOOD BARRIER?

Peepholes & Viewers
A good peephole or door viewer should cover a 180° angle, allowing you to see not only whoever is at the door but also anyone hiding nearby. It should also allow you to read any identification a caller may offer.

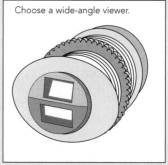

Choose a wide-angle viewer.

Never let someone into your home just because he or she flashes a badge. Police are required to show you a police photo-identification card, and you should ask to see it.

Door Chains & Blocks
A good door chain won't break or come apart from its screws when someone tries to force it. The mounting screws should be long enough to anchor the chain securely, preferably to a stud.

Door-blocking devices also offer good security. Some fit into a floor stop, others function like wedges and work on wooden floors and carpets.

WINDOW DEFENSE

It's a waste of time and money to install good locks on doors next to windows that need major repair. And no window security device is effective when a window's sash is rotten and its glass is loose.

Latches, Locks & Screens

Most window-latching mechanisms are weak and should be supplemented with secondary locks. Windows that you never open are best secured with penny nails placed in holes drilled into the sash. Screens and storm windows may deter or delay a burglar and should also be in good repair.

Basement Windows

Often ground-level basement windows are easy to kick in. Burglar bars work well to prevent this and are available in non-penitentiary horizontal or scroll designs. Look for bars that open from the inside, as they make window cleaning easier and allow for escape in an emergency.

LETHAL WEAPONS

Owning a gun may save your life or it may lead to your death or the death of someone you love. If you are thinking of buying a gun (or if you already own one), you should consider these points:

- Do you know how to handle a gun? If you don't, are you prepared to learn?
- Would you, in a crisis, be prepared to use lethal force?
- Do you trust yourself to make the right decision about when not to shoot?

If you do decide to buy a gun, you should get advice from an expert before choosing one. A handgun, for instance, fires more rounds before reloading than a shotgun. But a handgun is more difficult to aim and is less intimidating. On the other hand, a 12-gauge shotgun is so powerful that it can easily kill someone in another room.

NONLETHAL WEAPONS

There are two good nonlethal alternatives to guns: pepper sprays and Tasers (stun guns). But remember…if you reach for a nonlethal weapon and an armed opponent thinks you have a gun, you may get shot.

Pepper Spray

Pepper spray (more formally, *oleoresin capsicum* [OC] spray) is capable of incapacitating any attacker at a distance of up to 10 feet. It is favored by police departments and is more effective than Mace at disabling psychotics or people with an abnormally high pain threshold, such as those under the influence of the drug PCP.

Tasers

Tasers fire a dart attached to a thin wire and deliver an incapacitating, but nonlethal, electrical shock. Check with local police about local laws pertaining to any weapons.

Guard Dogs

Any barking dog in a house can easily deter an intruder. But if you want a dog that will be sure to defend you in the event of an actual attack, you should choose the breed with care and be prepared to have the animal professionally trained.

You should also be aware that good guard dogs—for example, Dobermans, German shepherds and rottweilers—can be so protective as to make social life difficult. In fact, some insurance companies will actually increase your homeowner's premium if you own a potentially dangerous breed.

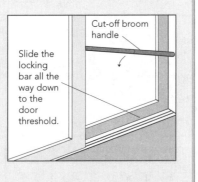

LOCK THAT WINDOW

Nails through pre-drilled holes in the frame lock a window tight.

Hole size should be a snug fit for the nail.

Windows that are not opened frequently: Drill a hole where the window sashes overlap to accommodate a nail or slim bolt. Do not use screws—you might have to open the window in an emergency. Position holes on both sides of the window for maximum security. Sliding bolt locks mounted on the window sash can also work, but are not as strong.

Sliding Windows (and doors): Cut a length of pipe or old broom handle to fit in the slider track at the base of the window or door. This will block the unit from sliding, even if the lock is breached. A hardware alternative is a security bar able to withstand up to 1,000 lbs. of force. They are made for windows and sliding patio doors. Look for *Master Lock Security Bars.*

Cut-off broom handle

Slide the locking bar all the way down to the door threshold.

CAUGHT IN THE ACT

If you think there's an intruder in your home, preserve your physical safety first! If you return home and find evidence that your home has been broken into, don't go inside. The intruder may still be there. If you wake up and hear an intruder in the house, you have three sensible choices:

- If you can, leave the house silently. When you're a safe distance away, call the police.
- If you can't get out, and if you have a safe room, go to it. Call 911.
- If all else fails, lie still and pretend to be asleep.

SAFEGUARD YOUR PROPERTY

Mark it up! If your property is stolen, you'll have a better chance of recovering it if it's engraved with your social security number. You can get engraving tools at hardware stores or borrow them from your local police department. You'll also fare better with your insurance company if you have a photo or videotape inventory of your valuables along with written documentation.

Best Hiding Places

No hiding place is perfect, but some are better than others.

Bedrooms and drawers are worst of all. Try the places below, but don't forget to leave a list of where items are hidden with a trusted friend.

In the kitchen, hide items in a stack of pots or in a box of powdered detergent.

In the basement or attic, use a discarded piece of equipment, a length of stovepipe or a pile of junk as hiding places.

In the garden, wrap items in plastic and bury them in the yard or in a potted plant outside or in the house.

How to Buy a Safe

Keep these things in mind when you shop for a safe:

- The most secure safes are floor models bolted to joists or wall studs. If you can't bolt it down, get a model that will be just too heavy for two men to lift.
- Combination locks are more secure than those requiring a key. The lock should have a device that freezes the bolt in the locked position if someone tries to drill it open.
- Get a fireproof safe that says internal temperatures will stay below 451°F—the temperature at which paper burns.
- Choose a safe that's big enough. Before you buy, put everything you'll want to store in the safe into a cardboard box. Then calculate the volume of the box and buy a safe with at least that much volume.

THE ALARMING TRUTH ABOUT ALARMS

What burglars don't want you to know. Homes without alarm systems are 20 times more likely to suffer break-ins than homes with alarms. More than 90% of crooks surveyed target homes without alarms, according to the *National Association of Police Organizations*.

Simpler technology makes alarm systems easier to operate, more reliable and cheaper to install than ever before. Relatively new wireless systems, based on motion sensors, can be effectively installed as do-it-yourself projects for between $250 and $750, depending on what options and controls are ordered.

Alarm-buying know-how means thinking ahead about what you are protecting. The average burglar steals about $1,000 worth of insured goods. Is a $1,000–$3,000 alarm worth it? If "life and limbs" are in danger from intruders, invest in a sophisticated system.

Dealer Installation
- High security level
- Lots of features; flexibility
- Monitoring service available
- Suited for a large home
- Cost: $1,000–$3,000

Do-It-Yourself System
- Reasonable security
- Limited features
- Simple operation
- For small home or apartment
- Cost: $200–$700

What Dealers Don't Want You to Know

- Sales reps usually have incentives to talk you into costlier components that you don't really need. Study the literature carefully; choose hardware that gives you the highest security for the least cost.
- Don't sign anything on the first visit—no matter what the bonus offer might be. Shop around. There's a lot of competition, and in the end, all dealer systems are about the same.
- Read the contracts carefully. Some sales agreements commit you, in small print, to buy monitoring services at monthly fees for up to five years. With others, payments don't cover the purchase, just monthly fees for equipment use.
- Avoid dealers not listed with the *National Burglar and Fire Alarm Association (NBFA)*, Bethesda, MD.

Brands & Sources

ADT	800-238-4636		Safety Zone	800-999-3030
Brinks	800-227-4657		Telko	800-888-3556
Linear	800-528-4454		X-10	800-675-3044

Plumbing Self-Defense

You seldom need a plumber. When you do, chances are that one won't be available for hours, or even days. Knowing a little more about plumbing than where the water comes in and drains out could save you hundreds of dollars in potential damage—and knowing how to intelligently address plumbing problems could keep you from being ripped off.

THE PLUMBING SYSTEM

Plumbing starts in your basement or utility room, where the water enters the home. You do not need to be a plumber to know the basics. Major leaks need immediate attention. Other than that, stopped toilets, dripping faucets and blocked drains may be the only plumbing problems that you will ever need to address.

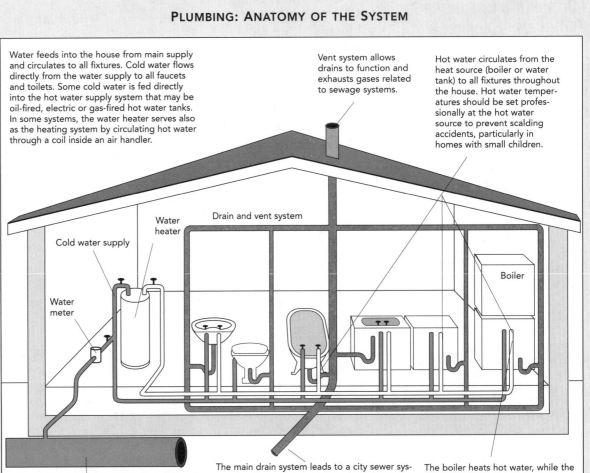

PLUMBING: ANATOMY OF THE SYSTEM

Water feeds into the house from main supply and circulates to all fixtures. Cold water flows directly from the water supply to all faucets and toilets. Some cold water is fed directly into the hot water supply system that may be oil-fired, electric or gas-fired hot water tanks. In some systems, the water heater serves also as the heating system by circulating hot water through a coil inside an air handler.

Vent system allows drains to function and exhausts gases related to sewage systems.

Hot water circulates from the heat source (boiler or water tank) to all fixtures throughout the house. Hot water temperatures should be set professionally at the hot water source to prevent scalding accidents, particularly in homes with small children.

Water heater

Drain and vent system

Cold water supply

Boiler

Water meter

Most water supplies come from a city water utility. Water enters from city utility and is metered where it comes into the house. The alternative is a **Well Water Supply** system that requires homeowner periodic attention (see p. 51).

The main drain system leads to a city sewer system. In some suburban homes where sewer systems are not installed, a **Septic Tank** is installed. Septic systems require homeowner maintenance that you should know about (see p. 51).

The boiler heats hot water, while the supply line feeds cold in and hot out. Inside the boiler is a coil that over time can become corroded and require replacement by a plumber.

Water from a municipal water supply requires no storage system in the house. If you have a well, water is pumped into a water storage tank. From there it's distributed by pipes into the water heater for heating and to the cold water supply.

The drain system is a combination of 2-inch (and larger) pipes that carry drain water and toilet water into the main waste pipe that leads to the municipal sewage system, or into a septic tank if you live in an area without a sewage system.

The vent system is a network of 2-inch pipes that attach to each of the primary drain pipes and vents through the roof. The purpose of the system is to provide air pressure to enable the drains to function, and to exhaust harmful sewage gases through the roof.

SHUTTING OFF THE WATER SUPPLY

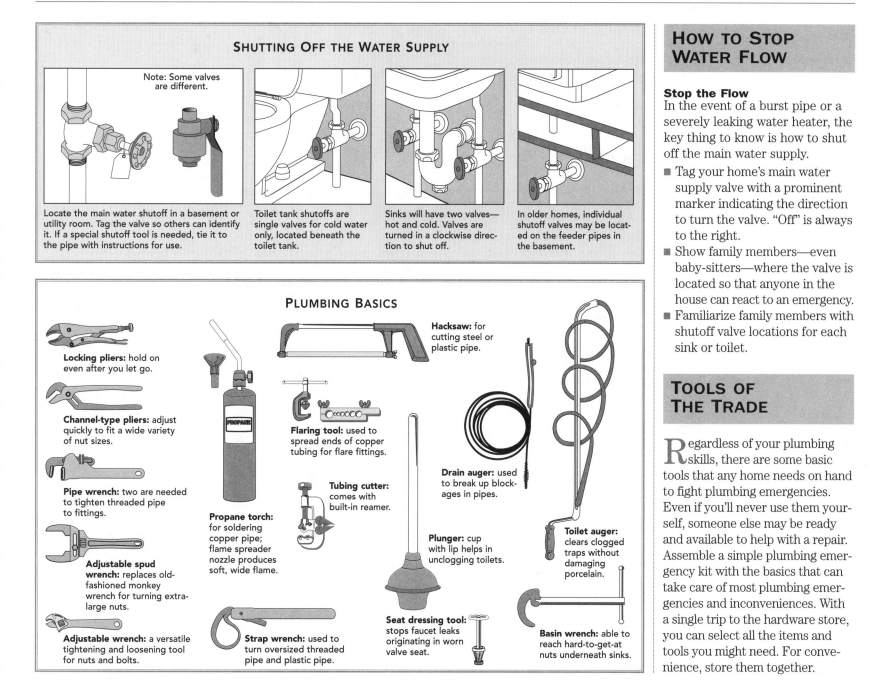

Note: Some valves are different.

Locate the main water shutoff in a basement or utility room. Tag the valve so others can identify it. If a special shutoff tool is needed, tie it to the pipe with instructions for use.

Toilet tank shutoffs are single valves for cold water only, located beneath the toilet tank.

Sinks will have two valves—hot and cold. Valves are turned in a clockwise direction to shut off.

In older homes, individual shutoff valves may be located on the feeder pipes in the basement.

PLUMBING BASICS

Locking pliers: hold on even after you let go.

Channel-type pliers: adjust quickly to fit a wide variety of nut sizes.

Pipe wrench: two are needed to tighten threaded pipe to fittings.

Adjustable spud wrench: replaces old-fashioned monkey wrench for turning extra-large nuts.

Adjustable wrench: a versatile tightening and loosening tool for nuts and bolts.

Propane torch: for soldering copper pipe; flame spreader nozzle produces soft, wide flame.

Strap wrench: used to turn oversized threaded pipe and plastic pipe.

Flaring tool: used to spread ends of copper tubing for flare fittings.

Tubing cutter: comes with built-in reamer.

Hacksaw: for cutting steel or plastic pipe.

Plunger: cup with lip helps in unclogging toilets.

Seat dressing tool: stops faucet leaks originating in worn valve seat.

Drain auger: used to break up blockages in pipes.

Toilet auger: clears clogged traps without damaging porcelain.

Basin wrench: able to reach hard-to-get-at nuts underneath sinks.

HOW TO STOP WATER FLOW

Stop the Flow

In the event of a burst pipe or a severely leaking water heater, the key thing to know is how to shut off the main water supply.

- Tag your home's main water supply valve with a prominent marker indicating the direction to turn the valve. "Off" is always to the right.
- Show family members—even baby-sitters—where the valve is located so that anyone in the house can react to an emergency.
- Familiarize family members with shutoff valve locations for each sink or toilet.

TOOLS OF THE TRADE

Regardless of your plumbing skills, there are some basic tools that any home needs on hand to fight plumbing emergencies. Even if you'll never use them yourself, someone else may be ready and available to help with a repair. Assemble a simple plumbing emergency kit with the basics that can take care of most plumbing emergencies and inconveniences. With a single trip to the hardware store, you can select all the items and tools you might need. For convenience, store them together.

41

EASY-TO-SOLVE PROBLEMS

The most likely plumbing emergencies you'll be called upon to attend are unclogging stopped or slow drains, and the occasional plugged toilet. Once in a while you may also want to change the washers in dripping faucets. In dire emergencies, such as frozen pipes—or worse, burst pipes—knowing how to shut off the water is the first defense against serious damage.

Repairs to minor leaks can be easily managed with tape and simple clamp devices available at any hardware outlet. Frequently, these repairs, particularly with commercial clamps, will last for years. But if a leak persists, you'll need more serious repairs. These can be made with relative ease using a propane torch and solder on copper pipes or special adhesives and fittings on plastic pipes.

Steel and older lead pipes require special equipment, such as thread-cutting tools. For the inexperienced, serious pipe repairs requiring the use of a torch are best left to a plumber.

LAME DRAINS

Blocked or Really Slow

If a drain leaves standing water in a sink or bathtub, and nothing obvious has been dropped down the opening, almost any chemical cleaner will dissolve the soap scum, old hair and grease that is causing the blockage. Brand names off the grocery shelf generally work well. Professional plumbers use heavy-duty chemicals, which you can purchase at plumbing supply outlets.

Really Blocked

Be sure that nothing serious has been dropped into the drain —wadded tissue, toys or, in the kitchen, utensils or excess cooking

LEAKING PIPES SOLUTION

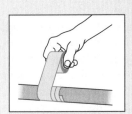
Control small leaks with multiple layers of electrician's tape.

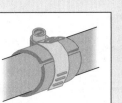
A spring clamp tightened over a rubber seal is a good temporary fix.

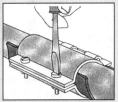
Special pipe repair clamp kits do an almost permanent job.

$ AVOID PLUMBER RIP-OFFS

1. See if a friend or neighbor knows a good plumber. If a neighbor has had recent work on their home, find out who did the plumbing.
2. Check the local *Yellow Pages* and newspaper classifieds.
3. Verify that any plumber you call is licensed and insured. Ask about hourly charges. If you can describe the problem, ask for approximate prices on major replacement parts. Then call a reputable plumbing supply house to compare prices.
4. Ask a local plumbing supply dealer to recommend a plumber. Then ask how long they've been dealing with that plumber.
5. Be prepared to describe what you think needs to be done in detail. That way the plumber can at least give you a ballpark number on the repair costs.
6. Check the business reputation with the Better Business Bureau. This will apply more for major work than minor repairs, but if you can't rely on any of the above sources, this is a good option.
7. If the problem is specific, such as badly clogged sewer lines, call a franchised specialist, like *Roto-Rooter*. Generally you can rely on nationally franchised businesses. Workers are trained and equipped for the task.

⚠ CAUTION: DRAIN CLEANERS ALERT

Chemical cleaners contain acids or alkalies. They are dangerous. Follow the instructions precisely and observe all the precautionary measures— especially, wear rubber gloves, clothing that you don't mind damaging (if the acid splashes) and eye protection, in the event of splashback. **Never mix two different types of chemical cleaners.** Avoid breathing the vapors while the chemicals do their work. Store drain cleaners well away from children's reach.

Trap toxic fumes with an inverted container over the drain.

DRAIN PATROL

Bathrooms equipped with mechanical drain stoppers in the sinks and bathtubs are notorious for slow drains. The stoppers must be frequently extracted to remove hair and grime build-up. Stoppers generally come out with a twisting pull upward. Sink models are held in place with a rod system. Loosen the screws on the rods to shift them out of the way to remove the stopper. The toughest part of this job is crawling under the sink.

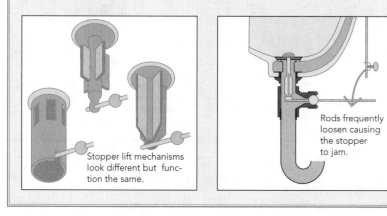

Stopper lift mechanisms look different but function the same.

Rods frequently loosen causing the stopper to jam.

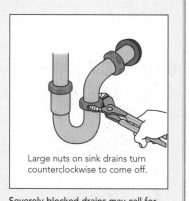

Large nuts on sink drains turn counterclockwise to come off.

Severely blocked drains may call for removal of the P-trap below the sink. Use wide-mouth pliers to turn the nuts. CAUTION: Wear rubber gloves and eye protection if chemical drain cleaners were used beforehand.

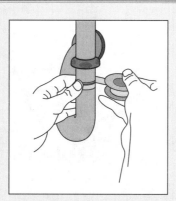

Corroded P-traps are easily replaced with new ones from the hardware store. Use plumber's tape or joint compound to seal the joints so they don't leak. Fill the sink, remove the plug and observe the trap for leaks.

waste. At the bottom of every drain (under the sink), is a U-joint or P-trap (so called because of its shape). It traps waste water to prevent sewer gases from entering the house through drains. Don't attempt to force debris down the drain with a coat hanger or screwdriver. In fact, such action could puncture the pipes. If commercial drain cleaner fails, use a plunger (see next page).

If All Fails

If previous efforts fail, you will need to try the mechanical route. Use wide-mouth pliers or a pipe wrench to unscrew the coupling nuts on the U-joint or trap beneath the sink. Turn counterclockwise to loosen. Wear rubber gloves and eye protection. Use a bucket to capture the water runoff.

Remember, all the water in the sink will come out that drain when you remove the trap. Generally, the worst of the blockage will be found in the trap. If it is badly corroded, get a new one at the hardware store.

Good idea: Have a new P-trap on hand before removing an old one with visible corrosion, as it will usually crack during removal.

Reassembled traps should fit snugly. Test for leaks by running the water while checking under the sink for drips.

Still Blocked

Now is the time to call a plumber or get a *drain auger* capable of reaming the drain pipes. Drain augers can be rented and cost less than a plumber. But chances are you'll use it only once or twice in a lifetime.

HARD WATER BLOCKAGES

Homes fed by mineral-rich well water are susceptible to pipe corrosion from lime, calcium and other deposits. Over time, this will cause slow or completely blocked drains. Generally, a regular treatment of commercial liquid drain openers will minimize the problem. If total stoppage occurs, use a drain auger or long-bladed screwdriver to scrape away corrosive buildup. Then use a plunger and firm water spray to disperse the debris.

JEWELRY DOWN THE DRAIN

Wedding rings and earrings frequently fall into sink drains. When this happens, don't panic. Avoid running water. Remove the drain trap. More than likely, the jewels are there.

If jewels fall into a garbage disposal, tape over the switch or turn off the circuit breaker. Use kitchen tongs to lift out the jewels. A small mirror and flashlight in the drain can help pinpoint the item while you fish with the tongs.

CLOGGED TOILETS

First, minimize the damage by not flushing a second time. Be patient. The water level will drop slowly, leaving room for you to clear the drain. If you know what is causing the blockage (e.g., a sanitary napkin or wad of tissue), attempt to pull the item up rather than force it into the lower drain where it might lodge more tightly. You can reach up the throat of the bowl (rubber gloves are probably desirable) and try to clear the blockage. Liquid chemical drain cleaners are not usually recommended for toilet stoppages.

Try a plunger if you can't dislodge the object. One with a tuck-in lip works best. Other designs generally give poor results and create a mess.

Be persistent—generally several forceful attempts are needed. *Warning:* Energetic use of a plunger can break the wax seal under the commode, causing a leak which will seep out from the commode base.

If the plunger fails and you have a closet auger, use it. If you do not succeed, a plumber or drain specialist will have to either remove the toilet or use a power auger.

PLUNGING THAT WORKS

Using a plunger: This would appear to be obvious. However, "plunger" is a misleading term because you really want the device to withdraw lodged drain matter, not necessarily force it down.

1. Be sure there's water in the sink or tub, enough to cover an inch or so of the plunger. If you have previously used chemical cleaner, run plenty of water to dilute the chemicals. Wear goggles and rubber gloves to protect against splashing, and keep curious children well back.
2. Plug the sink overflow opening with a rag to maximize the force of the plunger.
3. Secure a firm grip on the plunger, centering it over the drain. Force it up and down rapidly without pulling it from the water.
4. Strong tugging motion creates a vacuum and pulls debris up out of the drain, ultimately breaking up the blockage.

In the toilet: Follow the same principle, only pry out the folded inner cup on the plunger (if so equipped) to better fit the bowl opening.

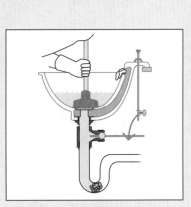

A plunger is most effective when there is 1 or 2 inches of water in the sink or tub. Wear gloves to protect from chemicals previously used to clear the blockage.

FROZEN WASTE PIPES

In extremely cold weather, consider a frozen drain as a possible cause of clogging before calling for professional help. Household waste pipes (sewer pipes) are larger and generally not prone to freezing unless they are located in a crawl space, external wall or unheated basement.

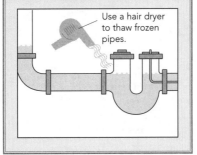

Use a hair dryer to thaw frozen pipes.

CLEARING STOPPED TOILETS

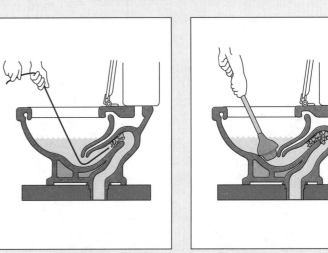

A clothes hanger with a bent hook at one end can be manipulated into the toilet opening. Wrap with an old sock to prevent scratching the porcelain.

A plunger, with the cupped lip inserted into the toilet mouth is effective, but messy. A plumber's auger works better for tough jobs.

TOILET TANK REPAIRS

Don't be daunted by toilet tank ailments. Although the innards of the tank may look complicated, the operating principle is simple and most problems are easy to fix.

All toilet tanks are fundamentally the same. Water fills the tank through a filler tube until it reaches a fixed level. A float valve controls the water level and shuts it off when the tank is filled. When the flush lever is depressed, it lifts the valve at the bottom of the tank and the water rushes into the toilet bowl.

The most common problems result from worn washers and seals, and parts that are corroded from years immersed in water.

Update Old Systems?

If your toilet system is 20 years old or more, most likely the tank components are the older, less efficient *float ball* and *ball cock* design. You may want to consider replacing it with a flush tank kit from a hardware or plumbing supply store. Such kits feature a tank fill valve design that requires no float arm or float ball. It takes about an hour to replace the assembly, and the kits come with clear, diagrammed instructions. It is generally less expensive to replace outdated systems with new parts.

EMERGENCY FLUSH

If the water is turned off for some reason, you can still flush your toilet one time since there's water stored in the toilet tank. After that, however, you can flush a toilet by simply pouring a bucket of water into the toilet bowl.

If authorities warn of a water shutoff, it's a good idea to fill the bathtub with water for such emergencies.

MORE EFFICIENT, LESS TROUBLE

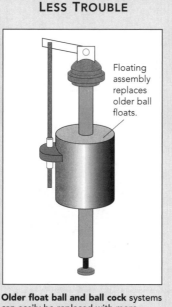

Floating assembly replaces older ball floats.

Older float ball and ball cock systems can easily be replaced with more efficient valve unit kits that do not use float arms. The kits come with clear instructions.

When toilets go wrong, here's what to look for...

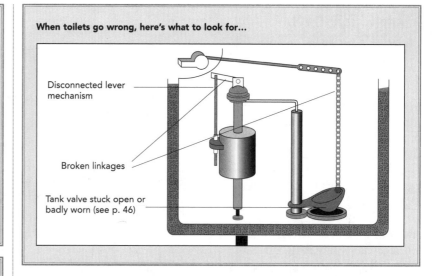

Disconnected lever mechanism

Broken linkages

Tank valve stuck open or badly worn (see p. 46)

TROUBLES WITH OLDER SYSTEMS

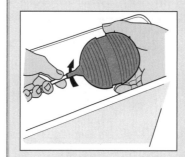

Seat washers wear and corrode.

Water won't stop flowing?
Open the tank lid. Chances are that water is running into the overflow tube. If so, the float device needs to be adjusted. Unscrew the float ball, turning counterclockwise. Shake it. If there's water inside, replace the ball. If not, replace it on the float ball rod. Bend the rod downward so the float ball shuts off water flow sooner.

If that doesn't work...
Chances are that the seat washer inside the plunger mechanism is badly worn. Keep track of how you remove the pieces to expose the washer so you can replace them in the same order. If parts are worn and corroded from hard water, consider replacing the whole valve assembly with one of the kits (pictured left). It is not a difficult task.

TANK & BOWL LEAKS

Other than *float valve* problems, the most common leaks in toilet tanks are caused by the *flush valve*—the opening in the bottom of the toilet tank that lets the water flow into the bowl. Usually, a leaky flush valve can be restored by giving it a good cleaning with steel wool or an abrasive pad. If the valve seat is corroded, or the *tank ball* rubber is cracked or worn, it will require replacement.

Simple Test for Valve Leaks

- Flush the toilet and wait until the tank refills. Pour a tablespoon of food coloring into the tank and wait several minutes. If the water in the bowl has changed color, the *tank valve* is leaking.

Kits can be obtained through a plumbing supply or hardware store. Knowing the toilet model is helpful, but not essential because the kits are universal. In general, plumbing supply houses are the best kit source.

- First, they are more likely to have parts for your model toilet tank.
- Second, the quality of the kits may be more professional—having brass parts instead of plastic.

FIXING LEAKING TANK VALVES

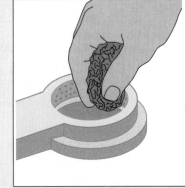

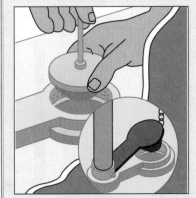

Turn off the tank water feed. Flush the toilet and soak up excess water with a sponge. Remove the flush valve (older models) turning counterclockwise. Newer models may have a hinged flapper valve. Clean and examine for wear and cracking.

Clean the valve seat with steel wool or fine sandpaper. Run your finger around the rim checking for corrosion, cracks or rough spots. The flush valve must fit snugly in the valve seat to maintain a watertight seal. If it's worn, replace both components.

REPAIRING TANK SEALS & WATER FEEDS

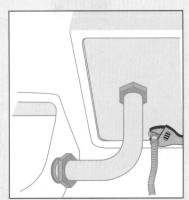

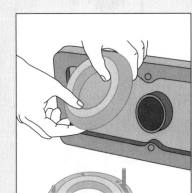

Older feed lines to toilet tanks are usually copper tubing. If leaking, replace the lines with newer flexible hoses. Buy kits for replacing the lines and the filler tube seals at plumbing supply houses or hardware stores.

Seals between the tank and the toilet bowl will leak over time. Sometimes simply tightening the bolts inside the tank will stop the leak. If not, remove the feed line and the bolts to replace the seals with a gasket kit. Also, use new bolts.

DRIPPING FAUCETS

Dripping faucets waste gallons of water every year. If left uncorrected/unrepaired they can cause damage that is expensive to fix. Repairs are not complex and require simple tools: screwdriver, oversized pliers and parts—washers, O-rings and seals found from any hardware store. These can be purchased as variety packs for fitting multiple faucet designs. Plan to work with one faucet at a time, turning off the individual water supply to the faucet.

Disassembly Tips

First, shut off the water. Most faucets have decorative caps that need to be pried off with a screwdriver to access screws. Once you remove the screws and pry off the handles, disassembly steps become obvious. Identify the damaged washer—usually it is dried, cracked or split. Select as close a match as possible from your variety pack and reassemble the fixture.

Single-lever faucets, generally found in kitchens, are more complex than regular fixtures. Before attempting the repair, identify the brand of faucet you have and visit a plumbing supply dealer for a repair kit specifically for your make and model. This is important because unlike regular fixtures, parts are not standardized from one fixture to another.

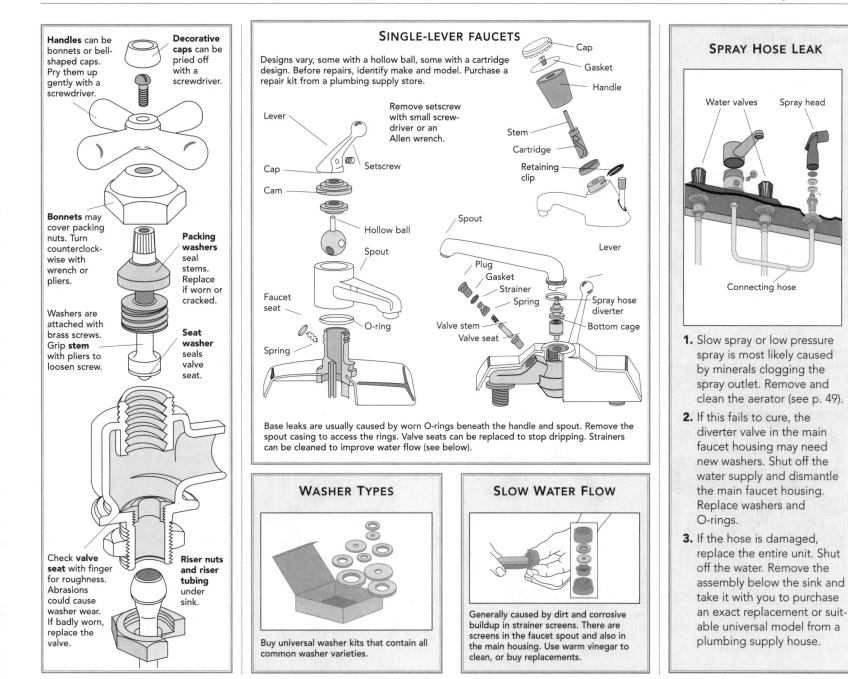

Handles can be bonnets or bell-shaped caps. Pry them up gently with a screwdriver.

Decorative caps can be pried off with a screwdriver.

Bonnets may cover packing nuts. Turn counterclockwise with wrench or pliers.

Packing washers seal stems. Replace if worn or cracked.

Washers are attached with brass screws. Grip **stem** with pliers to loosen screw.

Seat washer seals valve seat.

Check **valve seat** with finger for roughness. Abrasions could cause washer wear. If badly worn, replace the valve.

Riser nuts and riser tubing under sink.

SINGLE-LEVER FAUCETS

Designs vary, some with a hollow ball, some with a cartridge design. Before repairs, identify make and model. Purchase a repair kit from a plumbing supply store.

Lever

Remove setscrew with small screwdriver or an Allen wrench.

Cap

Setscrew

Cam

Hollow ball

Spout

Faucet seat

O-ring

Spring

Cap

Gasket

Handle

Stem

Cartridge

Retaining clip

Spout

Lever

Plug

Gasket

Strainer

Spring

Spray hose diverter

Valve stem

Valve seat

Bottom cage

Base leaks are usually caused by worn O-rings beneath the handle and spout. Remove the spout casing to access the rings. Valve seats can be replaced to stop dripping. Strainers can be cleaned to improve water flow (see below).

WASHER TYPES

Buy universal washer kits that contain all common washer varieties.

SLOW WATER FLOW

Generally caused by dirt and corrosive buildup in strainer screens. There are screens in the faucet spout and also in the main housing. Use warm vinegar to clean, or buy replacements.

SPRAY HOSE LEAK

Water valves

Spray head

Connecting hose

1. Slow spray or low pressure spray is most likely caused by minerals clogging the spray outlet. Remove and clean the aerator (see p. 49).

2. If this fails to cure, the diverter valve in the main faucet housing may need new washers. Shut off the water supply and dismantle the main faucet housing. Replace washers and O-rings.

3. If the hose is damaged, replace the entire unit. Shut off the water. Remove the assembly below the sink and take it with you to purchase an exact replacement or suitable universal model from a plumbing supply house.

FROZEN PIPES

In severe cold, especially in older, underinsulated homes, pipes can freeze. The symptoms are extremely low water flow or none at all. Freezing generally occurs where the pipes are the narrowest and the house temperature is the lowest. Basements and northern exposure walls are the usual areas. Isolate where the pipe is most likely frozen by testing water flow in various parts of the house and work from the frozen faucet back toward the suspect location of freezing.

Melt the Ice

Leave the faucets open. Use a heat lamp or hair dryer to warm the frozen area. Generally, this only takes a few minutes before the water is flowing. A propane torch is not recommended. It will melt plastic pipes and there's the fire danger.

Cold Weather Tip

Open faucets so water drips slightly during freezing conditions. This maintains sufficient water flow in the pipes to keep them from freezing. Pipes where the problem is constant can be wrapped with insulating foam or even special electrical tape to prevent freezing.

Prolonged ice formation in the pipes will cause them to burst, so it's critical to take action that will protect pipes that are most likely to freeze.

Steps for Extreme Cold

If severe cold is expected and you have pipes susceptible to freezing, consider:

- Running water into a tub to have available in the event of freezing.
- Turning on all faucets, then shutting water off at the main supply. This will drain pipes so they can't freeze. During the day, turn the water back on.

Permanent Cure for Freezing

Several quick techniques will prevent freezing. The easiest is to insulate with foam pipe liner that comes in various lengths and diameters. For pipes running through an outside wall location, it's best to use electrical heat tape—a broad band that works off electricity.

DISPOSAL DILEMMAS

Kitchen sink garbage disposals will jam if solid objects such as paper clips, large pits, cutlery, bottle caps or even jewelry lodge in the grinding mechanism. If the unit hums loudly but won't turn, something is stuck.

- Switch off the power for the unit—most are switched at the countertop or beneath the sink. **Never reach into the disposal with your hand, even with the power off.**
- Use a flashlight to check for the obstruction. If it's large, use pliers or kitchen tongs to lift it out. If you can't see anything obvious, the jam may simply be a small object.
- Use a broom handle wedged against the grinder to free the turntable. Once it turns, restore power.
- If this doesn't work, look for a red button beneath the sink at the bottom of the disposal. This is an overload switch. Push it in. If it clicks, it's reset. Try the power again. If it doesn't work, check the unit's circuit breaker.

Anti-jamming Systems

Some manufacturers install devices that reverse the grinding wheel to release jams. Check the casing of the unit (and the owner's manual) to see if such a device is installed. With the

QUICK FIXES FOR FROZEN PIPES

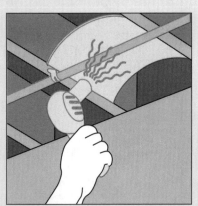

The freeze point is most likely near an elbow in the pipe located near an outer wall or area where there's a draft. With the faucet on, heat the pipe with a hair dryer.

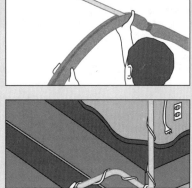

Insulate pipes prone to freezing with foam tubing from hardware stores. Or for extreme cold, wrap pipes with heat tape that plugs into an electrical outlet.

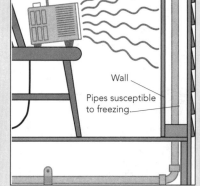

Pipes between walls will need prolonged exposure to a heat source. Place an electric heating unit close to the wall. Blow in insulation to stop future freezing.

power on, pressing the anti-jam button should free the impeller.

If you can't unstick the grind wheel, then it's time to call a professional.

Much more common is the provision of a hex wrench with the disposal. Insert it into the nut in the underside of the disposal and work it back and forth to release the jam.

Also, if a disposal has not been used for several months, it can rust up and may need to be replaced.

DISHWASHER DISTRESS

Most dishwasher failures don't need professional help. Save a service call by first going to the back of the owner's manual where troubleshooting charts take you step by step through common dishwasher ailments. Mechanical or electrical breakdowns generally occur in the pump or are belt

A SHARPER, FRESHER DISPOSAL

Freshen up and sharpen up your disposal with ice cubes and lemons. Treat the disposal to about 2 cups of ice and 1 cup of vinegar and turn it on. Add lemon (or orange) peels for a twist of freshness.

failures or solenoid switch problems. These need a professional. But poor cleaning, slow draining and water backups can, in most cases, be fixed by you.

Won't Switch On?
- Check the timer settings, that the door is properly latched and that the wall switch is on.
- Then check the circuit breaker or fuse.

Doesn't Drain or Slow Drain?
- Check the garbage disposal, where many dishwashers drain the waste water.
- Cycle the disposal if it's full.
- Also, check the filter in the bottom of the dishwasher. Most models have cuplike screens that become clogged with food debris over time.
- As a last resort, detach the drain hose where it flows into the sink drain or garbage disposal. The line must be clear and kink-free.

Leaks & Foam?
- Water and foam leaking out from around the door seal is the result of too much dishwasher detergent, or from the use of nondishwasher detergent, such as dishwashing liquid soap. Use a cup or glass to bail most of the water out and run the machine through its complete cycle.

DELETING DISH SPOTS

Most common dishwasher complaints are spotting and filming of glassware and dishes. This is not a machine problem as much as a hard water problem. Try this remedy:

➤ Wash and rinse spotted dishes as usual.

➤ Remove all silverware and metal items.

➤ Pour 2 cups of vinegar into a bowl and set it on the bottom rack.

➤ Do not add detergent.

➤ Run the spotted dishes through a wash cycle.

If the vinegar rinse fails, repeat the process using ¼ cup of citric acid crystals (from the drug store) instead of vinegar.

Citric acid crystals are also great for removing well water brown stains from the inside of the dishwasher.

DISHES STILL SOILED AFTER WASHING?

Check the hot water temperature and the water pressure. Too little or insufficiently hot water will leave your dishes dirty.

TOXINS IN YOUR WATER

Hot, moist air expelled by dishwashers, washing machines and showers can be laden with toxins like chloroform, benzene, trichloroethane and radon, according to Richard L. Corsi, PhD, associate professor of civil engineering, University of Texas at Austin. These compounds come from the tap water itself…and from detergents containing chlorine.

Self-defense: Have your water tested by a certified lab. To locate one, contact your state's water-quality department or the EPA's

CLEANING AERATORS & SHOWER HEADS

Remove the shower head with expansion pliers or a wrench that fits. Then use a pin and old toothbrush to clear mineral deposits and scum from the spray holes and vanes. Or try a product called *Lime-A-Way* to dissolve stubborn mineral and rust deposits.

Safe Drinking Water Hotline at 800-426-4791.

WATER HEATER WOES

Water heaters rarely rebel. They are among the most durable and reliable appliances, so chances are if your hot water cools, it's a minor problem that you can resolve without a plumber.

Tank in a Fuzzy Coat

A water heater is simply a water tank wrapped with insulation. Water flows into it from the main water supply and is heated by either electric elements—like oven elements—or a burner fired by gas or oil.

What Can Go Wrong?

Leaks develop, usually at the bottom where sediment and mineral deposits eventually eat through the tank lining. If such leaks occur, you need a new water heater and a professional to install it. Before you pay, however, check the warranty (sometimes labeled on a sticker on the tank). It may be covered. If it leaks badly or drains, turn off the gas, oil or electric heat supply.

Valve leaks are more easily fixed. Water heaters have two valves: one at the bottom to drain water and one at the top, a *pressure relief valve*. Water in the tank is under pressure similar to your household water supply, and if it becomes too hot, the valve is designed to relieve

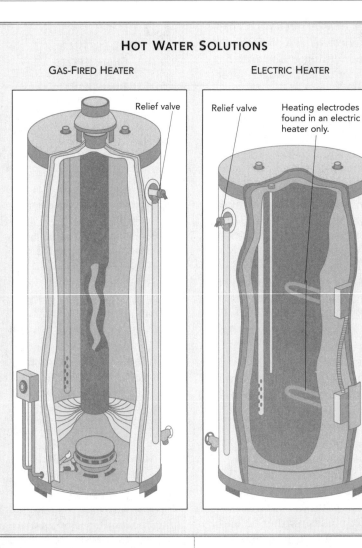

HOT WATER SOLUTIONS

GAS-FIRED HEATER — Relief valve

ELECTRIC HEATER — Relief valve — Heating electrodes found in an electric heater only.

pressure. Occasional leaking from the valve is not an immediate problem. Drain the tank via the drain valve in an emergency. Attach a hose and run it to a handy drain. **Caution: Opening any valve on the hot water tank will release dangerously hot water.**

Problems You Can Fix

Over time, heating elements, whether gas or electric, attract mineral deposits and lose their heating efficiency. If your hot water seems cooler than it used to be and the heater is several years old and your water is fairly hard,

then increasing the thermostat setting will often remedy the situation temporarily.

Suddenly Cold Water

Chances are the heating element is not doing its job.

- *Electric heaters:* First check the fuses or circuit breakers. If they've activated, reset them. If the problem persists, there's possibly a heating element problem. You will need to contact a plumber.
- *Gas heaters:* The pilot light may have extinguished. Check at the bottom for the bluish glow of the pilot. If none is visible, follow the printed instructions (on all gas water heaters) to relight the pilot.
  If the pilot reignites, you should hear a firm "whump" sound as the burner lights. If the burner won't fire up, there's probably a worn or damaged gas flow safety device, called a thermocouple. This is not a complex repair, but should be done by a professional.
  If there is a strong smell of gas, do not attempt to reignite the pilot light. Call the gas utility immediately.
- *Oil-fired heaters:* They generally have a red reset button on the burner unit. Push it in to try to restart the burner. Check circuit breakers and all switches before calling for your oil service company. The burner probably requires cleaning.

WELL WATER KNOW-HOW

Homeowners with wells should understand how to cope with their water feed system. Hard water, mineral pollutants, even high radon content can affect well water.

Test Water Regularly

Home kits for testing water for specific contaminants are available at hardware stores (see p. 17). For comprehensive testing, you need a professional lab. Municipal health authorities can recommend a laboratory or check the telephone directory. Many water treatment equipment companies will test water free, but will probably find contaminants. You will want to retest with an independent lab before investing in expensive equipment. Testing should be done every 12 to 18 months to verify that your drinking water is safe.

Well Knowledge

If household water pressure is diminishing, check the water pump circuit breakers. Then check the tank itself. Most tanks have a water pressure gauge that should indicate more than 30 pounds of pressure. Also, tap the tank to determine the water level. It won't be completely full since air pressure at the top is what forces water through the pipes. If the tank is less than half full, however, and you're experiencing low water pressure, the system probably needs to be purged—air let out of the tank to allow more water to enter. Or there's a pump problem, which requires a professional to repair.

SEPTIC SYSTEM SAVVY

Septic systems take the place of sewer lines in many suburban and rural communities. A large concrete tank is buried near the house. Into one side of the tank flow household waste water and sewage. Bacteria in the tank convert waste to nitrates, which flow out into leaching fields where they are converted to beneficial nitrogen.

- Paint products, strong chemicals and excessive bleach can kill the bacteria and seriously damage the system.
- Kitchen grease, coffee filters, paper towels, sanitary napkins and facial tissues must be kept out of septic systems. Grease and soaps form a layer of scum on the septic effluent surface and eventually will clog the system. Other "indigestants" form a sludge layer at the tank bottom, which over time can destroy the system's productivity.

Regular Cleaning, Longer Life

The average septic system should be pumped out every three years, and more frequently if more than four people live in the house. Regular use of a garbage disposal or laundry facilities means more frequent cleaning. In fact, garbage disposals are not recommended because vegetable fiber does not break down readily.

Septic systems need bacteria "charges" to work efficiently. A monthly tablespoon of dry yeast down the toilet is a cheap way to do this and just as effective as any product you can buy.

TEST YOUR WELL WATER

When You Live...	Test For...
Near a landfill, factory (old or new) or dry cleaning plant	VOCs (volatile organic compounds), pH, total dissolved solids, chloride, sulfate and metals
Close to underground storage tanks, or if the water has traces of gasoline	VOCs and petroleum contaminants
In mining or gas drilling areas	Iron, manganese, aluminum and pH. Also, chloride, sodium, barium and strontium
In an agricultural region	Pesticides, bacteria content, nitrates, pH and total dissolved solids

Septic Entry Pipe

Sludge and sediment needs cleaning every three years by professionals.

Exit pipe to septic field

If drains back up—especially on lower floors and basements—and there is a strong sewage odor present, chances are the tank needs an emergency cleaning.

Electrical First Aid

Electricity problems are best left to licensed electricians who know the local building code, have the tools and parts for the job and can keep you safely away from potential harm. There are times, however, when the problem can't safely wait for a professional to arrive. Some electrical tasks are so simple that even a novice, working with the power off and some clear instructions, can solve the problem. The information in this section is a handy guide to common electrical problems.

ELECTRICITY BASICS

Electricity enters your house through a main entry panel, usually a gray electrical box located in the basement or utility room. The main power wires from the utility company attach near the roof or in some cases reach the house via underground connections. In every case, the utility company wires feed through a utility company meter and from there into the home. Generally, meters are located outside to facilitate reading by the utility company in order to bill you. In apartment complexes or condominiums, meters are typically located in a central location.

The utility cables feed into the main entry panel, which in very old homes might still be a fuse box. In any home built within the past 25 years, the main panel will be a service panel, sometimes called a circuit breaker box. The purpose of the service panel is to distribute the flow of electrical power through your home.

ABOUT CIRCUIT BREAKERS

Circuits are the individual wires that feed electricity to a building and are rated at 120 volts or 240 volts. Multiple circuits are needed to power a house. The larger the house, the more circuits there are in the main power supply box. Large appliances such as stoves, ovens, dishwashers, refrigerators and clothes dryers each have a dedicated 240 volt circuit. Generally, lights and receptacles are

---

TURNING OFF THE POWER

The one thing you need to know about electrical power in your home is **how to shut it off in an emergency**. Every family member should know the location of the main service panel and the main switch as well as how to shut off individual circuits so that power to the entire home is not shut down because of a problem in a single circuit.

There are two basic systems: circuit breakers found in homes built within the past 25 years, and fuse systems found in older homes. Both systems serve the same purpose: they "break" the electrical connection between the main power supply and the individual circuits that feed electricity throughout the house.

---

combined into 120 volts circuits. These are divided among the different rooms and areas of the house. A living room with several wall outlets and overhead lighting may be serviced by a single circuit, while an adjacent room might have its own circuit. This configuration is the same for fuses or circuit breakers.

Why Circuit Breakers Trip

Circuit breakers and fuses serve as "emergency valves." These devices disconnect the circuit if the amount of power passing through a given wire is too much for the wire size, such as when too much power is demanded by lights or appliances connected to one circuit. For example, if you plug in an electrical heater with all the lights on, the extra demand in that circuit will heat up the wires. Circuit breakers sense the danger and shut the power off ("trip") that circuit. In older buildings, fuses "blow" or burn out.

This simply means that your electrical protection system is working. The purpose of circuit breakers and fuses is to safeguard against electrical overload which could heat up the wires inside the walls and result in a fire.

What Is a Short Circuit?

All current flows according to alternating pathways. Electrical cables consist of three wires: black, white, green or bare copper. The black and white wires carry power to the appliances, going into the appliance on one and out on the other. Shorts occur when the electrical current fails to follow its usual path inside the wire and instead chooses a shorter path through a faulty contact point. This causes the current to rise to a very high and potentially dangerous level instantly. If the copper surface of any of these wires touch one another, either through worn power cords or some other wiring

POWER SHUTOFFS YOU SHOULD KNOW ABOUT

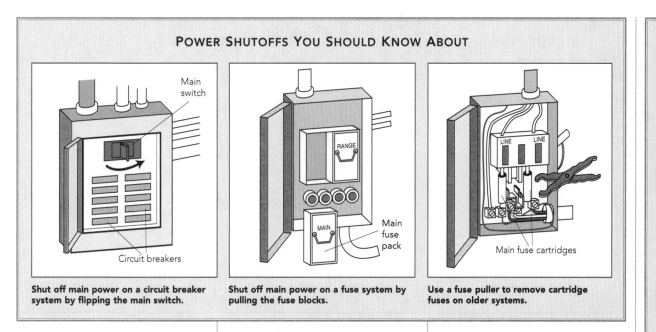

Shut off main power on a circuit breaker system by flipping the main switch.

Shut off main power on a fuse system by pulling the fuse blocks.

Use a fuse puller to remove cartridge fuses on older systems.

fault, the surge of heat causes the circuit breaker to react instantly, cutting off electricity to the affected circuit and preventing damage to the house.

WHEN CIRCUIT BREAKERS "TRIP"

If circuit breakers "trip," or fuses "burn," it indicates serious damage to one of the fixtures or appliances on the circuit.

- Check all lights and appliances for loose fittings or faulty switches.
- In particular, check extension cords for possible loose connections or exposed wiring. If there are cracks, brittleness

or burn marks in the wiring, replace the cord or a damaged plug.

Once you identify and repair the fault, reset the circuit breaker to the service position, noting if it holds or trips again.

Circuit Breaker Faults

It is unusual for circuit breakers themselves to fail, but if a breaker continues to trip and there is no obvious problem in the circuit, then the breaker itself might need replacing. Sometimes a faulty breaker will hum or crackle slightly. To change a breaker, the cover of the service panel needs to be removed and the **main power supply** must be shut off. This is best left to an electrician.

BLOWN FUSES

Older electrical systems are protected from overloading by fuses.

Fuse types are designed differently for each type of job they perform. Main fuses are cylindrical in shape and can have either bladed or cartridge-shaped contacts. Individual circuit fuses screw into sockets that are located in the main service panel.

A functioning fuse has a clear viewing window in which you can see the metal contact strip through which the current passes. When the fuse blows, the strip melts and breaks, often leaving a blackened viewing window.

CIRCUIT BREAKER RESETS

There are various types and styles of circuit breakers. Resetting them is usually a matter of pushing the switch back into position. With some models, it's necessary to push the switch all the way to the OFF position before putting it on again. Here are four models:

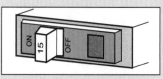

Tripped Position: Center. To reset: flip "off," then "on."

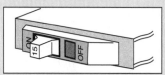

Tripped Position: Red flag showing switch to center. To reset: flip "off," then "on."

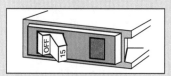

Tripped Position: Off. To reset: flip to the "on" position.

Tripped Position: Off. To reset: press in and release.

Follow Fuse Ratings

Fuses are rated by amperes, generally referred to as "amps." Most circuits are 15-amps or 20-amps. Larger appliances may draw as many as 30 amps. To avoid fire danger in a circuit, never replace a blown fuse with another fuse of a higher amp rating.

If your home is equipped with fuses, it is a good idea to keep a good supply of fuses of all ratings.

Circuit Breaker Fuses

Safety fuses with pop-out circuit breakers can be obtained at electrical supply houses. Such fuses offer the same convenience as circuit breakers (just press in the popped circuit button) and eliminate the need to keep a supply of regular fuses.

S-type Fuses

Some homes are equipped with fuses that will not allow you to insert a replacement with a higher amp rating. These safety fuses have two parts: the fuse itself and a socket that accepts the fuse. The socket is threaded into the normal fuse panel. The fuses then screw into the sockets. Each socket is designed to accept only a fuse of specific amperage. This way, there's never a danger of someone replacing a 15-amp fuse with a 20-amp fuse.

If you aren't ready for the expense of upgrading to a circuit breaker system, these S-type fuses are a safe alternative.

⚠ WIRE WARNING

If your electrical system is wired with aluminum or copper-clad aluminum wire, there is a higher risk of electrical fire than with conventional copper wiring. Heat expansion and contraction in aluminum wire is sufficient for the wire to work itself loose in switches and receptacles, making circuits susceptible to shorting. If your home is equipped with either of these wiring types, a safety check by a licensed electrician could avoid a serious problem.

SAFETY FUSES

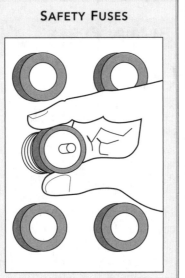

Safety fuses have pop-out "breakers" that can be reset. These fuses can replace regular fuses, saving the trouble of unscrewing and replacing fuses.

MAPPING CIRCUITS

Knowing which circuit breakers (or fuses) control which lights and electrical outlets is useful for emergencies. Most homes have circuits identified at the main power supply, noting various room areas covered by each circuit. If your panel box does not provide such information or if you want to detail the power routing to individual outlets and lights, here's how to do it.

Find a helper. Have that person walk from room to room with a small lamp or hair dryer, plugging the appliance into each outlet. You remain at the main panel.

As your helper plugs in the appliance, flip the circuit breaker off (or unscrew the fuse). As the power supply to each location terminates and can then be identified, mark it with a label.

Shortcut: Use an inexpensive walkie-talkie unit to communicate clear instructions to your helper. Or if you can't find an assistant, use a radio or vacuum cleaner to test each location. As you switch off the right circuit, the noise stops.

IS YOUR HOME SAFE?

If you find any hazards, check NEEDS FIXING and then have them fixed.

	TRUE	NEEDS FIXING
Electric outlets are not overloaded with lots of plugs.	☐	☐
Electric cords are in good condition.	☐	☐
Electric cords do not run under rugs or furniture legs or near hot appliances.	☐	☐
Electric appliances are used away from water.	☐	☐
People carry appliances by the handle, not the cord.	☐	☐
A multipurpose fire extinguisher is kept in the house.	☐	☐
All danger and warning signs are read and carefully followed.	☐	☐
Electric appliances that can get hot—such as heaters, toasters and light bulbs—are kept away from things that can burn.	☐	☐
Safety caps are inserted in outlets when small children are around.	☐	☐
Small appliances are turned off and/or unplugged when people leave home.	☐	☐
All extension cords, lights and appliances used outdoors are labeled for outdoor use.	☐	☐

Source: Electrical Safety World

ELECTRICAL TIPS & TACTICS

There are dozens of electrical chores you can accomplish on your own with a few general tools and clear instructions.

Once you have mastered how to shut down individual circuits in your home, repair and improvement jobs can be performed safely, potentially saving you a significant amount of money.

Moreover, electricians are not only expensive, but are difficult to secure for minor repairs.

The Right Tools Make It Easy

A few simple tools such as screwdrivers and pliers are basic. In addition you may want to consider some specialty items that make repair work faster and safer. In any event, these tools are useful to have available even if you are not going to tackle the repairs yourself.

Be Safe!

Finally, work safely. Double check that circuit breakers are off (or that fuses are removed). Use a **voltage tester** (see right) to check that no power is present in any wires you'll need to touch. Wear sneakers rather than leather-soled footwear.

ELECTRICAL TOOL BASICS

Here are the minimum tools and accessories to keep on hand for electrical troubles. Keep a small tool kit with all the items in one place. For electrical work, plastic-sheathed protective tools are recommended. Even if you aren't inclined to do the work yourself, it pays to have them on hand for repairs by others.

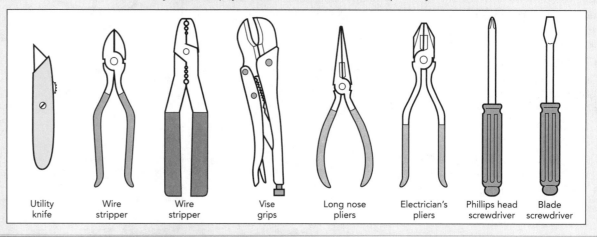

| Utility knife | Wire stripper | Wire stripper | Vise grips | Long nose pliers | Electrician's pliers | Phillips head screwdriver | Blade screwdriver |

TESTERS & CONNECTORS

NEON TEST LAMP

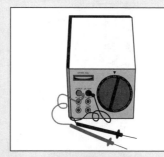

Basically two wires attached to a powered lamp tells you when power is present. Touching one wire to the positive side of a switch, the other to the negative side and if the lamp lights up, the power is on. Use it to test wires on any switch or fixture to be sure the power is off.

VOLTAGE/CONTINUITY TESTER

Voltage testers: Measures household and battery current. The tester is useful if you do any electrical work yourself. It meters the amount of voltage between two connections, such as a receptacle or light switch. It is also used for determining if there is electrical current (continuity) between wires.

WIRE NUT CONNECTORS

Connecting two or more wires in a fixture or outlet box is accomplished with wire nuts. These plastic nuts have interior threads which screw on and ensure greater contact. Important: Always be sure to twist together all wires before the nut is applied. It is also good practice to put electrical tape around the wire and the wire nut.

REPAIRING LAMPS & CORDS

If a lamp switch sticks, is loose or the bulb flickers when the light is turned off or on, chances are the switch is faulty or worn out.

- Unplug the lamp, check the cord carefully for breaks or bare wires.
- Plug it in and bend the cord back and forth every four to six inches. If there's no sign of cord trouble, the problem is probably in the switch.
- With the lamp unplugged, dismantle the lamp assembly, following the diagram.
- Check for loose or damaged wiring to determine what may have been causing the problem.
- If the cord is worn, consider replacing it now. Route the new cord through the fixture in the same manner as the old one was installed.
- When finished routing the new cord through the fixture, tie it off in an Underwriter's Knot, leaving approximately 2-inch leads.
- Strip the wires with wire strippers or a utility knife. Fix the "hot" lead to the brass screws on the socket, and the neutral lead to the silver screw.

- Then pull the cord down through the base. Make sure the insulator is properly seated covering the screws attaching the cord.
- Snap the upper section into the base. Plug in the cord and test the lamp.

BASIC LAMP ASSEMBLY: REPLACING A FRAYED CORD

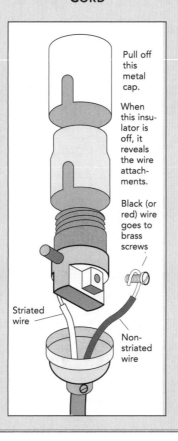

Pull off this metal cap.

When this insulator is off, it reveals the wire attachments.

Black (or red) wire goes to brass screws

Striated wire

Non-striated wire

UNDERWRITER'S KNOT

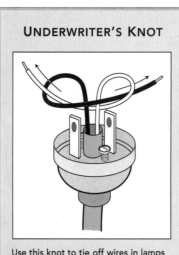

Use this knot to tie off wires in lamps and plugs. Pull the knot snug, then cut both ends to equal length.

REPLACING PLUGS

Appliances and light fixtures have only two basic plug types: flat and round. When plugs become loose, cracked or cause a short circuit, they should be replaced.

Unplug the fixture and use wire cutters to snip off the old plug.

Slip the cord into the body of the new plug and make the connections as displayed in the appropriate drawing on the right.

Polarized Plugs

Modern plugs are "polarized," meaning that one of the prongs is larger than the other. This ensures that the "hot" wire (usually copper) matches up with the "hot" side of an electrical outlet.

BASIC PLUG ATTACHMENTS

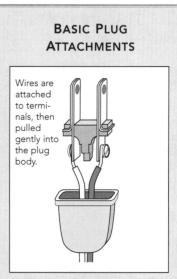

Wires are attached to terminals, then pulled gently into the plug body.

Flat cord plugs have a module that wires are attached to by screws.

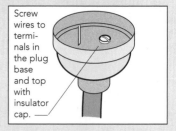

Screw wires to terminals in the plug base and top with insulator cap.

Round plugs need to have the wire knotted, then ends are twisted clockwise and screwed down.

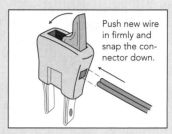

Push new wire in firmly and snap the connector down.

Quick-connect plugs have prongs inside that pierce the wires when the cap is closed.

SWITCH SAVVY

Changing a light switch is not complicated. With the circuit breaker turned off, there is no danger of electric shock.

However, if you find that the circuit breaker is indeed tripped, further checking is necessary to determine the location of the problem. In this case, calling an electrician would be the safest way to go.

Switch Basics

There are three basic switch configurations:

1. *A single-pole switch* controls one or more lights from one switch location. These are the simplest to work with.
2. *A three-way switch* allows lights or appliances to be controlled from two separate locations.
3. *A four-way switch* is used in conjunction with two 3-way switches to control lights and fixtures from yet a third location.

In most newer switches the wires are not attached to the terminal screws. Instead they are plugged into holes in the back of the switch. Release them by pressing a small-tipped screwdriver into the slot above the wire.

Should a wall switch fail, or in the event that you want to simply change the switch decor, you will need to know what's installed.

A, B, Cs of Switch Identity

- The first step: **Turn off the circuit breaker or remove the fuse** for the circuit on which you will be working.
- **Remove the switch plate by removing the screws, and expose the switch.** If two or more switches control the same lights, remove all the plates.
- **Verify the type of switch, single or three-way pole,** so you can purchase an identical replacement.

Read & Replace

Any new switch should be of the same amp and volt ratings as the one being replaced. Read the stamped information. CO/ALR means the switch can be used with copper or aluminum wire, while 15A-120V indicates amp and volt ratings. UL indicates code approval by Underwriters Laboratories.

Remove the two screws, top and bottom, that hold the switch in the electrical box. Then, gently pull the switch out of the box to expose the wires and terminals.

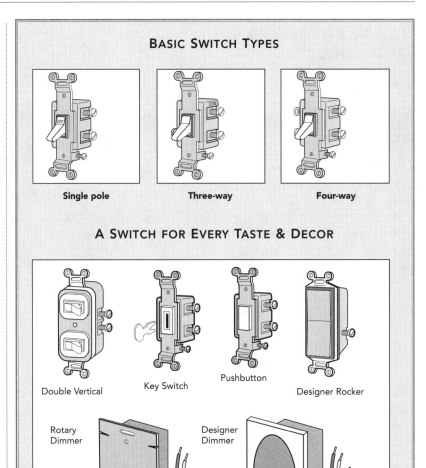

BASIC SWITCH TYPES

Single pole   Three-way   Four-way

A SWITCH FOR EVERY TASTE & DECOR

Double Vertical   Key Switch   Pushbutton   Designer Rocker

Rotary Dimmer   Designer Dimmer

There are many varieties of the three basic switch types. Some models are decorative (such as the rocker switch instead of a toggle), while others more pragmatic (such as internal glow lights to be viewed in the dark or "keyed" switches for security). Even audio-activated or motion-sensor switches can be used for convenience. Regardless of style and operation, the three basic wiring connection types remain the same—single pole, three-way and four-way.

CHANGING SWITCHES

You may want to replace a damaged switch or simply upgrade to a different style, such as a dimmer. Replacing an existing switch with a new one is easily accomplished and perfectly safe so long as you have turned off the power to the circuit.

Be certain not only that the replacement switch is the same type (single pole, three-way or four-way) as the old switch, and if possible obtain a replacement by the same manufacturer. Patent restrictions require each manufacturer to make physical changes in the construction of its switch. This means that sometimes connections are placed in different areas on the switch, which then requires a change in the internal wiring. The result can be a switch that looks quite different from the original even though it is wired to the same terminals as the switch it replaces.

If you would like to replace your single pole, "on-off" switch with a dimmer, you may do so easily; but be sure to get one with an on-off switch facility built in. As for applying a dimmer to a multiple-switching circuit using three- and four-way switches, you can get dimmer capability but must sacrifice the on-off capability unless additional hardware is added.

SINGLE POLE SWITCHES

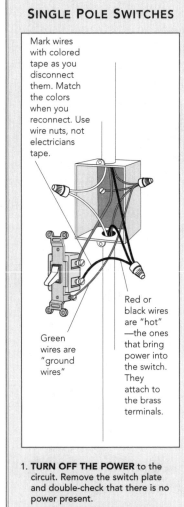

Mark wires with colored tape as you disconnect them. Match the colors when you reconnect. Use wire nuts, not electricians tape.

Green wires are "ground wires"

Red or black wires are "hot"—the ones that bring power into the switch. They attach to the brass terminals.

1. **TURN OFF THE POWER** to the circuit. Remove the switch plate and double-check that there is no power present.
2. Remove the switch from the connector box and draw a simple diagram indicating which power wires (black, white or red) are attached to which terminals on the switch. (Green or copper wires are grounds. They carry no power). Undo each wire and bend it away from the switch.
3. Reconnect the wires **in the exact same locations** as on the old switch.

3-WAY SWITCHES

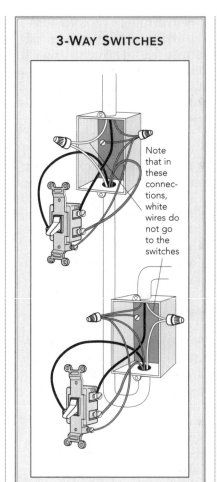

Note that in these connections, white wires do not go to the switches

Three-way switches are powered by 3-wire cable (black, white and red). Make careful note of which wire is attached to which terminal. A diagram is helpful.

1. **TURN OFF THE POWER** to the circuit. Double check with a tester to be sure. Note which part of the switch is the top.
2. Remove each wire from its terminal and bend it back from the switch. Tag the wires with tape to recall the exact terminal location.
3. Be sure the new switch is the same way up. Reattach the wires to the terminals. Test the switch.

INSTALL A DIMMER

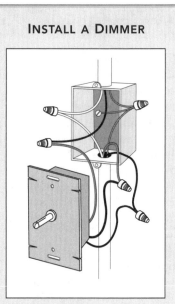

The dimmer must be compatible with either the single pole or 3-way/4-way switch it is replacing.

1. **TURN OFF THE POWER** to the switch.
2. Match the dimmer switch wires with the same color wires in the switch box.
3. Wires fasten with wire nuts provided with the switch.

On a 3-way or 4-way circuit, only one of the switches can be a dimmer.

Note: While a 3-way dimmer can and will provide dimming of the light, it will not by itself be able to provide actual switching from one circuit to the other. In other words, the switching function would have to be sacrificed if a dimmer by itself were added.

TROUBLESHOOTING OUTLETS

The duplex receptacles, or electrical outlets in your home seldom fail. They do get covered with paint, however. Occasionally an outlet might become worn and thus not hold a plug properly.

One of the most common reasons to change a receptacle would be to upgrade from an older two-prong type to a modern three-prong grounded outlet. This is, in fact, an important thing to do for safety reasons.

Replacing Older Outlets

If your home is older and the electrical outlets are not the grounded three-prong types, you may still have a grounding circuit available. In the past and currently, grounding is being provided by the metal of the conduit and that of the BX cable, and in the case of the plastic-covered cable, by the green or copper grounding wire.

Faulty Receptacles

If an outlet sparks when a cord is plugged in, that's an indication that the appliance is pulling a lot of current. If it shows blackening where the plugs go in, it is usually caused by a continual loose connection between the plug and the receptacle. Check to see if the current is appropriate and whether the item could be turned "off" before being plugged in. On the other hand, if the plug is loose,

THREE STEPS TO NEW OUTLETS

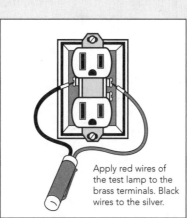

Apply red wires of the test lamp to the brass terminals. Black wires to the silver.

TURN THE POWER OFF that feeds the circuit. To be certain, either plug in a working lamp or test all wires with a neon test lamp before removing.

Pull the plug out of the electrical box to access the screw terminals.

Tug the fixture out of the electrical box. There are usually three wires, black, white and a green ground wire. Remove each of them and bend back.

If the plug wires are in holes, slip a small screwdriver into the slots to release the wires.

Modern outlet fixtures can be more easily installed by sliding the wires into the terminal holes. Black wires go to copper side, white to silver.

CHECK CIRCUIT INTEGRITY

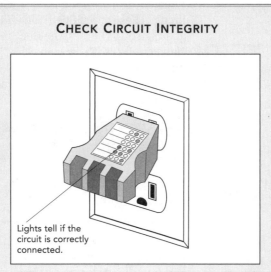

Lights tell if the circuit is correctly connected.

Useful: An outlet analyzer that plugs into receptacles (with the power on) and checks circuit integrity. Lights identify improper grounding or polarity. Available at electrical supply shops.

ORDER AN EASY HOW-TO VIDEO FOR UNDER $15

This video on electrical installation and connections is easy to understand and can help you...

- Understand basic electrical principles
- Run cable and install boxes, outlets, switches, lights and ground fault circuit interruptors.
- Make connections in boxes and service panels
- Install oven, microwave, fan and cooktop in kitchen
- Tie new wiring into existing wiring
- Understand 3-way and 4-way switches
- *Length:* Approximately 69 minutes

Order item #4008 from *www.hometime.com* or call 888-972-8453.

indicating poor physical contact or another reason, such as being very old and/or not having a ground terminal, then replace it. Replace receptacles with one of identical amp and volt ratings.

Be sure the circuit breaker is off (or the fuse removed). Use a voltage tester to be certain.

FIXING FLUORESCENTS

Fluorescent lighting fixtures can be a mystery because simply changing the lighting tube doesn't always fix a problem. This is because more can go wrong with fluorescent lamps than with incandescent. On the other hand, fluorescents last longer, burn cooler and cost less to operate than incandescent lights.

Fluorescent tubes contain a gas that glows when charged electrically. A phosphorus coating inside the tube glows when the tube is lit. Fluorescent tubes rarely burn out suddenly. When one won't light, wiggling it in the socket generally will get it started.

Which Tube for You?

There are three types of fluorescent tube: starter, rapid-starter and instant-start. The type is printed on the tube ends. You must replace tubes with the same type.

Replacement Technique

Double-pin tubes are rotated gently out of the rocker-type lamp holders. Push the new tube prongs into the slots and twist in either direction.

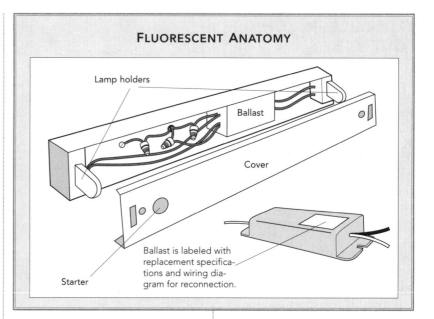

FLUORESCENT ANATOMY

Lamp holders

Ballast

Cover

Starter

Ballast is labeled with replacement specifications and wiring diagram for reconnection.

Instant-start tubes have a single prong. These are slipped one end at a time into the lamp holders. Handle tubes with caution. The phosphorus from a broken tube can irritate eyes, skin and respiratory system.

STARTER REPLACEMENT

The starter is a small cylinder tucked into the body of the lamp fixture, generally underneath the fluorescent tube.

If a new lamp fails to work, then the starter may be at fault. Remove it by turning counterclockwise. Replace starters with the identical rated unit.

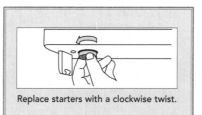

Replace starters with a clockwise twist.

BAD BALLAST?

Loud humming usually indicates a faulty ballast. After tubes and starter are replaced, if the fixture does not work, chances are it's the ballast. Turn the power off to the light and access the inside of the fixture. The replacement ballast must be the same size and type as the old one. Ratings are clearly marked

FIXING FLUORESCENTS

Symptom	Problem	Repair
Tubes flicker on and off. Erratic light.	Tube is burning out. Might also be cold temperature.	Gently wiggle the tube back and forth in the lamp holder. Replace tube. If cold, allow time to warm up.
Tubes new but won't start.	Bad or possibly faulty starter device	Replace the starter. Some have reset buttons to push. Starters twist out of the socket. If this doesn't work, replace the ballast.
Dark gray or black at ends.	Tube is burning out.	Replace tube.
Orange color at ends.	Internal filaments that heat the gas.	Allow a few moments to disappear. If persistent, replace the starter.
Buzzing or humming.	Faulty or worn ballast. Loose fittings.	Try tightening the screws in the fixture. Replace the ballast.

on the ballast label along with clear diagrams for rewiring the new ballast.

Tip: Don't mix the wires. Lay the new ballast on top of the old one. Disconnect and connect one wire at a time.

HANGING A NEW CEILING FIXTURE

The most complicated part of the job is getting the correct hardware. Underneath the old fixture lies an electrical box with a pair of screw holes that will accept most standard mounting hardware. If the fixture you want to install is new, chances are the manufacturer has included the right brackets for the weight of the fixture being installed.

Turn off the power to the fixture. Remove the screws anchoring the fixture.

- Undo the wire nuts. Test the wiring to ensure that no power is present.
- Remove all hardware associated with the old fixture.
- Install the fixture mounts for the new light connecting black wire to black and white to white. The green wire gets connected to the grounding terminal inside the box.

Ceiling Fans

The same installation procedures apply to a ceiling fan as to a light fixture. It is critical to use

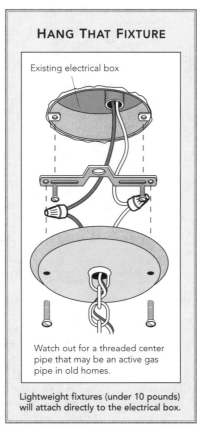

HANG THAT FIXTURE

Existing electrical box

Watch out for a threaded center pipe that may be an active gas pipe in old homes.

Lightweight fixtures (under 10 pounds) will attach directly to the electrical box.

hardware that will support the weight of the fixture. A primary consideration is whether the electrical box itself was properly installed in the ceiling so as to be certain that it will not detach and potentially injure persons below. Check for properly installed brackets holding the box to the ceiling studs, before installing any fan or heavy light fixture.

Generally, when you buy a ceiling fan, the manufacturer provides one or more universal

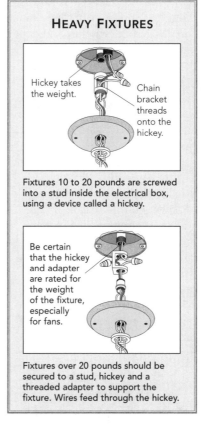

HEAVY FIXTURES

Hickey takes the weight.

Chain bracket threads onto the hickey.

Fixtures 10 to 20 pounds are screwed into a stud inside the electrical box, using a device called a hickey.

Be certain that the hickey and adapter are rated for the weight of the fixture, especially for fans.

Fixtures over 20 pounds should be secured to a stud, hickey and a threaded adapter to support the fixture. Wires feed through the hickey.

mounting brackets that allow attachment to the electrical box installed in the ceiling.

INSTALLING TRACK LIGHTING

The procedure for installing track lighting is very similar to hanging a light fixture. Here, too, the most complex part of the installation is mechanical, not electrical.

A track light fixture has a power module that fits under a standard ceiling light box. The power connections are similar, black wire to black wire, white to white, plus a green ground wire. The wires are connected to the power leads with wire nuts.

The track slips into the power module and carries power to the lights that are installed in the track.

There are many different designs, but they all operate on the same principle.

Tracking in a Straight Line

Turn off the power to the ceiling fixture.

- Install the track adapter plate over the ceiling junction box and attach the wires.
- Position the track adapter plate in the direction you want the track to run.
- Use a yardstick to pencil a line for the track to follow, so the track will be absolutely straight.
- Follow the manufacturer's instructions to anchor the track.
- Install the track lights and position for decor.
- Universal track adapter accepts a variety of fixtures.
- Check the packaging to ensure the cover plate hides the existing fixture hole and hardware.

Electrical Systems

While we can understand switching on a light and getting light or plugging in an appliance and having it work, there are dozens of electrical objects around us that appear to be completely baffling. Yet they can be easy to figure out and safe to work on as well as providing significant opportunity for savings if we do our own work.

TELEPHONE LINES & JACKS

The telephone man does not make house calls like he used to. Deregulation brought freedom of choice and reduction of service as far as many consumers are concerned. If you don't know how to install your own phone line, a new line could cost you anywhere from $50 to $100 for a technician.

The Only Shock: Price

Phone lines are powered by harmless low-voltage current—

so not only is it safe to work with them, but you can run them under carpets, behind window and door moldings or through the walls, floors or ceilings. Because the lines are small in diameter, you can install lines, jacks and phones with a simple drill, screwdriver and a visit to the hardware store.

Phone Connections

Almost all residential lines are 4-wire, "twisted pair" types. It only requires two of the wires to power your phone, so if you add another phone line in your home—say for a fax machine or a teenager—you don't need to wire the entire house. The telephone company will hook up the spare set of wires at your main telephone entry box, thus providing the signal for the new phone.

WALL PHONE INSTALLATION

If you buy a wall phone, you also will need a wall phone adapter. This is a device that fastens to the wall with regular drywall anchor. The adapters come with built-in modular telephone jacks and a universal faceplate. The telephone unit latches onto the faceplate.

Run the telephone cable up inside the wall or use telephone extension wires mounted on the wall with electrical staples.

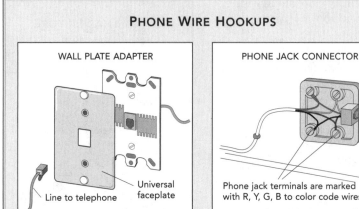

PHONE WIRE HOOKUPS

WALL PLATE ADAPTER

Line to telephone

Universal faceplate

If running wires from one part of the home to another, use telephone cable purchased from a hardware store. If lines are running from room to room, the flat telephone extension wire will do.

PHONE JACK CONNECTOR

Phone jack terminals are marked with R, Y, G, B to color code wires.

Residential phone lines have four wires: black, green, red and yellow. If you have a single phone line, two of the wires are used (usually red and black). For two lines, all four wires are used.

FIXING FAULTY PHONES

Problem	Repair
One phone & no dial tone	Check all cords for breaks, especially at the jacks. Try the phone at another outlet. If it is not the cord, try the telephone at a neighbor's home. If it works, contact the phone company regarding your line.
All phones dead	Verify with neighbors. In newer homes check for a "diagnostic" telephone jack at the phone service entry point. If you have such a jack, plug a phone into it. If a dial tone is present, the problem is in the home wiring. Check main service panel for loose or broken connections. No dial tone, contact the service provider.
Static on the phone line; erratic service	If you have a phone cord anti-tangle device, remove it. Damp weather conditions, local amateur radio, CB radio or nearby radio stations can cause interference. If persistent, install a modular filter obtained from a telephone service center.
Rapid busy signals	Usually indicates long-distance circuits are busy. Simply try later.

THERMOSTATIC CONTROL

Thermostats can affect your energy bills more than any other part of your heating and cooling system. Technological changes in thermostats in recent years have taken advantage of microprocessor computing to boost household energy efficiency.

If your home has a thermostat 10 years old or more, you can reduce your heating and air conditioning bills significantly with a single small investment and about 15 minutes of installation.

Programmable Thermostats

Replacing your old thermostat is a simple chore. There is no electrical hazard. Most operate on safe, 24-volt power already present in your old thermostat. Installation is simple. Only a screwdriver is needed, and all wires are color coded for foolproof setup.

Starting at about $40 (and going up to $200), programmable thermostats will adjust heating and air conditioning to different settings for day, night and when you're home or away. Before choosing a programmable thermostat, determine how many time/temperature cycles are best for your lifestyle. A typical pattern would be settings for waking hours, daytime during the week, daytime on weekends, evening cycles and sleep times.

EASY THERMOSTAT INSTALLATION

First, switch off the furnace at the main switch or circuit breaker. There is no danger of shock, but this will keep the system from engaging until the new thermostat is in.

Remove the old thermostat, carefully noting the wire connections. Follow the instructions on the packaging of the new unit, precisely connecting all the wires to their marked locations (red, green black, etc.). Plug or caulk the hole in the wall where the wiring enters the back of the thermostat. This will eliminate wall drafts that can cause the thermostat to operate erratically. Switch

WHAT A SMART THERMOSTAT CAN SAVE YOU

When it's cold: Lowering the thermostat temperature at night can save 15% to 20% on your heating bill. Lowering the thermostat during the day as well as night—up to 30% savings on heating bills.

When it's hot: By raising the setting from 75 degrees to 80 for eight hours a day, you can save up to 9%. Set temperature higher at night as well and save 11% to 15% on your cooling bill.

on the furnace and follow the thermostat manufacturer's instructions to program the new unit.

DOORBELLS & CHIMES

Doorbells and chimes work off low-voltage electricity, usually 6 to 10 volts. Newer models operate on 24 volts. A small transformer attached to an electrical box in the utility area or attic is the power source.

First, Check the Door Button

Remove the door button. Inspect for dirt or loose wires. Touch the two wire ends together. If the chimes (bell) work, replace the button.

If not, it's most likely the chimes. Remove the cover. There should be a shaft mechanism that may need cleaning and a drop of oil.

New Chimes Don't Ring?

You may have to upgrade to a 24-volt transformer. Compare the ratings on the old transformer with the requirements of the new unit. Transformers are connected to household 120 volt current, so **work with the power off**.

HOW SMART IS YOUR THERMOSTAT?

Feature	Benefit
Large digital readout	Can be easily read without eyeglasses on. Built-in lighting for night viewing is a great convenience.
Flexible scheduling	Offers cycling times for weekends as well as weekdays. Manual override for times when the schedule changes.
Senses outdoor conditions	Automatically adjusts for wall temperature so that heat goes on earlier when it's colder to bring room temperature to right level at correct time.
Power management	Combination of low-voltage coupled with battery backup, or battery powered with "low battery" indicator. Maintains programming data in a power failure. In addition, automatic daylight savings time adjustment.
Built-in instructions	Faceplate model with programming instructions on the plate. Instructions always handy.

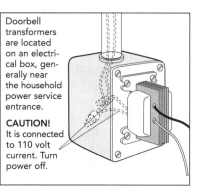

Doorbell transformers are located on an electrical box, generally near the household power service entrance.

CAUTION! It is connected to 110 volt current. Turn power off.

PREVENT FALSE ALARMS

Security systems reduce the risk of intruders, but they also create problems for police and fire departments. False alarms are becoming such a hazard that some local authorities are charging from $50 to $100 for every false alarm response.

Worse, many homeowners who experience frequent false alarms now leave their alarm systems off rather than run the risk of having them go off when nobody is home.

Batteries & Brownouts

The number one cause of false alarms during power failures and brownouts is a defective or depleted battery backup system. If the battery system for your alarm is four years old or older, replace the battery.

The Wind Factor

High winds can set off an alarm system by rattling doors and windows equipped with alarm sensors. Testing is simple: notify the alarm monitoring company that you are checking the system. Turn it on and go around the house shaking and attempting to open alarmed doors and windows. There should be a tolerance of about ¼ to ½ inch before the alarm activates. If it goes off to the slightest touch, that will be the problem sensor. Have the alarm company replace it.

Screen sensors are notorious for false alarms. Test all the screens by tapping them. Slight movement should not set off a door, window or screen alarm.

Glass Breakage Detectors

These devices require periodic recalibration which should be performed as part of your alarm system maintenance contract. Newer glass breakage detectors (in the past five years) will adjust themselves automatically to changing conditions.

MOTION DETECTORS

Spiders are a leading cause of motion detector activation. They nest behind corner-mounted detectors and occasionally creep across the front of it. What's small in reality appears big enough to alarm a detector with a spider crawling on its face. Other motion detector activators include:

- Open windows that cause curtains to flop in the breeze.
- Direct sunlight into the face of a detector at some point in the day, or a detector is facing out a window.
- An automatic fan, and even air blown by a heating or air-conditioning system, can activate sensitive detectors. Or an air vent that shifts a curtain could be the culprit.
- If the alarm falses regularly at about the same time of day,

check the house for all of the above environmental problems.
- If you recently shifted furniture or otherwise changed the environment, this is a likely cause of unexplained alarms.
- Dogs, cats and mice—anything likely to cause motion is likely to cause a false alarm.

CONTROLS & KEYPADS

If the alarm system is 10 years old or more, think about upgrading the control panel. New systems are highly computerized and incorporate numerous false alarm control measures. The biggest advantage of a new system is that it can allow every detector device in your home to be assigned its own zone. The advantage of a multizone system is that the control box identifies precisely which device caused a false alarm. This takes the guesswork out of troubleshooting and saves on service calls.

Easier, Better, Cheaper

Newer systems are reasonably priced and easier to install. Usually, the existing wiring can be used for the new installation. Keypad technology makes them easier to operate and overall they are more user-friendly.

House & Home

Basic Housekeeping

Safe Home

Security & Maintenance

Basic Housekeeping

Get Organized

Getting organized is a matter of managing time and clutter. A few simple tricks for managing your time, changing your habits and assigning family members responsibilities can change your life—starting immediately!

LIVE A NEATER LIFE

The first steps to home organization are for you to be organized yourself. Time management experts are all in agreement with one fundamental principle to better organization: make lists and work through them, crossing tasks off as you progress.

Prioritize Your Day

Make a daily or weekly To-Do list, assigning priorities—high, medium, low—to each task. You can have several "high priorities" to tackle in one day, but be realistic in times required and assign deadlines. Cross out each item as it's accomplished to give yourself a sense of forward momentum. You'll soon learn that listing is rewarding. The more you put on the list, the greater the satisfaction at day's end.

Manage Your Time

Before you begin lists, you must know where your time goes and how long it takes to accomplish various tasks.

Keep time logs of various tasks to identify time problems or time robbers. Usually, these are external, such as phone calls, drop-in visitors or other interruptions. Or, they might be internal, such as lack of self-discipline, procrastination, indecisiveness or failure to delegate. Set goals each day and strive to achieve them by minimizing interruptions. For example, use an egg timer to limit phone conversations, especially on busy days when your list is demanding.

Secrets of Successful Lists

Two lists are generally enough: a Master List and a Daily To-Do List. These are your basic time-management tools, but other lists are useful, too, and can save considerable time on repeat chores. For example, photocopy a master grocery shopping list with category headings like dairy, frozen, and so forth, including food and household items you shop for regularly. Keep your daily To-Do list manageable and don't be frustrated if you are unable to complete each task.

HOW TO BANK MORE TIME

➤ **Automate:** Purchase time-saving appliances such as microwave ovens, quality vacuum cleaners and other "tools" to shorten household chores.

➤ **Computerize:** Even if you are not computer literate, buy one for managing household finances, holiday card lists and even menu planning for parties and everyday recipe shortcuts.

➤ **Plan ahead:** For shopping trips, group errands together like grocery stops with dropping off cleaning, hardware store visits, picking up developed pictures and so on.

➤ **Shop wisely:** Buy at least two of goods like laundry detergents, toiletries, foods that last—any items that will save extra trips to the store.

➤ **Birthday cache:** Buy an assortment of birthday gifts and cards to avoid having to shop for each individual birthday. This applies especially for kids' birthdays when youngsters attend multiple birthday outings in a year.

➤ **Off-peak errands:** Don't go for hair styling just prior to holidays, banks on Fridays or paydays, medical appointments during peak hours.

➤ **Be first:** When possible, for scheduled deliveries, home repair calls, taking the car in for servicing. Call in advance to find out the least busy period in the day.

Use this list as a learning tool to gauge your future time more realistically. For example, if you allow one hour for shopping and it really takes two hours with travel time, adjust your next week's list accordingly.

Have one (preferably large) calendar in the house where everyone writes down scheduled appointments so that you are able to keep track of family schedules and prevent conflicts. Include pertinent family dates, such as birthdays, anniversaries and vacations. Don't forget school holidays, open houses, concerts, sports activities and meetings. Be sure to include medical appointments, house cleaners, gardeners and repairmen.

Put More Time in Your Day

Schedule household tasks. For example, paying bills and filing, correspondence, shopping, cleaning, doing laundry, and so on can all be done at regular times in the week. This will give you maximum efficiency, as well as save you time in the long run.

DAILY TO-DO LISTS

The Daily List differs from the Master List. First, you make it up the evening before. Refer to the Master List for controlling event items, such as appointments or outside commitments.

Time management experts recommend a "week ahead" planning session during a quiet spell over the weekend. One of the first items to list is time to plan your list. Itemize all the chores you'd *like* to get accomplished during the week to come. Alongside those chores, list the tasks which absolutely must be accomplished.

- Be realistic in scheduling your tasks and prioritize them from 1 to 4. Complete all of the #1's first.
- Put a time estimate alongside each task, or group similar tasks and allot time. For example, making four beds, allocate five minutes each.
- If you do not complete the previous day's list, roll items over to the current day.
- Don't become frustrated because you didn't complete all the tasks on the list. Instead, use more realistic time estimates to budget your future tasks more effectively.

When most people start using list techniques, they are amazed at how much time small chores take. By grouping tasks by function, you'll use your time more efficiently.

List by Function

Organize by function, listing appointments, shopping errands, return telephone calls; or by subject, shopping needs in a geographic area, questions for the doctor, and so on. Or you can plan your day around a project. For example, if you're decorating a room, you'll need to make plans for paint stores, wallpaper shops, hardware items and so forth. For big projects, plan at least a half day just to gather the tools and materials—probably mixed in with some other necessary stops on the way.

BEAT THE PAPER CHASE

- Go through mail as soon as you collect it. Separate bills from magazines, catalogs and flyers. Toss unwanted material immediately.
- Set up in-boxes or drawers for essential items, magazines (you want to read) and catalogs. Move bills and vitals to your desk area for later processing.
- When the catalog pile reaches the edges of the tray, toss the ones on the bottom. Chances are you'll never buy and a new one will come.

MASTERING THE MASTER LIST

- Make it a sturdy notebook, small enough to keep with you at all times in a handbag or briefcase. A notebook or professional organizer is a good investment.
- List everything you have to do.
- Enter items on the list as soon as they come up. You may not remember them later.
- Enter dates when tasks must be completed.
- Think of the list as a library inventory in which a manageable number of books/items are checked out and transferred to the daily to-do list.
- Don't organize or set priorities on the Master List. This comes later with the Daily To-Do list.
- Break down larger tasks into manageable pieces. For example, don't list: Prepare for children's school. Do list: Buy school supplies; plan school wardrobes; school books needed.
- Check your list each evening and enter tasks on the appropriate calendar day.
- Move several items to the Daily To-Do list, keeping watch on the time-tagged items.
- Delegate what you can to other family members, but enter the responsible's name and the deadline.
- It is usually confusing to mix home lists and business lists. Get a notebook with sections for work, home and long-term projects, such as decorating, vacation planning and so on.
- Don't forget to list life's pleasures and wishes: lunch with a friend, a trip to the aquarium, special events with family and even movies you want to see or rent.

Digital Time Management

- If computerization appeals to you, consider software to manage your schedule. Time organizer programs, such as *Sidekick*, have special features, such as built-in calendars and linked-activity capability, that automatically update Master Lists and Daily To-Do lists. Or, consider a product such as the *Palm Pilot* or other hand-held organizers. They let you maintain your day, month and even your life. But if you elect this route, be sure you are not the type who misplaces items; otherwise, your entire life-plan could get left behind somewhere.

TIME MANAGEMENT

Plan your time. Keep in mind your most productive and least productive times of the day, then plan your tasks accordingly. For example, if you have school children, the time getting them ready for school is fully allocated. Your most productive time may in fact be the hours immediately after they leave. Take on the hardest tasks first, during your most productive period, getting them out of the way while you're at peak performance.

Develop a handy and logical filing system for home tasks and business tasks so they're easier to do. This will save you even more time.

Attack clutter. Household clutter makes a home feel disorganized and is the number one cause of feeling overwhelmed.

Plan time for maintenance, not only of your vehicles but of household appliances as well. Furnaces, air conditioners, refrigerators and dishwashers are key appliances that need occasional attention, sometimes as simple as a good cleaning. If the appliances fail, it will inevitably be when you need them most. The time wasted procuring service and repair will likely be a hundred times more costly than attentive maintenance along the way.

Delegate the Obvious

Don't let family members off the hook. Delegate chores to everyone, starting with toddlers who can learn to put clothes in the laundry hamper. Have older children put on their own clothes, clear the table and put toys in designated spaces. Don't waste precious time being a slave to family members.

Establish Personal Goals

Start by asking yourself what you want more time for—reading, exercise, education, more quality time with family.

Then set specific goals of how and when you will manage to make more time for them. This won't happen overnight. You will have to make gradual adjustments in the pattern of your life and the lifestyle of your family.

Helpful: Time management experts suggest classifying activities as A, B or C, depending on importance. Often, the A tasks involve something you are doing for someone else. Keep yourself as a priority.

Best: Keep the A, B and C rankings for activities that are important to your life—and put an X next to those tasks that will help someone other than you.

Result: Being conscious of the activities that are important to your personal goals makes it easier to delegate tasks to others and concentrate your time on those tasks that matter most to you.

AVOID THE MADDENING CROWDS

1. **Make medical appointments** early in the morning or just after lunch to avoid the possible logjam effects later in the day.

2. **Carry your pharmacy phone number with you.** Ask your physician's office to call in any prescriptions to prevent waiting for them to be filled.

3. **Take an early or late lunch.** Avoid long lines and traffic.

4. **Get the first appointment** from home repair, installation or delivery people. You'll know when to expect them and they won't be held up by other jobs.

5. **Bank by mail or phone.** Avoid banks on the 1st, 15th and 30th of the month, all Fridays and during lunch hours.

6. **Patronize catalog businesses.** Most catalogs (or Internet) businesses deliver overnight for a slight delivery charge. Some items, like household goods, basic clothing, software and electronics, can be in your home within 24 to 48 hours, without the hassle of driving to the local mall. Frequently, prices are better, if not competitive, including the delivery charges.

GET THE CLUTTER OUT

The most difficult task in getting organized could possibly be getting started. The first rule in organizing your home: get rid of unnecessary clutter! This is a challenge to many of us pack rats; however, it is the only way to create an efficiently run home.

Starting off small and working your way up to the bigger challenges is the best approach. We all know our worst clutter-collecting culprit is our junk drawer. By following these simple steps, you will be able to master the junk drawer dilemma and move on to the bigger task of cleaning out the closets.

Make Piles

Create a pile for the following:
- Items you have not used in over a year (including those things that you have no idea what they are)
- Items friends have left at your home, which you've been meaning to return
- Newspaper articles or coupons that were thrown in the drawer for later use
- Forms waiting to be filled out
- Writing utensils that have been rolling around
- Take-out menus
- Miscellaneous business cards or phone numbers on scraps of paper lying in drawers

- Items that need to be readily accessible (keys, sunglasses, wallets, etc.)

Make Decisions

This is the moment of truth. Be brutally honest with yourself and ask the question, "Do I really need this?" If you have not used the item (or items) in the past year, then chances are, you won't. That fitness program application you got a year ago is not going to be used. This is the toughest part of the job. Just keep telling yourself "I can always get another one." In those special cases where you are sure that something is worthy of keeping but you never seem to use it (this is more pertinent with clothing), give it to a friend with the stipulation that you may want it back someday. The fact is, you'll never take it back, but this will relieve the anxiety attached with throwing away "perfectly good junk." Keep a garbage bag handy, and if possible (for those of you who tend to keep changing your mind about items you throw out), fill the bag with used coffee grinds or some other element that will prevent you from retrieving your throw-away items.

Make a Small Investment

Finally, you have a clean junk drawer full of pertinent stuff. Don't let all your efforts go to waste. Go out and purchase the three items that will prevent junk from ever accumulating out of control again.

The first item (or items if you have more than one drawer) is a plastic drawer organizer. The size and shape will obviously be dependent on its purpose.

Keep in mind you want something that will hold all writing implements, paper, sunglasses, keys, and so on in an organized manner. You will need a small three-ring binder for the take-out menus (in alphabetical order if you really want to impress your friends) and a small cork board to be hung on the side of your fridge or inside a frequently used cabinet door for your "temporary papers." Keeping visible forms that need to be completed or pamphlets that need to be read will prompt you to do the task sooner. A good rule is to throw out any papers if they hang on your cork board for more than a month.

Making It Permanent

All of the suggestions that have been presented here can work for any area of your home that tends to collect clutter. When cleaning out your garage or closets follow the same process of making piles, making decisions and making purchases. Substitute the appropriate organizers (plastic storage boxes for seasonal clothes, peg boards for tools in your garage, etc.).

Always ask yourself if something is really important enough for you to keep or else learn how to let go.

HOME OFFICE BASICS

Running a home is more like operating a business today than it has ever been. Organize an office space specifically for maintaining the business of running your home. This "office" needs to serve as command central for all planning, purchasing, travel, vacationing, home maintenance records, vehicle purchase and warranty records, home inventory control, insurance records and health and medical documents.

Vital family documents, such as birth certificates, passports, life insurance policies, mortgages and deeds, should be stored in a bank safe-deposit box or, at the very least, in a fireproof safe in your home.

Good Filing Habits

Create a filing system that makes sense for your lifestyle. Discipline yourself to use the filing system. This will make it easier to find information and accomplish your tasks more quickly and without frustration.

Having copies of all purchase transactions, whether for large items or smaller household furnishings, is vital. The more sub-files you have, the easier it is to maintain the business of your life. An insurance file, for example should be subdivided into Life, Health, Auto and Home folders.

FILING SOLUTIONS

➤ **Accordion files** are indexed files useful for filing paid bills and receipts, especially if you have a lot of paperwork. They can be purchased with either numerical or daily, weekly or monthly tabs.

➤ **File folders** with a tab for labeling can be removed from a drawer to carry papers.

➤ **Filing cabinets** are available in a variety of configurations and sizes. Even portable plastic files are better than no cabinet at all.

➤ **A household notebook** with rings can hold everything from repair listings to appliance and auto maintenance schedules, emergency phone numbers and doctors visits, to household inventory. Place appliance warranties and instruction booklets in freezer storage bags and hole-punch to place in the binder.

➤ **Photo albums** make excellent record keepers for medical information. The sticky peel-back sheets hold information and detailed backup records in one place.

➤ **Index card files** keep addresses, phone numbers and business cards. They are easy to replace when numbers change.

THINK COMPUTER

If you don't already have a computer, consider the value of owning one just to simplify your home "business" needs. Home-finance management programs, such as *Quicken* by Intuit, or *Money,* are simple to learn and save significant time in managing your household. Even if you have never used a computer, these home-management tools will quickly become indispensable.

In particular, the specialty features offered by some software programs, such as home inventory listings to organize and record all household assets, room by room, could prove invaluable in the event your home or property is destroyed.

Internet: Value in Itself

Popular-brand home computers come equipped for Internet access. If you haven't started using that medium by now, it is inevitable you will. Coupled with financial management information, judicious use of the Internet for planning family finance, travel and education could well offset the cost of the computer.

$ HOME-FINANCE WORKHORSE

Consider this list of chores a home-computer financial package can accomplish for your home-management strategy:

➤ Track bank account(s) activities and write checks for bill paying—usually faster than by hand once you learn how.

➤ Balance and reconcile your checkbook.

➤ Monitor credit card accounts, even allowing you to use the Internet to download credit card transactions directly from charge cards.

➤ Plan, track and monitor loan activities.

➤ Identify and locate tax-deductible items. (The savings from this feature alone may equal the cost of the computer.)

➤ Maintain irrefutable records to argue against the IRS.

➤ Track your investments, as well as providing direct Internet links to reports on stocks and mutual funds.

➤ Maintain home inventory files better than almost anything you might create yourself.

➤ Generate concise, clear reports on the status of all of the above, complete with graphs and charts.

BEST HOME OFFICE COMPUTER

Individual preferences in computers are personal and pragmatic. If you will be the only one using the computer and its primary purpose is finances and bill paying, then a laptop will probably be the right tool. The difference between a laptop and a desktop machine? In a word, size. Most importantly, visibility and the amount of space the computer may take up in your office. As far as performance goes, laptops are basically at par with desktop systems from the standpoint of disk storage space and operating speed. Essentially, there is no difference between what a laptop and a desktop machine can do. Bear in mind, however, that you'll want a printer also, and if your office is to be in a small corner of the kitchen, then a laptop better fits your needs.

What Do You Need to See?

If graphics, large type and lots of animated video are important to your computer use, then buy a desktop system. Desktop screens afford better viewing for Internet surfing and animated digital videos, as well as top clarity in working with numbers and graphics.

Pricing & Buying

If you are a first-time computer buyer, get some help from a friend who knows something about

---

SPACE & SIGHT SAVER

You can connect any laptop computer to a large video screen, giving you the best of both worlds: portability and small size, combined with big-screen performance.

---

the machines. Bear in mind that all machines basically do the same things (and contain essentially the same parts); the only serious considerations are reliability and customer service. Popular computer magazines regularly compare manufacturers' brands for reliability and customer service access.

Pricing is extremely competitive, so it pays to shop around. The best source for research is the Internet, where all leading manufacturers feature Web sites that do an excellent job of explaining features and advantages of different system configurations in detail—generally better than retail sales associates, who usually try to push a particular brand or model on you.

Another good source are specialty catalogs, such as *PC Connection* at 800-800-5555. Prices generally are better than retail, delivery is often overnight and sales personnel are knowledgeable.

Culinary Smarts

As the saying goes, "You are what you eat," and good food practice begins with the shopping cart. What you do with what you eat also matters. Proper preservation and preparation are the keys to sound nutrition and good health. Here are some food basics you may be overlooking, complete with tips and solutions proven by time, testing and taste. Armed with these basics, you can make a big difference in your kitchen's efficiency—and your family's health.

LABEL LOGIC

Knowledge is power, and that's especially true when reading food labels. The key phrase is "Daily Value." Checking the percentage of daily value can be more helpful than checking the amount the product contains. Why? The percent of daily value puts important nutrients on an equal footing in the context of your total daily diet.

For example, a food is low in sodium if it has less than 140mg of sodium. What may seem like a high amount—140—to some people is actually less than 6% of the Daily Value. On the other hand, a food with 5g of saturated fat could be construed as being low in that nutrient. But in reality, that food would provide one-fourth of the total Daily Value (20g) of saturated fat for a 2,000-calorie diet.

DECODE THE DATA

Once you learn the trick to decoding the nutritional information found on a food package or wrapping, the label makes sense.

The left side of the nutrition label lists the amount of various food constituents such as fat, cholesterol and sodium. To the right is the percentage of the daily recommended amount that this product provides.

Below this chart is listed the percentage of the Recommended Daily Allowance (RDA) of vitamins and minerals contained in one serving.

Daily values are the same for everyone for cholesterol, sodium and potassium. It is slightly confusing, however, because the daily values of fat, cholesterol and sodium are determined based on a diet of 2,000 calories/day, the amount needed by women in their 20s. Daily values for vitamins and minerals do not change. Values for vitamin A, vitamin C, calcium, and iron are generally the only ones listed because they are the most difficult to get in sufficient daily amounts.

Nutrition Facts

Serving Size 27 crackers (30g)
Servings Per Container about 15

Amount Per Serving

Calories 180 Calories from fat 80

	% Daily Value*
Total Fat 8g	**12%**
Saturated Fat 2g	**10%**
Cholesterol 0mg	**0%**
Sodium 240mg	**10%**
Total Carbohydrate 16g	**5%**
Dietary Fiber less than 1g	**3%**
Sugars less than 1g	
Protein 4g	

Vitamin A 0%	•	Vitamin C 0%
Calcium 4%	•	Iron 6%

* Percent Daily Values are based on a 2,000 calorie diet. Your daily values may be higher or lower depending on your calorie needs:

	Calories:	2,000	2,500
Total Fat	Less than	65g	80g
Sat Fat	Less than	20g	25g
Cholesterol	Less than	300mg	300mg
Sodium	Less than	2400mg	2,400mg
Total Carbohydrate		300g	375g
Dietary Fiber		25g	30g

MEASUREMENTS

Common Abbreviations

Tsp.	teaspoon
Tbsp.	tablespoon
c.	cup
pt.	pint
qt.	quart
pk.	peck
bu.	bushel
oz.	ounce(s)
lb.	pound(s)
sq.	square
min.	minute(s)
hr.	hour
doz.	dozen

Simplified Measures

dash	less than ⅛ teaspoon
3 teaspoons	1 tablespoon
16 tablespoons	1cup
2 cups	1 pint
2 pints (4 cups)	1 quart
4 quarts (liquid)	1 gallon
8 quarts (solid)	1 peck
4 pecks	1 bushel
16 ounces	1 pound

How to Measure Cups by Tablespoon

⅛ cup	2 tbsp.
¼ cup	4 tbsp.
⅓ cup	5 ⅓ tbsp.
½ cup	8 tbsp.
⅔ cup	10⅔ tbsp.
¾ cup	12 tbsp.
⅞ cup	14 tbsp.
1 cup	16 tbsp.

SHOP & EAT FOR HEALTH

If you eat right, you feel right. But what exactly is healthy eating? A balanced, healthy diet is critical to good health whether you are 2 or 92. All you have to do is plan your food shopping purchases and your eating habits around the Dietary Guidelines established by the US Department of Agriculture (USDA).

Variety Is the Spice of Life

Nutritionists recommend eating a variety of foods to get the necessary energy, carbohydrates, protein, vitamins, minerals and fiber.

You also need to balance what you eat with physical activity in order to maintain or improve your weight. You will also reduce chances of high blood pressure, heart disease, stroke, some cancers and the most common kind of diabetes.

Mix & Match

A healthy diet is a mixed one that includes plenty of grains, vegetables and fruits. These ingredients provide the vitamins, minerals, fiber and complex carbohydrates that help lower fat intake. A high fat intake is bad news, while a diet low in saturated fat and cholesterol appears to reduce the risk of heart attack and colon cancer. Use sugar, salt and alcoholic beverages in moderation to maintain good health.

ZEROING IN ON SUGARS

Want to cut refined sugars out of your diet, but not sure what they are? Besides sucrose—plain table sugar—beware of refined corn syrup and high-fructose corn syrup. These are widespread in processed foods such as fruit drinks and carbonated beverages, ketchup, "maple" syrup, soups and spaghetti sauces. Check labels for ingredients and calorie counts—in some cases, the count easily tops 100. Simple sugars are "empty" calories because, unlike complex carbohydrates (i.e., starches), they contain no other nutrients.

BREAKFAST, DON'T BANQUET

Good news for anyone who thinks breakfast is nothing more than an assault on the stomach: it doesn't take a big breakfast to do well nutritionally. You don't have to eat a lot to get a good start in the morning, but you do need complex carbohydrates (found in whole-grain breads, bran muffins and cereals) and protein (from lean meat, fish, low-fat cheese or milk). Carbohydrates give you quick energy, and proteins kick in to keep you going until lunch after the "carbs" are used up.

If you're looking for alternatives, here are 10 suggestions from nutritionists for the day's first—and most important—meal:

- Low-fat yogurt with fruit
- Natural peanut butter (oil skimmed off) on whole-wheat toast
- Low-fat cottage cheese with fruit
- Low-fat cheese with whole-grain bread
- Cereal and fruit with low-fat milk
- Banana or other fruit with low-fat milk whipped in a blender
- Tuna salad on whole-wheat toast
- Leftover chicken (skinless)
- Thinly sliced turkey with low-fat cheese

VEGGIES FOR BREAKFAST?

Are you in a doughnut or bagel rut in the morning? Why not make breakfast a power meal by adding some vegetables to your wake-up call? They can add balance and variety to breakfast.

- Start with 8 oz. of vegetable juice—V8 or tomato.
- Top an English muffin or bagel with hummus—the combination of bread and bean makes up a complete protein.
- Add chopped carrots, beans or zucchini to your cream cheese.
- Top your bagel and cream cheese with a thick slice of

tomato and a crunchy leaf of spinach or lettuce.
- Toss a handful of red or green peppers, spinach and broccoli florets into an omelet.
- Microwave a potato; cut it in half and scoop out some of the insides. Fill with low-fat cottage cheese; then top with chives.

GRAY BURGER OK

Ever wonder about that ground beef you just unwrapped?

As you begin to break up the red hamburger, you notice that the meat on the inside is gray. You wonder has it gone bad? No—as a butcher will tell you—it has lost its "bloom."

Ground beef turns red when it's exposed to oxygen. That's because myoglobin (an iron-containing protein that is found in muscle tissue) turns from its normal purple color to red when it absorbs oxygen.

Tightly wrapped meat gradually turns gray because it's no longer exposed to oxygen. The graying is more noticeable in leaner meat because lean beef has less whitish fat in it and fewer air pockets to hold oxygen longer.

In short, don't worry about the gray when you know the ground beef is fresh. In fact, that's how it should look cooked, too. Properly cooked, a hamburger should show no sign of "blooming."

HEALTHFUL FOOD PYRAMID

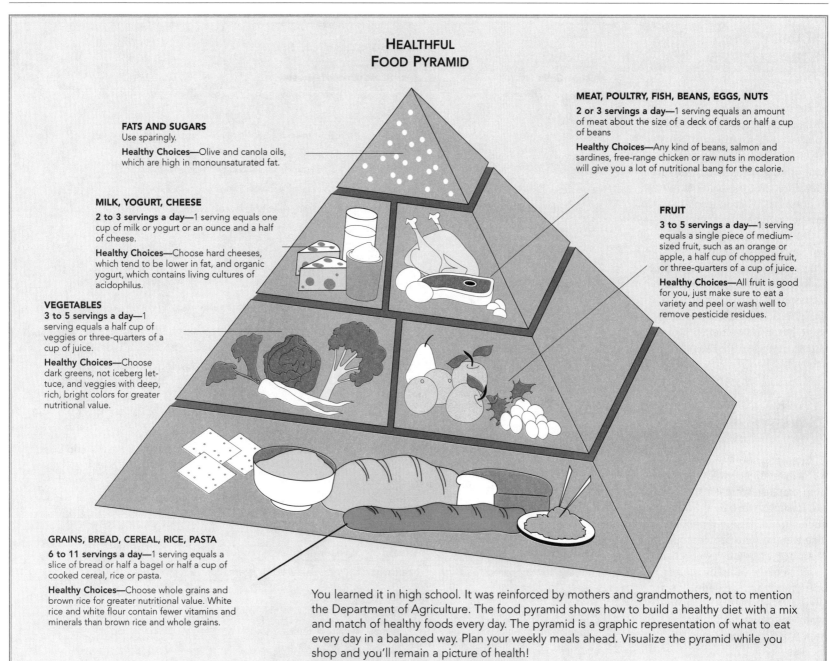

FATS AND SUGARS
Use sparingly.

Healthy Choices—Olive and canola oils, which are high in monounsaturated fat.

MILK, YOGURT, CHEESE

2 to 3 servings a day—1 serving equals one cup of milk or yogurt or an ounce and a half of cheese.

Healthy Choices—Choose hard cheeses, which tend to be lower in fat, and organic yogurt, which contains living cultures of acidophilus.

VEGETABLES

3 to 5 servings a day—1 serving equals a half cup of veggies or three-quarters of a cup of juice.

Healthy Choices—Choose dark greens, not iceberg lettuce, and veggies with deep, rich, bright colors for greater nutritional value.

GRAINS, BREAD, CEREAL, RICE, PASTA

6 to 11 servings a day—1 serving equals a slice of bread or half a bagel or half a cup of cooked cereal, rice or pasta.

Healthy Choices—Choose whole grains and brown rice for greater nutritional value. White rice and white flour contain fewer vitamins and minerals than brown rice and whole grains.

MEAT, POULTRY, FISH, BEANS, EGGS, NUTS

2 or 3 servings a day—1 serving equals an amount of meat about the size of a deck of cards or half a cup of beans

Healthy Choices—Any kind of beans, salmon and sardines, free-range chicken or raw nuts in moderation will give you a lot of nutritional bang for the calorie.

FRUIT

3 to 5 servings a day—1 serving equals a single piece of medium-sized fruit, such as an orange or apple, a half cup of chopped fruit, or three-quarters of a cup of juice.

Healthy Choices—All fruit is good for you, just make sure to eat a variety and peel or wash well to remove pesticide residues.

You learned it in high school. It was reinforced by mothers and grandmothers, not to mention the Department of Agriculture. The food pyramid shows how to build a healthy diet with a mix and match of healthy foods every day. The pyramid is a graphic representation of what to eat every day in a balanced way. Plan your weekly meals ahead. Visualize the pyramid while you shop and you'll remain a picture of health!

HANDY SUBSTITUTES

You're rushing through a new recipe or scrambling to prepare dinner, only to discover you're out of something. Before rushing to the corner market or abandoning the culinary adventure, look around—almost every kitchen has basic ingredients that can be used as substitutes.

Out of ketchup? One-half cup of tomato sauce and ½ cup of water, plus a dash of salt and sugar will do just fine. Or ¼ cup of tomato paste and ¾ cup of water with a dash of salt and sugar does the same job. For two dozen other substitutes, see the table on the right.

FAKE SWEETENERS?

Speaking about substitutes, will artificial sweeteners help you lose weight? In a word, no. Research fails to show that such substitutes help people lose weight. One problem: instead of eating artificially sweetened foods in place of high-calorie ones, many people simply add them to their diet. Also, such sweeteners don't suppress appetite—and some may even increase it.

SUBSTITUTION SECRETS

Recipe Calls for...	Substitute One of These...
1 tablespoon cornstarch	2 tablespoons flour **or** 1 ½ tablespoons of quick cooking tapioca.
1 cup of cake flour	1 cup less 2 tablespoons of all-purpose flour.
1 cup brown sugar	1 teaspoon imitation maple flavoring, and 1 teaspoon molasses, and 1 cup white sugar.
1 cup honey	1 ¼ cups sugar and ½ cup liquid (but it will be sweeter).
1 cup whole milk	½ cup water and ½ cup evaporated milk.
1 cup skim milk	⅓ cup instant non-fat dry milk and ¾ cup water.
1 cup heavy cream	⅓ cup butter and ⅔ cup milk.
1 cup heavy cream, whipped	⅔ cup well-chilled evaporated milk, whipped.
1 cup buttermilk	1 tablespoon lemon juice or vinegar added to sweet milk to equal 1 cup.
1 cup yogurt	1 cup buttermilk (but it will be thinner).
1 egg	2 tablespoons dried whole egg and 2 tablespoons water.
1 cup butter	⅞ cup solid shortening and ½ teaspoon salt (but not for pastry!).
1 cup melted shortening	1 cup salad oil.
1 teaspoon baking powder	1 teaspoon cream of tartar and ¼ teaspoon baking soda **or** ¼ teaspoon baking soda and ½ cup sour milk, buttermilk or molasses. Reduce other recipe liquids by ½ cup.
1 tablespoon fresh herbs	¼ teaspoon powdered herbs **or** 1 teaspoon dried herbs **or** ½ teaspoon herb salt. Reduce recipe salt ¼ teaspoon.
¼ cup bread crumbs	Make bread crumbs from stale bread or one slice toast **or** use ¼ cup dried corn cereal or another nonsweetened dried cereal crushed in a blender or processor.
1 clove garlic	¼ teaspoon garlic salt; reduce recipe salt by ⅛ teaspoon. **Or** ⅛ teaspoon garlic powder.
1 teaspoon allspice	½ teaspoon cinnamon and ⅛ teaspoon cloves.
1 teaspoon lemon juice	½ teaspoon vinegar (but flavor is different).
1 tablespoon prepared mustard	1 teaspoon dry or powdered mustard.
1 vanilla bean	1 teaspoon vanilla extract.
1 teaspoon lemon rind	½ teaspoon lemon extract (only for moist mixture).
1 small fresh onion	1 tablespoon instant minced onion, **or** 1 teaspoon onion powder.
⅓ cup cracker crumbs	1 cup bread crumbs.

Basic Kitchen Tips

The kitchen is the nerve center of any household, serving as "Action Central" for everything from food service to family communications. Here are some basic guidelines for the former, including tips on preparing and preserving food, as well as advice on dealing with the consequences— cooking odors, burnt food, cleanup and spoilage.

BANISH ODORS

- To prevent the odors of boiling cabbage or ham or cooking greens, add a teaspoonful of vinegar to the water in which they are cooked.
- To eliminate the odor of cooking vegetables, add some vinegar to another small pan of boiling water on the stove.
- To sweeten up a bad-smelling disposal, grind up ice cubes after every use. Or save lemon, lime and orange peel, and grind a little bit after using the disposal.
- Smoke odors can be cleared from a room in a few minutes by dipping a towel in equal parts of hot water and vinegar, wringing the towel out and walking around the room waving it gently.
- Keep a mint plant in rooms where there is an odor problem, like the kitchen, baby's room or bath. The mint absorbs stale odors and it looks nice too!
- A handful of dry laundry detergent placed in the bottom of trash containers (after cleaning) not only smells great—it deters flies and other insects.

BURNT FOOD REMEDIES

- If a stew has burned, pour the unburned portion of the stew into another pan leaving the burnt portion behind. Spices, such as pepper or chili powder, can then be added to the stew to disguise any burned taste.
- Most items that have been burned—like soup—can be salvaged if they are poured immediately into another pan without including the burnt portion from the bottom of the pot.

GET THE FAT OUT

When grease collects on top of soup broth, skim it with a piece of ice. The grease will harden and stick to the ice, making it easy to remove. Or place a piece of tissue paper on the top, which will absorb the grease. Likewise, a lettuce leaf brushed over the surface will act like a grease magnet.

To remove grease from cooked dishes, cool in the refrigerator. Remove the grease with a spoon after it has hardened.

OVEN TEMPERATURES

You've read the term "slow cook," but what does it mean to your oven? Here's a quick table that translates those cookbook ambiguities into usable numbers. Since most older ovens don't have accurate built-in thermometers, a separate internal oven thermometer is worth the investment.

Slow	300°
Slow moderate	325°
Moderate	350°
Quick moderate	375°
Moderately hot	400°
Hot	425°
Very hot	475°

MESS BUSTERS

Cookbook Cleanliness
When cooking from a cookbook, cover the book in a large plastic storage bag open to the page you are reading. This will protect the recipe from stains and keep the book open to the exact page!

Mixing Meat Loaf
When mixing meat loaf or sticky cookie recipes, cover your hands with small plastic bags to avoid the mess. Even better: mix the meat loaf inside a bag.

Clean Phone
Keep plastic bags handy when washing pans or cleaning the sink in case the phone rings. Put your hand in the bag and pick up the phone. No mess!

Recipe Protection
Cover your recipes with 2½-inch clear packaging tape. Instant laminate!

PREPARING FRUITS & VEGGIES

Fruit: Pick It Fresh & Keep It That Way
Pick fruit that isn't bruised, blemished or moldy.

Steer clear of fruit and vegetables wrapped in clear plastic wrap. They bruise more easily and deteriorate more quickly.

Refrigeration will slow fruit ripening, while placing fruit in a

SPEED RIPENING

An apple placed in a bag with the following soft fruits will ripen them quickly due to the fruits' exposure to ethylene gas which the apple gives off: avocados, bananas, kiwis, nectarines, peaches, pears and plums.

dark place will make it ripen much faster.

Fruits that will not ripen after harvesting: apples, cherries, grapefruit, grapes, lemons, limes, oranges, pineapples, strawberries, tangerines, and watermelons.

Stoning Fruit

To remove seeds from grapes, cut the grape slightly off center and remove seeds with the tip of a small knife or the end of a paper clip. Hold the grape up against the light to see the seeds.

To remove cherry stones, use the tip of a vegetable peeler.

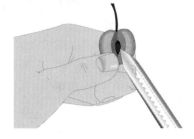

Skinning Fruit

Soft-skinned fruits, like peaches or apricots, are easily de-skinned by placing the fruit in a Pyrex bowl and pouring boiling water over the fruit. After 10 seconds, pour off the water and remove the skins.

Is It Ripe?

Apricots should be a soft, orange-yellow color and have a firm texture without bruises or soft spots. Refrigerate and use within four to five days.

Apples should be a bright color, with no broken skin and no bruising. They may be refrigerated and should last at least a week.

Avocados, regardless of what kind, should be slightly soft, but not mushy, if you intend to use them soon. Hard avocados will ripen in a few days at room temperature or quicker if placed with a banana peel in a plastic bag. Refrigeration stops ripening.

Bananas that are ripe have yellow skin with brown and black flecks. Bananas are great when brought home slightly green and allowed to ripen over a few days. Banana skins will darken if refrigerated, but the banana will not ripen anymore and its taste will not be affected.

Berries of any kind should be checked for mold, which begins quickly at full ripening. Check for crushed raspberries as they are very soft. Refrigerate berries unwashed until ready to use.

Cherries should feel firm, not soft or blemished, nor too hard. They should be medium to dark in color—the darker, the sweeter.

Refrigerate and eat cherries soon because they begin to deteriorate at full ripening.

Citrus fruit is at peak when it has finely textured skin and feels firm. Navel oranges are good for eating and are easier to peel. The sweetest juice oranges are Valencia, Temple and King.

Heating lemons or oranges in the microwave or under warm water will yield twice the juice for squeezing. Freeze the juice.

To peel an orange easily, heat it in warm water for three or four minutes before peeling.

To store a cut lemon, smear the surface with egg white to keep it fresh. Lemons can be frozen.

Grapefruit should be heavy for their size; if they are light, they may have dried out. Browning or greening of the peel does not affect their taste. May be refrigerated for several weeks, but warmer fruits yield more juice.

Grapes should be plump and firm, not faded in color, and have flexible stems. Allow to ripen at room temperature; then refrigerate to stay fresh for several days.

Kiwi fruit, when it is to be eaten in a day or two, should be light brown and slightly soft to the touch. Harder fruit will usually ripen in several days at room temperature.

Melons come in several varieties. *Cantaloupe* is a yellowish color when ripe, and the blossom end yields to soft pressure. Mushy cantaloupe is overripe and tends to mold.

Honeydew melons are ripe when they have a thick creamy white or yellow-white color and the blossom end yields to slight pressure. Harder, unripe melons (greenish white in appearance) will usually ripen in two days at room temperature.

FRUIT FRESHENERS

➤ Rinse strawberries before hulling, then drain on paper towels. Strawberries will become water logged if hulled first.

➤ Place the avocado seed in the guacamole. This helps keep it from getting brown before serving time.

➤ Freshly peeled apples will keep from browning if they are placed in water with lemon juice or ascorbic acid fruit-color keeper.

➤ To keep bananas from browning: pour a small amount of pineapple or lemon juice over them until serving time, **or** add a small amount of sherry.

MELON BOWL

To make a serving bowl out of a melon, cut a slice off the side (but not through to the fruit). Then lie flat on a serving platter.

Watermelon, when whole, should be light yellow on the underside that touched the ground and should be dull, not shiny. An unripe melon rind will be white to pale green in color. Fruit should be firm, not mushy. Refrigerate.

Nectarines that are ripe appear cream, red and yellow mixed and slightly soft to the touch. Look for fruit without green color near the stem, unless you want the fruit to ripen at home. Avoid bruised or mushy fruit.

Peaches should be firm, but yield to soft pressure. A red tinge does not indicate ripening, and green indicates that it is not ready to eat. Ripe fruit can be refrigerated for four to five days.

Pears should be somewhat firm to the touch, but a bit softer at the sides and near the stem when ripening. If purchased hard, ripen at room temperature.

Plums, whether red or dark purple, are best when slightly soft, not mushy or shriveled. Plums will ripen in a bag.

Pineapples are determined to be ripe by their aroma, dark green crown leaves and a firm and dry shell. Store away from direct sunlight and refrigerate when ripe.

Strawberries that are ripe appear bright red with no white color near the stem. White means the berries were picked early or are ripe but short on sun, which turns them red. Berries should be refrigerated, unwashed, with stems intact until ready to eat.

Tomatoes that are red and firm but yield to slight pressure are ready to eat. They lose their flavor when refrigerated.

SALAD SECRETS

Savory Suggestions

- *Before refrigerating vegetables,* remove leafy tops or the vegetables will deteriorate more quickly. Water destroys some vitamins, so do not wash any produce before putting away in a crisper except for salad greens. Other than mushrooms, vegetables that are tightly wrapped in plastic spoil more quickly.

TOMATO TIPS

Place under-ripe tomatoes in a drawer or another dark place away from direct sunlight. Sun makes tomatoes soft, but doesn't ripen them.

- *To prevent the soggy-salad-in-a-serving-bowl syndrome,* place an inverted saucer in the bottom of the bowl before you add the salad. The moisture will remain below the saucer and the salad will remain crisp.

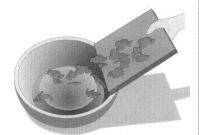

- *Soggy lettuce to start with?* Place lettuce in a bowl of water with 2 teaspoons of lemon juice and put in the refrigerator for one-half hour. Rinse and spin dry before serving.
- *Craving crisp celery?* When celery becomes wilted, place it in a pan of cold water with a slice of raw potato for a few hours.
- *Wilted lettuce?* Dampen lettuce with a sprinkle of cool water, wrap with a dishtowel and place in the refrigerator for an hour.
- *Brown lettuce leaves?* Tearing, instead of cutting, soft lettuce leaves will prevent brown stains. Make sure you tear bite-sized pieces.

VEGGIE POINTERS

- *Leave corn in their husks.* Leave peas and beans in their shells. Refrigerate peppers and onions. Keep fresh garlic from drying out for several weeks by peeling the buds and placing them in a jar and covering with cooking oil or vinegar. Refrigerate. The remaining oil is flavored nicely.
- *Peeling tomatoes.* Drop tomatoes (using a ladle so you don't splash and burn yourself) into boiling water for approximately 10 seconds. Then place in cold water. The skins will split and then are easily removed.

- *Slimy carrots?* Carrots that have a slight slimy feel are fine. Take a paper towel with a few drops of lemon juice and rub over the carrot. Rinse and use as you normally would.
- *Clingy corn husks?* Remove sticky silk from corn cobs after husking by rubbing the ears with a damp paper towel.

- *Turnip dirt.* Root vegetables (carrots, turnips, radishes, etc.) should be well cleaned. The green varieties should be soaked for a minute or two in cold water with ⅛ teaspoon of salt to retain freshness.
- *Tubers.* Onions, potatoes and other root vegetables and tubers should be stored in a cool, dry and dark place, such as a basket or wire rack that is ventilated.

COOKING VEGETABLES

Cut vegetables in small pieces and cook for as short a time as possible. Steam or add vegetables to already boiling water to preserve their vitamins. Keep the vitamin-rich water in which the vegetables were cooked, as well as leftover sliced onions, peppers and other vegetables. Freeze in separate plastic bags, ready for quick use in stocks and soups.

Boiled & Steamed Vegetables
- Steaming takes longer than boiling, but it's healthier.
- Add one teaspoon of lemon juice to corn when boiling. This keeps the color bright. Don't add salt—it toughens the corn kernels.
- Green vegetables will keep their color if boiled with a pinch of baking soda. Or keep the lid off the pan while cooking.
- Keep boiled cauliflower from turning yellow by adding lemon juice, vinegar or two teaspoons of milk to the water.

Dress Up Those Vegetables
After cooking vegetables, sprinkle with toasted chopped nuts or sunflower seeds, toasted sesame seeds, bacon bits or cooked ham. Alternatives: canned french-fried onions, fresh herb bits, crouton pieces, cut up hard-boiled egg bits.

Potato Tips
- To slice potatoes easily, first place the cutting knife in boiling water or over an open flame.
- A pinch of baking powder will make the potatoes lighter and fluffier. If they're soggy after adding milk (because they were overcooked), add powdered milk and they will become fluffy again.
- To bake potatoes quickly, boil them in salted water for 10 minutes and then put in the oven to complete baking at less than half the time. The water heats them through quicker than putting them in the oven cold. A microwave session of about three minutes per potato will also cook them quickly, with a finish in the oven for a crisper skin. A metal skewer through the potato will also speed up baking time.

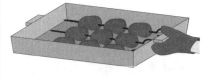

- Old potatoes will taste better with the addition of a little sugar to the boiling water. A teaspoon of vinegar will keep the potatoes light.
- Roasting potatoes will be crisper if the skin is rubbed with a little salt.
- For crisp baked potatoes, do not wrap in foil. Wrapping steams the potatoes and softens the skin. Simply scrub the potatoes and place them—still wet—on an oven baking rack.
- Don't toss out leftover baked potatoes! Dip them in water and rebake them for 20 minutes at 300°.

MEAT, POULTRY & FISH TIPS

Meat, poultry and fish comprise the protein portion of most people's diets (along with eggs and dairy, discussed in the next section). When choosing meat, know the definitions of Prime, Select and Choice cuts. The healthiest are lean and low in saturated fat and are labeled Select. Prime and Choice are higher in fat (and price, too), which makes them more tender and juicy.

Preparation
- Freeze meat, chicken and fish in the exact quantities you'll need to feed your family. This saves time and trouble. For example, freeze sufficient chopped meat for a meatloaf or enough patties for burgers, pork chops for one dinner, or stew beef for a soup portion.
- Freeze hamburger patties separated by wax paper to easily access what you need. Also freeze meatballs first on a cookie sheet and then remove to a plastic freezer container. You can then use what you need, when you need it!
- Always, for safety reasons, thaw meat in the refrigerator, never at room temperature. Never leave any meat, poultry or fish, cooked or uncooked, at room temperature for more

than two hours. Freeze meat and fish you won't be using within two days.

- Thaw frozen fish in milk in the refrigerator. This makes it taste like fresh fish instead of frozen. Use the milk for a sauce.
- Marinate meat in a sealable plastic bag for easy turning and easy cleanup. Just throw the bag away. You'll find you won't need as much marinade.

- Tough meat can be tenderized by marinating for one hour with a mixture of equal parts of vinegar and either cooking oil or stock.
- When grinding meat, add the ingredients (bread crumbs, onions, etc.) together in the food processor or the food grinder. Saves time and tastes better, too!
- Out of bread crumbs for chicken or pork chops? Mix stale bread and dry-mix salad dressing together. Add paprika and garlic salt for additional zing.

★ HOW TO USE A MEAT THERMOMETER

Insert the thermometer at the centermost and thickest part of the meat, taking care not to touch the bottom of the pan, the fat or any bones. When the meat reaches the desired temperature, push the thermometer a little deeper into the meat. If the temperature drops, the meat should continue to cook. If it stays the same, the roast is finished. It should be removed and allowed to stand covered for approximately 15 minutes before carving.

Seasoning Meat

Coat meat quickly and easily with bread crumbs or seasoned flour by placing the meat in a plastic bag with the mixture already in it. Shake the bag until the meat is coated. Easy cleanup: throw the bag away!

Cooking Meat

- Beef is ready to eat when the thermometer reaches 170°. And 160° to 170° for pork.
- Meat should be cooked at a high heat at first to seal in juices.
- Wait to add salt until the end of cooking—salt draws out the juices.
- Tender cuts of meat are best broiled, pan fried or roasted. Less tender cuts are better if slowly cooked in moist heat

(pot roasted, braised or in a stew).

- Cook a roast with the fat side up so the juices soak down into the meat, automatically basting it and keeping it moist.
- Meatballs won't fall apart if you put them in the refrigerator for 20 minutes before frying or boiling.

Frying Meat

- *Stop bacon from curling* by dipping strips in cold water before frying or by poking the pieces with a fork while frying.

- *Oil-free, no-stick hamburgers.* When frying hamburgers, sprinkle the pan with salt instead of cooking oil. The burgers cook in their own juices.
- *Sausages.* Prevent meat from spilling out of string sausages by waiting to separate them until they are almost cooked.
- *Prevent sausages from shrinking* by rolling them in flour. Roll off the excess.

Prevent Spattering

Place a pan lid a little askew over the frying pan to prevent grease splatters and the potential for burns. The meat will be more tender because the juices stay in. Even better: a metal colander works well by inverting it over the frying pan, allowing just steam to escape.

Quick Frying

Hamburgers cook quickly and evenly if you put ½-inch holes in the center of the patties. As the meat cooks, the holes will disappear.

Grilling Meat

- *Speed grilling.* Cut your cooking time by preheating the grill and its rack(s) for 10 minutes.
- *Save that juice!* Don't puncture meat or chops with a fork because that will release the tasty juices.
- *Use that heat!* Lining an outdoor grill with heavy aluminum foil will save heat by reflecting upwards and save on elbow grease when cleaning up.
- *Juicier burgers* are possible when you form the patties around chunks of cracked ice. The melting ice prevents overcooking on the grill.

Poultry Pointers

- *Poultry* is done when the meat thermometer reaches 180° to 185°.
- *Carving the bird* will be easier if taken from the oven and

SOMETHING SMELLS FISHY?

➤ Fish-fry odors are reduced when lemon juice is added to the fat.

➤ Before washing with soap, rub hands with lemon juice, salt or vinegar and rinse in warm water to keep fishy smell from setting.

➤ Remove fish odors from dishes and pans used to cook and serve fish by washing in vinegar.

allowed to stand. About 15 to 20 minutes for turkey, and 12 to 15 minutes for chicken.

■ *There's no difference* between fryer and roaster chickens when they weigh 3 ½ to 4 pounds, except the price (a fryer is usually less expensive).

■ *Save!* Buy whole frying chickens or turkeys and cut them into parts yourself, boning the breast for cutlets. It's much less expensive.

■ *Use tongs to turn chicken.* Piercing the bird lets out the juices.

■ *Duck and goose.* Prick duck flesh before roasting to drain fat, but don't do that to goose or it will be too dry.

Cooking Fish

■ *Baked.* A whole dressed fish needs about 6 to 9 minutes baking time per half pound at 350°. For pieces, place a layer of fish in an ungreased shallow baking pan and brush with melted margarine or butter. Bake for 4 to 6 minutes in a 450° oven per each half-inch thickness.

■ *Poached.* In a large skillet, add 1 ½ cups of water, wine or broth and bring to a boil. Add the fish and return the water to boiling. Reduce heat and simmer. Fillets and steaks take approximately 4 to 6 minutes per half-inch thickness; and 6 to 9 minutes per half-inch thickness if frozen.

Whiter, Firmer Fish

■ Add a touch of lemon juice to poached fish and it will be whiter and firmer.

■ Add a tablespoon of vinegar to stop fish from crumbling.

BAKING SODA CLEAN

Baking soda can remove those burnt-on stains in casserole dishes and pans. Apply plenty of soda, soak in hot water, then sponge off with a nylon sponge.

Baking soda sprinkled on cookware and rinsed with hot water removes cooking spray residue.

To deodorize food containers, pour two tablespoons into the container with hot water. Let sit until the smell is gone.

BEATING BACTERIA

240°	Temperatures—very high or very low—stop bacteria in its tracks. The time required to kill it decreases as heat increases.
212°	Canning temperatures for low-acid vegetables, meat and poultry in pressure canner. Canning temperature for fruits, tomatoes and pickles in water bath canner.
165°	Temperatures in this range prevent growth, but allow some bacteria to survive. This is the safety point for ground beef, which must be cooked throughout at 160°+ to destroy harmful bacteria, such as Escherichia coli (E. coli).
140°	Some bacterial growth may occur. Many bacteria survive. Temperatures in the 40° to 140° zone allow rapid growth of bacteria and production of some toxins.
60°	Some growth of food-poisoning bacteria may occur. Do not store meats, poultry or seafood in the refrigerator for more than a week.
40°	Cold temperatures permit slow growth of some bacteria that cause spoilage.
32°	Freezing temperatures stop growth of bacteria, but may allow it to survive. To check the accuracy of a food thermometer, fill a large glass with finely crushed ice, add clean tap water and stir well. Immerse the thermometer stem at least two inches into the mixture, touching neither the side nor bottom of the glass. The temperature should read 32°F. *Source: USDA.*

DAIRY: COOL IT

Dairy products spoil quickly and should be refrigerated. When adding cheese, cream, milk or yogurt to soups, stews, sauces etc., do so at the end of the cooking time to reduce the chance of curdling. Or, add a bit of the sauce or stew to the dairy product, mix and then return it to the remaining liquid. For a great low-fat substitute, use yogurt for sour cream and ricotta cheese for cottage cheese.

CHEESE TIPS

When cooking with cheese, remember that overheating and overcooking cause cheese to turn leathery and stringy.

Cheese melts quickly and blends easier if grated or shredded first.

Cheese is easier to grate and sticks less to the grater if chilled by placing in the freezer for 10 minutes prior to grating.

Moldy cheese? Cut off the mold using a knife that has been dipped in vinegar. Dip the knife after each cut. Vinegar kills mold so it won't come back as quickly as it does if you

QUICK, THAW THAT BUTTER!

Soften butter by placing an inverted warmed bowl over the butter plate. Use warm tap water to heat the bowl or heat the bowl in the microwave, filling it with cold water first.

just slice without the vinegar treatment.

Keep cheese fresh by putting butter on the edge of block cheese to prevent drying. Or put cheese, in its original wrapper, in a glass jar and close the jar lid tightly. Keeps a long time!

Store cottage cheese upside down in its carton. This keeps the surface from drying out and the cheese lasts longer.

USING CREAM, MILK OR YOGURT

Milk can be frozen, but cream can't!

To defrost milk place it in the refrigerator or put the carton in ice water, but don't defrost at room temperature.

Whipping cream will whip easier if you chill it first. Chill the bowl and beaters by placing them in the freezer for just a few minutes.

Cream won't whip? Whip a few drops of lemon juice into the cream gradually.

Out of whipping cream? Substitute one small can of evaporated milk and the juice from half of a lemon. The result will be stiff whipped cream.

Frozen yogurt. For a great dessert idea that's healthy too, put small yogurt containers in the freezer. Add diet soda over the top for a float! Freeze in advance for packed lunches. They will be partly defrosted by lunchtime.

Butter

Unsalted butter can be frozen indefinitely if wrapped and sealed airtight. Salted butter can be frozen for a short time in its original container.

Butter needs about 40 minutes prior to a meal to soften.

When sautéing vegetables or browning meat, add a bit of oil (olive or vegetable) to the pan to increase the threshold at which butter burns. Adds a bit of color too.

ADVICE ABOUT EGGS

Buy eggs from a refrigerated case, never at room temperature, to obtain the freshest quality. It's rumored that eggs stay fresher when stored large side up.

Should you buy white or brown? Neither is better than the other (the difference is in the breed of the laying chicken). It may help to remember which are freshest, however, if you buy white one week and brown the next.

YOLK MAGIC

- To separate egg whites from the yolk, place a funnel in a glass and break an egg into the funnel—the egg white will pass through and the yolk will stay in the funnel.
- Egg yolks will stay fresh for a few days if kept submerged in cold water in the refrigerator.
- Having trouble slicing hard-boiled eggs or with crumbling egg yolks? Just dip the egg slicer or knife in cold water to prevent crumbling. To quick-chop hard-boiled eggs, slice them in an egg slicer, then pick up the egg, turn it the other way around and slice it again.
- Crooked deviled-egg yolks? Keep yolks centered by stirring the water from time to time while boiling.

TIPS FOR COOKING EGGS

- To peel hard-boiled eggs, gently place in a pan of cold water for 5 to 10 minutes. Then crack the egg and roll it on a counter to break the shell into small pieces—the shell should then pop off.
- Is it hard-boiled or not? Spin the egg—if it spins evenly, it's hard-boiled; if it wobbles, it's raw.
- Poached coach: Add one teaspoon of vinegar to poached-egg water to keep the egg white from spreading and to help it cook over the yolk.

EGG WHITE WISDOM

- Beating egg whites? Separate the whites from the yolks about half an hour before and let sit at room temperature. This helps whites whip up to a greater volume. If you can't spare the extra time, place the eggs in a bowl of warm water for a few minutes before separating and beating.
- Want to make egg whites stay stiffer? Add slightly less than a teaspoon of cream of tartar to each batch of six or seven egg whites.

TURN LEFTOVERS INTO "LOVELIES"

Here are some tips on leftovers and what you can do with them, along with some ways to spice up your leftover meals.

Vegetables

- Keep salad and vegetable leftovers in the refrigerator for a few days in small plastic bags for later use in omelets and other salads. Don't forget to try wok-cooked leftover vegetables for a tasty Oriental dinner.
- Keep a freezer bag of salad, vegetables and even vegetable throwaways (the tops of scallions, the bottom and top leaves of celery stalks, endive, cabbage cores, slightly wilted beans, not-quite-perfect lettuce and spinach leaves) for use in soup later when you've accumulated enough leftover chicken gizzards, wings, hearts, etc., in another freezer bag. An inexpensive and delicious soup! Adding a little finely grated cheese to a thin soup improves the taste immensely, and don't forget that includes parmesan for an Italian flavor.
- Add vegetables together and combine with nonfat milk and spices in a blender to create a tasty nonfattening creamed soup. Dress it up with grated cheese and croutons.

Bread & Biscuits

- Leftover pieces of bread, biscuits, muffins, rolls and bagels can be frozen in a plastic bag or container. Not too many days later, bring them all out to accompany a meal as a wonderful assortment in the bread basket.
- Leftover French bread is great for homemade pizza. Slice bread in half horizontally, top with sauce and add your favorite Italian seasonings (oregano, garlic, onion), parmesan and shredded cheese (mozzarella is usually associated with pizza but any semi-soft cheese will do). Bake at 425° for 10 to 15 minutes until the cheese bubbles and begins to brown. Leftover meat can be added before baking too—be creative!

Rice Is Nice

- Add cinnamon, a small capful of vanilla extract, milk and sweetening to white or brown rice and warm in the microwave for a quick rice cereal.
- Leftover rice can be added to leftover chicken or turkey vegetable soup. It's a nice change from noodle soups.

COOKING ON THE WEB

www.allrecipes.com

http://busycooks.about.com

http://foodtv.com

www.foodweb.com

www.mealsforyou.com

www.kitchenlink.com

www.eatright.org
American Dietetic Association

www.switcheroo.com
The Cook's Thesaurus

www.ific.org
International Food Information Council Foundation
Answers questions about food allergies, general nutrition, food additives.

EGG ALERT

Raw or slightly cooked eggs (e.g., soft-boiled) should not be eaten by children, the elderly, diabetics, pregnant women, those with weak immune systems or liver disease, or anyone taking medication to reduce stomach acid.

Source: New York Times

Measure, Fix And Fasten

Here are a few critical odds and ends that help your day when you need to measure something and there's no ruler, fix something with innovation and fasten what has come undone.

ELUSIVE MEASUREMENTS

What did they do before inches, centimeters, pounds and gallons? People used their heads—not to mention fingers, feet and fists. The standard 12-inch foot, for example, belonged to the King. A finger snap was the smallest increment of time, and 500 bow-lengths equalled one earshot (about 660 yards). So if you need to measure and don't have the necessary gear, check the charts to find a handy substitute.

MEASURING WITHOUT A RULER

Length (rough approximations)
First joint of index finger = 1"
Width of fist = 4"
Hand-span (thumb to pinkie, extended) = 8"
Shoe (foot) = 12"
Elbow to finger tips = 18"

Close Approximations
3 aspirins = 1¼"
Full height of ½ gallon milk container = 9½"

Exact Lengths & Widths
U.S. penny = ¾"
U.S. quarter = ⅞"
The words "The United States of America" on the front of a $1 bill = 4"
The words "One dollar" on the back of a $1 bill = 3½"
The words "Twenty dollars" on the front of a $20 bill = 3¼"
Width of (standard size) "Bic" lighter = 1"
Width of a book of matches = 1½"
Cigarette (regular length) = 3¼"
Width of an audio cassette = 2½"
Two-penny nail (2d) = 1"
Three-penny nail (3d) = 1¼"
Four-penny nail 4d) = 1½"
Five-penny nail (5d) = 1¾"
Six-penny nail (6d) = 2"

Weight (close approximations)
Four U.S. quarters = 1 oz.
Ten U.S. pennies = 1 oz.
Four sheets of 8½" x 11" paper and one #10 (legal size) envelope = 1 oz.

TIME WITHOUT A WATCH

The smallest unit of time, one **brief instant**, = 0.013 seconds. (Sixty-four [or sixty, according to some] brief instants elapse during the snap of the fingers of a healthy individual.)
One hundred and twenty brief instants = one **instant** (1.6 seconds).
Sixty instants = one **moment** (1.6 minutes).
Thirty moments = one **period** (48 minutes).
Thirty periods = one **solar day** (24 hours).
Thirty solar days = one **lunar month**.
Twelve lunar months = one **solar year**.

HANG THAT PICTURE

Hanging pictures right the first time is made simpler if you cut a paper pattern the same size as the picture frame first. Pin the pattern to the wall for ideal positioning.

To get the hook in exactly the right place:
- Pull the center of the picture frame wire to its highest position. Measure the distance from the distance from the top of the frame to the peak of the wire.
- Mark the hook's position on your paper template. Once it's positioned on the wall, make a pinhole to mark the hook location.

HIDDEN HOOK HOLE

When hanging a picture on a wallpapered wall, cut a small "V" in the paper with a utility knife. Peel it back and insert the hook. If you decide to move the picture later, fold back the wallpaper and glue it on.

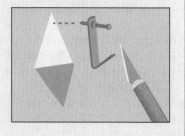

Multiple Pictures

To hang a collage of pictures, lay the frames on the floor in front of the wall area. Organize the arrangement that you're most happy with. Cut paper patterns as above and mark each individual pattern for the hook location.

Tape the patterns to the wall, check your spacing and arrangement. Then mark the hook locations accordingly.

HANGING WITHOUT A PATTERN

If you've just moved in and have to hang dozens of pictures, the "pattern" method is impractical. Instead, use a coat hanger to make a picture-marking tool.

■ Use wire-cutting pliers to cut out the bottom length of the hanger.

■ Make a finger loop at one end of the wire. Bend the other end at a 90-degree angle. Leave about 1-1/2 inches protruding.
■ File the tip of the bent piece into a point.
Use as directed.

FREQUENTLY FORGOTTEN FORMULAS

Area of a Circle
Square the radius and multiply by 3.14. Example: a circle with a diameter of 4 inches has a radius of 2 inches and an area of 22x3.14=4x3.14=12.56 square inches.

Area of a Rectangle
Multiply the length by the breadth.
Example: a rectangle measuring 2 ft by 3 ft has an area of 2x3=6 square feet.

Area of a Triangle
Multiply half the height by the length of the base (find the height by measuring a vertical line from the base of the triangle to the apex).

Acres in an Acre of Land
If the land is rectangular: Find the length and breadth of the land in feet, and divide by 5.5 to find the measurements in rods; multiply the length and breadth in rods and divide the result by 160 to find the number of acres.

If the land has parallel but unequal sides: Add the length of the sides or width and divide by two to get the mean length, and proceed as described above.

Volume of a Cube
Multiply the length of the three sides together. Example: a cube with sides of 3 inches has a volume of 3x3x3=27 cubic inches.

Celsius to Fahrenheit
In the Celsius system water boils at 100 degrees C, and freezes at 0 degrees C. To convert degrees Celsius to degrees Fahrenheit, multiply by 1.8 and add 32. Example: 100° Celsius = 100 x 1.8 + 32 = 180 + 32 = 212° Fahrenheit.

Fahrenheit
In the Fahrenheit system, water boils at 212 degrees F, and freezes at 32 degrees F. To convert degrees Fahrenheit to degrees Celsius, subtract 32 and divide by 1.8. Example: 212° F = (212-32) x 1.8 = 180/1.8 = 100° C.

Quick! What Is Your Age in Seconds?
It is the age of the Internet and if you are in need of a conversion factor, search on "conversion calculations," or look for *www.goconvert.com* or *www.convertit.com*. Or try *www.megaconverter.com* that even allows you to discover how many seconds old you are!

LOST BUTTONS, NO THREAD

It happens at the last minute when you're dressing for an important meeting or function. How to innovate? The obvious choice is a safety pin clipped from the inside of the garment. But if you travel with safety pins, chances are you travel with a sewing kit (an excellent idea). If you have neither, however, try one of these:

■ *Paper clip.* Easy to come by. Fold in two and push through diagonally opposed holes in the button (if the button is gone, just push through the fabric). Twist ends together.

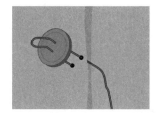

■ *Garbage ties.* The wire is thin and malleable but firm enough to pass through fabric like a needle. Strip off the covering and pass two ends through the button openings. Twist the tie on the opposite side of the fabric.
■ *Toothpick & dental floss.* The two could work together, but if in an emergency you have both of these, you probably have a sewing kit.

Multiply	By	To Obtain
centimeters (cm)	0.0328	feet
centimeters	0.3937	inches
cubic centimeters (cc)	0.06102	cubic inches
cubic inches (cu in)	16.387	cubic centimeters
footpounds	0.13826	kilogram meters
feet	30.48	centimeters
feet	0.3048	meters
feet	304.8	millimeters
gallons, Imperial (gal)	0.1605	cubic feet
gallons, Imperial	1.201	gallons, U.S.
gallons, Imperial	4.546	liters
gallons, U.S. (gal)	0.8327	gallons, Imperial
gallons, U.S.	231	cubic inches
gallons, U.S.	3.785	liters
grams (am)	0.03527	ounces
inches	2.54	centimeters
inches	25.4	millimeters
kilograms (kg)	2.205	pounds
kilogram meters (kg/m)	7.233	footpounds
kilograms per square centimeter (kg/cc2)	14.223	pounds per square inch
kilometers (km)	0.6214	miles
kilometers	3280.8	feet
liters (1)	0.22	gallons (Imperial)
liters	0.2642	gallons (U.S.)
liters	0.03532	cubic feet
liters	61.024	cubic inches
meters (m)	3.281	feet
meters	39.37	inches
meters	1.094	yards
miles (ml)	1.609	kilometers
millimeters (mm)	0.03937	inches
pounds (lb)	453.6	grams
pounds	0.4536	kilograms
pounds per square inch (psi)	0.07031	kilograms per sq. centimeter
square centimeters	0.155	square inches
square inches	6.452	square centimeters
yards (yd)	0.9144	meters

SIX TIES THAT BIND

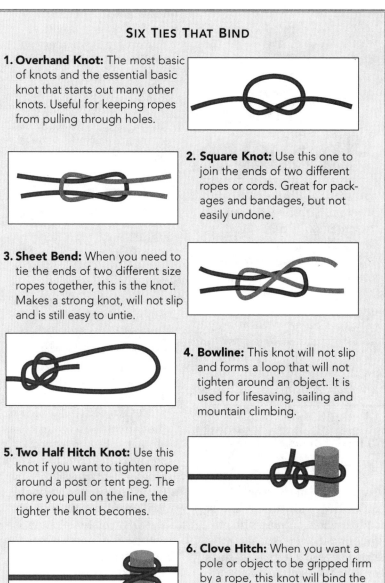

1. **Overhand Knot:** The most basic of knots and the essential basic knot that starts out many other knots. Useful for keeping ropes from pulling through holes.

2. **Square Knot:** Use this one to join the ends of two different ropes or cords. Great for packages and bandages, but not easily undone.

3. **Sheet Bend:** When you need to tie the ends of two different size ropes together, this is the knot. Makes a strong knot, will not slip and is still easy to untie.

4. **Bowline:** This knot will not slip and forms a loop that will not tighten around an object. It is used for lifesaving, sailing and mountain climbing.

5. **Two Half Hitch Knot:** Use this knot if you want to tighten rope around a post or tent peg. The more you pull on the line, the tighter the knot becomes.

6. **Clove Hitch:** When you want a pole or object to be gripped firm by a rope, this knot will bind the object so that it cannot turn or twist.

Solutions To Spots

No household challenge is visited more frequently than accidental spills and splashes. The most successful action is FAST reaction. Knowing what caused the stain, the tolerance of the fabric to different chemical and biological agents plus having the right solution to counter the staining culprit can keep you spot-free and save a bundle on prematurely discarded clothing.

STAIN BUSTER BASICS

One of the most frequent causes of discarded clothing and household articles is due to stains or damage to the fabrics caused by trying to remove stains. According to the Home Economics Department, Institute of Food and Agricultural Sciences, University of Florida, stain removal can be safe and effective when the following basics are observed.

Immediate Response

■ Rapid response is critical. Regardless of whether you plan to remove the stain yourself or have the fabric professionally treated, you must take some action before the stain has an opportunity to set. Fresh stains are easier to remove than old ones.

■ Blot or scrape off any stain substance immediately with soft tissue or paper towel. Depending on the fabric, it may or may not be wise to use water.
■ Read the product label before attempting to use any cleaning process. If you decide to take the garment to a professional cleaner, take it in immediately and be certain that they know exactly what caused the stain.
■ If you are going to attempt your own cleaning, ABSOLUTELY test your solution first on a non-exposed section of the garment.
■ Work from the inside of the garment to push the stain out rather than into the fiber. Do not rub but use a clean white towel on the face side of the fabric to blot the stain.

KNOW YOUR STAIN

There are five basic stain groups that are key to stain solutions.

1. Water-based stains can be dissolved with cool water and liquid detergents. Wine and fruit juices are in this group.
2. Oil or grease-based stains can generally be dissolved with a dry cleaning solvent, loosened with mineral oil and flushed clean with more solvent. These offenders include cooking oil, grease spatters and suntan stains.
3. Double-trouble stains such as meat juices, gravy and ice cream are both wet and greasy. They need to be treated in two stages; first as an oily stain, followed by water-based stain treatment.
4. Color food stains where you have to deal with first the greasy aspect of the stain with one treatment then separately apply treatment to eliminate the color.
5. Tough, tough stains, like tar, ink, mustard, coffee and paint need multiple applications of various concoctions. (See chart page 90). These include the "impossible" and unidentifiable stains, which include bio-stains from humans, pets, magic markers and so forth. The best approach is to treat them first as dry stains, then after airing, treat them as wet stains.

SPOT ACTION

Blot the stain immediately when it happens. Do not use water unless you are sure of the fabric's susceptibility to water staining.

Mark the stain location with pins or a piece of transparent tape. It may disappear when it dries. Read the fabric labels for care instructions.

Test any stain removal solution or chemical on a hidden section of the garment or fabric. Let it dry thoroughly to see the results before attacking the stain itself.

Turn fabric inside out to apply stain solution, forcing the stain out rather than in. Do not rub. Refresh the applicator often.

STAIN SURVIVAL KIT

Stains need immediate attention. Having the right products in place greatly enhances your chances of success. Packaging the right ingredients into a clear plastic container marked STAIN EMERGENCIES makes it easy for anyone in the household to react to a stain in an instant.

Absorbers

Paper towels Squares of blotter paper Squares of brown paper bag Absorbent cloth-like cheesecloth A fresh sponge	The first action with any stain is to absorb (not rub) it. Blotting paper or brown paper bag material absorbs grease stains. Applying the tip of a warm iron to brown paper on top of a grease stain causes the paper to blot the grease.

Scrapers

Old knife Spoon Old credit card	Thick deposits, like ketchup, mustard or honey need to be scraped off the fabric before any blotting or cleaning.

Applicators

Rubber gloves Cotton balls and swabs	For applying chemicals, harsh detergents or cleaning up bio-stains, rubber gloves are essential. For applying chemicals and solutions to fabrics, cotton and cotton swabs are a must.

Household Cleaners

Carpet shampoo Spray stain removers Specialty stain products Laundry detergents with enzymes Detergents without enzymes Clear vinegar, salt	Keep all commercial household cleaners and specialty products in the same emergency kit, separate from the supplies you would normally use. Small, labeled spray bottles are handy for the liquids.

Chemicals & Solvents

Ammonia Denatured alcohol Hydrogen peroxide Glycerin Turpentine Nail polish remover	Several of these items require a trip to the drugstore. Label the containers clearly and ABSOLUTELY store this kit out of the reach of small children.

STAIN REMOVAL TIPS & TECHNIQUES

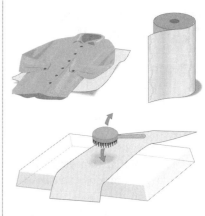

Stains on different materials need to be treated with varying techniques. Ketchup on carpets, for example, will require a different procedure than ketchup on a table linen or on clothing.

If a thick sauce such as gravy causes the stain, place the article on a smooth, hard surface and use a spoon or dull knife to scrape the surface.

Light back and forth strokes are sufficient. Avoid damaging the fibers, and do not use the "scraper" on delicate fabrics.

Soak and Sponge

Generally, with residue removed, treat most stains to a cold or warm water rinse. Never use hot water, it will allow them to set. Place the stained garment stain-side down on a white towel or otherwise absorbent material—paper towel will do. Use a separate piece of white absorbent material to brush the stain from the outer edges toward the center. Do not use circular motion. Change the position of the absorbing pad and sponging pad frequently so that the stain is absorbed and not redistributed.

Tamping & Blotting

Some stains respond better to blotting or tamping rather than sponging. A good tool for tamping is a white-bristled shoe polish applicator, new of course, used as you would a tack hammer tapping the stain out of the fabric. Place the material stain-side down on the surface of a casserole dish and tamp it out. For small spots on delicate fabrics use a toothbrush in the same manner.

CHECK YOUR ABCs

Check the Stain Removal A-Z table on page 90 to determine a recommended stain treatment such as soaking, the use of appropriate detergents, bleaches, solvents or other specialty items.

UPHOLSTERY & CARPET STAINS

Tougher fabrics usually recover and survive stain attacks better than clothing. The key is to take immediate countermeasures followed by more artful follow-up procedures as soon as possible.

Once the initial stain residue is controlled, shampoo both carpeting and upholstery back to normal. Depending on the age of the piece and the nature of the stain, it may become necessary to shampoo the entire carpet or furniture item. It is best to leave this level of "stain-busting" to professionals with the tools and materials specialized for the task.

RED WINE REMEDY

One quick first-aid fix for a red wine spill is to pour white wine on top of it immediately. The interacting wine chemicals neutralize the stain components of red wine. Sponge the two immediately with clear lukewarm water and a mild, soap-free detergent.

Beer & Alcohol

Any alcoholic beverage spill on a carpet or furniture must be flushed immediately with lukewarm water. A good soaking with soda water can neutralize the staining agents until the water arrives.

Liqueur Is Stickier

Sugars and colorings in liqueur tend to leave stains even after thorough flushing. Following the warm water flush, try a commercial stain-removing product if residue remains. If you can still see the stain, try using denatured alcohol to remove remaining coloration. *Caution:* **Test the alcohol on a hidden part of the fabric or carpet before application.**

Grease on a Carpet

This is easy to iron out, literally. Lay a patch of brown paper bag on the grease area, then apply the nose of a medium-heat iron to the location. The iron heats the grease and the paper absorbs it. Follow up with a commercial stain remover.

Furniture Dents in a Carpet?

Ice cubes placed on the indents in carpeting will lift the fibers. Brush the area with a firm bristled hair brush to complete the restoration.

A STAIN BUSTER'S GLOSSARY

BLEACHES
All-fabric
Safer than chlorine and oxygen bleaches, but less powerful.

Chlorine
Powder and liquid: For whitening, removing stubborn stains, deodorizing and disinfecting.
  Do not use on non-colorfast fabrics, or on wool, silk, mohair, leather or spandex; if used with an enzyme product, add near the end of wash cycle.

Oxygen bleach
For whitening and removing stains. Gentler than chlorine bleach; use with warm or (better) hot water for best results. Hydrogen peroxide, a disinfectant available at drugstores, can be used as a substitute for oxygen bleach. Do not use on non-colorfast fabrics.
  Never use chlorine bleach with ammonia, vinegar, cleaning fluids or rust-removers; in combination they can produce a toxic gas.

DETERGENTS
Heavy Duty
Granules: General purpose laundry.
Liquid: General purposes; good for pre-treating stains. *Tip:* use an old toothbrush to rub heavy-duty detergent into a stubborn stain.

Mild
Granules: For delicate fabrics.
Liquid: For hand washing only (produces too many suds for use in washing machines).

Non-phosphate
These are kind to the environment but can leave clothes dull and stiff; remedy this by periodically washing such fabrics in a non-precipitating water conditioner to release and eliminate detergent residue.
  Add detergents as the tub is filling, or dissolve in warm water and add to tub. Dumping detergent directly on fabrics may cause some colors to run.

ENZYME PRODUCTS
Used for pre-soaking and to enhance the cleaning-power of detergents; useful for heavy stains, good for biological stains such as vomit on clothing or carpeting. Wear rubber gloves when using enzyme products.

PRE-TREATMENT SPRAYS
Useful for heavy stains; they contain solvents, so spray just before adding to wash. Some plastic surfaces may be damaged by the solvents in pre-treatment sprays.

SOAP
Flakes, Granules: For lightly soiled and delicate fabrics. Produces scum in hard water.
  Bar soap: For pre-treating light stains and hand-washing. Soap produces scum in hard water. Avoid soap as a stain-remover for some fruit- and vegetable-based stains that contain tannin—it will set them.

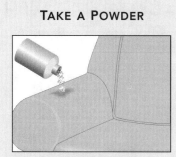
BIO-STAINS

Bio-stains are a gentle way of describing blood, sweat and vomit.

These affect their fair share of clothing, furniture and carpeting. Since these stains set harder over time, the sooner each is treated, the better the results.

Blood on Clothing

Wipe immediately with cold clear water. Follow with immersion of the article in cold, heavily salted water. Leave it set for at least 20 minutes. Follow with a soaking in a heavy-duty enzyme detergent before laundering as usual.

Blood on Furnishings & Mattresses

Sponge liberally with a heavy-duty detergent solution. A stiff brush may be helpful. If the stain persists, make a paste of water and baking soda. Apply and allow drying. Vacuum or brush it clear when dry.

Dried Bloodstains

These are tough and if all else fails, concoct a $\frac{1}{6}$" mixture of hydrogen peroxide and water with a few drops of ammonia. TEST ON A HIDDEN AREA of the article first. Avoid nylon fabrics.

Vomit Stains

You may want the rubber gloves for this. Scrape up the obvious as best you can. Then try the appropriate treatment:

- *Clothing:* Cold water rinse until the stain fades under gentle rubbing action. Soak and launder in heavy-duty enzyme detergent or follow normal laundry steps for the fabric.
- *Furnishings:* Sponge with a gentle warm water and ammonia solution (1-quart water, 1-teaspoon liquid hand detergent, 1-tablespoon ammonia). *Absolutely test this solution on an inside seam before using it on the stain.* Flush with cold water. An alternative is to mix a powdered detergent and water into a paste and apply directly to wet fabric. Once dry; use a commercial deodorizer.
- *Carpeting:* Brush with enzyme detergent in warm water with two capfuls of an antiseptic for odor control. Follow with a liberal amount of carpet shampoo.

STAIN REMOVAL A TO Z

Find your stain in the A to Z listings of the following pages.

- *Pre-treatment* suggests cleaning preparation.
- *Wash* suggests water temperature and detergents.
- *Special applications* offers tips for unusual situations.

Refer to pages 90–92 for the application procedures indicated by the bullets in the table.

Special Treatment Legend

❶ Ballpoint pen ink on suede can be removed by gentle sanding with fine-grain sandpaper.

❷ Candle drippings, wax or chewing gum: Place the garment in a freezer or apply ice cubes to the area. Break off frozen wax or gum then follow the suggested pre-treatment and washing procedures.

Although based on tests and research from reliable sources, the information contained on the following pages are recommendations only.

The success of the stain removal will depend on numerous factors, in particular, the type of fabric that is affected. Any solution must be tried on a part of the fabric that is normally hidden from general view.

STAIN REMOVAL A–Z

HOW TO USE THIS CHART

See page 89 for an explanation of terms used in this chart and details of special treatments.

- ● Pre-treat
- ■ Wash
- ▲ Special

Column groups: **PRE-TREAT** — Soak/Rinse [Water: Cold, Warm, Hot; Detergent: Enzyme, Mild; Bleach: All Fabric, Liquid Chlorine, Oxygen], Enzyme, Spray/Sponge [Solvent: Dry Cleaning, Petroleum based; Other], Rub In Heavy Duty Detergent. **WASH** — Water: Cold, Warm, Hot; Detergent: Heavy Duty, Mild; Bleach: All-Fabric, Chlorine. **SPECIAL** — Dry Clean, Dry Clean Only, NO Soap or soap-flakes, Other.

STAIN	Cold	Warm	Hot	Enzyme	Mild	All Fabric	Liquid Chlorine	Oxygen	Enzyme	Dry Cleaning	Petroleum based	Other	Rub In Heavy Duty Detergent	Cold	Warm	Hot	Heavy Duty	Mild	All-Fabric	Chlorine	Dry Clean	Dry Clean Only	NO Soap or soap-flakes	Other
ADHESIVE TAPE						●							●				■							
BABY FOOD	●								●						■								▲	
BALLPOINT PEN										●			●		■		■		■		▲			
BALLPOINT PEN ON SUEDE																								❶
BARBECUE SAUCE													●		■				■					
BEER															■	■							▲	
BEET ROOT JUICE				●	●								●											
BERRY JUICE															■		■						▲	
BLOOD	●			●										■									▲	
BUTTER													●			■								
CANDLE WAX										●			●				■		■					❷
CARBON PAPER										●				■				■						
CARROT JUICE					●	●														■				
CATSUP													●			■	■		■	■				
CHAP STICK													●						■					
CHEESE										●				■			■							
CHEWING GUM			●										●			■	■							❶
CHOCOLATE	●												●				■		■					
COFFEE															■		■						▲	
COFFEE WITH MILK	●														■		■						▲	
COLAS					·										■	■							▲	
COOKING FATS AND OILS															■	■								❶
CRAYON										●			●		■	■			■					
CREAM	●									●					■			■						
DEODORANTS													●		■	■								
DYES	●			●		●							●	■		■	■							

STAIN REMOVAL A–Z

Legend:
- ● Pre-treat
- ■ Wash
- ▲ Special

STAIN	PRE-TREAT Soak/Rinse Water: Cold	Warm	Hot	Detergent: Enzyme	Mild	Bleach: All Fabric	Liquid Chlorine	Oxygen	Enzyme	Spray/Sponge Solvent: Dry Cleaning	Petroleum based	Other	Rub In Heavy Duty Detergent	WASH Water: Cold	Warm	Hot	Detergent: Heavy Duty	Mild	Bleach: All-Fabric	Chlorine	SPECIAL Dry Clean	Dry Clean Only	NO Soap or soap-flakes	Other
EGGS	●													■				■						
FECES	●													■				■						
FELT-TIP PEN	●					●							●	■				■	■					
FLOOR WAX										●			●	■				■	■					
FRUIT JUICE																								
FURNITURE POLISH										●			●		■									
GLUE (WHITE)				●										■										
GRASS STAINS		●				●							●					■	■					
GRAVY													●					■	■					
GREASE										●			●			■	■							
GREASE (MECHANICS)										●			●				■							
GREEN VEGETABLES						●							●					■	■					
HAIR SPRAY													●					■						
ICE CREAM	●																	■	■					
INK (PERMANENT)		●				●							●					■						
INK (WASHABLE)																								
IODINE																		■						❶
JELLY	●																	■						
LIPSTICK										●								■	■					
MAKE-UP													●			■	■							
MASCARA										●							■		■					
MAYONNAISE																■	■							
MEAT JUICE	●																	■						
MILDEW				●														■	■					❶
MILK	●																	■						
MUD	●				●											■			■					
MUSTARD																		■	■					
NAIL POLISH																						▲		❷

STAIN REMOVAL A–Z

Legend: ● Pre-treat   ■ Wash   ▲ Special

STAINS	PRE-TREAT Soak/Rinse Water Cold	Warm	Hot	Detergent Enzyme	Mild	Bleach All Fabric	Liquid Chlorine	Hydrogen Peroxide	Enzyme	Spray/Sponge Solvent Dry Cleaning	Petroleum based	Other	Rub In Heavy Duty Detergent	WASH Water Cold	Warm	Hot	Heavy Duty	Detergent Mild	All-Fabric	Bleach Chlorine	SPECIAL Dry Clean	Dry Clean Only	NO Soap or soap-flakes	Other
OIL (COOKING)													●			■								
OIL (CRUDE)										●						■	■							
OIL (ENGINE)										●						■	■							
PAINT (LATEX)	●													■			■							
PAINT (OIL-BASE)																	■							
PERFUME																		■						
PERSPIRATION													●	■			■							
PINE RESIN										●			●					■	■					
POLLEN/TREE OR FLOWER										●									■					
PRESERVES: SEE JELLY																								
RUST															■									
SCORCH MARKS													●					■						❶
SHOE POLISH										●			●					■	■					
SMOKE/SOOT										●								■						
SOFT DRINKS																		■						
SUNTAN LOTION										●			●						■					
TAR: SEE (OIL, CRUDE)																								
TEA																		■						
TEA WITH MILK	●																	■						
TOMATO SAUCE													●					■	■					❷
TREE SAP										●								■						
URINE	●																	■						
VEGETABLE OIL										●						■	■							
VOMIT	●																	■	■					
WINE	●																	■						
WATER SPOTS																						▲		

Personal & Family

How to Be Healthy

**How to
Be Healthy**

**Coping with
Illness**

Body Power

Mind Power

Mind & Body …Simply Inseparable

Although we know that there is a powerful connection between our minds and our bodies, most of us aren't as adept as we could be at using that connection to improve our health. How can you harness the power of your mind to heal your body? And what effect does your body have on your mind? Read on for the answers to these questions, and to learn about the tools you need to function at your peak— day in and day out.

ALL ABOUT THE IMMUNE SYSTEM

We all know that having a strong immune system keeps us healthy and helps us recover quickly when we do come down with something. But what exactly is the immune system? And how does it work? Luckily, you don't have to be a doctor or a biologist to understand the basics of how your body protects itself.

The Immune System's Purpose

The most basic function of the immune system is to distinguish the body and all of its components from foreign and potentially harmful substances and organisms. Once it makes the distinction, its job is to destroy or neutralize anything that could compromise your health. You can take all kinds of medicine and try all kinds of treatments, but if your immune system isn't functioning normally, those efforts won't do you much good. Fortunately, the body has considerable natural defenses that protect it and help it recover when it is attacked.

Have you ever wondered what all of those immuno-related terms, such as antigens and antibodies, *really* mean? Fortunately, there are only a few concepts and terms with which you need to be familiar in order to understand enough to take charge of your immune system. First of all, there are two kinds of immunity—natural and acquired.

Natural Immunity

There are all sorts of structural and chemical barriers in the human body that prevent germs from invading and setting up house. Here are the main ones:

■ *Intact skin.* Most microorganisms cannot penetrate the body's skin on their own. If the skin is damaged, however, it is more susceptible to invasion.

■ *Mucus.* The function of mucus is to act as a trap for invading bad germs.

■ *Gastric acid and digestive enzymes.* These have two jobs: to break down food into tiny digestible pieces, and to break down germs.

■ *Antimicrobial substances.* These are substances made by the body, such as interferons, that serve to inhibit the functioning of invading microorganisms.

■ *Fever.* Although we tend to think of fever as the enemy, we are wrong. Specific cells in the body secrete pyrogens, which increase body temperature and inhibit the growth of particular microbes while enhancing the repair of damaged tissue.

■ *Natural killer cells.* These good cells cruise around killing microbes and tumor cells.

■ *Inflammatory response.* Redness and swelling, like fever, is viewed as a bad symptom, but once again, it's just the immune system doing its job. When an area is invaded, the blood vessels swell and become more permeable, allowing the body's defensive cells and substances to flood the area and overwhelm the enemy.

Acquired Immunity

In addition to the mechanisms listed above, an immune response can also be activated in reaction to invasion by a specific organism or any substance that the body perceives as foreign.

♥ BEST IMMUNE SYSTEM BOOSTERS

➤ Echinacea
➤ Astragalus
➤ Ginseng
➤ Maitake mushrooms
➤ Vitamin C
➤ Vitamin E
➤ Love
➤ Laughter
➤ Prayer
➤ Meditation and other relaxation techniques

⊘ WORST IMMUNE SYSTEM BUSTERS

➤ Stress and distress
➤ Untreated infections
➤ Alcohol and drug abuse
➤ Smoking
➤ Environmental toxins
➤ Poor diet
➤ Lack of sleep
➤ Excessive sugar intake
➤ Anger
➤ Depression
➤ Anxiety or chronic worrying

- *Antigens.* These are foreign invaders (such as bacteria and viruses) that stimulate an immune reaction in the body.
- *Antibodies.* When antigens enter the body, they are attacked by antibodies. Antibodies "fit" specific antigens, and may already exist in the body or may be manufactured in response to an infection.

When you have been exposed to an antigen for the first time, it takes a little while for the antibodies to build up. That is why you get sick. If the same organism comes to call again, it is tagged by the antibodies against it right away, marking it for immediate destruction by white blood cells. When you are immunized, or vaccinated, an antigen is artificially introduced into your body to stimulate the production of antibodies against it. These vaccinations can be quite effective, but do not appear to stimulate your body in exactly the same way as being exposed to the live organism does.

Signs of an Impaired Immune System

An immune system can be either underactive or overactive.
Signs of underactivity include:

- *Fatigue, low energy level or listlessness*
- *Frequent or repeated infections*
- *Slow healing*
- *Chronic diarrhea*

- *Overgrowth of organisms that our bodies would ordinarily destroy, such as yeast*

Signs of overactivity are:

- *Allergies*
- *Autoimmune diseases, such as rheumatoid arthritis*

The immune system can malfunction severely (as with AIDS) or, much more commonly, can become temporarily depressed. Stress is a major contributing factor to the depression of the immune system.

Building & Rebuilding Your Immune System

As with other parts of the body, you need to use your immune system in order to make it stronger and keep it in good working order. What does this mean in a person's day-to-day life? Give your immune system a chance to fight infections before you reach for pills that suppress the body's immune response. If you're running a fever, give it a chance to create an inhospitable environment for the invading organism instead of suppressing it with drugs. The fever has a purpose. If you feel that you must bring it down, then let it do its job during the day, and take medication to reduce the fever in the evening.

Do not overuse antibiotics. The body has a built-in ability to quash simple infections, such as those of the ear and bronchial tubes. Give your body a chance to build resistance to these organisms on its own. With antibiotic-resistant infections now reaching epidemic proportions, building an immune response to common infections is crucial, since there may be no effective medication available to treat them.

Watch out for steroid drugs like prednisone and hydrocortisone. They achieve their amazing

---

WHAT ARE GERMS?

We tend to think of infections as bacterial, but there are actually several types of microorganisms that can invade your body. The most common are bacteria, viruses, parasites and fungi (like yeast). Fortunately, your body's immune system has formidable mechanisms for preventing them from gaining a foothold. You can give your body a helping hand by limiting your exposure to potentially nasty bugs by observing the following simple rules:

➤ Wash your hands frequently, particularly after you use the bathroom and before you handle food.

➤ Thoroughly wash all fruit and vegetables; rinse meat, poultry and fish before cooking; and keep all cooking utensils and kitchen surfaces clean.

➤ Be especially careful to cover breaks in your skin, including burned areas. Ordinarily, germs cannot penetrate intact skin, but damaged skin is an open invitation to microbes. Keep the area clean and dry (germs love moisture), and cover it with a gauze dressing or bandage.

YOGA HELPS

Try this yoga exercise—called Child's Pose—a few times a day to strengthen your immune system:

From a kneeling position, bring your thighs together and sit on your heels, then exhale slowly while bending forward from the hips. Place your forehead on the floor and breathe deeply for 30 seconds. Focus on your breathing, then inhale slowly as you get to your feet. You should feel the tension flow out of your body.

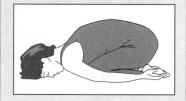

THE IMMUNE SYSTEM'S BATTLEGROUND

You may have heard of a technique called guided visualization. If you have an infection, for example, you might imagine little soldier cells swimming through your blood vessels blasting the invading bad bugs with weapons. Well, guess what? You actually *do* have an army, complete with an impressive arsenal, available around the clock. Here are the key players and how they take care of the bad guys:

Phagocytes: These are the notorious white blood cells that we hear so much about. They gobble up the miserable microbes trying to set up housekeeping in our bodies.

Memory Cells: These cells never forget a microorganism. They are left over from prior battles; when the body is invaded, they head over and attack bugs they've dealt with in the past.

Lymphokines and Interleukins: These secretions allow white blood cells to communicate with each other: "Hey, there's a spiky bad guy over by the liver that's been tagged by an antibody. Better get one of the T-cells to shoot his armor full of perforin, then get a phagocyte over there to mop up the debris."

Natural Killer Cells: Born killers, these cells cruise around searching for infected or cancerous cells and annihilate them by direct contact.

Antibodies: Contrary to popular belief, antibodies do not directly attack invading cells. What they actually do is "mark" bad guys for destruction—then phagocytes finish the job.

Perforin: This substance is secreted by some of the white blood cells and used to kill microbes by punching holes in their membranes.

results by suppressing inflammation—a normal immune response. The creams in particular *appear* innocuous, because people don't realize just how much of a drug is absorbed through the skin into the bloodstream. For example, consider the effect the nitroglycerin skin patch has on lowering blood pressure on chest pain due to heart disease. Rub calamine lotion on insect bites instead of using steroids, particularly for children, whose immune responses are still in the formative stages. Try to avoid using oral steroids on a regular basis—they should be reserved only for life and death situations.

Do not ignore minor infections. If you have symptoms such as swollen lymph nodes, recurrent cold sores or frequent sinus congestion, make a conscious effort to build up your resistance. Here are the steps to follow:

■ *Get plenty of rest.* In our society, there is a great value placed on pushing ourselves to the limit, working long hours and being highly productive. When was the last time you left work

AUTOIMMUNE DISORDERS

Sometimes the immune system incorrectly identifies healthy or harmless cells in your body as potentially dangerous and attacks them. This can result in chronic inflammation or even the destruction of vital organs. These conditions can be difficult to diagnose, and people may see many specialists before receiving the correct diagnosis. See a health-care professional if you ever have unusual pain in your joints or symptoms that you can't explain, such as blurry vision, fainting, unsteady gait or any type of partial or temporary paralysis. Although there is no cure for autoimmune disorders, they can all be treated. These disorders sometimes go into remission on their own, with the immune system suddenly "realizing" that it's been going after the wrong guys.

Rheumatoid arthritis. Unlike ordinary arthritis, in which constant mechanical friction wears away the cartilage between bones at the joints, with rheumatoid arthritis, the body actually attacks the cartilage and breaks it down.

Lupus. Systemic lupus erythmatosus often attacks the body on multiple fronts and can cause a characteristic butterfly-shaped rash on the face as well as symptoms of rheumatoid arthritis and kidney disease.

Multiple sclerosis. The body attacks myelin, which ordinarily covers certain types of nerve cells. Plaques then build up along the nerve fiber, interfering with the nerve's ability to send signals.

for a couple of hours to take an afternoon siesta? Well, while the siesta idea may be impossible to get your boss to agree to, it is important to spend enough time just resting so that your body can relax and repair itself. Begin winding down an hour earlier than you're accustomed to and read something light, such as a magazine or humorous book—whatever you find relaxing. Or create a relaxing ritual, such as an evening bubble bath. Everybody needs some down time, so make sure you get enough.

- *Don't overdo the partying.* Few things tax the body's systems like staying out late and drinking too much. If you only indulge once in a while, it won't kill you. But definitely avoid this form of recreation if you have any signs that you're not 100% up to snuff. And if you do go out, make sure you have a good meal, drink plenty of water and load up on vitamins that are depleted by alcohol, such as thiamine (vitamin B1) and vitamin C. Then make sure you get enough sleep the following night.

- *Eat healthy food.* Your body requires particular nutrients to fight infections and repair tissues effectively. Don't eat too many sugary foods—they tax the immune system. Fresh foods are the highest in nutrients, provided they haven't been sitting in the supermarket too long. Pick frozen vegetables rather than canned, and take vitamin and mineral supplements until you feel your best again.

- *Take immune-enhancing supplements.* There are particular supplements that appear to boost the immune function. Pay a visit to the health-food store and pick up tinctures of echinacea and astragalus. Take one dropper of each three times a day in a little water or juice. Stay with this regimen for up to four weeks and see if your symptoms abate. Don't take echinacea for longer without giving your body a rest—long-term use may actually depress immune function and the herb may lose its effectiveness. Avoid immune system enhancers if you have autoimmune problems, such as allergies, since the immune system is already hyperstimulated.

- *Reduce stress and pay attention to your emotional life.* Plenty of research shows that people who are stressed become sick more easily, more frequently, more acutely...and recover more slowly. Several studies have shown that students exposed to cold viruses are more likely to come down with a cold during final exams than at less stressful times. Being stressed changes the body's hormonal balance, making it more likely that invading organisms will gain a foothold. Read the following sections on having a sense of well-being, making friends and managing stress for techniques on how to improve your emotional state and develop a sense of serenity.

Create a Family Health Tree
Everybody has some strengths and weaknesses built right into their genes. Maybe you get frequent colds but never catch the stomach flu when everybody around you is sick with it. Think back over the past few years. What ailments do you tend to come down with? Are they the same ones that "run in your family"? You do not have any control over your genetic blueprint, but your diet, stress level, environment and other external factors are powerful determinants of whether you actually become ill. For example, you may have red hair, fair skin, freckles and a family history of skin cancer. But if you never sunbathe and always protect your skin with clothing, sunscreen and a hat when you go outdoors, your chances of getting skin cancer will be greatly reduced in spite of your genes.

It's a good idea to take stock of your family history in a methodical way. Make a list of any ailments that your parents and siblings suffer from. Divide the list into serious health problems

---

PSYCHO...NEURO...IMMUNO POTPOURRI

As impressive as it sounds, psychoneuroimmunology is just the study of the interconnectedness of your mind, nervous system and immune functioning. If you harbor any doubts that they are intimately connected, check out this potpourri of fascinating facts:

➤ In one study, a group of pregnant women with morning sickness were given syrup of ipecac (which makes you vomit) and told that it was a powerful drug that would get rid of their nausea and vomiting. The women *stopped* throwing up after they took it.

➤ In many cultures that believe in sorcery, people who had curses put on them died of no discernible cause other than their hearts ceased beating within hours or days of having been bewitched.

➤ Under hypnosis, people who were touched with cold metal were told that it was a burning iron and they developed blisters at the site.

(such as diabetes or heart disease) and less serious problems (such as seasonal allergies). Then move on to your grandparents' health problems, followed by aunts and uncles, and finally to your great-grandparents and cousins. For diseases that have a genetic component, the closer the person is to you in the family tree, the more likely it is that you will be susceptible to the same problems.

Bear in mind that just because a particular disorder occurs in your family does not necessarily mean that you are predisposed to it, only that the chances are higher. Similarly, the fact that certain disorders *do not* occur is no guarantee that you won't get them. For example, women with a family history of breast cancer are more likely to develop it, but most women who get breast cancer have no family history of the disease. So be sensible. Don't abuse your body with cigarettes just because nobody in your family has ever had lung cancer. Remember...you could be the first.

Once you have a general idea of your genetic background, you can take steps to protect yourself against health problems that seem to be common in your family.

HAVING A SENSE OF WELL-BEING

E ven though we've all heard the saying, "If you don't have your health, you don't have anything," most of us still think of the mind as having the greater power in the mind-body equation. But your body also exerts a powerful influence on your mind. That's why tending to both your physical and emotional health is crucial to a sense of well-being. Reducing stress to tolerable, even beneficial, levels is also key. But there are some misconceptions about the best way to achieve this. Relaxation techniques are all well and good; but if you're stressed out because you've overextended your resources and now the bills are due, the relaxation program won't do you much good. In other words, practical problems need

---

TIME FOR SOME CHANGES

Once you map out the changes you want to make in your life, there is a trick to staying on the new path—just don't get off it! What do we mean? Well, once you've made your plan, don't second-guess yourself if the going gets a little tough. It takes some fortitude to break bad habits and establish new ones. But you had good reasons when you started and they're still good reasons. It was a good plan when you formulated it and it's still a good plan. And don't let anyone else make you doubt yourself. They can make their own plans if they want to. Chances are you'll be living a new and improved life while they're still griping about theirs.

Most of all—*don't let yourself get discouraged.* Tiny steps in the right direction are still steps in the right direction, and they all add up...to a whole new life.

HOW TO SEE & BE THE "NEW YOU"

Do you know why horoscopes tend to be accurate...at least to some degree? Well, much of their predictive power results from the phenomenon known as the "self-fulfilling prophecy." You read the horoscope, it sounds appealing, and you subconsciously take steps you would not have otherwise taken, which then coincide with the horoscope's message. So how can you harness the power of this phenomenon to help you change your life? Easy. Simply visualize yourself feeling the way you would like to feel, looking the way you would like to look and living the way you would like to live. Make a habit of it and incorporate it into your daily routine. Here's how:

Have a vision. Picture the new you with those all-important details in place. Imagine yourself having finally lost those pounds, gotten a new hairstyle, gone back to school, become confident and relaxed, learned to react with patience instead of anger—whatever features of your lifestyle, personality or appearance you wish were different.

Fantasize on a schedule. Pick a time during the day (preferably two or three times), when you drop everything for five minutes, sit back, close your eyes and run your fantasy through your mind. Keep picturing the new you until it really begins to feel like you.

Include new-you people in your life. We're not suggesting that you drop all of your old friends, but get out and socialize with people who are living the way you would like to. If you want to be in better physical condition, don't just join the gym. Talk to the person on the treadmill next to yours. If you would like to learn more about classical music, go to concerts. Then strike up a conversation with the couple in front of you before the show begins. Before you know it, you'll have made a whole new group of companions for art show openings, plays, ski trips, kayaking or whatever else captures your fancy.

practical solutions.

We're so bombarded these days with advice on how to live well and feel well. But once you've figured out which changes you want to make, how do you go about unlearning years of bad habits without throwing your life into turmoil? Well, we're offering you a jump-start on a new life by separating the solid advice from the nonsense and providing an action plan for changing your life and feeling *good* about it!

How to Move a Mountain

Everyone makes resolutions about the changes they want to make in their lives. So what distinguishes those of us who achieve those goals from those who don't? Very simple—the people who succeed have a good, comprehensive plan that addresses all aspects of their lives, together with a frame of mind that allows them to view the work ahead as challenging rather than daunting. Never lose sight of what you're working toward and how much more contented you will be when you get there.

Here's a step-by-step plan that you can either follow exactly or customize to suit the requirements of your particular life. But in order to make the changes really happen, you must focus on each individual step without fretting over all the steps that will follow. Remember that old expression about moving a mountain one stone at a time? Even if at the end of a month's worth of effort you've lost only 2 pounds of the 20 you want to drop, you're still 2 pounds lighter than you were the month before and 2 pounds closer to your goal. The same is true of getting your home in order or improving your eating habits. Those small steps add up. Remember those 2 pounds? At the end of a year, they will add up to 24 pounds. Don't look left; don't look right. Don't allow yourself to become distracted or despondent. By the end of a year, all of those little steps will have added up to a whole new way of living.

Taking Stock of Your Day-to-Day Life

It is difficult to be in peak health when your daily life is in turmoil, so you will need to make an objective assessment of your home and work situations. Then make the changes that will help you create a comfortable and relatively stress-free environment for yourself. This is easier said than done, but probably is not as difficult as you think. It involves two basic steps: deciding what needs to be done and then doing it. Now, here are the all-important details.

Is Your Household Running Like a Well-Oiled Machine?

Probably not. But getting your house in order is easier than you think, and it's also extremely important to your sense of well-being. Many people believe that they're not happy or functioning well because they're low on serotonin, when the fact is that a messy life and a stack of unpaid bills would depress anybody.

Here are the basics of what needs to get done and how to make it happen:

■ *Clean up.* It's hard to feel good when your environment is unappealing, so make this a priority. If you have a little extra money, you may find it worthwhile to put your feet up and read a good book while somebody else does the dirty work... so to speak. Or you could make a deal with friends to help with their homes if they help with yours. It's much easier to get

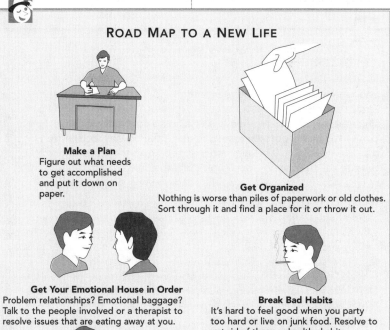

ROAD MAP TO A NEW LIFE

Make a Plan
Figure out what needs to get accomplished and put it down on paper.

Get Organized
Nothing is worse than piles of paperwork or old clothes. Sort through it and find a place for it or throw it out.

Get Your Emotional House in Order
Problem relationships? Emotional baggage? Talk to the people involved or a therapist to resolve issues that are eating away at you.

Break Bad Habits
It's hard to feel good when you party too hard or live on junk food. Resolve to get rid of those unhealthy habits.

Establish Healthy Habits
You have to replace the bad habits with good ones. It takes about a month to break a bad habit or establish a good one, so tough it out!

Follow Through
Don't give up. You'll need to be on top of yourself for a while to make sure that you don't slip back into your old ways.

through this kind of job with moral support and some good company. Depending on the level of grime that has accumulated, a glass or two of wine might not be a bad idea either. If you do find yourself going it alone, don't be daunted. Tackle one room at a time and clean the entire room, including the parts you think nobody will see.

HOW TO BE THE BOSS

Making lifestyle changes is an easy matter if you live alone, but what if you have a family? How do you get them to accept the new system? Since most of us prefer having a well-ordered life—particularly if someone else is willing to arrange it—this should not be a problem when it comes to initially organizing and cleaning the house. You may run into a little conflict later on when you start replacing the chips with grapes, but the key to success is to simply state the new order firmly and with confidence. If they want chips, they can go hang out at Grandma's.

When you put up the schedule, make sure that you assign chores. If there are tantrums over new responsibilities, explain the system and why it's necessary for everybody's well-being. Be clear about the expectations and the consequences, such as no television viewing, for failure to cooperate. Be firm, but not emotional, in your explanation. Children respond best when they sense that you are in control of the situation. Don't get sucked into having multiple discussions about the new system. Odds are that everybody understood it the first time, and anything else is just a delaying tactic.

Uncooperative spouses are a little trickier, and your best bet may be to just plead. Something along the lines of "*Pleeeaaaase* help me with this. I just want us all to be healthier and happier, and I'm trying to set up a system to make it happen," is hard to argue with. You might hear something like "I was happier when I could wash down breaded pork chops with soda for supper," muttered under somebody's breath, but few adults will want to try to support that statement in the course of a discussion. Since you're in the right, assume that you'll get grudging acceptance for your "Plan For A New Life."

■ *Get organized*. Use the same approach you used for cleaning the house to organize your bills, clean out the closets, sort through old papers and get the basement in shape. If you can afford it, hire a professional to do the initial work. In fact, organization specialists are now listing themselves in the *Yellow Pages* and placing ads in local newspapers. Otherwise, tackle one job at a time and don't worry about the ones you haven't got to yet.

■ *Make a schedule*. Once you have everything in order, you will want to keep it that way. The best system for achieving that is to maintain a master schedule and adhere to it. Set aside a particular time for paying bills, cleaning house, grocery shopping and every other activity that takes place regularly. Generate the schedule, put it up on the refrigerator or a bulletin board and then stick to it. Having a schedule will also help you realize how much time is really required to take care of a household, which many people underestimate.

JOY BEATS MISERY BY 2 TO 1

In a study that examined the impact of stress on immune system functioning, researchers found that the beneficial physiological effects of happy experiences (such as expressions of love) lasted for two days, while the harmful effects of negative events (such as having an argument) lasted just one day.

■ *Keep lists*. Keep a list of phone calls that need to be made, letters that need to be mailed, groceries that need to be picked up and every other small chore that needs to be taken care of. Then set aside a small block of time to attend to two or three things on the list every day.

■ *Take care of yourself*. Making time for activities that you enjoy and tending to your physical appearance are important determinants of your emotional health. It is particularly important to maintain your normal activities and good grooming when you feel down.

■ *Maintain the new order*. Put in the effort to keep things running smoothly and on schedule once the new system is in place. It may be tempting to let what seems to be small things slide, but the devil, as always, is in the details. A couple of dirty plates left on the coffee table in the living room may seem innocuous enough, but they become a signal that it's okay to start leaving cruddy stuff all over the place again.

How Habits Help & Hurt

It's an interesting fact that people who are creatures of habit live longer, healthier lives. Here's a fascinating tidbit: In a study measuring the effectiveness of a medication versus a placebo for the treatment of a medical condition, researchers found that people who took their placebo at the same time every day, according to the schedule, improved considerably over those who took the placebo erratically. Unfortunately for the makers of the medication, the disciplined placebo-takers also did better than those who got the study medication…but that's another story. The interesting

point here is that people who lead organized lives appear to be healthier, happier and more productive than those who go to bed, get up, go to work and eat on erratic schedules. Predictability is a form of security, and most people function at their best physically and emotionally within a secure and dependable framework.

EARLY TO BED, EARLY TO RISE MAKES A MAN HEALTHY, WEALTHY & WISE

There may be more to that old saying than you think—for two reasons. First, people with regular habits are healthier—the body seems to function best when it gets food, rest and exercise in a stable, predictable manner.

The second reason has to do with light and the body's natural rhythms. Back in the old days, we went to bed when it got dark and got up when it got light. Although it was born of necessity, it had some clearly beneficial effects on our bodies. When darkness falls, our bodies produce more of a hormone called melatonin, which induces sleepiness. As daylight approaches, our bodies produce less of it, which helps to wake us up and keep us wakeful.

By prolonging daylight through the evening hours with artificial and often bright light, we suppress melatonin production. In addition, many of us then keep ourselves awake with the help of a drug—caffeine, often in quite large doses.

Night-lights and electric clock lights don't help either. Even small amounts of light while you sleep will suppress melatonin production to some degree, causing you to sleep more lightly. Since melatonin production is also believed to boost immune function and inhibit the development of cancer, preventing your body from producing normal amounts of it is not a good idea.

Interestingly, some scientists think that a deficiency of melatonin may explain why children are going into puberty earlier than their grandparents did. If your children are hooked on their night-lights, it's a habit worth breaking. Let them fall asleep with it on, then turn it off.

Of course, not all habits are created equal, and not all habits are good. Just as the benefits of healthy habits (like eating green vegetables) accrue over time, the adverse effects of bad habits build up too. One day of smoking won't have any long-term effects, but a few years of smoking will. Take stock of behavior that you engage in on a regular basis, and then make sure that the habit is healthy, given the frequency. For instance, having a glass of red wine with dinner is a perfectly healthy habit, while five glasses with dinner is a perfectly *un*healthy habit.

How to Break a Bad Habit & Adopt a Good One

Changing habits is difficult and often requires formidable willpower. The good news is that the first few weeks are the hardest. Studies have shown that it takes about a month to break a habit or to establish a new one (which are really the same thing). If you can make it through that first month without breaking down, you're nine-tenths of the way there. That doesn't mean that you'll never have cravings, but at that point you have already proven that you can resist them. Be firm with yourself.

There is a secret to making and breaking habits that is the key to success: You must be able to picture yourself living happily without the habit you want to eradicate or with the one you

want to establish. Many people have trouble giving up bad habits like smoking or drinking because they cannot really imagine their lives without them. Or they may want to include more fresh vegetables in their diet, but can't really picture themselves not lining up at the drive-thru window at McDonald's. Take the time to visualize your new life. Fantasize about how wonderful it will be. Picture yourself healthier, more attractive and more in control of your life and destiny.

THE IMPORTANCE OF FRIENDS

Here's the bottom line: studies have shown that people who are lonely tend to have immune systems that don't function as well as those of people who are well connected. There are many reasons for this, not the least of which is the relief that any distraction provides from minor aches and pains.

But not all relationships are created equal. Being in a stressful marriage, for example, may be harder on an immune system than not being married at all. The key is to have a supportive social network. Just what does that psycho-terminology mean? Well, here are the benefits you should be experiencing from your interactions with other people:

■ *Having fun.* Not every event in your life has to be suffused with importance. Just cutting loose and relaxing reduces levels of stress hormones that compromise the functioning of your immune system. Make sure that you have at least one or two friends with whom you can be silly, if that's what you feel like doing.

■ *Receiving comfort.* Plenty of things don't go the way we'd like them to, no matter how blessed we are. If you have the kind of personality that allows adverse events to roll off your back, that's great. But if you don't (and let's face it, that's most of us), then having a non-critical, nonjudgmental shoulder to cry on is crucial. Half the time, just having a good cry and being able to vent is all that's needed to start feeling better.

If, as an added bonus, your friend gives good advice, so much the better.

■ *Liberation from loneliness.* Being alone is not necessarily a bad thing, and we all need some introspective time to ourselves periodically. But being *lonely* is a whole different kettle of fish. Being lonely is bad

FURRY FRIENDS ARE FINE

You don't necessarily have to love and be loved by other *people* in order to derive the benefits of close relationships. Plenty of studies have shown that people who own pets are happier, healthier and less likely to become clinically depressed than people who only have themselves to think about.

for you for the same reason that a sprained ankle aches more at night when everybody has gone to bed. When there are no distractions, even small things look big. Just having a certain amount of activity around you will keep you from being overly focused on small matters and will reduce the chances that you'll get depressed as well.

■ *Being taken care of.* Having emotional support isn't the only health benefit you get from

good relationships, of course. People who care about you will also encourage you to eat well, see a health-care practitioner when you're sick and tackle addiction problems like smoking. On a practical level, people who are close watch out for each other's health and well-being, prepare food for each other and, in their own ways, mother each other.

Bear in mind that although it is wonderful to receive love, attention, comfort and sympathy from

FOR SHY PEOPLE

Lots of self-help books are full of suggestions for how to make that first overture if you're shy. But what if your knees get so shaky at the thought of approaching a stranger that every tip you ever read falls right out of your brain? Forget trying to turn yourself into a Fearless Freddy. Simply put yourself in the line of fire of more assertive personalities and you'll have friends in no time. What do we mean? If you go where the people are (concerts, parties, plays), sooner or later someone is going to talk to *you* or maybe you can get yourself to talk to them. As an added bonus, people will get to know you as you really are…a little shy. Perfectly fine. Plenty of people value a more reserved and less aggressive personality anyway, so don't fret.

HOW TO MAKE FRIENDS

What if you've just moved and haven't made new friends yet? Or you realize that the people you've been associating with really aren't your type. Maybe you've had one too many late nights out…or maybe one too few. Or you've just never been that great at "connecting." How do you go about building a healthy social network ("good friends," in other words). Well, here's a formula:

Make a commitment. This is the first step to making any change in your life. Make sure that you want to include more friends in your life, and then make a plan to achieve it.

Figure out what you enjoy. This is easy. What do you like to do? A great determinant of whether you'll want to spend time with another person is finding out whether you have common interests. At least you'll know that you have a jumping-off point for a conversation and maybe some joint activities, too.

Go where the people are. You have to at least share air space with other people if you hope to make friends, so go to events, join clubs, go out with your coworkers after work. Even if they're not your greatest pals, you'll meet other people wherever you all end up. Odds are, once you're out among other people, you'll have a great time and meet some potential new friends and lifelong pals.

other people, you have just as much—if not more—to gain by giving it back. In fact, you can only have a truly intimate relationship—be it a friendship or a romantic love affair—if you experience and express as much concern for the other person as you receive. And it's the truly intimate, healthy relationships that lead to lasting happiness and a sense of contentment.

STRESS FACTORS

The late-20th-century phenomenon of being "stressed out" is really just the misapplication of a very basic human instinct—the fight or flight response. When we perceive a threat, our bodies pump adrenaline, our blood pressure goes up and our heart and breathing rates rise. In the blink of an eye, we're ready to either remove the enemy's head from its body or run a three-minute mile. This is very useful when you're out in the wild trying to turn some nasty critter into a family meal before it turns *you* into one. But it's not all that helpful in our present environment.

Unfortunately, the more primitive part of our functioning doesn't always do the best job of distinguishing a real physical threat (scary person with a knife approaching you in a dark parking lot) from an emotional threat (trail of pizza crumbs marking your child's movements through the house). Our bodies tend to create the same response in us: the release of stress hormones, causing higher blood pressure, tense muscles and the like. Although your body's response to the first situation is likely to be more extreme, the constant physical response to chronic irritations, like not getting along with your boss, can wear you down over time, making you more prone to depression, anxiety and illness.

So how can you take control of these reactions, deal with the irritants in a productive manner and reduce the primal reaction of your body? Fortunately, stress-related complaints are among the easiest to treat, provided you are willing to put in a little time and effort. For starters, give some of the ideas below a try.

Are You Revving Yourself Up?

Often we don't realize how many of our seemingly innocuous habits actually hyperstimulate our systems. Too much coffee can do it, of course, but so can those relaxing cups of caffeinated tea…if you have enough of them. If you've been having trouble relaxing, start by limiting your caffeine intake to no more than two cups a day—one in the morning and the other no later than 4 p.m.

Although some people find that exercising in the evening tires them out for bed, the more common reaction is to be in an alert state for several hours afterward. Try to get your exercise in before you go to work in the morning. Or round up a couple of coworkers to exercise with you at lunchtime. Exercising earlier in the day is actually a stress *decreaser*, since your heart rate and your blood pressure are lower after you finish. Stretching can relax tense muscles, stimulating a sense of calm.

Finally, watch out for that evening beer or glass of wine.

FIRST-STEP STRESS BEATER

Don't worry about being worried! When trying to reduce stress in our lives, we all have a tendency to focus on what we think are our problems and then try to figure out how to solve them. All of them. Right away. But don't focus on the little niggling things, and don't make a conscious effort to banish negative thoughts. Instead, put your energy into positive activities and ignore a less-than-optimum frame of mind. As you fill your life with such positive efforts, the worries and fears will gradually disappear by themselves.

TRY THIS FOR A MORE RELAXED ATTITUDE

Here is a yoga exercise—called The Corpse Pose—that is guaranteed to leave you feeling refreshed. Lie on your back with your legs and arms apart, feet turned out and palms up. Close your eyes and draw in a deep breath. Focus on breathing deeply and slowly for a few minutes. Don't consciously try to banish other thoughts; just let them flow in and out. If you just concentrate on your breathing, the thoughts will gradually subside. Repeat a few times a day, on the floor of your office if necessary.

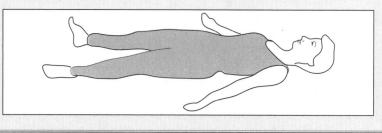

MEDITATION MAGIC

Not all of the popular practices of the 1960s were wacky. In fact, in some aspects, the hippies were really onto something. One of those is the practice of yoga or meditation, which actually includes several techniques that have been shown to slow you down, center you and ease away tension. That's because it combines controlled breathing and visualization with forcing you to sit still for a period of time (usually 20 to 30 minutes). The position shown below is the classic "Lotus," but you can meditate in any position you find comfortable. Resist any urge to enhance the relaxation effect with any popular controlled substances. The idea is to teach your body and mind to unwind themselves through using their own power. Here are the steps:

➤ Pick a peaceful, quiet place to meditate.
➤ Sit in a comfortable position.
➤ Pick a word ("mantra" in yoga-speak) to focus on.
➤ Concentrate on your breathing, repeating the mantra slowly in your mind.
➤ Visualize a beautiful light and open yourself up to it.
➤ Keep breathing in and out slowly, repeating the mantra and blending yourself into the light, for about half an hour.
➤ Slowly ease back into the world.

The half Lotus position

Keep the arms loose and relaxed at your side

Shoulders should be straight but relaxed

Palms up should be facing upwards

Back of one foot rests in crease between hip and abdomen

Alcohol has an initially sedating effect, but it wears off as you sleep. Then in the middle of the night, when you should be in your deepest sleep, your brain is over-active. That means you awake less refreshed, setting the stage for a stressful day.

Relaxation Techniques

Stress-related disorders are particularly responsive to the effects of controlled breathing, and most relaxation exercises rely on specific breathing techniques. Some rely on progressive muscle relaxation. Some people find that they have greater success with these methods under the direction of a teacher or health-care provider. Practitioners of the Alexander technique may be especially helpful. If you're the sort of person who is motivated by the camaraderie of a group setting, you might want to seek out a class—there are many these days. But first, try the simple relaxation recipe in the box to the left. With a little perseverance, you may be surprised at the results.

Other Relaxation Remedies

You don't have to resort to Valium or other tranquilizers to get some assistance with your stress levels. Although no chemical remedy should replace relaxation exercises for calming your nerves, there is some all-natural assistance available.

TIME TO DE-STRESS

There is quite a vast range of physical problems that can be either caused or aggravated by an overabundance of stress in your life and the accompanying stress hormones circulating in your body. Here's a small sampling:

➤ Anxiety
➤ Depression
➤ Tension headaches
➤ Digestive upsets
➤ Fatigue

➤ Insomnia
➤ Elevated blood pressure
➤ Neck and back pain
➤ Frequent colds and other infections

Research has even shown that people are more likely to have asthma attacks, develop heart disease and even die of a heart attack if they're too stressed. Just one more good reason to learn how to relax and manage your stress…before it has an even greater negative effect on you.

Here are a few botanical remedies to try:

- *Kava tincture*
- *Passion flower tincture*
- *Chamomile tea*
- *Valerian tincture or tea*
- *Hops tincture*

Laugh It Off

If mastering relaxation techniques sounds like a lot of work to you, there are other ways of releasing tension. Studies have shown that the simple act of laughing has a powerful effect on both your mind and body. You will have to make a concerted effort to infuse more of it into your life, but just like some of the other suggestions, you'll have plenty of fun trying.

HOW TO LAUGH

If you want to reap the full physiological benefits of laughter, you have to do it right. Snickering, sniffing and snorting as you try to repress the big guffaw simply will not do. It's the full-body, out-of-control, spasm-racked version that ultimately lowers your blood pressure and relaxes your muscles. If your friends and family hide their faces when you laugh in public, then you know you've got the hang of it. Better yet, get them laughing with you.

HOW TO TALK TO YOUR BODY

Mind-body medicine has been a catchphrase for about the last decade, but what exactly does it mean? Well, the aspect of it that most of us focus on is the concept that your mind can have a powerful impact on whether you get sick...and whether you get well.

As you begin to explore the possibilities, make sure you avoid the common pitfall of seeing mind-body effects as a one-way street, with your mind having all of the power over your body. A body that is poorly taken care of can put a real damper on your mental functioning, mood and overall health. Make sure that you eat well, exercise regularly and get plenty of rest. Be especially careful not to overdo it if you're not feeling your best. Many of us keep pushing to keep up with our daily routine even when we can sense that we're run down or are fighting off a cold or some other bug.

Here are some specific techniques that draw on the mind's considerable powers to bring about the healing response in the human body.

Get in Touch Using Biofeedback

Biofeedback is an ingenious therapy that gives you the ability to influence body functions that are ordinarily not under your direct control, such as blood pressure, heart rate and skin temperature. It is especially valuable for alleviating muscle tension that can lead to headaches, back pain, bruxism (grinding your teeth at night) and other ailments that are the result of stress. It has also been used with great success to treat high blood pressure, irregular heartbeat, ulcers, digestive problems and cold fingers and hands resulting from spasms of the blood vessels in the extremities (known as Raynaud's disease).

So how does it work? Biofeedback therapists use equipment that translates bodily functions like heart rate and muscle contraction into sounds and pictures. Sensors attached at different points on your body (painlessly!) transmit audio and visual signals (beeping sounds and flashing lights) to a monitor. If somebody were to tell you to lower your blood pressure, you would have no idea how to go about doing it. The beauty of biofeedback is that if the therapist tells you to slow down the beeping sound, with a little practice you can do it... even if you have no idea how you managed it. The speed of the beeps correlates with the level of your blood pressure. Afterwards, you practice at home without the feedback machine to duplicate the results on your own.

Considering the large amount of scientific data that supports the effectiveness of biofeedback techniques, it is surprising that it has not yet been fully incorporated into mainstream health-care choices. Definitely seek it out as a noninvasive way to manage chronic conditions like headaches and anxiety, particularly if you have been relying on medication to control your symptoms. It can even be useful for conditions such as impaired circulation in the feet of diabetics, who can be taught to raise the skin temperature in their toes significantly.

BIOFEEDBACK WORKS

Some conditions respond better than others to biofeedback. Here are the ones you're likely to get good results with:

- ➤ Anxiety
- ➤ Asthma
- ➤ Attention deficit and concentration problems
- ➤ Digestive upsets
- ➤ High blood pressure
- ➤ Incontinence
- ➤ Irregular heartbeat
- ➤ Migraines
- ➤ Muscle pain
- ➤ Stress disorders
- ➤ Tension headaches

Conjure Up a Lemon

If you're not convinced that what you visualize in your mind can cause a real physical reaction or sensation in your body, then you need to picture a lemon. Here's how this exercise in doubt removal works:

Sit back in a chair and close your eyes. Take a few deep breaths and let your thoughts flow in and out at random. After a minute or two, place a lemon in your mind's eye. Watch it turning around slowly, then imagine slicing it in half. Watch the sour juice shimmer on the cut surface. See yourself lift one of the halves to your mouth. Feel your teeth bite into the cut side, and let the juice run into your mouth. Squeeze the lemon half so that more of the juice and pulp are forced into your mouth. Now, admit it…you don't even need to sit back and go through the visualization to see what we mean. Because just by reading these words your mouth is already making excess saliva to dilute the lemon juice, and your mouth is already tense because of the assault of the extreme sour taste.

This is the mechanism on which mind-body therapies like biofeedback and guided imagery depend. After all, if you can use this power to cause saliva to flow, why can't you use it to relax blood vessels and lower blood pressure? The answer is, you can.

IMAGINE YOURSELF WELL

Guided imagery and visualization are hot topics for research studies these days because so many people claim that they work. These techniques have been used to fight everything from anxiety attacks to cancer, as well as to improve immune functioning. Guided imagery appears to be highly effective against pain, particularly chronic pain. It's definitely worth a try before you start experimenting with high-tech approaches. Here's a guided visualization exercise to work with if you suffer from any kind of chronic pain.

Lie back comfortably and allow your body to relax. Feel your arms, legs and eyelids becoming heavier. Let thoughts pass freely in and out of your consciousness; do not try to actively control them. After 5 or 10 minutes, or whenever you feel calm, focused and relaxed, visualize the part of your body that has been hurting. First picture it as red and hot, then imagine it in flames. Once the area is consumed by fire, imagine a person approaching with a huge, crystal-clear pitcher of cool water. Conjure up a person whose image is comforting to you. This could be a beautiful angel complete with wings, a middle-aged doctor or your mother—anyone whom you associate with an ability to heal. Imagine that person slowly pouring the water over the flames, over and over again, from an endless supply. Imagine the area cooled and soothed, then dry and healed, and finally…free of any discomfort and pain.

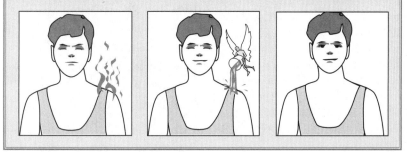

_i_

FOR FURTHER READING

Creative Visualization: Use the Power of Your Imagination to Create What You Want in Your Life
Shakti Gawain
New World Library

Secrets of Creative Visualization
Phillip Cooper
Samuel Weiser, Inc.

MAGIC & MIRACLES

More than priests or presidents, physicians in our society are the ones who we believe have power over life and death—they are the magicians of the Western world. But they don't act much like magicians anymore. In the eyes of many patients, doctors have turned into technicians and businessmen, losing their ability to be healers in the process.

But the desire for healers is primal, and the failure of doctors to address this need has created a void that many people are filling with alternative-care practitioners, treatments and remedies. What alternative medicine lacks in scientific evidence it makes up for in its emphasis on the tremendous healing power of the mind. A person's very state of mind can mean the difference between getting well and staying sick. That doesn't mean that you can cure any illness just by having a good frame of mind, only that it may tip the scales in your favor—often significantly.

Alternative-care practitioners spend more time with their patients, touch them more and reduce their feelings of isolation and despair. Those practices are part of the reason that psychotherapy is as effective as Prozac.

The Trouble with Statistics & Serious Illness

When given statistics about illness, most people tend to gravitate to the worst-case scenario. For example, if a woman in her 40s is told that her risk of having a baby with Down's syndrome is 1 in 50, she considers the likelihood of having a child with the disorder to be high. Yet, when people with pancreatic cancer are told that the chance of a cure is 1 in 50, they consider their odds of being cured to be low.

Statistics steal hope by implying that you'll be in the "big group." But the fact is that the person making the prediction doesn't know whether you have six months, six weeks or six minutes left to live. Doctors don't know how long a person will live; they only know the statistical probabilities for a particular illness. As with all of life's surprises, you are just as likely to be the recipient of a miracle—or beat the odds—as anybody else.

It's a good idea to have all of your affairs in order if you're diagnosed with a serious illness, but that's also a reasonable measure to take if you drive a car. Anything *can* happen, but that doesn't mean it *will*. Once you've taken care of any practical concerns, put all thoughts of death out of your mind. The more time you spend with other people instead of alone with your fears, the easier this will be. Problems are always formidable when it's dark and quiet, so avoid spending too much time by yourself.

Friends & Family

It's been shown over and over again that people with strong ties to others live longer and healthier lives. And now evidence is mounting that participating in support groups also helps people live longer when they have serious illnesses like cancer. Support groups are particularly helpful because they provide interaction with people who are having a similar experience and can empathize and share practical suggestions.

Maintain and strengthen your ties to family and friends, and don't feel guilty about imposing on their time or good graces. Most people want to be there for the people they love, so don't assume that you're intruding.

If you feel that seeing a therapist would help, then find one. Psychotherapy can be very helpful for reducing anxiety and working through the issues that having a serious illness raises.

Spirituality & Health

If you want to be happy and healthy, most cultures as well as scientific studies suggest that you develop and nourish your spiritual life. People define spirituality differently, but many hold in common a belief and faith in the power and inherent goodness of a higher being, which allows them to find beauty and peace in their daily lives. Looking out for the welfare of other people has also been shown to confer emotional and health benefits both to the helper and to the person being helped. It improves life for everybody in the community as well.

A sense of compassion, an ability to love and to forgive, and a sense that there is meaning to life beyond our day-to-day experiences are all key elements of having a serene outlook on the world. And it's serenity that is the key to emotional comfort, relaxation and inner peace.

Feel Better with Meditation

If you're not already meditating on a daily basis, you're missing out on a safe, easy strategy for better physical and emotional health, says Dr. Herbert Benson, President and founder of the Mind/Body Institute at Beth Israel Deaconess Medical Center in Boston. Study after study has shown that meditating for at least 10 minutes a day protects against anxiety and depression, headaches, heart rhythm disturbances, high blood pressure and premenstrual syndrome.

One common form of meditation involves repetition of a sound, phrase or motion…and passive disregard of intrusive thoughts. Walking, jogging, gardening or ritual prayer can be forms of meditation. These behaviors elicit a state of deep calm known as the relaxation response. That's the physiological opposite of the fight-or-flight response, in which emotional stress readies the body for lifesaving action by flooding it with powerful hormones.

PRAYING FOR HELP

About 100 controlled studies have shown that both praying and being prayed for have a positive effect on healing. You might expect the prayer's condition to improve—because of the beneficial impact on that person's state of mind. But, to the contrary, these studies have even shown an improvement in people who didn't know that others were praying for their recovery. In fact, in one study, a group of heart patients, for whom others had secretly prayed, had fewer complications than a comparable group of patients who had not received intercessory prayer. Even lowly lab rats who had been prayed for recovered faster than those who had not been the objects of prayer. And studies have even shown that microbes, like bacteria and fungi, grow faster when you pray for them, too.

Finally, people who are members of a religious faith—any faith—live longer and healthier lives than those who are not religious.

Minding the Body

Doing what you can to establish a healthy frame of mind may be critically important, but it doesn't mean that you can forget about the mechanical workings of the machine itself—the body. How to keep it in top running condition, what to power it with and what substances and practices to avoid are key elements of keeping both your mind and body in tip-top shape. Here's what you need to know about preventive maintenance.

KEEPING IN SHAPE

Although we tend to think of keeping in shape as having strong hearts (from aerobics) and strong muscles (from lifting weights), there's a little more to it than that. Your body is filled with chemical messengers known as hormones, which affect every body function, both physical and emotional. That's one of the reasons why exercising elevates your mood—physical activity causes your body to release endorphins. In fact, your nervous and endocrine (hormonal) systems are so interconnected that they're often referred to as the "neuro-endocrine system." So as you're struggling through your exercise routine, bear in mind that you will reap benefits far beyond improving your heart rate and muscle tone. And it may not be as painful as you think. Read on to find out why that's the case.

How Much Exercise Is Really Necessary for Good Health?

Although the standard of beauty in our country approves of clearly delineated muscles (even for women), you do not need to look like a magazine cover model in order to be in excellent physical condition and the peak of health. In fact, either being too thin or having overly bulky muscles is associated with other health problems, particularly in women. You do want to be in good enough condition to maintain a healthy weight, to be able to carry out reasonably demanding physical activities with ease and to keep your body's organs and systems in good working order.

Which Activities to Do?

What do you enjoy? Walking is fine, as is swimming. Gardening and aerobics classes are other options. Divide the activities into those in which you can participate every day (or almost every day) and those that are occasional or seasonal (such as skiing).

Now here's the key to being in shape: participate in activities *regularly.* It's not the sport you play occasionally that makes the most difference, no matter how intense it is. Rather, you need to spend 20 to 30 minutes a day, five or six days a week, doing something that gets your heart and muscles going. Study after study has shown that walking is fine exercise as long as the pace is brisk and you stick with it for a full half hour. The good thing about walking as exercise is that it doesn't require any other equipment or much fuss.

But whatever you choose, set aside the time for it, and then do it! Lunch hour at work is perfect. For example, a few minutes to eat and then a nice walk. Drag along a few office buddies—the camaraderie will keep you all going, and you'll all see the benefits.

Don't Overdo It

For those of us with a spare tire or two this may seem like a joke, but it really can be a serious problem. Young women are particularly susceptible to exercising in a way that's more

---

⭐ HOW TO STAY IN SHAPE WITHOUT ANY FUSS

Maintaining a healthy level of exercise does not have to be overly disruptive. It does not have to consist of complicated regimens and schedules that involve expensive personal trainers and hours of zealous and painful devotion. Here is all you need to do to make the low-key, life-altering change that will make you healthier and happier:

➤ Make the decision to exercise three or four times a week for about an hour or so.

➤ Create a time and space for the exercise. Set that time aside and make sure that everybody understands that you will not be available for any other activity during that time. Make it a part of your life—like bathing—that you simply cannot dispense with.

➤ Pick an exercise that you enjoy. It can be anything from mountain biking to walking to gardening. If you like the activity, you'll be more likely to stick with the program.

➤ Stay on track. The first month is always the most difficult because that's about how long it takes to form a new habit. After that, it will be part of your regular routine and you will feel out of sorts if you miss a day.

harmful than helpful. Here's an increasingly common and alarming scenario: A young woman with normal weight and fat distribution decides that she's not attractive because she can't see her hip bones protruding in front of her abdomen. First, she restricts her food intake. Then she starts running. Finally, she adds weight lifting. What's really happening to her body? Well, first of all, she's probably not eating enough food given her new, higher level of activity. Second, if she's replaced meat with lettuce leaves and carrot sticks, she'll be low on energy and deprived of some important nutrients. A restricted diet can also result in hormonal changes that disrupt the normal menstrual cycle. And increasingly, young women are being diagnosed with osteoporosis (thinning of the bones) which used to be seen almost exclusively in elderly women with small frames. Not to mention the fact that running is a particularly hard activity on the joints.

Solutions for Overweight

Assuming that you really do have too much body fat and less than optimally functioning cardiovascular and muscular systems, what's the healthy way to go about getting into shape? Well, not the way you might think— at least not initially. What do we mean? Do not start by restricting the number of calories you eat.

Instead, increase your activity level and wait a few weeks to see if you begin losing weight. Healthy food is packed with nutrients that your body needs, so don't eliminate your supply of these nutrients without trying to boost your metabolism first. Notice we said *healthy* food. So what's healthy? Read on…

BASIC DIET SMARTS

What should you eat? What should you drink? And does it really matter? Of course it does. Changing the way you eat is hard because breaking habits— often lifelong habits in the case of food choices—is difficult. But finding the strength to change the way you think about food has the power to change your whole life for the better.

Here's a thought to keep you going as you change your diet: It's not the foods that you eat once in a while that hurt you; it's the ones that you subsist on, day in and day out. In other words, if you happen to love hot fudge sundaes or sour cream and onion chips, you can still enjoy them… once in a while. Don't tell yourself that you'll never indulge in another sinful food. Just try to eat less healthy choices less often—only eat them on designated days—second Sunday of

the month for a giant portion of black forest cake, for instance, and Friday nights only for a medium bowl of chips. Here's another uplifting tidbit: As your day-to-day eating habits change, your craving for unhealthy foods will lessen. This is particularly true of well-balanced diets, which keep blood sugar levels stable. More about blood sugar later on, but remember resisting bad food *will* get easier.

How Much Does It Matter?

In case you're fuzzy on the details of why you need to eat healthy food, here are a few facts that should jar you into action.

■ *Poor diet is associated with diseases like colon cancer, hardening of the arteries and diabetes.*

■ *Low-quality food doesn't provide you with the nutrients that are necessary to maintain a high level of energy.*

■ *Unhealthy food doesn't supply adequate vitamins, minerals and other micronutrients necessary for growing and maintaining the body's vital structures, which can lead to conditions like osteoporosis (thinning of the bones).*

⚠ BEER-BELLY SURPRISE

Guess what? Beer really can give you a beer belly. Researchers aren't sure why, but excess calories that come from alcohol tend to decrease the waist-to-hip ratio in women (the tummy grows slower than the hips) and increase it in men (the tummy grows faster than the hips). Being heavy around the middle (apple-shaped) is associated with a higher incidence of both diabetes and heart disease.

♥ THE POWER OF CARROTS

You may remember your parents telling you that you had to eat your carrots or your eyesight would suffer, but what exactly is the connection? Well, carrots are extremely rich in beta-carotene, which the body converts into vitamin A. The body needs vitamin A for the synthesis of rhodopsin in the rods of the eye (among other things). The rods are the visual receptors that allow the eye to respond to low levels of light. If the rods cannot make a steady supply of rhodopsin, nightblindness results.

■ *People who eat poorly are more likely to be overweight, which is a risk factor for many diseases including heart problems and high blood pressure.*

Now, on to the details of how to approach powering your body properly and how to feed it the proper foods for fuel.

♡

EAT BY THE COLORS FOR OPTIMUM HEALTH

Here's what you should see when you look down at your plate: a palette of bright colors (and we don't mean the artificial ones that you find in Jell-O!). Pick dark, leafy greens over iceberg lettuce, rich red tomatoes over pale pinkish ones, and ripe, sweet, deep-orange peaches instead of hard, sour ones. Look below for a color key to the produce section of your local market, and enjoy the entire rainbow of nutrients at your next meal.

Yellow. In vegetables like squash, yellow equals carotenes. In lemon peel, it's the color of limonene, which may protect against some forms of cancer.

Orange. More carotenes, especially beta-carotene are found in orange foods, such as sweet potatoes, cantaloupes and carrots. Orange peel contains limonene.

Red. Tomatoes, strawberries, watermelons and other red fruits and vegetables are chock-full of lycopene, which may be a better cancer fighter than beta-carotene.

Green. Dark green vegetables are rich in carotenes as well as polyphenols, which may prevent certain cancers. Eat lots of broccoli, brussels sprouts and dark leafy greens.

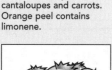

Blue/Purple. The dark purple-red color of grape skins indicates that they contain ellagic acid, which may prevent cancer and heart disease. Blueberries are full of polyphenols.

White. Cauliflower contains indoles (cancer fighter), while members of the onion and garlic family are full of allyl sulfides, which fight high blood pressure and cancer, and lower cholesterol.

Listen to Your Body, But Don't Be Fooled by It

Healthy eating is not about dieting and deprivation; it's about eating the just right amount of nutrient-rich food, nothing more and nothing less. Food is fuel. People who have a healthy approach to eating don't spend a lot of time thinking about food.

They eat when they're hungry, and they eat foods that will sustain them—like complex carbohydrates, protein and some fat—not sugary quick fixes.

Here are a couple of things to keep in mind as you reset your culinary clock:

■ *Are you really hungry?* We often mistake thirst for hunger, so before you assume that those hunger pangs really mean you're hungry, drink a glass of water. If you feel "hungry" within three hours of your last meal, you're also being fooled by your body. Have some water or a piece of fruit, then do something else to alleviate the stress or boredom that was most likely responsible for the hunger pangs.

■ *Build up your muscle.* We tend to focus our attention on eating as little as possible, but that's not necessarily a great idea. First of all, if you consume too few calories your body goes into "starvation mode," slowing down your metabolism. Fewer calories also mean fewer nutrients. Add a little weight training to your daily routine to boost muscle mass *and* your metabolism. You'll be able to eat a larger amount of food without gaining weight.

What Should You Eat?

Does it really matter where your calories come from? After all, your body turns everything it takes in into sugar for energy. So why not just live on strawberry tarts and ice cream to begin with? Well, you knew that we weren't going to recommend *that* because nutrition is about calories *and* micronutrients (like vitamins and minerals). So here's what you *should* be eating:

■ *Beans.* They provide high-quality protein and plenty of fiber. Use them in soups and salads.

■ *Fiber.* There are two kinds of fiber: soluble (e.g., in fruit) and insoluble (e.g., in whole wheat). Both types are important, but insoluble fiber may dramatically reduce the risk of colon cancer.

■ *Fish.* Healthier than meat and poultry, fish seems to protect against heart disease. Stick with deep-sea types, like cod and sardines, to reduce exposure to contaminants.

■ *Fruits and vegetables.* Full of vitamins, fiber, flavonoids and other micronutrients, fresh produce protects against heart disease, cancer and numerous other problems.

■ *Grains.* Whole grains stabilize blood sugar and reduce the risk of colon cancer by supplying the body with plenty of insoluble fiber. Replace simple carbohydrates, such as white bread, with complex carbs.

■ *Soy.* Soy products contain phytoestrogens, which may protect women from breast cancer and men from cancer of the prostate. Soy is also chock-full of high-quality protein.

What Should You Drink?

What you drink is just as important as what you eat. If you're getting a lot of your fluid intake from coffee and soda, you could be making better choices.

- *Water.* Water should be the mainstay of everyone's fluid intake—eight glasses a day or more. If your tap water doesn't taste great or if you think it's contaminated, get a filter or consider bottled water.
- *Juice.* You're better off drinking water and eating a piece of fruit than drinking juice, which concentrates the calories and eliminates the fiber. Juice that's been sitting around in cartons or bottles loses some of the vitamin content too. Many parents make the mistake of giving young children juice instead of water, which gets them hooked at a young age on the idea that beverages should be sweet. Give them water from the start instead; they'll be perfectly happy with it and healthier too.
- *Milk.* Milk is good for children, but its effects in adults are much less clear. In Finland, where adults commonly drink milk, heart attack rates are the highest in the world—in spite of the Finnish high-fiber diet. The culprit could be the raw milk sugar, because cultures in which adults eat cheese and yogurt (products where the milk sugar is fermented) do not have as high a heart attack rate.
- *Tea.* Tea is packed with flavonoids which may cut the risk of heart attack in half by making the blood less likely to clot. Flavonoids are also powerful antioxidants, which prevent cell damage and cancer. Both green and black teas appear to have similar effects, so drink the one that you prefer.
- *Wine.* A little red wine does appear to have a beneficial effect on the heart, but watch the amount—just one glass a day for women, two for men. Purple grape juice seems to confer the same benefits.

SODA: NOT JUST BAD FOR YOUR TEETH

Here's a 1-2-3 justification for giving soda the boot: Soda contains large amounts of phosphorus, which causes calcium to leave your bones and teeth. Less calcium makes these structures weaker. And if soda is replacing milk as a beverage, you could be getting a double whammy— less calcium ingested in addition to calcium being leeched from your bones and teeth.

So what *should* you say to your children who may be overly fond of soda? Remember, you're the parent. Keep it firm, simple and to the point: "Sorry, kids, but I just found out that too much soda can weaken your bones and teeth by causing them to lose calcium. From now on we're only having soda once a week and no more than two glasses apiece. You'll thank me when you're old and can still chew your own food and walk to the bathroom without having to holler for help."

And they will.

♥ SAFE ADDITIVES

Not every unfamiliar name on the list of ingredients should send you running. Here are some considered safe even by organic food purists:

- ➤ Citric acid and ascorbic acid
- ➤ Ammonium bicarbonate
- ➤ Malic acid
- ➤ Fumaric acid
- ➤ Lactic acid
- ➤ Lecithin
- ➤ Xanthum gum
- ➤ Guar gum
- ➤ Calcium chloride
- ➤ Monocalcium phosphate
- ➤ Monopotassium phosphate
- ➤ Annatto
- ➤ Carageenan

Handle Food Safely

Don't be complacent about food contamination just because you buy your groceries in a health-food store. Remember, bacteria and other organisms like organic produce just as much as you do. Here are the pitfalls you should avoid in order to protect your family and guests:

- *Wash the food.* This applies to everything, including "ready-to-eat" salad greens, as well as fruits and vegetables that you plan to peel. Fish, meat and poultry should be rinsed.
- *Don't pierce meat as you're cooking it.* You could be introducing bacteria into the interior, which may not get cooked thoroughly enough to kill the organisms.
- *Put food in the refrigerator.* Don't let prepared food sit out at room temperature for longer than two hours. Outdoors, keep food on ice or in a cooler, particularly dishes prepared with mayonnaise or meat, poultry, seafood or eggs.
- *Use different utensils.* Don't use the same knife or cutting board for meat as you do for fruits and vegetables.
- *Be meticulous.* Wash your hands, all utensils, cutting boards and kitchen surfaces thoroughly.
- *Wash your sponge.* It's a haven for bacterial growth.

SHOULD YOU BUY ORGANIC?

If you can afford the few dollars extra—yes. Although proponents of the use of chemicals and drugs in food production insist that they're safe, no one knows for sure. Even if they don't hurt you, they certainly don't contribute to good health, so stay away from them as much as possible. There are three major contaminants that you are trying to avoid:

Pesticides on the surface of the food. A thorough washing, particularly with lemon juice, will remove many surface pesticides. Peeling the fruit or vegetable is better, but wash it first anyway. Once you cut into the food, any residue left on the surface will be carried into the interior of the food.

Pesticides inside the food. No amount of washing or peeling is going to address this problem. Once the farmer sprays the crop, the chemicals are washed into the soil and are taken up by the roots of the plant. Buying organically grown produce is the *only* way to avoid this problem, and remember that grains are affected too. Buy organic cereals, bread and flour.

Hormones, antibiotics & other drugs found inside the food. To boost production, many American animals are fed drugs, many of which could end up being absorbed by the people who eat the products. Antibiotics fed to animals may be part of the reason for the increase in human antibiotic-resistant infections, and constant low-level exposure to antibiotics may also help account for the explosion of allergic conditions over the past 20 years. Hormones may also help explain the increase in weight of Americans during the same time frame. Some scientists think that ingestion of these hormones may be partly responsible for decreasing sperm counts and the increased incidence in fertility problems. These drugs don't only reach us via meat; in fact, toxins and medications are often stored or concentrated in the animal's body fat, making milk, cheese, butter, and other dairy products chemical warehouses. Buy only eggs, dairy products, meat and poultry that carry statements that the animals have not been given hormones or antibiotics. The safest products come from animals that have also been raised on organically grown feed.

Are you getting what you pay for? It's always possible to get ripped off, but products that state explicitly that they meet the California standards for organic produce are most likely to be free of the contaminants you're trying to avoid. If you're suspicious, you can have a sample tested by a laboratory or check with the Better Business Bureau or Department of Agriculture for complaints against specific companies.

BE SAVVY ABOUT SUPPLEMENTS

If you haven't already heard about it, there's an argument raging between those who believe that nutritional supplements are a key component of good health and those who think that they just result in incredibly expensive urine, or worse, that they're actually bad for you. The truth probably lies somewhere in the middle and depends on which substance you're talking about.

And, of course, vitamins and minerals are hardly the only supplements out there these days. You can buy everything from enzymes to amino acids to glandulars (whatever *they* are) to something called royal bee jelly… but should you? Read on to find out which supplements really help you and which ones just help the marketing geniuses or misguided minds who thought to pop them into pill bottles.

The Original Supplements— Vitamins & Minerals

There isn't any debate over whether vitamins and minerals are necessary for good health— they are. But there still is a debate over whether people who have a normal diet require supplements of these micronutrients.

Adding to the debate, the RDA (recommended daily allowance) may be the amount the body requires from all sources in order to prevent nutritional deficiency diseases, but many health-care practitioners believe that the recommended levels established by the RDA are too low for optimum health. In addition, vitamins and minerals may prevent or treat certain conditions when taken in

MONEY DOWN THE DRAIN?

For those of you who haven't heard, sanitation workers who clean portable toilets claim that tons of vitamin and mineral tablets make it out in more or less the same state in which they made it in, often with the brand name still intact. That's not great news, since it means that many of these pills are not being broken down, and the nutrients aren't being absorbed. Supplements are available in other forms that may be more absorbable, including liquids and powders.

You can make a powerhouse smoothie by mixing half of a banana, ice, orange juice and your choice of berries, together with the daily dosage of your vitamin-mineral powder, in a blender. It sure beats trying to swallow half a dozen pills…

higher doses. Then there's the matter of which segment of the population you're talking about. Elderly people, for instance, don't extract micronutrients from their food as efficiently as younger people do, so the elderly may get the most benefit from taking supplements. As long as you're not taking megadoses, you're unlikely to do yourself any harm and may even do yourself some good.

Here's a summary of the vitamins and minerals that have been making the news, along with some information you may not have heard.

Vitamin A

This is the vitamin that helps you see by maintaining night vision. Vitamin A also plays a role in the normal development of skin and certain other body tissues. If you take anything labeled "vitamin A," be aware that large doses (more than 50,000 IU a day) can be toxic. A safer bet is to take the precursors of vitamin A—the carotenoids. Precursors are substances that are used by the body to manufacture the vitamin. The advantage of taking mixed carotenoids is twofold. First of all, carotenes are water soluble, which means that any excess can be eliminated by the body. Vitamin A itself is fat soluble, and any excess is stored in the body, where it can reach toxic levels. Secondly, beta-carotene isn't the only carotene that's good for you,

and a supplement of mixed carotenes will supply you with a whole range of micronutrients, including lycopene (a powerful antioxidant that may help prevent cancer) and lutein (which may protect against vision loss resulting from macular degeneration).

B-Complex Vitamins

Though more exciting claims are made for some of the B vitamins than others, you should make sure that any supplement contains at least a small amount of each one. This is because, in some cases, the chemical interactions that occur between them are necessary for proper absorption.

Beyond that, you shouldn't take large amounts of any one B vitamin unless you are treating a specific condition or disease. If that is the case, be sure to consult a licensed health-care provider who has been trained in the medicinal use of vitamins.

- *B-1 (thiamine).* Thiamin makes energy available for the body, and a deficiency will result in particularly noticeable effects in brain function. Thiamine is selectively destroyed by alcohol, so drinkers should be especially careful to supplement their diets.
- *B-2 (riboflavin).* There have been no spectacular claims made for riboflavin, although some researchers say that it can

---

NUTRITIOUS FOODS

Regardless of whether you supplement your diet with vitamins and minerals, food should still be your primary source of micronutrients. There are several reasons for this, not the least of which is that we don't know how many substances natural foods contain that we haven't yet discovered, isolated and put into a pill. Secondly, many—if not most—micronutrients are more efficiently absorbed from the food in which they occur naturally. Finally, food provides you with other compounds, such as fiber and phytochemicals, which are necessary for optimum health and functioning.

Most of us know that meat is rich in iron and that oranges are full of vitamin C, but did you know that dark leafy greens are a better source of calcium than milk? Check below for other surprising sources of micronutrients.

Dark leafy greens. One cup of cooked collard greens contains more calcium than a cup of milk—360 milligrams versus just 300 milligrams. For a truly healthy delicious side dish, lightly steam your dark greens (spinach, collards or whatever), then toss them in hot olive oil with minced garlic. Voila! You're a continental chef.

Beans. All varieties of beans and legumes (like lentils) are known for improving digestive health and reducing the risk of colon cancer. But did you know that the isoflavonoids they contain may also protect against heart disease? And the soluble fiber they provide may lower cholesterol levels, further protecting against heart attacks.

Red Peppers. Four ounces of red peppers contain almost twice as much vitamin C as a cup of OJ, but that's not the only thing this vegetable has going for it. It's full of fiber and loaded with lycopene—a red pigment believed to be a powerful antioxidant and cancer fighter. Tomatoes and watermelon are rich in lycopene too.

Nuts. Nuts are good for you, but don't eat too many—they're high in calories. They contain monounsaturated and polyunsaturated fats (the good kind), some protein and ellagic acid and saponins, which may benefit the heart. Just two Brazil nuts a day supply the full quota of selenium—a potent cancer fighter. All nuts are healthiest eaten raw.

Eggs. Eggs have been so maligned that it's easy to think they're unhealthy, but nothing could be further from the truth. For just 80 calories per egg, you get high-quality protein, vitamin E and selenium. Just don't eat several a day or add bacon and buttered toast to the mix.

Tea. You wouldn't believe what this ages-old beverage is packed with. Try fluoride for starters. That's right, tea is good for your teeth and probably your heart too. The flavonoids found in tea make blood less likely to clot, possibly reducing the incidence of heart attacks. Flavonoids seem to cut cancer risk too.

act as an antioxidant, possibly interfering with the development of heart disease and cancer. But two other very important B vitamins—B-6 and B-9—can undergo the changes that make them useful to the body only if riboflavin is present. It's also one of the vitamins crucial for normal vision. Deficiencies can cause excessive sensitivity to light as well as itchy, sore, bloodshot eyes and blurry vision.

- *B-3 (niacin).* Here is one vitamin that can be both helpful and harmful simultaneously. Niacin got its good name because of its ability to lower

bad (LDL) cholesterol and raise good (HDL) cholesterol. Unfortunately, the amount of ordinary niacin required to achieve this effect can damage your liver. So try this only under a doctor's supervision. To treat high cholesterol safely with niacin, buy "flush-free" or "inositol-bound" niacin, a new and safer version of vitamin B-3.

- *B-5 (pantothenic acid).* This vitamin has exciting possibilities. Scientists now believe that pantothenic acid may help to detoxify dangerous manmade chemicals found in herbicides, insecticides and some drugs.

- *B-6 (pyridoxine).* There are some very exciting claims being made for the cancer-fighting and immune-boosting properties of vitamin B-6. These claims are being born out by scientific studies. Research has shown that B-6 boosts immunity in elderly people, and lab animals with cancer have experienced a slowing of tumor growth when given B-6. Don't exceed the recommended daily allowance of 50 milligrams, though, since too much of the vitamin can cause nerve damage.

- *B-9 (folic acid).* Folic acid is one of those vitamins that's been making headlines lately

because it appears to regulate the level of homocysteine in the blood. The presence of high homocysteine levels is associated with a higher incidence of heart disease and heart attacks. Folic acid also helps prevent certain birth defects and may also reverse a precancerous condition of the cervix, known as dysplasia.

Vitamin C

Perhaps more than any other vitamin, this much acclaimed micronutrient has been credited with everything from curing the common cold to reversing the aging process and erasing wrinkles. It can't live up to some of the more grandiose claims, but vitamin C does appear to be a powerful antioxidant and immune system protector. Although megadoses have been recommended for the prevention of everything from colds to cancer, lower doses do seem to have some clear-cut benefits. Take 1,000 milligrams at the first sign of a cold, and repeat the dose every few hours for the first few days. This regimen may shorten the duration of the cold and ease the symptoms, if nothing else. An interesting study from a region of China where cancer is prevalent shows that a small daily supplement of vitamin C together with a modest amount of vitamin E and selenium may make it less likely to get cancer.

VEGETABLE NUTRIENTS

Cooked vegetables sometimes provide better protection against cancer and heart disease than raw ones, according to Susan Southon, PhD, head, micronutrient section, Institute of Food Research, Norwich, England.

Cooking softens plant cells, allowing them to release up to 10 times higher levels of carotenoids and other antioxidants. But some nutrients, like vitamin C, are destroyed by cooking. Best: Eat a mix of fresh and cooked vegetables.

BONE BUILDER OR KIDNEY KILLER?

The first thing that comes to mind when we think of calcium is strong bones and teeth, but it's also crucial for maintaining a normal heartbeat, nerve and muscle function and blood clotting. Calcium also lowers blood pressure in some people. Calcium should be taken in a 2-to-1 ratio with magnesium. If you have trouble sleeping, try taking a combination calcium-magnesium supplement before you go to bed, as both minerals have a slightly tranquilizing effect.

Along with all of the beneficial effects of calcium are concerns that too much of it can cause kidney problems. In fact, excess circulating calcium may be deposited in the kidneys, causing kidney stones. However, research on the extent of the risk and what to do about it has yielded conflicting results. In fact, some studies have found a correlation between a *low* intake of calcium and the formation of kidney stones, with people who take in more calcium being at lower risk. All sides seem to agree that eating foods high in calcium does not increase risk. To be on the safe side, take your supplement with food, making it more likely that the calcium will be properly absorbed by your body.

Vitamin D

This is one of those vitamins that the body manufactures on its own simply by being exposed to the sun. In fact, just 10 minutes a day of midday sunlight supplies you with half of the recommended daily allowance. Vitamin D regulates the absorption and balance of calcium and phosphorus in the body, making it a key player in the formation of strong teeth and bones. It is also one of the substances that ensures normal muscle contraction and nerve function. Because vitamin D is fat soluble, excess amounts are stored in the body. If levels of vitamin D become too high, toxic effects can include heart, liver and kidney damage.

Vitamin E

Taking vitamin E has become very popular because studies have shown that it may lower the risk of heart attack by making the blood less likely to clot. It's also a powerful antioxidant and, in combination with vitamin C and selenium, may prevent certain forms of cancer.

Iron

This mineral, which you might think can only help you, is now being ingested in excessive and potentially unhealthy amounts. High iron intake has been associated with an increased incidence of heart attacks, and the fact that men have a greater amount of iron in their bodies (since women lose some through menstruation) may be part of the explanation for the greater incidence of heart attacks in men. Unless you have a proven deficiency, you should not take supplemental iron.

Magnesium

Magnesium, taken in combination with calcium (in a 2:1 ratio), can often be used to treat symptoms such as nervous tension, irritability, anxiety and insomnia. Magnesium may also provide protection against heart disease and help in the treatment of high blood pressure.

Potassium

Along with sodium and chloride, potassium helps maintain the balance of the body's fluids and is

---

ARE VITAMINS BAD FOR YOUR TEETH?

If swallowing big tablets of vitamin C makes you gag, don't think you're doing yourself any favors by opting for the chewable version. Just one 500-mg dose will make your mouth acidic enough to wear down the enamel, not to mention the fact that you're grinding the acid right into the grooves on the surface of your teeth—which is most vulnerable to decay. If you must use the chewable form (or have taken to using the new vitamin C chewing gum), be sure to brush and rinse thoroughly afterwards. And be especially careful about children's teeth. If your kids can't yet swallow tablets, buy supplements in liquid form.

MIRACLE MINERALS? OR... TOO MUCH OF A GOOD THING?

Just because a little bit is good doesn't mean that more is better.

Fluoride. A teeny tiny bit of fluoride makes teeth and bones a little stronger. Unfortunately, too much can cause a variety of problems whose effects may be mild or severe. Mild cases result in cosmetic defects of the teeth, including white patches, staining or a chalky appearance. Many children take fluoride supplements *and* brush with fluoride toothpaste (some of which they swallow) *and* drink fluoridated water *and* get semiannual fluoride treatments at the dentist's office *and* rinse with fluoridated mouthwash. Check your child's teeth regularly for blemishes, and reevaluate how much fluoride they're really getting from all sources. *Too* much fluoride can result in a serious condition called "skeletal fluorosis," which is an abnormal hardening of the bones, sometimes coupled with arthritic symptoms and nerve damage. A large amount of toothpaste can poison and even kill a child, but there is no hard evidence that long-term fluoride ingestion (in the amount you would find in a fluoridated water supply) causes cancer.

Chromium. This is one of those trace minerals that was long believed to play no useful role in our bodies. Now we know that it is critically involved in the metabolism of glucose and it increases the body's sensitivity to the hormone insulin, which lowers blood sugar levels when they are too high. It has been reported to have reduced the need for diabetes medication in some patients and may play a significant role in preventing and treating adult-onset diabetes. Claims have also been made for it as a weight-loss product, but there is no good evidence to support that. It is toxic in large doses, so don't try to lose weight by loading up on it. New research also suggests that chromium—particularly the popular chromium picolinate—may cause genetic damage. Don't take amounts over the recommended daily allowance, unless you are under the supervision of a health-care practitioner with expertise in the field of nutritional medicine.

also a key player in the transmission of nerve impulses, muscle contraction, heartbeat and blood pressure. A diet high in potassium-rich foods is associated with a lowered risk of heart disease and high blood pressure. Don't load up on supplements, though, because too much extra potassium can cause abnormal heart rhythms. The amount found in most vitamin and mineral supplements is fine unless you have kidney disease.

Selenium

An extremely potent—but only recently recognized—antioxidant, selenium, taken in combination with vitamins E and C, has been shown to reduce the risk of cancer. Selenium occurs naturally in Brazil nuts, and you can get the recommended daily allowance by eating just two of them a day.

Zinc

This mineral is essential to a properly functioning immune system and may also help shorten the duration of the common cold. Many avid supplement takers inadvertently jeopardize their body's use of zinc by not balancing it with their intake of calcium. Zinc absorption drops when calcium intake rises, so you need to take more zinc to counteract that effect. Also, take zinc at a different time of the day from your calcium supplement so that your body has more of a chance to absorb it.

FOR WHATEVER AILS YOU

Are you a confused consumer? Just when we finally get vitamins and minerals more or less sorted out, we discover that they're just the tip of the iceberg in the world of nutritional supplements. Some of the products you can buy these days sound great, but should you take them?

Be Careful with Hormones

Over-the-counter hormones, just like those available by prescription, have very powerful effects in the body and should only be taken under the supervision of a health-care practitioner trained in their use. Many people don't even realize that some readily available substances, such as melatonin, *are* hormones.

- *Glandulars*. The idea behind ingesting glandulars is that if your own glands are no longer producing optimal amounts of hormones and you eat concentrates of animal glands, miraculously—you're cured. But you're probably better off avoiding glandular material from animals. Your body's hormonal balance is extremely delicate and throwing a little ground thymus or pituitary gland into the mix can have far-reaching effects. Medical testing is necessary to determine whether you are actually deficient in a particular hormone and, if you are, the amount and means of supplementation must be calculated precisely. Don't mess around with this yourself.
- *DHEA*. This male hormone is supposed to be one of those "fountain-of-youth" supplements, but it may be more of a fountain of death. It almost certainly increases the risk of prostate cancer in men and of heart attack in women. Ironically, it may *lower* the chances of heart attack in *men*, and may also be of some benefit to people with autoimmune diseases, such as lupus. If you've heard something that leads you to believe you would benefit from taking DHEA, make an appointment with your doctor and take the information with you.
- *Melatonin*. This hormone is secreted by the pineal gland, located in the brain, and its job is to regulate the biological clock. The gland is stimulated to produce melatonin by falling light levels at the end of the day. Scientists have speculated that our use of artificial lighting in the evening interferes to some extent with the smooth functioning of this system. Many people try to combat insomnia by taking melatonin orally, but results have been mixed. Do not take any sleep aid, including melatonin, on a regular basis. Melatonin does appear to be effective for resetting the biological clock, when the problem is caused by jet lag. Since most people suffer the effects of jet lag only occasionally, taking the hormone for this purpose should be fine.

POWERHOUSE PILL FOR TIRED HEARTS

Coenzyme Q-10 is a vitamin-like substance with some substantiated benefits, particularly for people with congestive heart failure. CoQ-10 makes more energy available at the cellular level and seems to be particularly effective at improving the efficiency of cardiac muscle tissue. People without medical problems may be able to improve their aerobic endurance by taking the supplements. CoQ-10 may also benefit your gums, reducing the risk of gingivitis and helping to treat existing cases of gum disease. One hundred milligrams a day is a sufficient dosage for these purposes, but people with heart failure should take 300 mg a day in divided doses. Seventy percent of heart-failure patients who tried this regimen experienced a noticeable improvement in their symptoms within six weeks. CoQ-10 should be taken with a meal, since it is most efficiently absorbed in the presence of fat.

Protein—Is It Good, or Too Much of a Good Thing?

Many people swallow protein powders and mixtures of amino acids because they believe that doing so will help them build bigger muscles faster. Not only is this not the case, but you can actually harm your body by overloading it with protein and its derivatives. Most Americans already consume far more protein than they need— which is no more than four ounces a day *total* for the average adult. Excess protein can be hard on the digestive system, even damaging the liver and kidneys as well. If you want to increase muscle mass, the best way is to spend more time exercising.

Under certain circumstances, individual amino acids are used as medicines to bring about a particular effect. If you think you may benefit from taking supplements of a particular amino acid, consult a practitioner knowledgeable in their use. Here are a few of the more commonly used ones:

- *L-lysine.* Taking between 500 and 1,000 mg a day on an empty stomach may decrease the frequency of outbreaks of oral herpes (cold sores).
- *L-arginine.* People take L-arginine to build muscle mass, but bear in mind that you are tampering with the delicate balance of growth hormones in your body, which is not the greatest idea. Arginine also counteracts

the effects of lysine and may therefore trigger outbreaks of oral herpes in susceptible people.

- *Phenylalanine and L-tyrosine.* These amino acids are precursors of norepinephrine and, dopamine and for that reason, may help with depression and chronic pain. Be especially careful if you have high blood pressure because it may be aggravated by supplements of these substances.

⚠️

SEA MIRACLE OR SEA MUCK?

Blue-green algae is supposed to perk you up and pump you full of nutrients, too. But does the slimy scum really work? Well, maybe…if you don't mind possibly being poisoned in the process. Among the potential toxins found in blue-green algae is a liver toxin that is stronger than cyanide. It has a damaging effect on the nerves and brain, and is chemically related to cocaine. In fact, it may be the druglike effects of those substances that account for the feelings of euphoria generated by the algae. Apparently humans aren't the only creatures that have been drawn to the algae "high"—animals that feast on clumps of the stuff on the beach can't seem to get enough sometimes. Until they drop dead, that is.

HARMFUL HABITS

It's a sad fact that a lot of people will work hard to develop bodies that look great, then get all dressed up, go out feeling gorgeous and promptly pump themselves so full of drugs (yes, alcohol does count!) that they undo most of the good done by their diet and exercise routines. Not necessarily to their outward appearance—at least not right away—but to the internal workings of the body…where it *really* counts. Here's a rundown of the serious damage excessive partying can do to the body's most important parts:

- *Brain and nervous system.* If you think that drinking can't damage your brain, consider what too much alcohol does to your speech and coordination. In most cases, the effects on the nervous system are temporary,

but if you regularly overindulge, it's possible to permanently damage your functioning, including your ability to think and reason.

- *Digestive tract.* Alcohol is extremely irritating to the digestive tract, particularly the stomach, and can cause ulcers and gastritis.
- *Heart.* Long-term alcohol abuse can damage the heart muscle itself, causing congestive heart failure and other cardiac problems. And don't confuse having one glass of red wine with indulging in five margaritas. A little red wine may be good for your heart, but more alcohol than that may only *increase* your risk of getting other diseases.
- *Liver.* Your liver is the organ responsible for deactivating toxins that are circulating in your blood, which is why it is so specifically damaged by

---

⚠️

MEN & WOMEN & ALCOHOL

We may be able to dictate the laws of humankind, but not the laws of biology. When it comes to the adverse effects of alcohol on the body, women are hit much harder than men. You may think that this is due to the fact that women on average don't weigh as much, but that's not the whole story. Women also don't metabolize alcohol the same way. If a man and woman of the same weight consume exactly the same amount of alcohol, the woman will be more affected by it and the effects will take longer to wear off. Unfortunately, this also means that women are more likely than men to develop alcohol-related diseases, such as pancreatitis and cirrhosis, even after only moderate abuse.

alcohol abuse. It takes the liver between one and two hours to clear the alcohol from a single drink out of your system, so if you drink more quickly than the liver can act, alcohol circulates in your blood affecting your nervous system. Over time, the excessive toxin exposure may damage or destroy the liver, necessitating an organ transplant or causing death.

■ *Pancreas*. Many people either don't know or don't understand the devastating effects of pancreatitis (inflammation of the pancreas) on the body's

---

⚠ ALCOHOL LIMITS

No more than one drink a day for women; two drinks a day for men. If you overindulge once in a while, make sure that you have some food along with your drink. This will slow the absorption of the alcohol and moderate its influence somewhat. And bear in mind that more than about three drinks for a woman or five drinks for a man consumed over a couple of hours constitutes a binge, which carries particular health risks.

How much alcohol equals one drink? One glass of wine, one can or bottle of beer, one mixed drink and one shot of spirits are all equivalent.

---

ability to digest food. It is an extremely painful and debilitating disease that can result in long hospitalizations and surgical intervention. Women are more likely than men to develop this complication. There are cases on record of women with severe pancreatitis after only a few months of moderate alcohol abuse.

Does It Matter Which Poison You Choose?

If moderation in alcohol consumption is okay, why not an occasional hit of LSD or the odd snort of cocaine? Well, apart from the potential problem of ending up in jail, most illegal drugs have such potent effects that a single use can result in addiction, permanent disability or death. Cocaine, for example, has a nasty habit of killing people who didn't realize they had an underlying weakness in their cardiovascular systems. And more than one or two people who thought the electrical wiring in their brains was functioning just fine discovered that short-circuiting their entire cerebral setup with hallucinogens was easier than they had thought.

Between the chance of arrest, the possibility of addiction and the risk of death or disability that are part of the bargain with hard drugs, that glass or two of wine is probably your best bet.

FOREVER YOUNG

From pills to improve your brain functioning to creams to get rid of wrinkles, the promise of eternal youth is being marketed everywhere. So how do the claims stack up? Does any of it really work? Retaining your youth is really about being able to continue functioning mentally and physically the way you always have and to look good doing it.

WRINKLE RUB-OUT CREAMS

Before you shell out hundreds of dollars for expensive creams that are supposed to undo wrinkles once they're already in place, head to the nearest drugstore for the most effective wrinkle preventer of all—sunblock. And don't forget that smoking is a major cause of wrinkling, particularly around the mouth. That's because of the repetitive motion of sucking on the cigarette, which requires constant puckering.

Here's a selection of antiwrinkle ingredients, which you can find in both expensive creams and drugstore brands. It's the presence and concentration of these ingredients, rather than the price of the product, that determines their wrinkle-fighting capabilities.

Retin A. This chemical and its derivative, Renova, generally make for the most effective products, but you'll need a doctor's prescription.

Retinol. Creams containing this substance are available over-the-counter. They make skin feel smoother and softer, in addition to diminishing the appearance of fine lines.

Alphahydroxy acids, glycolic acid, fruit acids. These cause the top layers of skin to slough off, taking fine lines along with them.

Vitamin C. Concentrated vitamin C may yet turn out to be the best over-the-counter wrinkle remover.

If lotions and creams aren't making the grade, consider injections of collagen or Botox. Collagen plumps out the wrinkles, while Botox paralyzes the tiny muscles that can cause frown lines.

Here are the secrets.

How to Be Beautiful Forever

Have you ever looked at someone who was a little older and thought to yourself how incredibly attractive they were? How about Sophia Loren? Or Sean Connery? Not just "Not too bad for an older guy," but downright pins-and-needles, hotter-than-tamales *sexy*.

The truth is that what makes many people lose their attractiveness in their later years has nothing to do with lines in the face or gray hair at the temples. It's the loss of *vitality*—bright eyes, muscular strength, high energy and the constant indulgence in new ideas and activities—that can make you appear old and weary. You can work on your bags and wrinkles all you want, but the most important elements of what makes someone attractive never change. Here they are:

- *Self-confidence*
- *Varied interests*
- *Good health*
- *Attention to personal appearance*

Finally, how attractive do you feel? How many of us have known someone whom we felt was not particularly great looking, but who definitely acted like they were better looking than *we* thought they were? People who think they're good looking project that to others; if *you* think you're the cat's meow, others are more likely to think so too. So go ahead and strut a little.

Shaping Up the Shell

Just because your outward appearance is not as important as what you have going on inside doesn't mean that it doesn't matter at all. In fact, the way you groom yourself says a lot about how much self-respect you have. Here are some of the more reasonable things you can do to make the most of your

appearance without turning your life into a series of visits to the plastic surgeon.

- *Take care of your teeth.* Nothing will make you look older than your years faster than poor dental hygiene. Invest in a little cosmetic dental work and take care of your gums too.
- *Pay attention to the details.* Twenty-five-year-olds may be able to get away with messy hair and no makeup and still look great, but it doesn't work when you're in your forties or fifties. Pay attention to details, like your nails and skin and keep your hair color shade and makeup subtle.
- *Be a fashion maven.* Do you really want to be seen in public in old comfy clothes you wear around the house? It's easy

---

ℹ️ WHAT'S YOUR REAL AGE?

We've all known a "young" 60-year-old and an "old" 25-year-old, so…how do health, appearance, and demeanor reflect calendar age? To find out, go to *www.realage.com* and take the RealAge test. Or, go to a bookstore and pick up *RealAge: Are You As Young As You Can Be?* It gives tips on how to be more youthful.

---

for older people to look chic, so make an investment in a fashionable wardrobe. Ask your favorite department store about using the services of a personal shopper who will help you select the most flattering styles for your figure.

- *Stay strong.* Not only will you have more energy, but

working out with weights also reduces your risk of getting osteoporosis—one of the fastest ways to age. Any weight-bearing exercise (even walking) will build bone mass. Unfortunately, swimming won't, although it's still great for the cardiovascular system and easy on the joints too.

SUPER ANTIAGING SUPPLEMENTS

Nose: Zinc (preserves sense of smell)

Gums: Co-enzyme Q10 (improved circulation reduces gum disease)

Digestive Tract: Peppermint and chamomile teas (soothe the stomach and intestines, easing digestion)

Joints: Glucosamine sulfate (arthritis)

Blood Vessels: Ginkgo biloba, hawthorn, bilberry (varicose veins, strengthen blood vessels and improve peripheral blood flow)

Brain: Ginkgo biloba, vitamin E (memory, stroke); co-enzyme Q10 (microcirculation)

Heart: Co-enzyme Q10 (heart muscle, circulation); vitamin E (reduces blood clotting, lowering chances of heart attack); folic acid (counteracts homocysteine, which increases heart attack risk)

Bones & Teeth: Calcium, fluoride, vitamin D, phosphorus (density and strength)

Healers & Healing

What is a doctor? At his or her best, a doctor is someone who can figure out what's ailing you (diagnosis) and then help you get better (treatment). In our culture, when we think of doctors, we usually picture conventional medical (MD) doctors. But that perception is beginning to change as we incorporate more and more therapeutic approaches into our health-care system. Here's a summary of the options available to you today.

OLD-FASHIONED OR NEW-FANGLED?

With all of the choices now available, just deciding what kind of doctor you need and even whether or when you need one is a daunting task.

For most of life's day-to-day discomforts, choosing a traditional or "alternative" health-care option is fine, but bear in mind that if you have a more serious undiagnosed condition, you may have wasted valuable time by not having gotten more aggressive conventional medical treatment. It's a good idea to have a medical doctor (preferably one who is open to and knowledgeable about a variety of approaches to health and healing) or a properly trained and licensed naturopathic family physician (ND) check you out to make sure there's nothing serious underlying that sore neck or upset stomach.

A Matter of Philosophy

Why is there such a great divide between medical doctors and practitioners of complementary (traditional, natural or alternative) health-care practitioners?

It begins with a fundamental difference in the approach to health and healing. MDs specialize in emergency intervention and crisis management for specific conditions, while complementary-care practitioners focus on preventive care and a holistic therapeutic approach. Holism is the principle that you must look at a person's entire condition and improve all aspects of his or her physical and mental state in order to have optimum functioning and an enduring sense of well-being.

Having It All

You may feel that you need to decide which camp you belong in and then stick with only practitioners from a particular school of thought. But that's really not necessary. The truth is that each approach has its pros and cons depending on the situation, and there's no rule that says you can't choose a conventional approach to deal with one problem and a complementary approach to deal with another.

For example, have an MD remove an infected appendix surgically and an ND treat your recurring headaches using biofeedback and peppermint spirits.

Nor are the approaches mutually exclusive when it comes to treating the same condition. You can choose standard chemotherapy to treat cancer and still visit a complementary-care practitioner for guided imagery sessions to help boost your immune system.

How to Choose a Doctor

What we have in abundance now, which used to be in short supply, is choices. But…buyer beware. There are good doctors and bad doctors both within the conventional medical system and outside of it. Ultimately, you will live with the consequences of your choices, good and bad.

Choose your doctors and health-care providers with care by getting referrals from people you trust, checking credentials and insisting on an initial meeting. At that meeting, you will be able to ask questions and get a sense of whether you believe that the practitioner is intelligent, well-trained, compassionate and honorable. Pay particular attention to

WHERE'S THE SCIENCE?

Proponents of conventional medicine over traditional or alternative healing techniques often mention the lack of scientific studies available to back up many of those practices. But bear in mind that many conventional medical techniques and therapies have not been substantiated by scientific studies either. And, many folk remedies criticized by the medical establishment have turned out to have healing potential when finally studied. Apply your common sense to all recommended treatments— conventional and complementary. Ask whether the treatment being proposed could hurt you and why it is being advised. What are the alternatives? What are the risks? Don't be afraid to apply your powers of logical reasoning. Does the rationale behind the technique, therapy or medication make sense? If so, then proceed. But do so with caution. If your condition does not improve or if you notice side effects or other problems, then question your care provider about alternatives.

whether he or she seems interested in *you*. Scientific advances notwithstanding, the practice of medicine is still as much an art as a science. The best doctors have excellent intuition, which helps them make accurate diagnoses in cases where the cause is not clear-cut. Finally, make sure that the doctor does not seem rushed. Remember, you are paying for a professional service.

CONVENTIONAL MEDICINE

Although interest in alternative medicine has been increasing for the past 10 years or so, there are certain conditions for which conventional medicine is still absolutely the best approach. The most obvious of these involve life-threatening medical emergencies and serious physical trauma. The following includes symptoms and situations that should always send you straight to the nearest emergency room for conventional medical evaluation and treatment:

- *Severe cuts and bleeding*
- *Broken bones*
- *Bad burns*
- *Difficulty breathing*
- *Chest pain, or pain in your shoulder, jaw or hand*
- *Any unexplained pain or persistent discomfort, particularly if it comes on suddenly*

or you have never experienced it before.

- *Blurry vision, confusion, disorientation, paralysis or sudden weakness*

Emergencies are not the only situations in which you might want to opt for a conventional medical approach. Some conditions, such as epilepsy, may require treatment with powerful pharmaceutical drugs or hospital care, which only MDs can provide.

Other Conventional Practitioners

MDs are not the only ones who practice within the conventional medical establishment. In fact, with the increased attention being paid to controlling costs, you're increasingly likely to be seen by a nurse practitioner for a routine visit as by a doctor. Nurse-midwives deliver babies and provide routine gynecological care, and a

SHOULD DOCTORS GET PAID?

Here's a thought-provoking question: If a doctor fails to make you well, should you have to pay the bill? After all, if you don't succeed at your job, do you get paid? Well, before you ponder this for too long, consider this: In ancient China, doctors got paid only if their patients stayed healthy. Now that sounds fair, doesn't it?

nurse-anesthetist might be in charge of putting you to sleep and monitoring you while you're under if you have surgery. All of these practitioners, as well as registered nurses, physician's assistants and physical therapists, tend to be well-trained professionals.

When it comes to your emotional health, you have a variety of choices too. Psychiatrists provide psychotherapy and may prescribe medications for mental conditions and mood disorders. Licensed

clinical psychologists cannot prescribe medication, but undergo special schooling and are highly trained psychotherapists. Licensed clinical social workers and family therapists are also trained to treat emotional problems and can be very helpful. The most important criterion to apply when choosing a mental-health professional is whether or not you feel comfortable with the person. You will need to feel that you can share your deepest feelings and

LOOKING FOR A "NATURAL" FAMILY PHYSICIAN?

If you want a family doctor with a more "natural" approach to health care, you'll be pleased to know that you have a new option—properly trained naturopathic doctors (NDs) are now licensed as independent family-care physicians in 11 states…and counting. Naturopathic medical schools require a bachelor's degree and the same prerequisite science courses as conventional medical schools: biology, physics, general and organic chemistry, as well as courses in the humanities, social sciences and psychology. Naturopathic medical students spend four full years in graduate school, studying science for the first two years and clinical skills and natural therapeutics for the second two. NDs also study laboratory and diagnostic medicine and can order and interpret the results of X rays, blood tests and other diagnostic tests. Naturopaths do not practice in hospitals and will refer you to an MD if you have a condition for which you must be hospitalized.

Depending on the state in which they practice, naturopaths may deliver babies, perform minor surgery and prescribe naturally derived prescription drugs (like penicillin), in addition to providing a range of "natural" therapies, including spinal manipulation, acupuncture and homeopathic remedies. Although many naturopaths go on to specialize in a particular area of complementary care (such as Oriental medicine), by training they are the generalists of complementary health care, and will be able to advise you on everything from herbal remedies to reflexology to bee venom therapy.

BEWARE OF THE MIB

The Medical Information Bureau (MIB) is an organization that may have private information about your health and habits in its database of more than 15 million Americans and Canadians. The MIB releases your medical history to insurance companies that request it when you apply for a policy.

To find out if the MIB has information about you in its files, call 617-426-3660. If your records are in their database, order a copy of your report. It will cost $8.50 but will be well worth it, since you have the right to correct any misinformation it contains.

If the MIB does not have a record of information on you, take steps to protect your privacy. First, inform your health-care providers, in writing, that they are not to furnish any information about you to any organization, including the MIB, without specific written authorization from you. This includes your health insurance provider. Then, make sure that you do not give your social security number to any health-care providers or institutions. They do not need it. The only number required for their reimbursement is your health insurance policy number.

darkest secrets in order for the therapist to help you, so make sure that you trust him or her.

Chiropractors—For Spinal Manipulation

Chiropractors are not medical doctors, but they *are* experts at spinal manipulation. And popular practitioners at that—up to 10% of the U.S. population visits a chiropractor at least once each year. And that's no surprise, since at least one study has shown chiropractic therapy to be the most effective treatment for quick pain relief. Many conditions, such as chronic headaches, are linked to problems with spinal alignment, so chiropractors can help with a number of problems besides the usual low-back pain.

Be more wary of using chiropractic care to treat conditions like asthma, however. Some chiropractors like to bill themselves as primary-care practitioners, but spinal manipulation has not been proven to be an effective treatment for conditions that are not directly related to the skeletal system.

Bear in mind that simply being touched by a health-care practitioner makes many people feel better. In fact, touching the patient used to be considered an integral part of the healing process. Nowadays, however, medical doctors tend to touch their patients only for diagnostic purposes or to perform technical procedures.

BACK, NECK & HEAD PAIN

According to some studies, chiropractors seem to have the edge on pain when it comes to back and neck discomfort and headaches. One study found chiropractic treatment of acute back pain got people back to work within about a week versus three weeks when using conventional treatment. And the cost for the treatment that doesn't work as well? About twice that of chiropractic care for the same problem.

Chiropractors seem to do better at treating chronic tension headaches, too. In one fascinating study, headache sufferers were divided into two groups. Group one got chiropractic spinal manipulation; group two got standard drugs plus an antidepressant. At the end of the six-week treatment period, both groups were better, but 82% of the drug group had suffered side effects. A month after the treatment had ended, however, the drug group was back to square one—their headaches were just as frequent and severe as they had been before. But the chiropractic group was having fewer and milder headaches, even though they were no longer receiving chiropractic treatments.

Osteopaths—More Bone Specialists

sentence An osteopath is like a combination of a regular medical doctor and a chiropractor. Osteopaths are medical doctors who have specialized training in skeletal manipulation. Philosophically, they see damage to the skeletal structure as being at the core of many ills. However, they have extensive conventional medical training and practice in hospitals, and have the same rights, privileges and responsibilities as conventionally trained MDs.

TRADITIONAL MEDICINE

Every culture has its own traditional way of dealing with disease and death. For much of this century, our culture has followed the "scientific" approach, but many societies have philosophies of health and healing that are literally thousands of years old. And their techniques are still actively applied today (modern scientific data or not), many of them in societies where the people live long and healthy lives. Some, such as Ayurveda (the traditional medicine of India) and Traditional Chinese Medicine share a similar concept of maintaining the body and mind in a state of harmony for optimum health and well-being.

Ayurveda

The Ayurvedic medical system began in India more than 2,500 years ago. Around 80% of the population of India is still cared for by Ayurvedic practitioners, who believe that human beings must be brought into harmony with their environment. Based on tenets of Hinduism, Ayurvedic practices revolve around *prana*, the vital life force that energizes the body.

Ayurvedic practitioners, like most traditional doctors, are holistic in their approach. That means they're not interested only in the complaint that brought you to them. They believe that in order to treat a condition properly, they need to have a complete picture of your constitution and lifestyle.

To help you attain optimum health, the practitioner figures out your *prakriti*—your own unique balance of the three *doshas*, the *tridosha*. Here are the characteristics that the doshas represent:

- *Vatta* types are active, restless, anxious and creative
- *Pitta* types are intelligent, enterprising, critical and quick to anger
- *Kapha* types are relaxed, affectionate, indecisive and empathetic

Each individual has some characteristics of all three doshas, but one is generally dominant. The Ayurvedic practitioner uses your prakriti to determine which foods

---

⚠ AYURVEDIC ALERT

Be careful of the ingredients used in Ayurvedic medicines, which may contain toxic metals such as lead, mercury or arsenic. Although these substances have supposedly been "inactivated," that's a tricky thing to prove…and you don't want to get poisoned, naturally or otherwise.

---

you should eat, when you should sleep and other details of your daily habits—all designed to bring your doshas into balance.

Other aspects of Ayurvedic healing regimens are yoga and meditation, as well as a purification ritual called *panchakarma*. This purification process is not quite as charming as it sounds. It starts with steam baths and oil massages, then progresses to fasting, and finally on to rigorous enemas and induced vomiting. It sometimes includes bloodletting as well. Definitely intense and probably difficult to justify medically as well.

Traditional Chinese Medicine

Traditional Chinese, or "Oriental," medicine (TCM) requires a shift in perspective for those of us who are used to the Western approach to healing and how the body works. According to Chinese teaching, the body contains a network of pathways (meridians) through which the life force (*qi* or *chi*, pronounced "chee") flows. When the flow of bodily energy is disturbed, ill health results.

To maintain good health and a sense of well-being, *yin* and *yang* must also be in balance.

Yin represents the shady side of the mountain (a state of darkness and quiet), and yang represents the sunny side of the mountain (a state of light and activity).

Like many other healing traditions, TCM incorporates the use of herbs into its treatment of disease. However, the use of medicines and surgery is not at the heart of the Chinese approach to health and healing as it is in the West. Practitioners evaluate their patients from a holistic point of view, looking for signs that elements of their lifestyle are out of balance. They treat all aspects of what they perceive to be the impaired functioning—not just the complaint that brought the person to the doctor. Diet and nutrition, exercise (such as Tai Chi and other martial arts), stress reduction and massage are all cornerstones of Chinese medical treatment.

TCM includes several different techniques, not all of them as unusual as acupuncture. Although acupuncture gets most of the attention, actually herbs are used more extensively in TCM when active treatment is required. If you've been suffering from a condition that hasn't responded to whatever you've tried so far, consider making a visit to a licensed practitioner of this ancient healing art.

Although this treatment approach may at first feel alien, TCM has been shown to bring about good results.

♥ SHOULD YOU GIVE THOSE SCARY ACUPUNCTURE NEEDLES A TRY?

It depends on what condition you're treating. Western doctors aren't sure why acupuncture is so effective for some conditions, but it does seem to work well for nausea and pain, and perhaps for asthma and drug addictions as well. Being able to relieve nausea without having to take drugs is good news for pregnant women suffering from morning sickness and for cancer patients on chemotherapy who don't want to put their livers under any more strain (the liver is responsible for filtering toxins, including drugs). Acupuncture works well as a treatment for pain too, particularly low back pain, carpal tunnel syndrome, arthritis, headaches resulting from muscle tension and migraines. If you decide to try acupuncture, be sure the practitioner uses disposable needles.

COMPLEMENTARY MEDICINE

Many of the practices considered as "alternative" are really just techniques that can be used in conjunction with other treatments. Some are common sense (e.g., nice scents can lift your spirits; massage is relaxing), while others require a leap of faith or a new way of looking at health and healing. Here are some therapies to try for everyday ills or just to give your whole constitution a lift.

The Appeal of Aromatherapy

The most primal sense we have is our sense of smell. A whiff of a perfume you smelled on your great-grandmother when you were a small child can bring back a flood of memories buried for so long that you never knew you had them. Sexual attraction is thought to be driven at least in part by "pheromones," scents exuded by men and women that can cause a powerful sexual response. A person is unable to even consciously smell these aromas, yet they still generate a physical response.

Small wonder then that practitioners of natural, noninvasive healing techniques have turned to aromatherapy as a powerful tool for health and well-being. And they may be on to something good. In one interesting study, people who were trying to quit smoking had fewer withdrawal symptoms and less anxiety when exposed to the vapor from black pepper extract. Smokers who were exposed to the smell of mint experienced less anxiety, but their withdrawal symptoms were not reduced.

Massage & Other Bodywork Techniques

Massage usually feels great, but make sure that the person performing it is a certified massage therapist. If you're treating a medical condition with massage, it is possible to make matters worse by manipulating the muscles, bones and soft tissues. Don't have any kind of vigorous massage if you're prone to bruising or bleeding, and don't massage painful areas unless the cause of the pain has already been evaluated by a health-care practitioner who deems massage safe.

In any event, there are many types of massage therapy, known collectively as "bodywork." Here are some of them:

- *Alexander technique*. The goal of this therapy is to improve your posture, thereby relieving discomforts that are associated with poor spinal alignment. It may relieve tension headaches, back and neck pain, muscle spasms and whiplash pain.
- *Feldenkreis method*. This is a gentle therapy that improves flexibility, coordination and range of motion as well as posture and breathing. It may help people overcome physical limitations that result from an injury or chronic condition.
- *Hellerwork*. The goal of this therapy is to realign the body, using deep massage and movement therapy as well as therapeutic discussion. Hellerwork decreases tension and increases flexibility.
- *Myotherapy*. This deep-pressure massage therapy works "trigger points" to relieve muscle pain and tension.
- *Reiki*. In this technique, a trained practitioner places his or her hands over your body's energy centers to allow the healing energy to flow more efficiently. This technique is sometimes also referred to as Therapeutic Touch.
- *Rolfing*. This isn't just deep massage, it can really hurt. Proponents of the technique say that they're breaking up nasty adhesions that glue together the connective tissue enclosing muscles. Perhaps so, but be careful. In any case, many people who have suffered from chronic pain and stiffness have been helped by the treatment. As with all forms of deep massage, avoid it if you have a vascular disorder or are prone to bruising or bleeding.

Feet—Gateway to the Body?

Reflexology is one of the older healing techniques around, having been used as long as 5,000 years ago in China and more than 4,000 years ago in Egypt.

Reflexologists believe that points on the feet, ears and hands

---

HAND REFLEXOLOGY

Hand reflexology can provide quick relief for eyestrain, sore shoulders, stomach upset, neck pain, back pain and carpal tunnel syndrome, according to Bill Flocco, founder and director of the American Academy of Reflexology in Burbank, California.

A number of "reflex points" on the fingers, palms and backs and edges of the hands correspond to every part of the body. Applying pressure to these reflex points stimulates nerve impulses to help muscles relax, open blood vessels, increase circulation and allow in more oxygen and nutrients—key facilitators of healing.

To find a certified reflexologist in your area, call the American Reflexology Certification Board (ARCB) in Littleton, Colorado, at 303-933-6921.

Learn more about reflexology at the ARCB Web site: *www.arcb.net*. The site includes resources and an online referral to a certified reflexologist.

correspond to internal organs. By stimulating the proper point, you can trigger a healing response in the appropriate part of your body. Some reflexologists think that this energy flows along the same pathways, or meridians, described in Chinese medicine. Reflexology is generally regarded as safe, but avoid it if you have a vascular problem, such as phlebitis or deep vein thrombosis.

Wash Away the Pain

We all know how soothing a warm bath feels, but can water do more than just relieve stress? The answer is *yes*. Some women in labor have experienced significant relief from pain thanks to Jacuzzis now available in birthing centers. And warm, wet compresses can relieve everything from sore muscles to arthritis.

What about those spas we've heard so much about? Well, there may well be something to those healing springs and waters. Many substances are absorbed through the skin, so depending on the composition of the water, you may well be getting benefits beyond the comforting feeling of the water itself. Next time pain attacks, try using aromatherapy oils in a warm bath to relieve pain, alleviate congestion in your sinuses or chest and reduce stress and muscle tension.

Does Like Cure Like?

Homeopathy is a unique system of medicine whose cornerstone is the use of highly diluted remedies. Based on the concept that "like cures like," these remedies contain minute amounts of certain substances. In larger quantities, these substances can cause the same symptoms as the ones being treated.

Homeopathic practitioners evaluate their patients' demeanor and temperament, as well as details of their symptoms, extremely carefully because curing the ailment is dependent on picking exactly the right remedy.

A cold, for example, may be treated with any one of a dozen remedies depending on such details as whether the person feels better when sitting up or lying down.

For more on this subject, see "Homeopathic Medicine" in the next section.

⚠ DON'T TRY THESE TREATMENTS

In most cases, the worst thing that will happen if an "alternative" therapy doesn't work is that it won't have helped whatever ails you. You should be in pretty much the same shape you started out in, minus some money. But there are one or two less-than-innocuous therapies that you should steer clear of:

Colonics. Proponents of enema therapy claim that a lot of disease is caused by toxins trapped in the colon and even glued to the walls of the intestines. "Detoxification" is a favorite form of treatment for many alternative-care practitioners. In fact, your body has its own mechanisms for ridding itself of noxious material and interfering with that process often does more harm than good. The safest way to move waste out of the colon is to eat a high-fiber diet and drink plenty of water. Exercise speeds up the process too. Frequent use of laxatives and enemas can prevent your body from absorbing nutrients and interfere with the uptake of essential vitamins and minerals. Using huge volumes of water for enemas has also resulted in some deaths due to heart failure. Women should not douche either: douching disrupts the normal pH of the vagina and can spread infection up into the uterus as well.

Hydrogen peroxide. This is a fine disinfectant but lately has become a popular alternative therapy for everything from arthritis pain to killing "weak cells." Don't swallow hydrogen peroxide or allow it to be injected into your veins, no matter how much of a miracle cure anybody makes it out to be. Never use any hydrogen peroxide in a concentration greater than 3%.

MUSICAL MEDICINE

"Music therapy" is one of those great techniques that can't possibly hurt you. We all know that it sounds good, but can music actually make you well if you're sick? Results of scientific studies do indicate some quantifiable health benefits, including lowering blood pressure and stress levels, and relieving pain, too. In a study of women giving birth, those who listened to their choice of music used pain relief only 50% of the time versus 80% of the time for those who labored without audio-medicine. Another study documented fewer complications and a shorter recovery period for surgical patients who listened to music during operations performed while the patients were under local anesthesia. Ask your doctor about bringing music and headphones with you to any procedure.

For everyday stress or to relieve minor pain, recline in a comfortable chair and allow your eyelids, arms and legs to become heavy. Breathe deeply and slowly as you listen to the music. Although some people attribute particular power to the music of Mozart, the music most likely to be beneficial is the style you most enjoy listening to, so pick your favorite.

How to Choose & Use Medicines

With all of the pills and potions available today, how do you figure out what really works? Once you understand all of your options, the greater challenge is to figure out how to exercise that freedom of choice safely and effectively. The information here is meant to help you choose from among the different types of substances you can use to treat and prevent health problems.

MEDICINES TODAY— A VAST ARRAY

Just as our conception of a doctor has broadened over the past 15 years, figuring out what constitutes a "medicine" is no longer easy to do either. Here's a working definition: A medicine is any substance that you introduce into the body (by ingestion, injection, etc.) to treat or prevent a medical or emotional condition.

Medicines are often not innocuous substances, whether they're prescription pharmaceuticals, over-the-counter medications, or "natural" remedies such as herbs. It's a good idea to consult a health-care practitioner if you're planning to use a particular medicine for the first time. Conventionally trained MDs will be in charge if you need or want a prescription drug. Talk to a pharmacist or an MD if you're buying an over-the-counter pharmaceutical product. And consult an herbalist or a naturopathic physician (ND) for advice on how to treat conditions using herbal and other alternative remedies.

PHARMACEUTICAL DRUGS

Pharmaceuticals—whether they are by prescription or over-the-counter—are the most commonly used treatment in modern medicine. Most pharmaceuticals are highly purified substances, which make them powerful as well as fast-acting.

Prescription Medications

Unfortunately, prescription drugs are not just life savers… they can be life *stealers* too.

In fact, about 100,000 people a year die from using prescription drugs—more than are killed each year by car and airplane accidents combined. And more than one million people a year are hospitalized due to side effects from prescription drugs.

So how do you protect yourself? Follow these steps:

- *Double-check your prescription.* Mistakes happen all the time. Make sure that the name of the drug on the bottle matches the name on the prescription, which is the same one that you and the doctor discussed. Check the dosage too.
- *Ask for the package insert that comes with the medication.* Pharmacists often don't give out the insert along with the prescription, but inserts contain detailed information about side effects, precautions and other important warnings.
- *Be aware of the side effects.* Some side effects are harmless, but can be frightening if you're not informed—certain drugs can turn your urine garish colors, for instance. Still other warnings are critical, and may alert you not to take the drug if you have a particular medical condition, or to avoid certain foods or particular over-the-counter preparations. For example, a particular class of antidepressants called MAO inhibitors can cause a deadly increase in blood pressure if you eat aged cheese. Ideally, your doctor should inform you of such dangers, but that doesn't always happen. Make a point of asking both the doctor and the pharmacist about what side effects you can expect.

DON'T IGNORE SYMPTOMS

There is a downside to all of the great drugs you can get a hold of without a doctor's prescription these days—be they over-the-counter pharmaceuticals, herbal medications, homeopathic remedies or any other pill or potion. You could be masking a serious problem that requires medical attention. Gastroenterologists frequently see patients who have been suffering from indigestion or heartburn and have been treating the symptoms themselves with antacids and other stomach remedies, without ever suspecting that they have a serious condition like ulcers or stomach cancer. Even something as seemingly "emotional" as anxiety can be caused by thyroid dysfunction.

Think of symptoms that don't go away on their own as your body's way of telling you to see your doctor.

■ *Tell your doctor and pharmacist about other drugs.* Many medications interact dangerously. Make sure that both your doctor and the pharmacist are aware of all medications you take both regularly and occasionally, including over-the-counter drugs and natural remedies.

■ *Store as prescribed.* If the drug is supposed to be kept in a cool dark place, make sure that it's kept in a cool dark place. Many medications lose their effectiveness or undergo chemical changes when stored under the wrong conditions.

■ *Take as prescribed.* This may seem obvious, but you wouldn't believe how many people ignore directions that say "Take with food" or even "Take 3 times a day." In order for the drug to be safe and effective, it must be taken according to the instructions. Also, if the bottle says to take the entire course

MOLDY MIRACLES

Although we think of antibiotics like penicillin as medications that helped to define the era of so-called modern medicine, the use of medicinal molds dates back to ancient times. Around 1550 BC, an Egyptian physician quoted in the Ebers Papyrus stated that if a "wound rots…then bind on it spoiled barley bread." Both the Egyptians and the ancient Chinese used molds to treat all manner of external infections. In fact, the practice was apparently even more widespread: thousand-year-old mummies found in Africa had traces of tetracycline on them. However, the overuse of antibiotics over the past 50 years has led to an epidemic of bacteria that are resistant to them. Believe it or not, it wasn't until 1955 that their distribution was controlled by requiring a physician's prescription. Not that the new regulation did much to put the brakes on overuse—short-sighted doctors simply wrote billions of prescriptions for what were perceived as miracle cures for everything, including many viral infections, for which antibiotics are useless.

Unfortunately, about 20% of prescriptions for antibiotics are still being written to treat viruses. So where does conflicting advice about whether to use antibiotics leave us today? If you have a viral infection, you're better off taking steps to boost your immune system—getting plenty of rest, reducing your work load and taking herbs like echinacea, which boost the immune system by increasing the number of disease-fighting white blood cells.

MEDICAL SYMBOLS TO KNOW

Imagine this: your doctor's handwriting is neat enough to read, but you still can't understand what's on the prescription because of the abbreviations. If you've wondered why the code is so hard to crack, it's because most of the abbreviations are the shorthand version of Latin terms. If you're wondering why you even need to know what the symbols mean, here's why: People make mistakes…and more often than you'd think. The pharmacist will read the "scrip" and fill it, but it's your job to double-check and make sure you received the right dose of the right medication. While you're at it, tell the pharmacist about any other drugs or herbs you're taking, including over-the-counter preparations, to avoid dangerous interactions between substances. The pharmacy isn't the only place where you should do this kind of careful checking: don't forget the hospital, where medication errors are common. If you're not in any condition to watch out for yourself, have a friend or family member keep an eye on the details.

ac	before meals
bid	twice a day
c	with
cap(s)	capsule
daw	dispense as written (no generic or brand-name substitutions)
g, gm, GM	gram
gtt	drop
h	an hour
hs	at bedtime
mg	milligram (one-thousandth of a gram)
ml	milliliter (one-thousandth of a liter)
pc	after eating
po	by mouth
prn	as needed
qh	every hour
q2h	every two hours
qid	four times a day
s	without
stat	immediately
tid	three times a day
ut dict	as directed by doctor

of medication, be sure to do so. This is particularly important in the case of antibiotics because failure to complete the full course of treatment will allow drug-resistant bacteria to flourish and could leave you with an infection that is resistant to antibiotics.

■ *Adjust the dosage.* If you take a medication regularly, be sure to let your doctor know if you gain or lose weight, since it could affect the amount of medication you should be taking. Also, if you're on medication for a problem like heart disease or diabetes and hear of a fantastic natural treatment that you'd like to try, tell your doctor about it first. Some of these products do have effects and could potentially reduce your need for the pharmaceutical drug, leaving you over-medicated and more prone to adverse effects.

■ *Don't double-dose yourself.* Be careful if you use two forms of the same drug together, whether prescription or over-the-counter preparations— you could overdose. If your doctor writes you a prescription for anti-allergy medication, for instance, don't take it along with Benadryl from the drugstore because you feel you're not getting enough relief. Check with your doctor or pharmacist first.

■ *Don't use old drugs or other people's drugs.* These admonitions may seem obvious, but people ignore them all the time.

Over-the-Counter (OTC) Drugs

Many of us assume that drugs we can buy off-the-shelf without a doctor's approval must be safe, but that's not necessarily the case. Not only can those drugs themselves cause problems, but they can interact with prescription drugs, medicinal creams and ointments, herbal remedies, even the food you eat to produce unwanted effects. Did you know, for instance, that combining an aspirin a day with large amounts of vitamin E and a lot of garlic can make your blood dangerously thin? And combining a prescription blood thinner like Coumadin with vitamin E can cause serious bleeding. Make sure you let your health-care provider know about any and all drugs, remedies and supplements you take on a regular basis.

WARNING: WHAT NOT TO MIX

Ideally, your physician warns you of all potentially harmful interactions at the time a prescription is written, and the pharmacist warns you again when the order is filled. Unfortunately, it doesn't always work that way. Here's a list of some common interactions you should be aware of:

Grapefruit, grapefruit juice. Interacts with calcium channel blockers (heart medication) as well as antihistamines (including over-the-counter ones like Benadryl), and may cause serious heart problems. Also interacts with cyclosporin to cause confusion and trembling. These problems occur because a component of grapefruit appears to permit certain medications to be absorbed more readily, resulting in overdoses of drugs even when taken at the prescribed dosage.

Alcoholic beverages. Do not drink alcohol if you are taking any drug with sedative effects. Read the label! If it tells you not to drive, operate heavy machinery or drink alcohol, then don't! Alcohol will intensify the sedative and narcotic effects, making you drowsy…and possibly putting you to sleep forever by interfering with breathing and heart functions.

Bananas. You thought that the potassium bananas are packed with was good for you, didn't you? Well, it is…as long as you're not taking a class of heart drugs known as ACE inhibitors (like Capoten and Vasotec). The combination can lead to a dangerous buildup of potassium. And make sure you aren't taking potassium in your vitamin and mineral supplement either.

Caffeinated beverages. Don't consume caffeine if you take theophylline for asthma. Both substances have a stimulant effect on your body, and the combination can cause palpitations and seizures. Also avoid caffeine if you are taking the antibiotic Cipro, since this drug can boost caffeine levels in your body, causing shakiness and jitters. The same thing seems to happen when caffeine is mixed with Tagamet, Zantac, and Pepcid. Remember that caffeine isn't found only in coffee and tea, but also in many sodas (not just cola) and chocolate.

⚠️

OVER-THE-COUNTER DRUG PATROL

If you think that a medicine you buy right off of the drugstore shelf can't be strong enough or have enough side effects to hurt you, think again. A good rule of thumb for those drugs is to use them only occasionally, never regularly, except under the supervision of a doctor.

Aspirin and other nonsteroidal anti-inflammatory drugs, such as ibuprofen. These drugs can irritate the stomach lining and cause bleeding. If you must take aspirin regularly, stick with an enteric-coated version, which prevents the drug from being digested until it reaches the intestine where it is less likely to cause problems.

Acetaminophen (Tylenol). Taken regularly or in large doses, this drug can cause liver damage, especially if you drink alcohol. Even small amounts can intensify this effect.

Weight-loss drugs. Some weight-loss products contain ingredients that can drive up your blood pressure. Certain decongestants also have this effect, so never take the two together. Weight-loss drugs that contain stimulants give some people palpitations or jitters too.

Decongestants. Nasal sprays and drops that are used for longer than a few days can cause rebound congestion. When you stop using the product, your nose is stuffier than ever. The same thing can happen with drops that are supposed to "take the red out" of your eyes. Stop using them, and you look like you stepped out of a third-rate horror movie.

Laxatives. Regular use of laxatives can result in a loss of normal bowel function and cause dependence. Increase your intake of insoluble fiber—found in whole grains and cereals—instead. And a word of warning to people using laxatives as a weight-loss aid: chronic diarrhea can prevent your body from absorbing vital nutrients and can irritate the lining of the colon as well.

Hydrocortisone ointments or creams. These work by suppressing the normal immune response, which is something you really don't want to do. Plus, they are absorbed through the skin into the general circulation and may have far-reaching effects on the immune system over time. Also, any chronic skin condition should be evaluated by a doctor, since you may not be able to tell whether you're dealing with a fungal infection or skin cancer. Hydrocortisone just suppresses symptoms; it doesn't treat the underlying condition.

NATURAL MEDICINE

Herbs and foods that are being used for medicinal purposes are drugs. It is particularly important to reinforce this notion because when you buy herbal remedies in the health-food store, they are usually labeled as "nutritional supplements" and carry a recommendation to take a certain amount of the product daily in addition to the diet. This labeling is misleading and stems from the fact that manufacturers of botanical medicines are prohibited from making specific health claims for their products.

Are Herbal Medicines Safe?

There's been a lot of discussion about whether herbal remedies are safe, but the fact is that although there are some herbs that should be avoided (see box on next page), most are unlikely to harm you.

Talk about a double standard, though—toxic reactions to conventional medicines are currently responsible for one third of all hospitalizations. Can you imagine what the outcry from the medical establishment would be like if more than a million people a year had to be hospitalized because of adverse reactions to natural remedies?

i

HERBAL DRUG REFERENCE

Contrary to what you might have heard, a lot of scientific research has examined the safety and efficacy of herbal medicines. Unfortunately, most of it has not been conducted in the U.S. In part this is because pharmaceutical companies (which fund most of the drug research in this country) don't stand to make much money from the sale of herbals, since herbs cannot be patented. A great deal of research has been carried out in Europe, however, and in Germany in particular. The results of those studies are available in a document called the Commission E monographs, which outlines the uses and precautions for several hundred herbs. Commission E is the German regulatory body for drugs—the equivalent of our FDA (Food and Drug Administration). Now a well-respected U.S. publication, the *Physician's Desk Reference* (PDR), has used the Commission E monographs and the results of an exhaustive literature search of its own to compile the first "PDR for Herbal Medicines." It lists the indications for several hundred herbs, as well as precautions and side effects. An absolute must-have if you're planning to use herbs to treat yourself or your family. Make sure your doctor has a copy too!

This does not mean that you should be complacent about using "natural" medicines, however. Many of them *do* work, which means that, just as with pharmaceutical drugs, you need to watch out for side effects and adverse reactions. However, since their effects are usually milder than the effects of pharmaceuticals, the reactions are less likely to be serious as well.

Are Herbal Medicines Effective?

Now that we've addressed the question of whether herbal remedies can hurt you, we're left with the other question—can they help you? And if so, how much? As with any medicine, the answer lies in which condition you're treating and which medicine you're using. Although there are standard herbal treatments for some common ailments, visit a health-care practitioner who is an expert in natural remedies for guidance.

In order for herbal remedies to be effective, you must buy products that are potent. One of the drawbacks to the lack of regulation of natural remedies is that there is no independent body overseeing the quality of herbal products. Take the following steps to increase the chances that your natural medicine will be effective:

- *Don't buy loose, bulk herbs because dried plants of all kinds lose their potency if they sit around.*
- *Buy "standardized" extracts, which are guaranteed to contain a minimum amount of the herb.*
- *Use tinctures. The alcohol used to extract the active constituents of the herb preserves the herb's potency as well.*
- *Freeze-dried extracts are good, too. They are concentrated and stable, so they tend to retain their potency longer.*

If your doctor determines that you have an innocuous medical condition that you want to treat

---

NATURAL NEOSPORIN?

Medicines are not limited to substances that you swallow or inject; medicated skin creams and ointments contain drugs too. Skin rashes, irritations, burns and fungal and bacterial infections affect all of us at some time, but do you have to head for the nearest drugstore for treatment? Not necessarily. A perfectly effective remedy may be no farther away than your cupboard or refrigerator.

Honey. A medicine from as far back as Ancient Egypt, honey fights germs on two fronts. First, it kills bacteria by drawing the water out of them. Second, it disinfects wounds by using inhibine (an enzyme found in honey) to turn glucose and water into a well-known disinfectant—hydrogen peroxide. Honey mixed with lard has been used as an antibiotic ointment all over the world, including in Shanghai during the second World War, and is quite effective.

Wine and vinegar. Just in case you're thinking that it's the alcohol in wine that does the job…you're wrong. Actually the germ killer is a substance known as malvoside.

Garlic. Rubbing raw garlic on fungal infections like ringworm and athlete's foot works quickly, although it may irritate the skin slightly. Mix crushed garlic with a little vitamin E oil to take out the sting.

Other soothing substances for the skin are aloe vera, calendula and vitamin E oil. The best source of aloe vera is an aloe vera plant, which you can buy for just a few dollars. This will ensure you a fresh supply of the gel for mild burns. Just slit open a leaf and squeeze out the gel. Calendula is good for rashes and is available at health-food stores. Vitamin E oil helps speed healing and is great for chapping, too. Squeeze it out of a capsule or buy a small bottle of the pure oil. Make sure the color is amber, not pale, to be sure that it has not been adulterated with other oils.

HOMICIDAL HERBS

Not every leaf and flower offers up a quaint folk remedy. Some of them are good old-fashioned poisons. Here are the ones to avoid and why:

➤ **Ma Huang or ephedra**. Used for everything from asthma to nasal congestion to weight loss, this substance contains ephedrine, which can raise blood pressure, cause irregular heartbeat and make you nervous and jittery.

➤ **Comfrey**. This herb may indeed help wounds heal and broken bones knit back together, but unfortunately these wondrous effects may not happen before your liver is destroyed by the toxic pyrrolizidine alkaloids found in comfrey. Two other herbs—borage and coltsfoot—also contain these dangerous compounds.

➤ **Chaparral**. Supposedly great for treating cancer, colds, arthritis and pain, chaparral can cause liver disease and death.

Other herbs to stay away from include foxglove, life root, lobelia, sassafras, yohimbe, belladonna, germander, kombucha tea, pennyroyal, poke root, skullcap, wormwood and the Chinese medicine jin bu huan.

with herbs, be sure to have answers to the following:

- *What is the most absorbable form of the herb and how should it be taken?*
- *What is the proper dosage?*
- *How long should it be taken?*
- *What are the potential side effects of the herb and which drugs or foods does it interact with?*

Finally, remember that herbal medicines are *medicines*—not dietary supplements. Don't take them unless you are treating a specific condition. And stop taking them once the condition has resolved or if it becomes apparent that the herbal therapy is not working.

HOW TO TAKE A NEW DRUG SAFELY

Whenever you're treating yourself with a new over-the-counter medicine (whether it's a pharmaceutical drug or natural remedy), start with a small dose and watch carefully for allergies or any unpleasant reaction. Stop using the product and call your doctor if it causes nausea, vomiting, diarrhea, hives, rash or headache. Call an ambulance if you experience a sensation of swelling in your throat or have any difficulty breathing.

FOOD AS MEDICINE

Herbs aren't the only plants with a role to play in the treatment of illness. Lately, the role of food in the prevention of disease has finally been getting the attention it should have had long ago, and certain foods can be used to actually treat ailments too. Here are some:

Garlic. An all-purpose microbe annihilator, garlic kills bacteria, fungi and viruses. Take two cloves and get a good night's rest if you feel yourself coming down with something. Take two or three cloves a day if you're already sick, and take it regularly for a few weeks to fight off a persistent fungal or yeast infection.

Ginger. Ginger is highly effective for fighting nausea, morning sickness, motion sickness and all manner of digestive upsets. If you find the ginger too pungent, buy crystallized ginger candy, which is just as effective or take ginger powder in a capsule.

Cranberry juice. This juice (not diluted forms found in cranberry drinks) helps urinary tract infections. Drink several glasses a day to change urine pH and rid your system of unwanted organisms.

GOOD HERBS & WHAT THEY'RE GOOD FOR

It's relatively easy to put together an herbal arsenal that can help you fight most of the run-of-the-mill ills that you and your family are likely to encounter. Here's what you should have on hand:

Chamomile tea. A mild relaxant and excellent as a remedy for colic and stomach upsets, it can be safely used by children, too. Also, try chamomile tea bags on the eyes as a treatment for conjunctivitis. Place the tea bag in a little boiling water. When the tea bag has cooled but still warm, place over closed eyes, lie back, and relax with tea bags in place for 15 minutes two or three times a day.

Echinacea. It appears to work its magic by boosting disease-fighting white blood cells. Take it if you feel a "bug" coming on or if you have a cold, the flu or any kind of infection.

Feverfew. Take it to prevent and treat migraine headaches.

Kava. This is a heavy-duty anxiety-fighting herb.

Lemon balm. Excellent as a mild relaxant, it may also help fight the virus that causes cold sores.

Nettle. If you suffer from hay fever, you'll love this allergy fighter.

Peppermint spirits. It is excellent both for headache and upset stomach. For headaches, drip a little onto a folded tissue and rub across the forehead, on the temples and on the back of the neck. For tummies, put a few drops in a little water and swallow. Do not give internally to very young children.

Slippery elm. This soothes and coats the inside of your throat and intestines. It's great for sore throats and coughs, as well as diarrhea and other digestive problems.

Saint-John's-wort. This herb is as effective as pharmaceutical drugs for mild-to-moderate depression.

Valerian. It's the perfect herb for a perfect night's sleep. You can also try combining it with kava, lemon balm, hops or passionflower for even more sleep-inducing power.

White willow bark. This herb contains salicin, a precursor of aspirin. It acts more slowly and gently than the highly purified, fast-acting aspirin found at the drugstore, but it's also unlikely to upset your stomach or cause other side effects. Take it for mild fevers as well as aches and pains.

Wild indigo. It is particularly good for upper respiratory infections. Combine it with echinacea for sinus infections.

HOMEOPATHIC MEDICINE

Homeopathic remedies constitute a unique class of medicines that are particularly frustrating to conventional medical doctors and scientists. The theory underlying their use sounds ludicrous, and yet like so many other odd-sounding treatments, there is some evidence for their effectiveness.

Homeopathic medicines operate on the principle that "like cures like," rather like the "hair of the dog that bit you" theory of treatment. Of course, this principle is not unknown in conventional medicine. Two great examples are vaccines (in which you're inoculated with a component of the disease you're trying to avoid to stimulate an immune response against it) and allergy shots

(again, you're exposed to minute quantities of the substance in order to build up resistance). And although American doctors may consider homeopathic remedies to be absurd, French doctors do not. In fact, French pharmacies are required by law to stock these medicines and one-third of French doctors prescribe them.

Critics complain that by the time homeopaths have finished diluting the remedies, traces of the original substance can't even be detected. But does it have to be detectable to be effective? Although the results of scientific studies have not been dramatic, homeopathic remedies have been shown to be more effective than placebos—which means that they do appear to have some biological impact. Try them if you're bothered by a condition that is not dangerous. For best results, consult a practitioner trained in their

use, such as a homeopathic or naturopathic physician.

A POWERFUL PILL

You could make the argument —and a pretty convincing one at that—that one of the most effective all-purpose medications for garden-variety symptoms is the placebo. How can that be? We must first appreciate that as much as one third of the time when patients go to the doctor complaining of symptoms, no physical cause can be identified. That doesn't mean that there isn't one, of course, only that the doctor cannot detect one. Secondly, most conditions resolve on their own, and they end even faster when the victim believes that recovery is just a pill and some reassuring doctor's words away.

Not Convinced?

If you have any doubts about the power of your expectations to affect your physical responses, listen to this: A group of patients with stomach cancer was divided into two groups. One half were given a chemotherapy drug; the other half got a placebo. Now we all know that certain kinds of chemotherapy can make your hair fall out, right? Well, apparently sugar pills can, too…if you believe you're getting chemotherapy drugs. One third of the group on placebos experienced hair loss.

So is there a downside to sugar pills? Well…yes. Since pain is the body's way of alerting you that something is wrong, it's not a great idea to mask this symptom unless you're sure that its cause is innocuous. For example, if you suffer from angina (chest pain due to narrowed coronary arteries), the pain is your cue to take nitroglycerin, which dilates your blood vessels and restores blood flow to the heart muscle. In studies where patients got either active medication or a placebo, some of the patients on placebo stopped experiencing chest pain. But exercise stress tests showed that their hearts were not receiving enough blood, which meant that they *needed* an active medication.

IS LAUGHTER THE BEST MEDICINE?

We know that laughter makes us feel better, but why? Laughing raises endorphin levels (a feel-good hormone) and lowers levels of cortisol, which is released in response to stress. Laughter actually affects your body chemically, elevating your mood and boosting resistance and recovery in the process. It may not cure cancer, but…who knows? At the very least, anything that makes you laugh will distract you from what ails you, and we know *that's* good!

HOMEOPATHS OWE PIGS BIG

For decades, homeopathics have been enduring the accusation that their remedies work their magic thanks only to the placebo effect. But wait! Would pigs be happy with just any old pill? What about mama piggies whose teeny piglets were dropping like flies? In an intriguing study of a herd of sows who were suffering high miscarriage rates, 10 of the pigs were treated with homeopathic caulophyllum and had only half the stillbirth rate of 10 control sows. When the entire herd was treated, the stillbirth rate dropped from 20% to less than 3%. The homeopathic remedy was stopped, and the rate climbed to almost 15%. Once the sows were back on the medication, the rate fell back to less than 2%. Now, you must admit, that's pretty good.

Personal & Family
Coping with Illness

**How to
Be Healthy**

Coping with
Illness

Body Power

Mind Power

Emergency Scenarios

Only health-care professionals actually expect emergencies. But situations that require immediate action can and do happen all the time. Here's a variety of handy suggestions easy enough to recall in the scariest of scenarios. Learn them today, so that they're second nature when you need them.

DON'T FREEZE!

Many people panic in an emergency because they just don't know where to start. Do you go for help or stay with the victim? Should you perform CPR or wait for an expert? Don't let the urgency of the situation confuse you. Here are three words and an acronym that guarantee you will do the right thing in *any* emergency: **Check, Call, Care** and **ABC**. Memorize it: Check, Call, Care, ABC. Check, Call, Care, ABC. Say it over and over until it's second nature. This phrase will prompt you to take the right steps and take them in the right order.

Now read on to see what each of the components tells you to do.

Check

First, *check the scene* to make sure it is safe for you to approach the victim. Look for things like oncoming traffic, spilled chemicals, downed power lines or poisonous gas. If the situation is hazardous, do not approach the victim. Call your local emergency number immediately.

If the area is safe, *check the victim*. Start by asking if he or she is okay. If the person is conscious and talking, you can work together to figure out the problem and get help. Most likely the person will be able to tell you what's wrong. *Check for significant bleeding*, and apply firm pressure to any wounds that are actively bleeding.

If the victim is unresponsive, the acronym **ABC** (airway, breathing, circulation) will help you check for the right things in the right order.

- *Airway*. Unless you suspect a neck injury, tilt back the head and lift up the chin to open the airway. Look for objects in the mouth or the top of the throat that might be obstructing the airway.
- *Breathing*. Put your ear to the person's mouth and nose. Do you feel breath? Watch the chest for 15 seconds. Is it rising and falling? If the airway is open and the person is not breathing, you will need to perform mouth-to-mouth resuscitation or "rescue breathing."
- *Circulation*. Feel for a pulse by placing two fingers on the side of the neck just above the collarbone. Press lightly. Do not use your thumb which has its own pulse and may confuse you. If you cannot find a pulse, put your ear on the person's chest and see if you can hear a heartbeat. If you cannot detect one, CPR will be needed to restore circulation.

Call

Always call for an ambulance if the victim:
- *Is unconscious*
- *Is bleeding severely*
- *Is having trouble breathing or is breathing strangely*
- *Cannot be moved easily or without risking further injury*

Care

The type of care you should give will depend on the particular symptoms of the injury or illness. Read through the remaining topics in this section now so that you'll be prepared for an emergency.

SEVEN DEADLY SINS OF OMISSION

Don't freeze in an emergency because you're afraid of making a mistake or think someone else will take charge. Even if you just shout for more assistance you'll be helping.

Don't drive yourself to the emergency room. If you're sick or injured enough to be going there, you can't drive safely.

Don't remove an object that has caused a puncture wound. It may be preventing serious bleeding, or it may cause even more damage by removing it.

Don't hang up the phone on a 911 call. Dispatchers will let you know when they have all of the information they need and it's safe for you to disconnect.

Don't put a severed body part directly on ice. It may become frostbitten, which may prevent successful reattachment.

Don't postpone seeking prompt attention for a serious cut. Life-threatening blood loss can occur surprisingly quickly.

Don't ignore the potential seriousness of unexplained pain. People die every day because they ignore this warning sign. Any pain that you have never experienced before or that gets worse or fails to abate after a short period of time should be checked out.

OUT OF AIR

Although not all breathing problems are life-threatening, some have the potential to become so—often, quite suddenly. Take abnormal breathing seriously and watch the person like a hawk while you seek medical attention.

A surprise enemy in breathing troubles is simply the sensation of not being able to take in enough air, which triggers anxiety that makes the problem worse.

Reassure the person that he will be fine, and help him stay calm. This will ensure that his breathing is as regular and relaxed as possible.

When Every Second Counts

Breathing problems are among the most frightening of emergencies because it takes only 4 to 10 minutes for the brain to suffer irreversible damage if it is deprived of oxygen. This time period may be somewhat longer in extreme cold, such as if the victim is in an icy lake.

If you check an unconscious person and find that he or she is not breathing, check carefully for a pulse. Finding a pulse—even if it is a slow one—lets you know that blood is still circulating and, along with it, at least some oxygen.

It is possible to still have a pulse in the absence of breathing, but not the other way around.

Rescue Breathing

If an adult has stopped breathing, follow these steps:

- Shout for someone to call 911 while you attend to the victim or call 911 yourself if you are alone.
- Place the person on his back on the floor or on a flat, hard surface.
- Look in the mouth for any obstructions that you are able to remove. If the airway is blocked, no amount of rescue breathing will be effective. You'll know that the airway is obstructed if when you give the first breath, the air won't go in! If the airway is clear, the lungs will inflate and the chest will rise.
- Tilt the person's head back and lift the chin. If you think there might be a neck injury, lift the chin without tilting the head. Use your mouth to form a tight seal around the victim's mouth. Pinch the nose shut.
- Give two breaths. Breathe into the victim for two seconds per breath, then pause for three seconds to let air flow out again. Check for a pulse and see if the person has begun breathing. If there is a pulse but no breathing, continue rescue breathing at the rate of about one breath every five seconds. Check for a pulse and spontaneous breathing every minute (about 10 to 12 breaths). Continue mouth-to-mouth resuscitation until help arrives.

The technique is the same for children, except that they require one breath every three seconds instead of one every five seconds, and you will not need to blow with as much force to fill their lungs. Infants also require one breath every three seconds, but you must cover both the infant's mouth and nose with your mouth. Again, watch the force.

BE SAFE, NOT SICK

Most people are afraid of contracting the HIV virus during an emergency, but many other diseases and infections (such as hepatitis and tuberculosis) can be passed from one person to another during the administration of first aid. To protect yourself and the other person, keep the following items—known as "universal safety devices"—in your first-aid kits both at home and in your car:

Latex gloves. Wear them to prevent the exchange of body fluids that might contain dangerous organisms.

Airway bag. These devices, now widely available in pharmacies, allow you to perform rescue breathing without having skin-to-skin contact with the person you are reviving.

Goggles and plastic apron. These will protect you from splashes of blood from open wounds.

Of course these items may not be handy when you need them most, say if someone collapses at your feet in the supermarket. If your conscience requires you to provide assistance in spite of the risks, just do the best you can to avoid direct contact with any blood.

DON'T WASTE TIME

If someone is unconscious or in clear need of an ambulance and the cause isn't immediately obvious, don't spend a single second trying to figure out whether the person is a victim of a heart attack, poisoning or anything else. Just call for help, then treat the symptoms. If the victim isn't breathing, check the airway and do rescue breathing. If there's no pulse, perform CPR. If you can see bleeding, control it. But don't waste precious minutes diagnosing the condition…they'll do that at the hospital. Once help arrives, you can take a quick look around for any clues, such as weapons or empty pill bottles.

SIGN UP FOR CPR SCHOOL

If an unconscious person does not have a pulse, both circulation and breathing will need to be restored using cardiopulmonary resuscitation. CPR is mouth-to-mouth resuscitation (also called rescue breathing) plus chest compressions. The chest compressions replace the function of the heart, circulating blood that is now getting its oxygen from the rescue breathing.

CPR can be a lifesaver, but you must be trained in order to perform it safely and effectively. Call your local American Red Cross chapter or fire department for information on classes near you. The training takes only a few hours and the cost is usually minimal. The course includes not only CPR but also instruction on basic first-aid techniques for injuries and illnesses.

FIRST-AID MISTAKES

Even with the best of intentions, it's possible to hurt the person you're trying so hard to help. Here are a couple of absolute no-no's.

CPR alert. Don't perform chest compressions on someone whose heart is beating! This may sound obvious, but people have been killed by overeager first-aiders who didn't check the victims carefully enough to detect a heartbeat. Performing unnecessary compressions can cause a normally functioning heart to beat abnormally (arrhythmia), an extremely dangerous condition that can kill rapidly. To be absolutely certain that the person you are trying to save by using CPR actually needs the procedure, check for signs of circulation, such as breathing, coughing or movement. The American Heart Association no longer recommends a pulse check.

Stay where you are. Don't move an injured person unless you absolutely have to because of an imminent danger, such as fire or rising water. To avoid further damage, certain injuries *must* be stabilized before a person is moved. Although the most notorious of these are injuries to the neck and back, they're not the only reasons to stay put. Moving a victim of hypothermia (low body temperature) before the core body temperature has been elevated to at least 90 degrees Fahrenheit can cause irregular heartbeat and death. You can begin to warm up the person, but don't move him or her until you get the go-ahead from a health-care professional.

HEART ATTACK AID

Heart attacks are much less likely to be fatal than they used to be, but only for those who recognize the symptoms and get help *fast*.

Don't Ignore the Red Flags

The sensations that signal a heart attack can be unmistakable or barely noticeable. There are two tricks to surviving a heart attack: Don't ignore those minor symptoms, and don't think it can't happen to you just because you're young or in good physical shape. Here are the symptoms that generally are obvious:

- Severe or crushing chest pain that does not improve with rest or a change of position
- Shortness of breath or gasping that gets worse when lying down

---

SNEAKY SYMPTOM

Don't ignore a persistent, unexplained pain in your jaw, teeth or hand. Strange as it may seem, it's often the only sign that the heart isn't getting enough oxygen. Get it checked out. And if the first health-care professional you consult brushes you off, get a second opinion...fast.

- Chest pain combined with any of the following: severe anxiety, sweating, breathlessness, bluish lips or fingernail beds, or irregular or rapid pulse

Here are the symptoms that people tend to ignore:

- Pain or discomfort that radiates from the chest to the shoulders, jaw, arms, neck or hands
- Upset stomach, nausea or heartburn. If you are not prone to digestive upsets, be particularly alert. The onset of heartburn in someone who never gets it should always be checked out

If you develop any of these symptoms, call 911. Do not drive yourself to the emergency room—you could collapse along the way.

If you suspect that somebody else is having a heart attack, call 911, then keep an eye on the ABCs (airway, breathing, circulation). Ask the person if she carries nitroglycerin, a drug that alleviates chest pain. If so, help her take it. Do not drive the person to the hospital yourself. If she takes a turn for the worse, you won't be able to help her. If the person's heart or breathing stops, begin CPR while you wait for help.

Often people who have less dramatic symptoms will insist that they are fine and resist your attempts to get them to the hospital. There are a couple of ways to approach a person in denial:

- *Shock treatment method.* Point out that it's probably better to be embarrassed in the emergency room than lying dead in the morgue.
- *Guilt trip method.* Tell the person that you're worried sick, that you would never forgive yourself if it turned out to be anything serious, and so on. In other words, just guilt the person into it.

LET 911 FIND YOU!

Many communities have a system called "enhanced 911." This system allows emergency dispatchers to see the address and phone number of whoever is making a 911 call. That means that if you need help and can't talk, just dialing 911 will result in an ambulance or police car being sent to you. It's a particularly valuable service for young children, who may know that they should call 911 in an emergency but may not have memorized their address.

If the enhanced 911 system is not in place where you live, put your address and phone number near the phone so that callers can read it to the dispatcher. It's not unusual to "go blank" in an emergency and not remember information that is ordinarily second nature.

STROKE SYMPTOMS

Typically strokes are due to a clogged vessel in the brain or neck, in much the same way that heart attacks result from clogged blood vessels that feed the heart.

A small minority of strokes are the result of blood vessels bursting in the brain, which is much more likely to be fatal. Although we tend to be more familiar with heart attacks, strokes are almost as common and at least as debilitating.

Signs of Stroke

If a person exhibits the following symptoms, call 911. Watch the ABCs while you wait for help.

- Weakness, numbness or paralysis, usually on just one side
- Sudden headache
- Blurry vision or decreased vision in one or both eyes
- Loss of balance or coordination
- Disorientation and confusion
- Trouble speaking or understanding language

Sometimes, a person will experience a mild version of these symptoms or the symptoms will pass. Don't ignore this warning! Just as angina (chest pain) alerts you to heart disease, these pre-stroke symptoms—called transient ischemic attacks—are letting you know that you're at a greatly increased risk of having a stroke.

CHOKING VS. COUGHING

Help! Johnny is coughing his head off at the supper table. Mom starts thumping him on the back. Wrong! Dad yanks his arms high above his head. Wrong! We make all kinds of mistakes when we think someone is choking.

Is It Real Choking?

First you need to figure out whether the person is really choking. Coughing is not the same thing as choking. In order to cough, a person must be able to take in air—in other words, breathe. If you can breathe enough to cough, you're not choking—at least, not yet. In fact, forceful coughing is the most efficient way to dislodge an object from the throat.

A person is really in trouble if they can't talk or breathe, are wheezing or coughing very weakly, or have a red face and clammy or sweaty skin. When faced with genuine choking, don't delay.

CHOKING PREVENTION

What do you do if you suddenly find yourself choking and there's nobody in sight? Perform the Heimlich Maneuver on yourself, of course! Here's how to do it: Let yourself fall on a chair or table so that the edge hits your diaphragm, thrusting it up against your lungs. The weight of your body combined with the impact will force air out of your lungs and dislodge the obstruction.

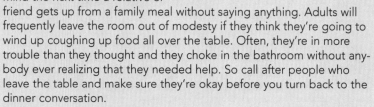

Speaking of choking alone, keep this little-known fact in mind the next time a relative or friend gets up from a family meal without saying anything. Adults will frequently leave the room out of modesty if they think they're going to wind up coughing up food all over the table. Often, they're in more trouble than they thought and they choke in the bathroom without anybody ever realizing that they needed help. So call after people who leave the table and make sure they're okay before you turn back to the dinner conversation.

What NOT to Do

Knowing what not to do is just as important as knowing what to do. Do not bang the victim on the back—a natural reaction. Doing so may dislodge the object, but since there is no upward force it will fall right back into the throat. Another favorite maneuver is pulling up the person's arms, which causes the person to take a deep breath. Unfortunately, it can also make the person inhale whatever is in the throat. Not the desired effect.

If the person can't breathe or talk, even to ask for help, it's time for the Heimlich Maneuver.

Don't Choke in the First Place

You can lower your chances of choking by keeping an eye out for the following risk factors:

- Dentures create a potential hazard by making it harder to tell whether food has been thoroughly chewed
- Any loss of sensation in the mouth increases the risk, so watch out for alcohol, which dulls the nerves that help you swallow
- Finally, don't eat too fast or talk, laugh or run with food in your mouth

---

HOW TO UNPLUG A BLOCKED AIRWAY

Heimlich Maneuver

Stand behind the person and put your arms around the waist. Reassure the person that you know what to do. Try to get him or her to relax. Make a fist with your thumb just above the navel but below the protrusion at the base of the chest. Do not bang this little bony tip—it might break and cause internal injury.

Make sure that your forearms are not in contact with the victim's ribs. Wrap your other hand around the fist and give five sharp upward thrusts in the victim's abdomen. If the victim is pregnant or very obese, try giving the thrusts in the middle of the chest. **Again, avoid that bone at the bottom of the sternum.**

'Heimlich' for Babies

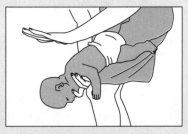

Slapping the back is correct, but here is how that whack on the back is supposed to be administered. Hold the child head down and give up to five sharp blows between the shoulder blades with the heel of your hand. Make sure you support the baby's head and brace your forearm against your thigh.

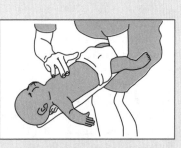

If this does not dislodge the object, you must give chest thrusts. Turn the baby over so that he is faceup but otherwise in the same position as before. Place your two thumbs in the center of the baby's chest a little above the bony protrusion at the base of the sternum. Give five sharp compressions.

UNIVERSAL CHOKING SIGN

It's human instinct to put your hands to your throat when you're choking. People the world over do it in exactly the same way. If you see this gesture and the person can't talk, you'll know that she can't breathe.

KINDS OF CUTS

The first thing to keep in mind when you see a lot of blood is that cuts that look like they're bleeding impressively are not always serious. And sometimes what is really a small amount of blood can look like an awful lot.

Little Cuts

Most cuts are close to the surface of the skin and therefore are not serious. These are the ones we see all the time, especially those of us with children.

Just apply pressure to the wound with a piece of gauze, and clean the cut with soap and water, rubbing alcohol or hydrogen peroxide. Protect it from dirt and further injury by covering it with a bandage, but take the dressing off at bedtime so that the cut gets some air. Bandages can trap moisture next to the skin, which bacteria thrive on.

Keep an eye on the cut until it looks like it is well healed. Have a health-care practitioner take a look at it if the cut becomes red or inflamed along the edges, develops pus or fails to heal.

Big Cuts

Deep cuts that have hit an artery or a vein are a whole different matter and require prompt attention. It's quite easy to lose a dangerously large amount of blood in a very short period of time. This is particularly true for children.

Ascertain where the cut is located. There are major arteries and veins that run along the inside of the wrist, the inner thigh and the neck, at the back of the calf and on the torso. Cuts that pierce or sever arteries spurt blood, while those that damage veins tend to gush. In addition, any cut that is very long or very deep is likely to bleed heavily, even if it didn't damage a large blood vessel.

If you're faced with a serious cut, don't waste time washing the wound. Just follow these steps:

- Using a piece of gauze, first-aid bandage or clean cloth, apply firm pressure to the cut. If the blood soaks through the material, place another dressing or piece of cloth over the first one. Do not remove the underlying bandages. Repeat this process if needed. Once the bleeding has slowed, apply a bandage and seek medical attention.
- If possible, elevate the cut above the level of the heart.
- If you cannot control the bleeding with pressure, you may be able to stop it by compressing the blood vessel feeding the cut between your hand and the bone under the wound.
- Using a tourniquet is a last resort. If you must apply one, see box at left and get medical help immediately.

Puncture Wounds

If the object that punctured the body is still in there, do not pull it out! Doing so may cause even more damage than has already occurred, and the object may be preventing severe bleeding by acting as a dam against severed blood vessels. If the object is embedded, see a health-care professional to have it removed and have the wound cleaned and dressed.

If the object that caused the injury is small and slips right out—like a nail—bear in mind that puncture wounds can be deep and that dirt and particles may have been rammed into the wound by the object, making infection a real threat. Be extremely careful about cleaning the wound and keeping the area clean. Visit a health-care professional at the first sign of infection.

Amputations

You might think that losing a limb in an accident would result in enormous blood loss, but generally that's not the case. In a complete amputation, the blood vessels constrict and retreat back into the limb, reducing the amount of bleeding. Shock is an enormous threat, however. So, in addition to keeping the victim calm, you must

---

TOURNIQUETS—HELP OR HAZARD?

If applying firm pressure and compressing torn vessels between your hand and the bone under the wound do not stop the blood loss, a tourniquet may be the only way to prevent life-threatening bleeding while you wait for help to arrive. But tourniquets can be dangerous because they stop all blood flow to the area beyond the point of the constriction. Only use one as a last resort. If you do apply one, be sure to follow these rules without exception:

➤ Once you put the tourniquet on, do not loosen it periodically to "let a little blood get to the tissues." Doing so could release dangerous blood clots into the bloodstream.

➤ Write down the time you applied the tourniquet on the person's forehead where it will be readily visible to medical personnel. This will let them know how long the tissues have been deprived of oxygen.

Apply the tourniquet like this:

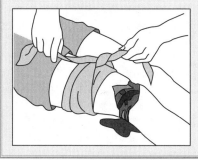 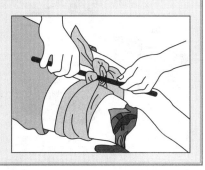

WRAP-AROUND BANDAGE

When a person has a puncture wound and the object is still embedded, the bandage must be applied so that it stabilizes the object, preventing it from moving around and causing more damage. Remember, do *not* remove the object.

Here's how it should look:

locate any body parts that became separated from their owner during the accident. Make sure they are transported with the victim no matter what their condition. Microsurgeons at the hospital will decide what is salvageable.

Here's how to take care of the amputated part:

- If necessary, rinse any dirt or debris off of the detached body part, but do not scrub it
- Wrap it in a piece of sterile gauze or clean cloth
- Put the wrapped part into a waterproof container, such as a plastic bag or a glass
- Place it on a bed of ice but do not bury it in the ice, which could cause frostbite

Internal Bleeding

Bleeding that takes place inside of the body is difficult to detect because there may be no obvious injury to alert you. Bruises are actually the most common form of internal bleeding and most are not serious. However, dangerous, even life-threatening, internal bleeding can occur for a wide variety of reasons. It may follow an accident or occur when blood leaks inside your body because of a problem such as an ulcer that has worn through the stomach lining. Here are the signs of internal bleeding:

- Cool, clammy skin
- Cold hands and feet
- Rapid pulse and dilated pupils
- Coughing or vomiting blood or material resembling coffee grounds

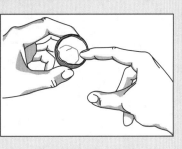

BAND-AGE OR BAND-EGG?

Here's how people from Ecuador handle a cut: Crack open an egg, empty it, and peel away the thin membrane that lines the inside of the shell. Place it slippery side down over the cut. The membrane will adhere to your finger and contract as it dries, pulling the edges of the cut together. Very creative, don't you agree?

BETTER CUT CLEANERS

Cotton balls are popular for cleaning cuts, but they are not the best choice. Tiny fibers may stay behind in the cut or get caught on the newly forming scabs. Use a lint-free material—such as gauze—instead.

- Stools that are black or that contain obvious blood
- Severe bruises or bruises that appear immediately

If you suspect internal bleeding, get medical help at once.

There is no first-aid measure that can alleviate this sort of bleeding, but that doesn't mean there's nothing you can do. The first thing to do is get help. Next, treat the victim for shock, which can result from any significant blood loss.

FISHHOOK FIX

If the entire barb of a fishhook gets embedded in the skin, don't pull it back out! The back end of the barb will tear the flesh, creating a much nastier wound. Instead, push it back through the skin in the same direction it entered, then snip off the barb and remove the hook from the body.

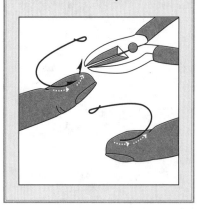

Tetanus Threat

Many people think that you only get tetanus from stepping on a rusty nail, but that's not the whole story. The spores that produce the toxin that causes tetanus live in dirt and soil, so any wound can become contaminated, no matter how you acquired it. Puncture wounds are particularly susceptible because they are relatively deep. Because tetanus is extremely difficult to treat once it sets in, it's extremely important to keep your tetanus vaccine up-to-date.

DEALING WITH SHOCK

We all know that a seriously ill or injured person can go into shock, and that shock is life-threatening and should be prevented at all costs. But what exactly is shock?

What Is Shock?

Shock is a condition that occurs when the body has suffered a serious injury or physical trauma that interferes with the ability of the circulatory system (the heart, blood vessels and blood) to deliver enough oxygen to the tissues for the body to function normally. Deprived of oxygen, cells begin to die and the organs stop working.

The body tries to compensate for the deficiency of the circulatory system by diverting blood flow away from less important parts (arms, legs and skin) to the vital organs—the brain, heart, lungs and kidneys. The process causes these symptoms:

- Pale, cool, clammy skin
- Rapid pulse
- Rapid or erratic breathing
- Weakness, faintness
- Restlessness or irritability
- Confusion or disorientation

Expect to see these symptoms in anyone who has been in an accident, and take the following steps to avoid shock or to minimize its effects if it does set in:

- Lay the person down

BUY A FIRST-AID PLANT

Question: What plant has leaves that contain a gel that helps burns, cuts and minor skin irritations heal faster?

Answer: It's the amazing aloe plant, whose cactus-like leaves are full of a substance that promotes cell growth. There are all sorts of expensive lotions that purport to contain some aloe, but why buy them? For just a few dollars you can have your own aloe plant and along with it a lifetime supply of pure, unadulterated aloe gel. If you get a sunburn, minor cut or rash, just break off a leaf and slit it open. Squeeze out the gel and apply it to the affected area.

- Prop up the legs about 12 inches to encourage blood flow to the vital organs, unless you suspect back or neck injuries
- Cover the victim with blankets or clothing and keep him warm
- Reassure the person that help is on the way and keep him calm

ALL ABOUT BURNS

Burns must be treated right away or they will get worse. Trapped heat continues to do damage even after the immediate cause has been removed. Burns can range from mild (first degree) to severe (third degree), and the treatment required depends on the burn's severity. Pain is not a good indication of the severity of the burn, since third-degree burns often destroy nerves and, therefore, the ability to feel pain in the area.

You should be able to treat first-degree burns yourself. Second-degree burns that are smaller than a quarter on a child and a

silver dollar on an adult can also be treated at home.

First-degree Burns

This is the category into which most sunburns fall. The skin is red, slightly inflamed and very tender. Immediately cool down the burn by running cool water over it for several minutes. In addition to preventing further damage, the cool water will reduce the inflammation and ease the pain.

Pat the area dry and cover it with a clean gauze dressing. The bandage will ease the pain by protecting the burn from air. After a day or so, apply pure aloe gel, which will help the burn heal faster.

Second-degree Burns

These burns are usually very painful and may swell. Often, there are blisters and the skin may look mottled. Sometimes the blisters break open on their own, but never open them deliberately. Once the protection of the intact skin is gone, the burn is susceptible to infection.

BURN DOS & DON'TS

Do
➤ Cool down the burn
➤ Prevent shock
➤ Reduce the risk of infection
➤ Relieve pain

Don't
➤ Pierce blisters
➤ Peel off burned skin
➤ Peel away any material that is stuck to the burn
➤ Put butter on a burn

As with first-degree burns, submerge the area in cold water—for up to half an hour if necessary. Then cover it loosely with a sterile dressing if it's small. If the burned area is larger, keep it in cold water while you seek medical help. If you see any signs of shock, treat them before you treat the burn.

LIGHTNING WOES

We've all heard that the chances of your hitting the jackpot are the same as the chances of lightning hitting you, but just what are those odds anyway? Well...if the population is 250,000,000 and about 400 people a year are hit, the odds are around 1 in 625,000—higher if you play golf or talk on the telephone during thunderstorms.

Of the 400 people hit, 100 die. Lightning can cause burns, broken bones, the loss of hearing or vision, damage to the nervous system and cardiac arrest. Victims may be confused, disoriented and suffer memory loss.

Take anyone who has been struck by lightning to the hospital. Even if they claim to feel fine, they should still be checked by a doctor, since being struck by lightning can cause the heart to beat abnormally.

Once the burn has begun to heal, you can apply aloe gel to it. Break open a capsule of pure vitamin E and spread that on the burn, too. It may help with the healing as well as reduce the scarring that sometimes follows second-degree burns.

Third-degree Burns

These burns are always serious and require immediate medical attention. Don't be misled by the lack of pain. The reason they don't hurt at the time of the injury is that the nerve endings have burned away. The skin is charred and white, and may look like a deep wound. If the burn was caused by caustic chemicals, call the poison control center after you call 911.

Run the burn under cold water, but watch carefully for signs of shock. This is a bit of a catch-22. You need cold water to cool down the burn, but exposing the victim to the cold can increase the chances of shock. If the burn is on an arm or leg, elevate it slightly to help the blood flow smoothly. These burns often swell, so remove any clothing or jewelry that may constrict the area. Cover the burn loosely with a sterile dressing while you wait for help to arrive.

Electrical Burns

Electrical burns often look small on the surface, but can cause serious internal injuries and may even make the heart stop beating. Look for two burns—one where the electricity entered the body and one where it left.

Make sure the electricity that caused the burn is turned off. *Never* try to pull a person away from the electrical current or you could be electrocuted, too. Run to the fuse box, turn off the power, then call 911. Treat the victim for shock and watch the ABCs. Be prepared to perform rescue breathing or CPR.

BATTERED BONES

Even when injuries involving bones, muscles, ligaments or tendons are not life-threatening, they must be treated carefully to avoid disability and impaired movement later on. Never move someone you suspect of having a neck or back injury unless the person is threatened by an even greater hazard, such as poisonous fumes.

Fractures

First aid for bone injuries consists mainly of stabilizing the site to control pain and prevent further injury. This is done using splinting techniques, which will vary depending on which bone is affected. There are four different types of fractures:

- *Simple.* The bone snaps cleanly into two pieces without breaking through the skin.
- *Compound.* In addition to the the bone, the skin is also broken. A sharp edge of bone may be poking through the skin, or the object that caused the injury may still be embedded.
- *Comminuted.* The bone is broken in more than one place. These fractures may be simple or compound.
- *Green stick.* The break does not go all the way through the bone. These fractures are much more common in children

---

USE PEAS FOR BUMPS & BLEEDS

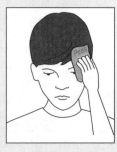

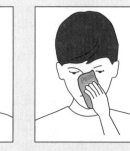

Forget those lumpy ice cubes and reach for a bag of frozen peas to control pain and swelling. They're ice-cold, already covered and contained, and will mold instantly to any body part. Use them for a bump on the head, a headache, toothache or abscess, and across the bridge of the nose for a nosebleed. The cold constricts the blood vessels, reducing swelling, bleeding and pain.

KNOCKED-OUT TOOTH RESCUE

Believe it or not, more than 90% of knocked-out teeth can be reimplanted. Follow the rules below to ensure that the process goes smoothly.

➤ Place a piece of rolled up gauze against the socket and have the victim bite down on it.

➤ Find the tooth and rinse it gently in running water to remove any dirt. Do not scrape off any pieces of gum tissue or skin.

➤ If the victim is an adult, have them place the tooth under their tongue and hold it there.

➤ If the victim is a child, place the tooth in a glass of milk.

➤ Go to the dentist immediately. If you are far from medical attention, replace the tooth in the socket yourself once you have rinsed it off. Then go to the nearest dentist or clinic.

because their bones are still somewhat "soft."

Sprains & Strains

We tend to think of sprains and strains as not being that serious, but they can be every bit as debilitating as a break.

- *Sprains* result from an injury to the ligaments, which hold bones together at the joint.
- *Strains* occur when tendons or muscles are torn or overly stretched. Tendons attach muscles to bone.

Unless you have an obviously minor injury, follow the same splinting procedures you would use for fractures and get medical help as soon as possible.

It may not always be clear whether you are dealing with a sprain or a fracture, since both involve varying amounts of pain and swelling. For a minor sprain, use an Ace bandage to keep swelling down. Aces are great, but be careful not to cut off blood flow. Ice packs also help reduce the swelling.

Dislocations

Dislocation occurs when a bone is displaced from its normal position in the joint. Suspect a dislocation if the limb is at an odd angle and the victim is screaming in pain. Unless you're out in the wilderness, don't try to pop the bone back into the joint yourself. The best you can do to relieve the pain is to take the pressure off of the joint. Carefully support or prop the affected limb and get medical help right away.

Safe Splinting

Splints are used to take the pressure off a break, immobilize an injury to prevent it from getting worse and reduce pain so that the victim can be safely moved. But before you start splinting, make sure you know the rules:

- Are you sure you need to splint? If help is on the way and you won't be moving the person yourself, let the experts do it when they arrive.
- If you do splint the injury, make sure you check the circulation in

the extremities before and after you put it on. Squeeze the fingers or toes and make sure the victim can feel the pressure. Check to see that the skin color is normal and that the skin feels warm. Recheck for feeling, warmth and color every few minutes while the splint is on.

- Splint the injury in the position in which you found it—do not try to make the limb look more "normal."
- When you splint the injured area, make sure you include the joints above and below the site of the break to keep the pressure off of the injury.

SPLINTS & SLINGS

How to Make a Soft Splint

You can use everything from towels to wooden boards as splints. Soft splints work particularly well on joints, such as the ankle. Pillows are an excellent choice.

How to Make a Hard Splint

Hard splints, which can be made from rolled-up newspapers, pizza boxes, even baseball bats, are best for the long bones of the legs and arms.

Use Your Body

You can use anything that stabilizes the injury—even another body part—as a splint. Fingers are particularly suited to "anatomic splinting" because they naturally lie side by side. Legs can also be successfully splinted together. Arms need to be splinted and cradled in a sling.

Take the Pressure Off

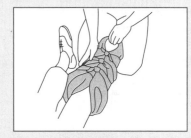

Take the pressure off any break or muscle sprain, even to the extent of resting it in a pillow or rolled-up sleeping bag. Secure the padding with ties. Elevate breaks or bad sprains and apply ice packs to control swelling, but do not leave elevated so long as to impede blood flow.

WATCH YOUR STEP!

Do you know which accidents are the deadliest? Most people get the number-one killer right—it's motor vehicle accidents—but the second one wrong. It's not poisoning or drowning or fires. It's falls! Although broken bones are generally only life-threatening in the elderly, falls can cause head and internal injuries in addition to broken bones. A particular hazard in older people with osteoporosis is the development of dangerous blood clots following a fracture. Pneumonia is also a common complication in the elderly.

POISONED! WHO DO YOU CALL?

If you think 911 is the number to call when you have an emergency involving poisoning, you're wrong...possibly even dead wrong. That's because it's the experts at the poison control center who can best tell you what to do immediately. Post the number of your local poison control center prominently near the phones in your house, on your list of emergency numbers and in your car. Obviously, call 911 if you don't have the poison center's number.

Should You Vomit It Up?

Good candidates for ejection include things like pills and medicines, which are not going to damage the body as they are vomited. If you are in doubt, do *not* induce vomiting. You should keep a bottle of syrup of ipecac in your first-aid kit to induce vomiting if the poison control center tells you to use it. Vomiting usually removes only about half of the poison, however, so after the victim throws up, you should administer activated charcoal to neutralize the rest of it.

Or Keep It Down?

Sometimes getting a substance that doesn't belong in your body out of it as soon as possible is not the best course of action. Cleaning products often contain acids or alkalies that can burn the throat terribly as they are thrown up. And petroleum products like kerosene and gasoline should not be thrown up because they can cause pneumonia. If someone ingests one of these substances, call your poison control center first, then 911 for an ambulance.

Beyond Drunk

The most abused drug of all—alcohol—can cause everything from garden-variety drunkenness to out-and-out alcohol poisoning. Here's how you can tell if it's time for a trip to the emergency room:

- Victim passes out and can't be awakened
- Irregular breathing
- Weak, irregular or rapid pulse
- Cold, clammy, pale skin

Be especially alert for vomiting as you wait for help. If the person throws up while unconscious, he could inhale the vomit and progress rapidly from "passed out" to "passed on."

Other drug abuse can have a wide range of effects depending on the type of drug. People are not usually forthcoming with information about drug abuse, so you may need to infer the problem from their behavior and appearance.

If someone is acting strangely, has either pinpoint or overly dilated pupils, and is excessively energetic, lethargic or angry, assume the worst and get help. Always check the ABCs and begin rescue breathing or CPR if needed while you wait for help.

WATER RESCUE

Saving a drowning victim is a two-step process. First you must rescue the person from the water, and then you must try to restore her breathing while you wait for more help to arrive.

Get the Victim Out of the Water

Rescuing someone from the water can be as simple as taking a baby out of a bathtub or as complex as using a human chain to reach someone who has fallen through thin ice.

If there is a lifeguard nearby, get his attention, since lifeguards have special training.

I CAN'T BELIEVE HE ATE THAT THING!

Adults are constantly amazed by what children will—and won't—put in their mouths. If even one tiny bit of sautéed mushroom slips past their little lips they'll throw a fit, yet a pint or so of bleach is perfectly palatable. Go figure. Assume that if it's guaranteed to kill you, little kids will eat it. **Keep hazardous substances absolutely out of the reach of children.** If you think this advice sounds obvious, bear in mind this sobering fact: More than 90% of poisonings occur in the home, and most of these involve young children. So even though we all know we're supposed to keep kids and chemicals apart, we're not doing the best job we could. Lock up all those household cleaners and medicines, and while you're at it, here are some poisons you might not have thought of:

Baby aspirin. One small bottle of 50 baby aspirin can kill a child. And as kids already know, they taste great! Hide them. By the way, never refer to medicine as "candy" to try to get kids to take it.

Iron tablets. These may not be as delicious as baby aspirin, but good taste is in the mouth of the beholder. Iron pills are kiddie killers. Lock them up.

Perfume. If it smells good, it must taste good...right?

Apple seeds. Most kids turn up their noses at the core, but for those who don't, the seeds can make them sick.

Although we tell our kids to be quiet all the time, when they actually are silent take it as a signal that something is wrong. They may be hiding because they're in the midst of doing something they know they shouldn't be doing or because they're absorbed in something fascinating, like Grandma's sugar-coated blood pressure pills. Check on any young child you haven't seen or heard for more than a minute or two.

Try to reach the person in trouble without actually getting into the water yourself. When people who can't swim get stuck in the water, they panic. And instinct tells them to grab onto anything that's floating—in this case, you. Unfortunately, you won't be floating for long. Look around for something you can throw to the victim and use it to reel the person in. Rope is ideal, but you can also hold out a sweatshirt, a log or even your leg as long as you can use your arms to hold tightly—very tightly—onto something solid.

Get the Water Out of the Victim

If the person is not breathing, you will need to perform mouth-to-mouth resuscitation, but the technique for a drowning victim is slightly different from regular rescue breathing.

- Turn the person on her side to drain out any water from the mouth and throat.
- Pinch the person's nose shut, then give four forceful breaths in the mouth. You need to give stronger breaths so that the air can get by any water blocking the breathing passages.
- Continue until helps arrives.

As you are performing mouth-to-mouth resuscitation, bear in mind that drowning victims tend to vomit when they begin to breathe on their own again. Brace yourself.

WHAT TO DO ABOUT BITES

Bites are dangerous primarily because of what they can transmit—generally venom, bacteria or other organisms. Wash bite wounds with exceptional care, but don't scrub them. Remember that all bites are puncture wounds, which are particularly susceptible to infection because they are so deep.

People & Other Animals

Believe it or not, a human bite is more likely to get infected than a bite that comes from a different mammal.

If you are bitten by an animal, find its owner if it has one. Seek medical treatment immediately if the bite is bleeding badly or if the animal is acting strangely.

ASPIRIN BITE ALERT

Do not give aspirin to someone in pain because of a bite that involved the injection of any kind of venom. Aspirin interferes with the ability of blood to clot, making it easier for the venom to spread throughout the body. If the pain is confined to the site of the bite, apply ice to control it. If the pain is more generalized, consult a health-care practitioner.

Otherwise, let the bite bleed freely for a couple of minutes, then wash it with soap and water for another 5 to 10 minutes. Finally, rinse it with an antiseptic solution like Betadine, which will help to kill the rabies virus. Cover it with a sterile gauze dressing.

Snakebite

There are only four dangerous snakes that live naturally in the U.S. Although people are terrified of being bitten by a poisonous snake, it's not as dangerous as you think—less than 12 of the 8,000 people bitten each year die. Most of those deaths occur in people who are already weak or sick or who are allergic to the venom. If you do wind up with a poisonous snakebite, call 911, wash the wound and keep the bite site below the level of your heart. If you travel in snake-infested areas where medical centers with anti-venin are not readily accessible, carry a snakebite kit.

By the way, if you think chopping off a snake's head will stop it from biting you, think again. Bite reactions can occur for up to 20 minutes after the head is detached.

Bees, Wasps & Hornets

The only real danger from these stings comes if you are allergic to

---

⚠ VENOMOUS AMERICAN SNAKES

Copperhead (adder). Adorned with a bold, dark gray design, copperheads are about four feet long and can be found from Massachusetts to Illinois as well as in the southern states.

Coral snake. Found in the Gulf states, Texas, New Mexico and Arizona, these snakes have black, red and yellow rings and are up to three feet long. Rather than striking and retreating, corals hang on and chew.

Rattlesnake. Responsible for 65% of poisonous snakebites in the U.S., this snake is found in all 50 states. It is up to eight feet long, has a light gray pattern and really does rattle before it strikes. Heed the warning!

Water moccasin (cottonmouth). This snake is gray and grows to be about four feet long. It lives in shallow lakes, slow-moving streams, swamps and on riverbanks in the southeastern states.

the venom. Symptoms of an allergic reaction include

- Hives
- Excessive swelling
- Nausea
- Difficulty breathing
- Bluish lips or face
- Shock
- Loss of consciousness

Allergic reactions can be life threatening, so if you see any of these symptoms, get help at once.

A normal reaction includes pain and swelling at the site of the sting, and possibly itching as well. If you can see the stinger, remove it with one quick scrape using a fingernail or the edge of a credit card. Wash the area and apply an ice cube to ease the symptoms.

1-2-3 Spider Bite Help

Though spider bites usually hurt, you may not realize you've been bitten right away. Even if you develop symptoms, you may not attribute them to a spider bite. If you ever develop unexplained symptoms like clamminess, excessive sweating and trouble breathing, seek help at once. A health-care provider may find the bite mark you missed.

If you know you've been bitten, keep the bite site lower than the heart and wash the bite with soap and water. Tie a strip of gauze snugly about three inches above the bite. If the area around the strip of cloth begins to swell, tie another strip three inches higher, then remove the first strip. This procedure may not contain the venom of the black widow, whose poison moves swiftly through the body. Fortunately, black widow bites are rarely fatal.

Bites from the Sea

It's not just the creatures running about on land and flying around in the air that want to inject you with their poison. They're waiting for you in the water, too.

- *Jellyfish and Portuguese man-of-war.* Wipe away any attached tentacles using a piece of cloth, then wash the area with alcohol, which neutralizes the toxin.
- *Stingray.* Heat neutralizes this sea creature's venom, so hold hot compresses on the injury or soak the affected area in very hot water. Unfortunately, the stinger itself is so large that it usually causes a laceration requiring medical attention. Sometimes the stinger is embedded and must be removed by a health-care practitioner.
- *Sea anemones and hydras.* Like the stingray, their toxins are neutralized by hot water, so soak the affected area in water that is as hot as possible.

Although marine life stings are rarely fatal and do not usually cause lasting problems, as with any bite, there is the chance of an allergic reaction or an infection. Get medical attention if you suffer anything more than a mild, transient discomfort.

BAD BUG BITES

Brown Recluse

The brown recluse spider is yellow or tan, has a dark, violin-shaped design on its back and is about a half-inch in diameter. It lives in nice dark places like wood piles and basements. It's fairly prevalent, so keep your eyes peeled.

The reaction to this bite usually takes two to eight hours to develop. Symptoms include pain, swelling, blisters, nausea and joint pain. The bite site may also become ulcerated and infected. Seek medical attention.

Black Widow

The black widow is most common in the Southwest. The nasty bites come from the female, who has a red hourglass design on the underside of her black, shiny body. Black widows are about three-quarters of an inch in diameter.

Symptoms of the bite include sharp pain, immediate redness, sweating, nausea, stomach and muscle cramps, chills and possible difficulty breathing. There is an antivenin available for black widow bites. Get medical help.

Tarantula

Believe it or not, this big hairy spider isn't as dangerous as the brown recluse or black widow. Tarantulas often hitch a ride over here in shipments of fruit that come from other countries—bananas are a big favorite.

The bite usually hurts, but not that badly, and is only dangerous if you are allergic to the spider's venom or if the bite becomes infected. So don't panic. Clean the wound carefully and call 911 if you experience trouble breathing.

Scorpion

Scorpions are most common in desert-like climates. They are not aggressive and most people get stung when they inadvertently step on them or touch them. Scorpions will often slip into a shoe for the night and when you get dressed in the morning...

Treat scorpion bites like you would treat spider bites. The signs and symptoms are similar. Some scorpion bites are life threatening, so seek medical attention right away. There is an effective antivenin available for scorpion bites.

Deer Tick

This tick can carry Lyme disease. Most prevalent in the eastern U.S., it can be as small as a poppy seed until it feasts on your blood. Another serious disease, Rocky Mountain spotted fever, is caused by another type of deer tick.

If you find an attached tick, remove it using tweezers. Grasp the body firmly at the base and pull gently until it lets go. Take it to the doctor with you for analysis. If you should get sick later on, make sure the doctor knows you were bitten by a tick.

WHAT MUST BE IN YOUR FIRST-AID KIT

Use a fishing tackle or tool box to store first-aid supplies. Keep them all together in one location and make sure that you replace items whose potency fades with time. You will need to have two of these—one to keep at home and one for the car.

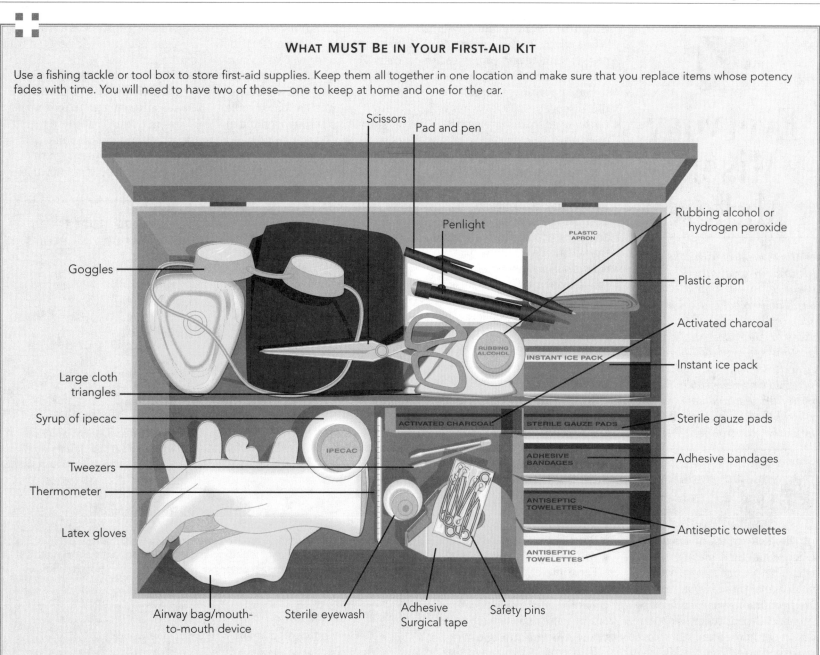

Scissors

Pad and pen

Penlight

Rubbing alcohol or hydrogen peroxide

PLASTIC APRON

Goggles

Plastic apron

RUBBING ALCOHOL

Activated charcoal

INSTANT ICE PACK

Instant ice pack

Large cloth triangles

Syrup of ipecac

ACTIVATED CHARCOAL

STERILE GAUZE PADS

Sterile gauze pads

IPECAC

Tweezers

ADHESIVE BANDAGES

Adhesive bandages

Thermometer

ANTISEPTIC TOWELETTES

Antiseptic towelettes

Latex gloves

ANTISEPTIC TOWELETTES

Airway bag/mouth-to-mouth device

Sterile eyewash

Adhesive Surgical tape

Safety pins

Everyday Misery Makers

It's the everyday ailments that doctors don't usually pay much attention to—like your not being able to get a good night's sleep or being plagued by headaches or allergies—that sabotage our sense of well-being, sap our energy and make us irritable and miserable. Read on to find out how you can control these conditions so that they don't control you.

NO MORE SNEEZING

Allergies and asthma have become the bane of modern existence. No one is sure why the incidence of these two interrelated conditions has increased so dramatically, but theories abound. Maybe our houses and workplaces are sealed up too tightly. Maybe a diet of processed food really isn't that great for the immune system. Who knows? By the time your nose is running and your eyes are itching, you're probably too sick to keep up with the latest scientific discoveries. Here's what you *really* need to know to get the relief you're looking for.

Just What Is an Allergy?

If your body reacts to a perfectly lovely item, say a strawberry, as if you had just been bitten by a king cobra, you are allergic to it. The body treats the substance as if it were a dangerous invader and mounts a full-fledged attack that causes the symptoms associated with allergies. You can be allergic to anything from poison ivy, which affects many people adversely, to apples, which don't affect many people at all. Don't mistake a food intolerance or sensitivity for an allergy, though; allergies have specific, well-defined symptoms. Here they are:

- *Hives*
- *Itching*
- *Nasal congestion*
- *Swelling*
- *Wheezing*
- *Skin rashes*
- *Anaphylactic shock (rarely)*

Food intolerances usually just cause some digestive upset, generally due to a deficiency in one or more digestive enzymes.

What Are You Allergic To?

If you suspect you have allergies, visit a specialist—known as an allergist or immunologist— to see whether this is in fact the case. The doctor will take your medical history and a history of your symptoms, and will perform a physical examination. Then he or she will go through a number of steps to see what could be disagreeing with your system. Depending on your symptoms, the doctor may perform the following tests:

- *Elimination and challenge diet*. First, all suspect foods are eliminated for four weeks. Symptoms should begin to disappear. Then foods are reintroduced one at a time over a period of several weeks or more until symptoms recur.
- *Scratch tests*. This traditional test for allergies involves placing a solution of the suspected allergen on the skin, then scratching the skin and examining the area 20 minutes later for signs of a reaction. The specialist usually tests for allergies to many substances at the same time in long rows along the back or arm.
- *Blood tests*. Some specialists think that scratch tests are not sensitive enough to pick up all allergies and that these tests sometimes indicate allergies that are not present (false positives). A blood test known as

---

FOODS MOST LIKELY TO INDUCE ALLERGIES

- ➤ Seafood
- ➤ Peanuts and other nuts
- ➤ Mango
- ➤ Papaya
- ➤ Strawberries
- ➤ Cow's milk
- ➤ Eggs
- ➤ Tomatoes
- ➤ Spinach
- ➤ Oranges
- ➤ Raspberries
- ➤ Wheat and wheat products
- ➤ Soy and soy products

SEVERE ALLERGIC REACTIONS

Although most allergies are more annoying than dangerous, severe reactions can result in a condition known as anaphylactic shock. If this occurs, call for an ambulance or get the person to the hospital right away. The symptoms include:

- ➤ Tightness in the chest and/or throat
- ➤ Difficulty breathing
- ➤ Swelling and/or reddening of the face and/or hives
- ➤ Bluish nailbeds or lips

the "amplified ELISA" may be more accurate and is generally covered by health insurance.

Fight Allergies Right

There are two types of actions you need to take to bring a problem with allergies under control. First you need to relieve those miserable symptoms. Then you need to make changes in your lifestyle habits and environment to keep the allergic reactions at bay.

If you choose to go the medical route for symptom relief, you will find plenty of effective prescription and over-the-counter medications to choose from. Be sure to ask your doctor about side effects.

What About Immunotherapy?

If reducing your exposure to allergens by controlling your environment doesn't do the trick or if your allergies are severe, you might want to try immunotherapy (allergy shots). Allergy specialists have a number of tools at their disposal to help you live in harmony with your environment.

In allergy desensitization, following a long period of complete avoidance, a small quantity of the allergy-provoking substance is slowly reintroduced. Allergy shots expose you to minute particles of the allergen to help you build up resistance.

Changing Your Life

Lifestyle changes will be needed to control exposure to airborne allergens—like pollen—and contact allergens, like wool or latex. Start with this change today: No more shoes inside the house. Take them off at the front door and go barefoot or wear slippers. And have your family members and friends take off their shoes too. Here's why: Shoes are extremely efficient allergen-dispersal tools. Any number of toxic substances, such as pesticide residues, and allergens, like pollen (not to mention dust and dirt), get tracked into homes on the soles of people's shoes. These are then spread very effectively from room to room, increasing the likelihood you and your family members could be exposed.

Clean House the Right Way

Start by getting rid of wall-to-wall carpeting. It makes an even cozier home for pet dander, dust mites and other allergens than it does for you. Once the carpeting is gone, you will be able to clean the floors properly, which will help keep dust (and therefore dust mites) to a minimum. Do this by first sweeping, then damp mopping. To keep dust down when sweeping, spray a rag with water until it is barely damp, then place it under the broom. Throw out your duster, which just provides free transportation for dust mites. Use a rag, lightly oiled or sprayed with water instead.

The next big enemy to eradicate is mold, which is responsible for an enormous percentage of allergic reactions. Get a dehumidifier for the basement and wash down any moldy surfaces with a solution of bleach and water.

⚠ ALLERGIES & CAVITIES

If you regularly take antihistamines and decongestants, watch your teeth. These drugs reduce the amount of saliva in your mouth, slightly increasing your chances of getting cavities. To *increase* your saliva production, chew sugarless gum. Be extra careful to avoid foods that promote decay, like sugary foods that stick to your teeth.

CELIAC DISEASE

One million Americans have celiac disease—and many have no idea they have it, according to Peter Green, MD, clinical professor of medicine, Columbia University College of Physicians and Surgeons. The disease is caused by an intolerance to gluten—the main protein in wheat, barley, rye and oats. The resulting intestinal inflammation hampers absorption of nutrients and can lead to diarrhea, cramps, anemia, osteoporosis, infertility and seizures. Once celiac disease sufferers eliminate gluten-containing foods from their diets, most begin improving within one week.

ALL-NATURAL ALLERGY FIGHTERS

Allergies are as old as the hills, and so are some of the weapons that can be used to fight them. You might want to try them. Many modern-day allergy sufferers swear by these natural remedies:

Nettle. This may be the best one yet for easing the congestion associated with hay fever. Look for the freeze-dried capsules—they're supposed to be the most potent.

Eyebright. This herb helps relieve itchy eyes.

Quercetin. This vitamin is supposed to restrict the release of histamine, which is responsible for the allergic reaction.

Bromelain. Found in raw pineapple, this enzyme is a potent anti-inflammatory agent.

The Joys of Spring

If you suffer from hay fever (seasonal allergic rhinitis), you know just how much fun it can be when those first spring plants burst into bloom...and your nose right along with them. Hay fever is the most common allergy and results from a reaction to pollen. In addition to the unpleasant symptoms of the allergic reaction, having hay fever makes the development of asthma more likely later on in life. Thus, allergy shots may be effective in reducing asthma attacks in hay fever sufferers. Some research suggests allergy shots may not be as effective in children.

As with all other medical conditions, an ounce of prevention is worth a pound of cure. So take these simple steps to prevent pollen from getting the best of you:

- *Use air conditioning.* Air conditioners not only cool the air, they also filter out pollen and some other airborne allergens.
- *Wear a mask.* If your powers of persuasion aren't good enough to get somebody else to mow your lawn for you, then wear a mask. You can get disposable ones at drugstores. Use it only once, and throw it away before you go back inside the house.
- *Take a shower.* If you've been out in nature—particularly on a high pollen-count day—shower as soon as you go inside to wash off the pollen. Don't forget your hair, which is a highly efficient pollen magnet.
- *Watch your timing.* Pollen levels are usually lower in the afternoon and on days that are cool and rainy. Listen to the weather forecast, and stay inside when pollen counts are high.

⚠️ AIRPLANE-SNACK WARNING

If you're allergic to peanuts, simply not eating them may not be enough to avoid an allergic reaction...if you're on an airplane. That's because the dust from open packets of peanuts disperses easily through the dry cabin air, yielding measurable levels of peanut allergens. If you have a severe allergy to peanuts, take an emergency epinephrine injector kit along with you when flying.

IS IT THE THING YOU LOVE?

Here's an interesting tidbit: If you suspect allergies, start by eliminating your favorite food and seeing how you feel a few days later. It's often the foods we crave that are the culprits.

IS IT HAY FEVER OR JUST A COLD?

You wouldn't believe how many people go through life with hay fever, thinking that they're just incredibly prone to colds. Since the symptoms are similar, here's how you can tell the difference:

Hay Fever	Respiratory Infection
➤ Thin, clear and watery nasal discharge	➤ Thick, yellow or green nasal secretions
➤ Fever never present	➤ Fever sometimes present
➤ Itching of the nose, throat and/or eyes common	➤ Itching rarely present
➤ Sneezing is prominent and often includes long sneezing spells	➤ Sneezing may occur, but is rarely violent or prolonged
➤ Symptoms can drag on for weeks or months	➤ Symptoms rarely last longer than a week to 10 days

If you're still not sure whether you're suffering from allergies or repeated respiratory tract infections, pay a visit to the doctor to rule out more complicated conditions that need to be more closely monitored, such as chronic sinusitis.

DESPERATE FOR FLOWERS?

Do you love fresh flowers but not the allergic symptoms they cause? Have a friend cut flowers and float them in a clear glass bowl or vase half-filled with water. Cover the top with clear plastic wrap. Secure the wrap (and hide the edges!) with a ribbon. As an added bonus, flowers can last for weeks in this controlled environment before finally wilting.

NO MORE WHEEZING

Asthma occurs when the airways constrict in response to a type of inflammation that can be brought about by allergies, lung irritants and infections or colds in susceptible people. Excess mucus formation contributes to the coughing and wheezing.

Triggers

The most frequent causes of asthmatic attacks are:

- *Allergies.* The most common allergens are ragweed, pollen, animal dander, dust mites, mold and insect remains. Sulfating agents are also major culprits and can be found in prepared foods and wine. Check labels and avoid products that list sulfur dioxide, potassium metabisulfate, sodium and potassium bisulfate, and sodium sulfite on the list of ingredients. All are sulfites.
- *Lung irritants.* The biggest offenders are smoke, gases, fumes and odors, such as perfumes and fresh paint.
- *Infections and colds.* Upper and lower respiratory tract infections can cause attacks by irritating and inflaming already sensitive airways. You might also want to get tested to see if you are infected with an organism called *Chlamydia pneumoniae.* The infection, which can be treated with antibiotics, may be present for years and cause asthmatic symptoms.
- *Physical exertion.* This is a very common trigger, and needs to be controlled up front with the use of an inhaler prior to exercising. The type of exercise you engage in can make a difference, too. Running or skiing are more likely to cause an attack than are walking on a treadmill or swimming. In fact, swimming is probably the best all-around form of exercise for asthmatics, since the humidity level and controlled breathing are easy on the airways.
- *Emotional distress.* Strong emotions like anger and fear can sometimes cause and often exacerbate an attack.
- *Air temperature.* Moving from a cold area into a warm area or from warm to cold may trigger an attack. Cold, windy air also causes asthmatic attacks.

Calm Is the Key

Although asthma is primarily a physical condition, it has a strong emotional component. Not only can strong emotions contribute to an attack, reacting with anxiety or panic—understandable though this may be—can make the attack worse. Because the airway constriction characteristic of asthma feels a lot like suffocation, the panic reaction is just as much an intuitive physical response as an emotional one.

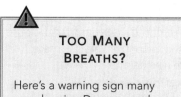

TOO MANY BREATHS?

Here's a warning sign many people miss: Do you need more than one breath to finish a sentence? If you're stopping midsentence to breathe, you might have asthma. Get your doctor to rule it out.

LITTLE-KNOWN ASTHMA SYMPTOMS

People are often surprised to find that those annoying symptoms they were attributing to being out of shape or having bronchitis are actually due to asthma. In fact, wheezing—the characteristic sound of asthma—only occurs in about half of those who have the disorder. Here are some of the other common asthma symptoms in disguise:

➤ **Coughing.** If you have a persistent cough, particularly if it occurs at night, and do not have an obvious explanation such as a cold, see your doctor and have asthma specifically ruled out as a cause. Coughing is the most common symptom of asthma.

➤ **Tightness in the chest, breathlessness, shortness of breath.** These symptoms occur as a result of the airway constriction and mucus secretions caused by inflammation in the lungs and airways.

➤ **Pain in the abdomen, chest, back or ribs.** Since people with asthma use the wrong muscles to breathe (breathing from the chest rather than the diaphragm), they often have pain or tenderness in these areas.

➤ **Anxiety.** A sensation or fear of suffocation can cause chronic anxiety in asthmatics. Health-care professionals often assume that a combination of anxious feelings and breathlessness are due to panic, but unless all possible medical causes have been ruled out, such an assumption could be dangerous. If you regularly experience that combination of symptoms, see your doctor.

MASSAGE YOUR WAY TO BETTER BREATHING

Here's an interesting finding: Children who received 20 minutes of massage from their parents each night at bedtime had fewer asthmatic attacks. The technique probably works its magic by reducing stress hormones, which are a known trigger of asthma attacks.

The best way to overcome this natural feeling is with deliberate controlled breathing, in addition to whatever medication is required. Relaxation techniques used to control anxiety attacks are also helpful.

Getting a Diagnosis

If you have a cough or cold that never seems to clear up, you should see a doctor and be tested for asthma. Wheezing should send you straight to the doctor; gasping for breath should send you straight to the hospital. Never use over-the-counter epinephrine inhalers—like Primatene Mist—without having been first evaluated by a specialist and given the go-ahead. These products do not treat the underlying inflammation, only the symptoms. So if the attack is more serious than you realize, you could find yourself on the brink of death.

Once you get to the doctor, he or she will evaluate you by taking a complete medical history, including a detailed accounting of your symptoms, and by performing a thorough physical examination and laboratory tests. These may include blood tests, X rays, allergy testing and spirometry (which measures air flow in and out of the lungs).

Management with Drugs

Drug therapy for asthma is now highly sophisticated and very effective. Here are the classes of drugs available and how they can help:

- *Bronchodilators.* These drugs relax the airways and relieve symptoms. However, they do not treat the underlying inflammation.
- *Anti-inflammatory agents.* The most powerful of these drugs are the corticosteroids, which attack the root cause of the asthma, namely the inflammation. However, they do not act immediately on the airways. Steroids can also have some negative effects if used in high doses over the long term, including glaucoma (from high-dose inhalers) and bone loss. Therefore, identifying and avoiding asthma triggers to reduce the inflammation is key.
- *Leukotriene modifiers.* These are the newest drugs in the arsenal and are very promising for people who have mild asthma that appears to be getting worse. They work to control the inflammation by changing the way your immune system reacts when the inflammation occurs.
- *Emergency drugs.* Drugs, such as theophylline, are used intravenously to restore breathing in severe asthma attacks.

Management with Herbs

Here are a number of nutritional supplements that either act to reduce inflammation, blunt the allergic reaction or ease breathing. Try them in addition to your other therapy or at a time when your symptoms are mild, in order to see if they work for you:

- *Licorice*
- *Ginkgo biloba*
- *Quercetin*
- *Bromelain*

⚠ SURPRISE CULPRIT IN ASTHMA ATTACKS

Be careful with aspirin and other nonsteroidal anti-inflammatory pain relievers if you have asthma. These drugs are responsible for quite a number of severe attacks, particularly in asthma sufferers who also have nasal polyps and experience bouts of sinusitis.

⚠ HEART DISEASE & ASTHMA DRUGS

If you have heart disease and asthma, heed this warning: only take beta-agonists (like albuterol) via a metered-dose inhaler. Taking the medication in pill or nebulizer form could cause a fatal heart attack.

★ LIQUID ASTHMA REMEDIES

If your asthma symptoms are not severe, give these liquid cures a try. *Warning:* Some are more palatable than others.

Coffee. This is a very effective remedy from way back. The caffeine in coffee and black tea has a mechanism of action similar to the asthma drug theophylline and can open the bronchial passages. A cup or two of strong coffee may well head off an attack if you drink it as soon as you feel symptoms.

Onion Juice. Perhaps not the most delightful drink, but effective nonetheless. Onion juice contains compounds that relax the bronchial muscles and stop them from going into spasm. Blend it with orange or carrot juice so that you can actually get it down, then hold your nose and do your best. It works!

Hot soup. This warm and soothing beverage will relax your breathing passages and may lessen the severity of an attack.

Parsley tea. Just pour very hot water over parsley sprigs, and in a few minutes you'll have your very own all-natural expectorant.

Watch out for this not-so-great natural remedy—Ma Huang. A powerful stimulant, Ma Huang does open airways. Unfortunately, it can also cause an irregular heartbeat and possibly sudden death. Try coffee instead.

Monitoring Your Breathing

Peak flow meters are great little devices that can be purchased at any drugstore. You blow into one end of a tube, and a gauge on the side registers the volume of air you exhaled. They come with a chart that shows you where your result falls on the spectrum and instructions on how to monitor your lung function.

Regular use of a peak flow meter allows you to assess the effectiveness of your treatment regimen and to detect asthma attacks early on.

Learn How to Breathe

Much has been made of breathing exercises for asthma sufferers —and with good reason. Breathing exercises have been shown to improve lung function and reduce the number and severity of asthma attacks. Although any breathing exercise routine should help to some degree, one regimen in particular seems to be especially effective: Eucapnic breathing. Also known as the Volitional Liquidation of Deep Breathing and the Buteyko Method, it has been used extensively in Russia, England and Australia with excellent results. Here's how it works:

Eucapnic breathing involves taking small breaths through the nose when you feel breathless, rather than trying to take giant ones. The goal is to do this while keeping your abdomen and diaphragm relaxed. This technique makes sense because people with asthma "overbreathe," throwing off the balance of oxygen and carbon dioxide in the bloodstream.

For an audiotape and manual that will teach you this breathing method, call 888-536-9574.

To order a videotape and manual, access the Internet and go to the following URL: *www.buteyko.com.*

Asthma & Allergies

Since many, if not most, asthma sufferers have allergies that trigger attacks, reducing exposure by controlling your environment is crucial to prevent attacks. Follow the same cleaning procedures appropriate for people with allergies. Don't open windows when the pollen count is high. Use air conditioning and an air filter instead.

Currently there is a lot of controversy about whether people who have asthma benefit from the desensitization shots that have been recommended for allergy sufferers. If you have a particular documented allergy that may be causing asthma attacks, you may want to go ahead and give the shots a try. However, one recent study of asthmatic children who had been given allergy shots to reduce their asthma symptoms found that the children did not derive any benefit from the shots.

⚠️

GAS TRAPS

If you've got asthma, gas is your enemy. People who cook and heat with gas experience more asthma attacks than those who don't. And having gas in your stomach isn't much better. It seems that the added pressure it places on the diaphragm can trigger asthma attacks. Self-defense: Use an electric stove, eat foods that are easy to digest and don't overfill your stomach.

HELP LINES & HOT SPOTS FOR ASTHMA & ALLERGIES

American Academy of Allergy, Asthma and Immunology	800-822-2762
Asthma and Allergy Foundation of America	800-7-ASTHMA
Indoor Air Quality Info. Hotline (Environmental Protection Agency)	800-438-4318
Support Groups Allergy and Asthma Network, Mothers of Asthmatics	800-878-4403
InteliHealth, Inc.	*www.intelihealth.com*
The Johns Hopkins University Asthma & Allergy Resource	*www.hopkins-allergy.org*

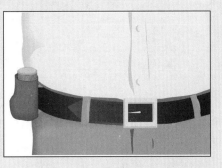

ASTHMATICS ON THE GO

This device, designed for runners and other athletes who need to carry inhalers but want their hands free, is perfect for kids too! Just attach the device to their belts and they'll never leave their medicine behind. Call 877-282-8070 or go to *www.allergy pack.com* to order.

DON'T WORRY, BE HAPPY!

Anxiety and depression are responsible for at least as much misery and almost as much disease as germs. These two disorders often occur together and most of us have to deal with a bout of one or the other at some point in our lives. The good news is that both respond well to the vast array of treatment options available today. In fact, the biggest hurdle to overcome on the road to recovery is recognizing the problem and then taking decisive steps to bring it under control.

Worrying Too Much

The nasty thing about anxiety is the way it can feed on itself, starting out as a small feeling of worry and building into a full-fledged panic attack. A certain amount of anxiety is nothing to be concerned about, and can be useful in resolving issues and getting things accomplished. It acts like a little fuel, the impetus for dealing with the cause of our discomfort. Too much anxiety is another matter altogether. So how can you tell whether you are experiencing productive stress or nonproductive anxiety? Read on to see where you are on the worry spectrum.

Generalized Anxiety Disorder

Unlike being hit with an occasional bout of worry, someone with GAD is almost continuously anxious and worried for a period of at least six months. Often he or she has some of the following symptoms as well:

- *Difficulty sleeping*
- *Aches and pains*
- *Headaches*
- *Stomachaches or other digestive upset*
- *Backache*

Panic Disorder

Many an ambulance has raced to the assistance of a person with all of the classic symptoms of a heart attack—chest pain, racing heart, difficulty breathing, anxiety —only to discover at the hospital that pure panic was the culprit. Although someone with a history of panic attacks may suspect that they are not dying, the symptoms are so overwhelming that they often find themselves in the emergency room anyway. Panic attacks can render the sufferer absolutely incapacitated because after a few episodes, simply the fear of having one can keep the person housebound.

The problem in controlling the symptoms is pinpointing panic disorder as the underlying cause and then persuading the person to accept the diagnosis and seek

IS IT YOUR MIND OR YOUR BODY?

Not all cases of anxiety are due to stress. Before you trade in your job and its financial security, pay a visit to the doctor for a complete physical. Describe your symptoms carefully, and make sure that all possible underlying medical causes are systematically ruled out. Don't let your health-care provider brush you off. Many don't take panic and anxiety seriously, so you will need to be responsible for seeing that you are thoroughly checked out. Make certain that you are tested for the following conditions, all of which can cause feelings of panic and anxiety:

➤ Heart disease, congestive heart failure and irregular heartbeat

➤ High blood pressure

➤ Thyroid problems

➤ Asthma

➤ Depression

➤ Diabetes

➤ Emphysema

➤ Pulmonary embolism

➤ Vitamin deficiencies

HOW TO STOP A PANIC ATTACK COLD

The best way to bring those scary sensations under control is to take action before the panic symptoms are full-blown. Remind yourself that as unnerving as the feelings may be, they are the result of a panic attack, not some dread disease. Then use the techniques below to control your breathing and heart rate:

Breathe in and out of a paper bag. This will increase the carbon dioxide level in your blood, which will slow down your breathing and prevent hyperventilation.

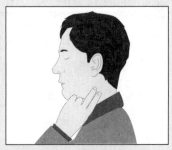

Place two fingers on the side of your neck just below your jawbone and press lightly until you feel a pulse. Apply gentle pressure for a minute or two to slow your heart rate.

treatment. Often, just being certain that panic disorder and not some life-threatening disease is responsible for the symptoms is enough to take the edge off of the attacks. Psychotherapy, support and reassurance are very effective. As with depression, combating loneliness is helpful in controlling symptoms. Fears can take on immense proportions when there is nobody else there to provide a "reality check." And just the distraction of having someone to interact with can keep people from letting their imaginations run wild.

If talk therapy and supportive interaction are not sufficient to control the attacks, there are a number of prescription medications that may effectively put an end to the symptoms.

Fears & Phobias

An unfortunate, but all-too-common consequence of panic and anxiety disorders is the development of irrational fears, or phobias. High on the list is agoraphobia, or the fear of open spaces. The term also applies to having a fear of leaving familiar surroundings or even one's own home. Sometimes panic and anxiety sufferers wind up housebound because of their fear of having a panic attack in public.

It's crucial to get help if you or someone close to you has developed this problem. The longer it goes on, the harder it is to treat. Cases of agoraphobia require the attention of a qualified mental health professional who will work with the person to control the feelings of anxiety, with medication if necessary.

Not all phobias are this dramatic, of course. The most common are associated with spiders, rats, snakes, public speaking and flying in airplanes. The trick is to confront and thereby neutralize the power of the phobia itself. This is best accomplished with the assistance of a therapist using a program of progressive exposure and desensitization.

When Worry Is Good

Believe it or not, a certain amount of anxiety is actually useful and spurs action that prevents even greater distress in the future. If you're worried about how you'll manage financially in your golden years, for example, you'll be more likely to take steps in advance to save for the future. Happy-go-lucky types often find themselves with stress and anxiety down the road because of their failure to take

---

BREATHING FROM THE BELLY

Learning how to breathe deeply and rhythmically is a well-known technique for controlling anxiety and may help with depression and asthma, too. Here's an easy way to strengthen your diaphragm and train yourself to breathe "from the belly" rather than high up in the chest:

Fill a one-gallon plastic bag with a few pounds of sand or dry beans and tape it closed. Lie down on a firm surface on your back and breathe deeply for a few minutes. Then place the bag on your abdomen and breathe, consciously pressing up against the bag with your belly as you inhale, letting it drop back down with exhalation. After five minutes, remove the bag and continue breathing deeply. Repeat the exercise twice a day for 15 minutes at a time.

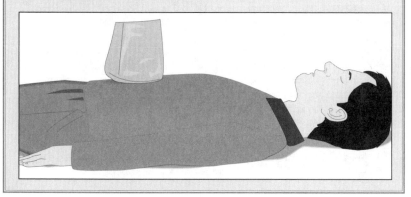

HERBAL REMEDIES FOR A CALMER YOU

You don't always have to resort to medications to relieve your anxiety. Try one of these soothing herbs and see if it does the trick for you.

Kava kava. Studies that compared this herb to a placebo given to anxious patients who didn't know whether or not they were getting the real thing proved it to be highly effective.

Valerian. This herb is particularly good if you have trouble sleeping because of your anxiety.

Motherwort. Consider taking motherwort if your anxiety makes you feel like your heart is pounding, skipping or fluttering. It's very effective at regulating the beating of your heart. But first, make sure your doctor has confirmed that your symptoms are due only to anxiety.

➤ **Passionflower, lemon balm, mistletoe, California poppy, chamomile, pasque flower and wild lettuce** are also worth trying.

steps now to ensure their future comfort and security. Try to assess your anxiety objectively. Are you worried about something legitimate, such as job security in an uncertain industry? If so, address the real problem and ignore the sensation of anxiety. The worry will lessen once you've taken steps to solve the underlying dilemma. If you're not sure whether your anxiety is justified, get the opinion of someone who you trust won't judge you.

Of course, it's not always easy to figure out what's wrong when you feel worried but can't put your finger on a specific cause. Enlist the help of a mental-health professional to help you rule out problems you might be suppressing, like an unhealthy marriage. If there really turns out to be "no good reason" for your distress, then it's time to explore the possibility that you have an anxiety disorder. You may also have an anxiety disorder if you have a genuine problem, but the level of stress that it causes is excessive.

The Fear of Illness

One of the most common anxieties is the fear of being or becoming ill. In fact, about 10% of people who see a doctor may have hypochondria. A much greater number experience heightened physical symptoms because of their emotional reaction to them. Unfortunately,

most cases of hypochondria don't get the attention they deserve because (1) patients are often unwilling to consider that the real problem may be emotional and (2) doctors don't take the disorder seriously. That's too bad, because about 70% of hypochondriacs obtain substantial relief from taking medication as well as from psychotherapy. So how do you know if you're really sick or just think you are? Here are the classic signs that the *fear* of illness is the real problem:

- *Fearing that you have illnesses whose symptoms you read or hear about*
- *Frequently asking for reassurance that you're not sick*
- *Obsessing about a particular disease or disorder that you're convinced you have despite having been given a clean bill of health*

- *Going from doctor to doctor and rejecting the diagnoses*

If these signs sound familiar to you, don't suffer. Visit a therapist and ask about the latest treatment options.

1-2-3 Anxiety Eradication

Taking charge of out-of-control feelings of panic and anxiety will require a concerted effort on your part, but it *can* be accomplished. Take the following steps:

- *Address problems such as job insecurity or a bad relationship that may be responsible for making you tense and anxious*
- *Sign up for a relaxation and stress relief program*
- *Get regular aerobic exercise, which boosts endorphins— the body's feel-good hormones*

- *Use herbs such as kava kava and valerian to help you relax when you feel particularly anxious*

WANT TO UNWIND?

Lava lamps aren't the only objects that have the power to induce a hypnotic stupor. Staring at a fish tank can do the trick as well. Although this might not be a great thing when you're supposed to be concentrating on your work, it's perfect if you're stressed out. In fact, studies have shown that watching fish swimming about in their aquariums is as effective as hypnosis or meditation in relieving the trepidation before a tooth extraction.

START AN INDOOR GARDEN

You might want to stock up on some greenery if you suffer from anxiety. A study in which anxious people stared at different objects found that looking at plants reduced anxiety levels substantially more than looking at the other objects.

STRESSFUL SWEETS?

We tend to think of sweets—like a luscious piece of chocolate cake—as soothing, but that's not always the case. Sweets can cause your blood sugar levels to fluctuate wildly, resulting in an emotional roller coaster of moodiness and anxiety. If you have a tendency to be irritable and nervous, try replacing sweets with high-protein foods that stabilize blood sugar levels, and see if your mood improves. Although you'll have to fight that craving with all your might initially, it will lessen as your body adjusts. Want to know what's even worse than plain old sweets for an irritable disposition? It's alcohol, which lifts you up and then slams you down. Avoid it like the plague if you're prone to anxiety.

By the way…although sugar may make you jumpy, *chocolate* may ease depression—*see* "Chocolate Therapy" on the next page.

FIGHTING DEPRESSION

Don't despair. No matter how bad you feel right now, hold this thought: Most people recover from depression within a short period of time, even without treatment. There are so many different treatment approaches available that even if your low mood is severe or persists, your chances of recovery are excellent.

Get to the Root of the Problem

Do you have a good reason to be depressed? Perhaps you've recently lost your job, gotten divorced or nursed a parent through a terminal illness. If you're not ordinarily depressed and have gone through a traumatic event, don't rush the healing process. The mind goes through a natural period of grieving and adjustment, typically lasting months, that is believed to be essential to long-term mental health.

Practical Worries Got You Down?

Financial problems, problems at work and other day-to-day stresses can lead to depression over time. Often, it's the sense that we have no control over our circumstances that is the biggest culprit. Inertia sets in and, before you know it, you're experiencing a chronic low-grade depression. If you know what's causing your dissatisfaction, making a change

is easier. Decide what you want, then devise an action plan to meet your objectives. Taking the first step is always the hardest. Once you're in the thick of it, the changes will take on a momentum of their own.

Unfortunately, what often happens is that by the time we realize that we're depressed, the underlying reasons may have become too murky to isolate. A few sessions with a therapist may help you figure out what's really at the root of the problem. Don't shy away from getting this kind of help. Therapists are trained to help you figure out your underlying needs, and can help motivate you to make the changes needed to restore a healthy balance to your life.

Too Much Time Alone

Loneliness is one of the biggest contributors to the current high rate of depression. Many people today live in a state of isolation unheard of even 50 years ago. With families and friends separating and people moving away for college, job opportunities or adventure, many of us find ourselves without companionship. And nothing will sink your emotional ship faster than sitting alone at home with your worries. New mothers at home with their babies, elderly people and some singles are all prime candidates for depression.

So what can you do about it? Clubs, library groups and support groups are all great ways to meet people. So are taking classes or

joining choirs. Find an activity that you enjoy—that's where you'll meet people who share your interests. Look into day care for elderly relatives, too. There are also many programs that will put older people in touch with each other.

How Low Is Too Low?

At what point is a blue mood a "real" depression? If you have no idea why you're sad and the low mood has persisted for longer than a couple of weeks, it's time to call your doctor or a mental-health professional.

SELF-IMPOSED MOOD ELEVATORS

If you'd like to laugh your way out of a depression (and who wouldn't?), try these activities in addition to your other therapy:

➤ Make yourself smile. Researchers have found that forcing yourself to smile will improve your mood. Make an exercise out of it. Relax your face into a smile every 15 minutes and hold the position for 30 seconds. Make sure the smile reaches all the way up to your eyes.

➤ Watch comedy on television or at the movies or listen to comedy on tape. Buy a portable tape player and play comedy tapes or other cheery recordings. Studies have shown doing so shortens the duration of depression.

The underlying mechanism? Scientists believe that smiling and laughing cause your brain to release its own natural mood elevators. You may not feel cheerful to start with, but by tricking your brain into releasing those chemicals, you can wind up with a genuinely improved mood.

CHOCOLATE THERAPY

Let's face it…if this does the trick for you, it's the way to go. Chocolate contains a substance that's chemically similar to the one responsible for putting that silly grin on the faces of people smoking marijuana. That compound, together with the stimulant effect of the caffeine, may make chocolate a decent choice for perking up a low mood. Try combining it with laugh therapy (rent a comedy video) and loneliness control (invite a friend over to watch it with you) for a truly pleasurable, mood-elevating combination strategy.

Here are some of the other signs that you may have a clinical depression.

- *Loss of interest in things that used to be important to you*
- *Loss of appetite or excessive eating*
- *Loss of interest in sex*
- *Insomnia or excessive sleeping*
- *Inability to concentrate*
- *Unreal or surreal feelings, known collectively as "derealization"*
- *Inconsolable crying or feelings of unbearable sadness*
- *Thoughts of suicide or of death*

If you or someone you know experiences suicidal thoughts or fantasies, get help right away—in the emergency room if necessary. With the wide range of medications and tools at our disposal, even the most severe depression can be treated effectively. Don't let someone slip away needlessly.

Is It Your Brain Chemistry?

Most experts believe that our personality and temperament are the result of a combination of our genetic makeup and our experiences. We all have a predisposition to react in a particular way to a given situation. But whether we actually do react according to our basic nature may depend on how our experiences have shaped our responses.

Today's drug therapy can alter brain chemistry and substantially improve mood and functioning. However, if years of unhealthy emotional reactions and responses have been built upon a less-than-optimum brain chemistry, you will need to unlearn those bad habits before you will see the total picture of your life improve. Many, if not most, people on antidepressant medication benefit from undergoing some form of talk therapy at the same time.

Talk Your Way Out of It

For all the hype that drugs and herbs have gotten in the fight against depression, talk therapy is just as successful as chemicals at restoring a normal mood. This may be because psychotherapy allows you to work through practical problems—like a bad marriage or insufficient income—which need to be resolved in order for you to be truly happy. Or the interaction with a "good listener" may be offsetting the loneliness that has lowered your mood. Some people benefit from exploring events in their childhood or past traumas that they believe to be responsible for their state of mind or personality.

Whatever the reasons, interaction with a trained therapist has proven benefits that have held up in study after study. Although many of us have an image of therapy as requiring years of lying on a sofa, in reality, even just a few sessions are often enough to do the trick. Sometimes all that's required is the reassurance that your ups and downs are well within the normal range and that you're not "crazy" or on the verge of going crazy.

Even if you are certain that medication is the best choice for you, never accept a prescription from a doctor who has spent only a few minutes with you. Although this is a frequent occurrence in today's cost-cutting environment, it is not in your best interests. A properly trained therapist should be able to accurately assess your state of mind and recommend the therapeutic approach that is likely to be effective.

How to Choose a Therapist

There are many kinds of mental-health professionals these days from psychiatrists and psychoanalysts to clinical psychologists, family therapists and marriage counselors, to clinical social workers. The best therapist for you is the one with whom you feel you have the best connection, provided that person has had formal training. If you wind up with a referral to someone you don't like, simply say, "I don't feel that we're

---

FOLIC ACID COUNTS

If you've been on antidepressants and haven't noticed an improvement, you might not be getting enough of one of the B vitamins—folic acid. Try adding a supplement that contains the recommended daily allowance of folic acid (400 mcg) to your regimen, and see if you notice an improvement. It may take a few weeks.

NATURE'S MOOD MODERATOR

So is Saint-John's-wort as effective for mild-to-moderate depression as the press claims? Absolutely.

Used for literally centuries to treat depression in Germany, it is considered front-line therapy there and it is prescribed before Prozac or any other antidepressant. It is most effective against mild or moderate depression.

Like other antidepressants, it may take a few weeks to kick in. But compared to antidepressant drugs, it causes fewer side effects. There has been some concern that it may cause hypersensitivity to sunlight and also reports of potential interactions with other medications. Among drugs that can interact are tetracycline, warfin, birth control pills and protease inhibitors used to treat HIV/AIDS.

connecting. Can you recommend somebody whose personality would work a little better with mine?" That's all. You don't have to be apologetic.

Fight Depression with Exercise

Force yourself! Getting started may be hard, but as soon as you get in the swing of exercising regularly, the benefits will give you all the motivation you need to keep going. Quite simply, exercise boosts the brain's production of endorphins—your built-in feel-good chemical.

Not only will you feel better emotionally, you'll be healthier and look better, too. There's nothing quite like looking great for boosting self-confidence and mood. If you're too embarrassed to run in public or join a gym, then buy an exercise video and pop it in the VCR at home. Just make sure you go through the program five days a week, preferably at a set time. Even if you think there is no time, spare yourself just a few minutes. Research has shown that eight minutes a day is enough to yield tangible results.

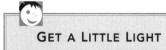

GET A LITTLE LIGHT

One particular form of depression, known as seasonal affective disorder (SAD), responds particularly well to light therapy. If you've noticed that you're always blue in the winter, SAD may be the reason behind it. Make an appointment with a therapist for an evaluation. The good news is that when sunlight is hard to come by, SAD sufferers can alleviate their depression by using a special light box. Your therapist will tell you where to find one.

HELP LINES & HOT SPOTS FOR ANXIETY & DEPRESSION

National Mental Health Association	800-969-6642; *www.nmha.org*
National Substance Abuse Hotline	800-821-4357
National Council on Alcoholism and Drug Dependence	800-622-2255; *www.ncadd.org*
The Mayo Clinic	*www.mayoclinic.com*
Intelihealth, Inc.	*www.intelihealth.com*
The Johns Hopkins University Medical Desk Reference	*http://webapps.jhu.edu/ jhuniverse/medicine/diseases*

MEDICINES FOR MIND & MOOD

The enormous amount of research conducted on depression has resulted in the development of drugs that can help almost anyone feel happier, calmer and better able to cope with life's ups and downs. There are drugs to treat anxiety and panic, manic depression and obsessive-compulsive disorder.

Depression. There are four major groups of drugs for depression: tricyclic antidepressants, monoamine oxidase (MAO) inhibitors, stimulants and selective serotonin reuptake inhibitors (SSRIs). All have advantages and disadvantages, and all have side effects. But all of them can get you back on your feet, too. Sometimes the dose can be gradually reduced over a period of weeks or months. Don't give up if the first medication you try doesn't work. It can take a little time to find the right medication and fine-tune the dosage.

Although the highly touted SSRI *Prozac* is very effective and has fewer side effects than the older antidepressants, it is not without its drawbacks. Up to half of the people who take it experience some loss of sexual drive or an inability to reach orgasm. Some researchers suggest that the supplement *ginkgo biloba* may offset these unfortunate side effects.

Manic depression. That old standby, *lithium*, is still the drug of choice for this disorder, although side effects need to be carefully monitored.

Anxiety. Old-fashioned benzodiazepines, like *Valium*, still work best in most cases of generalized anxiety disorder. *BuSpar* also works. If you are anxious due to an underlying depression, which is often the case, antidepressants may be effective as well.

Panic disorder. Two classes of drugs work for panic—*benzodiazepines*, like *Xanax*, and SSRIs, like *Paxil*. Phobias also respond to these medications as well as to the MAO inhibitors.

Obsessive-compulsive disorder. Though people with OCD are often not depressed, antidepressant medications seem to work best to control the condition.

Bear in mind that combining talk therapy with drug therapy is more likely to result in mood improvements that endure than using drug therapy alone. Resist the urge to develop a relationship with a mental-health professional that involves nothing more than 15-minute "status checks," where you have a quick conversation, get a new prescription and leave.

BACK PROBLEMS & RELIEF

Although around 80% of us suffer from back pain at some unfortunate time in our lives, there is no consensus on why this problem is so prevalent, nor on the best way to treat it. So, if you should find yourself with back pain that doesn't abate, you will need to arm yourself with information before you head into the fray. Here's where to start:

The Role of Muscles

Muscle strain may well be the leading cause of back pain, although many doctors are unfamiliar with the role of muscle-based back-pain therapy. How do your muscles go about torturing you in this way? Take a look:

- *Tension.* Both emotional and physical stress can cause pain due to prolonged contractions.
- *Spasm.* This type of intense muscle contraction is excruciating and almost impossible to relax through a simple force of will.
- *Trigger points.* Chronic muscle tension as well as injury can cause these small nodules of muscle tissue, which are extremely sensitive to pressure.

Back pain can also be caused by weakness or stiffness of the muscles. Since your muscular structure supports your spine, being in good physical condition

helps maintain the stability of your back.

When to Worry

Although most back pain is nothing to be overly concerned about, occasionally there is a more serious underlying cause. Here is what you should be on the lookout for:

- *Sudden pain.* If the back pain occurs suddenly and you can't connect it to a particular event, like just having lifted a heavy box, give your doctor a call.
- *Pain plus other symptoms.* If you are experiencing chest pain, difficulty breathing, difficulty urinating, fever, stomach cramps or any other troubling symptoms along with your back pain, call the doctor.
- *Pain that never ends.* If you have severe pain that has not lessened at all over a two- to three-day period, you need to have it checked out. Milder pain that persists beyond two weeks or so without abating also needs to be evaluated.
- *Radiating back pain.* Report any pain that travels down your leg or to other parts of your body. Also be on the lookout for pain that causes numbness or tingling in your fingers or toes.

How Long Should You Wait to See the Doctor?

If you feel like you are not improving at all, you should give the doctor a call to make sure that your problem isn't more serious

than simple muscle strain. In general, if you feel your mobility returning, you're probably better off being up and about.

Remember, the longer you're off your feet, the longer it will take you to recover. Doctors now generally recommend resuming gentle activity as soon as possible after your original injury.

Heat or Cold?

First ice, then heat. For the first two days, use ice packs to reduce the inflammation of the strain. Controlling the inflammation will help to control the pain down the road.

After a couple of days, apply heat. Heat reduces the pain and relaxes the muscles. A small towel soaked in hot water and then wrung out works very well. You will probably want to call on the services of someone else,

rather than twisting around to put hot and cold packs on your back. Chances are you won't be much good at twisting for a while anyway.

⚠ WALLET ALERT

Having your wallet stolen isn't the only good reason not to carry it in your back pocket. Depending on its position when you sit, its bulk may be positioning one hip higher than the other. Also, the pressure it exerts could bring on sciatic nerve pain. Always aim to distribute weight and pressure equally on both sides of the spine to keep it straight.

BEST EXERCISES WHEN YOU HAVE BACK PROBLEMS

If you're highly prone to back problems, some sports are much better choices than others:

Risky Choices: These sports involve movements that put a great deal of strain on your back:

- ➤ Bowling—twisting while lifting a heavy weight
- ➤ Golf—twisting while swinging a weight
- ➤ Tennis—sudden twisting and swinging of a weight
- ➤ Baseball, basketball, football—sudden twisting and jumping
- ➤ Weightlifting—enormous strain on lower spine and back

Better Choices: Perform these activities freely. They're great for the back:

- ➤ Swimming
- ➤ Cycling
- ➤ Walking
- ➤ Rowing
- ➤ Yoga

Natural Pain Relief

Wintergreen, birch bark, meadowsweet and white willow all contain the same anti-inflammatory and pain-relieving compound as aspirin, but in a milder form. You can also try mixing a drop or two of essential oils of sage, rosemary or thyme into vegetable oil, and then have someone massage it into the painful area.

Over-the-counter back pain patches are really quite effective. They contain menthol and/or camphor, both of which can relieve the pain by relaxing muscle tension.

Creams containing capsaicin may also be helpful. The main ingredient is the fiery compound found in hot chili peppers, and is thought to exert its effect by "tiring out" the nerve endings that transmit pain. It also works well for arthritis pain.

Rx Pain Relief

If you're ready for drugs that require a doctor's signature, there are some pretty potent choices. Many work to reduce inflammation and relieve pain, but some have side effects like drowsiness. Some can be addictive if taken for too long. In general, this type of drug use should be viewed only as short-term therapy, with a recovery and rehabilitation program already planned out.

Pin Relief

If you've tried everything short of surgery and have begun to despair, you may want to give acupuncture a try. Bear in mind that even if it relieves your symptoms, it probably is not getting at the source of the underlying problem unless your back pain is genuinely due to an excess or deficiency of *qi*. That's the body's life force—

HOT SPOTS FOR BACKACHE SUFFERERS

American Association of Orthopaedic Surgeons
www.aaos.org

American Society for the Alexander Technique
www.alexandertech.com

American Pain Society
www.ampainsoc.org

Dannemiller Memorial Education Foundation
www.pain.com

Nicholas Institute of Sports Medicine and Athletic Trauma
www.nismat.org

North American Spine Society
www.spine.org

National Network of Libraries of Medicine
http://nnlm.gov

Relax the Back
www.relaxtheback.com

HEALTH-CARE PRACTITIONERS—EXPLAINED

If you decide to take your problem to a health-care practitioner, you will have to decide which type to consult. Here are several good choices:

Family practice doctor or other generalist. Your own doctor will know your medical history, should be able to rule out a serious medical condition and can refer you to a specialist if necessary.

Orthopedic surgeon. This is the person you'll need to see if you are in that tiny percentage of people who absolutely has to have surgery.

Osteopath. An osteopath is like a combination of a regular medical doctor and a chiropractor. Osteopaths are MDs who have specialized training in skeletal manipulation. Philosophically, they see damage to the skeletal structure as being at the core of many ills.

Sports medicine specialist. If you developed back pain following a sports injury, you might be tempted to consult a sports medicine specialist. But watch out! Since sports medicine is not a certified specialty, any doctor can give himself or herself the title. Ask about experience and credentials.

Chiropractor. Although they are not medical doctors, chiropractors are experts at spinal manipulation. One study has shown chiropractic therapy to be the most effective treatment for quick pain relief.

Physical therapist. These health-care practitioners will work with you to improve your functioning and help you overcome problems such as bad posture. If you have undergone surgery, they will work with you during recovery and rehabilitation.

Massage therapist. Massage can feel great, but make sure that the person performing it is a certified massage therapist. It is possible to make matters even worse by manipulating the muscles and bones of the back in the wrong way.

Psychiatrist or psychologist. Nobody can say for certain what percentage of backache—or stomachache or headache for that matter—is due to anxiety or depression. But it is certainly at least a contributing factor in many cases. Even if you don't think you fall into that category, it's worth checking out if nothing else has worked. Not all cases of anxiety and depression are immediately obvious.

Acupuncturist. Acupuncture appears to be an effective treatment for a number of problems including back pain. It may be effective when nothing else has helped. Acupuncture is very safe and highly unlikely to do any harm.

the condition that acupuncture is supposed to remedy.

If your doctor has ruled out all potentially serious causes, approach acupuncture with an open mind. Many longtime backache sufferers have gained substantial relief this way.

Do You Need Surgery?

According to experts, surgery is required in only a tiny fraction of cases—perhaps as few as 1%. Make sure that you get at least two expert opinions and that you have exhausted all of the possibilities for less aggressive intervention before you agree to go under the knife.

STOP A SPASM

You can't will that excruciating back spasm to stop, so how *do* you get rid of it? Relax it away with this simple technique. Lie on your back, then draw your knees up to your chest. Put your arms around your knees and pull your legs snugly into your chest. Hold the position for a minute, then relax. Repeat the exercise as often as necessary to relieve the spasm.

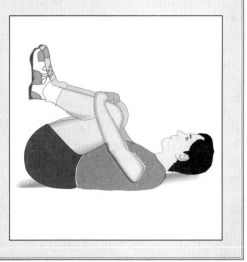

PICK A PERFECT PILLOW

We're so used to being told that what we find most comfortable is bad for us that you probably won't believe it's okay to have a soft pillow. It just needs to be firm enough to support your head and neck. Pull the pillow up off your shoulders though, and fit it under your neck. A soft feather pillow will accomplish this task perfectly. Don't buy a pillow that's so firm it lifts up your head into an unnaturally tilted position.

EXERCISE YOUR WAY TO A BETTER BACK

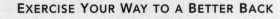

Single Knee Raise

Double Knee Raise

Single Leg Raise

Double Leg Raise

Partial Curl-up

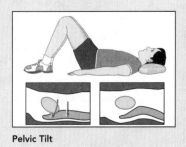

Pelvic Tilt

Sitting Bend

Hip Roll

PICK A PERFECT MATTRESS

Firm? Soft? Springs? Feathers? According to the experts, as with everything in life, moderation is the key. Pick a mattress that's reasonably firm, but not hard. Futons are actually fine—the problem is that most people don't fluff them up every day the way they should. A soft mattress on a hard board works well too. Let comfort be your guide.

HOW TO LIFT A HEAVY OBJECT

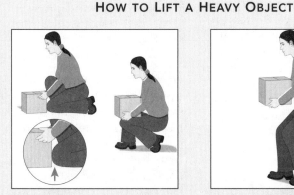

Kneel down in front of the object, and slide a corner up onto the front of your knee.

Keeping your back straight and upright, contract your abdominal muscles and lift the object straight up.

As your legs straighten out, keep your posture upright with your abdomen and buttocks tightly contracted. Hold the object up high. To avoid back strain, never carry anything low enough to be in front of your pelvis.

Be "load wary" even if you have only a small amount of weight such as shopping bags. Have the groceries packed in two bags so that you can carry the load equally balanced on either side of you to avoid pulling muscles.

BEST WAYS TO SLEEP

Tuck a pillow under your neck and another under your knees to sleep in this back-friendly "Lazy S" position.

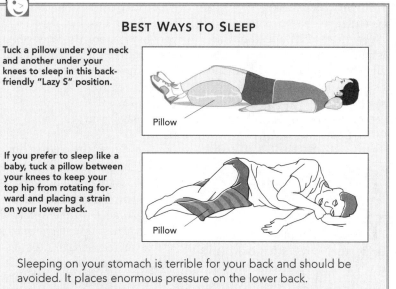

Pillow

If you prefer to sleep like a baby, tuck a pillow between your knees to keep your top hip from rotating forward and placing a strain on your lower back.

Pillow

Sleeping on your stomach is terrible for your back and should be avoided. It places enormous pressure on the lower back.

PROTECT YOUR BACK WITH PERFECT POSTURE

We're supposed to be standing *upright*, not slouching over. Unfortunately, many of us do slouch or slump, much to the detriment of our backs.

When you stand correctly, your head is balanced above your neck (not in front of it) and your chin is slightly tucked in. Your shoulders should be back and in a direct line with your hips, not bent over in front of the rest of your body. Your buttocks should be tucked in. Contracting your abdomen and buttocks will help you hold this posture.

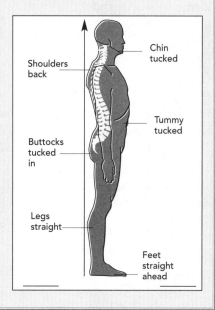

Shoulders back

Chin tucked

Tummy tucked

Buttocks tucked in

Legs straight

Feet straight ahead

Surgery is most likely to be successful if you have a damaged disk (seen on an MRI), together with numbness or tingling in the legs and pain that radiates down one or both legs. Surgery performed solely to relieve lower back pain is reported to be successful less than 60% of the time.

COLD REMEDIES

You know how the story goes… first a little sniffle, then a little tickle, then days of full-blown misery. We've all heard that there's no cure for the common cold, but you can do more than you may realize to cut that cold short and feel better *fast*! Here's the recipe:

Zinc

Zinc gluconate lozenges really do work. Scientists think that the zinc makes the tissues of the

ZINC LOZENGE WARNING

Bear this in mind while you're sucking on those popular *Cold-Eeze* lozenges: Zinc and copper work together in a 10:1 ratio. So for every 15 mg of zinc, you need to take 1.5 mg of copper. But don't exceed 100 mg of zinc or 5 mg of copper a day from all supplements combined.

nasopharynx less permeable to the cold viruses. In a recent study, people who took the lozenges cut the length of their colds almost in half compared with those who got a placebo.

Vitamin C

Vitamin C won't prevent a cold, but 1,000 mg every four hours at the first sign of the sniffles can reduce the symptoms. Drink lots of water when taking large doses so that you don't end up with a kidney stone. Give children liquid vitamin C rather than chewables, which can damage their teeth.

Chicken Soup

It helps! The steam and heat act as decongestants, loosening up secretions and clearing nasal passages. Clear liquids like water, juice and herbal tea also help to keep your secretions flowing. Drink six to eight glasses a day.

Garlic

Garlic kills bacteria and boosts the immune system. Swallow one chopped clove every few hours until you're feeling better, or take one to three garlic tablets a day.

Echinacea

This herb is a great immune-system stimulator and has been shown to significantly increase white blood cell count. Take either capsules or a liquid extract for up to one week at a time. Two other herbs, elderberry and goldenseal, appear to help fight colds too. Take them along with echinacea for a potent combo.

NOT HELPFUL FOR COLDS

Unfortunately, not every treatment really makes you feel better, let alone actually get better. And sometimes, the upside isn't worth the downside.

Antibiotics

Antibiotics just plain don't work on viral infections, yet doctors prescribe them 60% of the time for patients who come to see them with nothing more than a common cold. Unless you've developed a bacterial infection on top of your cold (such as bacterial sinusitis or an ear infection), resist the urge to walk out of the doctor's office with a prescription. Unnecessary antibiotics are not only ineffective and expensive, they also have side effects, and inappropriate use can lead to the growth of drug-resistant bacteria. Then, when you really need them, they may not work.

Multisymptom Remedies

What about all of those over-the-counter cold remedies? They

KIDS & COLDS

People catch more colds in the fall not because colder weather is on the way, but because the kids are back in school! Children contract and pass on the greatest number of colds by far, since they haven't been around long enough to have built up resistance to many of the more than 250 cold viruses that are out there.

do relieve symptoms, but have side effects such as drowsiness or nausea. Multisymptom products have the most side effects. Your best bet is to use a product that treats only the symptom that is bothering you and to take it at night when the side effects won't be so noticeable.

MORE THAN A COLD

Once in a while, a cold turns into something that really

⚠ BETTER OFF WITH A STUFFED-UP NOSE?

Be careful about using decongestants. Not only can overuse lead to rebound congestion that is very difficult to treat, but now doctors have linked excess use to strokes, too. Don't use decongestants if you have high blood pressure, heart disease or if you are at risk for stroke. And don't exceed the recommended dosage or use decongestants long-term even if you are in good health.

does need medical treatment. Here's how to tell when things have gotten serious enough to require a doctor's attention.

Stuffy Nose or Sinusitis?

Sinusitis is an infection of the hollow spaces around the bones near the nose, and often occurs following a cold. Nearly half of all cold-related cases of sinusitis clear up on their own, but if you have the following symptoms and they don't disappear within a few days, it's time to call your doctor:

- Yellow-green nasal discharge
- Fever
- Severe congestion
- Headache

Have your doctor determine whether the infection is bacterial before taking antibiotics, which only work on bacterial infections.

Sore Throat or Strep Throat?

A sore throat is often a feature of the common cold, but could also indicate a throat infection. Strep throat is caused by a type of streptococcus bacteria. Common symptoms include a severely sore throat, fever and swollen lymph glands in the neck. Have your doctor take a throat culture before you start on antibiotics. Many very painful sore throats are caused by viruses and will improve on their own as your body attacks the organism.

If the throat culture is positive, be sure to take the full course of prescribed antibiotics, even if you're feeling better. Otherwise, you are at risk for developing a very serious consequence of strep throat—rheumatic fever.

Just a Cough?

Occasionally, a cold goes into the chest and leads to bronchitis or pneumonia. These lung infections, which may be caused by either bacteria or viruses, can be quite serious, so see your doctor right away if you experience any of the following symptoms:

- Shortness of breath or difficulty breathing
- Chest pain
- Persistent cough, particularly if accompanied by chest pain
- Fever and chills

HOW TO NOT CATCH A COLD

Believe it or not, kissing is not a great vehicle for transmitting the cold virus! Thirteen pairs of college students participated in a study in which only one partner had a cold. The couples kissed intimately for one full minute, yet only one uninfected student later came down with a cold.

Although you don't want to be in the line of fire of a cough or sneeze, that's not the most common mode of transmission either. The viruses are propelled about three feet before they fall to the ground, where they are unlikely to be transmitted.

So how do those cold germs get passed around? On people's hands! Cold sufferers touch their mouths and noses, and then handrails, doorknobs and everything else. The virus sits there until another hand touches the same object, then it just hops aboard.

When that hand moves up to scratch a nose or rub an eye, the virus makes its way to the nasopharynx, where it invades the tissues.

To avoid passing your cold on to someone else, sneeze or cough into a tissue and throw it away; and always wash your hands with soap and warm water. To avoid catching one, wash your hands frequently, since you never know when you touched an object with the remains of a sneeze on it.

ACHY EARS

Earaches make children miserable, but trying to sort out the right thing to do is a constant

---

WHAT DO COLD SORES HAVE TO DO WITH COLDS?

Not much. Cold sores are caused by viruses, but not the ones that give you colds. To wind up with cold sores, you must first become infected with the herpes simplex 1 virus, which comes from the same virus family as chicken pox. The herpes simplex 2 virus, which causes genital herpes, also sometimes causes cold sores. The initial infection is usually accompanied by flu-like symptoms. Then the virus retreats to the nerves where it lies dormant until the next outbreak. The virus may flare up during periods of stress or in response to triggers like overexposure to the sun. Once the sores are well scabbed over, they are usually no longer contagious.

So how do you get rid of the unsightly sores? Keep them clean and dry, but don't cover them—they need to dry out. The prescription medicine acyclovir (brand name *Zovirax*) may help the sores disappear more quickly. The herb lemon balm also may be effective against the herpes viruses.

RELIEVE SINUS PAIN WITH ACUPRESSURE

Place your middle and index fingers next to the nostrils directly below the eyes and press upward.

dilemma for parents. Here are some tidbits that will help you help your child:

- *Antibiotics may not be the way to go.* Don't jump for the drugs. Unless your child is absolutely miserable and hasn't improved on his or her own after a few days, don't rush into antibiotic therapy.
- *Ease the pain.* There are a number of simple measures you can take to ease your child's discomfort. Try placing a warm compress over the ear to diffuse the pain. And to fight both the infection and the pain, make a trip to your local health-food store where you will find garlic oil with mullein leaves in it. The garlic is a natural antibiotic and the mullein acts as a natural anesthetic.
- *Wait on inserting ear tubes.* Unless your child has chronic pain and intractable ear infections, approach the idea of having tympanostomy tubes inserted with extreme caution. Placing the tubes is a surgical procedure requiring perforation of the eardrum. This hole is then held open by the tube, which could lead to scarring and eventual hearing loss. Ironically, one of the reasons often cited for placing the tubes is to avoid perforation of the eardrum due to infection. Proceed carefully, and be sure to get a second opinion.

FIGHT THE FLU

The most important thing to remember about influenza is that if you get a flu shot in the fall, you may be able to prevent the infection altogether. If you are diagnosed with the flu, there are now several antiviral drugs that have been approved by the FDA. These drugs can lessen the symptoms and shorten the duration of the flu, but experts are still debating whether most people should take these drugs, considering the cost and potential side effects. Fortunately, nature provides some all-natural antiviral substances that you can try if you and your doctor opt against drug therapy.

- *Echinacea.* This herb has well-documented antiviral properties. Take it three times a day with a little juice for one to two weeks.
- *Garlic.* If you can hold some down, garlic is an effective virus attacker. Try grating some into chicken soup. Two or three cloves a day is a pretty strong dose.
- *Take it easy.* Flu can be very nasty, so don't try to keep up your usual pace. Take in plenty of fluids to replace those lost through fever. Try ginger tea to soothe an upset stomach.

A Cure for the Flu?

The homeopathic remedy *Oscillococcinum* has gotten a lot of attention recently, in part because

NATURAL REMEDIES FOR COMMON COLDS

Congestion
- ➤ Chicken soup and hot tea.
- ➤ Take a hot shower—the steam heat will break up the mucus that's clogging up your nose and sinuses.
- ➤ If you prefer baths, put a few drops of eucalyptus oil into hot bathwater.

For the Adventurer:
- ➤ Old Polish remedy: Start with a cup of scalding hot milk. Add a tablespoon of honey, a teaspoon of butter and a teaspoon of grated garlic. Sip slowly…
- ➤ Old Eskimo trick: Plunge your nose into a big handful of soft snow. The sudden drop in temperature shrinks swollen nasal tissues.

Sore Throat
- ➤ Gargle with saltwater. One teaspoon of salt to a warm glass of water several times a day is just about the most effective remedy there is.
- ➤ If you have to watch your sodium intake, tea tree oil works well. Suck on lozenges or gargle with a solution of a few drops of pure tea tree oil in warm water.

Cough
- ➤ Licorice root tea suppresses coughs. Licorice-cayenne lozenges are also effective and work for a sore throat, hoarseness and congestion, too.
- ➤ Make thyme-honey cough syrup: Add 1 pint of boiling water to 3 tablespoons of dried thyme leaves. Let steep, covered, until cool. Strain, then add 1 cup of honey, stir well and refrigerate. Take 1 teaspoon an hour.

Headache
- ➤ Put your feet in a hot footbath while putting a cold compress on your forehead.
- ➤ Try a peppermint steam inhalation: Add no more than 2 or 3 drops of peppermint oil to 1½ quarts of boiling water, then breathe in the steam through your nose—if possible—for up to 15 minutes. Don't overdo it, as peppermint can burn.

Fever or Chills
- ➤ Ginger tea quells chills by creating a feeling of inner warmth. Don't take it within a few hours of bedtime though, since it's a mild stimulant.
- ➤ Two white willow tablets every three or four hours will help lower a fever. Do not use for children because of the possibility of Reye's syndrome.

clinical studies have shown it to be effective. Prepared from the heart and liver of the wild duck, it is safe to use both for children and adults.

HEADACHES— CAUSES & CURES

From anesthetic nose drops to biofeedback, headache treatments have come a long way since the days when state-of-the-art therapy consisted of drilling a hole in the skull to allow the pain to "escape." So don't suffer…just read on!

Headache Triggers

Averting a headache is often easier than curing one, so identify your triggers—then avoid them like the plague. Different headache types have different triggers, but some of the more common ones include stress, muscle tension, bright sunlight, eyestrain, lack of proper sleep, red wine and fluorescent lights.

Follow the Rules

If you feel a headache coming on, there are a few rules to follow regardless of the headache type or its cause:

- If you're going to take a pain-killer, don't wait. It's more likely to be effective if used at the first sign of a headache.
- Don't drink alcohol or eat anything sweet, both of which dilate blood vessels.
- Move out of bright light and away from loud noise.
- Do not watch television, read or do anything repetitive, such as knitting.
- Do not ride in a vehicle.

One Headache after Another

If you only suffer from an occasional headache, taking pain medication is fine. But if you get repeated headaches, you're better off finding more natural methods of relief. Often, lifestyle modification and the elimination of headache triggers are all that's needed. Using medication more than once or twice a week for an extended period can leave you with a nastier problem than the one you started with—rebound headaches that occur more frequently and are harder to treat.

What Causes Them?

If you always seem to have a headache, the first step is to attempt to identify the cause. Once you know the kind of headache you have, you can eliminate the triggers and target the most effective treatment. Sometimes headaches seem to be combinations of different types or otherwise resist classification.

CHASE AWAY STRESS

Muscular tension accounts for about 90% of all headaches, and appears to be primarily caused by stress. The pain from a tension headache is dull and steady and involves the whole head. Lightheadedness or dizziness may accompany the pain. Tension headaches can last from a few minutes to a few days.

THE MR. POTATO HEAD CURE

Don't laugh at this old Irish remedy—it really works! Wrap a bandana, scarf or gauze strip around your head, then slip in slices of raw potato against the spots where the pain is worst. Tighten the cloth around the potato slices and lie down in a dark room. Within an hour, the headache should be gone.

Nobody is quite sure how this method works its magic, but it may be by the restriction of blood flow to the head, activation of acupressure points or the astringent properties of raw potato drawing out heat or diverting blood flow away from the brain.

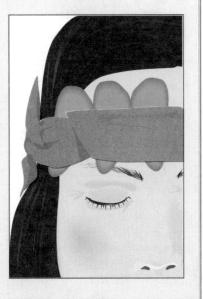

NATURAL RELIEF FOR HEADACHES

Massage Therapy has been found to reduce pain caused by tension and migraine headaches—but not cluster headaches. For a referral to a massage therapist in your area, see *www.amtamassage.org.*

Biofeedback uses devices that measure muscle tension and blood flow…teaches you to relax tense muscles…and boosts blood flow to your scalp, which can ease headache pain. For adults, 10 or more 30- to 60-minute sessions may be necessary to learn the technique.

Bothersome thoughts or a bad mood cause us to tense the muscles of the face, back, neck and shoulders—instinctively bracing us for a "fight." Add another trigger, like a rude cashier or a glass of red wine, and it's all over. Fortunately, tension headaches are the easiest ones to avert and to get rid of.

Your best bet for long-term control is behavior therapy aimed at reducing stress. If your problem is so severe that you have constant headaches, consult a behavioral specialist who can work with you intensively. If you get just occasional stress-induced headaches, practice these techniques for teaching your body how to relax:

- *Make faces.* Stand in front of a mirror and make all those hideously unacceptable faces you wanted to make at your second-grade teacher. The movement and stretching of the facial muscles forces them to relax.
- *Picture the pain.* Recline in a chair or lie down in a dark, quiet room. Close your eyes and picture a red light in your head in the exact same spot as the pain. Spend the next 5 to 10 minutes slowly dimming the light. The pain will be extinguished along with the light.

A GALLERY OF HEADACHE MEDICINES

If you choose to fight fire with fire, you will find that there is quite an arsenal at your local pharmacy. Here are the choices:

Acetaminophen (e.g., *Tylenol*). Works by blocking the impulses that transmit the pain message. Upside is that side effects of occasional use are rare.

Anacin. Combination of aspirin and caffeine. Caffeine's benefit is twofold. First, it enhances absorption of the pain medication so that you feel better faster. Second, it constricts blood vessels, which helps relieve headaches that are caused or exacerbated by dilated blood vessels in the brain.

Aspirin (e.g., *Bayer*). Don't turn your nose up at this original—it's still listed in the pharmacology books as the most effective pain reliever for uncomplicated headaches. Its downside is that it causes gastrointestinal upset in some people.

Excedrin. Here you go—all the big guns in one place. Aspirin plus acetaminophen plus caffeine.

Ibuprofen (e.g., *Advil, Motrin, Nuprin*). This drug is in the same class as aspirin, the NSAIDs (nonsteroidal anti-inflammatory drugs). It's a good one to try if aspirin works on your headache but upsets your stomach. All NSAIDs can cause digestive distress, but aspirin is worse than the others.

Ketoprofen (e.g., *Orudis KT, Actron*). This is similar to ibuprofen, but has a different chemical composition. Different people react to medication differently, so you may get relief from ketoprofen even though similar drugs are ineffective. Try it if ibuprofen doesn't work.

Naproxen Sodium (e.g., *Aleve*). Naproxen is similar to ibuprofen and ketoprofen. It does take a little longer to start working, but its effect lasts longer too.

HEADACHE RELIEF

When a headache starts, keep moving, says Dr. Roger Cady, director of Headache Care Center, Springfield, Missouri. Exercise produces painkilling endorphins and relieves stress. *Also:* Drink a caffeinated beverage to speed absorption of aspirin…massage your head and neck. *Guided imagery*—close your eyes…imagine water moving over you on a sunny beach, the waves easing tension. When you relax, picture your headache as an object. Turn it into liquid—and let it pour through your fingers.

MIGRAINES & CLUSTER HEADACHES

Overly dilated or constricted blood vessels in the brain can cause vascular headaches, such as migraines or cluster headaches.

The most common type of vascular headache is the migraine. Symptoms of a migraine include throbbing pain on one or both sides of the head, nausea, extreme sensitivity to light and sound, and sometimes visual disturbances such as flashing lights. Here are the more common migraine triggers:

- *Caffeine.* Found in coffee, tea, soft drinks and chocolate.
- *Fluctuating estrogen levels.* This is the biggest trigger for women's migraines. In fact, the estrogen-migraine connection probably accounts for why migraines are three times more common in women than men. Migraines tend to be their worst in the premenstrual phase of each cycle and during menopause. Unfortunately, trying to control the hormones using birth control pills is unpredictable. About one third of users improve, one third get worse and one third see no effect.
- *Alcohol.* Beer and red wine are the worst offenders,

probably because they contain tyramine, which is another well-documented trigger.

- *Scents.* Perfume, cigarette smoke and other odors can bring on a migraine.
- *Lighting.* Bright sunlight, glare, flashing lights and fluorescent lighting are implicated in many migraines. Try switching to incandescent bulbs instead of fluorescent ones if you think you may be sensitive to light. It's also a good idea to wear a hat or sunglasses outdoors.

Migraine Fighters

For many sufferers, there is simply no substitute for the most powerful drug they can get their hands on. If you fit into this category, stay with what works for you. But don't write off nonpharmacologic remedies without at least giving them a try. If you can control your migraines without medication, you will avoid the possible side effects and long-term dependency problems some people develop. Many who suffer from migraines have obtained relief from the following treatments:

- *Biofeedback.* A biofeedback practitioner can help you learn to divert blood flow away from your head by attaching temperature sensors to your hands to teach you how to warm them at will. Studies suggest that diverting the blood from your head to your hands can help relieve migraines.

- *Shower trick.* A cold shower, followed by a hot shower, followed by a cold shower.
- *Rebreathe your air.* Many migraine sufferers have gotten relief using a technique generally reserved for hyperventilation—breathing into a paper bag. Hold the bag over your mouth and nose and breathe slowly in and out for about 15 to 20 minutes. The higher carbon dioxide level can alleviate migraines.

Prevention May Be the Cure

Why wait until you actually have a migraine to do something about it? See which of these simple nutritional supplements work for you:

- *Feverfew.* This herb helps prevent migraines in many people, although it does not work for tension headaches. You can take it as a capsule, tincture or tea.
- *Niacin.* You may be able to head off a migraine by taking 100 to 300 mg of the nicotinic form of the vitamin. Take it at the first sign of a headache.
- *Magnesium.* This mineral is finally getting attention thanks to research showing that taking 400 to 600 mg a day may be helpful. A recent study found that 56% of the people who got magnesium supplements had fewer migraines. Only 31% of those who were given a placebo had fewer migraines. You'll need to take it for a month or two before you can tell if it's working.

MAGIC MEDICINES FOR MIGRAINE SUFFERERS

Many migraine sufferers don't realize what an extensive range of medications are available to fight these awful headaches. People respond differently to different medications. So if your headaches aren't helped by the first medication you take—don't despair! Just work your way up and down this list until you find what does work for you.

Bromocriptine. This drug may be useful in treating menstrual migraines when added to a medication that hasn't been effective on its own.

Chelated magnesium injection. This helps to relieve not only migraine but also cluster headaches.

Dihydroergotamine (DHE45). This drug is as effective as sumatriptan (below) and lasts for two days. Because it's injected, it is particularly useful when the vomiting that often accompanies migraines makes it impossible to keep down a pill.

Fioricet, Fiorinal, Midrin, Norgesic Forte, Wygraine. These are the old standbys that have been around for years. Don't write them off! They're comparatively inexpensive and highly effective choices for many migraine sufferers.

***Lidocaine* nose drops.** Lidocaine is the same anesthetic dentists inject to numb your teeth. In a small study, more than half of migraine sufferers who were given the nose drops felt significantly better within 15 minutes. Unfortunately, the effect was short-lived in half of them. The treatment may be best used to give immediate pain relief while waiting for another drug to take effect.

Methysergide (*Sansert*). This drug is often effective, but consider keeping it closer to the bottom of your list. Long-term use must be carefully monitored as it can scar the lungs, kidneys and heart.

Over-the-counter medications. Don't dismiss these as being too weak. They're very effective for many people, albeit in larger than usual doses. Check with your doctor.

Sumatriptan (*Imitrex*). Available in both self-injectable and pill form, it's being hailed as a "miracle drug" by migraine sufferers. Watch out if you have heart disease though—it works by severely constricting blood vessels and could precipitate an angina attack or worse.

Tylenol plus codeine. A combination of two old standbys that works well for many people.

- *Riboflavin.* Another potentially useful nutritional supplement is the vitamin riboflavin—or B2. Migraine intensity is relieved in some people with a dosage of 100 to 200 milligrams per day.
- *Antidepressants* (e.g., *Elavil, Prozac*). Tricyclic antidepressants (Elavil) have more side effects than SSRI antidepressants (Prozac), but appear to be more effective in preventing migraines. Both types need to be taken every day.
- *Beta-blockers* (e.g., *Inderal, Corgard*). Traditionally used to treat heart disease, these drugs help regulate blood vessel

ALL-NATURAL ASPIRIN

Aspirin's main pain-fighting ingredient, salicylic acid, is a synthetic form of salicin. Salicin occurs naturally in three herbs that you can find at your local health-food store:

➤ Black haw
➤ Meadowsweet
➤ White willow

These herbs are traditional folk remedies for headaches, fever and chills, and inflammation. So if you want aspirin, but not the upset stomach that often accompanies its use, try one of these natural "aspirin" herbs. Follow the directions on the package.

activity, decreasing episodes for some migraine sufferers.
- *Depakote.* This anti-epilepsy drug reduces the frequency of migraine attacks in half the people who take it.
- *Over-the-counter medications.* Try taking ibuprofen or a related anti-inflammatory drug for a week before your period to prevent menstrual migraines. Continue taking the medication until your period has ended.
- *Verapamil (Calan, Verelan).* Another heart medication, this drug also works well for some migraine sufferers.

Suicide Headaches

Migraines aren't the only vascular headaches around. While women get most of the migraines, men get hit with the other debilitating brain pain: cluster headaches. These headaches usually last for only an hour or two, but may recur several times a day, day after day. They can be even more painful than migraines and just as hard to control.

Researchers have found that smoking and napping are habits associated with cluster headaches, and advise sufferers to avoid both. In addition to steering clear of your triggers, there are a number of treatments that may be effective against these headaches:
- *Oxygen therapy.* Breathing pure oxygen for a few minutes works quite well for some people, so ask your doctor about

getting a tank of it to keep around. Because of the relief pure oxygen may provide, researchers recommend exercise as a way to control the headaches, since exercise results in a greater delivery of oxygen to the body.
- *Hot pepper spray.* Another effective remedy for some people is to spray capsaicin (a substance found in chili peppers) into the nostril located on the same side as the headache pain.
- *Nutritional supplements.* Try ginkgo biloba, which has been shown to improve blood flow in the tiny capillaries of the brain.

HEADACHES GALORE

Although tension headaches and migraines account for most head pain, they're not the only headaches on the block. And don't assume that the pain started in your head just because that's where it ended up. If you're a regular headache sufferer, make sure you rule out all of these possible culprits:

Tooth Trouble

Dental disorders like TMJ (temporomandibular joint) syndrome, cavities and abscesses can cause headaches. Also, if you grind your teeth in your sleep (bruxism) or clench them, talk to your dentist about being fitted

ASSORTED HEADACHE HELPERS

Drink a cup of coffee. Caffeine constricts blood vessels, reducing the throbbing pain of a headache. Taken at the first sign of pain, it may head one off altogether. No sugar though! Sugar dilates blood vessels, counteracting the caffeine benefit.

Put it on ice. Like caffeine, the cold temperature of an ice pack will reduce the inflammation of the blood vessels in your head. It's an old-fashioned remedy, but it works!

Bring on the hot peppers. In one study, 75% of headache sufferers who rubbed capsaicin cream (Zostrix), derived from hot peppers, in their noses felt better.

Run hot and cold. Sit in a hot bath while holding an ice pack to your head. The hot water will relax your muscles, thereby relieving tension. The heat will also dilate the blood vessels everywhere except your head, diverting blood flow away from the site of the pain.

with a mouthguard. If you're not sure about nighttime grinding, ask your partner or have a friend listen in on you one night.

From Top to Toe

Believe it or not, your feet can hurt your head. Make sure your shoes fit properly and that structural foot problems, such as bunions, receive the proper treatment. Problems with your feet can also throw off your posture, which can cause headaches, too. Rule out back and neck trouble if you can't pinpoint the cause of your head pain.

Watch Your Eyes

Visual disorders or eyestrain should be ruled out if you're a frequent headache sufferer. If your eye-care professional recommends corrective lenses, wear them! And wear sunglasses, too. It's easy to underestimate the strain that sunlight and glare can put on the facial muscles. People tend to squint without realizing it, thereby setting the stage for a whopping headache.

Eat Right!

Low blood sugar is a very common culprit. Eat regularly and snack a little between small meals if you need to. This will keep your blood sugar levels more consistent, and will also help with the energy swings and irritability caused by fluctuating blood sugar levels.

Look for food sensitivities, too. If you get headaches often and can't figure out why, tyramine could be at fault. Cut the following tyramine-rich foods from your diet and see whether your headaches are eliminated: alcohol, aged cheeses, chocolate, sour cream, onions, citrus fruit and fresh-baked products that contain yeast. Hot dogs and cold cuts, which are loaded with nitrites, could also be to blame.

Finally, eliminate the flavor-enhancer MSG (monosodium glutamate) from your diet. It's most commonly associated with Chinese food, but check the labels on packaged foods, too.

One More Cup of Coffee?

Caffeine constricts blood vessels, which can give you a headache. Conversely, if you miss your daily dose, the blood vessels will be more dilated than usual, which can also cause a headache.

If you want to kick the caffeine habit, reduce your intake by about 20% a day until your consumption is where you want it to be. If you get a withdrawal headache anyway, drink a little coffee at the first sign of pain. You may be able to avert a full-blown headache without having to consume too much caffeine.

The Horrible Hangover

Too much alcohol can cause the notorious hangover. Take these four steps before you crawl into bed to lessen the impact of the alcohol in the morning:

■ *Take two Alka-Seltzer tablets.* The aspirin will help stave off the inevitable headache, and the sodium bicarbonate will offset the digestive distress.

■ *Drink black coffee (if this won't keep you awake).* No, this will not sober you up, but the caffeine will constrict the blood vessels in your brain, lessening the chances of an unbearable headache. Alcohol dilates the blood vessels, which contributes to the headache. Also, caffeine enhances the effect of the aspirin in the *Alka-Seltzer.*

■ *Drink one or two large glasses of water.* Alcohol causes dehydration, which contributes to nausea and headache.

■ *Have a snack to help stabilize your blood sugar levels...if you think you can manage one.*

⚠ FREEZING-COLD HEADACHES

Remember the last time you had an "ice cream headache"? Here's the latest theory on what causes this head pain: The back of the palate contains nerves that control the dilation and constriction of blood vessels. These nerves stretch into the head. When very cold substances touch this area, they stimulate the nerves to make blood vessels in your head dilate, which causes severe head pain. The pain passes a couple of minutes later when your palate has warmed up.

To protect yourself, make sure you take in cold food and drink near the front of your mouth. Also, watch out for those practical jokers who might present you with a "brain-freeze straw"—an item designed to place cold liquid at the very spot guaranteed to give you that one-minute migraine.

■ WHEN TO WORRY

Although most headaches are nothing to fret over, once in a while they're the result of more than just a bad day at the office. Here's when you should call the doctor:

➤ The headache is unlike anything you have ever experienced before.

➤ Pain is sudden and severe.

➤ There are other symptoms, such as blurred vision, numbness, dizziness, confusion, loss of memory or inability to speak clearly.

Also call your doctor if you develop a new pattern of headaches or if your usual headaches become stronger or more frequent.

GET A GOOD NIGHT'S SLEEP

We all spend the occasional night tossing and turning, but what is merely a passing annoyance for most of us is a nightly battle for an unlucky few. Here's what you need to know to take back the night.

Why Does It Happen?

You would think we'd have a clear answer to a problem that affects about 70 million of us, but not so. People usually fall into one of two categories: those with initial insomnia, who have trouble falling asleep, and those with secondary insomnia, who have trouble staying asleep.

Insomnia can have many causes, and getting to the root of it helps pinpoint the most effective treatment. Among the possible reasons for sleepless nights are:

- *Anxiety*. We've all lain awake worrying at some point, but for some people anxious tossing and turning becomes one of those hard-to-break habits.
- *Depression*. A case of the blues may keep you awake temporarily, but clinical depression can create a serious disruption of sleep patterns.
- *Restless legs syndrome*. This neurological disorder isn't serious, but it can definitely make your nights miserable. Most

cases occur after the age of 40, and result in an almost irresistible urge to move the legs.
- *Sleep apnea*. This is a condition in which a person actually stops breathing during sleep. They then awaken gasping for breath. Often, the sufferer is not even aware of these awakenings.
- *Medical conditions*. This may sound odd, but don't assume that your insomnia is due to a sleep disorder. All kinds of medical problems—bladder problems, heart disease, asthma and others—can cause you to awaken during the night. So before you start pouring lavender oil on your pillow, pay a visit to the doctor. He or she will be able to rule out medical causes, as well as medication use, as the

source of your sleeplessness, Make sure you mention any over-the-counter medicines you may be taking. Many of these can rob you of a good night's sleep.

How Much Sleep Do You Really Need?

Although there is no one correct answer, most adults do not get as much sleep as they need. The consensus among sleep experts is that most people require at least seven hours of restful sleep to function optimally, and that many people need eight or nine. If you regularly need an alarm to wake you up in the morning, sleep through the alarm or have to drag yourself out of bed in the morning, you need more sleep. Also, go to bed earlier if you tend to get drowsy during the

day or drift off without intending to—say, at work or while driving.

And don't let your teenage children persuade you that they don't need as much sleep as the "little kids." Most teenagers need 10 hours of sleep or more.

Although some people swear by a quick afternoon nap, don't even consider it if you're having trouble sleeping at night.

Sleep Hygiene

"Sleep hygiene" is a term coined by experts to describe good sleep habits—those that lead to dependable, restful sleep.

⚠️ SOME DRUGS KEEP YOU AWAKE

No, this does not refer to the kind of medication you buy in a dark alley. Any number of over-the-counter and prescription drugs do more than they're supposed to, delivering a sleepless night in addition to their beneficial actions. Here are the drugs to watch out for:

- ➤ Painkillers that contain caffeine (check labels—many over-the-counter drugs contain caffeine to boost the pain-killing effects)
- ➤ Cold and allergy remedies that contain the decongestant pseudoephedrine
- ➤ Appetite suppressants
- ➤ Many antidepressants
- ➤ Beta-blockers
- ➤ The antiseizure medication phenytoin (*Dilantin*)
- ➤ Thyroid hormones

SURPRISING SLEEP SABOTEURS

You've probably figured out that coffee is not a great sleep inducer. But did you know that eggplant can keep you up, too? Here are a few other pep pills you may not know about:

- ➤ Tomatoes
- ➤ Potatoes
- ➤ Bacon
- ➤ Cheese
- ➤ Spinach
- ➤ Chocolate
- ➤ Sausage
- ➤ Sugar
- ➤ Ham
- ➤ Sauerkraut

All of these foods contain a substance that causes the release of a brain stimulant.

Here are the basics:

- Go to bed at the same time each evening and get up at the same time each morning, even on weekends.
- Get the right amount of sleep for your body. If you only need seven hours, don't sleep for eight. If you need eight, don't try to get by on six.
- Don't go to bed on a full stomach. The digestive process itself keeps many people up. Also the pressure of a full belly on the diaphragm may keep you from taking deep and restful breaths.
- Don't drink coffee, tea or other caffeinated beverages within six hours of bedtime.
- Don't smoke in the evening.
- Don't exercise within six hours of going to bed.
- Do take a hot shower or bath an hour or so before bedtime.

Nightmares & Night Terrors

Although regular nightmares usually only occur in children under the age of six, up to 50% of adults experience an occasional nightmare. Frequent nightmares in anyone over age six are believed to be the result of an emotional problem, and they should be referred to a therapist for evaluation and treatment of the underlying problem.

So what's the difference between night terrors and nightmares? Night terrors occur during the first two-thirds of the night when we experience non-REM (rapid eye movement) sleep. Nightmares happen during the last third of the night during REM sleep. A person experiencing a night terror will often scream, twist, sweat and breathe heavily, as well as appear to be in terrible distress. But in the morning, they will have no recollection of the event. Someone who has a nightmare will often wake up, remember details of the dream and want to be comforted. Experts say it's fine to wake somebody having a nightmare, but a person having a night terror will only become disoriented if woken.

LIGHT OR NO LIGHT?

If your body is hypersensitive to light, even the tiny amount emitted by your clock radio may be disturbing your sleep. To rule light out as the cause of your insomnia, try plugging up every little light leak in your bedroom and see if it helps. Place a rolled-up towel under the door and turn the radio to face the wall or drape a piece of cloth over it.

TO DRINK OR NOT TO DRINK . . .

Since alcohol can be both a sedative and a stimulant, many people are confused about whether it helps or hurts efforts to sleep soundly. It hurts. A drink at bedtime may help you relax at first, but it will fragment your sleep later on when the effect wears off.

And here's a warning sign you may not have recognized: If a single drink tends to hit you particularly hard, you may not be getting enough sleep at night.

ALL-NATURAL RECIPE FOR A RESTFUL NIGHT

A peaceful night may be as close as the nearest health-food store.

Vitamins & Minerals

Deficiencies of calcium, magnesium, copper, iron, zinc and the B vitamins can all contribute to problems with sleep, so make sure you take a vitamin and mineral supplement that provides the recommended daily allowance. In addition, calcium and magnesium are particularly soothing. Try taking 800 mg of calcium and 400 mg of magnesium with a glass of warm milk an hour or so before you plan to go to bed. Make sure you don't take more than 1,200 mg a day of calcium and 600 mg a day of magnesium from all supplements combined.

Herbal Remedies

Valerian, California poppy, kava kava, passionflower, skullcap, lemon balm and hops all help you sleep. Start with valerian, and work your way down the list. Try each herb for three nights until you find the one that does the trick for you. You can also buy preparations that contain more than one of these sleep aids. If none of the individual herbs works for you, try combining them for an extra-potent potion. If your sleep is being disrupted by chronic, low-grade pain, Jamaican dogwood may be particularly helpful.

Chamomile Tea

Your grandmother may have suggested this old insomnia cure, and with good reason. Drink the tea in the last half-hour before retiring to soothe away the day's tensions.

Lavender Essential Oil

Try sprinkling a drop or two on your pillow or in your bathwater at night. Lavender may exert its soothing effect by slowing nerve impulses, thereby inducing relaxation.

If you take any of the following medications and are having nightmares, talk to your doctor.

- Beta-blockers
- Tricyclic antidepressants
- Nasal sprays
- Sleeping pills

Snoring

Snoring results from a partial obstruction of the airway and can have many causes, including large tonsils or adenoids, limp tissue or poor muscle tone, or an overly long, soft palate. Structural problems, like big tonsils, are beyond your control, but other factors are not. Here's what you can do to take control:

- *Don't drink alcohol in the evening if you have a tendency to snore.* Alcohol causes muscle relaxation, which makes it more likely that the tissues of the throat will sink into the airway, causing snoring.
- *Lose weight.* Extra fat on the outside of the body also means extra fat on the inside, which further narrows the airway. Sometimes, losing weight is all that's needed to get rid of snoring altogether.
- *Sew a ball into the back of your pajamas or nightgown.* You are far less likely to snore if you sleep on your side, because

the throat can't collapse on itself the way it does if you sleep on your back. If you roll onto your back in your sleep, the hard object should send you rolling right back onto your side.

- *Tip up your bed.* Place a brick or two under the headboard of your bed. Like sleeping on your side, having your head elevated helps prevent the structures and tissue of the throat from collapsing back over the airway.

Sleep Apnea

The same process that causes snoring also causes sleep apnea, but the blockage is severe enough to actually close the airway. The person generally will awaken gasping for breath. All of the self-help measures appropriate for snoring may help relieve sleep apnea, but this condition often requires additional measures such as CPAP (see box, lower left).

In the most serious cases, surgery may reduce the size of the structures in the throat or enlarge the opening of the airway.

Chemical Rest

If it seems that simply taking a pill and sleeping like a baby is too good a scenario to be true...that's because it is too good to be true. First of all, sleeping pills may

---

KILLER PILL

Have your doctor make sure you don't suffer from sleep apnea before you start taking sleeping pills, or you might sleep like a baby...forever. Sleeping pills may prevent a person with sleep apnea from waking up if their airway becomes closed off by the soft tissues of the throat. Ordinarily, a sufferer would awaken gasping for air in time to prevent suffocation.

⚠ DO NASAL STRIPS WORK?

Nasal strips, which have become quite popular, do open up the nasal passages quite effectively, so they could conceivably relieve snoring caused by nasal congestion. The trouble is that most snoring is caused by an obstruction in the throat, not the nose.

RELIEF FOR SLEEP-APNEA SUFFERERS

Continuous positive airway pressure (CPAP) is an effective way to relieve the strain on the respiratory system of a person with sleep apnea and ensure that they get a steady supply of oxygen.

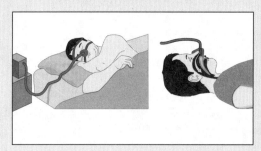

WHY DO WE SNORE?

Normal breathing passage and open airway.

Structures relax causing snoring.

Structures collapse, causing sleep apnea.

cause, of all things, insomnia. This often occurs because these medications interrupt the normal sleep cycle. There are several types of sleeping pills, both prescription and over-the-counter.

- *Benzodiazepines.* This class of drugs is available only by prescription, and includes drugs like *Halcion*. The benzodiazepines are habit-forming and can cause terrible rebound insomnia when taken every night and then discontinued. Users may also experience anxiety the day after taking them. These drugs are best taken only occasionally to cope with a particularly bad night.

- *Ambien.* This drug works like the benzodiazepines, but doesn't cause the same degree of rebound insomnia or next-day anxiety.

- *Drugstore medications.* What about over-the-counter medications like *Sominex* or *Unisom*? These are just antihistamines, ordinarily used to treat allergies. One of their side effects is that they make you drowsy, hence their usefulness. They're not as effective as the benzodiazepines, but you can become just as dependent on them. Some antihistimines, like *Vistaril*, are available with a prescription. Doctors sometimes prescribe these drugs for insomnia, but they're not the best choice.

- *Sedative antidepressants.* This is another example of making use of a drug's ordinarily unwelcome side effect. Antidepressants like *Elavil* cause drowsiness as a side effect, and therefore make decent sleeping pills. The doses given to combat insomnia are not sufficient to treat depression, however.

Losing Your Grip?

Many people with insomnia worry that sleep deprivation will cause them to lose their minds. Although there are some cases on record of people seeing flashing lights or hearing noises after long periods of sleeplessness, these symptoms are not indicative of insanity. The converse is true, however: almost all emotional and psychiatric disorders can *cause* insomnia.

ARE YOU SURE YOU HAVE INSOMNIÀ?

You may not have insomnia even if you think you do... even if you're *sure* you do. This is one of the first exercises a specialist is likely to have you perform:

Place a piece of paper and pencil and a clock next to your bed. Once you go to bed, jot down the time every 10 minutes until you fall asleep. That's all.

You wouldn't believe how many blank sheets of paper these specialists see. Often, people think they're awake when they're really dreaming.

SHOULD YOU TAKE MELATONIN?

Melatonin has been touted as the miracle cure for sleeplessness, but is it all it's cracked up to be? Here's the theory: Melatonin is a natural hormone secreted by the pineal gland that plays a role in regulating the sleep-wake cycle. When there's plenty of light, production of melatonin is suppressed. When it gets dark, the body makes a lot of it. You also feel sleepy. So the melatonin production is regarded as the cause of the sleepiness. Although it appears to work for some elderly people whose melatonin production has fallen off dramatically, it does not appear to be particularly helpful for anyone else. It may be more effective in combating jet lag than insomnia. There have not been any reports of serious adverse affects, so you may want to try it. Bear in mind that it is a hormone, not a vitamin or mineral, and may therefore turn out to have effects on the body or mind that are as yet unknown, especially if used regularly for a long period of time.

HELP LINES & HOT SPOTS FOR SLEEP DISORDERS

American Academy of Sleep Medicine
507-287-6006; www.asda.org

Int'l Sleep Products Association
703-683-8371;
www.sleepproducts.org

American Sleep Apnea Association
202-293-3650; www.sleepapnea.org

National Sleep Foundation
202-347-3471;
www.sleepfoundation.org

LULLABY & GOOD NIGHT

In a study where people were given tapes of music to listen to before going to bed, researchers found that all but one of the participants fell asleep faster and slept longer after having listened to the tapes. When the scientists took away the bedtime music, the insomniacs tossed and turned again.

The Killer Diseases

Heart disease and cancer are the two illnesses that claim the most American lives. But thanks to discoveries about the connection between lifestyle choices and health, together with the development of new drugs and advanced surgical techniques, we're developing better tools to both treat and prevent these dreaded conditions. Getting on this lifesaving bandwagon requires information and the willpower to make changes in the way you live every day. Read on to find out how to make the right choices in your life. Then, just do it— today!

HEART CENTRAL

More of us die from heart disease than from anything else, but what exactly is it? In spite of its name, heart disease is not a disease of the heart, but of the blood vessels. It can lead to both heart attacks and strokes. Coronary artery disease isn't the only cause of heart trouble, however. Heart failure, irregular heartbeat, burst blood vessels and diseases that affect the valves of the heart account for just as much illness. Read on for a description of the various disorders, how to avoid them and what to do if you find yourself with symptoms.

CARDIOVASCULAR DISEASE

Most of us think of heart attacks when we hear the term cardiovascular disease, but strokes cause almost as much illness and death. Both are the end result of a disease process that has taken place over many years, often over a lifetime. You can intervene at any point in this process and take steps that will help you avoid a medical crisis. Here's what you need to know.

What Is Heart Disease?

Heart disease is a disorder of the coronary arteries, which supply blood to the heart. Medical thinking on the precise mechanism behind this problem seems to be in constant flux, but the basic facts are: Following injury or damage, fatty deposits build up on the inner walls of the coronary arteries, restricting the supply of blood to the heart. Arteries that have these deposits of plaque are neither as wide nor as pliable as healthy blood vessels. As the disease progresses and the constriction worsens, signs that the heart muscle isn't getting enough oxygen to function well often develop. These may include:

- *Angina pectoris* is a chest pain that occurs because the heart is not getting enough oxygen-rich blood. It usually comes on after some form of exertion.
- *Shortness of breath* may accompany everyday exertion, such as walking up stairs.
- *Dizziness, lightheadedness and fainting* can also be signs that the heart isn't getting an adequate supply of blood.

Are You at Risk?

Certain conditions and lifestyle choices predispose you to heart disease. Many of these are "modifiable risk factors," which means that there are things you can do to reduce their effect. Others are due to your genetic makeup and are not in your control.

- *Having the wrong genes.* This is truly unfortunate, and is the biggest factor of heart disease. But just because you have a family history of heart disease does not mean that you are programmed to die young. In most cases, heart disease develops because of a complex interaction between genetic makeup and lifestyle habits. Having the wrong genes simply means that you need to be extra-vigilant about controlling any other risk factors and you should have your doctor begin monitoring you at a younger age.

FIRST WARNING OF HEART TROUBLE

A particular form of chest pain called angina pectoris is a strong signal of underlying coronary artery disease. Here are the signs of angina pectoris:

➤ Chest pain that comes during exercise, on cold windy days, after heavy meals and in times of stress

➤ Pain is most commonly located behind the breastbone, and may be perceived as pressure or tightness

➤ Sometimes the pain occurs in the arms, neck, jaw, back, teeth or hand

The pain of angina is similar to that of a heart attack, but generally subsides with rest. Don't try to "rest away" the first episode of it though, or you may be ignoring an important signal. For many heart attack victims, the heart attack itself was the first warning they had. Always seek professional medical care at any sign of this type of pain.

■ *Having unhealthy habits.* Most people know what these are, and realize that changing bad habits requires some willpower. Quit smoking, eat foods that are low in saturated fat and eat large amounts of fresh fruit and vegetables, maintain a reasonable weight and get a moderate amount of exercise. A person does not have to join the local gym. Taking a daily 20-minute walk is almost as beneficial.

Other conditions associated with a high incidence of heart disease include high blood pressure, high cholesterol levels and high homocysteine levels. Diabetes is particularly hard on the cardiovascular system. If you have diabetes and, for some reason, are not being closely monitored for signs of heart disease, ask your doctor why. In such cases, you will need to work with a specialist to manage all of your risk factors.

No discussion of cardiovascular disease would be complete without an emphasis on the dangers of smoking—one of the main contributors to the development of cardiovascular disease. More than 200,000 deaths a year are caused by the impact smoking has on cardiovascular health. In fact, smokers are about twice as likely to have a heart attack as non-smokers. If you can't quit on your own, talk to your doctor about smoking cessation treatments.

UNUSUAL PHYSICAL INDICATORS

We all know of at least one physical characteristic that puts a person at risk for heart disease: obesity. But did you know that there are other, subtler associations? If you have one of the signs shown below, take steps to reduce all other risk factors, such as smoking or poor eating habits. And get regular screening tests and checkups.

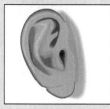 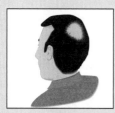 

If you have creased earlobes, watch out! Having one affected earlobe may raise your chances of having heart disease by as much as 33%, while two creased earlobes ups the risk by 77%.

Baldness isn't so great for the heart either. Two types of baldness seem to be predictors of heart disease: rapid balding and loss of hair in the "Friar" pattern shown above.

Are you an apple or a pear? Putting on weight around the middle (the way some men do) is an indicator of higher risk. Heavier hips may not be very chic, but then neither are heart attacks!

SUPER-EASY WEIGHT-LOSS & EXERCISE PROGRAM

Dieting and exercising don't need to consume your life for you to lose weight and improve your cardiovascular fitness. Here's a two-part weight-loss and exercise program that just might change your life—and your looks.

Three-quarters diet. Keep on eating whatever you're used to, but eliminate about one quarter of the portion. In love with that salami sandwich? Prepare it the way you usually do, then cut it into four equal pieces, and get rid of one of them. Want to eat popcorn? Fine. Make your usual portion, then get rid of one quarter of it. Used to having a can of soda with that? Pour a fourth of it out before you begin. You'll barely notice the difference because your diet won't have changed, but you will have chopped 25% of the calories out of your daily eating. Once you've lost a few pounds, you may be more motivated to make other healthy changes, like replacing half of the salami in your sandwich with healthy green things. Don't be discouraged by what appears to be slow weight loss. Losing just 2 pounds a month will leave you more than 20 pounds lighter at the end of a year.

Ten-minute exercise plan. Now that research has shown that even 10 minutes of exercise provides health benefits, you don't need to plan your life around an exercise routine. Pick out 10 minutes in the morning and 10 in the afternoon or early evening, and spend that time walking up and down a flight of stairs in your home. Go as fast as you can. If you don't think it will make you sweat, just try it. Live in an apartment or house with no stairs? Speed-walk back and forth in the longest hallway you have access to for 10 minutes twice a day. Not only will this small amount of activity get your heart working, but doing it regularly will speed up your metabolism, which will help burn calories more quickly. Perform this activity in conjunction with the Three-quarters Diet, and within a few weeks you may actually feel like pricing those high-fashion workout outfits or investing in a mountain bike.

THE LOWDOWN ON HIGH FAT

For all of the fuss over cholesterol, most people who have heart attacks have normal cholesterol numbers.

That doesn't mean that cholesterol doesn't play a role in heart disease, only that the interaction is more complex than it may initially appear.

At the same time, for people who are clearly at high risk for heart attacks and strokes, reducing high cholesterol may cut the risk of dying by as much as one-third. So what's the story?

The key lies in knowing about the different components of your blood lipid profile, or the fats in your blood. There are two bad

elements (low-density lipoprotein, or LDL cholesterol, and triglycerides), which damage blood vessels, and a good element (high-density lipoprotein, or HDL cholesterol), which protects your vessels from heart disease.

When you have your cholesterol measured, make sure that your doctor gets a breakdown of the different levels of each of these components. A normal overall level of total cholesterol could still mean you're at risk for heart disease if your LDL cholesterol

and triglycerides are high. And a total cholesterol level that looks quite high may be perfectly healthy if a disproportionate amount of it is HDL cholesterol.

Although medication may be required for poor blood lipid profiles that don't respond to lifestyle

changes, you can often create a dramatic improvement by changing your food choices, losing weight and exercising.

New Killer on the Block

Until recently, bad cholesterol was thought to be the most dangerous thing floating around in

ARE AVOCADOS ALL BAD?

Although avocados have gotten a bad name for being packed with fat, the critics haven't noticed that it's the healthy monounsaturated kind. Another healthy food on the high-fat hit list is nuts, which naturally contain monounsaturated oils and vitamin E—both of which are good for the heart. Just stay away from the ones that have been roasted in unhealthy oils.

FIGHT HEART DISEASE WITH FOOD

In addition to eating a diet rich in fresh fruit and vegetables and low in fat, particular foods may provide specific benefits to the cardiovascular system by turning thick, sticky blood into thin, slippery blood. That's good for the heart because it decreases the chances of blood clot formation, which is a major cause of heart attacks. Here are the good choices:

➤ Red wine

➤ Purple grape juice

➤ Ginger

➤ Onions, garlic, shallots, scallions and chives

➤ Turmeric (a spice)

Vitamin E is also a highly effective blood thinner.

BUTTER OR MARGARINE?

For years the conventional wisdom was that margarine had to be better for your heart than butter because it consisted of polyunsaturated oil rather than saturated animal fat. The problem is that the process by which liquid polyunsaturated oils are magically transformed into a solid butter-like mass produces substances called trans fatty acids, which abound in packaged and processed foods as well as margarine. And unfortunately, trans fatty acids seem to be even worse for you than saturated fat. So what should you do?

Olive oil. Monounsaturated oils are clearly the best for your heart. Use olive oil whenever possible in place of other oils.

Canola oil. This is another monounsaturated oil. Use it when the flavor of olive oil is too distinctive for whatever dish you're preparing. With its milder flavor, it's the best oil for mayonnaise. You can find mayonnaise made with canola oil at your local health-food store, and it tastes just like "real" mayonnaise.

Flaxseed oil. If you don't eat a lot of fish, consider adding flaxseed oil to your diet. It's a rich source of the same omega-3 fatty acids that make fish so good for your heart. You can find it at health-food stores, but make sure it's been stored in the refrigerated section, since it has a tendency to become rancid. It's great on salads.

Butter. If you absolutely must have some, there are a few ways to enjoy the flavor without overdoing it.

Especially when the butter is cold we tend to take off big chunks with the butter knife. Instead, use a cheese slicer to get ultra-thin slices.

If only the flavor of real butter will do for your popcorn, heat a mixture of half canola oil and half butter. Since the canola oil is so mild, the combination tastes like melted butter.

Finally, remember that fat is fat. Even the ones that are good for you contain 100 calories per tablespoon. Use them in moderation.

your bloodstream…at least as far as getting coronary artery disease was concerned. But now scientists are beginning to think that may not be the case. High levels of an amino acid called homocysteine may turn out to be even more of a threat, damaging arterial walls and setting the stage for the development of those deadly plaque deposits.

If that hypothesis proves to be correct, vitamin therapy could be immensely useful in the treatment of heart disease. Three of the B vitamins—B6, B12, and folic acid—help the liver keep homocysteine levels in check. Low levels of folic acid, in particular, are associated with high levels of homocysteine. According to a recent study, taking supplements of these vitamins may cut your risk of heart disease in half. How much should you take? Make sure that you're getting at least the recommended daily allowance from your multivitamin.

COMBAT HIGH BLOOD PRESSURE

High blood pressure is a main cause of stroke and contributes to kidney disease, heart disease and heart failure. Ideally you should have consistent blood pressure readings of 120/80 or lower. The higher number is the "systolic" pressure—the pressure when the vessel is contracting to pump blood. The lower number is the "diastolic" pressure—the pressure when the vessel is relaxed between contractions.

Unfortunately, there aren't usually any symptoms, which is why hypertension is termed the "silent killer." In extreme circumstances, you could experience headaches, dizziness and even seizures. But your blood pressure should be brought under control long before you begin to have such severe symptoms. Here are the options:

- *Stress reduction.* Although relaxation exercises may not bring about a dramatic reduction in blood pressure, a decrease of just a few points is often all that's needed. Used in conjunction with other measures, the effect may be more pronounced. Concentrate on deep breathing exercises.
- *Exercise.* Studies have consistently shown that although exercise temporarily boosts heart rate and blood pressure, the long-term effect is a reduction both in blood pressure and heart disease. If you already have high blood pressure, avoid lifting more than a few pounds of weights, which puts greater stress on the vessels.
- *Medication.* Sometimes medication is the only way to bring blood pressure down to safe levels. There are four major types of drugs that accomplish this—diuretics, angiotensin-converting-enzyme (ACE) inhibitors, calcium-channel blockers and beta-blockers.

Each medication has its own particular benefits and drawbacks, which you should discuss with your health-care provider.

Once a drug is recommended, ask why your doctor has suggested that drug over the others. If your doctor prescribes a calcium-channel blocker, specifically ask whether it is a sustained-released formulation. The short-acting versions of some of these drugs have been cited as a possible *cause* of heart attacks.

The Great Salt Debate
We all know that we're supposed to keep our blood pressure

★ DOUBLE-CHECK HIGH BLOOD PRESSURE READINGS

If you're told you have high blood pressure (hypertension) based on readings taken in the doctor's office, unless it's sky-high, insist on monitoring your blood pressure at home before accepting the diagnosis. Home blood pressure monitors are available at most pharmacies. Take your blood pressure three times a day for at least a week, then report the findings to your doctor. If the home readings are normal and your doctor wants you to take medication to lower your blood pressure anyway, make sure you get a second opinion. It is very common for people to have artificially elevated readings at the doctor's office—a phenomenon known as "white-coat hypertension." This occurs when nervousness causes an increase in blood pressure. Occasionally, the opposite is true and feelings of security caused by the presence of health-care professionals result in a temporary decrease in blood pressure.

■■ ANXIETY AND DEPRESSION CAN LEAD TO HIGH BLOOD PRESSURE

People with normal blood pressure who initially rated highest in anxiety and depression were 69% more likely to be treated eventually for hypertension.

Self-defense: If you feel anxious or depressed, consult your doctor, warns Bruce S. Jonas, PhD, behavioral scientist, Office of Analysis, Epidemiology and Health Promotion, Centers for Disease Control and Prevention.

in check by reducing our intake of salt. But is it true? Is it even healthy? Since the answers vary depending on the results of the study du jour, what's a confused hypertensive to do?

Before you try the low-sodium approach, increase your intake of potassium, which counteracts the effects of sodium. Most of us think of bananas, but oranges, cantaloupes and baked potatoes are great sources of potassium, too. An adequate intake of magnesium and calcium is also necessary to regulate blood pressure. Many scientists believe that the problem isn't too much sodium, but rather an inadequate intake of potassium, calcium and magnesium

needed to balance out the sodium.

If you "salt to taste," the amount of salt that you actually need to add may have been distorted by years of overuse. To find out how much you *really* want, don't add table salt to your food for two weeks. Then, start salting, but use just a little and see if the lesser amount does the trick. You should find that somewhat less salt than you used before is just as satisfying. And some foods—like corn— which have a flavor that is masked by salt, may taste great without it. Observe your blood pressure. If it's lower than it was, stick with less sodium.

Finally, don't go crazy trying to eliminate sodium from your diet.

Your body actually requires sodium to survive, and severe restrictions may actually cause heart attacks.

HEAD OFF A HEART ATTACK

Coronary artery disease and hypertension often result in a "cardiovascular event," otherwise known as a heart attack or stroke. Fortunately, if you have a heart attack nowadays, your chances of surviving it are much higher than they used to be— but only if you get to the hospital quickly. If you even *think* you might be having symptoms of a heart attack, get to an emergency room immediately. The worst thing that can happen is that they'll send you home again. If you do turn out to be having a heart attack, your prompt action

might have saved your life. Doctors need to do their work early on in the process, both to save your life and to minimize damage to the heart muscle so that you're not incapacitated by heart failure or other problems down the road.

What Is a Heart Attack?

Heart attacks—or myocardial infarctions—occur when the blood supply to a portion of the heart muscle is cut off. Unless the blood supply is restored quickly, the area of the heart that is being deprived of blood will die. Blood flow interruption is most likely caused by:

- *Plaque.* Sometimes the fatty deposits themselves are the problem. If the buildup becomes severe enough, the entire opening of the artery can close up, thereby depriving the heart of blood. Or a piece of plaque may break away from the artery wall and travel

---

SYMPTOMS NEVER TO IGNORE

Many people who suffer heart attacks die because they underestimate the severity of seemingly mild symptoms or delay getting help. Here is a list of symptoms you should *never* ignore:

➤ Chest pain that doesn't improve with rest or a change of position

➤ Shortness of breath that gets worse when lying down

➤ Chest pain combined with any of the following: anxiety, sweating, breathlessness, bluish lips or fingernail beds, irregular or rapid pulse

In addition to the warning signs above, get the following symptoms checked out, particularly if you have never had them evaluated by a health care professional:

➤ Pain or discomfort that radiates from the chest to the shoulders, jaw, arms, neck or hands

➤ Upset stomach, nausea or heartburn

➤ Persistent unexplained pain in your jaw, teeth or hand

For more on heart attacks, see "Heart Attack Aid," page 136.

ASPIRIN AID

You've heard about how great aspirin is at reducing the risk of having a heart attack by thinning the blood, right? Well, one of the first steps doctors are likely to take if you show up in the emergency room with a heart attack is to give you blood thinners to dissolve existing clots and reduce the chances of new ones forming. Thinner blood is also easier for the heart to pump.

Now, some doctors are saying that getting a jump-start on the process may not be a bad idea. So if you think you might be having a heart attack, take an aspirin right away. Just make sure that you tell the doctors about it when you get to the hospital.

through the vessel toward the heart. The plaque can then lodge along the way, obstructing the artery.

- *Blood clot.* Coronary artery disease causes arteries to become less elastic, which makes them more prone to injury. The artery wall may develop little splits or cracks. The body's response to this is to form a blood clot, which covers the injured area. This blood clot can then break off and occlude a vessel, thereby impeding the blood flow in the same manner as a traveling piece of plaque.

Much less commonly, heart attacks may be caused by burst blood vessels—known as aneurysms—and spasms in the coronary arteries.

What Next?

Once you've had a heart attack and your condition has been stabilized, you may need to undergo further testing and treatment. This may include the following:

- *Cardiac catheterization.* In this procedure, the cardiologist threads a catheter into the coronary arteries either to visualize their condition or to actually eliminate a blockage. First, a special dye is injected, which allows the doctor to locate the blockage. Once he or she can see what's going on, a decision will be made as to

whether to perform bypass surgery, balloon angioplasty or just prescribe medication. In cases of multiple blockages or blockages that are difficult to access with the catheter, bypass surgery may be recommended. If there are one or two accessible areas of narrowing, the doctor may perform balloon angioplasty. This is a procedure in which a "balloon" is inflated inside the narrowed area to press the plaque tightly against the arterial walls. Although this procedure is effective for most patients, in one-third of cases the arteries close up again within six months. Inserting a wire mesh stent into the area reduces this risk. Ask your doctor about using one.

- *Coronary artery bypass graft.* CABG is the procedure a surgeon uses to bypass diseased sections of arteries with pieces of blood vessels taken from another part of your body.

Making significant lifestyle changes after surgery will often greatly improve the chances for

long-term success. Not everybody who has a heart attack needs to undergo surgery. Often the recommendation to perform surgery has more to do with the training and personal preferences of the doctor than an absolute medical necessity dictated by the circumstances. How do we know this?

BIORHYTHM RISK

If you work at night, watch your heart! People who work a regular 9-to-5 day have only half the rate of heart disease as night shifters. If you must work odd hours, minimize or eliminate any other risk factors you may have.

SEE YOUR DENTIST & YOUR CARDIOLOGIST

Nasty fats aren't the only bad things living in your bloodstream—bacteria and viruses may be camping out in there, too. And there is now some substantial evidence to suggest that they may play a greater role in the development of heart disease than previously thought.

One of the herpes viruses (cytomegalovirus) has been implicated in heart disease, as has an organism known as *Chlamydia pneumoniae*, which is sometimes responsible for respiratory illness. And don't forget the bacteria that cause gum disease, which may get into the bloodstream via little cuts or ulcers in the mouth. Once these organisms are in the blood vessels they may damage artery walls, replacing smooth, slippery surfaces with rougher, scarred ones that are more conducive for plaque formation. On the plus side, some researchers think that the widespread use of antibiotics over the past 50 years may also be partly responsible for the decrease in heart attacks because they destroy these bugs along with their original target.

ASK FOR A WARM OPERATION

Patients who are kept warm during surgery have cardiac complications about 1% of the time. Patients who are not kept warm have cardiac problems about 6% of the time. So should you even have to ask to be kept warm?

Unfortunately, the answer is yes. To increase your chances of being a member of the healthier group, ask your surgeon to make sure you get heated intravenous fluids during your operation. Also, ask to have a forced-air heater trained on your body. Feel free to add it in writing to the informed consent sheet you will have to sign prior to surgery.

If the surgeon has the nerve to complain that the heater will make the operating room too hot, gently point out that his or her level of discomfort is unlikely to be anywhere near yours, no matter what the temperature.

Because in Europe, where medical management is preferred over surgical intervention, heart attack victims are just as likely to live as long as American victims. It simply makes sense to get a second opinion.

Many American doctors prefer surgery because they believe

CONTROVERSIAL TREATMENT

If you want to walk right into a hotbed of controversy, try talking to your cardiologist about chelation therapy.

Chelation therapy involves the intravenous infusion of a substance called EDTA, which binds to metals in the blood, thereby removing them. Proponents believe that these metallic elements increase free radicals, leading to plaque buildup on arterial walls. They point to studies that show improved blood flow and fewer symptoms after chelation therapy. Doctors argue that those benefits could be the result of lifestyle changes or other therapy that has accompanied the chelation therapy.

In any case, it doesn't appear to make matters any worse, although it's not cheap. Be sure to read everything you can find, both for and against the treatment, then apply your powers of logical reasoning.

that it improves the quality of life (that is, once you've recovered from the trauma of the surgery!) by producing better blood flow to the heart muscle.

Surgery is not without risk, however. You can die during the surgery and there is a significant incidence of stroke in the month following the procedure. So, keeping this in mind, what are some of the other options?

■ *Medication therapy.* Often, neither bypass surgery nor balloon angioplasty is required following a heart attack. And sometimes surgery is not recommended because the patient has other health problems that make the procedures too

risky. Several medications can reduce the risk of another heart attack, including beta-blockers, cholesterol-lowering medications and blood thinners. Nitroglycerin—a drug that improves blood flow to the heart muscle by dilating blood vessels—may be prescribed for angina. Medication to lower blood pressure may be ordered as well.

■ *Lifestyle modification.* Doctors are beginning to recognize the powerful effect that changes in your day-to-day habits can have on heart disease. Stop smoking, take a daily walk, decrease your intake of unhealthy fats and increase your consumption of fresh fruits

and vegetables. If you're overweight, find a weight-loss program that you can live with and apply all of your willpower to make sure you stay on it. Work on your personality, too. The research appears to show that states of hopelessness and despair are even worse for your heart than anger and hostility. Dieting and change of lifestyle usually lend to change of attitude. Although people with aggressive Type A personalities have an increased risk of heart disease, they're not as badly off as the roll-over-and-die types! It's the people who know how to relax who have the lowest risk of heart disease.

FROM HEART DISEASE TO HEART ATTACK

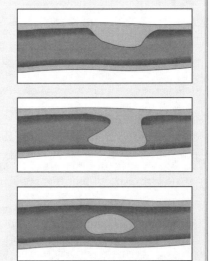

Fatty deposits build up as plaque on the artery walls, constricting the vessel. The rate and level of the deposits depend on diet, lifestyle and family medical history. If your family has a history of heart disease, you need to visit your doctor regularly.

Plaque ruptures, injuring the vessel wall and triggering the formation of a blood clot. At this stage you might be experiencing chest pains, shortness of breath and other symptoms. Regular doctor visits can sometimes provide advance warning.

Blood clot breaks off and travels downstream, blocking the flow of blood to the heart muscle. At this stage, the symptoms of heart attack [see p. 176] are usually evident. You should seek immediate medical attention.

LAUGH SOME MORE

Reach for that TV remote control or head for the nearest comedy club. Hearty laughter results in a temporary increase in blood pressure, followed by a sharp decrease...the same benefit conferred by exercise. Double your heart attack risk reduction by exercising *and* laughing.

STROKE PREVENTION KNOW-HOW

Strokes usually occur for many of the same reasons as heart attacks, and in much the same manner. The main difference is that in cases of stroke, it's part of the brain that loses its blood supply. There are two major types of stroke: those that are caused by blockages, and those that are caused by burst blood vessels (hemmorhagic strokes). The latter are less common and more deadly.

Often there are warning signs that a stroke may occur. If you have high blood pressure, you are at particularly high risk and should be closely monitored by your health-care provider. If you are experiencing any of the following symptoms, you may be having a stroke. This is an emergency and calls for an immediate trip to the emergency room.

- Weakness, numbness or paralysis, usually on just one side
- Sudden headache
- Blurry vision or decreased vision in one or both eyes
- Loss of balance or coordination
- Disorientation and confusion
- Trouble speaking or understanding language

Also be on the lookout for transient ischemic attacks (TIAs). During these attacks, the diminished blood flow to the brain causes symptoms of stroke, but the symptoms come and go.

At the Hospital

Once you're at the hospital, doctors will determine the cause of the stroke. The most common strokes, which are caused by blockages, may be treated with clot-busting drugs, just as heart attacks are. Surgery may be required to remove a blood clot. Once your condition is stable, a program of therapy will be designed to help you regain whatever function may have been lost. Depending on the location of the stroke, you may have trouble with the use of your limbs, with speech, with memory or almost anything.

What Next?

Sometimes the plaque buildup that increases the chances of stroke occurs in the arteries of the neck, and doctors may recommend surgery to clear away this plaque. They may also prescribe aspirin to keep the blood thin and reduce the risk of future strokes caused by blood clots. Blood thinners do, however, slightly increase the risk of having a hemmorhagic stroke.

Preventing Strokes

Following a diet and exercise program that's good for your heart will also protect you from most strokes. In addition, you must be vigilant about monitoring and controlling blood pressure, which is a big risk factor for stroke. Don't smoke, which constricts blood vessels and increases the incidence and severity of many forms of cardiovascular disease.

HEART HELPER OR HEART HURTER?

To drink or not to drink…it's been a moral dilemma for centuries, but what's the bottom-line effect on the health of your heart? The short answer is that it depends on what you're drinking and how much. Red wine clearly seems to exert a beneficial effect, probably by thinning the blood and possibly by the effect of antioxidant compounds acting on free radicals. A small amount of alcohol also relaxes you, which is good for the blood vessels and your mood. More than a little, however, and the problems start. Moderately high amounts raise blood pressure, increasing the risk of heart disease and stroke. And the extra calories add extra weight. Heavy drinking can actually damage the heart muscle itself, possibly leading to heart failure. And women must be especially careful, since they are unable to process alcohol as efficiently as men.

So what constitutes "moderate drinking"? About one drink a day for women and two for men. A drink is defined as a glass of wine, a beer or a shot of straight spirits.

THE LOVE DRUG

Did you know that heart attack survivors who live alone are twice as likely to die within a year as those with partners? That men who don't feel loved by their wives have twice as much angina pain as those who do? That study after study have shown that people who feel lonely, isolated or unloved get sick more often and die at a younger age than people with strong social ties?

So what are you supposed to do—you either have close family and friends or you don't, right? Wrong. None of the studies have shown that these connections need to fit a particular mold; they just need to exist between you and a person or people whom you see frequently enough for regular companionship and in whom you feel comfortable enough to confide.

So if you find that you've become isolated, make an effort to meet new people and fill up your evenings and weekends with activities that include them. Remember, you won't just be reducing your own chances of illness and early death…you'll also be helping your new companions reduce theirs.

WHEN YOUR HEART FAILS

Heart failure occurs when the heart muscle—most commonly the left ventricle, which sends blood to the entire body—is too weak to pump as strongly as it should. As a result, blood backs up into the heart, and fluid then builds up in the lungs and the rest of the body. The heart gradually becomes enlarged, making it even less efficient. What causes this weakening of the heart muscle?

MIRACLE IN A BOTTLE?

Although there are plenty of nutritional supplements with no hard science to back up their effectiveness, coenzyme Q-10 seems to be an exception. CoQ-10 enhances energy at the cellular level, improving the heart's ability to pump blood. Although its most dramatic effect occurs in patients with heart failure, it can also be helpful for those with coronary artery disease or other cardiac problems.

Patients undergoing bypass surgery should take it both before and after the procedure. The daily dosage is 2 mg of CoQ-10 for every 2.2 pounds of body weight.

- *Coronary artery disease* can cause heart failure because inadequate blood flow adversely affects the heart's pumping ability. In addition, a heart attack may leave the heart muscle less able to pump efficiently. Many heart attack survivors go on to develop heart failure. In fact, our success at saving heart attack victims is partly responsible for the increasing incidence of heart failure—the only form of cardiac disease on the rise.
- *High blood pressure* can cause heart failure because it forces the heart to pump harder to circulate the blood. It also increases the risk of having a heart attack.
- *Defects of the heart or valves* may also be responsible. If one or more heart valves fail to open or close completely, the heart has to pump harder to keep the blood circulating quickly enough and to try to prevent blood from pooling in the chambers.
- *Bacteria and viruses* may attack the heart and cause either inflammation or actual damage to the muscle.
- *Thyroid disease, anemia and alcoholism* can all cause heart failure.

Most people are not aware that they have heart failure until one or more of the following symptoms send them to the doctor:
- *Breathlessness.* This symptom generally occurs at night or during exercise or periods of physical exertion. Fatigue and an inability to engage in previously tolerated levels of exercise are also warning signs.
- *Swelling.* Ankles and feet are the most noticeable external areas of fluid retention. Watch out for sudden weight gain. Fluid can also build up in the lungs, causing difficult or labored breathing.

ANOTHER HELPER

Omega-3 fatty acids lower blood pressure and improve blood flow by thinning blood and reducing clotting. They may even lower cholesterol and help remove fatty buildup from artery walls. Good fish sources are tuna, sardines, herring, salmon and mackerel. Avoid fish oil supplements though, which may be contaminated. Nonfish sources of omega-3 include flaxseed and walnuts.

A FEAR ATTACK?

Can you be "scared to death"? Afraid so. Although it's rare to actually die from the biochemical effects of fear on your body, it can happen. Here's how: When faced with terror or sick anticipation, the body produces adrenaline. Adrenaline puts your body into a hyperalert mode, so that you can be as ready as possible to either run or fight. Your heart rate and blood pressure can soar, which in vulnerable individuals could precipitate a heart attack or fatal heart rhythm.

Another effect of the fear is that your blood thickens, presumably to guard against uncontrolled bleeding if you should be injured in a fight. This is great if you have to do battle, but it does increase your risk of heart attack by increasing the chance of blood clot formations. The "thick-blood phenomenon" might also help explain why Type A personalities—who use adrenaline for fuel—are more likely to get heart disease.

So what should you do if you feel the fear? In a crisis, take slow, deep breaths to restore a more normal heart rate as quickly as possible. At the same time, assess the situation so that you can figure out what to do to solve the problem. If, because of stress, you suffer from a chronically high level of adrenaline, be diligent about following a relaxation program. And eat foods that thin your blood, such as ginger and garlic.

■ *Arrhythmias.* Often the heart will race or beat irregularly. If you experience either one of these symptoms and the sensation does not pass quickly or passes but then recurs, visit your doctor to rule out a serious cause.

There are different treatments for heart failure, depending on the underlying cause.

■ *Medication.* There are some highly effective drugs available that work either by relaxing blood vessels, reducing the fluid buildup, or acting directly on the heart muscle to improve its efficiency.

■ *Surgery.* Heart transplant used to be the only option for patients with severe heart failure, but a doctor from Brazil has developed a procedure that looks promising. During the operation, a section of the left ventricle is removed, making the heart smaller, thereby improving its efficiency. Currently one-quarter of the patients who undergo this procedure die, but that may be partly because only the sickest patients are candidates for this experimental operation. So far the ones who survived the procedure, however, have been doing remarkably well.

GRAB BAG OF HEART TROUBLES

Coronary artery disease may be the single biggest killer of Americans, causing nearly 500,000 deaths a year. But other cardiovascular diseases account for nearly another 500,000. Heart failure is responsible for many of those deaths, and the disorders described below cause most of the rest.

Arrhythmias

Abnormal heart rhythms result from a malfunction of the heart's built-in electrical system. This can be controlled either with medication or by having a pacemaker/defibrillator implanted. We all have occasional irregular heartbeats, and they are almost never anything to worry about. However, make sure you report repeated episodes of palpitations to your doctor, and seek help immediately if they are accompanied by dizziness or fainting. If you're not aware of having palpitations but often feel faint, dizzy or excessively tired or lethargic, also call your doctor.

Diseases of the Heart Valves

Valves are flaps of specialized tissue that prevent blood that is being pumped from flowing back into the area that it's being pumped away from. If one of the heart valves is defective or damaged, the doctor may hear a "murmur" through the stethoscope. This is the sound of blood flowing through a faulty valve. Many people have heart murmurs, but most of the time they don't affect functioning or require treatment. In more severe cases, oxygenated blood may be delivered too inefficiently to support normal activity. Surgeons may then recommend replacing the faulty valve with an artificial or porcine (that's right—from a pig) one during open heart surgery.

> ⚠️
> ### PACEMAKER ALERT
>
> If you have an implanted pacemaker regulating your heartbeat, don't hold a cell phone within six inches of your chest. The microwaves given off by some cell phones can cause the pacemaker—and therefore, your heart—to malfunction.

> ### SHOULD YOU WORRY IF YOUR HEART HOPS, SKIPS & JUMPS?
>
> Palpitations are often frightening, but are they serious? We all experience the occasional "skipped" beat or fluttering sensation, and these are generally innocuous. More prolonged periods of a racing or pounding heartbeat may be due to anything from simple stress to a life-threatening arrhythmia or tachycardia. If you have frequent episodes, ask your doctor to examine you carefully to rule out more serious conditions (such as thyroid problems or anemia). If he or she gives you a clean bill of health but your symptoms persist, see a cardiologist who may be able to identify a cardiac condition that a general practitioner has missed.
>
> Exhaust all other possibilities before you accept a diagnosis of stress. Health-care professionals are often quick to blame it for many symptoms they can't explain, particularly when they occur in women. You will need to be your own advocate and insist on having a complete workup performed by a specialist. Always see a doctor at once if palpitations are accompanied by nausea, dizziness or lightheadedness.
>
> So now for the big question...can your heart really "skip" a beat? Yes, a skipped beat is usually nothing more than a heartbeat that's occurring just a little too early to be in sync with the other beats. To reduce the incidence of skipped beats, take several deep, full "belly" breaths and avoid caffeine, alcohol and nicotine, all of which can induce or aggravate palpitations.

So what is "mitral valve prolapse?" The mitral (or bicuspid) valve separates the left atrium of the heart from the left ventricle. It is supposed to keep blood that is being pumped from the atrium into the ventricle from flowing back into the atrium. If the tissue flaps that make up the mitral valve slip slightly out of position or don't fit together tightly, blood may seep back into the atrium. If your doctor hears the heart sounds characteristic of this condition, or an ultrasound shows the problem, antibiotics may be recommended for dental and surgical procedures. Although the chances are still small, damaged heart valves are more likely to become infected if bacteria are introduced into the bloodstream.

Aneurysms

An aneurysm is an area in a blood vessel where the wall is thinner than it should be. The pressure of the blood volume then causes it to bulge out at that spot, further weakening the structure. The bulge may be filled with fluid or clotted blood. Symptoms vary depending on where the aneurysm is located. If it's in the abdomen, you may experience throbbing and pain; if it's in the chest, you may have pain, breathlessness, coughing or throat discomfort. Brain aneurysms generally cause no symptoms unless they burst. Report any unusual symptoms to your doctor and always get help immediately for sudden excruciating pain. Aneurysms can burst, causing severe internal bleeding. If caught before they rupture, they can usually be repaired. Once they burst, rapid surgery can save the lives of about half of the victims.

Spasms

Sometimes blood flow to the heart muscle is restricted by spasms in the arteries. If you suffer from angina but don't have any evidence of blockages, spasms may be to blame. Medication can control the condition, but a proper diagnosis is essential.

HELP LINES & HOT SPOTS FOR CARDIOVASCULAR DISORDERS

American Heart Association	800-242-8721; www.americanheart.org
National Stroke Association	800-STROKES; www.stroke.org
Cardiac HealthWeb	www.bev.net/health/cardiac/
HeartInfo.org	www.heartinfo.org

ALL-NATURAL PRESCRIPTIONS FOR A HEALTHY HEART

Not all substances that act positively on your heart and blood vessels were born in a chemistry lab. Here's a summary of what can be found at the health-food store and their purported benefits:

Calcium and magnesium. Magnesium plays a key role in the relaxation of smooth muscle, which makes it an extremely useful tool in relaxing muscle spasms of the heart and arteries. This mineral has also been shown to have a direct positive effect on certain types of arrhythmias. It should be taken in a 1:2 ratio with calcium. Take 400 to 600 mg a day of magnesium together with the corresponding 800 to 1,200 mg of calcium.

Coenzyme Q-10. CoQ-10 improves the functioning of the heart muscle by improving the generation of energy at the cellular level. It's particularly useful in cases of heart failure.

Folic acid. Make sure you get 400 mcg a day of folic acid to neutralize the harmful effects of homocysteine, now thought to be a key cause of coronary artery disease.

Ginkgo biloba. Most of the great press about this supplement has centered around its positive effects on memory. But ginkgo brings about those benefits by enhancing blood circulation, which also improves the functioning of the cardiovascular system.

Motherwort. This herb is available both in capsule and tincture form, and may slow and regulate the beating of your heart. If you seem to suffer from frequent palpitations and your doctor has ruled out a serious underlying cause, try this.

Niacin. High doses of niacin (2,000 to 3,000 mg a day) are quite effective at lowering cholesterol, but have side effects like flushing and skin rashes. Slow-release formulations reduce those effects, but not without introducing a problem of their own—elevated liver enzymes. Treat this supplement like a prescription drug and talk to your doctor before you add it to your regimen.

Potassium. Although we often think of sodium as the culprit in high blood pressure, a lack of potassium in your diet is just as likely to be the problem. That's because these two minerals balance each other out. Add baked potatoes and orange juice as well as bananas to your diet. In addition to its role in controlling blood pressure, potassium, like magnesium, is key to the regular beating of the heart. Heavy drinkers need to be particularly certain about taking supplements, because drinking depletes potassium.

ANTIOXIDANTS VS. FREE RADICALS

Implicated as a major player in the development of both heart disease and cancer, free radicals have been getting a lot of attention lately. And we've been hearing how antioxidants can offset the ill effects of free radicals. Of course, none of us wants to admit that we really aren't sure what free radicals and antioxidants are, so...read on.

Free Radicals

Free radicals are oxygen molecules that are missing an electron, which causes them to race about in your body, stealing replacements from other molecules.

This process may damage both the healthy cell's membrane and its genetic material, predisposing it to cancerous changes. This process also speeds up the oxidation of harmful LDL cholesterol, hastening its accumulation on artery walls and contributing to the development of heart disease.

Free radicals don't jump on-board your body the way bacteria and viruses do. They're made by your body continuously during the process by which the oxygen you breathe in is used to create energy. But exposure to unhealthy substances can promote the formation of too many free radicals for your body's antioxidants to counteract. This increases the chance that healthy cells will suffer free-radical damage. Free-radical promoters include toxic chemicals, radiation, ultraviolet sunlight and pollution.

Antioxidants to the Rescue

Antioxidants protect other cells in the body by offering one of their own electrons to the unstable free radicals, so that they don't need to steal them. Some antioxidants are made by the body itself, while others come from nutritional sources. Your best bet is to eat a variety of fruits and vegetables and take nutritional supplements as well. Don't rely only on supplements because scientists can't be sure which components of the foods are having the most beneficial impact. For example, we know that tomatoes are rich in vitamin C and that vitamin C is a potent antioxidant. So it might be reasonable to assume that you could replace the power of the tomato with a vitamin C pill. But we recently learned that the lycopene in tomatoes may be one of the most powerful antioxidants yet discovered. There is surely plenty we haven't learned yet.

Here's a list of antioxidants that are available in supplement form:

- *Coenzyme Q-10*
- *Beta-carotene*
- *Ginkgo biloba*
- *Grapeseed extract*
- *Lycopene*
- *Pine bark extract*
- *Selenium*
- *Vitamin A*
- *Vitamin C*
- *Vitamin E*
- *Zinc*

HOW TO GET MORE FROM BETA-CAROTENE & LYCOPENE

Although nobody's writing off beta-carotene as a potent antioxidant, there may be an even more concentrated one hiding in your refrigerator—lycopene, which is found in tomatoes, watermelon, red peppers and strawberries. Beta-carotene makes fruits and vegetables yellow or orange, while lycopene makes them red. A recent study found that the incidence of cancer was significantly lower in people who ate at least seven servings of tomatoes a week. One tomato equals one serving.

Flying in the face of the old recommendation to eat your vegetables as close to their natural state as possible, it turns out that the cooking process helps break down the fibrous walls, making greater quantities of lycopene available to your body. Pasteurized tomato juice (which has been heated), tomato sauce and tomato paste are concentrated, usable sources.

Along the same lines, lightly steaming carrots may make the beta-carotene more available to your body. Don't boil the vegetables in water though, because you'll be pouring most of the nutrients down the drain. Cooking them well in soup or stew is okay because you'll be eating the liquid. Lycopene seems to be best absorbed in the presence of fat, so an old-fashioned pasta sauce made with cooked tomatoes and a little olive oil may be the best way to go.

ANTI-RADICAL FOODS

Taking antioxidants in pill form may be a reasonable supplement to a healthy diet, but it's not a substitute. Since we probably aren't even aware of the existence of many of the antioxidants yet, they're only available in their natural form—food. Here's a list of excellent natural sources of antioxidants:

- Carrots
- Tomatoes
- Broccoli
- Cabbage
- Spinach
- Onions

All fresh, whole fruits and vegetables contain plentiful amounts of antioxidants, so eat your favorites. If possible, buy them organically grown so that you don't offset any of their anti-oxidant benefits with pesticides, which promote free radicals.

CANCER—CAUSES & CURES

Perceived as just about the scariest disease around, cancer isn't really a "disease" at all. It's a process that occurs in more than 200 diseases collectively known as cancers. Although they bear the same classification as a cancer, each of these diseases is very different, and some pose more of a threat than others.

Don't assume the worst before you have all of the facts about your particular form of cancer. Most are treatable and many are curable. As with so many of life's trials, your biggest enemy may be your fear of cancer in general, rather than the facts of your specific situation.

If It's Not a Disease, What Is It?

Cancer itself refers to deranged cell growth that includes the following features:

- *Uncontrolled growth.* Cells multiply in the body all the time, but there are built-in mechanisms that prevent this growth from continuing beyond a certain point. Cancer cells are resistant to these controls. So what distinguishes a benign (noncancerous) tumor from a malignant (cancerous) one? After all, benign tumors may also continue to grow until they are removed. In addition to

uncontrolled growth, malignant tumors must also have the following two characteristics:

- *Ability to invade neighboring tissues.* Cancer cells have a peculiar ability to grow into the surrounding tissues by producing special enzymes that break down the barriers between the cells. That's why noncancerous tumors usually feel so distinct from the surrounding tissue, while malignant tumors feel "fixed" or attached. This type of invasion allows the cancerous tumor to interfere with the functioning of those healthy cells, which can ultimately cause the affected organ to fail. But why can't you just remove the cancerous tumor and have that be the end of the problem? Often you can—if you discover it early enough. But cancers have a third feature that helps them guard their survival.
- *Ability to spread to other parts of the body.* Cancerous cells can also break off from the original site of development,

travel to other parts of the body, and set up housekeeping. This process is known as metastasis, and often it occurs even before the original tumor is discovered. In addition to these features, some cancer cells produce substances, such as hormones, that affect other parts of the body.

What Cancer Does

As some cells become cancerous, they make a lump that burrows into neighboring tissues, and they spread elsewhere to make more lumps.

LESSON FROM CHINA

Although researchers have had a hard time proving that any single nutrient prevents cancer, the combination of beta-carotene, selenium and vitamin E was found to be effective in a large-scale, long-term study conducted in China.

Almost every cell in your body has a function that contributes to your health and survival. The problem with cancerous cells is that not only do they not have useful jobs, but also by killing or crowding out healthy cells that do have jobs, the cancer cells prevent your body from functioning normally. This can cause

EIGHT WARNING SIGNS OF CANCER

If you notice any of the following signs, pay a visit to your health-care provider right away. Even though these symptoms are by no means proof of a serious illness, they are common characteristics of many cancers. Early detection usually improves the chances of a cure.

1. A change in bowel or bladder habits
2. A sore that doesn't heal
3. Unexplained bleeding or discharge
4. Discovery of a lump
5. Difficulty swallowing or ongoing indigestion
6. Change in the color, size or shape of a wart or mole
7. Persistent dry cough or hoarseness
8. Unexplained weight loss, especially if it occurs in conjunction with fatigue

THE MIRACLE OF REMISSION

Although it's rare, sometimes, for no apparent reason, a diagnosed, documented and authenticated case of cancer just goes away on its own. Most of these cases occur in four rare types of cancer—kidney cancer, melanoma, neuroblastoma and choriocarcinoma—but there have been instances of spontaneous remission for every known cancer. Remission probably occurs because of a sudden reactivation of the immune system.

organs that must work in order for you to survive (like the brain or the liver) to be unable to perform their vital functions. Cancerous growths can also perforate tissues inside the body, causing internal bleeding and other serious problems.

What Causes Cancer?

Two factors interact to create an environment conducive to the development of cancer. You don't have any control over the first factor, but you do over the second.

■ *An inherited predisposition or tendency for a particular cell type to become cancerous.* This is the one you can't control. Cells vary in their levels of susceptibility to becoming cancerous. For instance, although many people smoke cigarettes, not all get lung cancer. Some people's lung cells just have greater resistance to undergoing abnormal change. Occasionally, an actual inherited defect is responsible for an abnormally high degree of susceptibility. Two genes—BRCA1 and BRCA2—are thought to be responsible for some familial breast and ovarian cancer. These factors account for about 5% or 6% of all breast cancer. A gene known as RB1 causes a cancerous tumor, called retinoblastoma, in the eye of up to 95% of children with defective copies of the gene.

■ *A trigger or triggers.* This is the factor you do have some control over. Having cells that are predisposed to becoming cancerous usually isn't enough to cause them to actually become cancerous. In most cases, you also need something to trigger the malignant changes. And depending on the level of inherited susceptibility, it may take more or less exposure to the trigger for cancer to occur. For example, a fair-skinned person (who is likely to have an inherited predisposition to skin cancer) may only need to have had two bad sunburns and to have spent a total of 100 hours sunbathing (trigger) to get skin cancer. A dark-skinned person may be able to tolerate three or more times that level of exposure without ill effects. Of course, since you don't know—in most cases—what your inherited level of susceptibility is, it's safest to avoid all known triggers. For example, you don't know whether your lung cells are programmed to be able to handle 50 years of Marlboros or only 5. It's probably not worth the risk to find out.

Preventing Cancer

Although there are no guarantees that you won't get cancer, you can certainly reduce the chances. Discuss your risk factors with your health-care provider, then eliminate as many triggers as you can from your day-to-day life. Make sure that you undergo the appropriate screening tests for your age and medical history. The details of whether and when to have some of these tests is controversial, so make sure you arm yourself with information from both sides of the debate. Once you've done that, don't shy away from using your intellect to decide whether you think the test makes sense for you. Even the scientists don't always agree on which tests are beneficial.

Treatment Options

A diagnosis of cancer is not a death sentence by any means. Today's treatments are not only highly effective against many cancers, but easier to tolerate as well.

FIGHT CANCER WITH PHYTO-FOODS

Phytochemicals are compounds found in plants that appear to reduce the risk of cancer. But, because we don't know which components are responsible for the beneficial effects, only a few of the perhaps hundreds of phytochemicals have been isolated and incorporated into nutritional supplements. By taking a pill instead of eating the plant, you'll be missing out on all of the cancer-killing compounds yet to be discovered.

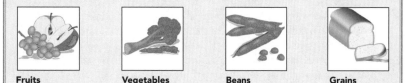

Fruits   **Vegetables**   **Beans**   **Grains**

CANCER TYPES

The following words often appear as part of the name of a form of cancer. Most cancers fall into one of the following four categories:

Carcinoma. Carcinomas develop in the soft tissues, such as the internal organs, skin, glands and mucous membranes.

Sarcoma. Sarcomas affect the bones and the tissues associated with them—muscles and connective tissue.

Leukemia. Leukemias are cancers of the blood forming white cells of bone marrow and lymph nodes.

Lymphoma. These occur in the lymphatic system, usually in the lymph nodes and the spleen.

- *Surgery.* In many cases, surgery is all that's required to eradicate a cancer. If the tumor is detected early and hasn't spread, surgical removal may be the end of it, if the cancer is deemed to be "non-agressive" by a pathologist (a doctor who specializes in studying tissues). Often, surgery is followed with either radiation therapy or chemo-therapy. This is the safest option for tumors that tend to have a high recurrence rate or have already spread. Surgeons will often remove lymph nodes that are close to the site of the tumor and some adjacent tissue and have them examined for signs of cancer. This provides information about whether the cancer has spread.

- *Radiation.* Today's radiation therapy is highly sophisticated and involves administering pre-cise doses to specific locations. Although we usually imagine a big X-ray machine delivering the zaps, radiation therapy sometimes involves implanting radioactive seeds directly in the tumor. This method concen-trates the dose where they're needed, while reducing poten-tial damage to healthy tissues.

- *Chemotherapy.* This treatment is effective against many forms of cancer, but presents the same challenge as radiation: how to kill the cancer cells while dam-aging as few normal cells as possible? One new technique for accomplishing this involves injecting the chemotherapy drugs into the tumor in a base of collagen that turns into a solid once it's in place. This reduces the unpleasant side effects patients usually experience. Ask your doctor to find out about it.

DON'T TAKE ANTIOXIDANTS?

...but only while you're under-going radiation treatments or chemotherapy. That's because the antioxidants will protect the cancer cells along with the healthy ones. Since one way radiation and chemotherapy kill dividing cells is by gener-ating free radicals, taking antioxidants will offset some of the benefits of these treatments.

!

CHEMO CAUTION

There's a fine line between the amount of chemotherapy it takes to cure you and the amount that can kill you. Check your dose every time it's administered to make sure it correlates with the amount pre-scribed by your doctor. Even some of the most respected cancer hospitals have been known to make these errors—with deadly consequences.

CANCER PHASES

Remission. Spontaneous remissions are those in which the cancer completely disappears on its own. Other remissions may be partial or complete. In the former, the cancer regresses but does not disap-pear. In a complete remission, physicians can find no signs of cancer.

Recurrence. If cancer is found following a remission, you are having a recurrence. The longer you have been in remission, the lower your chances of recurrence. Rates of recurrence vary greatly depending on the type of cancer and how advanced it was at the time of diagnosis.

Cure. When you have been in remission for a long enough period of time that the chances of recurrence are calculated to be extremely low, you are said to be cured. The time frame varies depending on the type of cancer. Some cancers rarely recur after two years in com-plete remission, others recur commonly within a 10-year time frame.

BREAST CANCER SCREENING

Mammograms
Hormone replacement therapy (HRT) can affect mammogram results, according to David Dershaw, MD, director of breast imaging, Memorial Sloan-Kettering Cancer Center, New York City. Supplemental estrogen makes breasts unusu-ally dense and lumpy for a small percentage of women. That makes tumors hard to spot. *If you're on HRT:* Ask your doctor about stopping it 12 weeks before the mammo-gram. Otherwise, tell the tech-nician that you're on HRT. *Caution:* Do not go off HRT without your doctor's consent.

Laser Breast Cancer Screening
A new, painless screening test generates a three-dimensional image without compressing the breast and without radia-tion, reports Jennifer Harvey, MD, associate professor of radiology, University of Virginia Health System, Charlottesville. It may help detect tumors that are not clear on a mammo-gram. The test may also pro-vide more effective imaging of dense breasts, which are hard to image with mammog-raphy. The technique is being tested by the Food and Drug Administration.

Experimental Treatments

Sometimes the conventional treatments—surgery, chemotherapy, radiation—don't work well enough to cure you. If that turns out to be the case, you may have more options than you think.

■ *Experimental treatments.* The difference between experimental and alternative therapies is that the former are being researched by mainstream scientists, whereas many of those same researchers consider the latter unlikely to be effective. Experimental therapies have either not yet been approved for treatment of cancer at all or have been approved only for particular cancers. For example, bone marrow transplantation is considered to be an effective treatment for leukemia, but is still experimental in the treatment of advanced breast cancer. Biologic therapy is also under investigation, and includes the use of monoclonal antibodies, interferons and interleukins. Angiogenesis inhibitors—agents that prevent cancer cells from establishing or maintaining their blood supply—are also under investigation. So far, only mice with cancer have benefited, but humans may well be next.

■ *Clinical trials.* Experimental therapies are evaluated by a rigorous process that culminates in what are known as clinical trials. During this phase, the treatment is tested in humans. There is an expectation, based on the results of laboratory research and animal experiments, that the therapy will be reasonably safe and effective. If your form of cancer has not responded well to other treatments, consider enrolling in a clinical trial of an investigational therapy that targets your disease. You can get information about clinical trials by calling major cancer centers.

■ *Alternative therapies.* This is a tricky area. If your doctor tells you that conventional medicine has nothing more to offer, then presumably you have nothing to lose but your money by trying unproven remedies. But replacing effective techniques with these "cures" is another story altogether. Ask to speak to other people who have undergone the therapy. Find out what the success rate is for someone with your type of cancer at your stage of development. Make sure you read the fine print in any contract you sign with a practitioner. (That's good advice no matter what kind of health-care provider you're dealing with.) Finally, don't disregard the healing power of hope and faith. Regardless of whether a particular treatment has an actual biochemical ability to heal you, if you believe that it does, then it just might.

FISH-CURE COMPETITION

Here's the problem with turning your nose up at something that sounds too silly to be true...it might be true. That may well turn out to be the case with the notorious shark cartilage cure for cancer—although not in the form available at health-food stores.

A component of shark tissue is now believed to counteract the "angiogenic" properties of cancer cells. These angiogenic properties allow cancer cells to establish their own blood supply. If cancer cells didn't have this property, they wouldn't be able to grow.

Unfortunately, the scientists responsible for this latest research are claiming that *their* shark cartilage isn't like the other shark cartilage. They call their shark cartilage a drug, and so on. You get the idea. They're right to make a distinction between their more purified form of the fishy substance and the currently available products; but it just goes to show that there may be a grain of truth in even odd-sounding alternative remedies.

MAJOR CANCER CENTERS

Although there are many exceptional physicians and treatment centers, a few around the country offer cutting-edge treatments and are absolutely up-to-date on the latest research.

If you're not already being treated at a major center, it's a good idea to contact one of the top treatment centers listed below. Ask for the newest research information, including any clinical trials that may be under way. Then make sure your doctor is aware of any advances. Your health-care providers can also contact these centers directly with questions.

Memorial Sloan-Kettering Cancer Center. New York. 800-525-2225; www.mskcc.org

University of Texas M.D. Anderson Cancer Center. Houston. 800-392-1611; www.mdanderson.org

Dana-Farber/Partners CancerCare. Boston. 800-320-0022; www.cancercare.harvard.edu

Johns Hopkins Oncology Center. Baltimore. 410-955-8964; www.hopkinscancercenter.org

Mayo Clinic Cancer Center. Rochester, MN. 507-284-2511; www.mayo.edu/cancercenter

Clinical Cancer Center at Stanford. Stanford, CA. 650-498-6505; http://cancercenter.stanford.edu

MORE CANCER MUST-KNOWS

Although there are more than 200 different cancers, some are vastly more common than others. Here's what you need to know to protect yourself from some of the ones that occur most often.

The Basics About Breast Cancer

If all of the advice and information about breast cancer that makes it to the airwaves were in agreement, we'd all know what to do to prevent this common disease. But, unfortunately, even the experts disagree on fundamentals like mammography screening. So what do we know for sure?

- *Risk factors.* About 5% to 6% of breast cancer is attributed to the action of inherited genes called BRCA1 and BRCA2, which also cause ovarian cancer. If several women in your family have had breast and/or ovarian cancer, you can have yourself tested for the gene. For those with no direct genetic risk factors, a high-fat diet and high alcohol consumption appear to increase risk. Having a full-term pregnancy prior to age 30 is protective, as is breast-feeding for a minimum of one year. The benefits of these practices are greatest when women are youngest, with the effect slowly diminishing, until it disappears altogether in the early 30s. It is believed that pregnancy and breast-feeding cause breast cells to mature into a state that is less vulnerable to the effects of cancer triggers. People have occasionally speculated about whether there is a connection between wearing a bra and the development of breast cancer—there isn't.

- *Self-exam.* Breast self-exam is usually considered a mainstay of screening because most lumps are still discovered by women themselves. You will need to know how your body normally feels, so check your breasts carefully every month. Choose a point midway between menstrual periods when your breast tissue will be at its smoothest. Examine them during a bath or shower—the warm water will relax your muscles, and the soap will make it easier to feel smaller lumps. You can also buy a gel-filled pad that you place over your breast when you perform the exam, which makes the lumps easier to feel. Most malignant tumors occur in the upper outer quadrant of the breast. Most lumps are not serious, but always have a new one checked out by your doctor.

BREAST CANCER & TAMOXIFEN

Taking tamoxifen to head off breast cancer may be all the rage right now, but it's not an innocuous preventive measure. The drug has been used for 20 years to reduce the risk of recurrence in women who have already been treated for breast cancer and has been moderately successful. The problem with giving it to healthy women is the side effects, which may include menopausal symptoms like hot flashes and an increased risk of uterine cancer. The best candidates for preventive tamoxifen therapy are probably postmenopausal women with a family history of breast cancer and who have had hysterectomies. Premenopausal women who have the BRCA1 or BRCA2 gene may find the risks of therapy a palatable alternative to prophylactic mastectomy (having both breasts removed to prevent them from becoming cancerous). Either way, deciding to take tamoxifen requires a lot of investigation and careful thought.

A second drug—raloxifene—may turn out to be more promising. Until now used to treat osteoporosis, raloxifene may reduce the risk of breast cancer without increasing the risk of uterine cancer.

Other risk reducers include cutting down the fat in your diet, avoiding excessive alcohol, losing weight, stopping smoking and getting regular aerobic exercise.

OVARIAN CANCER NEED-TO-KNOW

Ovarian cancer is notoriously deadly, because it's usually already at an advanced stage by the time it's diagnosed. Here are some specific risks and risk reducers:

Avoid using talc. Don't dust your lower body with talcum powder. Tiny particles can travel to the ovaries where they can cause cancerous changes.

Take the Pill. Birth control pills may reduce the risk of ovarian cancer by as much as 40% by suppressing ovulation.

Breast-feed your babies. Pregnancy and breast-feeding reduce cancer risk by suppressing ovulation for a period of time. Long-term, uninterrupted ovulation is a risk factor for ovarian cancer.

Test for CA125. If you are experiencing any unexplained gastrointestinal symptoms, bleeding between periods or lower back pain, have your doctor perform a blood test for CA125. The level of this protein is elevated in women with ovarian cancer.

- *Mammography.* You may have heard the recent furor over whether screening mammography saves lives. Premenopausal women usually have dense breast tissue that makes it difficult to visualize lumps using mammography. In women over the age of 50, mammography is more useful. Although many doctors remain wedded to guidelines that recommend mammography for younger women, the evidence that it saves lives in those under 50 isn't as strong.

- *Treatment.* If you find yourself with breast cancer, the plan of attack will depend on the size and location of the lump and whether the cancer has spread. The most important first step you can take is to make sure you're being treated by a doctor who cares for at least 30 breast cancer patients a year. Research shows that you'll live longer in the hands of a doctor experienced in treating breast cancer.

What About Cervical Cancer?

Cervical cancer is among the most preventable and treatable of cancers. If you want to protect yourself, first consider this fact: Cervical cancer is almost unknown in nuns and is extremely common among prostitutes. It's not sexual activity itself that appears to be the risk factor, however, but the sexually transmitted diseases that are an all-too-frequent consequence. The biggest villain appears to be the human papilloma virus, which causes genital warts. The changes the virus causes in susceptible cells can trigger the development of cancer. This is one more good reason to practice safe sex, though condoms are a less than perfect way to prevent a genital wart infection.

Fortunately, early detection of cervical cancer leads to early cure almost 100% of the time. The best screening test is the Pap smear. But there are still some other important factors that might affect the results of your Pap smear. What you need to know:

- *Timing.* Schedule your Pap smear and pelvic exam for two weeks after the start of your period, midway between two cycles. Postmenopausal women can have the test done at any time. Don't douche, have sex or use yeast medication or any other vaginal products for two days before the test.

- *Laboratory errors.* Believe it or not, somewhere between 5% and 25% of slides are misread. To reduce the chances that your test will be incorrectly analyzed, tell your doctor that you want your slides sent to a lab that uses either Autopap or Papnet technology.

⚠️ SIGNS OF LEUKEMIA

If your child complains of pains in his or her legs or you notice some limping that doesn't pass within a few days, pay a visit to the doctor. These are common first signs of leukemia in children. Others include:

➤ Fatigue or lethargy

➤ Anemia and pale skin

➤ Breathlessness

➤ Bruising and/or bleeding

➤ Petechiae (little purple spots on the skin of arms and legs)

Also, if your child just doesn't seem "well," make sure the doctor orders a blood test.

Preventatives for Colorectal Cancer

Although poor eating habits aren't the only cause of cancers of the colon and rectum, something about our high-fat, low-fiber American diet certainly seems to be a trigger for those who have a genetic predisposition. Scientists are almost certain of this fact, in part because immigrants who come from countries with low rates of these cancers get

---

COLONOSCOPY VS. SIGMOIDOSCOPY

Colonoscopy picks up more early signs of colon cancer than sigmoidoscopy, according to Dr. Philip S. Schoenfeld, head of the gastroenterology research section at the National Naval Medical Center in Bethesda, MD.

Colonoscopy allows doctors to inspect the entire three- to four-foot length of the colon, whereas sigmoidoscopy reaches only 25 inches. A study of 300 people who received a sigmoidoscopy found that 5% had advanced precancerous polyps and 20% had early precancerous polyps too high in the colon to be found by sigmoidoscopy, but detectable by colonoscopy.

♥ RARE VS. WELL-DONE

If you like your steak rare, you can indulge yourself without any guilt. A recent study found that people who ate meat cooked well-done had three times the rate of stomach cancer as those who preferred it rare or medium rare. Cooking it to the well-done stage is thought to be responsible for the formation of cancer-causing substances.

them at the same rate that we do once they adopt our lifestyle. Here are some things to keep in mind as you make your food and exercise choices:

■ *Fresh fruits and vegetables* contain vitamins, minerals and other substances that protect us from free-radical damage. Beta-carotene, lycopene, selenium, calcium and vitamin C may be particularly beneficial. But don't rely on supplements alone for these nutrients. Whole foods contain many other beneficial compounds not available in pill form.

■ *Fiber* keeps food moving through the colon quickly, preventing carcinogens from staying in contact with the bowel wall for too long a period of time. Fiber also prevents constipation, which reduces inflammation and irritation of the colon and rectum, both of which are risk factors for colorectal cancer.

■ *Exercise* speeds up your metabolism, including the rate at which food moves through your digestive tract.

■ *Fat* moves slowly through the colon, and much of the most damaging fat—the saturated kind—is found in red meat, which is difficult to digest. Make sure you eat plenty of fruits, vegetables and fiber along with any meat to help move it through your system more quickly.

STEP-BY-STEP GUIDE TO AVOIDING CANCER

Since susceptible cells usually require an extra push before becoming cancerous, you can reduce your risk by avoiding the known triggers.

Alcohol. Heavy drinking depresses the immune system and actively contributes to the development of cancers of the mouth, liver and breast. Have no more than one drink a day if you're a woman and two drinks a day if you're a man. And don't drink in binges.

Poor diet. An unhealthy diet deprives your body of nutrients that fight the growth of cancerous cells. A poor diet may even include foods that are considered to be cancer promoters. Avoid processed foods, and eat a diet that includes lots of fruits and vegetables.

Tobacco. All tobacco products cause cancer, not just cigarettes. Pipes, cigars and cigarettes cause mouth and throat cancer in addition to lung cancer. Chewing tobacco causes cancer of the mouth. And smoking contributes to many other cancers as well.

Toxins. You can't avoid all toxins, but try to minimize your exposure by avoiding anything your common sense tells you may not be healthy. If you're not sure about the safety of an item that's part of your daily life, do some research.

Stress. Chronic stress can compromise the functioning of your immune system, possibly affecting the body's natural ability to fight cancer. If do-it-yourself relaxation techniques don't help you unwind, sign up for a program that provides hands-on guidance.

Sunlight. Too much sun causes skin cancer, and may contribute to other types of cancer, too. Overexposure to ultraviolet light is thought to suppress the immune system, compromising its ability to control the growth of cancerous cells.

FOODS THAT FIGHT PROSTATE CANCER

It's now clear that a low-fat diet helps prevent prostate cancer. In addition, certain foods are beneficial, says Dr. Duane Baldwin, former chief resident urologist, Loma Linda University School of Medicine, Loma Linda, California.

➤ **Allicin.** Use garlic in pasta sauces and stir-frys.

➤ **Citrus fruits.** Oranges, lemons, etc., are loaded with *pectin*, a fiber that fights cancer.

➤ **Gluten.** In a recent study, men who ate gluten-based meat substitutes were two-thirds less likely to have an elevated level of PSA (prostate-specific antigen).

➤ **Omega-3 fatty acids.** *Sources:* Salmon, mackerel and other cold-water fish.

➤ **Selenium.** In a recent study, men who took selenium supplements had a lower risk for prostate cancer. *Good source:* Brazil nuts.

➤ **Soy.** Tofu, tempeh, miso and other soy foods contain *genistein* and other isoflavones, compounds that retard the growth of cancer cells.

➤ **Tomatoes.** They're rich in *lycopene*, a pigment that develops anticancer properties once it's been cooked.

Skin Cancer Risks

Sunlight, we've learned, is quite dangerous, with the thinning ozone layer implicated as a major contributing factor. So what's the best way to protect yourself?

- *Know your body.* Check your skin regularly for new marks, moles or warts, as well as any changes in preexisting spots. Get someone you know to check your back and the backs of your legs and arms. Don't forget your scalp. Skin cancers are less common in areas protected from the sun by hair, but they still occur occasionally. Check everywhere! Melanoma—the deadliest form of skin cancer— sometimes makes its appearance as a black spot under a fingernail or toenail.

- *Stay out of the sun.* Clothing and sunscreen can only provide a measure of protection. Stay in the shade when the sun is at its strongest, between the hours of 11 a.m. and 3 p.m.

- *Protect your skin.* White or light-colored clothing and a hat are your best protection. Don't rely on sunscreen alone. It has not been in use that long— it may turn out that it doesn't provide as much protection as is thought. Finally, don't forget to protect your eyes with sunglasses. Make sure that they're dark enough to do the job and that they filter out both UV-A and UV-B rays.

- *Pass on the tanning salon.* Although they're often touted as being safer than the real thing, tanning beds are just as bad for your skin as too much sunlight. If you want to have a golden glow, use sunless tanning creams. These creams have been refined to the point where they'll give you a natural-looking tan without that orange undertone. Don't forget that years of tanning not only dramatically increase your chances of getting skin cancer, but also lead to less-than-delightful leathery looking skin and premature wrinkling as well.

Excessive exposure to sunlight isn't the only cause of skin cancer. Keep an eye on any area of skin that has been damaged, such as by burns and skin ulcers.

SKIN CANCER TYPES

Basal Cell. These cancers are very common and highly curable. In most cases, basal cell cancers do not spread to other areas, but they can cause a lot of damage to the skin if they are not removed.

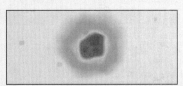

Squamous Cell. Although still highly curable, squamous cell cancer is somewhat more likely to spread than basal cell. Most commonly it spreads to the lymph nodes or lungs. All skin cancers, no matter how innocuous they appear, should be removed promptly.

Malignant Melanoma. Unlike other skin cancers, melanoma is extremely dangerous because it is invasive and highly likely to spread. Melanomas may have already burrowed deep into layers of underlying tissue, while still appearing small on the surface of the skin.

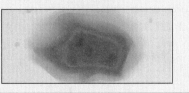

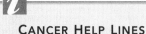

CANCER HELP LINES

National Cancer Institute
800-422-6237
www.cancer.gov/cancer_information

American Cancer Society
800-ACS-2345
www.cancer.org

MINIMIZING YOUR SKIN CANCER RISK

➤ **What is your hair color?**
Blond or red ....4 points
Brown ....3 points
Black.............................1 point

➤ **What is your eye color?**
Blue or green...............4 points
Hazel............................3 points
Brown ....2 points

➤ **When exposed to one hour of summer sun, you...**
Burn and sometimes
　blister ....4 points
Burn, then tan..............3 points
Tan ....1 point

➤ **How many freckles do you have?**
Many............................5 points
Some ....3 points
None ....1 point

➤ **Where is your job?**
Outdoors......................4 points
Indoors & outdoors.....3 points
Indoors ....2 points

➤ **Has anyone in your family had skin cancer?**
Yes ....5 points
No..................................1 point

➤ **Where did you live before age 18?**
Southern states ....4 points
States in the middle
　of the country ....3 points
Northern states ....2 points

Scoring:
10 to 15............below-average risk
16 to 22............average risk
23 to 25............high risk
26 to 30............very high risk

No matter what your risk, have a dermatologist examine your skin once a year.

RED FLAGS FOR COMMON CANCERS

Breast: presence of a lump, discharge or bleeding from the nipple, thickening of the skin, an "orange peel" appearance, itching, redness, a sore or inverted nipple, presence of a lump in the armpit

Cervix: bleeding between periods, bleeding during sex

Ovary: abdominal or pelvic discomfort, bloating or distension, irregular periods or bleeding between periods

Uterus: vaginal bleeding, bleeding between periods, cramping or abdominal pain, bloating

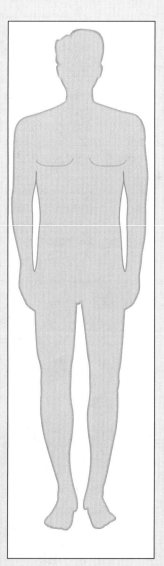

Bladder/Kidney: blood in the urine, pain on urination, frequent urination, lower back pain

Bone: pain or ache in a specific area, often accompanied by tenderness, swelling or warmth

Brain: repeated or severe headaches, seizures, paralysis, sudden change in personality, difficulties with speech, vision, or balance

Colon/Rectum: change in bowel habits, rectal bleeding, black or tarlike stools, presence of black grains that look like coffee grounds in the stool, abdominal pain or distention, weight loss

Leukemia: pale skin, pain in bones and joints, bruising, nosebleeds, fatigue, weight loss, repeated illness

Lung: persistent cough, coughing up blood, shortness of breath, chest pain, upper back pain

Lymphoma: enlarged lymph nodes, fevers, night sweats, loss of appetite, weight loss, itching

Stomach: mild stomachache, fatigue, loss of appetite, weight loss, indigestion or pain after eating

Throat: hoarseness, sore throat, difficulty swallowing, coughing up blood

Thyroid: presence of painless lump in the middle of the neck

Prostate: difficulty passing urine, blood in the urine, pain in the lower back, pelvis or thighs

Penis: presence of lump or sore (usually painless), painful urination, swollen lymph nodes in the groin

Testicle: presence of a lump, an enlarged testicle, pain or discomfort in the scrotum or testicle

Bear in mind that in many, if not most cases, these symptoms do not signal the presence of cancer. And in most cases of cancer, only one or two of the symptoms will be present, not the whole list.

Personal & Family

Body Power

How to Be Healthy

Coping with Illness

Body Power

Mind Power

Exercise

Research shows that a key to a longer and happier life is regular exercise, both aerobic (for endurance) and resistance (for strength). Set aside time at least three or four days a week for brisk walking, cycling or other moderately intense exercise. Here's all you need to know to get—and stay—in shape.

ARE YOU IN SHAPE?

The key to getting in shape and staying fit is to develop your own fitness regimen, or Personal Exercise Plan (PEP).

The goal of any exercise program is to create a long-term plan that works—one that is safe and enjoyable regardless of the season.

How fit are you? Have you been inactive in the past six months? Be realistic about your starting point. For a quick assessment of your overall condition, try these three simple tests. Ratings apply to a relatively fit, middle-aged individual.

1. How many sit-ups can you do comfortably in a minute? (Do them with your arms folded in front of your chest and your knees bent.) The answer will help you estimate the strength and endurance of your abdominal muscles. If you can't do at least 20 sit-ups in a minute, your strength and endurance may be poor; 20 to 29 is considered fair condition; 30 to 39, good; and 40 or more, excellent.

2. How many push-ups can you complete in a minute? (Remember to keep your arms and legs as straight as possible when you do them.) This is a test of your upper body's muscular strength. Less than 16 push-ups a minute suggests poor condition; 16 to 23, fair; 24 to 39, good; and 40 or more, excellent.

3. How fast can you walk a mile? Test your legs and aerobic capacity, using a school track (the standard is 440 yards or one-quarter mile).

Be sure to do some stretching beforehand, and maintain a comfortable pace. You should be able to carry on a normal conversation while walking—if you're out of breath, slow down. Your goal should be to walk a mile in 17 minutes (that's 3.5 mph) or less (see box).

Based on the time it takes you to cover a mile, consider yourself in one of these three categories as you launch your PEP program:

ONE-MILE WALK TEST

Minutes	MPH	Fitness
12 or less	5.0	Excellent
15	4.0	Good
17	3.5	Average
20	3.0	Fair
24 or more	2.5	Poor

20 minutes or more—*beginner*
17 minutes—*intermediate*
15 minutes or less—*advanced*.

Note: Before you begin any exercise or weight-loss program, be sure to check with your physician—particularly if you have a history of personal or family health problems.

FIND YOUR TARGET HEART RATE

With an estimate of your fitness level, you can begin to monitor your heart rate to ensure the best—and safest—results from exercising.

Your exercise activity should be intense enough to raise your heartbeat between 60% (beginner level) and 80% (advanced level) of your maximum heart rate (MHR), depending on your current condition. Working the heart will cause it to pump faster, adapt to a greater workload and become more efficient.

Raising your heart rate during physical activity is the key to improving your cardiovascular health. When the heart works harder, it raises the pulse rate to a target range, eliciting what is know as the "training effect." This is an exercise zone high enough to stimulate desirable physical adaptations, such as making the heart a stronger pump, increasing the number of capillaries and improving the oxygen-carrying capacity of the blood. But it is also a level of physical exertion low enough to prevent potential coronary problems, as well as premature fatigue and the pain typically experienced by competitive athletes.

Once the pulse rate reaches the target range, the real benefits of exercise begin. To calculate your target range, first subtract your age from 220 (beats a minute). This is your maximum heart rate. Then multiply your MHR by .6 and then by .8 to establish your target heart rate range (THR). If you are 40, for example, your THR would range from 108 to 144 (220 - 40 = 180 x .6 and .8); at 45, it would be 105 to 140.

To be sure you're getting the benefits of exercise—without overdoing it—check your pulse immediately after your workout (assuming the activity has lasted 20 minutes or more). It should fall in a target range that reflects your age and fitness level (see table on the opposite page).

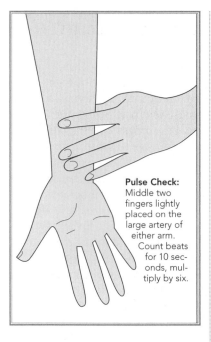

Pulse Check:
Middle two fingers lightly placed on the large artery of either arm. Count beats for 10 seconds, multiply by six.

HOW TO CHECK YOUR PULSE

A normal heartbeat is 70 to 72 times per minute. After physical exercise, it can be double that, depending on your age and fitness level. To check your pulse, place two fingers from one hand on the inside of the opposite wrist, at the radial artery, and press gently. Count the beats for 10 seconds and multiply by six to determine your heart rate for one minute. To measure the "training effect" of exercise on your heart, be sure that your workout has lasted more than 20 minutes before taking your pulse.

EXERCISE: THE HEART OF THE MATTER

Maximum Heart Rate (MHR)*		Fitness Level: Target Heart Rate Range		
		Poor-Fair 60%-65% MHR	Average-Good 70%-75% MHR	Excellent 75%-80% MHR
Age	BPM	BPM	BPM	BPM
25	195	117-127	136-146	146-156
30	190	114-123	133-142	142-152
35	185	111-120	130-139	139-148
40	180	108-117	126-135	135-144
45	175	105-114	123-131	131-140
50	170	102-111	119-128	128-136
55	165	99-107	116-124	124-132
60	160	96-104	112-120	120-128
65	155	93-101	109-116	116-124
70	150	90-98	105-113	113-120
75	145	87-94	102-109	109-116

*MHR = 220 minus your age. Do not exercise at more than 80% of this rate.
BPM = beats per minute (pulse).

WHAT'S THE BEST EXERCISE?

For well-rounded fitness, alternate or combine several types of low-impact, aerobic exercises that you enjoy. The most popular include jogging, fitness walking, bicycling and swimming. Other options include hiking, cross-country skiing, aerobic dancing, in-line skating, rowing, canoeing and kayaking. All are excellent for controlling weight, developing aerobic capacity and building stamina. From a fitness standpoint, however, each offers benefits and drawbacks. Here's a look at the pros and cons of the most popular workout activities:

Jogging & Fitness Walking
Benefits: Strengthens heart and legs and aids breathing. Excellent stress reliever. Walking has low injury potential. Minimal equipment needs (sturdy shoes). No special skills required. Easily becomes a "life sport."

Drawbacks: Does little to build upper body—proper arm swing helps, but weights or striding poles are required for serious upper body workouts. Jogging can be jarring—compared to walking, it has a higher impact on muscles and tendons, bones and joints.

Bicycling
Benefits: Excellent for strengthening and toning leg muscles. Firms up buttocks faster than jogging or walking. Minimal impact on bones and joints, although it puts more demand on hips and knees than jogging or walking does.

Drawbacks: Does little to build upper body or strengthen bones. Can create tension in the back, shoulders as well as the neck. Requires special equipment. Can be hazardous.

Swimming
Benefits: Exercises all major muscle groups of the body. Buoyancy minimizes impact on bones and joints. Builds overall endurance and strengthens the cardiovascular system. Swimming with a kickboard is an excellent way to build up legs. Best strokes for workouts are backstrokes, butterfly and crawl. Excellent stress reliever; can easily become a "life sport."

Drawbacks: Does little to build muscles or strengthen bones. Requires special skills. Can be inaccessible.

Rowing, Canoeing & Kayaking
Benefits: Excellent for building upper body. Strengthens abdominal, arm, shoulder and back muscles. Rowing (sculling) builds strong leg muscles. Also a good stress reliever.

Drawbacks: Requires special skills and equipment. Inaccessible. Canoeing and kayaking provide little or no benefit to leg muscles.

HOW MUCH IS ENOUGH?

Your exercise program should incorporate three factors: frequency, intensity and duration. Depending on how often you work out during the week, you should exercise for at least 20 to 60 continuous minutes at a time. The benefits of sustained exercise range from improved aerobic capacity and cardiovascular conditioning to stronger muscles and bones, better weight control and relief from stress.

If you have been inactive, focus on time, not distance. Start by simply *walking* regularly—15 to 25 minutes, three days a week—for the first few weeks. Increase the intensity and duration as you feel comfortable. Your age and fitness level should determine how hard you exercise.

To achieve optimum benefits without overdoing it, your workouts should be intense enough to raise your target heart rate to between 60% and 80% of maximum (see table on previous page). To get the full benefits of exercising, you should maintain your target heart rate for at least 30 minutes. Exercising within your target range for 30 minutes or more at least three times a week is the secret to achieving and maintaining fitness. For best results, many physiologists

BURNING UP THOSE CALORIES

Activity	Calories/Hour
Running 10 mph	1,200
Running 8 mph	975
Cross-country skiing	900
Jogging 6 mph	600
Walking 4 mph	300
Swimming	300
Walking 3.5 mph	270
Walking 3 mph	240
Canoeing 2.5 mph	230
Bicycling 5.5 mph	210
Strolling 2.5 mph	210

recommend 45-minute workouts four or five days per week.

WALKING: ALL GAIN, NO PAIN

There are many reasons why walking for fitness is America's most popular form of exercise. In simplest terms, it is an activity that can be pursued almost any time, anywhere, with anyone, at no cost. It demands little skill or practice, and other than comfortable footwear, it requires no special equipment. And, assuming that you're in relatively good health, the activity is virtually risk-free.

As with any program involving your health, however, check with your doctor before you begin—especially if you're over 35,

seriously overweight, have been inactive or have a family history of heart disease.

How beneficial is walking as an exercise? It all depends on your goals for getting fit and staying fit. Fitness is the ability of the body to withstand physical stress and to perform at an optimum level without injury. Being "physically fit" means that you have:

1. A strong heart and healthy lungs

2. A low ratio of body fat to lean body mass (18% to 22% in women, 15% to 18% in men)

3. Sound bones and strong, flexible muscles

4. Good posture and balance

As a low-impact aerobic exercise, walking can improve your fitness in all four of those areas. It provides the cardiovascular benefits that aerobic dancing, jogging, running and bicycling provide—without the injuries.

Biomechanically, walking is different from other exercise because one foot is always on the ground, reducing the impact on your body. When you run, for example, you land with a force equal to four times your body weight. When you walk, the impact is equivalent to only one and a half times your weight.

In short, fitness walking is ideal for strengthening your cardiovascular system, losing and controlling weight, toning muscles, boosting stamina and reducing stress.

GETTING STARTED

You're not alone if you're a bit daunted by the thought of suddenly making exercise a consistent part of your life. Most people confess that they have little energy to spare, especially for a workout. But experience shows that regular exercise actually gives you more energy, not to mention a greater ability to deal with normal daily stress.

Regardless of your age or current fitness level, set aside some time today to take a walk—even if it's only for 10 or 15 minutes. Consider it the first step in your new fitness program.

WHY WALKING WORKS

Why walk? Here are a dozen benefits of fitness walking. It...

➤ Strengthens the heart
➤ Improves circulation
➤ Reduces blood pressure
➤ Expands aerobic capacity
➤ Promotes lasting weight loss
➤ Strengthens muscles and bones
➤ Improves posture
➤ Increases stamina
➤ Reduces stress
➤ Boosts morale
➤ Enhances sleep
➤ Builds self-esteem

WHAT IS A "BRISK" PACE?

A realistic goal for walking workouts is to cover a mile every 15 minutes (that's 4 mph), for 45 minutes or so. For most walkers over 40 years old, this pace will raise the heart rate to 120 or 125 beats per minute—an appropriate level for sound cardiovascular health.

In order to stay motivated keep in mind these five pointers:

1. Maintain a positive attitude. Don't ask yourself *if* you'll walk today—but when.

2. Choose your own pace. Set realistic goals in terms of time and distance, and reward yourself for achieving them.

3. Walk with a companion. It will not only make the activity more fun, but it will give you a strong incentive to keep each other motivated.

4. Add variety. Routine needn't be synonymous with monotony. Change the course of your walks each day. Try "theme" routes—outdoor art, buildings, landscaping, neighborhoods.

5. Keep a log. Jotting down your progress will help you keep a focus on fitness. It's also rewarding to watch time and distance go up, while your waistline and stress level go down.

WARM UP & WORK OUT

Regardless of your fitness level, every exercise activity of more than 20 minutes should include these three phases:

1. Warm-up
2. Workout
3. Cool-down

Ideally, with a workout phase of at least 45 minutes, your total exercise period will span an hour, including warm-up and cool-down. Plan to spend six or seven minutes warming up beforehand. This includes strolling for a few minutes and then pausing to do a few gentle stretches. Besides loosening your muscles and joints, warming up also increases circulation in your muscles and allows your heart rate to rise slowly, avoiding unnecessary cardiovascular strain.

Repeat the procedure after your exercise, slowing down to a stroll and then stopping to stretch while your flexibility is at a peak. This will help prevent your muscles from tightening up and allow your heart to return gradually to its normal resting rate.

S-T-R-E-T-C-H

Warming up with a few stretches can make all the difference in how effective your

10 POSTURE POINTERS

For better—and healthier—posture whenever you're strolling or walking, remember these 10 tip-to-toe body positions:

➤ Head erect, eyes forward
➤ Shoulders pulled back, but relaxed
➤ Back straight
➤ Stomach pulled in
➤ Buttocks tucked in
➤ Body weight balanced over hips
➤ Hands turned inward, with fingers open and relaxed (like holding an ice cream cone)
➤ Arms swinging naturally, with about a 90-degree angle at the elbows
➤ Knees bent slightly
➤ Feet shoulder-width apart, toes pointed straight ahead

workouts become. To warm up, try these six simple stretches (do each at least four or five times, holding for 10 to 20 seconds):

1. Neck stretch and shoulder shrug. Standing with your body relaxed, drop your head forward until your chin touches your chest. Slowly turn your head, moving your chin to touch your right shoulder. Then, turn your head to the left side, touching your chin to the left shoulder.

After four or five repetitions in each direction, stand straight and relax. Then, lift your shoulders toward your ears and let them drop six or seven times.

2. Hip flex and roll. Stand straight with your hands on your hips, and rotate your upper body in a circular motion. After four or five repetitions in each direction, stand comfortably with your feet shoulder-width apart. Now extend your right arm over your head and bend your torso to the left. Hold for 20 seconds or so, then repeat the stretch using your left arm and bending your torso to the right. Repeat five times.

3. Quad stretch. To loosen your quadriceps (the large muscles in front of your thighs), stand on your left leg by holding on to a stationary object with your left hand. Bend your right leg behind you and grab your right foot with your right hand. Pull the foot upward until you feel a slight tension in the front of the right thigh. Hold for 20 seconds, and then repeat with your other foot.

4. Hamstring stretch. Rest the heel of one foot on a wall, bench or other raised surface slightly below waist level (your heel should be two or three feet off the ground). Keeping your knees and back straight, slowly lean forward from your hips and reach for your toes. Grab your forefoot or ankle and pull yourself toward your toes. You should feel a slight pull in the back of your leg. Hold for up to 20 seconds, without bouncing. Repeat with the other leg and foot.

5. Calf flex. Stand facing a wall or other support with one foot behind the other. Point your toes forward and place your palms on the wall. Lean forward with your weight on the rear heel, keeping the heel on the ground and the

CONQUERING MUSCLE CRAMP

A cramp is an involuntary muscle contraction, usually caused by dehydration, fatigue or improper stretching before or after exercise. For relief, think opposites. Greater tension in one group of muscles causes the opposite muscles to relax.

If a muscle in the back of your leg "seizes," tense the muscles in the front of the leg. If you suddenly experience a cramp in your right calf, for example, hold your right leg down with your left heel and flex the leg by pulling against the heel for about 20 seconds.

Common in thigh, calf or foot muscles, a cramp should last only a few minutes. Don't ignore it, however—it could lead to a muscle spasm that lasts several days. Treat soreness with a gentle massage and hot bath.

back knee straight. Lean far enough to feel a stretch in the upper calf. Hold for 10 seconds and then relax. Switch legs and repeat.

6. Ankle roll. Stand on your left leg, with your right leg raised slightly in front of you and toes pointed straight ahead. Gently rotate the right foot at the ankle, making circles, 10 times in each direction. Repeat, standing on your right leg and rolling your left ankle. For extra ankle flex, alternately tap the back of your heel and the tip of your toes on the ground.

With proper warm-up and stretching, your body will be prepared for the workout phase, or core, of your exercise program.

DOES FITNESS FIGHT THE FLU?

Worried about flu season? Check with your doctor or local medical center about an annual shot. Protection is especially important for young children and the elderly. Vaccination does not always prevent the flu, but the shot can diminish its severity.

Those in good physical shape—athletes especially—may think that they have greater resistance to colds and flu than the average, out-of-shape person. Unfortunately, they're wrong.

There are things you can do to protect yourself from colds and flu, but exercise seems to make little difference. Here are a few common questions people ask about fitness and the flu.

- *What causes the flu?* Flu is caused by a virus spread from person to person. When people who have the flu cough or sneeze, they expel thousands of virus particles into the air. The virus is so small that it can stay aloft in minute droplets—until you inhale them or pick them up from surfaces you touch. Colds are also caused by viruses, but the symptoms are usually confined to the upper respiratory tract and don't include high fever.

- *Why do I keep getting the flu? Why can't I build up a resistance?* Unlike other viruses, the flu actually changes from year to year. After a bout of the flu, you do build up immunity to the virus that made you ill—but when the virus changes the following winter, that immunity will have no effect against it.

- *If I get the flu, is it a good idea to exercise?* It's best to stop exercising when you have a fever or muscle aches that accompany the flu. If you have a mild virus that causes a cold with congestion, sneezing and dry cough, but no fever or aches, you can safely keep up your exercise routine.

WHAT'S YOUR WALKING SPEED?

To determine your walking speed, find the duration of your walk in the left-hand column below. Then move across the table to the column indicating the distance of your walk. The figure on the intersecting dotted line is your speed in miles per hour.

Example: If you walk three miles in 50 minutes, your speed is 3.6 (a pace of 3.5 or more is considered "brisk").

Time (min.)	Distance (miles)					
	1	2	3	4	5	6
20	3.0	6.0	9.0	NA	NA	NA
30	2.0	4.0	6.0	8.0	10.0	NA
40	1.5	3.0	4.5	6.0	7.5	9.0
50	1.2	2.4	3.6	4.8	6.0	7.2
60	1.0	2.0	3.0	4.0	5.0	6.0

HOW DIFFERENT SPORTS RATE

- *Best for cardiovascular fitness:* Cross-country skiing, hiking (uphill), ice hockey, rowing, running, stationary biking.
- *Moderately effective:* Basketball, cycling, downhill skiing, in-line or ice skating, racquetball, soccer, squash, swimming, tennis (singles), walking.
- *Nonaerobic:* Baseball, bowling, football, golf, softball, volleyball.

⚠

SETTING THE PACE: BEWARE WEAR AND TEAR

The Pitfalls....

➤ Looking down instead of ahead

➤ Leaning forward too much

➤ Keeping hand(s) in your pocket(s) or moving arms away from body instead of swinging close to sides

➤ Pointing toes outward instead of straight ahead

➤ Pushing off from the ball of foot instead of toes

...and the Penalties

➤ Harder breathing, back pain, poor posture, shorter stride

➤ Poor posture, poorer balance, muscle tension, back pain, energy loss

➤ Loss of rhythm, poorer balance, wasted energy

➤ Shorter stride, loss of momentum

➤ Loss of propulsion, shorter stride

⭐

BOTTOM LINE'S DO-IT-YOURSELF EXERCISE-WALKING PROGRAM

Week	Time (Min.)	Distance (Miles)	Pace* Min./mi.	MPH	Frequency Days/wk.	Goals for Week Hours	Miles
1	48	2.0	24	2.5	3	2.5	6.0
2	60	3.0	20	3.0	3	3.0	9.0
3	60	3.5	17	3.5	3	3.0	10.5
4	60	3.5	17	3.5	4	4.0	14.0
5	68	4.0	17	3.5	4	4.5	16.0
6	68	4.0	17	3.5	4	4.5	16.0
7	67	4.5	15	4.0	4	4.5	18.0
8	67	4.5	15	4.0	4	4.5	18.0
9	75	5.0	15	4.0	4	5.0	20.0
10	75	5.0	15	4.0	5	6.2	25.0
11	90	6.0	15	4.0	5	7.5	30.0
12	90	6.0	15	4.0	5	7.5	30.0

***Pace is approximate and should be geared to maintaining your heart rate at 70% to 75% of its maximum (maximum heart rate = 220 minus your age).**

BOOST WALKING WORKOUTS

Simple as walking is, there are basic techniques for maximizing the benefits of your workouts.

1. Start in the proper position. Stand with your feet parallel, shoulder-width apart, and toes pointed forward. Your head should be erect, with your shoulders pulled back but relaxed and your back straight. Look four or five yards ahead. Your arms should bend at the elbow, forming a 90-degree angle. Your palms should be turned inward, hands open and relaxed (as if you were holding an ice cream cone). Pull in your stomach, tuck in your buttocks and bend your knees slightly. You're ready to walk!

2. Put a swing in your stride. From the basic starting position, take one step forward by raising your left foot and planting your left heel while you push off with the toes of your right (now rear) foot. Keep the rear leg straight. With your head erect, eyes looking forward, shoulders back and stomach in, swing your upper right arm forward and your left arm back. Your upper right arm should be parallel with your forward or left leg, and your left arm should be extended back and parallel to your rear leg. As your forward foot hits the ground, straighten it, but not completely, until your whole foot touches the ground. By using your whole foot, you will make full use of all the leg muscles to absorb the impact (which is 1.5 times your body weight!). Then, start the rear leg swing by pushing off with the toes. Use your front leg muscles (thigh and shin) to guide your leg as you pull it straight under your body. Shift arms so that the forward arm swings back freely and the back arm swings forward.

3. Strike at the heel. Walking is a heel-to-toe proposition. Land on the rear outer edge of your heel with your toes pointed upward at a 40- to 45-degree angle to the ground so that the forward moving foot makes contact with the ground at the heel, not at the midfoot or ball of your foot. When you do this, your foot should be at a 90-degree angle with the shin.

4. Roll forward in a natural rocker motion. Once your heel strikes the ground, roll forward on the outer edge of your foot until you reach your toes. The round outer edge of your foot acts as a rocker bottom for what amounts to a series of continuous "forward falls" (which, biomechanically, is all that walking really is). You are now ready for the toe-off. Roll onto the ball of your foot and push off with your toes before you break contact with the ground.

5. Breathe in rhythm with your arm swing. Because walking is an aerobic exercise, proper breathing technique is as important as stride or arm swing. Practice breathing in on the right arm swing and out on the left swing. Breathe deeply through your nose, as if sniffing a rose. Concentrate on using your diaphragm, not your chest, keeping your shoulders back and relaxed.

PACING IS IMPORTANT

If you are just beginning aerobic workouts, pace yourself to exercise at 60% to 65% of your maximum heart rate (MHR) for the first four or five weeks. Move up to 70% to 75% MHR as your fitness level improves and the higher intensity becomes comfortable.

If you're walking for exercise, you'll find that you have to work harder and stride faster to reach your target heart rate.

Build your pace gradually, and by the twelfth week or so you could be cruising at 80% of your MHR—and close to 4 mph (i.e., 15-minute miles).

Walking at 80% of your MHR and 4 mph for 30 minutes is intense exercise. However, it's a reasonable objective if your primary fitness objectives are aerobic capacity and cardiovascular conditioning.

DESIGN YOUR OWN PROGRAM

To establish an exercise regimen, set specific fitness goals—for example, weight loss and control, improved cardiovascular health, muscle toning, reduced stress or speed walking for sport. Here are tips for tailoring an exercise program to your needs:

■ *Exercising for weight loss and control.* If losing weight is your chief objective, think distance rather than speed. Slow your pace (and your heart rate) and go for longer time and distance. By expanding the duration of your workouts, you'll log more miles and burn more calories. Walk for an hour at 3 mph, for example, and you'll cover 3 miles and burn about 250 calories. Walking for half an hour at 3.5 mph, you would log 1.8 miles and burn only 150 calories.

Your body begins to burn fat most effectively after about 30 minutes of uninterrupted exercise. While a 20-minute walk may be beneficial, it will not be as conducive to losing weight as a longer outing— even if you cover the same distance by walking faster.

There are several ways to increase the intensity of a workout, and therefore its caloric expenditure. The most obvious is to incorporate slopes, steps and stairways into your route. The climbing segments will accelerate your heart rate temporarily and will also boost caloric burn by as much as 50%. Walking with poles or handweights (a pound or two at most) will provide similar effects. The same is true for walking in sand, shallow water or high grass.

To optimize weight loss and add variety, alternate the duration and frequency of your workouts weekly, changing their intensity daily. For example, walk for 45 minutes on three days one week (making sure one day includes a few hills or stairways) and try 30-minute walks four or five times the next week (with added intensity on two of them). The distance won't differ significantly—in each week you will cover between 6 and 8 miles. The key is time—the longer you walk or work out, the more calories you'll burn. It's that simple.

Note: Conditioning is a consistent proposition. So what happens when you have to skip a week or two? For every week you miss because of vacation or illness, allow one week to return to your full exercise regimen.

■ *Exercising for better cardiovascular health.* If your main objective is to strengthen your heart, lungs and circulatory system, build your exercise program around shorter, more intense workouts. If walking is your workout choice, for example, plan on three or four weekly sessions of at least 20 minutes nonstop, at faster speeds (4 mph or more) and higher heart rates (70% to 80% of maximum). Add longer, slower segments for duration and to round out the regimen.

In addition to increased aerobic capacity and greater physical stamina, your measure of success will be decreased heart rates at a specific speed. At 4 mph, for example, you may initially find that your heart rate is 140. With cardio-conditioning, it could drop to 125 or less.

Similarly, as your program progresses, you will discover that it takes greater effort— more speed—to get your heart to pump 140 beats a minute. In fact, to reach either a specific heart rate or 80% of maximum, eventually you may have to do more than simply pick up your pace. Your options? Climb steep steps or hills; walk in water (from ankle to knee deep), sand or tall grass; polewalk (i.e., use ski-like poles) or carry light handweights.

You're on target whenever you have to work harder to elevate your heart rate.

■ *For peak fitness, try speed walking.* If you're fit in terms of your weight and cardiovascular conditioning, try speed walking to maximize your workouts. Speed walking provides the ultimate package of benefits: high heart rate, significant caloric burn, maximum aerobic efficiency and a full-body workout. Consider the satisfaction of striding smoothly and comfortably at 6 mph—and burning more calories than a jogger or runner. At 6 mph (10-minute mile), a runner expends about 650 calories, while a speed-walker burns about 730.

You can begin mastering speed walking in about the third month—or about three or four weeks after you start topping 4 mph regularly (see "Bottom Line's Do-It-Yourself Exercise-Walking Program" on p. 203). But don't assume that training for 5 or 6 mph is just a matter of walking faster and farther on each workout. The best approach—one that involves a variety of speeds—is to commit to four or five days a week, divided into easier, harder and longer workouts. To begin, test yourself over a two-mile course (one mile is too short for a true indication of fitness). How fast can you cover two miles? The answer (which should be less than 30 minutes) will give you a base pace.

RULES OF THUMB FOR FITNESS WALKING

1. Walking for fitness means walking at least three times a week for more than 20 minutes, at your target heart rate.
2. If you're out of breath and can't carry on a normal conversation while walking or exercising, slow down—you're overdoing it.
3. If you can't repeat the same distance at the same pace the next day, take a break—you're walking too far, too fast, too soon.
4. It's okay to take a day off between workouts, but don't take off more than three days—you'll risk losing all you've gained in conditioning.
5. If you've been relatively inactive, it will take your body about three weeks to adjust to a new fitness regimen.
6. For long-term weight loss, a pound a week is the most sensible goal.
7. A pace of 3.5 mph (17-minute mile) or 4 mph (15-minute mile) is all it takes to optimize the benefits of walking.

STEPPING OUT AT 3 MPH

One way to estimate how fast you're walking is to count the number of steps you're taking per minute. If you're less than 5 feet 6 inches tall and you take 110 to 120 steps per minute, your speed is about 3 mph; at 130 to 140 steps per minute, it's 4 mph.

If you are more than 5 feet 6 inches, 105 to 115 steps a minute is about 3 mph, and 125 to 135 steps a minute is about 4 mph. (If you're applying the clock, remember that 3 mph amounts to a mile every 20 minutes, and 4 mph is a mile every 15 minutes.)

Walking at 3.5 to 4 mph is considered "brisk" and constitutes a sound workout pace for proper conditioning.

SEVEN STEPS TO STAYING POWER

Worried about sticking to your exercise plan? Try these seven simple incentives:

1. Fun. First, find an exercise program or workout that you enjoy. If the exercise is something that you always dread, you're not going to stick with it.

2. Convenience. Pick an exercise that fits your lifestyle—something that doesn't require a lot of extra effort (e.g., don't buy special equipment you can't afford or travel to sites not easily reached, such as a club or pool several towns away).

3. Schedule. Start with little notes or visual reminders until the exercise becomes part of your routine. Make an appointment

with yourself so there's always time in your schedule to do it.

4. Timing. Try mornings. Exercising is a great way to start the day, and you'll get it done and out of the way. If you're not a "morning person," try lunch breaks or an end-of-the-day regimen that becomes something you look forward to.

5. Frequency. Exercise at least three times a week, for 30 minutes, incorporating activities that strengthen your muscles and cardiovascular system. Activities such as brisk walking, jogging, cycling, swimming and recreational sports are all valuable workouts.

6. Psychology. Get psyched. Recite the benefits of exercising regularly. By doing something you enjoy and doing it consistently, you'll feel better about yourself. You'll also see tangible results— weight loss, stronger muscles, more stamina, easier breathing, less stress. Dwell on the positives. Feel the pride, and reinforce the positive attitude by rewarding yourself for reaching certain milestones.

7. Moderation. Don't burn yourself out in the first few weeks. Depending on your level of fitness and physical activity in the past year, build up gradually to a better conditioned body. The key to exercising is consistency, not intensity. Go for the long haul— you can't compensate for past inactivity overnight.

HOW TO DEAL WITH PAIN

Exercising does have its downside. Pains and strains can strike joints and muscles. Repeated stress and shock to the body can cause stretched or torn ligaments and muscles, painful bruises and various arthritis-like conditions. Although the best solution may be to eliminate the activity that causes the problem, consider that a last resort.

As any exercise physiologist or trainer will tell you, it's important to heed early symptoms and treat any injury as soon as it develops to keep it from getting worse. Serious injuries occur when you ignore the first signs that a joint or muscle area is vulnerable. These symptoms include:

- Redness and swelling
- Pain in the elbow, radiating through arm down to wrist (tennis elbow)
- Dull or moderate pain behind the kneecap (runner's knee)
- Pain at the bottom of the kneecap
- Pain along the shin (shin splints)
- Pain with overhead motions (shoulder bursitis)
- Aches in the lower back, especially pain that radiates into the legs (sciatica)

When you experience any of the above symptoms, take these three steps:

1. Try RICE: *Rest* (temporarily discontinue the activity), *Ice* (apply cold to the affected area), *Compression* (wrap the area in a bandage) and *Elevation* (keep the leg or arm raised).

2. Switch to a different activity temporarily. Substitute an exercise that doesn't place stress on the same joint or muscle area. If you do resume the old activity and still feel some slight discomfort, warm the area before your workout and afterwards apply an ice pack.

3. If simple measures do not bring relief, consult your doctor.

AT-HOME EQUIPMENT OPTIONS

Convenience and privacy are the two biggest benefits of buying home exercise equipment. It eliminates traveling to a gym, waiting in line, worrying about weather conditions and having the world watch while you work out. Assuming that you are somewhat familiar with the equipment and have the space to store it, here's the latest on the home workout scene, with four-point summaries of the most popular equipment currently on the market:

Stationary Bike
Pros: Stable and very easy to use. Particularly suited to simultaneous reading or TV viewing.

Cons: Can tire muscles before cardiovascular functions. Benefits legs but does little for upper body. Can be very boring.

Features: Look for models with easily adjustable resistance, sturdy pedals and a seat height and saddle that will accommodate your body size. If you are worried about your back, try a recumbent model.

Cost: Basic units, $200 to $900. Top of the line, $1,200 to $3,500.

Treadmill
Pros: Requires greater balance and more concentration than a stationary bike, making it more challenging and motivating. Adjustable inclines and speeds on motorized units provide built-in incentives to "keep pace."

Cons: Consumes space, not easily stored. Assembly can be difficult. Belt can be too small and narrow for your natural stride. Motorized models can be dangerous without stable rails or sufficient belt length. Also noisy.

Features: Nonmotorized units fold for storage. In motorized models, look for an adjustable incline up to a 10% grade and speeds up to 10 mph. Higher priced models offer electronic resistance and programs as well as feedback.

Cost: Basic units, $200 (nonmotorized) to $1,000. Top of the line (motorized), $1,500 to $3,500.

Ski Machine
Pros: Excellent workout, plus high caloric burn with very little

discomfort. Benefits upper and lower body muscles, as well as cardiovascular conditioning.

Cons: Requires a good sense of balance and coordination. Takes some practice at first.

Features: Adjustable resistance. Higher priced units can be programmed and feature monitors with LED (light-emitting diode) displays.

Cost: Basic units, $200 to $600. Top of the line, $700 to $1,200.

Stairclimber
Pros: Great for strengthening thighs and hips. Provides more intense cardiovascular workout in less time.

Cons: Provides little benefit to upper body. Can lead to knee problems. May be difficult to get legs moving at the same speed. Takes time to adjust to machine's intensity.

Features: Motorized units can be set to different intensities, with electronic feedback. Higher priced models feature hydraulic systems for smooth, quiet operation.

Cost: Basic units, $300 to $700. Top of the line, $2,000 to $3,500.

Rowing Machines
Pros: Provides well-rounded workouts for shoulders, chest, arm and leg muscles. Involves more muscles than bikes, climbers or treadmills. Excellent aerobic conditioner.

Cons: Can cause back problems, possible knee strain. Can be extremely boring.

HOW TO BUY HOME-EXERCISE EQUIPMENT

Before buying any piece of home-exercise equipment, take these four steps:

1. Test equipment at the store. If you're ordering by mail, find a friend, local club or "Y" with similar units for a tryout. Go shopping in your sweats and try at least a 5-minute workout on several models to determine which ones are comfortable and enjoyable.
2. Check safety features. Are mounts and dismounts easily accommodated? Are there belts or revolving components that may be hazardous to small children?
3. Consider buying more than one piece of equipment. Switching back and forth between machines provides different benefits and helps beat boredom.
4. Check the *Yellow Pages* and ads in the sports section of your newspaper to locate local sources. And don't overlook the possibility of buying used equipment at a local consignment shop, specialty store or through classified advertisements.

Features: Some models are portable and stowable. Top-of-the-line units are equipped with electronic feedback.

Cost: Basic units, $150 to $300. Top of the line, $500 to $900.

BE SAVVY ABOUT STATIONARY BIKES

A stationary bicycle can provide excellent aerobic workouts—even better than a road bike. But don't assume that you can just hop on and pedal to your heart's content. To avoid pain or injury, follow these pre-workout pointers:

■ Check with your doctor, especially if you have any heart, knee or leg problems.

■ Raise the seat on your cycle high enough so that in the downward position, your foot just reaches the pedal with your knee slightly bent. This is the proper mechanical position for any cycling, whether stationary or over the road.

■ Always warm up and cool down with your bike set on a low resistance level. After a 3- to 5-minute warmup, set a constant pedal speed and increase resistance to your chosen level of difficulty. Cool down with a lower resistance setting for 3 to 5 minutes.

■ If you're not already in shape, start at 65% of your maximum heart rate (220 minus your age). If your heart is beating faster than that, then you're probably overdoing it. As you become more fit, gradually work up to 80% of your maximum heart rate.

■ Start cycling in 10-minute sessions, gradually increasing to 15, 20 and 25 or more minutes per session as comfortable. A gradual buildup over a period of weeks helps prevent injury to muscles and joints.

SECRETS TO A GOOD EXERCISE SHOE

Before you buy a pair of shoes for exercising or sports, check the footwear's basic features. Biomechanically, for example, walking differs from running—and the shoes for each are designed accordingly. Look for these basic features when shoe shopping:

■ *Flexibility.* With each step, a walking shoe should flex to at least 45 degrees between the heel and the walking surface. That's because its sole is thinner, with flex channels or grooves across the bottom. A running shoe shouldn't bend much beyond 30 degrees without some straining. It is designed for the smaller flex angles that occur while running. Bend the walking shoe with your hand to test its flexibility. If it's too stiff, it could be a shoe that will strain your lower leg muscles.

■ *Support.* In a walking shoe, your heel should feel like it's cradled in a cup. That's because it is. The shoe is designed to prevent side-to-side rolling. With its built-in arch support, it also provides more stability. In a running shoe, your feet will ride higher and feel less stable. That's because there's more cushioning and fewer support features designed to cradle your heel.

■ *Cushioning.* A walking shoe should give you a feeling of firm cushioning, with no tender spots at the ball or heel. The name of the game is shock absorption. In a walking model, you don't want to hit bottom, but you also don't want to sink in rather than roll forward. A running shoe should seem spongier. That's because it's designed for pounding and flatter-footed landings.

■ *Profile.* Compare a walking and a running shoe by placing both on a counter or other flat surface. The distinction between the two should be obvious when you look at their profiles. The walking shoe should have a natural, heel-to-toe curve, or rocker shape. Neither the heel (which should be beveled) nor the toe should touch the surface. The running shoe should have a flatter profile. Also, look for rounded, roomy toe space in the walking model, and a more receded (slanted downward) or tapered toe in the running version.

- *Interior.* Check the lining and insole. Look for breathable, absorbent materials. Check for seams and rough spots inside the shoe. The footbed or insole should be contoured, padded and, preferably, removable for drying out or replacement.
- *Weight.* Light is right. Your best bet is a shoe that weighs 8 to 14 oz. Pick up a canvas boat shoe or leather loafer in one hand and hold a walking or running shoe in the other. You should feel a distinct difference.

GETTING EXERCISE SHOES THAT FIT

Once you've checked the basic features of footwear, deciding which pair to buy comes down to three factors: fit (comfort), style and price. Wear your workout socks when you try on shoes (remember, your feet expand when you exercise). And don't be surprised to find that you move up at least half a size when buying shoes for exercising.

If you're not sure about the fit when buying a pair of shoes, stand in your socks on a piece of paper and trace around your foot. Compare the outline of your foot with the sole of the shoe. If it seems too short or too narrow,

try a larger size or different model. There should be half an inch (a thumbnail's width) between your large toe and the tip of the shoe.

To check width, examine the shoelace holes. When the shoe is snugly laced, the holes should be about a thumb's width apart. If the distance is greater or less than that, chances are it's not a good fit. (What about models with Velcro straps instead of laces? Not a good idea! Laces allow shoes to conform to your feet at a number of points; Velcro straps hold, viselike, as your feet expand.)

Always try on both shoes to be sure both feet are served. And, once you've worn the shoes for a while and found that they work, buy another pair just like them. By alternating pairs you'll not only prolong the life of the shoes, but you'll give them extra airing out and drying time between wearings.

HOW TO FIND BARGAIN FOOTWEAR

They used to cost about $20 and were called sneakers. But those days disappeared more than a decade ago. Exercise and athletic shoes now carry exotic names and tags that often exceed $100. It's not impossible, however, to find quality footwear in the $50 range. Here are some pointers to help you:

- *Shop around.* Prices in sporting goods stores and specialty shops are generally higher— by 20% to 40%—than in department stores. Call different kinds of stores to compare prices before you buy. If you do end up shopping in a specialty store, ask about any discounts it may extend to members of a local health club or group to which you may belong.
- *Buy at the right time.* Most major shoe makers (e.g., *New Balance*, *Nike*, *Reebok*, *Saucony*) introduce new models in January and July. That creates great bargains in December and June, when retailers slash prices on old models to make room for new stock.
- *Check mail-order and dis- counter catalogs.* If you know exactly what brand, model and size you want, mail order can save you 20% or more off retail prices—even with the additional $3 or $4 in shipping and handling charges tacked on.
- *Consider resoling.* Be sure you need a new pair of shoes (most pairs should last anywhere from 300 to 500 miles). Do the pinch test: Hold the heel with your thumb on the inside of the shoe and your index finger on the sole, then squeeze. If your fingers bounce back and leave no indentation, your shoes are

still in good shape. If the treads are worn, perhaps new soles are all you need. Check with a local shoemaker, or try *Resoles.com.* (714-751-0272), which resoles walking, running and tennis shoes for less than $20.

TAKING STOCK OF SOCKS

Silk socks are definite no-nos for exercising. And cotton socks may be great for lounging, but during workouts, the socks' tendency to retain moisture can lead to blisters and other foot woes. Look for synthetic fibers, such as acrylic or polypropylene blends, that whisks away perspiration. Among popular sports hose are the activity-specific brands *Thor-Lo*, *Ultimax* and *Wigwam*.

It's hard to get fit if you're not wearing the right size socks. Socks that are too tight can cause broken or even black toenails, and socks that are too loose will bunch up, creating blisters. When checking the label, note that sock sizes are different from shoe sizes. When in doubt, choose a size that is at least one larger than your shoe size.

For the best fit, podiatrists recommend socks with heel and toe pockets. Called *reciprocated* socks, they won't bunch up.

GETTING INTO THE RIGHT GEAR

Beyond proper footwear, what should you wear to work out? It all depends on the season and the temperature. Go layered, loose and comfortable. Your body generates a lot of heat when you exercise. Even in cold weather, you don't have to dress as warmly as you would for normal activities. (Rule of thumb: You should feel a slight chill when you first step out to work out.) A few layers of clothing will act as insulation to keep you warm during the early stages of exercising. As you begin to feel hot, you can strip off one or two layers.

Fabrics play a key role. Given its absorbency and comfort, cotton works well year-round. If you're worried about whisking away sweat, count on acrylics—particularly in socks. Look for *Orlon* and polypropylene. Wool blends, fleece and polyester pile are excellent insulators (skip wool, though, if you're concerned about moisture—it gets wet and stays wet). And what about down? It's still an incredible insulator—particularly at temperatures below zero. Trouble is, down loses its insulation properties when wet. New synthetic fillers, such as *Hollofil, London Fog nrg2000, Polarguard, Primaloft, Thermolite*

Plus and *Thinsulate,* rival down for warmth in less extreme temperatures. These synthetics are also quick-drying in wet conditions and much less bulky.

For outer layers, choose high-tech, breathable fabrics—they're lightweight, wind-resistant and waterproof or water-resistant. Nylon is a good wind breaker, but don't count on it for water resistance or breathability.

And finally, in addition to comfort, go for safety. Choose light-colored apparel when possible. In darker clothing, look for reflective features—logos, strips and panels that will reflect in the dark.

WHAT ABOUT WEIGHT LIFTING?

Whether you're lifting free weights or using a machine, use a weight or setting that lets you do 8 to 12 repetitions comfortably. If you find yourself struggling to get past five, the weight is too heavy. If you complete 10 without feeling any fatigue, the weight is too light. Experiment with each dumbbell or machine to get the right setting. You can adjust the weights upward from time to time—as long as it doesn't invite injury or discouragement.

Weight lifting is an anaerobic activity that will build your strength but do little to improve your cardiovascular fitness.

EXERCISES FOR A STRONGER BACK

Strengthening your back and stomach muscles is the best protection against back injury. Here is a series of four exercises that can help you do that. However, if you have a back problem, don't overdo any exercise (soreness is a sign to cut back), and check with your doctor before starting any exercise program.

- *Bent-knee leg lifts.* Lie on your back with legs bent and arms at your sides. Bring one knee as close to your chest as you can, while extending the other leg. Alternate the legs.
- *Flexed-knee sit-ups.* In the same position you started in for the leg lift, sit up slowly, bending forward, starting with your head. Lift up six to 12 inches and do not overarch your back.
- *Knee-chest leg lifts.* Work from the bent-knee position, with a small pillow under your head. With your hands, bring both knees up to your chest, tighten the stomach muscles, and hold that position for a count of 10.
- *Back flattening.* Lie on your back, flex your knees and put your arms above your head. Tighten your stomach and buttock muscles and press your lower back hard against the floor. Hold this position for a count of 10, relax and repeat.

DESKBOUND? STAY FIT AS YOU SIT

Here are four head-to-toe exercises that you can do at your desk to keep yourself mentally alert, tone your muscles and relieve strain:

1. Head circles. With your chin resting on your chest and your shoulders down and relaxed, drop your head forward and slowly move your chin toward each shoulder. Then lift your chin up, looking at the ceiling. Repeat this exercise five to six times.

2. Torso twist. Raise your elbows to shoulder level and slowly twist around as far right as possible. Then reverse. Do 10 to 12 turns each way.

3. Stomach slimmer. Sit erect, with your hands on your knees. Exhale, pulling your abdominal muscles in as far as possible. Relax, and inhale. Exhale as you draw in your stomach again. Repeat 10 to 20 times.

4. Heel and toe lift. Lean forward with your hands on your knees. Lift both heels off the floor, strongly contracting the calf muscles. Lower your heels and lift your toes high toward your shins (although unachievable, aim for a 45-degree angle between the top of your feet and your shins). Repeat these two-lift movements 12 to 15 times.

Repeat all four twice a day.

FIGHTING ATHLETE'S FOOT

Wet socks and damp shoes can cause athlete's foot, a painful peeling and itching ailment that can be as persistent as it is unpleasant. It's caused by fungi that live on your feet and need only a warm, damp environment. For protection, soak your feet for 15 minutes in warm, soapy water after exercising, then dry thoroughly—especially between your toes. (A half-cup of white vinegar in a pan of warm water will also do the trick.) Because athlete's foot is contagious, use paper towels, so you can discard them. Once your feet are dry, apply talcum powder.

For powders, liquids and creams that fight athlete's foot, look for brands such as *Desenex*, *Lotrimin* and *Tinactin*. If the malady is between your toes, use a liquid rather than a powder. For the bottom of your feet, use *Tinactin*.

Finally, avoid wearing the same pair of shoes two days in row, so the resting pair can dry out completely between wearings.

BEAT DIABETES

The results of a study of 21,000 male physicians indicate that exercising once a week reduces the risk of adult-onset diabetes (type II) by as much as 23%. Vigorous exercise two to four times a week lowers the risk of developing diabetes by 38%; and at five or more times a week, the risk is cut by 42%. The results, reported in the *Johns Hopkins Medical Letter*, also show that lack of exercise contributes to one of every four cases of type II diabetes.

1,060 IS PAR!

A round of golf burns about 1,060 calories—if you walk and pull your clubs on a cart for 18 holes. That's the equivalent of running six miles, according to kinesiologists at Purdue University.

CHECK THE OFFICIAL WAISTLINES

The National Institutes of Health recommends that you check your waist circumference, which is a gauge of abdominal fat. A girth of more than 35 (female) or 40 inches (male) may mean an increased health risk if your body mass index (BMI is between 25 and 29.9 (i.e., you're overweight) or is more than 30 (obese). See page 213 for how to calculate your BMI.

For more information on the government's weight guidelines and BMI chart, go to *www.nhlbi.nih.gov/ guidelines/obesity/bmi_tbl2.htm*.

FIT FACILITIES: IS THE GYM A GEM?

So you've decided to join a health club or gym to get in shape. There are many options, from elite private training facilities to hard-core bodybuilding groups set up in storefronts. Which you choose ultimately depends on how much privacy you want and on your pocketbook. Still, there are certain criteria that can help you size up any health and fitness facility:

- *Cleanliness.* Overall impression should be "clinically clean": near spotless flooring and no stained mats, piles of dirty towels or sloppy bathrooms.
- *Bright lighting.* Facility is well lit. Look for incandescent bulbs—they're easier on the eyes than fluorescent.
- *Proper ventilation.* The air should feel cool and smell fresh, not sweaty (i.e., walking into the facility is not tantamount to getting hit in the face with a stuffy blanket).
- *Ample space.* Besides being uncomfortable for workouts, a crammed layout is unsafe.
- *Well-maintained equipment.* Check the benches, belts and mats. Surfaces should not be torn or worn. Also note storage —is the equipment well positioned and organized, including the free weights?
- *Professional staff.* The staff should be obvious (i.e., easy to spot), available and eager to assist. Look for a ratio of no more than 25:1 (at least one trainer on duty for every 25 members). And be sure to check trainer certification. Thumbs up for those with any advanced degree in exercise physiology or physical therapy. Look for nationally recognized credentials from organizations such as ACE (American Council on Exercise), ACSM (American College of Sports Medicine), AFAA (Aerobics & Fitness Association of America) or NSCA (National Strength & Conditioning Association). And give an extra thumbs up if the club belongs to IHRSA (International Health, Racquet & Sportsclub Association).

HOUSEWORK WORKS

Who says housework isn't work? Consider these fitness facts documented by exercise physiologists at Arizona State University:
- Scrubbing and waxing floors demands as much energy as walking 3 mph or cycling 5 mph.
- Climbing stairs is the equivalent of playing doubles tennis or jogging 5 mph.
- An hour of housework (vacuuming, making beds, washing windows) can burn 240 calories.

There is a sport shoe for every occasion it seems and it makes sense to have more than one pair if you are active. Athletic shoe specialists will match your sport with the best foot attire. There are differences in shoe engineering design for walking, running, basketball, tennis and so on, but the simple basics must be present in any shoe you buy—especially if you are going for bargain prices.

ANATOMY OF A SPORTS SHOE

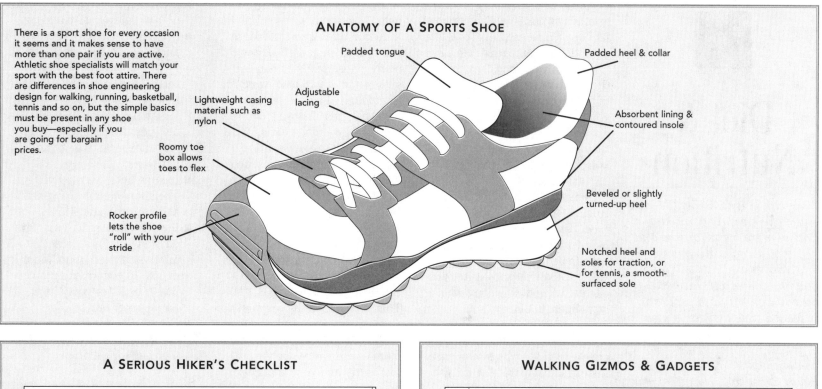

Padded tongue

Padded heel & collar

Adjustable lacing

Lightweight casing material such as nylon

Absorbent lining & contoured insole

Roomy toe box allows toes to flex

Beveled or slightly turned-up heel

Rocker profile lets the shoe "roll" with your stride

Notched heel and soles for traction, or for tennis, a smooth-surfaced sole

A SERIOUS HIKER'S CHECKLIST

- Adhesive Tape
- Antiseptic Cream or Liquid
- Bandages/Band-Aids
- Dog-Repellent Spray
- Elastic Ace bandage
- Flashlight
- Foot Powder
- Insect Repellent
- Moleskin
- Pain Reliever
- Plastic Water Bottle
- Pocketknife
- Shoelaces (extra pair)
- Sunscreen Lotion
- Reflective Bands or Patches
- Waterproof Matches
- Whistle

WALKING GIZMOS & GADGETS

Carry the gear to make walking more fun, and safer, too. Plan your hike and equip for the terrain, as well as whatever nature might offer.

Diet & Nutrition

What can you eat to get the most out of exercise? A balanced diet. Eating more fruits, grains and vegetables and cutting down on fats, sugars and salt will give you all the energy you need. Starting an exercise program is a good time to change your diet. After all, if you're going to get fit, why not make other commitments to your health? Before drastically changing your diet, however, talk to your doctor or a licensed nutritionist.

EATING WELL PAYS OFF

Staying fit means eating well, watching not only what you eat but how much. A diet low in fat (30%), moderate in protein (15%) and high in carbohydrates (55%) is best.

Limit the fat you consume to 30% of your total daily calories, avoiding saturated fats (found mainly in meat and dairy products) as much as possible. Each gram of fat equals nine calories. To determine the percentage of calories from fat in your foods, multiply the grams of fat by nine and divide by total calories (check your food labels for quantities). For example (from a container of "low-fat" milk): 5 grams of fat x 9 = 45, divided by 120 calories = 38% fat calories.

One of the best secrets to controlling fat intake is substitution (see "Savory Substitutes," p. 213). Low-fat cooking and eating do not have to be bland. There are a variety of low-fat substitutes you can use without forsaking your taste buds. In place of sour cream, for example, try fat-free sour cream, nonfat yogurt or cottage cheese blended with lemon juice. Instead of using oil to sauté, use fat-free commercial chicken broth, fruit juice, wine or sherry.

For baking, count on high-flavor ingredients such as fruits, vanilla and rum and orange extracts. Add pureed fruit instead of oil, butter, margarine or shortening.

CALORIES: HOW MANY DAILY?

When it comes to weight loss, diet pills and fad diets—including the currently popular high-protein regimen—seldom bring lasting weight loss.

Worse, they can damage your heart, liver and kidneys. The best thing for lasting weight loss is smart food choices. So, how many calories should you consume each day to lose weight? One pound of excess fat equals 3,500 calories. To lose a pound, therefore, you must eat 3,500 fewer calories than your body needs to maintain its present weight. Your net loss should be a weekly—not daily—proposition. By reducing daily intake by 500 calories, you can lose a pound a week (500 x 7 = 3,500).

Note: Don't go overboard. It is dangerous to drop your daily calorie supply to less than 1,000. That is an unhealthy regimen that should be supervised by a medical professional. *Best bet:* Stick with a more conservative goal—you'll feel better and your chances of making the weight loss last will be better as well.

SIX-POINT DIET CHECKLIST

Dieting can be dangerous. Crash diets and other quick-loss remedies don't last. Losing and controlling weight is a long-term proposition that should incorporate proper eating habits and regular exercise. A healthy weight-loss program should:

- Provide at least 1,200 calories a day to meet your nutritional needs.
- Include foods you like in terms of taste, preparation and cost.
- Provide a negative caloric balance (not to exceed 500 to 1,000 calories per day lower than the recommended intake) that results in gradual weight loss without metabolic abnormalities. Maximum weight loss should be two pounds per week.
- Include behavior modification to eliminate poor eating habits and improper nutrition.
- Include exercise at least three days a week for at least 20 to 30 minutes at a minimum intensity of 65% of your maximum heart rate (i.e., 220 – your age x .65 = target heart rate).
- Establish new eating and physical activity habits that can be followed for a lifetime.

WHAT SHOULD YOU WEIGH?

As a guideline for your appropriate weight (within 5 to 10 pounds, depending on your age, gender, body build and fitness level), take the number of inches you are over five feet, and if you're a female, multiply that number by five and then add 100; if you're a male, multiply by six and add 106.

Example: A woman who is 5 ft. 4 in. tall should weigh about 120 pounds (4 x 5 = 20 + 100 = 120).

SAVORY SUBSTITUTES FOR LESS FAT

Watching your weight can be more a matter of substituting food items rather than giving them up. Here are examples of quick ways to cut calories and fat.

Forget... One Serving	Cal./Fat (g)	...and Try One Serving	Cal./Fat (g)
Butter or margarine	100/12	Butter substitute	4/0
Ice cream	265/14	Ice milk	185/6
		Nonfat yogurt	90/0
Sour cream	125/12	Nonfat sour cream	30/0
Whole milk	140/70	1% fat milk	105/2
		Skim milk	85/0
Cooking oil	120/14	Cooking spray	2/1
Doughnut	175/10	Corn muffin	42/1
Potato chips (1-2 oz.)	150/10	Plain popcorn	50/0
Beer or cola	150/00	Sugar-free cola	0/0

ARE YOU OBESE? CHECK YOUR BMI

One of the many new guidelines for evaluating obesity in adults is body mass index (BMI). According to the National Institutes of Health, you're overweight if your BMI is 25 to 29.9, and you're obese (i.e., your fat tissue is excessive) if your BMI is 30 or more.

To calculate your BMI, divide your weight in kilograms by your height in meters squared. To get your weight in kilograms, divide your weight in pounds by 2.2. To get your height in meters squared, divide your height in inches by 39.37, then multiply that number by itself. (Alternatively, you can also calculate BMI by multiplying weight in pounds by 703 and dividing that figure by height in inches squared.)

If you're 5 ft. 10 in. and weigh 190 lb., for example, your BMI is 27.2 (190 divided by 2.2 = 86.36. And 70 divided by 39.37 = 1.78. Then 1.78 x 1.78 = 3.17. And 86.36 divided by 3.17 = 27.2).

If your BMI falls above 25, there's no reason to panic. However, it could be an indication that it's time to lose a little weight. For most people, 5 to 10 pounds will do the trick.

(For a quick estimate, see "What Should You Weigh?" on the previous page.)

HOW TO LOSE TWO POUNDS A WEEK

Everything you do, including sitting and breathing, burns calories. The average adult expends about 2,400 calories daily. A pound of fat tissue is equivalent to 3,500 calories. Thus, if you cut your caloric intake by 500 calories a day and consume only 1,900 daily, you could lose about a pound a week (500 x 7 = 3,500).

Now add the exercise factor. If you walk an hour each day at 5 mph (an advanced 12-minutes-per-mile pace), you could burn about 500 calories more. That makes 3,500 a week, or another pound. In short, you could burn 7,000 calories a week, or two pounds, by cutting back on your calories and exercising. In 12 weeks, you could shed as much as 24 pounds.

Chances are you would prefer a less demanding exercise regimen —say three or four times a week, at a slower pace. Then your weekly weight loss would be less than two pounds. The essence of exercising to lose weight is duration (time) and distance, not speed. Burning an extra 350 calories each time you walk 3 miles could eliminate 1,400 calories if you do it four times a week. And with a 500-calorie cut in your daily diet, you could realize almost a pound and a half a week (1,400 + 3,500 = 4,900 calories).

PACING TO BURN CALORIES

MPH	Calories Burned/Hr.
2.0	175-200
2.5	200-250
3.0	250-300
3.5	300-350
4.0	350-400
4.5	400-450

Based on 150-lb. individual walking at 0% (level) grade. For every 15 pounds over or under 150 pounds, add or subtract 10%.

HOW TO AVOID DEHYDRATION

When exercising, don't forget your body's most essential nutrient: water. You can survive for weeks without food, but only a few days without water. When you are exercising or dieting, you need more water than usual. Here are some guidelines:

1. Drink before you feel thirsty. Five to eight 8-oz. glasses of water per day (i.e., two quarts) should be your norm. If you're overweight, drink more—an extra glass for every 15 pounds of excess weight.

2. Drink cold water. It helps eliminate waste faster and reduces the body's core temperature.

3. Increase water consumption in hot and humid weather, when you perspire more.

4. When active at higher altitudes, such as when you're skiing or hiking, drink more water than usual. Thin, dry air causes dehydration. (This is also important whenever you travel by plane.)

5. Avoid beverages containing caffeine—it's a mild diuretic and may contribute to dehydration. It's the same for beer, wine and other alcoholic drinks.

WATER IS WHERE IT'S AT

You're all wet! About 50% to 70% of you is water. It courses through your veins and sustains your organs. It's in your bones—in fact, water is in every cell in your body.

Except for "sugar-free" drinks, all beverages contain various nutrients and fuels. Some contain sugar, some have salt and some provide vitamins and minerals. But by far the most important benefit from any beverage comes from water. That's why exercise physiologists recommend water as the single best drink before, during and after a workout.

Medical research shows that water serves four crucial functions in the body:

1. Air conditioner. Water helps you keep cool three ways —by evaporating from the skin as perspiration, by circulating in blood near the skin and by evaporating from your lungs when you breathe.

Drinking sufficient water is critical to the process that keeps the human body from overheating. It is also crucial in winter: A U.S. Army study showed that people who were dehydrated in the cold had skin temperatures that were 20% below those who were given adequate water.

2. Garbage collector. Water plays a key role in eliminating waste, moving solid waste through the intestines and allowing the kidneys to function.

3. Lubricator. Water is the body's natural lubricant, allowing your joints to move freely and your organs to operate properly. Without enough water, even your eyeballs have trouble functioning (they can't swivel in their sockets).

4. Energizer. Thanks to its positive charge, the very presence of water allows other chemical reactions to take place in the body. Enzymes and hormones, for example, dissolve in water and react with one another. Without sufficient water, your body has trouble breaking down fats to use them for energy. That's why dieters and exercisers need extra water.

Surprisingly, drinking and thirst do not go hand in hand. If you simply drink enough to slake your thirst, you're probably still underhydrated. And if you wait until you're thirsty to start drinking

water, you're already too dry. Every healthy adult should consume 5 to 8 large glasses—about two quarts—of noncaffeinated, nonalcoholic liquid every day. Regular exercisers should drink even more. If you exercise an hour a day, you should drink three quarts of water instead of only two. If you're jogging or walking for exercise, drink at least two ounces of water for every mile you cover.

CHOLESTEROL: GOOD VS. BAD

Cholesterol is the main blood fat in your arterial plaques. It has two primary components— high-density lipoprotein (HDL), or "good" cholesterol, and low-density lipoprotein (LDL), or "bad" cholesterol. The good kind—HDL — carries cholesterol away from the arterial walls and deposits it in the liver, which excretes it. The bad kind—LDL—deposits cholesterol on the lining of the coronary arteries, eventually forming plaque.

When you get a cholesterol reading, check your HDL and LDL levels, using these benchmarks:

- Total cholesterol should be below 200.
- The ratio of total cholesterol to HDL should be less than four (the lower the better).
- LDL levels should not be allowed to creep over 120.

HDL— KEEP IT HIGH

It's not clear how much diet can override individual genetic influences on HDL cholesterol. But research shows that eating monounsaturated fat—such as that found in almonds, avocados and olive oil—tends to keep HDL levels high. Studies also suggest that HDL can be raised by eating garlic, raw onions, vitamin C tablets, fatty fish and alcohol (possibly one reason a little alcohol may reduce heart disease). Exercise also boosts HDL.

Unfortunately, low-fat diets usually depress HDL, which is why some nutritionists recommend higher fat diets with olive oil rather than extreme low-fat diets. The real danger, all nutritionists emphasize, is saturated fat, which raises blood cholesterol and increases clotting. A 3-oz. sirloin steak, for example, has about 19 grams of fat (about 70% of calories), more than half of which are saturated. Shrimp, on the other hand, is very low in fat—4 ozs. has only 1.2 grams of fat, or 10% of calories. In short, given a choice between fish or beef, opt for the seafood!

Note: Foods labeled "cholesterol-free" may still contain highly saturated fats, such as palm oil or coconut oil, which can raise the blood's cholesterol level.

Personal & Family
Mind Power

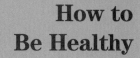
How to
Be Healthy

Coping with
Illness

Body Power

Mind Power

How to Be *Really* Smart

Believe it or not, being smart has nothing to do with Ivy League schools and everything to do with understanding the way people think and why they do the things they do. Being intelligent is one thing...being smart is something altogether different—and, in the long run, a better predictor of success. So what's the difference? And how do you get yourself from bright to brilliant?

TYPES OF INTELLIGENCE

What is intelligence? We used to think that a high score on an IQ (intelligence quotient) test meant you were intelligent, smart, even brilliant—and likely to succeed, too. Now we know that's not necessarily the case. IQ tests measure only specific abilities and assume a certain environmental background and set of experiences. But the truth is that people are intelligent in different ways, and we *all* have weak spots in our mental functioning as well—Harvard grads included.

It's all well and good to be able to learn information quickly and retain it well, but how well can you apply it? Do you have common sense? How well do you bounce back from setbacks? Do you think up creative solutions when unexpected problems arise? The answers to these and other questions—more than any IQ score, however spectacular—will predict your real-world intelligence...and your ability to succeed.

Here are the different types of intelligence and what they involve:

■ *Analytical intelligence.* Analytical thinkers are good at assessing problems and solving them. They judge ideas and concepts objectively, without a great deal of emotional involvement. They react to errors by correcting them, not by agonizing over them.

■ *Creative intelligence.* Here are our poets, artists and inventors. Creative types are not intellectually constrained to building on what already exists—they rewrite the book every time, coming up with new and innovative ideas.

■ *Practical intelligence.* It's all well and good to be full of creative ideas, but you still need to implement them in order for the bud to become a flower. That's where practical intelligence comes in. Practical thinkers know how to make something useful emerge from a dream. And they're good at separating the good dreams from the pipe dreams, too—to figure out whether an idea can make that all-important leap from cool concept to practical reality.

■ *Emotional intelligence.* Probably the most accurate predictor of success and happiness is a person's emotional IQ, which reflects how well one reacts to failure, interacts with others and processes life events. Do you berate yourself when you come up short? Or figure out where you went wrong and try again? Do you toss and turn all night over your worries? Or decide to look at them with a fresh eye in the morning and get a good night's sleep?

THE VALUE OF EMOTIONAL INTELLIGENCE

If you want to increase your emotional intelligence, you have to stop agonizing over life's day-to-day problems.

Here's a mental exercise to go through whenever you find yourself brooding: Ask yourself what the absolute worst possible outcome could be. In most cases, it's nothing dramatic, let alone disastrous. If you get fired from your job, you're being freed up to explore a new opportunity. Financial troubles? It's a chance to reevaluate your spending patterns and priorities and make changes that will ensure greater long-term security.

People with high emotional intelligence don't fret. Look for the challenge in the change, and rise to the occasion.

FOR FURTHER READING

Emotional Intelligence, Daniel Goleman, Bantam Books, Inc.

How to Think Like Leonardo Da Vinci: Seven Steps to Genius Every Day, Michael J. Gelb, Dell Publishing Company, Inc.

The Complete Idiot's Guide to Improving Your IQ, Richard G. Pellegrino and Michael J. Politis, Macmillan General Reference

Leadership IQ, Emmett C. Murphy, Mass Market Paperback

Test Your Lateral Thinking IQ, Paul Sloane, Sterling Publishing

A BETTER BRAIN, A KEENER MIND

What is the difference between your mind and your brain? There are two sides to mental functioning—the structure, substances and physical events (the brain, nerves, electrical impulses, hormones) and consciousness, feeling and reasoning (the mind). In order to be at your brainy best, both your brain and your mind need to work at an optimum level. Almost anyone can advance from good to superior with some willpower and a plan. You can improve your brain, make it function more efficiently and make it more versatile and more creative. But how?

Fueling the Brain

Just as with every other part of your body, your brain doesn't work at its peak unless you power it properly. First, exercise. Getting a good blood supply to the brain is crucial to optimum functioning. Exercise achieves this by circulating a large volume of blood quickly and improving peripheral blood flow. This encourages your body to create more capillaries, which increases the oxygenation level of the brain. A better blood supply also leads to an increase in the size, or surface area, of the brain. Coupled with lots of intellectual exercise, physical exercise will improve your mental capabilities. Choose a form of aerobic exercise that you enjoy and stay with it—at least 20 to 30 minutes three or four times a week.

A healthy, well-balanced diet is crucial, too. Macronutrients (sugars, fats and proteins) and micronutrients (vitamins and minerals) help fuel the brain with energy that can be used immediately. They are also necessary to maintain the health of the structures of the brain, nerves and blood vessels.

Develop Your Mind Muscle

Being a good learner may not guarantee success, but an agile mind that absorbs and processes information quickly and accurately certainly doesn't hurt. You'll be happy to know that you don't have to be born brilliant; those skills can be developed. So how do you do it?

- *Get organized.* It's very difficult to be productive in the midst of clutter, including emotional clutter. Get your environment in order and deal with any issues that might be holding you back.
- *Figure out what you want to do.* Take a personality and career path test and dabble a little in some areas you've never explored to see if you have a hidden talent or interest. If you

TRY SOMETHING NEW

Every time you learn something, new circuits are created in the brain. Don't fall into the trap of thinking that only young pups can learn new tricks…brain cells can form new connections at any age. Challenge your brain. Just because you weren't good at math as a child, for example, doesn't mean you won't find it fascinating—and be great at it—now.

haven't explored a subject, you know nothing about it.
- *Be self-disciplined.* Once you've settled on a new activity or line of work, stick with it and give it your all. Come up with a plan for how to become more expert. Once you begin to enjoy some success, the satisfaction of achievement will no doubt fuel your momentum.

HOW TO SUCCEED

Getting great grades in school certainly makes you feel good, but academic success isn't any guarantee of real-world success—at least not by itself. So just how do you measure success? Successful intelligence involves achieving the right combination of analytical, creative, practical and emotional intelligence, then using it to live a productive and emotionally stable life filled with interesting activities, challenging intellectual pursuits and close and loving personal relationships. For those of you who think that money is tied to greater happiness, think again. Several studies have shown that winning the lottery is just as likely to lead to divorce or depression as it is to make you happy. The happiest winners seem to be those who give most of the money to loved ones and make the fewest changes in their own lives.

IMPROVING YOUR MEMORY

Since there's a pill for everything these days, there must be one to help you remember things better, too. Right? Well, maybe. The herb ginkgo biloba does seem to help, but mainly for people whose memories are compromised by a medical problem. There's still no hard evidence that it helps the average person become any swifter. Ginkgo seems to work by improving the circulation of blood in the brain. Your best bet for improving your memory is still practice. Try exercises, such as memorizing poetry, to improve your skill.

You & Your Children

We all want our children to do well academically, because we tend to equate success in school with success in life. But good grades are only half the story when it comes to having a secure future. You want your child to develop a versatile mind, high moral standards, good intuition, a big heart and the ability to withstand adversity. But how do you help your children become good—truly successful—adults?

INTELLECTUAL DEVELOPMENT

What does it take for your children to develop to their fullest potential? Maybe not what you think. It has become very popular for parents to start "teaching" their children even before they're out of the womb, but is the practice sensible or just silly? Certainly babies seem to be particularly drawn to their mothers' voices, most likely because it's a familiar sound—though no longer muffled. Beyond that, it's difficult to say whether babies would benefit from having stories or music sent through speakers via their mother's belly to their tiny ears.

Early Development

What happens *after* the baby is born is much more important, but hyperstimulation isn't necessary for optimum development. You want your baby to be a bundle of joy, not a bundle of nerves. So what should you do to aid your baby's development?

- *Talk to your baby.* Face-to-face interaction and direct eye contact are the best ways to teach your baby how to communicate verbally. Many new parents make the mistake of not talking to their new babies because the babies can't talk back—at least not yet. Babies, however, are particularly receptive to higher pitched voices, repetition and rhyming sounds. In almost every culture in the world, mothers instinctively raise their voices, look directly at their babies and say the same phrase two or three times. "Look at the little doggie, look at the little doggie, Maggie." This system is perfect for teaching babies how to speak.

- *Play music.* Almost all babies love music, and certainly music develops a specific part of the brain. Children who hear a great deal of complicated music (like classical) and who learn how to play an instrument also seem to be better at math. Playing an instrument also develops dexterity and fine motor coordination. Although children should be listening to music from birth, they can't learn to play an instrument before they have developed a certain level of coordination—at perhaps the age of five or six, depending on the child. Don't push it too early in the hope that they'll get a jump-start on all the other kids on the waiting list for a hard-to-get-into preschool.

- *Cuddle, cuddle, cuddle.* Babies need to be touched, smiled at, held and cuddled *a lot* in order to develop normally. You may have read recently in the news that children adopted from orphanages in countries where they did not receive enough attention don't bond normally

★ BEST BEDTIME RITUAL

We all know that reading is one of the keys to the development of an active intellect, but how can you make it part of your child's daily ritual? Set bedtime at a half hour before you want your kids to go to sleep, then let them read in bed. Make sure that each child has a reading light and let them choose books that appeal to them. Read stories to children who are too young to read to themselves, but don't let endless story time become a tactic for delaying lights out. Tired children don't learn as well and have less energy than kids who are well rested. And to reinforce the idea that reading is fun and worthwhile, make sure your children see you doing plenty of reading.

with their adoptive families, are often destructive and disruptive and don't know how to give or receive affection. These emotional skills are just as important to your child's success and happiness in life as intellectual skills, and possibly more so.

- *Provide "toys."* Babies who are developed enough to hold or grab an object like playing with toys. But what's a toy? Although many parents spend scads of money on "educational" and expensive toys for infants, you certainly don't need to. Anything that holds the baby's interest will do. A good old-fashioned wooden spoon and metal bowl is wonderful, if you can stand the noise. A whole stack of pots will keep your toddler entertained for hours.

TV & Computers

Once your baby is a few years old, you might find that you can't get him or her away from the TV or video games. We've all heard the horror stories, but how detrimental is it *really*? Well, that depends on how many hours a day, as well as the type of entertainment. Actively screen the shows your children watch, and forbid programs that feature inappropriate material, including not just sex and violence, but also adult themes, off-color humor and racist or sexist jokes.

Let your children choose a favorite show or two for pure entertainment, but restrict the major portion of their viewing to shows about nature, science and history. If that's all they get to watch, they'll find it entertaining soon enough.

What about the computer and video games kids love so much these days? They're not as bad as you might think. Many of the computer games are educational in one way or another, and they improve children's fine motor coordination, too. Don't let them download games from the Internet unless you've checked the content carefully first. Video games are good for coordination, but again watch the content. Many are violent. Select games that require children to develop skills beyond those related to violence and war.

Frequency is the key issue with all electronic entertainment. One hour a day is more than enough, and perhaps a couple of hours a day on weekends.

Healthy Pastimes

So what *should* kids be doing with their time? They could be developing their minds, building healthy relationships, contributing to the running of the household and enjoying life. Here are some suggestions:

- *Spend time with siblings, friends, and family*
- *Talk to faraway friends and relatives on the phone*
- *Play games*
- *Play outdoors*
- *Read books*
- *Draw, paint, and make craft projects*
- *Invent crazy things that don't work and make a big mess*
- *Build things*
- *Play with toys*
- *Do homework*
- *Help out around the house and yard*
- *Help neighbors*
- *Take care of a pet*
- *Grow plants*

EDUCATION TAPES FOR YOU & THE KIDS

Need to learn a new language, new subject, or just become more literate? Get in the habit of listening to educational tapes while you drive or take the bus or subway to and from work. The practice doesn't have to cost a fortune either. Your local library probably has an extensive collection of books on tape. If you need to learn about a topic that you can't find in book-on-tape form, read the material into a dictaphone, then listen to it as many times as necessary to master the information. You'll benefit twice: once by reading it aloud, and again by listening to it.

If you have kids, play tapes of classic literature. You may think that the stories and language will be beyond their level, but as they listen to more difficult material, their vocabulary and language ability will improve to meet the challenge. They'll get caught up in the plot and will soon be demanding to go for car rides just so that they can find out what's going to happen next in the story.

ARE BOYS REALLY BETTER AT MATH?

And girls with words? Well… in general, yes. Contrary to politically correct thinking, it probably doesn't have all that much to do with sexist expectations or upbringing. Part of the difference can be traced to the fact that male and female brains are physically not identical. Add to that the effects of different hormones for each gender. High math performance seems to be tied to high testosterone levels, whereas high estrogen levels are related to high verbal scores. Women also do better on tests of fine motor coordination, while men are better at spatial tasks. Of course, these differences do not apply in individual cases; they are only generalities. Since we all have unique hard-wiring in our brains, there are plenty of great women mathematicians and men who are prize-winning writers.

SOCIAL & EMOTIONAL ISSUES

Being brilliant at school is all well and good, but learning how to relate to other people is of utmost importance. Learning how to love and nurture is all about learning how to help other people, therefore helping family and friends is a key step in a child's emotional development. Encourage kindness, and avoid exposure to violent television shows and video games, particularly those that combine the violence with humor. If kids think it's funny to see a person blow up today, who knows what they'll think is okay tomorrow?

Learning to Be Considerate

Most children need to learn to be helpful, to develop a sense that they are part of a community. Young children are often naturally helpful because they like to feel grown up. Parents frequently make the mistake of discouraging children who are at this stage of development from helping with cooking and cleaning because they can't work quickly and often make a bigger mess than the one that was there originally. Children end up feeling discouraged. Then, later, when *you* think they're old enough to help out, they can't be bothered. Instead, assume that even tiny toddlers can do something more useful than drawing on the walls, and give them little jobs. Increase the responsibilities as your child gets older. When you need something done, state what it is nicely, but be firm.

Here's what kids should be able to manage around the house:

- *Toddlers.* These little ones can fetch and carry—put dirty diapers in the garbage and get clean ones, bring you a paper towel to wipe up a mess and so on. They can also pour and stir when you're cooking, and they love anything that involves food preparation.
- *Middle-aged kids.* Five-to-nine-year-olds can handle chores like setting the table, dusting, vacuuming, loading and unloading the dishwasher, putting away groceries and anything else that doesn't have an element of danger to it.
- *Big kids.* Ten-to-12-year-olds should learn how to cook, do the laundry and generally perform household chores like cleaning the bathroom to a nearly adult level of skill, although it may take them a little longer.
- *Little adults.* For the purposes of household work, teenagers are adults and should generally be able to cook simple meals, do the laundry, clean up, mow the lawn and wash the car with a minimum of fuss. If they have grown up in an environment where their cooperation has been expected and appreciated, they will take on at least some of those tasks naturally and without being asked.

Remember to express your gratitude! Just because you expect all members of the family to help out, doesn't mean you shouldn't thank them when they do. And make sure they see *you* working, too!

BENEFITS OF A PET

Having a pet to care for is one of the best ways to teach a child how to be responsible. In fact, it's a perfect model for friendship and family life. The child cares for the creature and gets love and happiness in return. There's plenty of work, but love, laughter and companionship, too.

Resist the urge to pick out a pet for your child. It's really an adoption and your child is most likely to bond with a critter of his or her own choosing. So unless the choice is completely unreasonable, try to be open-minded. Once the pet comes home, insist that your child feed and care for it.

And don't fall into the trap of giving the pet away if your child's level of care isn't what it should be. Just keep sending him or her out to feed, pet or brush the animal. Your child will likely transcend fear, lethargy or whatever was preventing his or her participation in the pet's care. Eventually both the bond and the habit of caring for the animal will develop, and your child will have learned a valuable lesson about how to love.

HOW TO MAKE CHILDREN FEEL GOOD ABOUT THEMSELVES

There's a lot of talk these days about making children feel "special," and a lot of emphasis is being placed on getting kids to talk about themselves and their feelings. Not all experts agree on this approach to developing a strong self-image though. Just like adults, children feel good when they do the right thing, make the right choices, and experience success. Telling your child that he or she is special after failing a history test just isn't going to have the same effect as helping your child figure out what went wrong, addressing the real problem and then having him experience success on the next test. Children feel good when they succeed, so concentrate on helping them address their weak spots—we all have them—and remind them that you work on your problems, too. *Then* they'll feel good.

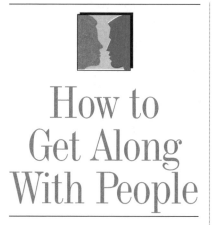

How to Get Along With People

People are social beings by nature—not loners. In fact, study after study has shown that people who are socially isolated get sick more often and more severely, and they die at a younger age than people who live, work and play with others. But getting along with others can sometimes be a real challenge. Here are some pointers for a healthier social life.

INTERPERSONAL COMMUNICATION

The art of communication has less to do with making yourself understood by other people than it does with understanding what others are trying to convey to *you*. If you master how to listen, then people will be receptive to what you have to say when you begin to talk.

How to Listen

Listening to others is a great skill. Here are some basics:

- *Look directly at the person's face and make eye contact.*
- *Smile, but not continuously or inappropriately.*
- *Sit or stand at the same level.*
- *Lean forward toward the speaker.*
- *Pay close attention. Don't look away, stare at your hands or fiddle with an object.*
- *Pay attention to the speaker's body language.*
- *Make sure that the person has finished speaking before you begin speaking or turn away.*

How to Be Charismatic

Now for the other half of the equation—how to get people to listen to *you*. People are most likely to be receptive to your ideas if you're easy to talk to. Never talk down to people, even if you are considerably more knowledgeable about the topic being discussed than they are.

People need to feel respected. Whatever it takes, make a serious effort to remember people's names. Use word associations or rhymes, whatever works.

If you're at a gathering and have forgotten somebody's name, discreetly ask someone else whether they can give you the person's name. If the worst happens, and you end up having to introduce someone whose name you've forgotten, smile and say, "I'm so sorry. I recognized your face right away, but I'm terrible with names."

Be kind. Don't let little annoyances get on your nerves enough to affect your good manners and friendly disposition. Offer compliments. Smile often when you're speaking and ask about a person's job, family and hobbies. People are interesting and you'll naturally build up a group of friends. Offer help and don't turn it down when it's offered in return. Lasting relationships are built on give-and-take.

BODY LANGUAGE PRIMER

A great deal of information is conveyed by the way we use our bodies. We are all very sensitive to the cues that come from body language, whether we realize it or not. In fact, hand and facial gestures are key components of our communication system and interact with words to convey meaning.

Open Arms & Hands: Convey openness and honesty. Folding your arms in front of your chest sends a negative signal and puts up a barrier between you and the person you're speaking to.

Relaxed Face: Furrowed brows, clenched teeth and tight lips are all signs we know well. But watch out for a lopsided smile— it's less likely to be sincere than a more natural side-to-side grin.

Eye Language: Watch for eyes that don't smile along with the mouth. And here's another clue that's more subtle, if you're watching that close: If a person's pupils dilate when they smile at you, they're genuinely happy; if you see the pupils constrict, watch out!

Lower-Body Language: People who are tense and want to appear relaxed concentrate on their upper body and face. Look at a person's legs and hips if you want the real story. If their arms and face are relaxed, but their legs and feet are tensed or crossed, believe the legs.

CAN YOU SPOT A LIAR?

Probably not as easily as you might think. Many people think that nervousness is a sure sign that a person has wandered too far from the truth, but that's often not the case. People can easily become jittery when they're under suspicion or unjustly accused. So what are some better barometers?

➤ Listen to the story. Does it make sense? Some scenarios are simply impossible, no matter how convincing the storyteller. Ask for details and pose questions. The more a liar has to speak, the more likely it is that contradictions will emerge.

➤ Look for subtle body language that reduces the person's exposure, such as bringing a hand to the face, standing sideways instead of facing you and leaning backwards rather than toward you.

Anyone who thinks they have a lock on how to spot a less-than-honest character should think again. Even seasoned bloodhounds like police detectives and judges can't always accurately separate fact from fiction. And pathological liars and sociopaths are notorious for being able to fool even lie detector machines.

EMOTIONAL CONTROL

Here's where we need to make the distinction between feelings and behavior. Controlling your feelings is nearly impossible, but how you react to them is something that—with a little practice—you can learn to modify.

How to Get Angry

Anger is felt by all of us at one time or another. That feeling of rage wells up, and before we know it, we're banging doors and slamming down phones...then wishing that we hadn't. Here are the rules for fighting fair and not having to wake up to regrets.

■ *Think before you speak.* It's nearly impossible to take back hurtful comments made in the heat of an argument. A spirited discussion about why the laundry didn't get done can easily degenerate into a tirade of personal insults.

■ *Focus on the issue at hand.* Don't bring up countless irrelevant complaints. An argument about whether to spend tens of thousands of dollars on a new car is not the time to discuss why his dirty socks are always on the bedroom floor. Stay with the topic at hand.

■ *Walk away.* If heads are hot and no progress is being made toward a resolution, leave. If you're the one losing control, stop talking and say that you need to take a walk to cool off. If it's your opponent whose grip has gotten a little shaky, say that you'll continue the conversation once he or she is calmer.

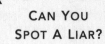

HOW TO STAY MARRIED

The key to a long marriage is not only lots of moonlit walks on the beach and romantic dinners. It's also about staying with the idea. In fact, being committed to the commitment is more likely to ensure a long-lasting relationship. Why is that? It's because feelings, like anger and infatuation, are transient, but principles endure. If divorce is a last-resort option for you, you're more likely to work on resolving your problems. Many couples go through emotionally rough periods when one or both partners feel neglected or misunderstood, but if both people are willing to try the wait-and-see approach, chances are that it will turn out to have been just one of the many emotional ups and downs that occur in every long marriage. Many people divorce believing they'll live on a constant high with another partner, only to discover that every relationship has its peaks and valleys.

STRONG RELATIONSHIPS

Positive social encounters not only benefit the immune system and cardiovascular system but also lower one's sensitivity to pain, according to Dr. Edward Hallowell, instructor in psychiatry at Harvard Medical School.

How to forge better connections with the people around you...

■ *Make connecting with others a priority.* Most of us place such a high priority on family and work obligations that we often fail to take advantage of opportunities for connecting with others.

■ *Connect in person.* Keeping in touch by phone, mail or e-mail isn't nearly as powerful as connecting face-to-face.

■ *Establish connection rituals.* People who get together regularly to play cards or share a round of golf tend to develop deep, mutually supportive relationships.

■ *Build on the connections you already have.* Look up a long-lost friend...reconcile with a family member with whom you've argued...set aside one night a week so you and your spouse can resume "dating."

■ *Prune away negative connections.* It's easier to hold onto good friends if you avoid people who treat you badly.

Travel Tips & Skills

Safe, Secure and Healthy

Plan, Pick
& Pack

**Airlines
& Airports**

**Driving
Self-Defense**

A New Look at Travel

Traveling for business or pleasure is an increasingly hectic, complex and frequently dangerous affair.

Arm yourself with these insider suggestions and know-how that help you choose where to go, how to get there, how to avoid trouble and how to survive the journey safely, sanely and financially sound.

MAKE TRAVEL TIME PRODUCTIVE

When you are well organized for it, travel time can be at least as productive as office time. Many professionals find it more so because they aren't distracted by phones and other interruptions.

Planning Is the Key

If you think you never take the right things on a trip, chances are you do not feel well organized in your office either.

To make business travel easier to plan, first work on straightening your office, so that finding the necessary papers to bring on a trip can be done quickly and efficiently.

In her book, *Taming the Paper Tiger*, author Barbara Hemphill of Hemphill & Associates offers these filing ideas for efficiency on the road:

Once you have absorbed the content of a document, make appropriate notes in your planner or calendar, which will always be with you, and then toss or file the original document.

The goal of filing is to develop a system that enables you to retrieve particular documents when needed. Try keeping separate action files and reference files, perhaps in different colors. Action files would be things like *call…discuss…write.*

For reference files, think of the circumstances under which you might need the information…or the first word that might come to mind. Be specific. Effective organization is as much about knowing what to get rid of as it is about knowing what to keep.

Examples: If you would want the document or file when writing a speech, file it under *Speech Ideas*. If you occasionally visit clients in Chicago, keep a generic *Chicago* file, with information on hotels, restaurants, contacts, and so on, as well as a file for the specific Chicago client.

Keep a file index, in alphabetical order, with cross-references to files that contain related material. Make several copies of this index so that you will have one to take with you on the road. You should always travel with a file marked *To be filed* (when back at the office).

STAY IN TOUCH WHILE TRAVELING

Travel with a cell phone for convenience and necessity. There are also many services that will page you, or even notify your cell number, if a fax is waiting. You then have the option of telling the service to send the fax to the nearest fax machine or to a modem number for your laptop computer. See *www.efax.com.*

A headset is an invaluable accessory. Most cell phones today have a headset jack, and a headset allows you to write with one hand while holding a pad with the other.

Keep Track of Messages

Stay organized by entering critical information in your calendar/planner. Then flesh out all the details in a separate notebook that is just for telephone messages.

Some computer printers are compact enough to take with you, but if you rarely print, the extra weight isn't justified. Usually you can gain access to a printer at a client's office, a hotel's business center or a nearby copy shop, many of which are open 24 hours.

Be sure to pack blank floppy disks (to transfer files to another computer) and your Windows (or other operating system) installation disk (in case you have to use a borrowed printer and need to install the appropriate drivers).

WHAT TO TAKE ALONG FOR BUSINESS

Avoid the embarrassment of a client visit where you don't have a key piece of information. Before you leave, think through what you are likely to need.

➤ Make a list of things you have actually used, or needed, on previous trips. Add items that relate to your current visit.

➤ Carry a series of individual files—one for each client, each city, each project. Use a briefcase that affords easy access to files in confined spaces.

➤ Check out portable filing systems that can be hung on a hotel room door.

SHOCK-FREE TRAVEL

Vacations and business trips are always much more enjoyable when you anticipate and avoid any unpleasant surprises.

Here, from Betsy Wade, *New York Times* columnist on travel, are some of the biggest travel snafus and the steps to take to avoid them and enjoy your trip to the fullest.

Locate Your Passport

Find your passport and look at the expiration date. If it expires within the next 12 months, get started on renewing by mail. You can renew as early as you like. If it expired in the last two years, file immediately.

Renewing your passport by mail is quick and efficient. It's also $30 cheaper and considerably less stressful than requesting a rush at the last minute. The *National Passport Information Center* can be reached at 888-362-8668. For the latest updates on dangerous destinations, check the State Department's Web site at *www.travel.state.gov*.

For Short Flights

Short trips will probably have no food service. The number of amenities will likely be even less if you have connecting short flights.

Take along food that will travel well, not spill and can be eaten cold.

Find Out About Inoculations

Yellow fever, dormant in the U.S. since the 1920s, suddenly claimed an American life in 1996. If you plan an exotic trip, check with a travel clinic. You might also check with the Center for Disease Control at *www.cdc.gov/travel* on the Web, or call 877-FYI-TRIP.

Even if you plan only a few domestic ventures, ask your doctor about your personal record of inoculations. If it is lost, assume that your shots are 10 years out of date and start over. At a minimum, the "childhood vaccinations"— diphtheria, tetanus and whooping cough—should be boosted.

When Packing, Include Your Sports Shoes & Bathing Suit

Fitness facilities are more common than ever, even in small hotels and on ships. On the Celebrity Cruise's *Galaxy*, for example, passengers work out in a health club with more machines than many land-bound clubs.

You can easily build a "fitness itinerary" by accessing popular hotels and resorts over their Web sites, where fitness centers are described in detail. Some even include pictures of the equipment and facilities.

Nonsmoking Facilities

If you are sensitive to smoke, ask for a smoke-free hotel room and a smoke-free rental car. The car rental companies, notably Budget and the American Lung

---

INTERNET TRAVEL ADVISER

Travel planning freedom. That's what the Internet offers. You can choose destinations, pick packages, study cruise ships, view airlines' schedules, book tickets and even bid on airfares, hotel rooms and car rentals. The Internet enables you to become your own travel agent, but it takes time and practice to learn it enough to work in your favor. There are thousands of travel-related Web sites. Every airline, cruise operator, hotel chain and major travel agency has its own site. Try a site like *www.travelocity.com* to get an idea of what's available. Another excellent site is *www.priceline.com*. Or enter an airline name (or cruise line, agency, etc.) in one of the search engines. Or simply enter "travel" and a destination. You'll be flooded with information. Surf the sites and be sure to save the ones that help you most under "Favorites" in your Web browser. Experienced Internet users save all the major airlines' schedules under the Favorites menu for quick access.

Want help with Web sites? Try *Travel Planning Online for Dummies, 2nd Edition*, by Noah Vadnai (IDG Books). It describes the best of the best travel Web sites including those with city plans, restaurant guides, hotel guides and even information on where to find the best travel commentaries on the Internet.

Power Web sites. Airlines and hotels publish last-minute special deals on their Web sites, but you have to hit every site to find the deals. Try *www.travelzoo.com*. This free service surfs the Web each week and compiles deals from major airlines into a single report that gets delivered to your e-mail box as a newsletter. Another site— *www.webflier.com*—also monitors airline offers. The site also offers a variety of "hot" travel sites on the Web so you can get the best deals. The well-known travel guide, *Frommers*, also has a newsletter available at *www.frommers.com*.

Physically challenged travel. Ever try to get a taxi that can accommodate a wheelchair? This Web site will help: *www.projectaction.org*. It's operated by *National Easter Seals* and offers facilities and transportation information to make travel easier for physically challenged individuals. *Feature service:* an Accessible Traveler's Database listing airport, hotel and transportation facilities that accommodate special-needs travelers.

All-inclusive travel? Typing "all-inclusive+vacations" into your Web browser will bring almost 200 vacation planning Web sites alive on your screen. Shop the Web for agencies that sound best to you, then call to determine how they gather information on the resorts they sell. If they don't visit and inspect, call one that does.

Association have cooperated to replace cigarette lighters with plastic plugs bearing a red "no smoking" sign. This is a preference your travel agent or the rental company should enter on your personal record, so it will be requested every time. If you are a smoker, be sure you know what you are getting into. With a few exceptions only—Amtrak, for example—most places ban smoking completely.

Driving in New Places

Plan to rent a vehicle with a computer navigation system. These cars are now more common, particularly in the Hertz and Avis fleets, although they cost more. Ask your travel agent to add this choice to your basic profile, too. Most of these cars have display screens on the dashboard showing maps and arrows, plus a voice-prompting system. The devices take advantage of the Global Positioning Satellite to tell you where you are. They are well worth the extra cost.

Create a 3-by-5 Card to Save Your Wits in an Emergency

Write down your doctor's home number or beeper number, the same for your dentist and the number of a neighbor you expect will be at home. If you do not know what to dial to reach your long-distance company, add them to the card. Clip to the card photocopies of your eyeglasses prescription, the front two pages of your passport and your credit card numbers. Do not carry this in your wallet.

Tickets Too Good to Be True Usually Are...

If a ticket price quoted in a tiny newspaper ad seems way too low, it is. You may get into a bait-and-switch situation, where you could be burned by a fraudulent consolidator.

To be safe, ask your travel agent to sell you a consolidator ticket or a bargain fare. The markup the agent will charge is a small premium to pay for dealing with someone you know and can trust. Also, pay with your credit card for added consumer protection. (see "Arm Against Air-Ticketing Problems," p. 233).

Prudent Advice

Travel security expert Peter Savage, author of *The Safe Travel Book* cautions...

Know what to expect. Check with the State Department for worldwide travel warnings and bulletins at 202 647-5225...or online at *http://travel.state.gov.*

Purchase an emergency medical assistance and evacuation policy. Prices start at a few dollars a day for two weeks of coverage. Check with your life and/or health insurance agent.

FIND THE RIGHT TRAVEL AGENT

Travel agencies used to be a dime a dozen, but that is changing. Airlines (and the Internet) are making the travel business more challenging and less profitable by cutting back on the commissions paid for airfares.

This is making travel choice both more complicated and more expensive for consumers. Many travel agents now charge fees for services that used to be free. Some who started charging fees in recent years are bumping up those charges to customers in order to maintain margins.

If you don't feel you're getting the service you're used to from a travel agent, chances are you're not. But with tougher competition in the market, you have more leverage than you think.

Personal or Business

Most agencies have corporate clients to ensure a steady flow of business. The more corporate clients an agency has, the better your chances for more flexible service.

The best place to start your quest is with friends and business colleagues who travel frequently. Gather one or two references from them and then launch an interview campaign.

Key Questions to Ask

- Has the agency been in business long and is it in good standing with the local Better Business Bureau? Is the agent a member

AIRLINE CLUB MEMBERS GO TWICE THE DISTANCE

Airline club memberships are a valuable tool for frequent travelers. Ranging from $200 to $400 annually, memberships are entrées to the relatively quiet private lounges in busy airports. You can store your bags, work, communicate, sleep and drink all the free coffee you can handle.

Now that almost every airline has partnered up with competitors, your club membership goes twice as far. You can use it with all the carriers in the alliance, regardless of which you're flying with.

Biggest benefit: Club ticketing agents can check you in without lines, and handle booking arrangements and upgrades quickly and efficiently. If you're bumped at the gate or enduring a cancelled flight, run, don't walk, to the nearest private lounge to get rebooked on another flight, even with an alternate carrier.

Special item: Most clubs sell day passes for $20 to $50. This might be well worth the cost during an unexpected, long delay.

of the American Society of Travel Agents?

- How many agents does the agency have and how are they trained? Will you be assigned a specific person to handle your account?
- Is there a 24-hour hotline in case you need to change your itinerary at the airport after business hours or on holidays?
- Who are some of the corporate clients? How long have they been clients?

⚠ TRAVEL AGENTS' SECRET

Travel agents make money from commissions. In recent years airlines have reduced commissions on flights. The total number of travel agencies declined immediately following the reduced commission structure, but now there are more agencies than ever according to the *American Society of Travel Agents*. To compensate for lower commissions, most agencies now charge service fees to clients, but you can get them waived, especially if you are a good customer not requesting a lot of ticketing changes. Ask your agent about waiving fees. If they don't cooperate, consider booking your own fare directly with the airline or over the Internet.

- Does the agency work with a preferred airline and what fare concessions will it be able to negotiate? More importantly, what is the agency's relationship with your preferred carrier?
- Ask the same questions about hotel chains. Some larger agencies who regularly book corporate hotel accommodations have special rate structures with some chains.
- How computerized is the agency? Do the agents use computer software to scan airline reservation systems for lowest fares? Does the agency have its own Web site? Are agents savvy about using the Internet for destination research?
- Does the agency charge service fees? If so, for which services? Are the fees waived for frequent travelers (such as corporate travel)? If so, point out that family travel generally requires fewer schedule changes. Also, ask if the fees get applied per ticket or per booking.
- Get the fee policy in writing and ask to be notified when there is a change.
- No matter how much you trust your travel agent, consider doing independent price searches on the Internet as a way of keeping tabs. If you find better prices, call this to the attention of your agent.

🕐 MINIMIZE HOLIDAY TRAVEL HASSLES

Traveling during holiday seasons can ruin the best of occasions. During the peak seasons almost 50 million travelers jam airports and hotel facilities. In winter, there are weather problems to contend with, leading to inevitable flight delays. Overbookings are at their highest, and on-time arrivals at their lowest, while both passengers and airline personnel are thin on patience. Here's how to avoid the hassle:

Ticket intelligently: This is not a time to seek bargain seats, or yours may be left in the terminal. Instead, book well in advance at a regular fare. It may cost a little more, but your chances of being stranded go way down. Reconfirm your ticket 24 hours ahead of flight time and show up at the counter a good two hours (more for International flights) ahead of departure. Most airlines will give your seat up if you are not at the gate at least 10 minutes before departure.

Beat the pack: Don't just show up at the airport early—be a day or two early. Arrange your schedule so you're traveling ahead of the pack. Also, book the earliest flight possible. According to DOT (Department of Transportation), flights before 9:00 am arrive on time about 80% of the time. Always allow time for road congestion around the airport.

Travel light: Very light. Send gifts and clothing via UPS or Federal Express. All you need is a carry-on. This eliminates concerns about lost luggage or bags that make it to connections that you may miss.

Plan to fly: When you book your ticket, get a schedule of other flights that leave before and after yours. Track other carriers as well. If there's a delay or cancellation, at least you have another option to try. A cell phone is your best tool in a crowded airport filled with delayed passengers. Experienced business travelers enter the phone numbers of competing airlines' reservation systems as well as a hotline number for their corporate travel agency.

Don't fly standby: Even if you feel lucky. Chances of snagging a standby seat during the holiday season are low. Most passengers do show up, so the "no-show" ratio drops and there is greater demand. If you have to get somewhere on a specific date and time, sacrifice and pay the full fare to ensure that other plans aren't spoiled. Also as much as possible, choose nonstop or direct flights.

Don't give up the seat: Airlines notoriously overbook during peak seasons. If you have an assigned seat, think three times before giving it up—unless you are very, very flexible. Free future travel is fraught with restrictions, and even a gate agent's guarantee of "next flight" seating could be disrupted by weather or equipment problems.

Frequent-Flier Facts & Fiction

The airfare wars have had some advantages for the more than 60 million travelers enrolled in frequent-flier programs. Mileage award programs have extended to hotels, rental car companies, credit card purchases, telephone solicitors and banking transactions. You can even get "points" for having cavities filled!

AIRLINE MILES & MYSTERIES

Even though the major airlines gave more frequent-flier awards in the past year than in previous years, it's still difficult to book a free flight. Whether it's fewer seats available or simply more people flying, the award seats are a precious commodity. Experts say keep trying, be flexible about dates and times and try partner airlines. It's well worth your while to become educated about your frequent flier memberships.

What Airlines Won't Tell You

Airlines want to sell seats, not give them away—even if they owe you. Do not expect the air carrier to encourage you to use up frequent-flier miles, especially on well-traveled routes. The *Department of Transportation* is taking a more active role in determining airline policies and procedures related to frequent-flier programs. They are looking at whether carriers are diligent in communicating information on seat limits and program changes to members.

If you don't feel you know enough about your airline's frequent-flier program, contact the frequent-flier club service center.

Who to Call

- *American AAdvantage:* 800-882-8880
- *Continental OnePass:* 713-952-1630
- *Delta SkyMiles:* 800-323-2323
- *Northwest KLM WorldPerks:* 800-447-3757
- *United Mileage Plus:* 800-421-4655
- *US Airways Dividend Miles:* 800-872-4738

CHOOSE THE RIGHT PLAN

Before you join the first frequent-flier program that offers an enrollment form, take stock of the features that matter to you and your travel habits. While your goal is to earn free travel as quickly as possible, bear in mind that every program is different and some carriers offer their members better awards and more seat availability than others.

Where you travel and how often frequently impacts your choice of program. Obviously, the airline that serves your travel cycles most conveniently is the one you will want to join as a frequent flier.

FIVE KEYS TO THE RIGHT PROGRAM

Partners. Take a close look at the partnership programs that each carrier is affiliated with. Bear in mind that for an average frequent traveler, more than 30% of the total miles earned come from affiliations with credit cards, hotels, banks and telephone companies. The more partners an airline has, the faster your miles add up.

Award choices. Check out the award choices. An ideal program should offer awards to places you are likely to travel. Not all airlines fly to all locations or have the most efficient itinerary.

Elite level. Most frequent fliers aspire to move up to the gold and platinum levels of their membership. This allows them to take advantage of such perks as inexpensive or free upgrades and priority baggage handling and check-in. Airlines frequently alter their policies, especially on upgrades from discount or certain economy fares, so be sure to keep abreast of any changes with your preferred carrier.

Rules and conditions. Rules

BEWARE OF AGENCY OVERRIDES

Your travel agent may not tell you, but many agencies collect preferred carrier fees from airlines. Some industry critics call them "kickbacks." These overrides benefit the agency and could be harmful to you. For example, if a travel agent has an override scheme with a particular carrier, the agent may favor that carrier, even if it means urging you to take a less desirable flight or an inferior seat, like a middle seat or one at the rear of the aircraft.

Don't fall for the ruse. Know your travel agent's preferred airline, and better yet, state clearly your choice. Check alternate carriers yourself, if necessary. Otherwise, you'll be traveling to your destination on your travel agent's favorite airline.

change all the time. Remember that nearly all airlines have "blackout" periods—peak travel times during which they sell few or no discounted seats to popular destinations. Previously, many programs, with the exception of Southwest, TWA and US Airways, also had expiring miles to limit their long-term liability. Some airlines reserve the option of terminating your account if no mileage has been deposited within 18 consecutive months. Also, find out if the program allows you to transfer awards to others, especially if you are a high-mileage traveler, racking up more miles than you use.

Minimum mileage. If your travels take you on a lot of commuter flights, check that minimum mileage will be credited to your account regardless of the flying distance. Most carriers award 500 minimum miles. TWA and America West offer 750-mile minimums.

Best of all: Mileage programs are here to stay. Join them!

TRAPS & PITFALLS

Most members convert their miles for free coach tickets, upgrade programs or pay full price for catalog merchandise. This is okay if your miles are going to expire before you are able to use them. Experts agree that the best way to redeem miles, which are worth about two cents each, is to use them for

international flight upgrades. These are usually the best values for your miles, and you'll really appreciate the extra legroom and amenities on these longer flights. Here's some practical redemption tips:

■ *Award seats.* You can earn frequent-flier miles not only by flying, but by dining out, getting your car waxed, calling long distance and even refinancing your house. Getting an award redemption seat on an airline, however, calls for extreme flexibility in departure and arrival dates. Popular destinations are frequently booked almost a year in advance and more.

Solution: Try booking to an alternate airport. This is especially a good idea when traveling to Europe during peak summer months. Or consider traveling at unpopular times, like late at night or midday on a Tuesday or Wednesday. Keep trying—more often than not seats open for frequent fliers several days before departure.

■ *Upgrading.* It's no secret that more people want to upgrade than there are seats available. With more than three trillion frequent-flier miles hovering over the market, free seats are in demand. Seat capacity is growing at only 3.4% a year, while frequent-flier miles are climbing between 11 and 18%.

Solution: Chances of an up-

grade are better if you're an elite, or preferred, club member. Only three million travelers qualify for those programs, and they get first dibs on seats.

■ *More information:*
Travel Discount's Frequent Flyer Programs
www.traveldiscounts.com/ discount/airlines/freqfly.htm;
Travel.com
www.travel.com/aviation/ airline/alff.htm;
FrequentFlier.com
www.frequentflier.com;
Web Flyer
www.webflyer.com;
ClickRewards
www.clickrewards.com

TRAVEL AGENTS WON'T TELL YOU THIS

Unpublished fares, which may include Internet tickets, convention and group airfares, package deals and direct sales tickets, are frequently exempted from mileage giveaways.

Watch your travel agent. Many of them use consolidators to secure cheap deals. You may not find out that your fare didn't count for mileage until you get a blank statement for the trip. Save the surprise and ask if the fare qualifies for miles before you buy the ticket.

AVOID FREQUENT-FLIER HASSLES

Here are the biggest frequent-flier program hassles, and how to keep from being disappointed. These suggestions are from frequent-flier guru Randy Petersen, publisher of *Inside Flyer*, a newsletter that tracks the major airline programs, and author of *The Official Frequent-Flier Guidebook* (AirPress/$14.99).

Expired Miles

To be eligible for a free domestic ticket on nearly any airline, you generally need 25,000 miles in its program. Yet travelers often miss free flying opportunities because their airlines' miles have expired before they could be used.

While business travelers may not have to worry about expiration dates, since they are constantly earning miles, "infrequent" frequent fliers have trouble accumulating enough miles within a set period to earn a free ticket.

Solution: Try sticking with airlines whose miles don't expire.

Today, more and more airlines do not require that you redeem your miles within a set period.

If your miles are about to expire, you can often redeem them for a coupon good for one free domestic economy class ticket. This coupon may give you all an additional year to make a specific booking.

No Seats Available

When you "buy" a free ticket with 25,000 miles, you are actually buying a discount ticket. All discount tickets, whether paid for or awarded through frequent-flier programs, are capacity controlled, meaning the airline only makes a set number available on each flight. Unless such seats are available when you make your reservation, you may be out of luck.

Solution 1: If you really want to leave on a particular date and you have many miles in your account, consider using more than 25,000 miles. On many airlines, if you trade 40,000 miles, "standard fare" seats become available to you.

Solution 2: To improve your chances of getting a seat for 25,000 miles, make reservations as far in advance as possible, between three months and six months before your departure date. Some international travelers book as much as one year in advance.

Also, be flexible about your flight dates and times, if possible —Two flights close together in time, may have very different seat allocations.

"Blackout" Dates

On heavy travel days, airlines will not allow you to use 25,000 frequent-flier miles to purchase a discount ticket. Blackout dates vary by airline. Check your carrier.

Solution: Instead of planning your vacation and then trying to make airline reservations, establish a range of dates on which you are willing to depart and return. Then see which dates are available for an award ticket.

Again, you can always pay a premium in miles to get around a blackout date. Most carriers will charge you at least 40,000 miles for a domestic coach ticket and 70,000 miles for international flights during a blackout period.

Tickets Not So Free

More than 30% of the so-called free tickets have additional fees for services such as express mail or electronic ticketing.

Those fees must come out of

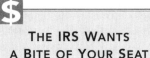

THE IRS WANTS A BITE OF YOUR SEAT

Congress passed a 7.5% excise tax on frequent-flier miles as part of the budget balancing tax relief act.

Since airlines sell their programs to partners, like banks and car rental companies, the tax gets passed on to the buyers. Only Hertz appears to be passing the tax along to customers, although it's only pennies on your bill.

Ask your bank, hotel or credit card company if you're paying any taxes you don't know about for frequent-flier miles.

Good news: Experts believe it's doubtful that frequent-flier miles will be taxed as personal income, despite the fact that the IRS has been trying to do that for several years.

your pocket and cannot be paid in miles. What's more, there is sometimes a cash charge if you want to change an award ticket.

Solution: Plan ahead and order early. Stick with your travel plans once you've reserved an award ticket. If you've purchased the ticket months in advance, you probably don't need it sent to you by expensive courier services.

In general, don't incur extra charges on an otherwise free ticket.

⚠ AIRLINE PARTNERSHIPS THAT WORK AGAINST YOU

Just because airlines like Cathay Pacific, Quantas, Singapore Airlines and others are listed as partners in your frequent-flier program, don't assume you'll get miles awarded by traveling with them, specifically if you fly economy class. Many such carriers refuse to transfer miles to their U.S. program partner. Check first, then fly.

Earned Miles Not Registered

As many programs become more loyalty programs, the ways in which you can earn miles (other than by flying) are increasing.

Unfortunately, these programs may not always credit you for the miles you deserve. Even experienced travelers have found that mileage for car rentals, hotel rooms and other such bonuses is missing from their frequent-flier account balance statements.

Solution: Keep track of the miles you earn in a "mileage checkbook." Whenever you earn miles through a partnership program, log the amount into your book. Also, make copies of any receipts for purchases that earned you miles, and keep them in a separate folder.

When your frequent-flier statement arrives, compare the number of miles you've earned to the amount you have been credited. Nowadays, with most programs, you can also check your account on-line. If there's a discrepancy, submit copies of your receipts as evidence, and ask to be credited for the missing miles.

Miles to Nowhere

Many people who have saved their miles for a once-in-a-lifetime vacation have been disappointed to find that their airline dropped service to that destination.

Example: Continental and Northwest Airlines stopped flying to Australia after years of service there. Frequent-flier milers planning to go to Australia were disappointed.

Airline alliances change often. If you are saving miles for a flight to an exotic location on your carrier's partner airline, there's no guarantee that service will be offered in the future.

Solution: It's better to use the miles you have now, rather than save them for the long term. But if you've already been saving for a specific destination on an airline whose miles do not "time-out," continuing to save isn't without hope. Even if your carrier terminates service to a particular destination, it is highly likely that the airline will bring in another

MANAGE YOUR MILES

➤ Don't trust airlines to keep track of your frequent-flier miles. Keep a ledger of miles and points as you earn them and use them.

➤ Save boarding passes and passenger coupons of your tickets until your mileage statement arrives.

➤ Regularly match your statement against your ledger. If you find a discrepancy, contact the program's service center.

ELITE MEMBERSHIP MILEAGE ALERT

When you travel with international carriers, the miles you accumulate probably do not count toward elite or preferred club membership status. Code-share airlines (two different airlines that serve the same route but share passengers) seldom count air miles toward gold and platinum status.

partner or even reinstate the destination.

Example: Travelers disappointed when Continental stopped flying to Australia can now get there again with their miles on Continental's Malaysia Airline partnership.

HIGH-MILEAGE CREDIT CARDS

Every major U.S. airline has teamed up with a bank to offer credit cards to frequent fliers. Usually, these cards have annual fees. Interest rates may vary, but they are seldom the lowest available.

More Miles per Dollar

The idea is simple: Customers use the card to make everyday purchases. Each dollar spent earns a frequent-flier mile.

Downside: Most of these card programs have a cap of 60,000 miles a year.

Travel & Entertainment Cards

The well-known ones are *American Express (Amex)* and *Diners Club.* They offer the same benefits as the affinity credit cards, but have fewer restrictions.

Both cards offer the same advantages over bank cards:

■ Miles can be applied to any airline of your choice.

■ There's no expiration on the miles you earn.

Downside: The cards carry a hefty annual fee—as high as $300 for an *American Express Platinum* card. Amex has also started taking miles away if the card balance isn't paid each month. (A $15 service charge will reinstate them.)

AWARD BONUSES

■ Mileage awards can never be sold, but they can be given to another person for free. Check the rules.

■ Many airlines give extra bonus miles for certain routes, but they may not give them automatically. Look for promotions, and read the fine print.

Ticketing Tactics

It's a traveler's market when it comes to buying tickets. Travel agents are competing for your dollar, the Internet is exploding with Web sites that offer travel data and airlines are making it easier than ever to plan your own flight and handle your own ticketing.

TRAVEL AGENT ANGST

The role of the travel agent is changing. Severe commission cutbacks by the airlines are forcing agents to become more competitive in taking care of clients. Although they charge fees for services that used to be free, a good agent will work harder for your business than ever before.

The Internet offers you ticketing independence. Virtually every airline has its own Web site, offering fast, efficient ticketing service.

What you don't get easily, however, are the comparative flight schedules and fare comparisons that are available through a professional agent. Also on the Internet, hundreds of travel Web sites offer a multitude of travel packages.

If you prefer having a travel agent do the legwork, it pays to have some idea of the multitude of options that are available. Be aware that agents don't always know (and sometimes won't tell you) what options you really have for cheaper travel.

Know Where the Deals Are

The key to getting the best deals in ticketing is to know where the deals can be found. If you don't have access to the Internet, the weekend newspaper travel supplement is crammed with bargain rates.

For more sophisticated travel planners, consider subscribing to one of the many newsletters catering to travel and travelers. Among the best:

- *Best Fares* (12 issues, $60): 800-635-3033; *www.bestfares.com*
- *Consumer Reports Travel Letter* (12 issues, $39): 800-234-1970; *www.consumer-reports.com*
- *Frequent Flyer* (free bi-weekly online newsletter): 800-323-3537; *www.frequentflyer.oag.com*
- *InsideFlyer* (12 issues, $36): 800-767-8896; *www.insideflyer.com*
- *The Ticket* (free): 404-261-8455; *www.travelskills.com*

WEB SITE TICKETING TOOLS

Few things are changing travel habits more than the Internet. Most airline sites now let you book not only air travel, but car rentals and hotels, too.

www.aa.com: *American Airlines* site offering information on schedules, fare quotes, gates, times and reservations. A membership feature allows access to "super saver" fares and special deals.

www.Iflyswa.com: *Southwest Airlines* site offering "ticketless travel" plus the usual airline fare and schedule data. The site is also available by accessing **www.southwest.com.**

www.ual.com: *United Airlines* site offers discounts for Web site users.

www.delta.com: *Delta Airlines* provides on-line domestic and international booking through its site, along with other flight information.

One-stop shopping is everybody's goal, but there's always a better deal outside an air carrier's dedicated site…here are the hottest:

www.travelocity.com: This site gives you access to the same information as travel agents, allowing you to make your own travel plans.

www.ITASoftware.com: This is another site that lets you find out all about fare options.

www.4airlines.com: This site allows you to find the lowest priced airfares, vacation packages and even weather report links.

http://travel.yahoo.com: Supported by the search engine *yahoo.com*, it offers flight pricing, car rentals, hotel rooms and more. *Hot feature:* Book a vacation based on personal activities or interests.

www.webflyer.com: This site offers information on flights and last-minute supersavers as well as how to purchase miles. The IntelliTrip feature lets you enter a flight number and track an aircraft's progress on the screen.

www.expedia.msn.com: Here you can access "fare finder." You enter your departure point along with a preferred arrival date and time, and it will indicate your choices. "Fare compares" will get you the lowest price, while "saved itineraries" gives you a detailed description of your travel plans.

www.priceline.com: State your best price and it will locate a carrier. If the ticket is available, you can purchase it on-line. This site is expanding to include all traveling expenses and even mortgages.

www.cheapflights.com: While the name sounds enticing, this site may or may not have the cheapest flights. It is worth a look to compare. Flights can be booked through an agent on-line or by phone. If you want the services of an agent, this site gives you a list of them.

TEMPTING FARES

You may be tempted by low fares on overseas tickets found in the travel section of your newspaper. Many of these fares are offered by consolidators, companies that have contracts with certain airlines for wholesale tickets and sell them at discounts that range from 20%–50%. If you are sure about your travel plans—generally these tickets are non-refundable and usable only on the issuing airline—you may reap good savings. Check whether they can earn mileage.

STUDENT FARES

US Airways offers a student Advantage Program with savings that include a one-time discount of $20 on a qualifying US Airways fare and up to four travel certificates that include discounts of 15% on two roundtrip, coach fares over $175. In addition, Student Advantage members will receive 5,000 bonus Dividend Miles with online booking and 500 Dividend Miles for every subsequent online booking.

Student Advantage serves the need of college students by providing information on current events and discounts on travel and related products.

For more information, visit the Student Advantage Program on the US Airways website. For more information by phone, call 877-2JOIN-SA (877-256-4672).

SENIOR FARES FARE WELL

If you're 62—in some instances, 65—and ready to go traveling, there are no better deals available for seniors than those offered by the airlines.

Older travelers get favored status when it comes to flying. Most airlines have special programs and clubs for seniors, as well as senior coupon books—all to encourage active retirement travel.

Time on Their Side

Unburdened by work schedules, seniors have the flexibility to travel frequently and on flights that don't conflict with peak traffic. Furthermore, seniors tend to plan their travel well in advance.

To qualify for senior fares and programs, you'll have to be able to prove your age, both when you arrange ticketing and at the time of travel.

Cash in with Senior Coupons

On most airlines, seniors qualify for an automatic 10% discount off any nonsale tickets they purchased from the air carrier.

But a big saver for seniors is coupon books which offer some of the best deals in air travel. Major U.S. airlines sell coupon books—usually four tickets that equal round-trip tickets to anywhere in the continental U.S. and parts of Canada or the Caribbean for under $300. This is about as good as fares get—even when they are on sale.

Companion coupon books allow a second person, regardless of age, to accompany a senior who is traveling with a coupon.

Rules for Coupon Use
- Coupons must be used within a year of purchase.
- Reservations need to be made at least 14 days in advance. If you're impulsive, you can fly stand-by with a coupon.
- No minimum stay is required.
- One-way or round-trip is optional.
- In Florida, US Airways allows seniors to fly round-trip on a single coupon.

- US Airways also allows grand-children to accompany seniors using coupon tickets.

When Senior Coupons Make Sense

Major U.S. carriers sell senior coupons. So for the trips you might make, pick the carrier that best serves your destinations.

If you anticipate less than two trips a year, you're probably better off flying a regular fare with the usual senior discount.

The prices of airline coupon books vary. But service, surcharges and some rules vary more. The determining factor in your choice will be whether the air carrier serves your travel needs with routes and schedules you're likely to use.

Frequent-flier miles are awarded by most carriers to coupon book holders for every flight they make.

⚠ ARM AGAINST AIR-TICKETING PROBLEMS

Use your credit card to protect yourself against consolidator fraud. For example, if a consolidator issues you a fraudulent ticket, it could be confiscated at the gate. If this happens, your credit card purchase gives you an edge. How? Federal regulations stipulate that you do not have to pay for a service charged to your credit card if the service was not received.

Purchasing consolidator tickets through a travel agent is a good way to protect yourself, too. The agent will be the liable party should there be a problem. It's always prudent to check out a consolidator with the local Better Business Bureau or consumer protection agency.

Most reputable consolidators sell only through travel agents. They advertise in the newspaper and are prevalent on the Internet. A good consolidator: *Unitravel*, 800-325-2222; *www.unitravel.com*.

Be sure to enroll.

In general, coupons are a better deal on longer flights.

Check Out Senior Clubs

Some airlines have special Senior Clubs. The clubs are generally open to members 62 and up, although some begin at age 55. They offer a variety of travel bonus packages that can be very competitive with regular published fares.

Join the Right Club

As with coupons, the club you join will depend not so much on price and policies as it does on where the airline flies and how often you'll use the membership.

Some clubs allow younger companions to fly with you using the same advantages.

Key Club Highlights

Primary services offered by the clubs are "zoned fare" programs, where seniors can fly for bargain fixed fares within designated geographic zones, for example, the Northeast.

Both Delta and United offer major concessions to first-class and business travelers.

Each of the airlines charges annual fees, with options for lifetime membership fees that range from under $100 to several hundred dollars depending on the membership you select.

- Continental Airlines, *Freedom Flight Club,* 800-441-1135.
- United Airlines, *Silver Wings Plus,* 800-720-1765.

Continental Airline's Freedom Flight Club is considered the most flexible of all the senior clubs. It offers up to 20% off all fares at all times without seat limits, zoned travel or blackout dates. Its annual fee of $75 allows travel to all 50 states. For $125 a year, you can "club" international. The age limit is 62 and up.

TIRED OF SOLO TRAVEL?

Traveling alone can be fun and full of surprises, but also can be lonesome and expensive! Single supplements for packaged trips can sometimes double the cost. Solo travelers looking for companions might try Travel Companion Exchange. It costs $59 for a trial membership. Call 631-454-0880 or visit their Web site at *www.whytravel alone.com.*

Hint for a Woman Alone

Be aware of the local customs. If local tastes demand it, be sure to wear longer skirts, cover your shoulders (and possibly your hair), wear loose-fitting clothes and do not show too much bare skin. See *www.journeywoman .com* for a list of most nations and their standards of dress, or visit *www.hermail.net* for a directory of women from 35 countries who are ready to offer advice.

EMERGENCY TRAVEL

If you need to be by a close family member due to illness or death, all the airlines have bereavement fares. Such fares are generally 50% of the full fare, usually for domestic flights only.

Most airlines will also waive advance purchase requirements on such fares.

To take advantage of such special rates you'll need to provide a doctor's note and hospital information. In case of death, the name and number of the funeral home is generally acceptable. If you are unable to gather all the information ahead of your flight, you can get the discount after the fact by submitting paperwork within a reasonable time of returning home.

The rules vary from one airline to the next, so check with more than one carrier before you commit. Sometimes a regular unrestricted fare is better than the fare allowance for illness or death. Also look at *www.priceline .com* or a consolidator, or use mileage awards.

TINY TOT TRAVEL

Infants can travel free using an empty seat if the plane isn't filled. If the plane is full, the baby must be held by a guardian. Airlines offer infant half-fares if the baby occupies an approved infant safety seat. However, infant seats are in short supply and not always available. Half-price fares for infants do not apply if you are using senior coupons.

If you're flying during peak travel times with an infant, the safest bet is to purchase a seat for the baby to ensure your own comfort.

Rules Regarding Child Seats

The Federal Aviation Administration (FAA) recommends, although it isn't mandatory, that an approved Child Restraint Seat (CRS) be used. Acceptable seats will be labeled as certified for vehicles and aircraft.

A CRS has to occupy a window seat and may not be used in an exit row. The seats must be tightly fastened in place using the aircraft seat belt.

Infants and children under 20 pounds should be placed in the seat facing backwards. Children between 20 and 40 pounds can travel facing frontward. Children over 40 pounds are safe in standard aircraft seating.

The Art of Packing

Packing is more than throwing clothes in a bag and hoping it arrives on the same flight as you. Knowing what to pack and how can make the difference between a great trip and a loathsome journey. Here is what you should look for—and more important, how the pros keep organized from one packing to another.

DON'T PACK VITALS

The first thing to remember about packing is what to leave out of your suitcase. Passports, visas and other travel documents are obvious. Travelers' checks and other valuable documents should be with you at all times, including any special medical records you might need in an emergency.

Carry-on Contents

What should go into your carry-on bag? Most people overlook vital

---

MEDICATION SAFETY VALVE

If you are traveling in a foreign country and depend on medication, make a precise list of the drugs you need and carry it in a safe place. The list should include your pharmacy telephone number and the prescribing doctor's number as well.

---

medication. Be sure to include at least a two-day supply of medications just in case your checked-in luggage does not arrive at the same time.

Experienced business travelers include toiletries, socks and underwear in their carry-on, as well as amenities to make a long flight more comfortable. Bring along bottled water, aspirin for headaches and lip balm to combat the dry high-altitude air. Toothbrush and toothpaste are also welcome items at the end of the trip.

Forget the Family Jewels

Experienced travelers forgo jewelry altogether, especially when visiting countries where it might be conspicuous and draw unwanted attention. No matter how secure the luggage locks appear, do not pack any jewelry, travel tickets, passports or vital documents into anything but a carry-on bag that stays with you at your seat. If you must bring

jewelry, opt for simple, plain and understated items.

WRINKLE-FREE PACKING

If your travel is more than overnight and the occasion calls for multiple dress-up outfits, you will want to pack a single large suitcase as efficiently as possible.

According to the authors of *Packing, Bags to Trunks* (Knopf), the tissue or plastic bag method is effective.

■ Place tissue paper or plastic bags between each layer of clothing. This lets garments slide rather than rub.

■ Interlock belts and run them along the circumference of the suitcase. Place trousers waist-

band to waistband with the legs left to hang outside the case. Add a layer of tissue to the surface.

■ Place blouses and shirts face-down folded, using a long fold to turn up the bottom of the garment a third to avoid a mid-belly crease. Add more tissue.

■ Suit jackets turned inside out (see diagram). Roll up ties and tuck them inside jacket pockets. Add another tissue layer.

■ Now the pant legs. Fold them over the top. Add more tissue. On top of that add sweaters and socks laid out flat, not rolled.

■ Shoes, stuffed with underwear, go into bags (plastic or fabric) and get stuffed in the sides of the bag along with the toiletry kit. Everything else, carry on.

HOW TO FOLD A SUIT JACKET

Here's a wrinkle "minimizer" for jackets in a suitcase:
1. Hold the jacket facing you and slip your hands inside the shoulders.
2. Turn the left shoulder inside out (but not the sleeve).
3. Place the right shoulder inside the left shoulder. The lining is now on the outside with both sleeves inside the fold.
4. Fold the jacket in half; slip it inside a plastic bag and into your suitcase.

Secure Rooms

The next best thing to getting there is staying there. If the room isn't right, the trip isn't right, whether you're on business travel or leisure time. Here's a primer on getting the right room for the right price and avoiding rip-offs in the process.

BEST ROOMS, BEST RATES

Hotels are becoming more like airlines. You can "deal" your way into rooms in much the same way as you bargain for airline seats—even more so.

Deals at the Desk

The "safest beds" are in hotels that provide comfort, convenience and economy. Experienced travelers ensure all three by negotiating deals at the front desk. You can save anywhere from a few dollars up to $50 a night off the regular room rate simply by asking for a better price. Negotiating at reservation time is helpful. Ask for the "corporate rate," even if you are on vacation with family. Every hotel has a special rate for business travelers and if you can produce a business card, you can get either a discount or a room upgrade.

Rack Rates vs. Credit Cards

Most business credit cards automatically gain you a discount when you reserve. Similarly, automobile club memberships and AARP affiliations qualify you for cheaper rates. Despite those "given" discounts, you can do even better by asking.

In a recent *Consumer Reports* survey of travelers, one third of the 55,600 participants asked for discounts at the front desk. About half, in fact, did get a lower rate.

$

PHONE CALLS TO AVOID

Use a credit card or prepaid phone card to make calls from your hotel room. Even better, use the lobby payphones. This is especially critical when traveling in Asia or Europe where some hotels mark up calls 25 to 35%. Many hotels block special access calling-card lines, such as AT&T, MCI and Sprint, in order to line their own pockets. If you plan to make calls while away, ask about the hotel's calling policy at reservation time and certainly at check-in.

ROOM SAVVY FOR PERSONAL SAFETY

Don't get harmed in a hotel incident. Even the most reputable of hotels have their fair share of crime in the halls. To ensure maximum safety, follow these hotel safety advisories:

1. When entering a room alone for the first time, prop the door open with your bag and check the closets and bath to make sure you're really alone. Check the hall to see that no strangers are lurking.
2. Check that all doors and windows are locked, that sliders have safety bars in place and that adjoining room doors are locked.
3. Use the peephole before opening the door to anyone—be it maid or maintenance. If you cannot confidently identify the person as a hotel employee, call the front desk and verify that the person should be there.
4. Make it a habit to lock and dead-bolt your door every time you go into the room, especially following room or maid service.
5. If the room has a safe, as many hotels do, lock valuables inside at all times. If there is no safe, use the safe-deposit box of the hotel. They are free, safe and fireproof.
6. Use only the main entrances to exit and enter the hotel, especially at night. Do not open your door while alone with a stranger close enough to force his way in behind you.
7. Give your key or passcard to no one and do not accept help opening a difficult door from someone who is clearly not a hotel employee.
8. Avoid drawing attention to yourself in public areas with lavish jewelry, large supplies of cash or bundles of packages.
9. For women traveling alone, consider the merits of having your bags delivered to your room versus the security of not allowing anyone to identify your room number.
10. If you arrive by car at night, park where it is light or take advantage of valet parking.

SURF FOR SAFE CITIES

If international travel is in your future, government-sponsored Web sites and telephone services issue warnings on global terrorism and places to avoid. Go to *www.state.gov/www/global/terrorism* to track terrorist hot spots or *www.travel.state.gov* for news events on hot spots. No Internet access? Call 202-647-5225.

PART 3

Plan, Pick
& Pack

Airlines
& Airports

Driving
Self-Defense

Travel Tips & Skills

Airlines & Airports

Airport Travel Smarts

Every air journey begins and ends with an airport. This is where you begin your "negotiations" with the airlines for a comfortable experience. Here's a series of smart traveler guidelines that will guarantee a safe, hassle-free arrival.

WHY GET TO THE AIRPORT EARLY?

■ *You can navigate check-in more easily.* Lines are getting longer at airports—it isn't your imagination. Airlines are reporting record yields, which means that more people are traveling than ever before. New security measures—checking photo IDs against tickets, questioning travelers about packing or carrying packages for strangers—add time to check-in as well.

Curbside check-in may become a thing of the past.

■ *Allow for clogged security checkpoints.* Expect more delays at the X-ray machine, as more sophisticated devices flag more suspicious items. Security staff may take more time to perform hand searches and interviews as well. Nowadays, you may pass through more than one checkpoint.

■ *You won't lose your assigned seat.* Several airlines have instituted new rules concerning the point at which passengers with reserved seats are deemed no-shows, and the seat is released to standby passengers. It used to be 10 minutes before "pushback." United and Alaska airlines have changed that to 20 minutes; Northwest and some others to 15. If you don't lose your seat altogether by being late, you may lose your reserved seat, which means you're most likely to get relegated to a dreaded middle seat.

■ *You won't miss your flight.* Several international carriers shut the door at the airline gate 10 minutes before the flight is set to depart. No amount of negotiating, crying or begging will get you on board, even if the plane is still parked at the gate.

■ *You'll be closer to the head of the line if there is a problem,* and you will have time to make

alternate plans. If there's a gate change, you won't have to run to the new gate. If there's a flight cancellation, you'll be among the first to be rebooked —before the gate agents have dealt with all the other frustrated travelers.

■ *Flying is stressful enough.* Many experienced travelers get to the airport with an hour to spare, and board relaxed and ready for the trip. A bad experience can ruin your whole day, short or long flight.

AVOID AIRPORT HASSLES

When you buy a plane ticket, you enter into a contract with the airline, which promises to deliver what you paid for— provided you follow its rules. Those rules, called the "Contract of Carriage," can be provided by the airline. Essentially, the contract says that if you do not follow the rules, your ability to seek compensation in the event of an inconvenience is severely limited.

■ *Reconfirm your flight within the designated 72 hours.* If you don't, you could be bumped. The smaller the airline, the more important it is to reconfirm and get a confirmation number or the name of the agent you speak with.

DON'T BE LATE

Standby passengers who arrive before the deadline may have a better chance of getting on the flight than someone with a reserved ticket who arrives late.

■ *Check for schedule changes.* If the airline changes the departure time of the flight and you end up missing it, the airline is not responsible.

■ *Know your check-in deadline.* If you arrive late, the airline is permitted to give away your seat. If you arrive close to the deadline, get your name into the airline's computer as fast as possible, since passengers are bumped in reverse order to which they are entered— last in, first out. For domestic flights you usually have a

---

CREDIT-CARD AIRFARE

Protect yourself! Pay for airline tickets by credit card. If you end up in a dispute with the carrier, you may have recourse through your credit card company. Federal regulations state that services secured by credit card don't have to be paid for if you don't receive the service.

one-hour deadline, and a half hour if your seat was assigned in advance. For international flights, it is usually two hours, sometimes three.

DELAY STRATEGIES

Like turbulence and lost baggage, flight delays are an irritating fact of travel life. They result from any number of reasons: bad weather, air-traffic congestion, security concerns, maintenance problems, a delayed incoming flight.

And because airlines do not guarantee their schedules, they're not required by law to rearrange your schedule. It's up to the traveler to somehow manage when delays or cancellations occur.

What to Do in a Delay

- Dash to the closest phone as soon as you hear. Do not stay in the line at the counter or the gate unless you're at or near the head of the line. Experienced travelers carry a cell phone with the airline reservation number and travel agent's number. Call your travel agent's emergency hotline number listed on your itinerary. You could be rebooked on another flight in a matter of minutes.
- If your agency doesn't have a hot line, if you booked a ticket directly through the airline or if you booked a ticket through

the Internet, call the airline's reservation department. You'll know within a minute or two if there are any seats available on any carrier, and you can book it and be on your way. If you're lucky you may even get to your destination at about the same time as you originally planned.
- If you do stay in the line, work with the gate agent. Stay polite, calm and friendly. Ask about your options. Don't hesitate to flaunt your frequent-flier status. The computers at the gate have up-to-date availability information. Make sure you ask about endorsing your ticket on another carrier if the one you originally booked can't accommodate you.
- Remember that gate agents are facing dozens of frustrated,

often belligerent people whenever there's a delay. How you behave toward them is likely to be reflected right back.

Experienced travelers also advise that the best defense against flight delays involves several common-sense preemptive moves: Always get to the airport early, for one. A lot of frequent travelers time their airport arrival for early check-in and use the wait time catching up on phone calls or business reading.

GATE AGENT ETIQUETTE— YOURS

Gate agents are empowered people, especially in times

of crises—like overbooking and other delays.

They can give free upgrades, change seating assignments, waive various fees, settle small claims and endorse your ticket to another airline. You may have to be persistent and you must be prepared with documentation.

Be courteous and friendly. In a bind, the agents are doing the best they can for everybody, but try to engage them. A smile is your most powerful tool, plus some acknowledgment of the great job the agent is trying to do.

Be quick about explaining your problem or request. There are people behind you, and pressure is mounting all around you.

Stay Above It All

Be patient. Even if your problem can't be resolved to your

satisfaction by ground staff, you can contact the airline after the fact.

AVOIDING DELAYS

Seasoned travelers fly early in the day. Most early flights leave on time, and if a flight is canceled, there's always one coming after, so rerouting as a standby passenger is an option.

Also, later flights are more susceptible to the ripple effects of early flight delays caused by weather and heavy air traffic.

Nonstop flights are best. There's little point in catching an early flight in one city just to be dumped in a hub city at a high traffic time. If you have to make a stop, try to choose an airport that has low traffic volume (see "Airports to Avoid," p. 246). Remember: "Nonstop" is not the same as "direct." A direct flight may have stops and is susceptible to ground delays.

Know the Code

Airlines constantly monitor flights for on-time arrivals/departures on various routes. Ask your ticket agent to advise you on the one-digit code indicating airline on-time records. On-time means no more than 15 minutes late.

The on-time scale is from 0 to 9. A flight coded as a 2, for instance, is on time between 20% and 30% of the time, while a flight designated with an 8 is on time between 80% and 90% of the time.

By booking the right flight on the right airline, you can increase your odds of averting an unwanted stay at the airport.

DELAY RECOURSE

Delays generally fall into two categories: those due to weather and air traffic, and those due to the airline itself. If weather or air traffic is holding up your flight, there is little you can do. But in cases where the airline is responsible for your delay because of equipment failure or lack of an aircrew, you generally have recourse.

If you're delayed, find out why. Go to the departure board and see if flights on other airlines are also delayed. If they are, then there is probably an air traffic or weather problem. But if your flight is the only one delayed, find out why by calling the airline's toll-free number or asking the gate attendant.

The airline should inform passengers of the cause of the delay and let them know what options are available. If the delay is not due to bad weather or air traffic congestion, it could be time to inquire about "Golden Rule" 240.

RULE 240

Rule 240 requires the carrier to cover all additional expenses accrued in getting you to your destination via another carrier in cases of delays unrelated to weather and air traffic problems. Confirm that the delay is not due to weather or air traffic. Tell the agent that you cannot wait, and mention the rule. The agent is obligated to code your ticket for the next available flight, with any carrier. Agents will probably try to book you on their airline. Make sure to ask them to check flights with other carriers.

If your flight is canceled, the same rule applies, unless you're using certain frequent flier or discounted tickets. To find out if Rule 240 will apply to your ticket, contact the airline's customer service representative— before you leave on your trip.

If you're stranded overnight, airlines commonly offer hotel rooms, meal vouchers and sometimes a phone and fax allowance.

WHEN TO GET BUMPED

Airlines are required by law to ask for volunteers before bumping ticketed passengers. It may be worth volunteering depending on the answers to the following questions:

1. Will the airline get you a confirmed seat on the next flight, regardless of the airline?

2. What amenities will they give you until your flight is ready?

3. What are the restrictions on a free ticket they may give you?

Volunteers may be offered a free round-trip ticket. Make sure that this is what they're offering, since airlines may make an initial offer of a standby or space-available ticket, which can be troublesome to use.

Free "bump" tickets don't acquire frequent-flier miles, so members of frequent-flier programs should ask for travel vouchers to put toward future flights on that airline. The flights these vouchers are used for can accrue miles. Vouchers should be worth at least the amount of the original ticket.

If an airline is having trouble getting volunteers, it usually offers additional incentives. These can include cash, more travel vouchers, meal vouchers, free long-distance phone calls and passes to the airline club to wait for your flight. If you're on an overbooked flight where they're looking for volunteers, and you know that there are other flights to your destination soon after this one, volunteer, get your perks and take the next flight out.

When Not to Get Bumped

Sometimes you may be bumped against your will. In that case, you may be entitled to "denied boarding compensation." The amount will depend on the length of the delay, the price of your original ticket and whether you followed the airline's rules.

If you're on time and get bumped anyway, ask to be rebooked on the next flight out. If they get you to your destination less than one hour late, they owe you nothing. If they get you to your destination between one and two hours late (between one and four hours for an international destination), you are entitled to the cost of your one-way fare, up to $200. If you're more than two hours late (four hours international) or if the airline doesn't make alternate arrangements, you are entitled to twice the one-way fare, up to $400. If they try to give this to you in the form of a ticket voucher, you can insist on money. Also sometimes the original ticket can be used again or submitted for a refund.

That is the minimum the airline is required to do, but if you feel

Airline	Voluntary Bumps 2001*	Involuntary Bumps 2001	Bumps/ 10,000 Travelers 2001	Bumps/ 10,000 Travelers 2000
US Airways	65,589	1,357	0.31	0.67
American	103,966	1,937	0.35	0.44
America West	40,010	604	0.39	1.27
Northwest	58,054	1,557	0.40	0.43
Delta	135,690	4,544	0.65	0.34
Continental	54,383	2,599	0.87	1.44
United	120,191	5,499	1.00	1.64
Alaska	25,922	1,567	1.47	1.53
Southwest	63,289	9,215	1.63	1.84
American Eagle	1,463	270	1.88	3.74
TWA	30,440	3,303	2.01	3.11
Total	**698,997**	**32,452**	**.83**	**1.08**

THE BUMPIEST AIRLINES

Statistics cover January–September 2001, from the U.S. Department of Transportation.

Of nearly 392 million passengers on the 11 top carriers monitored by the *Department of Transportation,* more than nearly 700 million took an incentive payoff to volunteer their seat. Just over 32 million travelers lost their seats despite wanting to stay on board.

You can monitor airline performance data on the World Wide Web at *www.dot.gov/airconsumer.*

LOST & STOLEN TICKETS

Airline tickets are similar to negotiable documents. Taking these steps will help you get a refund or a new ticket if yours is lost or stolen.

➤ Make a copy of your ticket, and carry it separate from your actual ticket when you travel. At the very least, make a note of your confirmation number. (It may be on your itinerary or credit card receipt.)

➤ Although there is generally a "lost ticket fee" of around $70, your ticket will be reissued at the ticket counter in the airport.

that you were seriously inconvenienced, you can demand—and often get—more than the compensation you were offered. If you intend to seek more compensation, make sure not to cash a settlement check or use a ticket voucher you may have received. If you do, you waive your rights to demand more.

Sometimes you're just not owed anything. If you didn't meet the check-in deadline and you don't have a confirmed reservation, there may be nothing you can do. This may also apply if the flight is a charter, if you're using frequent-flier tickets, if the aircraft has 60 or fewer passengers or if the airline substituted a smaller plane than it originally planned to use. There is more variation with international flights coming to the U.S. and flights between foreign destinations. They may bump you even if you do everything right.

FLIGHT STATUS ONLINE

Most major airlines now provide up-to-the-moment flight information through their Web sites. You can check the status of arrivals and departures and, often, gate information as well. Some will even beep you on your PC, cell phone or pager if a flight is delayed. Go to *www.fly.faa.gov*.

CARRY-ON RULES

Airlines are enforcing the two-bag-per-passenger carry-on rule.

Most airlines are placing "sizer boxes" near check-in counters, and any baggage that doesn't fit must get checked.

Size allowances vary subtly by airline. *US Airways*, for example, requires that overhead bags be no more than 10" long x 16" wide x 24" across, and that underseat bags must measure no more than 8" x 16" x 21". Garment bags are limited to 45" x 4" x 23". Airlines are even getting tough on purses—anything over 18" x 12" x 4" is considered a carry-on.

Different Lines, Different Rules

Because airline requirements differ (and airport personnel have different tolerances for exceptions), you may find yourself having to check your carry-on item on a connecting flight.

Many domestic commuter airlines allow only one carry-on bag. Other bags are left with baggage handlers on the ramp.

Many international carriers are allowing only one carry-on bag.

Baby strollers are not permitted on aircraft. They can be checked at the door of the boarding ramp where they're tagged. At destination, they can be claimed at the jetway.

WHO'S WHO OF BAGGAGE WOES

Airline	Traveling Passengers	Baggage Complaints	Complaints/ 1000 Travelers
Alaska	11,677,193	34,988	3.00
US Airways	51,990,955	200,896	3.86
Delta	86,927,813	357,429	4.11
Northwest	45,403,924	190,139	4.19
America West	19,272,838	81,254	4.22
Continental	36,146,307	155,127	4.29
American	63,987,895	294,110	4.60
Southwest	73,494,713	350,712	4.77
United	67,722,438	343,485	5.07
TWA	20,442,249	129,910	6.35
American Eagle	11,308,947	83,253	7.36
Total	**488,375,272**	**2,221,303**	**4.55**

The chances of actually losing a bag during air travel are rather slim. The most common complaints are misdirected and delayed luggage, articles stolen from luggage or bags and luggage or contents damaged through rough handling.

The top-11 U.S. airlines carried nearly 490 million passengers in 2001. Of those passengers, 2.22 million filed a mishandled baggage report. You were least likely to have a baggage problem with Alaska Airlines according to these Department of Transportation statistics.

Baggage self-defense: Don't pack valuables such as cash and jewelry. Carry them with you. Luggage locks are easily opened, so cameras and electronic gear are susceptible to theft and breakage.

➤ Do not pack valuable documents, travel papers, tickets and tour vouchers. And keep your car keys with you, too.

➤ Don't overstuff your bags. This puts stress on the zippers and seams, inviting serious damage in rough handling. If you must overstuff a bag, wrap a belt around it to ensure that it won't pop open in transit.

➤ Put a name and address tag inside the bag as well as on the outside. Be sure to include a number where you can be reached at your destination.

➤ Mark your bag with distinguishing tape or ribbon so that you can quickly spot it at the baggage claim area.

Source: US Department of Transportation

LOST LUGGAGE SAVERS

Carry a photo of your suit-case(s). This will come in handy if your luggage is lost, you're suffering from jet-lag and in a foreign country where you will be unable to explain the subtleties of teal and taupe ripstop nylon.

Or try the *Unlosable Luggage* service offered by *Travel Smart* (www.travelsmartnews.com). With your subscription (under $30), you get a set of decals for your bags. The decals carry a prominent toll-free number that can be called 24 hours a day from anywhere in the world. Airlines or individuals calling that number report the location of your bag. When you call in to report the loss, bingo, you and your bag are back together again.

LUGGAGE SAVER TIPS & TRICKS

So many things can happen to checked baggage that many travelers prefer to use only carry-on bags. Today, most airlines— domestic and international—limit the passenger to one piece of carry-on luggage (plus a small pocketbook). Check the specifics of your airline.

Carry-on Tips from the Pros

There are a lot of tricks that will let you get everything you need into a carry-on. Garment bags, for example, can be used to carry a lot more than a suit or a dress. You can usually get away with more during off-peak hours and in large planes. Boarding early will ensure that you can find a place for all your stuff.

Check-in Luggage Protection

Try to pick a direct flight— ideally nonstop—because the chances of losing your luggage greatly increase if you have a stop along the way.

Make sure you check in on time, because if you're late, your lug-gage may miss the flight you barely made. It is essential that your name, home address and the address at your destination be tagged onto your luggage. Also, put the information inside your luggage, in case the tags get torn off by mishandling. Make sure you get your baggage stubs and check that your baggage is labeled correctly. Rip off old airline tags.

Beware of going over the lug-gage weight or size limit—you'll have to pay extra. Also, baggage allowances vary for transatlantic flights, intra-European flights and others. Check your route and the allowances allowed on each leg.

Insurance Options

Most airlines offer "excess valu-ation," which is a form of baggage insurance. For one or two dollars for every hundred dollars of cov-erage, the airline accepts liability for damage to checked luggage, with $5,000 as a common ceiling.

DON'T FORGET YOUR MEDICINE

Naturopathic physician Jamison Starbuck, ND, suggests some natural remedies to pack in your medicine kit. Most are available at health-food stores....

Calendula, an effective topical antiseptic and wound medicine. Buy a liquid preparation — either a tincture or glycerin-based formula — and put it in a small spray bottle. Use for cuts, scrapes, insect bites, and burns, including sunburn.

"Rescue remedy," a Bach flower remedy, helps curb mild anxiety, such as fear of flying, homesickness or stress. Place four drops on the tongue, or in two ounces of water — up to four times a day. Safe for children and adults, and won't interfere with prescription drugs.

THE NEW WORLD OF TRAVEL

In the aftermath of September's events, travel may be safer than ever. Unprecedented airport secu-rity, reinforced cockpit doors, sky marshals, increased police pres-ence in major cities and height-ened public awareness all promise increased security.

Here are some ways to cope with delays, frayed nerves, and most of all, your fears.

- Don't give in to fear. We take acceptable risks (driving to work, playing sports, eating in restaurants) every day. Instead of being paralyzed by risk, try to understand and minimize it.

- Stay vigilant. Watch for unusual activity especially in airports. If you notice anything unusual, call the authorities immediately.

- Be patient with new delays, security checkpoints, baggage searches, and inconveniences. This is the price of our safety. Smile, cooperate, and appreci-ate the efforts required to make our skies safe.

- Incorporate travel delays into your schedule. Get to the air-port extra early, set up camp at an uncrowded gate, and use the time to make cell phone calls, read mail, pay bills, or prepare for meetings.

GETTING THROUGH AIRLINE HUBS

Hubs bring a lot of travelers to places they don't want to go.

Nonstop vs. Direct

When you buy your ticket be sure you understand the difference between *direct* flights and *nonstop* flights.

Unless you're flying coast-to-coast, finding a *nonstop flight* from a major city to a smaller city is increasingly rare. But if you can find a nonstop, take it. You will save at least 1 to 2 hours, reduce the chances that your baggage will be lost and not have to worry that you will miss a connecting flight. Not to mention the safety factor of one less landing and takeoff.

Direct flights, believe it or not, don't go direct to where you want to go, but stop at a hub somewhere. The advantage of a direct flight, is that you don't have to get off the plane when you land at the hub. You won't be able to miss your second flight, and there is much less risk of baggage loss.

Know Your Hubs

If you fly a lot, you'll be in one or more of the 15 major hubs at least several times a year. Knowing which ones to avoid and when to avoid them could save you a lot of travel grief.

If you can't fly direct from San Francisco to Philadelphia, for example, you have the option

ATLANTA INTERNATIONAL AIRPORT

BOSTON-LOGAN INTERNATIONAL AIRPORT

MIAMI INTERNATIONAL AIRPORT

CHICAGO INTERNATIONAL AIRPORT

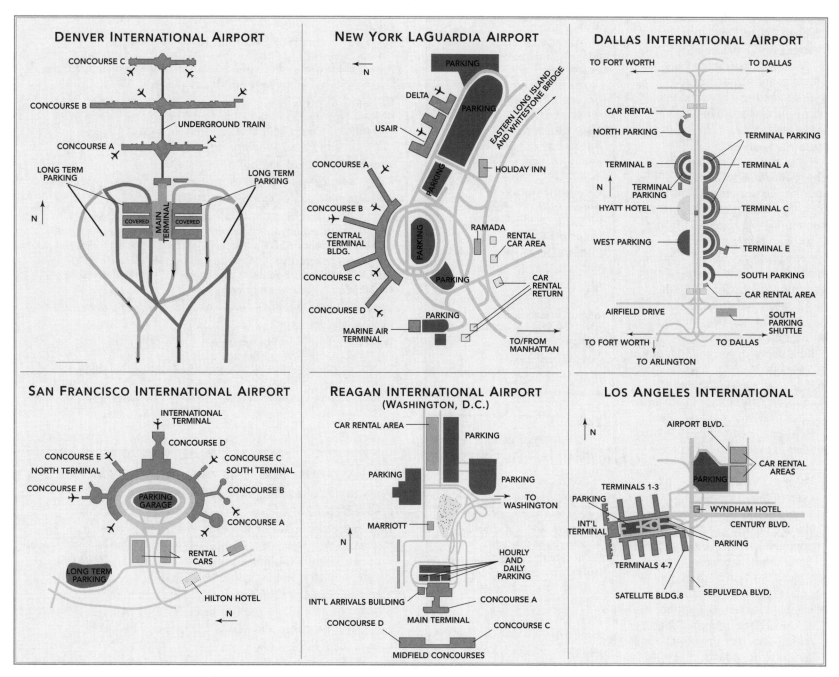

DENVER INTERNATIONAL AIRPORT

CONCOURSE C

CONCOURSE B

UNDERGROUND TRAIN

CONCOURSE A

LONG TERM PARKING

LONG TERM PARKING

COVERED

MAIN TERMINAL

COVERED

N

NEW YORK LaGuardia AIRPORT

N

PARKING

DELTA

PARKING

USAIR

EASTERN LONG ISLAND AND WHITESTONE BRIDGE

CONCOURSE A

HOLIDAY INN

PARKING

CONCOURSE B

CENTRAL TERMINAL BLDG.

PARKING

RAMADA

RENTAL CAR AREA

CONCOURSE C

PARKING

CAR RENTAL RETURN

CONCOURSE D

PARKING

MARINE AIR TERMINAL

TO/FROM MANHATTAN

DALLAS INTERNATIONAL AIRPORT

TO FORT WORTH

TO DALLAS

CAR RENTAL

NORTH PARKING

TERMINAL PARKING

TERMINAL B

TERMINAL A

TERMINAL PARKING

HYATT HOTEL

TERMINAL C

WEST PARKING

TERMINAL E

SOUTH PARKING

CAR RENTAL AREA

AIRFIELD DRIVE

SOUTH PARKING SHUTTLE

TO FORT WORTH

TO DALLAS

TO ARLINGTON

SAN FRANCISCO INTERNATIONAL AIRPORT

INTERNATIONAL TERMINAL

CONCOURSE D

CONCOURSE E

CONCOURSE C

NORTH TERMINAL

SOUTH TERMINAL

CONCOURSE F

CONCOURSE B

PARKING GARAGE

CONCOURSE A

RENTAL CARS

LONG TERM PARKING

HILTON HOTEL

N

REAGAN INTERNATIONAL AIRPORT
(WASHINGTON, D.C.)

CAR RENTAL AREA

PARKING

PARKING

PARKING

TO WASHINGTON

N

MARRIOTT

HOURLY AND DAILY PARKING

INT'L ARRIVALS BUILDING

CONCOURSE A

CONCOURSE D

MAIN TERMINAL

CONCOURSE C

MIDFIELD CONCOURSES

LOS ANGELES INTERNATIONAL

N

AIRPORT BLVD.

CAR RENTAL AREAS

PARKING

TERMINALS 1-3

PARKING

WYNDHAM HOTEL

INT'L TERMINAL

CENTURY BLVD.

PARKING

TERMINALS 4-7

SATELLITE BLDG.8

SEPULVEDA BLVD.

of using several other hubs—Chicago, Dallas/Fort Worth, Denver or St. Louis, among them. If Chicago is experiencing one of its famous winter storms or spring thunderstorms, don't go there—unless you like to camp in the airport.

Reroute Yourself

Try changing to another flight, one that arrives well behind the weather. Or in a crunch, see if your travel agent can shift you to another carrier who flies through a hub with better weather.

Keeping an eye on the weather channel just ahead of a trip can give you a picture of where the flight delays will occur. Some other tips for hub planning:

- Don't book the last flight out. If it's delayed, you will be stuck overnight.
- If you do get delayed, try rebooking through your travel agent's 24-hour hot line. The local gate agents will be tied up.
- Always travel with alternate schedules for other airlines. Professional travelers keep a copy of *OAG Pocket Flight Guide* in their travel case. (issued monthly, order by phone, 800-DIAL-OAG, or via the Internet at *www.oag.com*).
- If the delay is due to equipment failure, you may be entitled to compensation by the airline. Ask to see the airline's delayed flight policy. They're required by law to provide it.

AIRPORTS TO AVOID

Several major airports—all hubs—are being rehabilitated for the anticipated explosion in air travel in the next two decades.

New York/JFK
Annual traffic: 31 million
Project cost: $4.4 billion
Completion: 2002

Chicago/O'Hare
Annual traffic: 70 million
Project cost: $1 billion
Completion: 2003

Dallas/Fort Worth
Annual traffic: 60 million
Project cost: $3 billion
Completion: 2004

Miami International
Annual traffic: 35 million
Project cost: $5 billion
Completion: 2004

Source: Airports Council International.

CHEAPER FLIGHTS AT SMALLER AIRPORTS

Go to *www.priceline.com*. Enter your location and destination. Before the name-your-own-price service tells you anything about money, it will give you a list of airports within two hours' driving distance from your destination. You can then search on Priceline or elsewhere for low-cost flights to specific airports.

Herbert J. Teison, editor, Travel Smart, 20 Beechdale Rd., Dobbs Ferry, NY 10522.

HOW TO FILE A COMPLAINT

If you want to put your complaint about an airline on record with the Department of Transportation (DOT), you can:

Call: *202-366-2220*
Write: *Aviation Consumer Protection Division U.S. Department of Transportation, Room 4107, C-75 Washington, DC 20590*

E-mail: *airconsumer@ost.dot.gov*

If you write, include your address and a daytime telephone number with area code, so the agency can contact you.

DOT uses its complaint files to document the need for changes in consumer protection regulations and, if necessary, as the basis for enforcement action. DOT publishes monthly reports on the number of complaints received about each airline. Reports also have airline statistics on flight delays, bumped passengers and mishandled baggage. Available on the Internet at *www.bts.gov*.

Safety issues are handled by the Federal Aviation Administration (FAA):

Call: *800-255-1111*
Write: *Federal Aviation Administration Aviation Safety Hotline, ASY-300 800 Independence Ave. S.W., Washington, DC 20591*

LOW-COST BOOKLETS FROM THE GOVERNMENT

Plane Talk: A series of fact sheets on air topics
Frequent-Flier Programs: Tips on avoiding baggage problems
Defensive Flying: Public Charter Flights, Transporting Live Animals, Passengers with Disabilities
Kids and Teens in Flight: When children fly alone
Consumers Tell It to the Judge: Small Claims Court tactics
Your Trip Abroad: Primer on customs, shots, insurance
A Safe Trip Abroad: Precautions against robbery, terrorism
Travel Tips for Older Americans: Tips for senior travelers
Visit: www.access.gpo.gov

High-Flying Health

Once you're on the aircraft, you've already survived the most hazardous part of your journey—the ride to the airport.

Flying is routine for millions, but for some it poses health aggravation because of air pressure changes, reduced oxygen availability and irritation of existing sinus or cold-related conditions. And then there's the flight demon—jet lag.

In this section, you will learn how to combat jet lag, sit right, eat properly and arrive in style.

IN-FLIGHT EAR PAIN

Ear pain is a common problem. It is most likely caused by barotitis, aka aerotitis, which is usually most acute when the plane descends and the air pressure in the cabin is greater than the pressure in your middle ear.

Air is forced into the middle ear through your eustachian tubes. If they're blocked because of a cold, allergies or sinus infection, you could be in for some head-splitting pain—or worse, a ruptured eardrum.

What can you do? Use a nasal decongestant spray with oxmetazoline hydrochloride or similar agent to keep your eustachian tubes clear, or take an over-the-counter antihistamine 20 minutes before takeoff.

Also try the Valsalva maneuver, gently forcing air through your nose while keeping your nostrils pinched shut and your mouth closed. (It's the same method scuba divers use as they descend underwater to equalize the pressure in their ears.) Do the maneuver every minute or so as soon as the plane starts to descend.

AIRSICKNESS

To anyone who's gotten motion sickness on a bumpy commuter flight bucking a storm, those bumps that may have seemed so amusing when you were a kid suddenly don't appear so funny.

Caused by a turbulent ride (as well as by anxiety and excitement), sickness is experienced in aircraft just as it is in boats and cars.

Because most aircraft fly above bad weather, airsickness is now an infrequent ailment affecting an estimated one in a thousand passengers. But a prolonged bumpy ride can upset the labyrinth mechanism of the inner ear, causing nausea.

If you feel sick, it's important to keep your head as still as possible on the headrest and keep your eyes closed.

Tendency Toward Airsickness

If you're prone to airsickness, avoid fried and fatty foods before a flight, as well as alcohol and smoking.

Before takeoff, keep away from salty, high-fat or dairy products as they may make you nauseated. Other remedies:

- A preflight dose of Dramamine may be effective, but only if it is taken a few hours before take-off. The active ingredient tends to make you both sleepy and dry out your mucous membranes, so make sure you stay awake long enough to drink at proper intervals.
- You may also want to sit at the window. Some motion sickness sufferers find some relief in staring at a fixed object like the horizon or, on a cloudy day or at night, the wing. Try sitting near the wing, too, since there is less motion there than elsewhere on the plane. It's bumpiest in the tail section.
- A seat near the galley or lavatories is not a good idea. Explain your problem to the flight attendant and chances are that a move to a less vulnerable seat will be arranged.

COMBATING JET LAG

Jet lag affects travelers flying east-west or west-east, in which they change time zones faster than their body clock can reset itself. Biological rhythms have a program of around 24 hours, and jet lag is the failure of the body to adjust its own routine to a clock that may, for instance, bring darkness—and bedtime—10 hours earlier or later than usual. Most travelers suffer from the syndrome, some acutely.

Jet Lag Symptoms

Symptoms of jet lag can include intense fatigue, headaches, irritability, digestive problems, insomnia, sleepiness, dizziness and a foggy head. Jet lag at its worst may cause disorientation and wild mood swings. While none of these is terribly threatening, all are uncomfortable, and can make the first few days of a holiday or business trip a misery. The effects of jet lag seem to be greater on eastbound flights than on westbound. Reactions can be slowed for two days following a 10-zone trip westward, and for three days after a similar eastward trip.

Losing Your Senses

Research suggests that cognitive function may be impaired by jet lag, which is why many companies advise their traveling executives to rest before planning high-level meetings. Some companies ban their executives from making major decisions within 24 hours of a 5-hour time change. It's also why vacationers should think twice about renting cars (especially if you'll be driving on the left when you're not used to it) or hitting the ski slopes, until you've given your body a chance to recover.

Set Your Watch

At least one airline instructs its crew to keep their watches on home time, regardless of what time zone they are in. The most cautious medical advice is that one full day of recovery is needed for each five-hour time change. Travelers should try to go to bed as near as possible to their usual bedtime on the first night after arriving.

The short-stay traveler, such as the businessman continually on the move, is most at risk from jet lag. The long-stay traveler on holiday has enough time to acclimatize. Babies up to three months seem to be unaffected.

Jet lag researchers at university clinics, often in conjunction with NASA and the Air Pilots Association, are studying the use of light boxes now commonly used in the treatment of Seasonal Affective Disorder (SAD). Exposure to the light, which simulates sunlight, is believed to help speed up the so-called "phase adjustment" process. Some frequent travelers take

TEN KEYS TO CONQUERING JET LAG

Jet lag: Some people are blissfully unaffected, others find it takes days (or longer) to adjust to a new time zone. While there's not much you can do to eliminate it, there are some things you can do to minimize its effects.

➤ Take nonstop flights. You'll spend less time getting there and have more time to adjust once you are there.

➤ Get on the plane rested. Don't try to build up a sleep deficit, assuming that fatigue will help you to readjust to a new sleep schedule faster.

➤ Set your watch to the time zone at your destination as soon as you board the plane. Then follow your routine as if you were at the destination. Some professionals, however, feel it's better to leave watches on the home time zone. Experiment to see what works best for your body.

➤ Keep yourself hydrated. Many of the symptoms of jet lag—headache, crankiness and gastric discomfort—are caused or exacerbated by dehydration.

➤ Stay away from alcohol. Besides its diuretic (and dehydrating) effect, it disrupts natural sleep rhythms.

➤ Get out in the sunshine. Natural light stimulates the pineal gland, which helps regulate circadian rhythms.

➤ Get some exercise. A brisk walk or a light workout at the hotel health club (even calisthenics in your room) will make you feel better and may help you readjust faster. Better yet, begin exercising on the plane, doing stretches and calisthenics at your seat, and getting up every hour or so to walk a bit. Some airlines, including *Northwest* and *Lufthansa*, have exercise videos and/or pamphlets that show you stretches and movements you can do aloft.

➤ Use naps judiciously. If you're flying east on an overnight flight—for example from the U.S. to Europe, you may be tempted to take a long nap after you arrive. Experts advise that a nap should not last longer than three hours. Otherwise, you'll have trouble falling asleep that night.

➤ Take a shower during layovers. Not only will it freshen you up, but it boosts circulation and pampers fatigued muscles.

➤ Take it easy when you first arrive. Remember, it takes your body one day per time zone crossed to adjust.

⚠ JET LAG MYTH

The "Jet Lag Diet," popularized several years ago, which advocated eating certain foods at certain times of the day and fasting at other times, beginning three days before your flight, has been thoroughly debunked by sleep researchers. A controlled study by the U.S. Army actually found that the practitioners had a harder time adjusting than the nondieters.

melatonin supplements instead, but doctors are divided in their opinions on its effectiveness. Another jet lag remedy, aromatherapy, uses essences that enhance alertness when you should be getting up and out, and others encouraging relaxation when you should be sleeping.

DON'T FLY WITH A COLD

When you have a bad cold, your eardrums can be damaged in flight. Why? When the mucous membranes in your head are inflamed from infection, it's harder for air to enter behind the eardrum to equalize pressure. Worst case scenario: pain, temporary hearing loss, even the eardrum bursting inward.

In fact, *British Airways* prohibits its personnel from flying with a cold or ear infection.

What can you do if you simply must fly? Reduce the swelling of the eustachian tube with decongestants, starting several days before departure, before the flight and an hour before landing. While in the air, exercise the muscles that open the eustachian tube: chew, swallow, wiggle your jaw, open your mouth very wide, pinch your nostrils while blowing air out your nose.

For serious sufferers, earplugs fitted with ceramic filters control the flow of air entering the ears to facilitate the adjustment to pressure. Contact *Cirrus Health Care Products*, 800-327-6151.

WHEN ARE YOU TOO SICK TO FLY?

Most of us fly even when we're ill, assuming that postponing travel is more trouble than it's worth and that aspirin will fix it.

The problem is that flying with a fever, head cold and other minor illness can make the condition worse, or at the very least, lengthen your recovery time.

When to Ask Your Doctor

Certainly following any surgery you must consult with your doctor before a trip. This would apply to anyone having a chronic disease or illness that could result in an in-flight medical emergency.

If you do travel with a medical condition, take all precautions to avoid dehydration. In addition:

- Wear a special medical bracelet or keep an identity tag handy that describes your medical condition.
- Don't travel without special medications or medical devices that you may need. Keep them in a carry-on case—not in your checked luggage.
- Have your doctor furnish names and numbers of physicians in the cities you'll be visiting.
- Carry pertinent medical records, or a summary, listing all medications you are taking for your condition.
- Have an extra supply of medication with you, especially for international travel. Don't get stranded without your pills.

HOW TO DEAL WITH LEG PAIN

One in a thousand people develop clots in their legs from sitting for extended periods of time.

The condition, called Deep Venous Thrombosis, or DVT, causes painful swelling, cramping and redness in the calves or other parts of the legs. The symptoms aren't always immediate. They can show up several hours or even days after a long flight.

Other symptoms include chest discomfort, coughing or noticeable vein swelling.

AIRPLANE HEADACHES

About 30% of air travelers suffer from ear-splitting or head-splitting pain when their plane takes off and/or descends. That's without the added torment of a head cold or allergies (sinus congestion exacerbates the problem).

To the rescue: EarPlanes, a disposable earplug developed by the *House Ear Institute* in Los Angeles and tested on Navy pilots. The plugs, which consist of a ceramic filter tucked in a silicon tube, slow the rate of air pressure changes on the eardrum. They're available at most chain drugstores, on travel Web sites and from travel accessories catalogs like *Magellan's*. For information on the devices, and for names of retailers, contact *Westone Laboratories, Inc.*, in Colorado Springs, at 719-540-9333, 800-582-4771 or online at *www.earmold.com*.

If you get "crampy" on a long flight, you should consult your doctor. And the next time you fly:

- Avoid medication that impairs blood circulation
- Wear loose clothing and footwear
- Make a habit of walking every 30 minutes or so
- Sit straight so as to avoid putting pressure on the lower back and legs
- Use your carry-on as a footstool to relieve leg pressure
- Don't fall asleep for extended periods in the same position
- Increase your water intake dramatically, which should also help keep you walking in the aisles

FIGHT BACK PAIN

You can wrench your back even before you board, just by using bad form getting your suitcases in the car. What you can do: use wheels whenever possible, even if you feel dorky doing it. Pack two lighter bags instead of one really heavy one. Spend the $1.50 for a Smarte Carte.

Watch How You Lift

Be especially careful when loading and unloading your carry-ons out of overhead bins. You can do severe damage to your lower back if you're not careful.

Once airborne, get up and move around at least once an hour,

because sitting in a cramped chair can put stress on your spine and strain your back muscles.

Use a pillow to support your lower back and/or elevate your knees above your hips by putting your feet on a briefcase, carry-on bag or a stack of magazines. This takes some of the load off the small muscles along your spine.

PREGNANT TRAVELERS

Unless you're having a high-risk pregnancy, traveling while you're pregnant poses no special health risks, either for mother or child. Still, special precautions are advised.

Always discuss your travel plans with your physician before you make any reservations.

Think twice about traveling to third-world countries. Many immunizations and medications routinely recommended for travelers to developing nations are either unsafe or haven't been adequately studied in pregnant women.

Malaria poses a special risk—it may result in a more severe infection—and increases the risk of miscarriage, stillbirth, and premature birth.

Some antimalarial drugs, like chloroquine, may be safely taken during pregnancy. Others, including doxycycline, may not.

If you get traveler's diarrhea, do not use antibiotics unless directed by a doctor. Care should also be taken in using any over-the-counter medication. Talk to your doctor about which ones to bring with you, since pharmacies in other countries may carry unfamiliar products or different formulations than the ones you usually use.

Time Your Travel

The best time to travel during pregnancy is during the second trimester, when you're less likely to have morning sickness and fatigue and you're not yet very big. During your first trimester, you may be more affected than usual by motion sickness. Check with your doctor before taking any motion-sickness medication, even if it's over-the-counter.

Don't travel anywhere during the last six weeks of pregnancy. It may precipitate labor, and you don't want to be away from home when you're about to deliver.

When on board:

Always wear your seat belt. Belt extensions are available if the belt is too tight.

Travel in loose-fitting clothing. Dehydration and cramped quarters compromise circulation, so don't add insult to injury by wearing anything tight.

Do isometric exercises and walk around the cabin every hour or two—it'll keep swelling to a minimum. But be aware that it still

INFANTS IN THE AIR

Because infants don't always react well to being in an airplane, anything you can do to ease their flight will be doubly appreciated—by your child and you, as well as your neighbors.

One trick is to feed them during ascent and descent. Since babies don't know to swallow or yawn to reduce ear pain from cabin pressure, feeding them will force swallowing.

You cannot bring a car seat onto an aircraft unless it will fit into overhead storage. New model, dual-purpose infant carriers, however, are permitted if they carry the FAA sticker approving the seat for air travel.

Not all flight personnel are familiar with the newer rules. You may have to point out that the seat is FAA approved.

may be tough to get your shoes back on.

Support your lower back with a pillow, and prop your feet up on a suitcase or stack of magazines.

Carry your own bottled water and healthy snacks.

Carry your medical records with you, and always bring your doctor's name and telephone number. Get references for doctors at your destination, just in case.

FLYING THE TOXIC SKIES

As if concerns about crashes and terrorists aren't enough, now there's increasing concern about the quality of cabin air. The Centers for Disease Control, which has been studying the issue for several years, recently found that several people caught tuberculosis after sitting near an infected passenger on a long flight. Flight attendants are being studied for the effects of consistent exposure to secondhand smoke as well.

Why the Concern Now?

While previous generations of aircraft pumped in only fresh air, planes built since the 1980s provide a 50-50 mixture of fresh and recirculated air. At any given time, about half the air in a cabin is recycled and half is fresh. Manufacturers claim this air is safe, since it passes through the same high-efficiency particle (HEPA) air filters used in hospitals.

But in a 1986 study, the National Academy of Sciences found that current equipment barely provides minimum acceptable air quality on planes with full passenger loads. And filters that aren't properly maintained can become dirty and ineffective. They also do not filter out viruses.

Dry Air & Disease

Dry cabin air makes a particularly hospitable environment for all sorts of unwanted airborne pathogens. Prolonged exposure to dry air irritates nasal passages, and cracks in membranes invite infection.

If there are vents about your seat, open them. The airflow will grow cooler with altitude, so layer accordingly.

Ask the flight attendant to set the fresh air system all the way up since the equipment may not be set at its maximum level on flights with few passengers.

Fly first or business class if you can. Fewer passengers and more space in the front of the plane means fresher air. Also, the front of the aircraft is better ventilated.

If you're flying near someone who's coughing and sneezing, see if you can change your seat.

"Bacteria essentially slide off wetness," says Dr. Herbert Patrick, a respiratory specialist at Thomas Jefferson University Hospital in Philadelphia. Also do whatever you can to keep hydrated.

DEHYDRATION DANGER

Many of the symptoms of jet lag—or any discomfort after a long flight—have less to do with crossing time zones than the fact that you'll arrive dehydrated. Cabin air has actually been tested (by Boeing Company) at less than 10% humidity, making it considerably drier than the Sahara Desert. (Optimal comfort falls around the relative humidity factor of about 50%.)

What to Do

- Don't board thirsty or very full. Digestion requires a lot of fluid.
- Take in 8 ounces of fluid, preferably water, for every hour in the air. So for a 5-hour flight, drink a quart of water.
- Don't rely on the beverage cart. Use your own bottled water or unsweetened juice.
- Avoid caffeinated beverages. That means coffee and certain soft drinks, which are also high in sodium.
- Stay away from alcohol, a diuretic, which may actually speed up the dehydration process.
- Pass on the peanuts and pretzels—both of which have too much salt.
- Keep your skin moisturized. Use a light moisturizer (many models, who fly constantly, swear by Kiehl's products, available by mail order or at department stores). Spritz your face every so often with a bottled mist sprayer (Evian makes a good one) or even a plant mister.
- Prevent your nasal passages and sinuses from drying out by applying a little oil (almond, jojoba, olive or plain mineral) inside your nostrils.
- Humidify the air periodically by breathing through a damp handkerchief.
- Continue taking in fluids after landing, since it may take a few days to totally rehydrate yourself. Also, a good soak (in the pool, the sea or a bathtub) the day you fly will help.

⚠️

PESTICIDE PERIL

Many countries require all airlines entering their airports to spray aircraft with pesticide. Some carriers spray empty planes; others do the fumigation with passengers in their seats. The practice is controversial—the U.S. Department of Transportation, for one, is lobbying to stop it worldwide—and may have adverse effects for passengers who have respiratory ailments and/or heightened sensitivities to any or all of the toxic chemicals in the sprays.

Countries where spraying is routine: Argentina, Australia, Barbados, Fiji, Grenada, India, Jamaica, Kenya, New Zealand, Panama and Trinidad. You may also encounter it on flights between the U.K. and India and Kenya.

Source: U.S. Department of Transportation.

Comfort Aloft

There is more to safe flying than simply arriving at your destination. Air travel has both physical and mental impact.

Finding a "safe seat" on an aircraft, particularly on a long flight, means seating for the most comfort, the greatest safety and the highest value for your travel dollar.

Scheduled airlines in North America and Western Europe use less than a dozen aircraft models. Interior designs are fundamentally the same, and comfort and safety features relatively standard. But knowing the ins and outs of professional air travel can determine a better outcome for your journey—whether it's for business or pleasure.

RIGHT SEAT, RIGHT PLANE

C hoosing an airline is usually a matter of destination,

BREATHE EASY

Air, or the lack of it, is the major comfort (and safety) factor in jet travel. With the plane flying between 30,000 and 40,000 feet, cabin air is maintained at the equivalent of being at 5,000 to 7,500 feet on the earth's surface. Air is thin. The body is getting less oxygen. This can lead to headaches, blurry vision, light-headedness and fatigue. Concentrate on deep, slow breathing to minimize effects.

2. Flying Smart
If business is your travel purpose, the better air and comfort of business class are essential to arriving relaxed and overcoming jet lag in the shortest possible time. Many big companies insist on 24 hours rest before executives launch into work.

1. The Right Class
First class and business class offer wider seats and more ventilation since the air volume is about three times higher than that in the regular cabin. (Pilots have it best in the cockpit where the ventilation is 10 times higher than in the econo-my section.)

4. First Row Seats
Bulkhead seats offer superior leg room and no forward seat to reclin in your lap. These seats are best fo traveling with infants, children and physical deficiencies. Downside: arr rests, which shift out of the way in other seats, cannot be moved, so stretching out for sleep (or obesity) is not an option in a first row seat. Also, underseat bag storage can be problem on a full flight.

t Row Seats
e are prime seating
e savvy traveler
xtra leg room, but
nean extra respon-
y. You must be will-
nd able to open the
in an emergency.
cally impaired per-
and children are not
o sit in these rows.
l the rows in front
t rows. The seat
don't recline.

5. Swelling Limbs
Body tissues expand with altitude.
This is because of increased tissue
absorbency of nitrogen gas. Body
parts can expand by as much as
20 to 35% at prolonged altitudes
between 30,000 and 40,000 feet.
Feet swell (wear loose shoes), rings
choke blood to fingers (remove
jewelry) and tooth filings swell,
especially amalgam fillings susceptible to internal air bubbles.

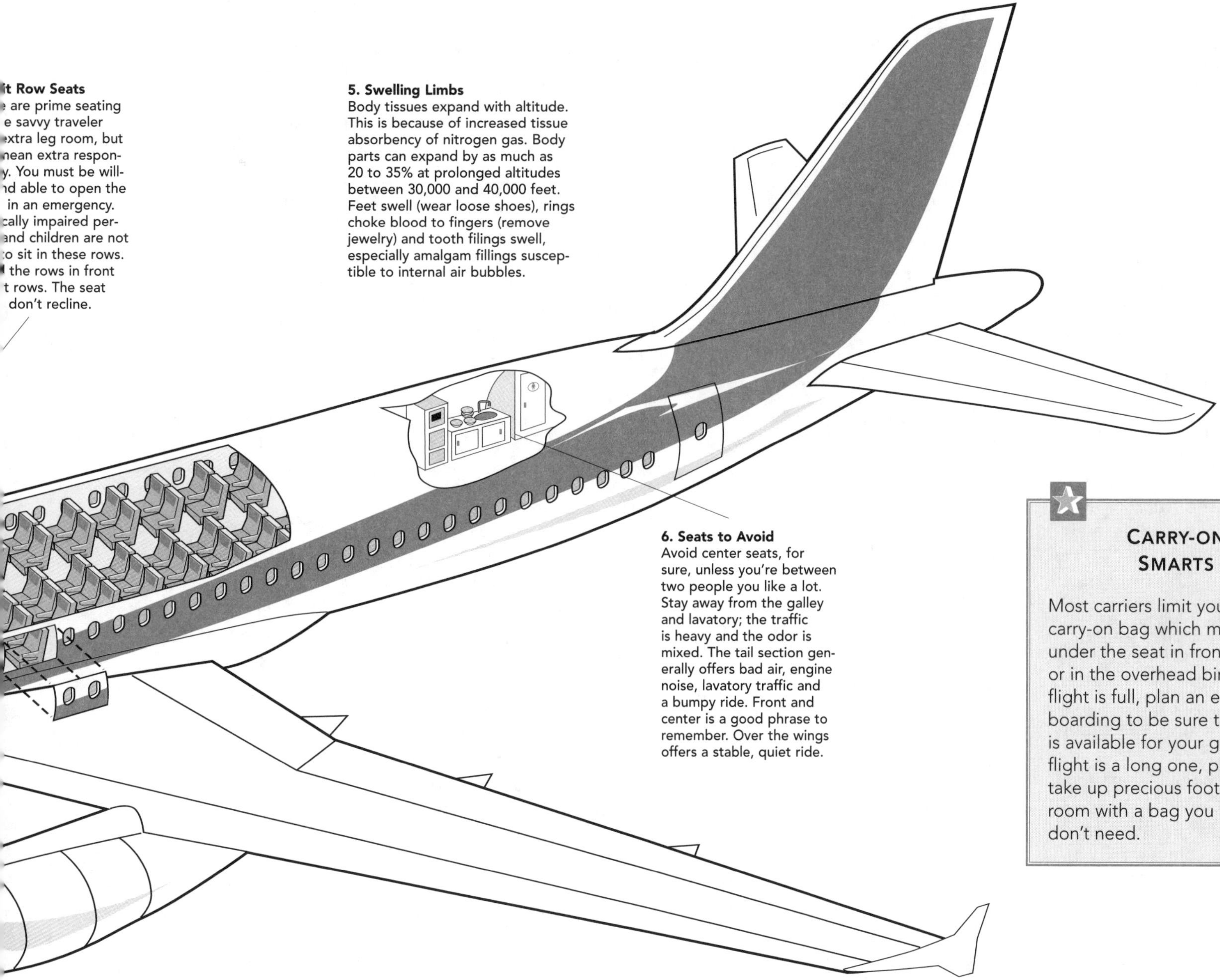

6. Seats to Avoid
Avoid center seats, for
sure, unless you're between
two people you like a lot.
Stay away from the galley
and lavatory; the traffic
is heavy and the odor is
mixed. The tail section generally offers bad air, engine
noise, lavatory traffic and
a bumpy ride. Front and
center is a good phrase to
remember. Over the wings
offers a stable, quiet ride.

CARRY-ON SMARTS

Most carriers limit you to one
carry-on bag which must fit
under the seat in front of you
or in the overhead bin. If the
flight is full, plan an early
boarding to be sure that space
is available for your gear. If the
flight is a long one, plan not to
take up precious foot and leg
room with a bag you really
don't need.

timing and price. Getting the right seat is a matter of planning and frequently negotiation.

Aircraft are designed for minimum comfort. Marketing staff are assured by statistics that passengers are more interested in airline reliability, such as on-time arrivals and low fares. While true for short-range travel, the longer hauls do tend to use larger aircraft which offer less cramped seating arrangements than flights of an hour or less.

Choose a Big Plane

If you're large of frame and have a distance to travel, definitely seek out a nonstop flight that supports equipment like the Airbus A-300 to 600s, and the 767-200s and 300s. In some cases, but rarely on domestic flights, Boeing 747s and Lockheed L-1011s are still being used and they're fairly roomy.

Worst Seats in the Skies

Every airline has them: seats that don't recline. There are an estimated 77,000 airline seats in America's scheduled fleet that don't tilt back.

The airlines really don't want you to know about these seats. Most claim that they don't show them in their computer. Even your travel agent doesn't know.

Essentially, any seat in front of an exit row will not recline for obvious safety reasons. Similarly, seats at the very rear of the aircraft seldom recline because they are butted up against the bulkhead.

AIRLINE CUSTOMER RANKINGS

Here's how the top 11 U.S. airlines stacked up in 2001 in terms of consumer complaints to the Department of Transportation. Criticism covers flight delays and cancellations, baggage handling, customer service and disputes over fares and frequent-flier miles.

Top-10 U.S. carriers

Airline	Complaints	Passengers	Complaints per 100K Passengers
Southwest	281	73,742,867	0.38
Alaska	174	13,667,526	1.27
American Eagle	204	11,973,856	1.70
US Airways	1,049	56,146,174	1.87
Northwest	1,065	54,171,658	1.97
Delta	2,021	93,386,645	2.16
Continental	952	42,779,867	2.23
American	1,964	78,115,155	2.51
TWA	528	20,791,995	2.54
United	2,448	75,453,979	3.24
America West	729	19,576,031	3.72

Statistics for foreign airlines don't take into account the number of passengers carried, so the rankings reflect only the number of complaints registered. The bigger the airline, the higher the complaint number.

Foreign Carriers

Carrier	Total Complaints	Carrier	Total Complaints
Air France	221	Mexicana	45
Alitalia Airlines	177	Allegro	40
British Airways	148	Sabena	39
Air Canada	86	TACA	38
Lufthansa	74	Virgin Atlantic	33
Air Jamaica	65	LACSA	30
KLM	52	Aero Mexico	27
SwissAir	49	Iberia Airlines	27

Roughly 10% of a plane's economy seating won't recline. The worst aircraft are the 747s (all those exits). The Boeing 777s and the Lockheed L-1011s have the fewest nontilts.

Worse Yet

No one ever wants a middle seat. The aircraft offering the least number of those are Boeing 767s and the Airbus A-300s. The MD11s, Boeing 747s and DC-10s have more middle seats in coach class than do other aircraft.

Seating near the galleys is noisy and disturbing, particularly on a long flight. Needless to say, seats across from the lavatories have their own charm—eventually every passenger on board will be hovering over your seat during a long flight. If sitting near the bathroom isn't appealing, then your chances are better on a 747, DC-10 or a Boeing 777 where there are fewer seats near lavatories than on an Airbus, MD-11 or a 767.

The hands-down winner of worst seats would be a middle seat that doesn't recline and is located directly across from the lavatory

BUILD YOUR OWN SAFETY MARGIN

Today's airline hub routes make it impossible to avoid the commuter lines. But you can minimize risk:

➤ Avoid commuters when the weather at your departure point or destination is really bad. For example, thunderstorms, tornado warnings, heavy snow or fog conditions.

➤ Be particularly cautious during winter in the northern climes where "icing in the clouds" is a flight hazard. Airplanes (and pilots) do not like ice. Flying in icing conditions is not as much a problem for large jets as it is for smaller propeller-driven aircraft.

➤ Travel in off-peak hours when pilots and air traffic controllers have more time and less air traffic delays. At least one crash in recent years was a result of an aircraft icing while "holding" to land.

Slow Down

Pilots have the pressures of schedules and flight operations to contend with. Although every plane leaves the gate at the pilot's discretion, there may be times when your discretion and schedule have more latitude than the pilot's. If weather is bad, wait a day or two if you can.

with the only window view being the leading edge of an engine.

COMMUTER AIRLINE SMARTS

It is a matter of record that commuter airlines have a higher fatality rate than the larger carriers. Nevertheless, your chances of being involved in a fatal air crash, even on a commuter carrier, are still less than one-half a chance in a million!

Commuter aircraft are more dangerous than larger airliners for a number of reasons. The planes are smaller and fly at lower altitudes than jet carriers. This makes commuters more susceptible to weather related problems, whereas the big jets fly above the weather. Secondly, commuter aircraft do not have the same level of sophisticated navigational weather-avoidance and backup systems that are standard on full-sized jets.

Finally, commuter lines, even though they are affiliated with major scheduled carriers, are not necessarily maintained to the same standards as the regular airlines. Pilots, too, tend to be less experienced than those of full-sized jet aircraft. Also, the high-technology flight simulators available for the big jets do not exist for all of the various craft flown by the commuter lines, so pilot training is not as thorough, particularly for emergency procedures related to equipment failures. In fact, the primary cause of commuter air crashes since 1986 has been "pilot error."

How Safe Are They?

Commuter planes are increasingly safer. More demanding traffic and schedules are bringing improvement to the industry. Since 1986 there have been no commuter fatalities attributed to equipment failure, whereas in the 1970s aircraft deficiency resulted in fatality rates exceeding one in a million.

HOW SAFE ARE OUR PLANES?

Much safer than they were 15 years ago, despite the tragic crashes we hear about. Passenger numbers have jumped from 300 to 650 million, but the number of fatalities per one billion flight hours has been cut in half.

About 74% of U.S. air carrier accidents in the past 10 years are the result of crew errors or maintenance oversights. Only about 10% of aircraft crashes were caused by a failure of the aircraft systems.

Statistically, even if the aircraft themselves were absolutely failsafe, 9 out of 10 fatalities would have occurred because of human error.

Source: American Institute of Aeronautics and Astronautics.

COMMUTER AIRLINES

The top-20 commuter lines employ a variety of aircraft types that connect hub routes to feeder airports. Many popular models are foreign-built with American-made engines and navigational systems. Increasingly, carriers are adding smaller jets to the commuter fleet with improved performance, comfort and safety.

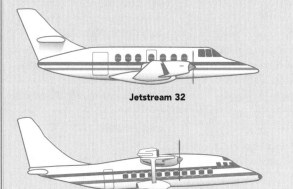

Jetstream 32

Shorts 360

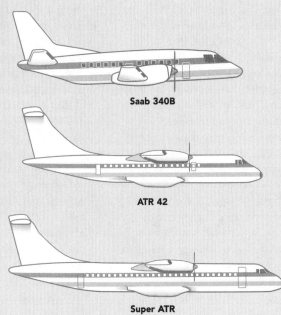

Saab 340B

ATR 42

Super ATR

SAFETY REMINDERS

Leading security expert William McCarthy, PhD of Threat Research Inc. offers the following advice for people who travel within the United States.

- *Be alert to risks.* Best advice: Live your life as usual, but increase your awareness of what is going on around you.
- *Watch your surroundings* as you walk down the street or enter a building. Be aware of the people and events around you. Don't daydream.
- *Avoid points of vulnerability.* When you enter a building—to be safer—put as much brick-and-mortar as possible between you and the outside walls. Don't linger in the lobby. The area of greatest danger is near big plate glass windows of buildings, stores and airports. If possible, keep a reinforced cement column between you and the glass.
- *Beware of mail bombs and biological agents* that might be sent through the mail. Best advice: If you get a suspicious package, don't open it.
- *Consider a package suspicious if it…*
  - is addressed to someone who doesn't exist.
  - carries an unfamiliar return address.
  - carries excessive postage.
  - is stained.

- *Very important:* If you are suspicious of a letter or parcel, leave it unopened, clear the area and call for help.
- *Never be embarrassed about calling the police.* If it is a false alarm (based on legitimate suspicion), no harm is done—but if there is a bomb, failing to call the police can hurt or kill. Best advice: If you notice a suspicious package or object in your workplace, make an immediate effort to find out how the package got there. If you don't get an answer that satisfies you by the end of the day, call the police. Don't go home for the night without resolving your worry.
- *Warning:* Never remain in the vicinity of an unattended package or suitcase left in a public area.

… and Overseas

Benjamin Weiner of Probe International, Inc. offers this advice to the international traveler:

- *Think carefully about where you go.*
- *Reduce your risk:* Some countries pose greater risks than others. A country may be an avowed foe of the US or something may be happening now that makes a country a high-risk place to visit.
- *Keep up with current events* so you know the latest political, economic and social hot spots. Your travel agent or business

travel department should know the latest State Department warnings on areas to avoid or contact the US State Department at 202-647-5225 or the embassy or nearest consulate of the country. Helpful: Travel warnings from the State Department are available online at *http://travel.state.gov/travel_warnings.html*.

- *Plan when to go.* Terrorist acts are most likely to occur on symbolic days. Take into account religious holidays, ethnic observances and national days.
- *Be a security-smart traveler.* Join an airline club for a relatively safe place to wait for your flight. Travel light, with everything in one or two bags.
- *Be as inconspicuous as possible.* Best advice: Dress quietly. Wear a business suit or sports clothes in muted tones. Don't wear religious symbols. Avoid clothing with logos of American colleges or sports teams. Don't wear flashy jewelry or an expensive watch. Helpful: Your luggage should not have any American symbols or logos of American companies. It must have an ID tag, but put your identification into the holder backward. If the luggage is lost, the tag will be taken apart to learn your identity. Otherwise, anyone looking at your ID tag will see only a blank card.
- *Be a street-smart traveler.*

Avoid street demonstrations and political gatherings.
- *Be polite and soft-spoken wherever you go.*
- *Visit high-profile tourist attractions during off-peak hours.* That will not only help keep you safe, it will let you see the sights when the crowds are the thinnest.

IMPORTANT WEB SITES

➤ State Department's Bureau of Consular Affairs (*www.travel.state.gov*).

➤ British Government foreign office (*www.fco.gov.uk*).

➤ Abe's Travel Safety Guide (*www.travel-safety-and-health.com*).

➤ Foreseeable Risk Analysis Center (*www.frac.com*).

➤ Bureau of Transportation Statistics (*www.bts.gov*). Important travel statistics including accident, on-time, and delay information for common carriers.

➤ Federal Aviation Administration Traveler Briefing (*www.faa.gov/apa/traveler.htm*)

…and Health

➤ Travel Health Online (*www.tripprep.com*). Country-specific health and safety information.

PART 3

Travel Tips & Skills

Driving Self-Defense

Plan, Pick & Pack

Airlines & Airports

Driving Self-Defense

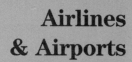

Safe Driving, Better Driving

Every year, over 40,000 Americans are killed in car accidents, and many more are injured. The majority of accidents are caused by human failure: judgment errors, traffic violations and drinking and driving.

DRIVE BETTER, LIVE LONGER

Most Americans stop learning how to drive as soon as they get their license. Too often those rudimentary skills aren't up to the demands of today's high-performance cars, congested streets and super-fast roadways.

Luckily, many of the techniques taught at the *Bob Bondurant School of Driving* in Ontario, California to race-car drivers can be readily applied by amateurs.

The first principle is smoothness. The easy flow of the vehicle down the road through imperceptible accelerating and breaking not only makes for a fluid ride, but also makes for a safe one. Visualize the ideal movement of your car like a steel ball rolling through a glass chute.

How to Be a Smooth Driver

How do you get that degree of smoothness? Through complete control! Make all your movements *slow and progressive*.

Start with posture. The driver should be sitting upright, buttocks hard against the back of the seat.

Hands should be on the wheel at the 9:00 and 3:00 positions, with each thumb falling naturally to either side. No other grip will enable the driver to hold the wheel during a front tire blowout or to make an instantaneous change in direction.

Roll, Don't Tromp

When accelerating, roll the side of the foot onto the accelerator with just enough pressure from the ball of the foot to increase the engine speed. Plopping the whole foot down on the pedal generates excessive thrust and the car will lurch forward. Introducing and releasing gasoline requires a gentle foot.

To maintain smoothness, don't accelerate until you've determined that the lane you are merging into is clear. That means don't tailgate the car ahead of you and then make an abrupt turn out.

Brake with Balance

If you have an older car without ABS (antilock braking system), then you will need to brake with the same attention to control. The ideal to keep in mind is to balance the chassis on the wheels to get a solid "grab" from a patch of rubber on each wheel. Brake too hard and the chassis will pitch forward, unloading the rear wheels, requiring the driver to oversteer to keep the rear end

HOW TO MANEUVER "FISHTAIL" SKIDS

1. Without touching the brake, take foot off the accelerator. Allow car to slow naturally.

2. Steer in whichever direction the back of the car is sliding. Do not overcorrect.

3. Hold the steering direction until the skid lessens, then smoothly straighten the wheel.

4. When the car is straightened, gently reapply acceleration increasing speed slowly.

from coming around. Release the brakes just as gently.

WEATHER HAZARDS

Your best defense if you find yourself having to drive in bad weather is to *slow down*.

Ice Conditions

When a cold front turns rain into snow, wet roads can become unexpectedly icy. The road is most slippery when the temperature is around 32°F. That is danger time! Such weather tends to occur early in the season, when drivers haven't yet fully adjusted to winter driving.

Reduce the chance of skidding by being very careful when you brake or accelerate. If you do skid, follow the steps in the illustrations on skidding.

Beware of Black Ice

Black ice is ice that blends into the road visually. It is particularly dangerous because you can't see it. Be on the lookout in areas where there is an absence of sunlight (such as underpasses or in the shadows of tall buildings).

Remember, ice forms first and melts last on bridges.

SAFE IN THE RAIN

Rainy road conditions significantly reduce traction. Your car needs a minimum of four seconds stopping distance between it and the car in front of

you. Light rain can be even more treacherous than heavy storms, since a slight amount of water mixing with oil and dirt on the road makes the surface very slick.

Rain-Ready Action

Make sure your window wipers are in good condition.

Apply a rain repellent to your windows. These products cause rain to bead up and roll down your windshield quickly, significantly improving visibility.

Once you're out in the rain, turn on the car lights to make yourself more visible. Turn on the defroster to improve your own visibility. Whenever possible, try to drive in the tracks of the car ahead of you.

In areas with a lot of wet roads, install rain tires. The Goodyear Aquatread is a good one.

■ When driving through deep water, go slowly so you don't splash water in the engine, which can cause the motor to stall. Worst case, it will cause hydrostatic static lockup and damage the engine. Avoid deep puddles, which can hide potholes.

■ Hydroplaning occurs when a wedge of water rises between the tires and the road. The tires then lose contact with the surface of the road, making it impossible to control the car. This happens more often when tires have less than one-eighth of an inch tread

depth or are improperly inflated. A sudden burst of acceleration also increases the possibility of hydroplaning. Do not brake.

Finessing Fog

■ Turn on your low-beam headlights, especially at night when the glare-back of high beams actually reduces visibility.

■ Drive at reduced speed. Watch the edge of the road or the center line. The white line on the right-hand side of the road is called the "fog line" and is meant to provide navigation in heavy fog.

■ Turn on your emergency flashers and keep to the inside lane on the highway.

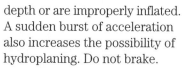

FRONT WHEEL SKID CONTROL

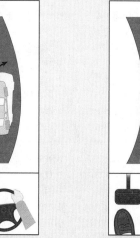

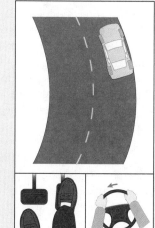

1. Release accelerator and do not touch the brake. As speed decreases, so will severity of skid.

2. Straighten front wheels to line up in the direction that the front of the car is heading.

3. When grip is restored, move back to the left-hand side of the road and gently accelerate.

- Keep the radio low, or off, and a window cracked to listen for cars and especially large trucks.
- Run the defroster on high to keep the windshield clear.
- Wear light sunglasses to see better in the glare created by fog.

BLIZZARD SAFETY

On a long drive, get to a motel and wait it out. If you do get caught in the open highway, your best bet is to pull over to a safe spot off the road—well off the track of snow removal equipment.

- Stay with your car, as it's easy to become disoriented on foot. Limit engine use to conserve fuel. Run the engine with downwind windows cracked.
- Periodically clear the snow away from your tailpipe each time you run the motor for heat.
- Savvy snow country drivers keep storm parkas, hats, gloves and even sleeping bags in the trunk.
- Cell phones are saving more road travelers every day. Don't leave home without one.

Snow Know-how

In snow, you will need 3 to 12 times the stopping distance required on dry roads. The lighter your car, the more distance you will need.

Snow tires improve both traction and stopping performance significantly. Experts recommend snow tires on all four wheels to maximize safety, particularly when it comes to stopping power on frozen road surfaces. Almost all new cars come equipped with radial tires which offer superior gripping performance in rain and to some degree, snow. But radial, tires are not snow-configured unless marked M&S (mud and snow) on the sidewall. Chains are even better—they cut stopping distance on icy roads in half.

SNOW DRIVING

Driving fast in snow conditions is easy but it is almost impossible to stop quickly. To stop, reduce your speed by at least half and double the distance between vehicles. The biggest mistake made by sports utility vehicle (SUV) drivers is assuming that because they can go in the snow, they can also stop faster. Not so. Stopping conditions on snow-slicked roads are the same for both two-wheel and all-wheel drive vehicles.

Braking. Light, gentle pressure on the brakes is essential to avoid sliding into a skid. Cars equipped with ABS (antilock brakes) afford greater control in snow than ordinary brakes. If you are driving a non-ABS-equipped car, braking on snow and ice should be done with quick pump actions on the pedal. Jamming down hard on the brake pedal will cause the wheels to lock and set the vehicle into a spin.

SNOW BANK ESCAPE TECHNIQUES

Unless you have an all-wheel-drive vehicle, remember that a rear-wheel-drive car has to push the car out of a snow bank while a front-wheel-drive car has to pull it out. Obviously, the wheels need to be free to do the job.

➤ Before you start the motor, turn your wheels from side to side to push away the snow from the sides of the tires.

➤ Clear as much snow as possible away from the wheels (keep a shovel in the trunk during winter months).

➤ Let the motor warm up, then, with the car in a lower gear, step on the accelerator and apply pressure slowly and steadily to give the tires a better grip. Gunning the engine will make your wheels spin quickly, digging the car further in.

➤ Rock the car gently back and forth, shifting between reverse and drive to build momentum. *Warning:* Rocking can wreck transmissions. When rocking, be sure the tires stop moving before changing direction. Do not shift into drive while the car is rolling backward and vice versa. Pull out of the bank completely once the car starts moving.

➤ The National Safety Council advises keeping a bag of cat litter in the trunk to sprinkle in front of the driving wheels for added traction. You can also buy plastic devices which can be easily wedged under snowbound wheels for superior traction.

EXTREME DRIVING

Tornadoes. Don't try to outrun a tornado. They move at 70 miles per hour. If one is very close, leave your car for a safe building or, in the worst case, lie flat in a ditch or gully.

Hurricanes. Be prepared with a full gas tank so you can evacuate if a warning is issued. Avoid driving on coastal or low-lying roads because of the threat of flooding. Get out early.

Earthquakes. Avoid bridges, overpasses and any structure that may have been damaged by the tremors. Remain in your car. It's safer than getting out and trying to find safety.

Rising waters. The force of the current of swiftly running water on a badly flooded street may pull your car off to the side. Ease off on the gas, don't brake and steer away from the current.

If you get caught in a flash flood and the engine stalls, get out of the car immediately, as the car might get swept away. Carry small children and link hands with adults.

CARS & FLOODS

Why, during storm conditions, do we see so many people being rescued from their vehicles? Because cars do not float well, and some drivers are fooled into thinking they can make it through.

If you drive into floodwater at high speed, the effect is almost the same as hitting a wall. Water is thrown into the engine compartment, the vehicle stalls and you're stuck. If you must drive in flood conditions, pay close attention to road contours, there may be water where the road dips. Night flooding is particularly hard to see, so exercise extreme caution and drive at slow speed.

If you encounter flooding and must enter, try not to be first. Watch the person ahead of you to see if they make it. Do not follow a utility vehicle if you are in a car. There's a big difference in height and ground clearance.

As a rule, once water reaches mid-point on your wheel hubs, you're in deep enough and should withdraw. If you do decide to press on, drive slowly but steadily, in a low gear to keep the engine at high revs so water won't creep into the exhaust.

Once out of the water, drive with your foot lightly on the brakes to dry them out.

ESCAPE FROM A SINKING CAR

➤ A car will sometimes float on deep water and that is the time to get out. If you have a sunroof, use it to escape. Or open a window and crawl out. That is the best escape route.

➤ If you run into water, the first thing to do is unlock the doors. Remove seat belts and switch on the lights. Battery or electric window motors will fail when wet, especially with seawater. Act fast!

➤ If the car is submerging rapidly and window escape is impossible, bring small children close to you. Avoid opening the doors. Wait until the water pressure inside the vehicle equals that outside.

➤ Stay near the top of the car so you can breathe the remaining air while you try to open the doors. Exit holding the hands of any passengers.

1. If the car is truly submerging and you are unable to escape by window or sunroof, immediately unlock the doors. Do not attempt to open them yet. It will allow water to rush in too quickly and you may not be able to escape.

2. Remain calm and reassure passengers. Release all seat belts and get them out of the way.

3. Turn on the head lights to be seen by rescuers.

4. Lift children out of car seats and keep their heads up near the roof where there is more air.

5. Allow the water inside to equalize pressure with the water outside in order to open the door. Then exit.

Driving With the Big Rigs

We share the roads with large trucks every day and they are dangerous. Those big rigs can weigh upwards of 80,000 pounds and range from 40 to 100 feet long in triple-trailer combinations. When large trucks are involved in accidents with cars, 98% of the fatalities are the people in the cars. If you drive, know how to handle yourself around trucks.

BIG RIG REALITY CHECK

If your car and a huge truck are involved in an accident, chances are, statistically, that the cause will be a driving error on your part. According to the *National Highway Traffic Safety Administration (NHTSA)*, 72% of all fatal car-truck accidents are caused by the motorist.

Ultimately, every driver must realize that 80,000 pounds of steel hurtling at speeds up to 70 mph or more along the highway is not safe to be around, let alone toy with.

STOP & GO POWER

Car drivers understand that semitrailers cannot stop as fast as cars traveling the same speed. But what is the stopping distance? The *Insurance Institute for Highway Safety (IIHS)* says that a car traveling at 55 mph can stop in about 133 feet. A loaded tractor trailer at the same speed requires 196 feet to stop. That assumes the truck's brakes are not overheated from heavy traffic conditions, which would lengthen the stopping distance.

Reaction Time

The *National Safety Council (NSC)* warns about reaction time: the amount of time it takes to get your foot on the brake. Given that an alert driver's reaction time is about three-quarters of a second, that adds about another 60 feet to stopping distance at a speed of 55 mph.

What About Brake Lag?

Brake lag is the time required for brakes to achieve maximum stopping power. Cars have hydraulic brakes with low lag factors. Tractor trailers have air brakes, which are slightly slower, adding many feet to the stopping

distance. NSC studies show that a fully loaded tractor trailer running at 55 mph with hot brakes will travel 335 feet before coming to a complete stop.

No matter whose statistics you choose to accept, a car that drives in front of a big rig on the highway better be way out in front.

SHIFT & TURN

Tractor trailers generally have to move to the left as a first step to making a right turn or

conversely, for a left turn. That is especially true on city streets.

Unprepared car drivers misinterpret the lane shift as the beginning of a left turn. They assume they can pass on the right (a taboo with all trucks) and get trapped between the truck and the curb as the truck makes its originally intended turn.

Turn Signals Tell the Tale

If you are behind a large truck, watch the turn signals. Believe what they are telling you and leave lots of space. Most truck

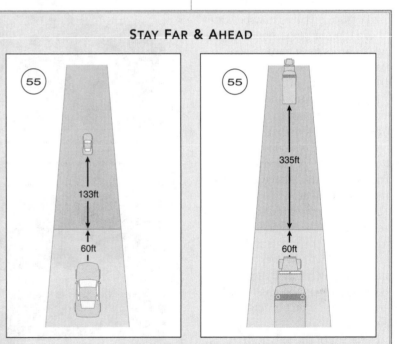

STAY FAR & AHEAD

55 — 133ft — 60ft

55 — 335ft — 60ft

Most drivers gravely underestimate stopping distance required at highway speeds. Reaction time to hit the brakes carries you 60 feet or more before even beginning to stop.

If you are not at least 400 feet ahead of a large truck traveling at 55 mph, you are in danger. A good defensive driving measure is to stay well out in front, change lanes or allow the truck to pass you.

drivers are polite, good drivers and will signal their moves.

NEITHER NIMBLE NOR QUICK

Since trucks can't move around on the highways as easily as cars, professional drivers give themselves and other motorists as many options as possible. For

BEWARE OF BOBTAILS

"Bobtails"—tractors without their trailers—may look more agile than when tethered, but the facts indicate otherwise. Fatal accidents involving bobtails are 13 times higher than for tractors pulling trailers. It takes almost as long to stop a tractor running without its trailer as it does a fully loaded rig. Without the trailer's weight, a bobtail has reduced tire-to-pavement contact area, compromising braking and steering.

example, a truck in the center lane of a highway isn't "hogging" the road. Rather, the driver is doubling the options in case he has to swerve left or right.

Hard braking in a tractor is far more likely to result in a jack-knife (where the trailer skids 90 degrees to the tractor) or an overturned trailer.

Bad Place to Hang Out

If you are going to pass a big rig, get it over with quickly and efficiently. Do not hover around the back wheels, especially if there's a slow vehicle in front of the truck. Should the truck have to brake suddenly, the trailer is very likely to swing into your lane and a mere bump will send you off the road.

The best technique: Stay behind the truck until the road ahead of you is clear enough to pass the entire length of the truck.

Be alert. Accelerate briskly, making certain the truck driver knows where you are. If you can see his face in his mirror, he can see you.

Get by quickly and leave the trucker plenty of room before signaling to change lanes.

Stay Out in Front

Don't let trucks crowd your bumper. Keep your speed up or move into another lane. On downhill runs, truckers like to gain momentum for the uphill side. Your best bet is to stay out of the way. Remember, any "argument" with an 80,000-pound vehicle is weighted in their favor.

WINTER DRIVING TIPS

You can minimize problems you face driving in nasty

weather, says Bob Cerullo, a certified master mechanic and owner of VINS Motor Service Corporation in New York.

Antilock Brakes (ABS)
In a skid

On ABS-equipped cars, the ABS system senses a skid and automatically pumps the brakes to stop. But many drivers continue to pump the brakes—which causes the ABS to stop functioning and makes the car unable to stop.

Safer: When you feel a skid starting, press down the brake pedal to allow the ABS to stop the car, and keep pressing. Don't let grinding and growling sounds—which are normal—make you release your foot.

Important: On non-ABS-equipped cars, pump the brakes to help control the car and prevent a skid.

Hydroplaning

On a wet road, tire treads may not be able to grip the pavement or flush aside water.

In cases such as this, tires sit on top of a thin film of water, like a water ski atop the surface of a lake. This is called "hydroplaning"—and when it happens, your car is out of control. Your steering wheel won't respond.

Safer: On wet pavement, slow down to 35 mph or less before curves. Brake gently. Avoid abrupt starts.

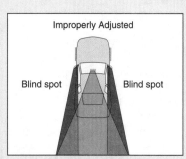

MIRROR IMAGE

Improperly Adjusted

Blind spot   Blind spot

If you can see your rear fender in your side-view mirrors, you are leaving serious blind spots for traffic overtaking your vehicle.

Properly Adjusted

Adjust all three mirrors so that what is visible in each one slightly overlaps what you can see in your main rear-view mirror.

Properly adjusted mirrors allow continuous tracking of an overtaking vehicle from your rearview angle into your peripheral vision.

Crash Strategies

Safe driver or not, each year your chances are one in five that you will be affected by a car crash. Oddly, Americans perceive their chances of being in an accident as only one in a thousand. Drivers who have been ticketed for moving violations—about 10 to 15%—are twice as likely to be involved in a crash. So, your first defense is to overcome the notion that "it can never happen to me."

NO ACCIDENT

Safety experts don't refer to crashes and collisions as accidents. The reason? Around 95% are preventable.

With more motorists driving more vehicles more miles, there is considerable stress associated with being on the road. As busy people try to make up time in their cars, they tend to drive more aggressively, show less tolerance for other people and be less prepared to anticipate driving mistakes.

The number one cause is inattention. Four out of every 10 drivers involved in a crash did nothing to try to prevent it from happening. Because of inattention, they didn't see the collision coming.

Inattention Factors

Inattention comes in different forms. Fatigue. Lighting a cigarette. Fiddling with the radio. Talking on a telephone or CB. Disciplining misbehaving kids in the back seat. Cell phones are attributed to so many accidents in Europe that some countries mandate that drivers pull over while on the phone—or risk a ticket.

As you grow older, aging becomes a factor in inattention. Cognitive processes slow down. Information is processed more slowly. Mental distractions are more common and devoting the level of awareness required for driving becomes more difficult. It is more difficult to see objects in areas of low-light contrast (e.g., seeing a pedestrian crossing the road at dusk).

Speed Kills

The number two cause of accidents is speeding or driving too fast for conditions. There is an increase of almost 30% in the number of crashes that occur on rainy or icy days, when road traction is reduced by slippery conditions. In the past few years, as posted speed limits have been raised, the number of crashes has increased. In states where the limit was raised from 55 to 65 miles per hour, 15 to 30% more crashes have occurred.

Drugs & Alcohol

Driving while impaired accounts for a large number of crashes. The law considers you impaired when your Blood Alcohol Level (BAC) reaches 0.10%. Some states are lowering BAC to 0.08%. According to the Highway Loss Data Institute, drivers with BAC above 0.15% on weekend nights are 380 times more likely to die in a car crash than nondrinkers.

Alcohol and drugs dull a driver's skill, as do many prescribed medications. The public's awareness of the danger of driving and drinking has increased, but for certain groups, particularly males between the ages of 21 and 40, there has been no decline in the rate of driving incidents associated with the use of alcohol. The same is true for drivers over 65.

The good news is found among drivers aged 16 to 20, where the proportion of fatal injuries involving alcohol has declined since 1980.

The number of drug-impaired crashes, particularly in large urban areas, has increased by about 20% in the past few years.

Other Causes

Other major causes of crashes include disregarding traffic control devices, such as stop signs and stop lights. In residential areas, it is estimated that 90% of all drivers fail to come to a complete stop at signs. Failing to yield the right of way is another cause of accidents.

WHAT TO DO IN A CRASH

The first step to take is prevention. Rid yourself of the notion that "it can never happen to me."

Although Americans perceive the chance of being involved in a crash to be slight, statistics prove otherwise. Now is the time to think about the actions you will take at a crash scene, not in the traumatic moments following an accident. Be prepared, especially in those vital 15 to 20 minutes before help arrives.

Before Police Arrive
■ *Secure your vehicle.* Put the car in "Park." Turn off the

THE SAFEST COLOR

Light-colored single-tone cars are safer than dark ones. They have significantly fewer accidents because they stand out from their surroundings so other drivers notice them better. The safest car color is greenish-yellow—then cream, yellow, white. **Least safe colors: red and black.**

LOOK, LISTEN, THEN STOP TO HELP

It's an unpredictable world. Some people appearing to be in trouble are really looking to *make* trouble—for you. People standing by the roadside flagging you to stop are usually an indication of an emergency, but not always. Be careful. They may not really need your help—instead, they may have criminal intent.

➤ Pull well ahead of the person or stalled vehicle. Approach with caution, looking for signs of an accident. Skid marks and broken glass are clues to seek. Carry your cell phone with you if you have one. At night, a flashlight is a must.

➤ From a safe distance, ask the person what happened. If there's no clear evidence of a crash, dial 9-1-1 and report that someone has flagged you down.

➤ Know where you are before you leave your vehicle, either by identifying a mile marker or mentally noting the last exit sign you passed.

➤ If there's the slightest doubt, or if you are alone and there appears to be more people than one at the troubled vehicle, err on the side of caution. Make a note of the location and drive on to secure help.

vehicle. Activate four-way flashers. Check for injuries. If the car is on a major highway or road, particularly at night, get out and stand away from the vehicle. Take immediate action to warn other traffic of the danger ahead. Injured persons should not be moved, but those able to get clear of the car need to do so.

■ *Check the other vehicle.* Ask if the driver and passengers are OK. Say nothing about the accident to indicate fault or blame. Let the police figure it out later, and even then, say as little as possible. Remember, you'll be in shock and not totally clear in laying or accepting blame. Be polite, concise and keep your temper.

■ *If there are no injuries,* keep the accident scene safe from other traffic by waving off vehicles with a flashlight or setting road flares if you or a passerby has them. If possible, move vehicles to the safest area of the road. A mistake most people make is to stand in or near the roadway to wave off oncoming traffic. Don't put yourself between your disabled car and the vehicles traveling on the road. Instead, stand away from your car.

ACTION CHECKLIST

Although the specifics depend on the jurisdiction where a collision occurs, there are general legal and administrative principles that apply to all scenes of an accident.

Your first obligation when you are driving a car involved in a crash or a collision is to stop as near to the scene as possible. This does not mean that you should leave your car in the path of oncoming traffic or in the middle of an intersection.

In most jurisdictions it is permissible to move the car off the roadway if it can be driven. The only exception is when somebody has been injured (*Note:* There are still some jurisdictions where vehicles must remain unmoved until a police officer arrives, but these are becoming fewer).

Get the Facts

■ *Exchange required information.* Obtain information from the other driver(s) and passengers. You'll need their names, addresses, telephone numbers, and for the driver, automobile registration number and insurance company. Drivers must show their driver's license when it is requested.

■ *Unattended vehicle.* If you hit one or otherwise damage property, try to locate the owner. If you can't, attach a written notice, leaving your telephone and license number. In the note, be specific about the damage you caused and its precise location on the vehicle. Examine the vehicle for other damage that you did not cause and include it in your note. Be sure to keep a copy of the damaged vehicle's license number and the exact time and location of the incident.

DON'T GO WITHOUT A FLARE

A savvy driver has flares, also called fuses, in the trunk. You are far more likely to need them than a first-aid kit. Buy flares and practice using them. You might not be able to read the instructions in the dark.

Position three flares to channel the flow of traffic from right to left, away from your car. Place the first flare 300 feet behind your car in line with the right fender. Place the next flare, 100 feet back, in the middle of the car. Place the flare closest to the car, 10 feet back, just outside the left bumper.

Other valuable safety items include emergency flashing lights, strobes and reflector triangles. They are especially useful during the bright daylight, and they don't burn out in a short time, as flares do.

- *Witnesses.* Get the names and telephone numbers of any witness and ask them to note the damage you caused versus any other damage.
- *Police notification.* You are required to notify the police if your vehicle is involved in a collision that results in death, personal injury or minimum property damage (the minimum amount, usually several hundred dollars, depending on the jurisdiction). It is always advisable to notify the authorities. The officer's report may be of use should there be liability claims.
- *Formal reporting.* You are required to file a formal written report if you are the driver of a vehicle involved in any collision that results in injury or damage greater than a minimum amount. You will have several days to submit it to the appropriate state or local agency. Failure to do so can result in license suspension. The reports, which can be obtained from local police departments and insurance companies, are generally confidential and cannot be used as evidence in civil or criminal trials pursuant to the collision.
- *Insurance reporting.* Generally, any incident requiring a report to the police needs to be conveyed to your insurance carrier. Chances are good that your policy requires it and the failure to comply may jeopardize your coverage.
- *Liability.* The owner of a vehicle assumes financial responsibility for the driving actions of others permitted to use their vehicle. In many cases, both the driver and the owner may be liable because of injuries to others.

EMERGENCY CARE

Life-threatening traffic crashes are distressingly common. Every person in the U.S. can expect to be in or witness a traffic crash at least once every 10 years. Whether you are directly involved, or the first one there, your actions can save lives.

Call 9-1-1
Immediate response can be critical. That means recognizing the warning signs of an emergency, which rarely look as dramatic as in the movies. Signals include a vehicle blocking the roadway; other vehicles slowing or stopping; a vehicle off the road in a ditch, field or ravine; smoke coming from a vehicle; broken or cracked windshield or glass on the pavement, a broken guardrail or fence.

Contacting Emergency Medical Service (EMS) is the fastest way to get medical help to a crash victim. Dial 9-1-1 as soon as possible. Tell the dispatcher what happened, the location of the emergency (landmarks, mile markers, nearest intersections or exits), and the number of victims. Don't hang up until the dispatcher hangs up (often they can provide instruction on how to care for the victim until the ambulance arrives).

While Waiting for Help
In attending to the victims, pay special attention to dangerous hazards like electrical power lines and hazardous chemical or fuel spills. Never ignite flares around leaking gasoline or diesel fuel.

Ask the victim to turn off the ignition of the car (or turn it off yourself). Ask bystanders to stand well off the roadway. Onlookers with emergency training will assist without your having to ask. If their skills exceed yours, let them take the lead.

Do not move or allow victims to move unless there is immediate danger like fire or oncoming traffic. Treat victims as though every

> **⚠ SPEAK NOT**
>
> What to say and what not to say: *Do not argue, accuse anyone, admit fault or sign any statement except as required by police.* You cannot be forced at the crash scene or the police station to give an opinion about the cause of the accident. You have the right to consult an attorney before making any statement.

bone in their bodies is broken and they have spinal injuries.

Avoid heroics. The goal of Bystander Care is to help the victims survive until professional medical help arrives.

Bystander Care Basics
1. *Check for consciousness.* If a victim is not moving or talking, tap the victim on the shoulder and ask, "Are you OK?" Failure to answer may mean the victim's airway is blocked.
2. *Open the victim's airway.* Without tilting the head back, lift the victim's chin.
3. *Check for breathing.* Place your ear next to the victim's mouth and nose to listen and feel for breathing. Watch for the chest to rise and fall.
4. *Report to EMS.* Be prepared to tell EMS which victims are most badly injured.
5. *Render first aid if you know it.* Otherwise, use commonsense practices. If someone is bleeding badly, for example, apply pressure to the bleeding area with your fingertips. If pressure does not seem to slow or stop the bleeding, press harder over a wider area. (*Note:* Protect yourself against diseases carried by blood by wearing disposable latex gloves, using several layers of cloth or gauze pad, using waterproof materials such as plastic or having the victim apply the pressure.)

DEER ALERT

Deer strikes are one of the most threatening animal hazards in North America. More than 1.5 million deer collision reports are filed each year and scores of thousands more are estimated to go unreported. According to the *Highway Safety Information System (HSIS)*, in Michigan alone, 99.7% of all accidents with an animal involve deer.

Deer Accidents

Deer strikes account for about 300 human deaths a year and more than 30,000 injuries. Insurance companies will pay out more than one billion dollars in damage claims caused by vehicles hitting or swerving to avoid deer.

CHANGING A TIRE IN THE DARK

A dark highway is not a good place to fumble and learn tire changing, especially if your car is a new model with unfamiliar jacking equipment. A tire-change drill for yourself and family members can pay off, especially if it's conducted in your driveway instead of on a rainy highway, at night, which is when many tires go flat. Have everyone who drives your car practice tire changes.

Secrets of Deer Evasion

The best defense is to know where deer tend to hang out, such as around wooded areas and park sites. Avoid driving in these areas, but if you must, be mindful of:

- *Time of day.* Crashes involving animals occur most frequently at night and early morning. The greatest number occur between 4 a.m. and 6 a.m. and between 6 p.m. and 11 p.m.—basically, at dusk and at dawn.
- *Mating season.* Significantly higher deer-related crashes are reported in the month of November because this is deer mating season.

At the first sign of deer on the roadside, slow down and assume other deer are close by. On a highway, traffic permitting, drive in the lane furthest away from where a deer might leap out.

CAR SAFETY

As vehicle weight decreases, the number of occupant deaths rises. Driving a bigger car improves your chances of surviving a crash, according to the *Insurance Institute for Highway Safety*. This is especially true of the bigger, heavier sport utility vehicles (SUV). When an SUV side-impacts a car, for example, chances are 27 to 1 that a death will occur. That compares with 6 to 1 if an automobile hits another car on the side.

WHAT EVERY SAFE TRUNK SHOULD CARRY

First-aid kit. It should include large gauze dressings for trauma accidents; disinfectant, bandages and blankets for serious care-giving; even latex gloves in the event you encounter profuse bleeding in a victim unknown to you. In Europe, where there is a more realistic perception about the danger of driving, 70% of drivers carry first-aid kits. In the U.S., the number is less than 5%.

Powerful flashlight. This is mandatory. The preferred model would have a rugged steel-cased body as is used by many police departments, both as a light source and an emergency tool capable of smashing car windows. Laser lightbulbs shine brighter and farther. Check batteries regularly and keep the light with you in the vehicle on long night trips.

Flares. Flares or alternative reflectors can be set up on the road behind you in case of a night breakdown or tire problem. Also, a powerful spotlight that plugs into the car lighter provides excellent lighting in an emergency or tire change situation.

Fire extinguisher. It really is foolish not to carry one since a quick spritz could save your car and possibly even your life. If the car is on fire, stop well off the road as soon as possible and get out of the vehicle. Do not lift up the hood (unless armed with a fire extinguisher). Lifting the hood feeds circulating air to the engine, making it more likely that a fire will ignite or an existing fire will worsen. Remember, cars that catch fire do explode. In particular a fire near the fuel tank should be dealt with immediately. Use an extinguisher or get as far away from the vehicle as possible.

Shop for Safety

You can purchase safety features in a car, much as you can performance features. Many cars have the same safety features, but some are better to have than others. Head restraints, for example, can be far more protective if they are fully adjustable than restraints that have minimal positioning controls. Antilock brakes are becoming a standard and having them on all four wheels is critical. Similarly, all-wheel disc brakes are safer than disc brakes on just the front of the vehicle.

Speed Trap

Speed is a major contributor to traffic fatalities and accidents in general. Millions of perfectly safe drivers with accident-free records are guilty of speeding at one time or another. There are times, however, when speeding tickets are issued to the wrong driver, at the wrong time, for the wrong reason. If you're one of those, what can you do?

SPEEDING TICKETS: PAY OR FIGHT?

Speeding tickets are inevitable, especially if you do a lot of highway driving. If you do not depend heavily on driving for your livelihood or if you have managed to avoid tickets during a lengthy driving career, the simplest option is to pay the ticket. In most states, you acknowledge guilt by signing the back of the ticket and mailing it to the governing jurisdiction along with your check for the fine.

Fines

Depending on which state you are in, and the speed at which you are accused of traveling, fines generally range from around $100 to several hundred dollars. The size of the fine may play a big role in your decision to fight the ticket. The fine itself may not matter to you, but most states mark your driving record with speeding violations. Insurance companies monitor those records. A speeding ticket triggers an increase in your insurance rate that generally exceeds the cost of the fine, and the surcharge remains on your policy rates for two or three years. To avoid that, it might pay to fight the ticket to either win or at least have the charge reduced to avoid a mark on your driving record.

Cost of Defense

You can defend yourself readily against a speed charge or you can hire a lawyer. If you choose the latter, it's best to hire an attorney from the jurisdiction in which the charge is filed. That way the attorney will be familiar with the local procedures and temperament of the court. Cost for such a defense can range from $200 to $800 (depending on location). As there is no assurance of winning, it is best to include the amount of the fine as well when assessing your costs.

Self-defense saves the expense of a lawyer, but will require your time. Consider not only the time

(and travel) you will have to take away from business, but also how much work needs to be done in preparing your case. You will not win by walking into court and saying you did not do it. You need to prove that the arresting officer's claim is wrong, inaccurate or inconclusive.

Chances of Winning

Whether or not you win will depend on the method used to stop you: radar, laser gun, observation by air or ground patrol or an estimated speed clocked by a patrol car. Also relevant is the local court's track record concerning speeders, which you can learn by telephone interviews with a local attorney in planning your defense.

Decision to Fight

It probably pays to fight a ticket if your driver's license could be placed in jeopardy or if your insurance carrier might place you in a high-risk pool. Fighting an out-of-state ticket may be pointless, however, especially if that state does not have the capability of marking your driving record. Many bordering states do exchange traffic violation data. Check with local state highway authorities to see if a ticket in another state can show up as a mark on your record.

Fighting on Principle

Few people can be bothered fighting a speeding ticket. The court system is chaotic, time-consuming, wasteful and often

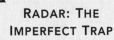

RADAR: THE IMPERFECT TRAP

Radar is fallible. So are the officers who use it. So if you plan to contest a speeding ticket, be mindful of these common radar-fouling entities:

➤ Aircraft operations, such as landing/taking off
➤ Bridges and overpasses
➤ Electronic equipment in nearby buildings
➤ Metal buildings and structures
➤ Metal road signs and guardrails
➤ Neon signs
➤ Parallel roads
➤ Police cruiser electrical equipment
➤ Police cruiser motion
➤ Power lines or transformers
➤ Radio and microwave towers
➤ Security system installations
➤ Weather, rain, snow or extreme heat
➤ Welding equipment

If you are ticketed for speeding by radar and plan to fight the ticket, go back to the scene of your alleged infraction and note the presence of any of the above items. It could contribute to your defense. Write the police authority who issued the ticket inquiring about the effect of any listed items.

unfriendly. States count on revenue from traffic violations and don't like to see accused traffic offenders getting off in the courts. New York State, for example, "taxes" motorists approximately $40 million annually, most of that from accused speeders. But enough traffic fighters can beat the system. In Connecticut, for example, beleaguered traffic courts were so glutted with people fighting traffic tickets that legislators were forced to halt the practice of marking driving records if accused speeders pay by mail. Furthermore, traffic ticket fighters who win their cases cost the states more money in bureaucratic expenses than they receive from the imposed fines. So if you want to get even, fight the ticket!

STOPPED BY THE POLICE

Few events are more frustrating than being pulled over for a traffic violation. How you react can determine the severity of the fine or whether you get a ticket or a warning.

If you are traveling in a local municipality, chances are good that you can "earn" a warning by being pleasant and cooperative. Above all, do not argue. On the highway, particularly away from your home state, being professional and cooperative is prudent

behavior. State troopers tend to be less lenient and more into the business of issuing tickets than are local police authorities.

Getting Pulled Over

Generally, a police officer will signal you to pull over by using flashing lights and sirens. Use your 4-way flashers to let the officer know that you are complying. Do not slam on the brakes or make abrupt lane changes. Take your time, slow down gradually and drive until you reach a safe part of the road to pull over. Your safety and that of your passengers come way ahead of the officer's desire to issue a summons. Pull well over to the right, as far from the traffic flow as possible.

What to Say, What to Do

Sit quietly as the officer approaches your vehicle. Don't volunteer anything. Respond to the officer's questions truthfully. Address him directly and politely, using the term "officer." If you are asked if you knew how fast you were going, say you aren't sure (which is true, because you don't know how fast he clocked your vehicle). And say no more. There is no need to admit to speeding. The officer knows how fast he thinks you were going. You are not obligated to confess. Make no excuses or arguments. The officer has heard them all and chances are that you are being recorded. Any statements you make to the officer can be used against you.

Passengers should remain silent with their hands in plain view. There is very little conversation needed in the issuance of a traffic summons. You will be asked very quickly for your license and registration. Tell the officer where each one is located (in your wallet, purse or in the glove box). Retrieve each slowly. Fast movements make police nervous, and traffic stops are among a policeman's most dangerous duties. Be cooperative and cordial, but no joking. Put the officer at ease. If

---

★
WHAT TO DO WHEN YOU ARE PULLED OVER

➤ Stay in your car unless requested to exit
➤ Turn off the radio or CB
➤ Turn off any radar detectors (don't try to hide them)
➤ Remove your sunglasses
➤ Extinguish any smoking materials (in the ashtray)
➤ Remove gum you may be chewing
➤ Leave your seat belt fastened
➤ Roll down your window
➤ Turn on the interior light (if it's night)
➤ Don't rummage around for your license
➤ Rest both hands on the wheel in plain view

---

you open the glove box for example, leave it open. It shows you have nothing to hide.

Ask Questions, if Able

As you give the officer your identification, ask if you might question the method employed to clock you. If the officer is of a mind to respond, ask the location of the cruiser when he first spotted you and measured your speed. Was the cruiser in motion or stationary? Was the engine running or off? Was air conditioning being used in the cruiser or other radio equipment? In particular, was he transmitting? Ask to see the speed recording unit and your vehicle's speed measurement. Find out if he was using a feature called "instant-on." Determine the brand and model number of the speed device, and ask when it was last calibrated and by whom. Make note of the officer's answers. If he refuses to answer, make note of that as well. It is unlikely that an officer will cooperate with this dialogue, but if he's agreed to answer questions, there's no harm in trying. And if he refuses cooperation, you can cite his attitude in court.

While the Ticket Is Being Written

Take notes. While the officer writes about you, you write about the officer. Write down any comments he made about why he stopped your vehicle or how he tracked you. Write about your traffic position at the time you were clocked and when you first spotted the cruiser. Be mindful of the traffic pattern around you at the time of the stop. Note the location where you were stopped and the exact time. Write down the mile marker on the highway where you stopped and the mile marker where the alleged infraction occurred. Be sure to note any unusual terrain (overpasses, high tension wires, hills). Note road and traffic, weather and light conditions.

Final Words

The officer will return your license and registration. He will also give you a summons, which will advise how you might pay or elect to contest. Depending on your behavior in the process, the officer may have downgraded the speed at which he claimed to have clocked you. At this point make certain you have his name correct, his shield number and the time of the event.

FIGHTING THE TICKET

A ticket for speeding! Should you fight it? The answer is yes if the following are true:
- The ticket is issued in your home state
- You have pleaded guilty to one or more recent moving traffic violations in your home state (generally within three years)

- You are ticketed in a state that shares traffic violation data with your home state

The answer is probably no if the ticket is issued in a state away from home that does not report speed violations to your state.

Common sense should prevail. It is usually not worth the time, energy and money to fight a speeding ticket that will not have an impact on you other than the fine.

If your insurance rates are going to be increased or if you are in danger of having a license suspension, then you should invest in arguing the case. The best way to do that is to hire a lawyer from the jurisdiction where the ticket was issued.

Do-It-Yourself Defense

If winning is critical to maintaining your license, and you believe you were singled out unfairly for a speeding ticket, defend yourself.

To win, you will need either to cast doubt on the arresting officer's speed estimate or contest that the speed-measuring equipment was improperly used, not calibrated to specifications or used in an area of high electromagnetic interference (which adversely affects radar).

Arm Yourself

You first need to prepare a defense. You will need records related to the arresting officer and the equipment used to trap you. The police will not be cooperative, so you will need to issue a subpoena. Do this by contacting the Clerk of the Court at the address on the back of your summons. Ask for the procedures and contact addresses. A local attorney may even assist you for a modest fee.

Issuing a subpoena for evidence may seem excessive for a traffic ticket, but it demonstrates your

SUBPOENA LIST

There are three elements of evidence you will need from the police:

➤ Speed-measuring equipment maintenance record
➤ Arrest officer's records
➤ Patrol car's maintenance records

level of intent to mount a serious defense. A subpoena for evidence necessary for your defense can also challenge the police. If they do not provide the evidence you request, you can ask the judge to dismiss the case. The judge may not agree to dismissal, but ultimately the evidence you subpoena (at least some of it) will be provided so you can marshal a defense at a subsequent hearing.

RADAR: NOT ALWAYS RIGHT

Police radar operates on microwave radio signals to compute the speed of approaching vehicles. Blips in microwave signals caused by other radio transmissions and even the police vehicle's air conditioning system can cause false readings on the receiver. That could result in a ticket to fight.

Radar will compute the speed of larger vehicles before registering cars. Be skeptical if you get a ticket while driving in traffic with lots of trucks.

The Business of Living

Money Smarts

Money Smarts

Savvy Deals

Retire Richer

Banks, Bankers & Banking

Go for the gold! Don't settle for bronze or silver when it comes to getting the most out of your bank. Convenience and compatibility are important, but service, security and savings pay off in the long run.

COMPARISON SHOPPING

No matter how long you've done business with a bank, it pays to call around and see what's available from other banks in the area. For example, all banks are now trying to increase their earnings through added fees. Just the fees for a common checking account can cost you several hundred dollars annually, net of any interest you may earn on that account. So, it's wise to shop around for the lowest fees.

If you qualify as a senior citizen, ask if they offer free checking. If not, it may pay to switch to another bank. Many banks offer special "membership accounts" to anyone over 50 years old. It may involve a minimum monthly fee—but no minimum balance or charge for checks—which is often offset by the interest earned on the account. Other benefits are also available, such as a free safe-deposit box and free travelers checks.

Ferret Out Avoidable Fees

People go out of their way to get an extra eighth of 1% on a CD, and then pay their banks much more than that in fees. Some tips for negotiating and minimizing fees:

- *Use a small bank.* A small bank will be more flexible in negotiating fees and interest rates because it needs your business to attract new customers and grow. If a bank employee won't negotiate fees, ask to speak to an officer. Most senior personnel will make an effort to satisfy you, especially if you are a good customer.
- *Avoid overdraft charges.* Ask your bank to "red flag" your account and call you if it is overdrawn. Most small banks will give you until 3 p.m. the same day to cover the overdraft, saving you the high charge and the embarrassment of a returned check.
- *Ask that minimum-balance requirements be waived.* Many banks will waive those requirements if you insist. If not, consider a credit union, which usually is cheaper and offers better service. For more information, call the *Credit Union National Association* at 202-638-5777.
- *Refuse unnecessary products.* Banks can be intimidating when offering extra services. For example, if they agree to give you a car loan, you might find it difficult to refuse the hugely overpriced credit, life and disability insurance that is added to the loan. Even worse, you may not realize that because the insurance cost has been added to the loan, the premium is subject to a finance charge.

$ CHECKLIST FOR CHOOSING A BANK

While convenience is important, don't make location the only reason you select a particular bank. Think service—beyond checking and savings accounts. Visit several banks before you decide, and speak with a new accounts representative. Use this checklist as a guide:

➤ Is the bank financially sound (i.e., well capitalized) and federally insured. (Is the FDIC—Federal Deposit Insurance Corporation—symbol on the door)?

➤ How wide a range of services is offered? Does the bank offer loans, mortgages, checking and savings accounts, certificates of deposit, safe-deposit boxes, financial and estate planning, direct deposit?

➤ What's the minimum deposit required for a savings account?

➤ What does it take to qualify for a free checking account?

➤ What other fees, interest rates and penalties apply? Especially check non-interest-bearing and interest-bearing checking accounts and automatic-teller-machine transactions.

➤ Is there reader-friendly written material available on services offered, interest rates and service charges?

➤ How many bank officers are available to answer your questions?

➤ How do the bank's fees and interest rates compare with other banks in the area?

➤ Is there 24-hour account access by telephone? Is it all voice-operated or will you be able to speak with a representative?

➤ Does the bank provide online banking options, and what are the charges?

BANKING PROTECTION

Don't make the mistake of thinking that a *Federal Deposit Insurance Corporation (FDIC)* symbol on the bank's door means that all transactions are insured for up to $100,000. Some facts you should know:

- If you have several accounts at a bank, you may not be covered for the total value. For FDIC purposes, an individual account is determined by adding up each account held under a common name or Social Security number. For example, if you have a savings account of $50,000 and a CD for $60,000 at the same bank, $10,000 is uninsured.
- Joint accounts held by the same persons are only protected up to $100,000, regardless of whose Social Security number appears on them. If you and your wife have two joint accounts totaling $150,000, then $50,000 is uninsured. Avoid this by using both individual and joint accounts: If you have an individual savings account and a joint account with your spouse, each account has full protection up to $100,000.
- You cannot increase the limit of coverage by depositing funds in different branches of the same bank. Diversify your accounts among several banks.

- IRAs and Keogh accounts are added together for purposes of coverage limits. If necessary, roll over sufficient amounts to other institutions.
- Mutual funds and other investments made through a bank's broker are not protected.

Safe Deposit Safety

Banks usually don't insure safe-deposit boxes for theft. If they do, it's very difficult to collect because you can't prove the box's contents. You could have a bank officer sign a safekeeping receipt each time you visit to confirm the contents, but this sacrifices your confidentiality and doesn't guarantee coverage. *Best bet:* A home safe. Models that exceed the fire safety of a bank vault cost less than $250, and losses are covered by your homeowner's insurance. List each item in a policy rider.

Not Recommended

- *Trust departments.* Banks are known more for their mismanagement of trust money than for astute investment advice. You can probably do better with a trust accountant or trust attorney.
- *Bank-sponsored mutual funds.* Most are load funds that carry a sales commission of up to 8%. And most banks offer a limited selection of funds. By doing research, you can find many well-managed funds with good histories and invest in them without paying a sales load.

CHECK YOUR BANK'S INTEREST RATES

To be sure your money makes money while it's in the banker's hands, check these seven points and use the table as a guideline for evaluating your bank.

- ➤ Does the bank pay interest from day of deposit to day of withdrawal?
- ➤ Does the bank pay interest only on the lowest balance during the quarter?
- ➤ How is interest compounded?
- ➤ Does the bank have any "dead days" (days at the end of a quarter when interest is not paid)?
- ➤ If you make a withdrawal or close the account before the end of the quarter, will you lose interest?
- ➤ Are there penalties for an inactive account?
- ➤ Is there a monthly service charge?

$50 COMPOUNDED AT 5%

Year	Annually	Semi-annually	Quarterly	Monthly	Daily
1	$52.50	$52.53	$52.55	$52.56	$52.58
2	63.81	64.00	64.10	64.17	64.20
10	81.44	81.93	82.18	82.35	83.43
20	132.66	134.25	135.07	135.63	135.90

BANKING RESOURCES

- ➤ Comptroller of the Currency, U.S. Treasury Department, 250 E St. SW, Washington, DC, 20219, 202-874-4700. Compliance management division handles consumer complaints against national banks. Web site: *www.occ.treas.gov/org.htm*
- ➤ Federal Deposit Insurance Corporation, 550 17th St. NW, Washington, DC 20429, 800-934-3342. Provides information on deposit insurance and FDIC institutions. Web site: *www.fdic.gov*
- ➤ Institute of Consumer Financial Education, P.O. Box 34070, San Diego, CA 92163, 619-239-1401. Information on state banking authorities. Web site: *www.financial-education-icfe.org.*
- ➤ Veribanc, P.O. Box 461, Wakefield, MA 01880, 800-442-2657. Rates the financial strength of banks. Web site: *www.veribanc.com*

Loan Wisdom

We are so accustomed to using credit to purchase everything from houses to clothing that we rarely give it a second thought. Well, think again and become a smart borrower.

BORROW SMART

Here are five areas for driving a harder bargain with a lender to save as a borrower:

Credit Cards

Demand a better deal. Credit card issuers are fiercely competing for your business. If you have a good payment record, they won't risk losing you to a competitor. You can lower the rate on your card debt from 15% to 9%, or even 7%, for six months, just by asking. You can also take advantage of mail solicitations if the rates are low. But be sure a low rate applies for at least six months. It's not worthwhile to transfer a balance for less than that.

Read the fine print on statements carefully to find out when interest will be charged—and at what rate—on any outstanding balance. "Buy now and owe nothing for six months" sounds great, but in six months, you might still owe the entire balance on everything you've charged. And if you can't pay, you may be charged interest retroactively—typically at a super-high rate of 20% or more.

Home Improvement Loans

Borrow only as much as you need. It's safer to borrow a specific amount for a specific purpose than to take as much as your bank will lend you. If you need $5,000, don't borrow $15,000. The rate on home equity loans rises as interest rates generally rise. Some people who took out loans in the past few years find it difficult to make their payments when rates are up.

College Loans

College loans are abundant and relatively easy to get. Many are federally subsidized, but have dollar limits and must be renewed annually while still in school. An advantage is that you will qualify for a special interest deduction on your taxes. There is also a 6-month grace period after graduation before payments begin.

If traditional college loans are too expensive, then consider alternative sources for finding money for higher education.

Borrow cheap by taking a home equity loan or tapping your 401(k). Interest on a home equity loan of up to $100,000 is tax deductible. Interest on a 401(k) loan is typically one or two percentage points above the prime rate. When you borrow from your own 401(k), you're paying off the loan—including interest—to yourself, but you must repay the loan within five years. Otherwise the Internal Revenue Service will consider it a distribution from your retirement account. The IRS will then demand income taxes on the full amount, plus a 10% early withdrawal penalty if you are under age 59½.

Car Loans

Don't talk financing until you have negotiated the price of the car. Dealers often quote a higher price if they know how you plan to finance the purchase, or that you plan to lease rather than buy. When you're ready to buy, shop around from your local bank to AAA to find the best interest rates on a car loan.

Mortgages

Some experts suggest paying down your mortgage as much as you can. Just an extra $50 a month applied to your loan principal can make a big difference—you'll save nearly $40,000 in interest for each $100,000 borrowed. Yes, you will have a lower tax deduction, but a taxpayer in the 27% tax bracket, for example, would see a net gain of just over $29,200 per $100,000.

Others suggest taking that extra $50 each month and investing the money for a higher return, while preserving the mortgage interest deduction.

Either way, evaluate your options and do what's best—and safest—for you.

ELEVATE EQUITY

When applying for a home equity loan, home appraisals are always lower than the market value appraisal. The bank wants protection in case of a default. If you want a larger loan than the appraisal will allow, have your home appraised independently. That can be done through a real estate agent. Ask for a Comparative Market Analysis, a report on your home in relation to others in the area. Also get an estimate of your home's fair market value. Then call the bank with the new information and for reconsideration. If the bank is uncooperative, go to a new bank. The second bank will likely be more flexible because its appraiser won't feel comfortable deviating greatly from the information you provided.

Credit Preservation & Restoration

Credit cards are a convenience we have come to rely on—for travel, restaurants, everyday purchases. No cash, no checks, just one bill at the end of the month. But the convenience can be costly if not managed properly. It pays to be savvy about fees, interest and obligations.

CREDIT CARD KNOW-HOW

N ever have so many companies issued so many different credit cards with so many different features as now. There are more than 20,000 MasterCard and Visa programs—in addition to the cards offered by American Express and Discover. How to get the best deal?

First, consider your spending habits: If you pay your bill in full, shop around for the lowest or no annual fee. If you carry a credit balance from month to month, look for the lowest interest rate.

Second, compare competing credit card solicitations. Save the ones you get in the mail and clip ads for a month. By going through them all at once, you won't get confused trying to remember different interest rates and fees. *Key:* Look for a box of fine print at the end of each solicitation. By law, the issuer must disclose the card's interest rate and annual fee, whether the rate will increase after a set period (such as 90 days) and by how much, and whether the card carries any additional fees.

Third, if you like everything a card has to offer, and particularly if you have a good credit rating, try to negotiate with your current card issuer (if you have one) or the new one for an even better interest rate and/or annual fee. Play the competition. Mention the lowest rates you have been offered and ask if an issuer will match them or do better.

Check Your Credit

Before you apply for a loan, make sure you have a healthy—and accurate—credit report. Call the major credit reporting companies for a copy of your credit report: *Experian* (888-397-3742) and *Equifax* (800-685-1111).

Carefully examine them for problems and mistakes.

Even if you don't plan on applying for a loan, you should check the accuracy of your credit report, just in case you might need it. For example, many auto insurance companies and landlords use credit reports to determine the riskiness of applicants.

Your Best Reference

Major credit cards whose charges you have been paying on time can be your best credit reference—even better than a mortgage or car loan. That's because home and car loans are secured, while your credit-card payment record demonstrates your reliability when paying off unsecured debts. But don't overdo it. Banks will view a timely payment record on two or three credit cards in your favor, but they may hold it against you if you have too many cards, if your cards are always charged up close to your credit limit or if you take out a new card and immediately run it up to its limit.

IF YOU GET RID OF A CARD...

If you decide to get rid of a credit card, ask the credit card company to report to credit bureaus that your account has been closed. They won't do it unless you ask because they hope you will resume using the card. If you leave old accounts open, you may have difficulty getting a loan or a mortgage. When a lender looks at a credit report and sees multiple credit cards, he worries that you may default on a loan, since you look like you could easily become overextended.

IF YOU TRAVEL...

When you travel and use your credit card overseas, the issuer may charge a conversion fee. The fee to convert charges in foreign countries is usually 1% of the charge. Check to see if your issuer does charge and, if so, determine if the card offers enough benefits in other areas to make up for that drawback. Otherwise, shop around for another card to use for foreign travel.

IF YOU CHARGE A LOT...

Specialty cards, such as frequent-flier cards and automobile-rebate cards, can be good deals for you if you charge a lot. For example, you usually have to charge $25,000 a year on a frequent-flier card to earn a free ticket. But if you travel a lot and pay your balance in full every month, the card's annual fee is worth it.

PLAY THE COMPETITION

Competition has become so hot in the credit card business that it is foolish to pay 18% interest or an annual fee. Many card issuers now charge 12% for conventional cards (purchases only, not advances). A few credit cards are under 8%. AT&T's Universal card stimulated the no-annual-fee trend. New cards introduced since then have gone beyond no fees to offering users extra incentives such as free air travel, gas purchase rebates, and credit toward the purchase of a new car—even mortgages.

CONSOLIDATING CREDIT

Many credit card issuers advertise an attractive low rate if you agree to transfer your debt from other cards to the new one. That can be a good deal, but check to see if you will be charged for the service. When you agree to consolidate debts, a credit card company uses cash to pay off your outstanding balances and may charge you for the cash advance. If the company does charge a fee, consider whether it is worth it. If not, shop around for another company that will do it for free. Or, if you carry a balance through a

bank, call and ask for the lowest rate possible. Competition among bank cards has forced many banks to make special deals to hold on to customers. *Example:* A New York bank recently cut a customer's 16.8% rate to 8.9% for 12 months, provided he transfer at least $1,000 worth of debt from another card. The bank also waived the transfer fee.

But be certain that you really are getting a better deal. Check the fine print for the interest charges and hidden penalties.

COSIGN CAVEAT

Parents often cosign credit cards or other loans to obtain credit for their children. But parents should be aware that creditors in most states are not required to notify cosigners when a borrower exceeds a credit limit or falls behind on loan payments. Thus, a cosigning parent can become liable for overdue payments and penalties without ever knowing there's a problem —and the parent's credit rating will be affected as well. If you do cosign a loan, monitor payments and monthly statements closely. *Even better:* Consider having the child cosign your credit card. That way, the child will have access to the credit line while monthly statements come directly to you.

DO YOU NEED THE BELLS & WHISTLES?

Beware of credit card "bonuses" designed to lure new customers. They may not be of any value at all.

Purchase protection. New purchases will be insured if damaged, lost or stolen within a certain time period. Apart from the time-consuming paperwork involved if you want to file a claim, many issuers require that the item be warranteed/registered, that you tried "in good faith" to correct the problem with the merchant, and that the purchase was made within 100 miles of your mailing address.

Credit card insurance. This is in the event that you lose your card or are unable to pay your bills because of a disability. Consider, however, that you are automatically protected from excess charges if your card is stolen.

Rebates. The value here depends on your level of monthly charges and future needs. Some companies offer cash rebates—about 1% of what you spend, but usually you have to spend at least $500 to get a rebate. Other companies offer rebates of up to 5% on car purchases, gasoline or other items. Consider if you want to be tied down to a certain brand of gasoline or really intend to buy that make of car.

CREDIT CARD RESOURCES

➤ Federal Trade Commission, 6th St. and Pennsylvania Ave. NW, Washington, DC. 877-FTC-HELP; *www.ftc.gov.* Credit Practices Division oversees credit-related issues; provides free copies of consumer brochures.

➤ Consumer Information Center, P.O. Box 100, Pueblo, CO 81009. 888-878-3256. Offers numerous publications on choosing and using credit cards, the cost of credit and how to build a good credit history.

➤ CardTrak, P.O. Box 1700, Frederick, MD 21702. 800-344-7714. Provides information on currently available credit cards of all kinds.

➤ "Tips on Customer Credit," Council of Better Business Bureaus, 4200 Wilson Blvd., Arlington, VA 22203. 703-276-0100. Brochure explains types of credit, credit cards and credit reports.

Basics of Investing

Even for financial wizards, investment decisions can be daunting. What to buy in stocks and bonds? Mutual funds? What to look for in the future? Lacking a crystal ball, the best approach is to be savvy about where you put your money. Here's how 50 bucks buys a million, and more.

IFFY ECONOMIC INDICATORS

Investment bankers watch economic reports from the government and industry associations in making investment decisions. So should you. But you must know which ones to pay attention to as the basis for serious decisions. Here are eight indicators many investors consider badly flawed:

- *Retail sales.* The Commerce Department samples retailing establishments to compile this report; but it doesn't sample enough to do the job accurately.

- *Unemployment rate.* The Labor Department does a good job counting employed people but a bad job counting people seeking jobs.

- *Producer prices.* This is no longer useful as a predictor of future inflation. The current focus on cost-cutting rather than raising prices means higher prices may not be reflected in the marketplace.

- *Consumer prices.* Measurements don't keep up with rapidly changing consumer tastes. And there's no adjustment for improvements in quality when reporting seemingly "inflationary" prices.

- *Personal income.* This can't be accurately tracked. Month-to-month changes can be distorted by such things as an increase in Social Security payments or a big farm subsidy payment.

- *Consumer savings.* The government takes personal income, subtracts personal spending, and assumes we've saved the rest. This misses the fact that we buy stocks, bonds and houses, which appreciate in value—an important component of net worth ignored by this report.

- *Money supply.* How can you separate out the U.S. money supply when financial markets are as globally integrated as they are today? This so-called indicator also overlooks shifts in how people hold their money balances—from bank accounts, which count in the money supply, to mutual funds, which do not count in the money supply.

- *Gross domestic product.* This is not necessarily timely. There are often significant revisions (whole percentage points) after the report is out. Also, GDP stats fail to take into account that unsold inventories will cut into future growth. Better to look at final sales (published with this report) as a guide to underlying momentum in the economy.

TRUSTY ECONOMIC INDICATORS

The seven reports that can best help you keep up with the economy:

Durable Goods Orders

These numbers, particularly new orders for durable goods, are accurate, not subject to major revision and very useful for forecasting the economy.

Supply Delivery Times

From the National Association of Purchasing Management's monthly report, these figures are a good indicator of both production and employment. As the economy strengthens, it takes longer for new orders to get filled; then more people must be hired.

Industrial Production

Although this report, from the Federal Reserve, has some shortcomings in measuring production in high-tech industries, it remains a valuable indicator of an important part of the economy.

Nonfarm Payrolls

Published as part of the unemployment report, this is a good indicator of people actually at work (nonfarm).

Monthly Motor Vehicle Sales

These come from the automakers and are timely and accurate.

BEWARE OF ONLINERS

A lot of excellent investment advice is available online—but scam artists also operate in that unregulated environment. Use computer networks to collect data that will help you form your own opinion. Beware of hype and promises delivered over a network. **Don't:**

➤ Assume that bulletin boards police those who make claims through them.

➤ Rely on advice received from any person who hides his or her identity.

➤ Believe any claims about "inside information" or "pending news releases."

➤ Overlook the conflict of interest that exists when a person who touts an investment also sells it.

Housing Starts

Accurate and seldom revised, this report counts the number of new homes started each month and the number of permits to build new homes in the future.

Commodity Prices

These are very sensitive to demand pressures and can give you a clue, early on, as to when there might be a pickup in inflation. They can be found in *The Journal of Commerce* (18 industrial commodities) or Commodity Research Bureau publications (prices for both industrial and agricultural commodities).

NARROW SHORT-TERM LOSSES

Investors can significantly narrow their losses in the short term and enhance their gains in the long term with a well-diversified portfolio. Here are four pointers:

The Past Is Rarely Prologue

The people with the biggest losses are those who spend too much of their assets on last quarter's or last year's high fliers or "hot" sectors. That doesn't mean you shouldn't invest in those areas; it means you shouldn't spend too much money chasing rainbows that don't end in pots of gold.

Play the Field

Diversification covers a lot of ground. Cash is OK as part of a

---

FIRE YOUR MONEY MANAGER WHEN...

➤ He or she strays from stated goals: for example, promised to invest in growth stocks but begins to invest in value stocks.

➤ There is a high turnover in the manager's firm. That reflects instability— plus new employees shouldn't get their education at your expense.

➤ Your objectives change and your manager's expertise doesn't meet your needs.

Key: It's hard to fire a friend, so keep your relationship with your money manager strictly business.

---

diversified investment strategy, but if you're totally into cash, you'll win occasionally but lose most of the time. Diversify between stocks and bonds, and between types of stocks and bonds. A reasonable allocation is 60% in stock funds, 40% in bond funds.

Stick with Stocks

A well-diversified portfolio includes four major stock market sectors: aggressive growth, growth and income, small-cap funds (invests in shares of small-growth companies) and international funds. Ideally, you would want 100 shares of stock in each of 10 to 12 different companies, allocated among the four stock categories.

Ladder Bond Maturities

On the bond side, a well-diversified portfolio includes three categories: tax-exempt municipals, corporates, and treasuries. Your bond funds should be further diversified by laddering maturities— long-term, intermediate and short-term. For example, instead of a long-term municipal bond

---

fund for maximum yield, consider an intermediate or short-term municipal fund. That will reduce your yield a little, and reduce your risk a lot. Don't place a heavy bet on any one maturity. *Remember:* The higher the yield, the higher the risk.

MATURE BONDING

It's wise to shift investments from stocks to bonds at a gradual rate as you grow older. The percentage of your portfolio invested in stocks should equal 100 minus your age. So if you are 55, you should be 45% invested in stocks and 55% invested in bonds or cash. *Rationale:* Over the long run, stocks consistently outperform bonds. You'll need this extra income for retirement. Meanwhile, the money you keep in bonds will meet your short- and medium-term cash needs, letting you maintain your stock investments long enough for them to recover from any short-term mar-

---

ket drop and protecting you from ever having to cash in your stocks while the market is low.

50 BUCKS BUYS A MILLION!

A survey of high school students revealed that they waste at least $20 a week, or $80 a month, on things they really don't need—snacks, candy, video games, and so on. If that's true of kids, think about how much you must waste. If you could harness that money— or even just $50 a month—and use it to start a regular investing program, you would be well on your way to becoming a millionaire or more.

Strategy: Invest $50 each month in a few major companies that have long histories of rising earnings and dividends, and reinvest your dividends. If your money grows at 13% to 15% annually (which is the rate at which the proven companies have appreciated since World War II), the earnings potential of your portfolio would be:

➤ After 10 years: $12,500 to $14,000

➤ After 20 years: $54,900 to $70,700

➤ After 30 years: $198,900 to $300,000

➤ After 40 years: $817,000 to $1,570,000

P/E RATIO MYTHS

Price/earnings (P/E) ratios have little to do with whether a stock is a good or bad buy. Many analysts recommend stocks with low P/Es as cheap and warn that stocks with high P/Es are expensive. But history shows otherwise. From 1953 to 1995, the stock market had an average P/E of 15. But the top-performing stocks of that period started with an average P/E of 20 and ended with an average P/E of 45.

In recent years high-tech stocks have had wildly fluctuating, and in some cases, astronomical P/E ratios—when the market changed quickly, many investors did very well with them, until 2000.

Reality: Firms with low P/Es often have them simply because they are poor stocks, while firms with high P/Es usually have demonstrated superior prospects. The simple truth is that most firms have P/Es that fairly reflect their value.

FUTURE WINNERS

Investors who want to do well over the next few years will have to change the way they think about the U.S. economy. Because consumers are more price conscious than ever before, the economy will not be led by consumer goods industries, as it has been in the past. Instead, stock market analysts predict that today's market will be dominated by the following investment trends:

- Companies that specialize in capital goods—especially in the machinery and machine tool, electrical equipment and construction industries—will show sustained earnings growth. Low-cost producers in the specialty steel and construction engineering areas will also be attractive for investors.
- Companies that specialize in technology will still do well. Telecommunications equipment—cellular and cable—and computer software companies will be in the forefront.
- Small companies will show great growth potential. Look for niche companies with innovative services and technologies.
- The outsourcing industry will benefit from corporate cost-cutting trends and should expand rapidly. This includes companies that provide computer services, temporary office help, legal and accounting help and building security and maintenance.
- International investing will be very important to the success of an investor's portfolio as the export of capital to emerging markets increases. One approach is to invest by dollar-cost-averaging in mutual funds that have major stakes in Southeast Asia and South America.
- Companies that cater to older Americans will remain strong. Prosperous companies will include those that provide security services and long-term health-care facilities.
- Food providers will grow as the world's standard of living continues to improve. This will boost the fortunes of companies specializing in agribusiness. Fertilizer companies, farm machinery manufacturers and bioscience firms will experience the benefits.

MUTUAL FUND SMARTS

What's in a Name?
A mutual fund's name doesn't necessarily reflect its investment strategy. For example, one

SIX STEPS TO STOCK IMPROVEMENT

Whether you're thinking about investing in stocks or you're an old hand in the market, here are six pointers that will help you multiply your earnings:

1. Invest in proven winners—companies whose dividends per share have increased each year for at least 10 consecutive years. You can pick out these companies from *Value Line* or *Standard & Poor's*, available in most libraries.

2. Invest in at least five to eight stocks, each in a different industry. The diversity will help your portfolio deliver consistently high results and cushion it during downturns in different sectors of the economy.

3. Make sure each company has a dividend reinvestment plan (DRP) that does not charge a commission and sign up for it. A DRP uses your dividends to buy additional shares rather than sending them to you, thus adding to the value of your portfolio.

4. Make sure each company has an optional cash payment plan, which allows you to buy additional shares directly through the company without paying brokers. You can mail the purchase price for the new stock directly to the company.

5. Consider using a discount broker—commissions are typically 50% lower than those charged by full-service brokers. Don't worry too much about commissions, however. After you buy your first shares through the broker, you'll make future purchases directly with the companies.

6. Don't sell your stock unless you need the money—or unless a company is no longer paying higher dividends per share each year. If you need to sell stock, it can be done through the company.

growth-and-income fund yielded only 0.5%, which is about the lowest yield of any mutual fund with the word income in its name. The Securities and Exchange Commission requires only that 65% of a fund's assets be invested according to the strategy outlined in its prospectus. Before you invest, make sure the fund invests in the kind of securities you want to own. If you already own the fund, is it still investing the way you want it to?

■ *Foreign securities.* A fund may have more foreign securities than it publicizes. Even though many funds state that their stakes in foreign securities are limited to 10% of their portfolios, that may not take into account American Depository Receipts (ADRs), listings by foreign companies on U.S. stock exchanges. While ADRs can be great investments, they also mean more foreign risk. Analyze all the holdings in your fund—including ADRs—to determine the percentage tied to foreign markets.

■ *Hidden taxes.* You may owe taxes on mutual funds, even if they don't do well. When funds buy and sell stocks frequently, often there are capital gains. That means there are taxes to pay on those gains—even if the fund performed poorly for the year. For example, one growth-stock fund with a negative 6.7% return paid $1.08 per share in

capital gains, which was 10.2% of its price per share. Funds that trade a lot are best bought for an IRA, since the capital gains are tax-deferred.

■ *Management.* More and more mutual funds are using "teams" to manage their assets, which means you never know who is the brains of the operation or whether you should pull out your money because the person behind the fund's success has left. Call the fund at least once a year and ask who is responsible for investing the money. If it's a team, ask for the name of the leader and inquire about his or her experience.

FIVE WAYS TO REDUCE MUTUAL FUND RISKS

Mutual funds can be excellent investments, but many people are confused by the growing number of choices and troubled by the market's volatility. Here are five strategies for reducing your risks:

1. Avoid smaller funds. Funds that have assets of less then $200 million tend to either perform well or be major disappointments. Managers often take big chances, hoping that a heroic performance will attract new investors. Sometimes that strategy works, but it can also backfire, making this type of fund extremely risky.

2. Avoid funds with high expense ratios. High expenses—greater than 1% for a stock fund and 1.5% for a bond fund—reduce your profits and, in some cases, mean more risk. Managers often take high-risk chances to produce higher returns to justify expenses.

3. Pay close attention to bond-fund maturities. Bond-fund investors can cut risk by buying funds with shorter maturities. Long-term bonds are hit much harder than short-term bonds when interest rates rise. Seek a risk/reward balance by buying a bond fund with a variety of maturities.

4. Diversify intelligently. Don't simply seek safety by investing in more funds. Six funds can be as risky as one if they all have the same investment style. Buy stock funds that have different investment philosophies (e.g., value, growth, equity income) and that invest in different-sized companies (e.g., small-, mid- and large-cap stocks).

5. Buy at least one fund with significant international exposure. By investing in a fund that invests abroad, you are limiting your risk if the U.S. market falls. Many domestic funds have sizable international holdings, some as much as 20% in foreign stocks.

INVESTMENT RESOURCES

➤ Securities and Exchange Commission, 450 5th St. NW, Washington, DC 20549. 800-SEC-0330. Regulates stock and bond markets; offers free publications for investors. Web site: *www.sec.gov.*

➤ American Association of Individual Investors, 625 N. Michigan Ave., Chicago, IL 60611. 312-280-0170. Provides publications, conferences and seminars on investing in the stock market. See their Web site: *www.aaii.com.* Customer Service: 1-800-428-2244.

➤ North American Securities Administrators Association, 10 "G" St. NE, Suite 710, Washington DC 20002. 202-737-0900. Securities enforcement agency with offices in every state; offers free publications on how to avoid scams and frauds. Web site: *www.nasaa.org.*

Smart Money Management

With a little effort, you can save a bundle when you buy everything from big-ticket items to toiletries. Go for discounts. Clip coupons. Change your lightbulbs. Join a food co-op. Here's how to s-t-r-e-t-c-h those dollars and make smart money management part of your daily routine.

PHONE FOR PRICE QUOTES

You can save big money on appliances, furniture and large equipment by calling a "price-quote" company—a firm that offers brand names at substantially discounted prices. Many consumers don't know about price-quote companies because they spend little money advertising. To find one in your area, look in the *Yellow Pages* for the item you want to buy. You will often find promotions touting "top brand names" at "wholesale prices." Comparison shop for the best deal. When you call, the salesperson will want to know the specific item you want, the manufacturer, model number and other details.

Here's a sampling of price-quote companies who deliver nationwide:

- *Cedar Rock Furniture* (Box 515, Hudson, NC 28638, 828-396-2361) carries all major furniture at up to 50% below retail.
- *Nationwide Auto Brokers* (29623 Northwestern Hwy., Southfield, MI 48034, 800-521-7257) will send you a form (for $11.95), which shows the operational equipment available for the car you want. Then they arrange delivery with a local dealer. You save $150 to $4,000 by having the broker negotiate a price break that eliminates the sales commission.
- *CMO* (2400 Reach Rd., Williamsport, PA 11701, 800-233-8950) offers brand-name computers like IBM, Epson, and Hewlett-Packard, as well as systems and software at savings as high as 40% off retail.

REAPING REBATES

True or false: Sending in rebate offers is too time-consuming and not worth the money. False! Rebate offers include cash refunds, coupons for future purchases and free merchandise or premiums. You have to pay postage, but while the value of coupons averages 50¢, refunds are commonly $2 to $5 or more. Savvy rebaters take particular pleasure in a "triple play"— a purchase involving a sale, a coupon and a rebate. For example, your detergent costs $3.99 and goes on sale for $1.99. You use your $1 coupon, for a net cost of 99¢. Then you send in for a $1 rebate. Your detergent was free!

Rebating involves some paperwork, but once you get the hang of it, you'll know what to look for: rebate forms on supermarket bulletin boards or shelves, proof-of-purchase seals on rebate products, and rebate receipts from stores advertising a net price "with rebate."

It pays to subscribe to a newsletter that publishes lists of offers. One newsletter, *Refundle Bundle* (Box 140, Centuck Station, Yonkers, NY 10710), for example, has about 400 offers per issue, with information on refunding and filing forms.

SHARING SAVINGS

- *Share tools & time.* Organize exchanges and bargaining co-ops with friends and neighbors. You buy the snowblower; they buy the leaf blower. When contracting for services, nego-

DOLLAR-STRETCHING SHOPPING

Here are simple ways to trim your shopping bills:

- ➤ Don't buy health and beauty products at the supermarket. They're cheaper at discount drugstores.
- ➤ Buy store-brand film from retail chains, such as Target and Kmart. Their 35mm film is made by 3M and other high-quality manufacturers. The cost is 25% less than Kodak or Fuji.
- ➤ Buy products that come in refillable containers—laundry detergent, shampoo, household cleaners, fruit juices, even pens. The refills are much cheaper than replacing the product each time.
- ➤ Shop off-season. Time your purchases for seasonal sales. Buy a winter coat or suit in January or a lawn mower in August.
- ➤ Ask if a store or service will accept other stores' or services' coupons. Many, particularly services such as dry cleaning, do this, but do not advertise it.
- ➤ Go for senior discounts, if eligible. Many stores issue senior discount cards that allow cashiers to subtract as much as 5% to 10% off the bill. Some set aside one day a week for senior discounts.

tiate a neighborhood group discount. On equipment rental, see if a neighbor wants to split costs.

- *Barter for services.* Handy with graphics? Are you an accountant? Whatever your talents, offer your services in exchange for those you need. Design flyers or trade tax preparation for lawn care, TV repair, computer lessons, health club fees.
- *Share rented videos with friends & neighbors.* Most video stores allow two days for a rental. One household gets it one day, and another household the next day. You split the cost.

- *Share a newspaper subscription with your neighbor.* You read it in the morning, for example, and your neighbor reads it in the evening. Share magazine subscriptions, too.

GO FOR EXTRA DISCOUNTS

Take an extra 5% discount off any major purchase!

Next time you buy a dishwasher, stereo or new coat, use your credit card as a bargaining chip to receive a special "insider's discount." Just offer to pay the merchant in cash —in exchange for a 5% discount.

Credit cards typically cost merchants 2% to 7% of your charge, and they may have to

PENNY-PINCHING AT HOME

Lights. Use fluorescent bulbs. They are more expensive, but last 14 times longer than incandescent bulbs and use 75% less electricity.

Dryer. When weather permits, hang clothes out to dry. If you don't use your electric dryer six hours a week, you can save $190 a year.

Washer. Use the cold water setting for washing. Most detergents can clean your clothes just as well in cold water as in hot or warm water. At $13 per person per month to heat water, you can rack up big savings on your family's utility bill.

Bathroom. Put a water restrictor in your shower head to reduce water flow up to 50% without cutting down on water pressure.

Living room. Keep fireplace flues closed when not in use to save up to 10% of your home's heat.

Outdoor lighting. Use fixtures that turn on and off by motion detector.

wait to get their money. Given the opportunity to receive payment immediately, many retailers will welcome your offer.

If you can't get a break on the price, ask if the merchant will "throw in" extra items to go with your purchase, such as head phones to go with a stereo. Also, ask about upcoming sales. If one is starting soon, many stores will give you the sale price early rather than risk losing your order.

SUPERMARKET SAVVY

- *Buy vinegar* rather than expensive specialty products for cleaning around the home. A mixture of half water/half vinegar

is just as effective for cleaning windows, bathrooms, kitchens and carpets. *Other uses:* clearing drains (handful of baking soda followed by a half cup of vinegar) and killing sidewalk or driveway weeds (full strength).

- *Buy store brands.* Most are of comparable or even superior quality to name brands. You can save 30% or more every time you shop. *Exception:* If you have a coupon that makes a name brand cheaper.
- *Buy generic brands.* They provide substantial savings, especially on cereal and canned goods.
- *Avoid costly weight-loss products.* Curb your appetite (and get nutritious fiber) by eating an apple before meals or as a snack. A baked potato with nonfat yogurt and chives does just as well.
- *Check the supermarket's circular* before you shop and plan menus around sale items or double-coupon promotions.

CLIP THOSE COUPONS

Shrewd coupon clipping pays off. Conscientious clippers save at least 25% on supermarket bills. Here are some strategies of a Pennsylvania woman who saves $1,200 a year on groceries:

- *Set aside time to clip and file.* The best time to clip is just before you go shopping—make a list and match coupons to your targeted purchases. Clipping and filing can take up to 10 hours a month, but you save $10 an hour in income. It's a job for which you make your own hours and answer only to yourself.

- *Use all available resources.* Supermarket flyers are the best source for easy clipping and in-store special sales. Daily newspapers (especially Wednesday and Sunday supplements) and women's magazines (*Good Housekeeping*, etc.) have coupon sections.

Respond to market surveys about your purchasing preferences when they offer to send you coupons (appropriate to your needs).

- *Keep your files organized and up-to-date.* Set up a portable filing system, such as an expandable, accordion folder, and index coupons by product category (dairy, beverages, cleaning products, etc.). Periodically check expiration dates so you don't miss out on savings on items you intend to buy. Take your file with you to the supermarket for unexpected bargains.

COUPON STRATEGIES

Watch for sales. When prices are marked down, you increase the value of your coupon.

Don't get locked into brand loyalty. Store brands are often comparable or even superior to name brands and can save you 30% or more if you have a coupon. Check unit prices, however. You may have a coupon for a name brand that makes it cheaper than a store brand.

Buy ahead. When you find a good deal on items you know you will use—such as toilet paper, bar soap and laundry detergent—stock up. In the long run, such big purchases generate significant savings.

Look for double and triple bargains. Shop in stores that double manufacturers' coupons. If you have an in-store coupon for the same item, you can use that, too—for triple savings. Also look for deals that offer "buy one, get one free" or "buy one, get another product free."

Give yourself an incentive. Bank your coupon savings for a special purpose. Make achieving your goal an incentive to clip, clip, clip!

WHAT GOES ON SALE WHEN

January	February	March	April	May	June	July	August	September	October	November	December
Appliances	A/C units	Boys' and	Fabrics	Handbags	Bedding	A/C units	Back-to-school	Bicycles	Cars (outgoing	Blankets,	Blankets,
Baby carriages	Art Supplies	girls' shoes	Hosiery	Housecoats	Boys' clothing	Appliances	specials	Cars (outgoing	models)	quilts	quilts
Books	Bedding	Garden	Lingerie	Household	Fabrics	Bathing suits	Bathing suits	models)	Fall/winter	Boys' suits,	Cards, gifts,
Carpets, rugs	Cars (used)	supplies	Painting	linens	Father's Day	Children's	Carpeting	China,	clothing	coats	toys (after
China	China	Housewares	supplies	Jewelry	specials	clothes	Cosmetics	glassware	Fishing	Cars (used)	Christmas)
Glassware	Curtains	Ice skates	Women's	Luggage	Floor	Electronic	Curtains,	Fabrics	equipment	Lingerie	Cars (used)
Holiday cards	Furniture	Infants'	shoes	Mother's Day	coverings	equipment	drapes	Fall fashions	Furniture	Major	Children's
Costume	Glassware	clothing		specials	Lingerie,	Fuel	Electric fans,	Garden items	Lingerie,	appliances	clothes
jewelry	Housewares	Laundry		Outdoor	sleepwear,	Furniture	A/C units	Hardware	hosiery	Men's suits,	Christmas
Furniture	Lamps	equipment		furniture	hosiery	Handbags	Furniture	Lamps	Major	coats	promotions
Furs	Men's	Luggage		Rugs	Men's	Lingerie,	Furs	Paints	appliances	Shoes	Coats, hats
Lingerie	apparel	Ski equipment		Shoes	clothing	sleepwear	Men's coats		School	White goods	Men's
Overcoats	Radios			Sportswear	Women's	Luggage	Silver		supplies	Winter	furnishings
Pocketbooks	Silverware			Tires, auto	shoes	Men's shirts	Tires		Silver	clothing	Resort &
Preinventory	Sportswear			accessories		Men's shoes	White goods		Storewide		cruise wear
sales	equipment			TVs		Rugs	Women's		clearances		Shoes
Shoes	Stereos					Sportswear	coats		Women's		
Toys	Storm					Summer			coats		
White goods	windows					clothes					
(sheets, tow-	Toys					Summer					
els, etc.)	TVs					sports					
						equipment					

YOU & YOUR PHONE BILL

Take advantage of consolidation and "equal access" in the phone wars. You have a choice about which long-distance service to use, and now, even local telephone service can be offered by an out-of-state carrier.

- *Choose a service that offers the cheapest rates for your calling pattern.* Look at last year's telephone bills to see where and whom you called and how long you talked. If you make a lot of long-distance calls, a minimum monthly rate won't matter to you. If you make only a few long-distance calls, however, the minimum charge might be higher than your average phone bill.

- *Check for volume discounts.* Some companies have a minimum monthly usage requirement and/or volume discounts. If you make only a few short calls each month, it will be hard to justify a monthly minimum. If you call long distance a lot, then a volume discount might offer significant savings.

Rounding off the number of minutes per call can add as much as 10% to your phone bill, especially if you make a lot of shorter calls. Choose a company that rounds to the tenth of a minute rather than the full minute.

ENERGY COST CUTBACKS

Every electrical appliance in your house offers opportunities for curbing energy use and increasing savings. To be savvy about how much you can save, you have to know what your appliances cost to run. Here are estimated costs based on the average electrical rating for the appliances, using a current cost of 12.0¢ per kilowatt-hour (kWh). On the surface, it may seem that some of your appliances don't cost all that much to run. Cumulatively, however, all the little charges add to your monthly electric bill.

Lightbulbs
- 18-watt fluorescent (1,250 lumens)–0.2¢/hour
- 75-watt incandescent (965 lumens)–1.0¢/hour

Living Room
- Cable TV converter–1.54¢/month
- Color television–1.7¢/hour
- Computer–2.2¢/hour
- Stereo–1.2¢/hour
- Vacuum cleaner–7.2¢/hour
- VCR–0.4¢/hour

Kitchen
- Coffee maker–2.4¢/pot
- Dishwasher–14.4¢/hour
- Freezers–$18.24/month (frost free)
- Frying pan–14.4¢/hour
- Microwave –1.2¢/5 minute
- Ranges:
- Surface unit–18¢/hour
- Oven–60¢/hour
- Refrigerators–(frost free)
  16.5-18.4 cubic ft.–$12.00/month
- Toaster–13.2¢/hour

Laundry
- Clothes dryer–30¢/half hour
- Iron–13¢/hour
- Washing machine–4¢/load
- Water heater (off peak)–$12.96/person/month

Bedroom
- Clock–16.8¢/month
- *Electric blankets:*
- Twin–7.2¢/night
- King–11.6¢/night
- Sewing machine–0.9¢/hour
- Waterbed heater–$11.40 to $17.28/month

Bathroom
- Hairdryer–0.6¢/5 minute
- Razor–0.5¢/month
- *Showers (5 min.):*
- Regular head–32.9¢/shower
- With restrictor–13.2¢/shower

Comfort
- *Air conditioners:*
- 8,000 BTUs–12¢/hour
- 12,000 BTUs–18¢/hour
- Dehumidifier–3¢/hour
- Humidifier–2¢/hour
- *Heating systems:*
- Hot air–$14.68/month
- Hot water–$10.97/month
- Portable heater–(1,500 watts)–18¢/hour
- Pool/well pump–1 H.P. motor–12¢/hour

Source: Association of Home Appliance Manufacturers.

Medical Money Matters

Until recently, medical care was one area where most people were afraid to look for bargains for fear they would compromise the quality of their treatment. In this day and age of soaring physician and prescription costs, you can't afford not to shop around. Top-notch care may be available for less than you think.

VISITING THE DOCTOR

Do you really have to see your doctor—and pay for the cost of an office visit?

Before you make an appointment talk to your doctor on the telephone. Describe your symptoms. Let the doctor decide if he or she needs to see you. If you have a severe head cold, for example, and you're not running a fever, the doctor may simply recommend rest, fluids and aspirin.

If you have a follow-up appointment after an illness and you feel completely recovered, inform the doctor. Likely the appointment is unnecessary.

Don't assume you need an appointment to get a prescription. If it's a problem you've had before, and your doctor is familiar with it, ask if he or she might call in a prescription or a refill over the phone.

Negotiate Doctors' Fees

Nearly all doctors cut their fees, but you have to ask. Negotiate directly with the doctor. Think of your visit as a business transaction—you are paying for a service. Doctors can't afford to lose customers. Call around to find out what other doctors charge. Naturally, you don't want to bother with haggling over fees when you're sick, so arrange all this in advance if possible. Here are some negotiating examples:

- If your insurance doesn't cover 100% of a procedure, ask your doctor to reduce the fee to the amount your insurance will cover. Some are already under contract as a "preferred provider" prepared to accept 80% of their normal fee.
- Ask for a discount for paying cash for office visits and other services. Billing and filing claims create a lot of paperwork for doctors, and often they will offer discounts for cash.
- Ask for quantity discounts for regular treatment of a chronic condition, such as allergies.
- Negotiate a flat price for a procedure that might require several office visits.

Shop Prescriptions, Too

Ask your pharmacist about cost-cutting measures for prescriptions. For example, if you are able to buy a 90-day supply of drugs rather than three 30-day supplies, you may pay only one copayment instead of three. Also, generic drugs can cost significantly less than brand names. Some insurance companies have special arrangements with mail-order pharmacies, which can lower your medication bills. If your insurance company doesn't offer such an arrangement, a discount pharmacy is likely to have lower prices.

CARE–"FREE"

Take advantage of free health care. Shopping malls and drugstores offer everything from free eye exams and flu shots to screenings for high blood pressure, diabetes and cancer. The same tests can cost more than $200 in a doctor's office.

State and local health services, as well as senior citizen agencies, often provide free clinics and services, such as flu shots. There is normally no income restriction for participating. Call your local health agent to find these programs.

Hospital, university and other medical research studies offer free care to participants. If you qualify for a particular study, you will likely get a thorough physical and regular checkups for the duration of the study—free. Requests for participants in such studies are advertised in newspapers. Or ask your doctor or local hospital for referrals.

MORE SAVINGS

Read your insurance policy carefully. Know exactly what's covered. Submit claims for everything for which you can expect reimbursement. People often assume they can't get reimbursed for incidentals—the small lancets diabetics use to obtain blood samples, for example—when many policies do cover such items.

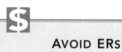

AVOID ERS

Avoid emergency rooms. In a true emergency, heading for the ER can save your life. But using the ER for nonemergency care is very expensive. You'll pay up to 10 times more than if you got the same treatment in your doctor's office.

Scrutinize your hospital bills. They are notoriously inaccurate and they favor the hospital 80% of the time. Before surgery, many items are placed in the operating room in case the doctor needs them. Patients are mistakenly billed for them even if the doctor never uses them. Check with your surgeon to find out if he or she used all the supplies and medication you were billed for. If not, ask the billing department to reduce your bill accordingly.

HEALTHY HEALTH CLUBS

A health club or sports center is a good deal only if you can use it often and safely—and get your money's worth. What to look for:
- Convenience to either your home or your office (15 minutes or less away).
- Hours that suit your schedule.
- Trained staff to help you set fitness goals designed for your own needs and to supervise your safe mastery of the equipment. Look for college degrees in physical education or certification from the *American College of Sports Medicine* or the *Institute of Aerobic Research*.
- Enough equipment (cardiovascular as well as weights) in good working order so you don't have to wait to work out.
- A trial membership, preferably for three months.

- A refund policy if you become disabled or have to move.

If a health club meets those criteria, you will likely use your membership often and the fee will be justified. The best bargains in health clubs are often at the local YMCA or YWCA.

HEALTH CLUB WARNING SIGNS

Health clubs are now regulated in many states, but the regulations vary and don't always protect the public from a club going into bankruptcy. To protect yourself, avoid clubs where:
- You are pressured to sign up that day. You should be able to take a contract home and study it.
- You are offered a lifetime membership for a hefty fee (this is illegal in many states).
- You see equipment not being used because it is out of service and no attempt is being made to fix it. Also, pool areas are not kept clean and free from mildew and mold (you should be able to see the bottom of the pool).
- The staff has no recognized credentials and you don't get good vibes talking to them or other members of the club.
- The local *Better Business Bureau* has complaints against the club. It's always wise to call the Bureau and check on a club before you join.

MEDICAL DEDUCTIONS NOT TO MISS

Dependent Deductions

Even though you may not be able to claim a personal exemption for your contribution to the support of relatives because of their income, you can still deduct any medical expenses you pay on their behalf—if you provide more than 50% of their support. Instead of giving a relative cash to pay medical bills, pay them yourself.

A person who is claiming a dependency exemption for a parent under a multiple support agreement with other relatives should also pay the dependent's medical expenses. *The reason:* In determining the qualification for the exemption, the payment of medical expenses is treated as part of the dependent's support. The payment is also deductible as a medical expense. That is, you get a double tax benefit for the same payment—a dependency exemption and a tax deduction.

Take off Your Glasses

Prescription eyeglasses are tax deductible if you need them to do your job. To qualify, the glasses must have been customized for the workplace and unsuitable for general use. *Tip:* Have the optometrist write "occupational use only" on the lens prescription. The deduction is taken as a miscellaneous expense, subject to the 2% miscellaneous itemization limits on Schedule A.

Miscellaneous Medical Deductions

Medical deductions have been allowed for the following:
- Apartment rent when the apartment was rented for an ailing dependent because it was cheaper than hospitalization
- Elastic stockings recommended by a doctor for a person with varicose veins
- Fluoridation device installed at home on the recommendation of a dentist
- Hair removal through electrolysis performed by a licensed technician
- Mattress and boards bought solely to alleviate an arthritic condition
- Mobile phone to enable a person who has heart disease to immediately call a doctor in an emergency
- Telephone calls made long distance to a therapist for psychological counseling
- Reclining chair bought on a doctor's advice to alleviate a heart condition
- Stop-smoking and alcohol-recovery programs

Managing Senior Assets

You may not be a senior citizen yet, but it's never too early to start thinking about managing your assets for the future. There are pitfalls to avoid and benefits to take advantage of. The goal is to secure your financial future and those of your children and grandchildren.

ESTATE TAX TRAPS

Many seniors underestimate the cost of estate taxes because they believe the $1 million estate tax exemptions in 2002 will protect them, or because they know they can pass assets tax-free to a spouse. Traps:

- Your estate may be pushed far over the $1 million amount by overlooking such assets as life insurance proceeds, the value of retirement accounts and appreciation in the value of your home.
- Passing all your assets to your spouse can be a costly mistake because he or she will be able to pass no more than $1 million to the next generation tax-free, while the two of you could plan together to pass a combined $2 million.

Three Ways to Avoid Tax Traps

These basic strategies can help you avoid estate tax traps:

- Have your life insurance owned by your spouse, a child or a trust benefiting family members. You can provide the money to pay the premiums through annual tax-free gifts.
- Make double use of the $1 million exemptions by passing up to that amount of your assets to children directly. Or use a trust that pays income to your spouse for life and then distributes its assets to your children, while leaving the remainder of your assets to your spouse. The $1 million exemption will be available for both your disposition of property and for your spouse's disposition of property.
- Use gifts to cut your estate. You can make annual gifts of up to a dollar limit ($11,000 in 2002) to as many separate recipients in the family (e.g., your parents as well as your children) as you wish, free of gift tax. The limit is $22,000 if the gift is made jointly with your spouse.

Tax savings are impressive even if you are widowed or divorced. An individual with four married children and 10 grandchildren can give the children, their spouses and their grandchildren $198,000 a year with no tax.

Another way to use gifts to cut your estate is to give assets that will appreciate in value— shares of growth stocks, for example. Any future appreciation would be taxed only when the recipient sells the stock.

REVERSE GIFTS TO ELDERS

When older family members have less than $1 million in assets, a reverse gift can save hefty taxes. You make gifts to family members of income-producing assets that have appreciated in value. When they die, the assets will pass back to you or other family members with stepped-up basis—revalued for tax purposes at market value— so potential gains tax on their appreciation is eliminated.

Gifts of income-producing assets to family members in lower tax brackets, such as children over age 14, can further cut family income taxes.

PASSING IRAs TO HEIRS

Most people leave their Individual Retirement Accounts (IRAs) to their spouse. But if your spouse is adequately provided for, you may want to leave some or all of your IRA money to your children or grandchildren. You get the greatest mileage from an IRA that you leave to your grandchildren or other beneficiaries who are much younger than you. The benefits:

- The IRA will continue for a long period—50, 60 or even 70 years, depending on the grandchild's age and the payout method selected.
- Earnings in a traditional IRA will accumulate on a tax-deferred basis for that period of time. This can add hundreds of thousands of dollars to an IRA.

There's a substantial income-tax saving in leaving a traditional IRA to a low-bracket grandchild rather than to a spouse. A spouse will pay income tax on IRA payouts at the 30% rate or more. But once a grandchild reaches age 14, income is taxed at his or her rate, not the parents' rate.

There's an estate-tax saving. The IRA assets and their growth over the years will not be included in your spouse's estate.

Note: The most you can give to your grandchildren is $1 million (adjusted annually for inflation). After that, gifts to grandchildren are subject to a generation-skipping tax.

SUPPORTING AN ELDERLY PARENT

If you are self-employed, consider employing your parents in the business. Jobs they can do might include writing monthly checks, managing a piece of real estate or investigating investments you are considering.

Special Concern

If your parent is under 65 and receives Social Security benefits, he or she will lose $2 of Social Security for every dollar earned over a certain amount. One way around this is to set up an S corporation with the parent as stockholder. The dividends paid out of the S corporation do not diminish

TAX-FREE FAMILY TREE

Try a "Grandparent Trust"

Consider setting up a "grandparent trust"—that is, a trust for the benefit of someone you are not legally obligated to support, even though the income is in fact used for support purposes. When the trust's income is used to provide support for a grantor's grandchild, it is not taxed to the grantor. Further, the trust principal is not included in a grantor's estate, so your tax situation benefits from such an arrangement in that respect.

The grandchild also benefits, receiving support he or she otherwise might not receive. And so does your immediate son or daughter, who has been relieved of the obligation of providing support for offspring. If you set up a trust with a third party, such as a bank, serving as trustee, and the trustee has the authority in its sole discretion to use trust income for the support of a person that you must support, such as your wife or minor child, the IRS does not regard you as the owner of the trust fund.

Help Pay College Costs

Grandparents who want to help out with college costs can get a special tax break. When payments are made directly to the university for the child's education, the amounts are not subject to gift tax rules.

Social Security payments. Of course, once the parent reaches 70, no earnings affect Social Security payments.

Caution

The *Social Security Administration* has authority to look beyond the facade of a business enterprise and determine the true situation. If it finds that the corporation was established solely to avoid deduction of Social Security benefits, it can impose deductions against benefits.

BENEFITS OF EARLY RETIREMENT

Collecting Social Security early can pay off. Even though benefits are reduced, they'll usually add up to more in the long run.

Example: If full benefits are $750 per month for retiring at age 65, you can get reduced benefits of $600 a month by retiring at age 62. You'd have to collect full benefits for 12 years to make up the $21,600 you'd receive during the three years of early payments.

WHY SELL NOW?

With so much emphasis on getting equity out of your home, more banks can be expected to offer some form of Reverse Annuity Mortgages (RAMS) to seniors. Basically, the bank lends you the value of your home; the amount advanced, plus interest, become the principal of the loan. Payments to the bank are deferred until the sale of the property or from the borrower's estate upon his or her death.

While reverse loans allow seniors on fixed incomes to realize the equity buildup in their homes without having to sell, essentially you are giving away your home— at least a big share of the equity you've built up over the years— to the bank to stay there. Diluting your (and your heirs') hard-earned equity in your home should be a last resort.

For younger seniors with a longer life expectancy, the monthly income from a reverse mortgage probably won't be enough to make much difference and, because the interest compounds over a long period, it becomes a very expensive way to borrow.

Better: Sell to your children and let them pay you $300 to $400 monthly. Or sell to an outsider under an agreement that allows you to live there as long as you wish.

The Business of Living

Savvy Deals

Money Smarts

Savvy Deals

Retire Richer

Secrets of New Car Deals

Getting a new car is terrific fun. Shopping for a new car is filled with dread and intimidation. A few buying tips can make new car buying less of a hassle—thanks to readily available buying facts and even hot competition of Internet car buying. Most important, you, the buyer, have access to knowledge that offers a critical edge when dealing with the dealers. Here's how to prepare for the purchase and drive away satisfied.

CHOOSE YOUR CAR, PICK YOUR PRICE

Know what you want. The very first step is to decide which vehicle will serve you best. Only then can you arm yourself with knowledge to tackle the dealers. Remember, they sell cars every day. You buy one every few years.

Determine the make and model, then do your homework.

- *Research your choice.* Read what the experts say. *Consumer Reports, Car & Driver,* and *Road & Track* are three excellent information sources.
- *Decide the dealer's profit.* You can determine what you want to pay the dealer by learning the difference between "dealer invoice," what the dealer pays for the car, and the MSRP (Manufacturer's Suggested Retail Price), also known as the "sticker price."
- *Determine the value of your trade.* Know what your current car is worth. This should be a part of your research. Look up prices of used vehicles in one of the used-car pricing guides.
- *Know the dealer cost of optional equipment.* Again, you decide how much profit you want to give the dealer.
- *Arrange advance financing.* A bank or credit union may give you a better car loan rate than the dealer. Always investigate your options.
- *Check with your insurance carrier.* The car you want may carry extra costs to factor into your calculations.

DETERMINE THE DEALER'S PROFIT

The car's primary sticker lists certain charges. (Ignore smaller stickers indicating dealer extras, sometimes called AMUs or ADMUs—additional dealer mark-up, waxing, pinstriping and so on.)

MSRP or "sticker": The price the manufacturer would like you to pay.

Base price: What the dealer (sometimes) pays the manufacturer for the car. Determine if any dealer incentives are active.

Invoice price: What the dealer pays the manufacturer for the car, including the optional features.

Fair markup to you? Figure 2% to 3%—$300-$500—for cars in the $15,000 range, and up to $2,000 or more for luxury vehicles.

Model bargains: Sometimes dealers are forced by distributors to accept slow sellers in the model line. These vehicles are often luxury cars accompanied by manufacturer-to-dealer rebate incentives. Dealers will sell these vehicles at "cost" and make money off the incentive. If your research uncovers dealer incentive rebates on a particular model, you might snag a bargain.

You decide what profit you're going to allow the dealer by researching prices and knowing what he is making on the deal. Then, shop for a dealer who you believe deserves to profit from your business.

RESOURCES

Consumer Reports New and Used Car Price Service: 800-933-7700
For $12 order a report that includes invoice price, sticker price plus invoice and sticker price for all options; plus a listing of factory rebates to car buyers, and factory rebates to car dealers. *Also included:* Advice on how to use the information in negotiating a deal. Also online at *www.consumerreports.org.*

AUTOSPEC: 900-288-6773
The call is charged to your phone bill at $2 per minute. You get all the same information as the other sources plus a free faxed printout of the report, which you can use to negotiate.

Newsstand Information
Edmund's New Car Guide and *Pace Buyers Guide* (about $6) give current prices for most makes, models and years of cars and trucks. Used-car editions generally go back 10 years. Also provides useful 800 numbers for essential price comparison reports.

BE A DEALER'S NIGHTMARE

A car dealer's bad dream is a knowledgeable shopper who:

- *Knows exactly* what he or she wants in a particular model
- *Understands the difference* between sticker price and dealer cost and knows how showroom pricing works
- *Has researched the real value* of his or her trade-in and is expecting a realistic price, or is selling the old car elsewhere
- *Does not want to waste time* with sales people who "aren't authorized" to close the deal
- *Knows there's a factory incentive* that gives the dealer much more room in price negotiation
- *Speaks knowledgeably* about the regional availability of the car she or he wants
- *Has the financing* to close the deal—today, if they can come to terms, but is not in a rush
- *Knows where the competition* is located and probably hasn't been there yet
- *Shows a willingness to "walk"* if the deal isn't making financial sense (starting with the trade-in allowance)

DEALER TRICKS & TACTICS

Defend yourself against pressure sales tactics by recognizing when they're being applied and knowing how to counter them. Sales people know that statistically less than 5% of customers who "walk" ever return. Use that information in your favor; don't take these ruses:

- *"This is the last car left. Don't know when another like it will come in."* If the deal is in your control and the price is within reason, take the car. If not, say, "I won't be pressured like that. Let's get the price right and I'll take it."
- *"What will it take to close this deal today?"* Know what a fair price is (from your homework), respond with a fair deal offer. If they keep asking, you keep responding with the same message. Eventually, they'll get the point and stop asking.
- *Laying on the guilt* by asking if you're serious about buying the car or telling you the sale is necessary to their job. Remember, this is a "button-pushing" ploy.

Tell them you are serious about the deal at the right price—nothing less.

- *Blaming the boss* by claiming they have no authority. Just say that you want to deal with the person who has authority rather than waste your time.
- *"If we agree to this point, will you buy this car today?"* Tell them "no," but also tell them it will work in their favor toward your decision.
- *"If we can get this car for you with these options, do we have a deal?"* Never agree to a deal based on this ploy. Tell them that those are the options you prefer, if they can get them in a vehicle at your fair price, it will help with your decision.
- *Delaying tactic.* Don't let it happen. If you're asked to wait while they check something, get up, walk around, drift toward the door, leave the building. Tell the sales person you have an appointment. Stay in control of the negotiation pace.
- *"There's a delay in checking your credit."* Smile. Tell them your credit is perfect and to give you a call when they have themselves sorted out. Walk. They'll run after you.
- *Don't get "trapped"* by "lost" keys or mislaid titles. Take an extra key for the dealer to use in test-driving your trade-in and surrender only a *copy* of your title.

SEVEN AIDS TO NEW CAR CHOICES

Make two columns on a page and list key specifications important to your vehicle needs. Add up your "wants" vs. "needs" to make a choice.

1. How will you use the vehicle? For commuting, hauling, recreation (sports car), improving your social status (luxury car), sales calls? Do you travel long distances?

2. What are the key characteristics? Economy, luxury, power, interior space, trunk space, seating and number of doors?

3. List the options that you *want* in one column and those you really *need* in another. Air conditioning is probably a must if you're in the car a lot, but do you really need an expensive antitheft package? What engine size do you need—6 or 8 cylinders? How important are power seats?

4. Review your answers. For example, if economy is important and you need a vehicle with lots of room, maybe a van makes more sense than a car. Or, if you drive mostly alone, a 2-door may be suitable; but if you're in sales and drive clients, then a 4-door is a must.

5. List your performance preferences. Do you want speed, handling and agility or off-road towing and hauling capability?

6. Select a make and model before you visit dealers. Talk to friends. If you aren't certain about a particular model, rent one for a day to really find out how much you like it.

7. Read the reviews and test drive reports on the vehicle that appeals to you. Also see if there have been any recalls.

SURF THE NET, BUY A CAR

Car shopping and buying over the Internet is growing at an alarming rate. *Auto-by-Tel Corp. (www.autobytel.com)*, just one of the online companies selling cars, processes 60,000 car customers monthly to its nationwide network of 2,000 (and growing) dealers.

How It Works

Car shoppers are directed from an Internet dealer's menu page to the vital information—sticker price, dealer cost, transport charges, and so on. Customers fill in a detailed purchase request listing make, model and optional equipment. The Internet dealer forwards the details to an accredited dealer nearest you. That dealer must contact you within 24 to 48 hours with a low, firm, no-haggle price.

Why It Works

The dealer's cost in the sale is slashed significantly. A dealer's typical cost per vehicle is $820 in personnel expenses and $295 in marketing expenses, according to the *National Automobile Dealers Association (NADA)*. Those costs account for about 60% of a dealer's operating expenses. Selling through the Internet drops those numbers. In fact, participating dealers claim to sell more cars at about 70% of the normal cost.

Financing & Insurance

Strategic alliances are forged between Internet dealers and key players in finance and insurance. *American International Group (AIG), General Electric Auto Financial Services* and certain banks all participate in providing total service financing, insurance and car lease transactions.

Downside

You still have to deal with your trade-in, but all the vital pricing statistics are available on the Internet. Place an ad in your local paper for best results.

AUTO WEB SITES

Find car safety information, news, statistics, advice, maps, Internet links.

Car Talk
http://cartalk.cars.com

Mr. Traffic
www.mrtraffic.com

U.S. National Highway Traffic Safety Administration
www.nhtsa.dot.gov

Nutz and Boltz
www.motorminute.com

Auto Answers
www.autoanswers.com

Motor Trend
www.motortrend.com

CHOOSE YOUR MAKE & MODEL: DRIVE IT OFF THE INTERNET

If your next car does not involve the Internet, chances are that you will be losing money in the sale—new or used. The nation's largest auto dealer chain, *AutoNation*, sold $1 billion worth of new and used cars in 1999. They project that by 2005 the Internet will account for 15% of their auto sales. If knowledge is power, consumers reign high in new and used car purchases with the wealth of information provided by the scores of Web sites offering classifieds, test drive reports, new and used car pricing guides, recall records and even title history records to track a vehicle's history. For example, was the car ever written off because of flood damage or accident? Here are some of the key sites to track in your next auto sale or search:

www.kbb.com   *Kelley Blue Book* provides new car and used car prices. It has been used for decades by the dealer industry to quote new car prices and used car values.

www.edmunds.com   An excellent resource site by Edmunds, the 30-year-old publisher of new and used car guides. Good site for consumer information, road tests, repair reports and safety information. Features access to a nationwide test-drive tour where you can actually track test your choice of 120 new vehicles.

www.imotors.com   Shop online for a used car by make, model, color and price. Then have it delivered through a certified dealer.

www.carpoint.msn.com   Microsoft's Web site for the new and used car markets. Lets you specify the vehicle you want in your geographic area, then ties into dealer locator database to find the car you want. Also ties into *Kelley Blue Book* listings for used car prices. A good site if you want to set a fair market price for your existing car in your market area.

GOING DOWN...

Used car prices have leveled off after years of declining and are forecast to climb slightly this year, according to industry experts. *Reason:* The cost of a new car has increased an average of 2.8 percent over the previous year and used-car prices climb in lockstep with new-vehicle prices.

In addition, the number of off-lease cars will decline in 2001 for the first time in 10 years, causing a shortage of the most desirable used vehicles resulting in higher prices.

Used-car buyers usually have until the end of July before prices will increase dramatically as the market reflects more new-vehicle price increases and extremely short supply of two, three and four year old off-lease models.

Used Cars: Good Sense, Big Savings

If you want a great deal on a car, buy a used one. New cars depreciate about 15% to 20% the moment you drive off the dealer's lot. By the end of the first year, some new cars are worth only half their original value. Also, used cars don't carry the extra charges of a new vehicle—transportation costs, dealer prep charges and costs for added accessories or special features, like a leather interior. Here are tips on what to look for in a previously owned auto—and where to find the best deal.

USED CARS: BETTER THAN EVER

It used to be that if you had a rich person's tastes and a poor person's wallet, you'd shop for a used car. Not anymore. First,

---

MILEAGE MATTERS

High mileage matters. The assumption behind used car pricing is that the average vehicle is driven 15,000 miles a year. If the mileage is greater, you should get a discount of 20 to 25 cents for every mile exceeding the 15,000 per annum. Similarly, you should be prepared to pay more for a car with less mileage.

Buyer beware: Odometer tampering persists despite severe penalties for dealers caught tampering with mileage. About three million of the used cars sold each year have had their odometers "fixed." *Average rollback:* 30,000 miles, enabling dealers to skim up to an extra $750 from the unsuspecting buyer.

Source: National Highway Traffic Safety Administration.

---

there's big savings in late-model used vehicles.

- *Manufacturer's warranties may still apply* to low-mileage vehicles. And extended warranties can be purchased at reasonable prices.
- *New cars lose as much as 50% of their value* at the end of one year on the road, yet they're hardly broken-in. You get far greater value for your money in a used car than in a new one.
- *Used is cheaper.* Title fees, taxes and insurance are usually less. Plus you pay no fees for dealer prep or transportation charges— all items that have zero resale value when you buy new.
- *Used cars are available.* There are a multitude of cars coming off leases written 36 months ago. Plus the growth in car rental fleets is feeding the market regularly.

- *Attractive financing,* competitive with rates for new cars, now exists for the used vehicle market.
- *New sales strategies* (see "The New Super Lots") make "used" as good as "new." Well, almost.

SHOP MONEY FIRST

Unless you're flush with enough cash to buy the car you want, start with the car loan first. Usually you will find the best loans with your own bank. Knowing exactly what you can afford to spend will speed and simplify the purchase and reduce haggling, too.

Know Your Prices

Check used car prices in the *National Automobile Dealers Association (NADA) Used Car Guide*, available in bookstores or at newsstands. Another excellent

source is *Edmund's Used Car Guide* or *Pace Buyer's Guide*. Such guides fix prices for used cars (new cars, too) and tell you which discounts should be taken from the "offering price" for high mileage, and which premiums you should expect to pay for optional extras that may have been added when the car was new.

THE NEW SUPER LOTS

The mushrooming numbers of cars coming off lease are spawning new mega-car lots for used vehicles. Springing up near many metropolitan areas, these huge used car businesses sell only used cars at "no haggle" prices. You'll find acres of handpicked previously owned vehicles that have passed a rigorous 100-point mechanical and safety check before being included in the dealer's inventory.

Designed for convenience and risk-free car shopping, these operations take advantage of computerized inventory and dedicated customer service practices— including child-care services and golf carts to view the cars.

Examples: *CarMax*, launched by *Circuit City*, and *Driver's Mart Worldwide*—both opening in major metropolitan areas with expectations of hundreds of superstores in the next year.

TAKE A TEST DRIVE

I t's hard to believe, but more than 60% of used car buyers never take a test drive. Many assume that doing so triggers opportunity for the dealer or owner to start pressuring them. Take a test drive—or walk away from the deal. Try every knob, button and option. Listen for odd noises. If there are any problems and you still want the vehicle, include in the contract that the problems must be fixed before you put down any money.

Show Up in Daylight

Plan your test drive on a good-weather day so you can see any dings, dents and ripples (indicating a body repair) in the car's finish. Bright sunlight will reveal spots that have been repainted.

Bring a small flashlight. Check under the car for signs of oil leaks, especially in the transmission area. Drive the car forward, then get out and check for signs of leaking where it was parked. Beware of the seller who has the car all warmed up and waiting for you and parked away from its normal station.

Plan a Test Route

You want to test all aspects of the vehicle's performance.
- Make sure you drive a route that includes hills, bumpy roads, curved roads and a stretch of highway driving.

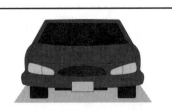

Frame alignment. Step well back from the car and look along the sides for mis-alignment of the wheels or ripples in the side panels that indicate crash damage.

Shock absorbers. Push down on the corners of the car to test the shocks. There should be a firm up-and-down motion with no bouncing effect.

Check wheels with the car elevated. There should be no looseness in the bearings.

HOW TO TEST DRIVE A USED CAR

Check under the hood and under the car. Look for oil leaks and any signs of damage to the frame or any new parts that may indicate a repair.

Start the engine. Let it warm up. While waiting, check for leaks again. Test the brakes, power steering, lights, turn signals, emergency brake, windshield washers, wipers, air conditioning and other accessories.

In the car, with the hood and windows open, put the car in drive, then reverse, listening and feeling for any looseness or thumping in the transmission or other parts of the drive train.

Depress the brakes fully. If the pedal sinks low and feels mushy, chances are the brakes need replacement. Check the brake reservoir to see if the fluid is still topped off. Close the hood and check the latching mechanism. You're ready to drive.

On the road, accelerate smartly. Listen for any strange noises and roughness in the engine or transmission. Do a brake test to see if the car pulls left or right. Steering should be smooth, the car should run straight without tugging left or right.

Drive briskly over a bumpy road. The vehicle should feel solid with minimal bounce. In a parking lot make full turns left and right, listening for sounds in the front suspension.

On a hill, accelerate to strain the transmission and engine. Both should perform smoothly.

On a highway, accelerate into the traffic flow. Check the exhaust in the mirror—there should be little or none. If there's bluish smoke, go home. Test passing and handling ability. Does the steering shimmy at speed?

At the end of the test, check for leaks again. If all seems well, you've done the best you can short of a mechanic's inspection.

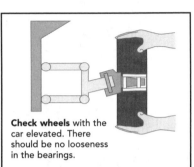

9. Check all lights including high beams, turn signals and brake lights. Check wipers and washers. Check chrome for signs of sprayed paint (signs of a paint job and possible repair).

8. Under the hood, examine the radiator for signs of leakage, corrosion, rust. Test connecting hoses; they should feel firm with no soft spots. Hose connections must be free of corrosion. Coolant level should be at the correct level.

TEN STEPS TO SIZE UP A USED CAR

10. Inside, check the seat fabric for unusual wear, stains, tears in the backs of seats. How worn are the brake pedals, accelerator, driver seat? Do they indicate possibly higher miles? Check ceiling fabric for water damage, especially with sunroof vehicles. Test all windows. Sit quietly. Is there an odor? Does it feel right? If all is a go, start the test drive.

1. Show up while the sun shines. Have a rag or towel to kneel on for under-vehicle inspection and something to clean your hands with. Stand away from the car and approach it slowly. Look for dents or ripples along fenders, hood, trunk. Check for variations in paint finish plus any cracks, peeling chips or rust spots.

2. Walk around the car. Check glass for cracks, pitting or rock strikes. In the trunk, lift the liner and look for any color mismatch or rust in the tire well. Check the spare tire. Check rubber trunk seals for tightness and rubber texture. Trunk lid should fit evenly, latch easily without slamming.

3. Open gas cap door checking for rust signs. Press your weight down on the rear fender trying to bounce the car. Response should be smooth. If it bounces, suspect bad shock absorbers. Wipe a finger in the exhaust pipe. The result should be carbon and water, not oily. Test exhaust for tightness.

4. Check door seals for wear, distortion, dry or cracked rubber. Examine inside hinges for rust. Note door dings and check the paint. Look underneath the vehicle with a flashlight. Note any unusual rusting or oil leakage around the transmission.

5. Examine the tires for wear, distortion, tread depth (try the "quarter test," see next page). Grab the front tire at the top using both hands. Test for any sign of looseness in the wheels.

6. Do an oil check. Chances are there's fresh oil, in which case, unscrew the oil cap. The inside should be clean, not slimy. Run a finger around the rim of the valve cover. It should be clear (apart from oil). If it's slimy and jelly-like, there may be a problem.

7. Belts should be tight with no signs of cracking, fraying or whiteness on the edges. Battery terminals clean with minimal corrosive buildup. Check the battery compartment for rust. Check brake fluid reservoir for signs of leaking or low fluid level.

- If the vehicle is a sports utility, plan to test it off-road and use the all-wheel drive.
- Watch, feel and listen for all the symptoms listed in the box (page 294). Pay particular attention to whether the steering tugs to the left or right when braking.

After the Ride

Perform another walk-around with the engine running and hood open. Look for leaks again. Listen for sounds of fan belt chafing or valves clicking. If anything seems amiss, make notes.

NEGOTIATING THE NEW PRICE

After the test drive and inspection, go over your notes with the seller. Deduct from the asking price any repairs or replacements that you feel you need to do to bring the car up to your level of expectation. Figure in the following:

- Tire replacement, if justified. Negotiate for all four tires and a spare, if the vehicle's worn.
- The cost of any repairs that are needed, such as brakes, wheel alignment or non-functioning accessories.
- The cost of any bodywork or paint work that you would want to have done, or replacements of carpeting, floor mats, etc. or repairs to damaged seat coverings.

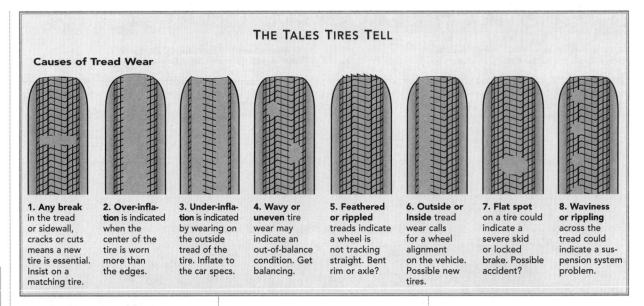

THE TALES TIRES TELL

Causes of Tread Wear

1. Any break in the tread or sidewall, cracks or cuts means a new tire is essential. Insist on a matching tire.

2. Over-inflation is indicated when the center of the tire is worn more than the edges.

3. Under-inflation is indicated by wearing on the outside tread of the tire. Inflate to the car specs.

4. Wavy or uneven tire wear may indicate an out-of-balance condition. Get balancing.

5. Feathered or rippled treads indicate a wheel is not tracking straight. Bent rim or axle?

6. Outside or Inside tread wear calls for a wheel alignment on the vehicle. Possible new tires.

7. Flat spot on a tire could indicate a severe skid or locked brake. Possible accident?

8. Waviness or rippling across the tread could indicate a suspension system problem.

WHEN TIRES ARE WORN...

Tires will be one of the most expensive replacements on a used car. They can also tell you something about the mileage of the car and how well the owner maintained the vehicle. Carefully examine the tires and have the dealer or owner replace faulty ones displaying any of the characteristics in the chart on this page.

Dealers obviously have more leeway than a private owner when it comes to switching tires. It is not unreasonable to negotiate a new set of tires on a vehicle with high mileage whose treads are badly worn.

Telltale Tires

If the wheels shimmy during your test drive, or if the car pulls to the left or right, chances are the vehicle's wheels aren't properly aligned or balanced. Close tire examination of the front wheels can confirm both these problems and if either exists, negotiate new tires, alignment and balancing.

QUARTER CHECK FOR TIRE DEPTH

Quick test for tire tread wear. Insert a quarter, head-side facing you into the tread. Acceptable tread depth should reach half-way between the coin's edge and the nose of the head.

Buying New Tires

Tire prices vary widely among tire distributors. Generally, you can expect better prices for popular brand name tires through specialty tire outlets.

- Service stations and car dealerships may charge a premium, and don't always carry the brand best suited to your vehicle.
- Try to buy tires similar to the original equipment on the vehicle and never mix radial tires and non-radials on the car.

Sidewalls Tell the Story

Tire sidewalls carry vital information on tire specs. The owner's manual lists tire specs that must be matched or exceeded when replacing tires. Read the specs, and don't let some "dealer special" put danger between you and the road.

Leasing A Car

Leasing a car makes sense if you want to drive a new or expensive model, but don't have the money or desire to own the car. Leasing is an especially good deal if you do not plan to keep the car for more than five years, do not drive more than 15,000 miles a year, and are careful not to damage the car. But while leasing is generally less expensive than buying a car, many people end up paying more than they should. Before you sign a contract, be sure to check the small print regarding down payment, insurance charges, mileage allowances and term length.

TO LEASE OR NOT TO LEASE

Leasing a car makes sense if you tend to change cars frequently and don't put more than 12,000 to 15,000 miles a year on a car. It also may make sense for business purposes if yours is a profession that requires a specific type of vehicle in day-to-day business. A contractor, for example, may want to look at the advantages of leasing a light truck as a business expense.

The Pros of Leasing
- *Low down payment* or no down payment making the car you really want more affordable with feature options you might not get if you were buying.
- *Lower monthly payments,* generally, than if you were purchasing the car outright.
- *New vehicle* every three years giving you the luxury of a new car with new warranties, so you're protected against the expense of major repairs.
- *You maintain* pace with automotive technology which is changing rapidly. You'll always be driving the safest, most efficient vehicle available.

The Cons of Leasing
- *When it's over, it's over.* You have to either turn the car in or buy it out of the lease. It also means you'll be going through the new car purchase process every three years. Worst, you don't own a car after 36 months of payments.
- *Dealers love leases.* It makes cars more affordable, but more importantly, buyers have not yet learned how much it pays to haggle in a lease. Amazingly, consumers somehow equate leases with fixed pricing and they simply roll over for any deal offered.
- *Leases are more complicated,* so dealers can hide more profit. If you plan to lease, recognize that there are a whole new set of negotiating skills involved—otherwise, you stand a good chance of being taken.
- *You have to negotiate two prices.* First, the cost of the car, second, and equally important, the residual value of the car after the lease ends.
- *Security deposits* are necessary with a lease. Though not anywhere near as high as a down payment on the car, you still need to plan on at least one month's security payment. Argue if it is any higher.
- *Lease processing fees.* Some dealers will insist on paper processing fees for the lease. Refuse these. They are making money on the financing in any event. Threaten to walk and this fee will disappear faster than you can.

⚠️

BUYER BEWARE OF "WEAR & TEAR"

When negotiating a lease, take extra time to clarify the dealer's "wear and tear" policy before you sign. There is no set standard or industry definition for "wear and tear," and a misunderstanding at the beginning can be costly when the lease expires. Dents in the frame, dog hair or food stains on the seats all add up. Ask about specific types of damage and have the dealer put the repair costs in writing.

➤ **Tip:** Some leases actually state that the car is to be returned in virtually the same condition that it is delivered. Dealers love this one. It gives them a license to steal at the end of the lease, because they determine the level of wear. Arrange a lease with a company whose policy is more intelligent.

➤ **Tip:** Have any "wear and tear" repaired yourself. An independent mechanic or repair shop will charge you less than the dealership.

➤ **Tip:** Never take a lease for longer than 42 months and preferably 36 months or less. Otherwise, you end up making costly repairs that are not covered by the warranty.

CHECK THE ADS

Most car-leasing ads stress low monthly payment in large type. In smaller lettering, you may find that you have to make a down payment of several thousand dollars to get that low rate and that the lease may run for longer than you think—30

USED CAR LEASING

The overall reliability of cars has increased to the point that leasing can be arranged for most high-end luxury cars. This is especially appealing if you want to drive a late model luxury car such as a Mercedes, BMW, or Lexus, where the model designs don't change from year to year.

Negative: Residual prices are frequently so high that you could be driving around in a new car for the same cost of a used luxury car. It's a matter of preference.

months, for example, rather than the customary 24 months, so you may wind up paying additional interest charges. Read print ads carefully and in the case of TV or radio ads, call the 800 number that is now legally required to be announced in the ad to learn about all of the lease's details.

KNOW THE PRICE

Most people are unaware that they should negotiate the total price of the car before discussing their intent to lease. In fact, only about 10% of people looking to lease bother to haggle, compared to 75% of those who plan to buy. Haggling is smart

because lease payments are based on the car's total price. Find out the dealer's cost of the car, call competing dealerships to find the lowest prices, and check leases from various finance sources to find out who has the lowest rates. Only then should you discuss the monthly lease payments and other terms of the contract. Ask for the lowest monthly payment available without adding any money to the down payment.

CLOSED-END VS. OPEN-END LEASE

Closed-end leases fix the value (residual) of the vehicle up front. This is an agreement between you and the lessor on what the price of the car or truck will be when the lease period ends.

Most leases today are, in fact, closed-end. If you have the option for an open-ended lease, which means the value of the car is established based on its appearance, market condition (and dealer's whim), decline it.

BUY MORE MILES

The number of miles you expect to drive and what you actually will drive over two to three years probably will be different. About 40% of people who lease cars take 12,000-miles-per-year deals, and

most of these people exceed the limit, resulting in higher mileage costs. One excess mile costs 10¢ to 15¢ if you don't buy up front. Buy in advance, however, and the per-mile cost is only 8¢ to 9¢. If you don't use the excess miles, the fee is usually refundable.

GET GAP INSURANCE

When leasing a car, buy a gap-insurance policy. Monthly lease payments do not cover the total cost of the car. If the car is stolen or totaled in an accident, your auto insurance policy will only cover its market value. You will still owe the borrowed amount on the lease. Gap insurance makes up the difference. Be sure to ask the dealer or financial institution where you are leasing about this insurance before signing the papers.

OPT TO PURCHASE

Many leases include an option to buy the car for the residual price specified in the lease—that is, the amount of money expected from the sale of the car at the end of the lease period. This can be a good deal. Many leased cars are currently selling for more than their residuals.

RESOURCES & REFERENCES

➤ *Automotive News, Crain Communications,* 1400 Woodbridge Ave., Detroit, MI, 800-678-9595
➤ *Center for Auto Safety,* 2001 S St. NW, Washington, DC, 20009, 202-328-7700
➤ *Consumer Reports Annual Auto Issue, Consumer's Union,* 101 Truman Ave., Yonkers, NY 10703-1057, 914-378-2000
➤ *Consumer Reports New and Used Car Price Service,* P.O. Box 549027, Chicago, IL 60654-9027, 800-232-3470
➤ *Kelley Blue Book Used Car Guide,* Box 19691, Irvine, CA 92623, 800-444-1743
➤ *NADA Official Used Car Guide: Retail Consumer Edition, National Automobile Dealers Association,* 8400 Westpark Dr., McLean, VA 22102, 800-544-6232
➤ *Buying a New Car, Federal Consumer Information Center,* Dept. 301J, Pueblo, CO, 81009, 888-8PUEBLO
➤ *Shopping for a Safer Car, Insurance Institute for Highway Safety,* P.O. Box 1420, Arlington VA 22210, *www.highwaysafety.org/ vehicle_ratings/sfsc.htm*
➤ *The Insider's Guide to Buying a New or Used Car,* Betterway Books, Cincinnati, OH, 800-289-0963

PC Shopping Strategies

Now more than ever owning a computer makes sense. Finally, computer engineers are figuring out that computers and people need to communicate. Systems have become more reliable and software more interchangeable. Challenges today are focused more on understanding how the software works and not needing to know how the machine works.

WHO SHOULD BUY A COMPUTER?

If you write letters and checks, own a home, manage a family, go to school or have children who will be attending school, a personal computer is more of a necessity than a luxury.

Moreover, computers are less expensive than ever and easier to use. If you give careful thought

to how you might use one, a computer can free more time for you by taking over much of your routine household management, particularly in keeping track of finances.

Another good use for a computer is to inventory household items for security purposes. Home inventory software is a part of some programs such as *Quicken* financial software (under $50). In the event of household disaster, this application alone could be worth many times the cost of the computer.

How much you pay for a personal computer (PC)

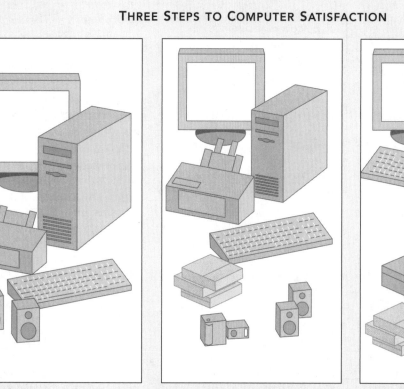

THREE STEPS TO COMPUTER SATISFACTION

Buy a packaged system including a computer, keyboard and monitor equipped with a CD-ROM, sound card, speakers and internal modem. Hard disk size and memory will suit most startup needs. Add an ink jet color printer and basic software. You'll be able to handle letter writing, desktop publishing, household finance and check writing and also access the Internet.

As skills develop, add more sophisticated software, such as a suite containing word processing, a spreadsheet program and perhaps a database package. Adding a black & white laser printer will speed printing, especially if you print off the Internet. By now you'll know whether emphasis will be on games for your system, educational programs or business applications.

At this stage of computing activity you will probably be ready for an upgrade to a larger, faster system equipped for the particular interests of your household. A scanner will probably be justified for a broader graphics capability and you'll want to take advantage of technology advances in faster chips, increased memory, higher speed modems and DVDs.

depends on what you will be using it for and how many "extras" you think you will need. Today basic computers can start as low as $500. Generally, the higher the processor speed, the larger the hard disk space, and the greater the amount of RAM memory, the higher the price. Larger or flat-screen monitors also cost more.

As you shop around, you will find that a well-equipped, name-brand computer with a monitor, a CD-ROM drive, a backup capacity, and a keyboard will range from $900 to $2,500. Sometimes you can also get a printer or scanner as part of the deal.

Prices are constantly falling as competition increases and new models supplant old ones (often purchased at a bargain). Notebooks, or portable computers, can be more expensive—up to $1,000 or more than a desktop model.

SHOP RIGHT, BUY SMART

C omputers are everywhere and the array of prices can be confusing. But you don't have to be an experienced computer user to take advantage of the extremely competitive market.
- Your best bet in buying a computer is to visit a local computer superstore to learn all you can about various models, features and speed. Then obtain a

PURCHASING TIPS

➤ Pay for a computer with a credit card. It gives you some protection if things go wrong. Some credit card companies will even go to bat for you if you have problems with a major purchase such as a computer.

➤ Buy over the Internet. All computer catalog retailers have sites, as well as all manufacturers. The dot-com purchase gives you more information than most superstores and retailers. Out-of-state purchases are usually free from state tax and the information you obtain is reliable.

popular computer catalog from a computerized colleague and order a system over the phone or over the Internet.
- You will save paying tax on the system since the order, in most cases, comes from out of state.
- The prices, even without considering the tax-free advantage, are very competitive and the equipment is essentially the same with plenty of name-brand representation.
- You don't have to lug the system home. It will be delivered, in many instances, the next day.
- Setting up is no more complicated than if you carry a box home from a retailer and open

it. Connections are clearly marked and most catalogs, like *PC Connection* (800-800-5555), have a special hot line you can call to help you through the setup phase.

Top Mail-Order Brands
Companies you may have heard of—*Dell Computer* (*www.dell.com*) and *Gateway Computer* (*www.gateway.com*)— sell almost exclusively by mail order. They have an excellent record for delivering computers that set up easily right out of the box. The instructions and customer support are good, and the systems are well priced and backed by strong warranties.

Superstores
The prices are competitive. There are a variety of name-brand systems, including the store's own systems. If you experience problems setting up, these superstores are not always equipped to provide phone assistance. Plus, you have to pay local sales tax on the purchase and carry it home.

Electronic Stores
Prices are competitive, but don't look for too much help or advice. They are better at pricing special brand-name packaged systems.

Specialty Shops
They offer the most help and advice on what to buy. They generally have a narrow choice of brand-name packages, but the best prices are on their own nonbrand systems which can be good buys.

TOP BRANDS

These computer brands are available in a wide selection of retail outlets, superstores and catalogs. The better known brands tend to cost more, but that doesn't necessarily mean better computer performance. Customer support is the critical factor to consider. Ratings for customer service are offered by popular computing magazines. Product performance reports are consistently good for each of these companies.

➤ Apple Computer
Cupertino, CA.
800-MY APPLE

➤ Compaq Computer
Houston, TX. 800-345-1518

➤ Dell Computer
Dallas, TX. 800-472-3355

➤ Gateway Computers
Vermillion, SD. 800-846-2000

➤ Hewlett-Packard
Palo Alto, CA. 800-752-0900

➤ IBM Personal Computer
Somers, NY. 800-772-2227

➤ NEC Technologies
Boxborough, MA.
800-632-4636

➤ Packard-Bell Electronics
Westlake Village, CA.
800-733-5858

➤ ACER America
San Jose, CA. 800-733-2237

THE RIGHT PROCESSOR

How can you be sure that the computer you buy today will be able to run tomorrow's software?

Start by choosing the right processor—the PC's "heart." While older PCs were locked into their original processor, newer Pentium computers (for *Windows*®) and Power PCs (for *Macs*) are easily upgradable and can readily accommodate more powerful chips as they become available. The faster the processor, the better. If money is a problem, buy a PC that has an upgradable processor, and upgrade later when additional cash is available.

SUPPORT HARD DISK SPACE

Be sure to buy adequate hard disk capacity—the place where the computer files get stored. The rule of thumb among experienced computer users is that you'll always need 10 megabytes (MBs) more storage capacity than your current hard disk provides. These days, with operating systems like *Windows* and *Mac OS*® gobbling up dozens of megabytes of space, and even modest applications requiring up to 30MB of capacity, your best bet is to buy a PC with at least ten gigabytes (GB, about 1,000 megabytes) hard disk.

Manage Memory

A PC should have at least 32 megabytes of random access memory—or 32 MB of RAM. To run many of the new software programs, 64 MB of RAM is recommended. Your computer should have enough slots to expand RAM to at least 128 MB, and preferably 256 MB, not too far down the road.

MAC OR PC?

Your choice matters less today than ever and will continue to become less of an issue as new technical and software agreements are forged by the makers of both types of systems. PCs now have 90% of the computer marketshare; MACs, 10%.

➤ PCs tend to be faster than MACs. They're also less expensive with greater business software availability.

➤ MACs were originally considered easier to use than PCs, but new Windows® software has leveled the playing field.

➤ MACs dominate the graphics design, architectural and typography fields, but are weak in business and general applications.

➤ MACs are more expensive. Software programs are limited compared to PCs. Some software outlets no longer carry MAC applications.

➤ MACs are more compatible with PCs than ever. There's software that can make a MAC work like a PC. New model MACs are also available with built-in PC processor boards.

➤ *Bottom line:* If you're new to computing, buy a PC. You'll have more options.

LOOKING AT MONITORS

Don't buy just any old monitor. Pay close attention to the monitor's "dot pitch"—the spacing between the screen's color phosphors. Dot pitch typically ranges from 0.21 to 0.39 of an inch. The smaller the pitch, the sharper the image and the less the eyestrain.

Monitors come in various sizes, with the most popular being 15, 17 and 19 inches. If you intend to do a lot of desktop-publishing work, a 19- or 21-inch screen might be important. Otherwise save a few hundred dollars and opt for a 15- or 17-inch display. Their basic performance is comparable to the 19-inch monitor.

PONDERING PRINTER OPTIONS

Black and white? Color? Ink jet? Laser? Your choice of a printer depends on what you want to use it for. If you want a color printer for graphics (signs, cards, presentations, etc.), cost is definitely a consideration: a good quality ink jet printer can be purchased for $200 to $500; a color laser printer will set you back $3,000 or more.

If you don't need color and will be printing a great deal of text, you should consider a black-and-white laser printer, which generally prints twice as fast as ink jet models. Prices start at around $375. If you won't be printing a lot of text, however, you can get a black-and-white ink-jet model for as low as $150 and even less. Many companies have stopped manufacturing black-and-white ink-jet printers because for another $50 or so, consumers are buying color models, and the black-and-white printing quality is as good. At today's prices, having more than one printer is a viable economic consideration. Select a good quality laser printer for letters and such and a separate printer entirely for color work.

The Business of Living
Retire Richer

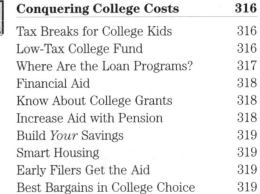

How to Ax Your Taxes   327

Home-Buying Tips & Selling Traps 332

Estate Planning Know-How   341

Future Plans

No matter what your age, it's never too early to plan for your financial future. The sooner you begin, the better off you will be in your golden years to enjoy the fruits of your labor—rather than struggling to make ends meet. Here's how to plan ahead and generate savings that will pay off when you retire.

RETIREMENT DREAM LIST

The most common mistake in retirement planning is waiting too long to plan. We are so pre-occupied with the pressures of ongoing financial commitments—household expenses, mortgage, car payments, credit card debt, college tuitions—that we put off today thinking about tomorrow.

Draw up a "dream list" for your retirement years. Be realistic! It's human nature to want many things, but goal setting makes you decide what's most important.

Think about:

- *Financial obligations.* If you have a mortgage, when will it be paid off? If you are sending children or grandchildren through college, when will those payments end?
- *Lifestyle.* Do you want to be able to take expensive vacations? Eat out frequently? How often will you want to buy a new car?
- *Residence.* Will you sell your home? What will you purchase or rent instead? If you plan on moving, how expensive is it where you want to live? Will state and local taxes be higher or lower?
- *Work plans.* When do you plan to retire? Will you continue to work—full-time or part-time? If you plan to continue working, how will it affect your Social Security benefits?

PLAN WITHIN YOUR MEANS

An old a rule of thumb said retirees needed about 75% of their pre-retirement, after-tax income. For example, if your current annual after-tax income is $50,000, you'd need 75% of that, or $37,500 in annual retirement income. But, what you need will depend on how you plan to spend your retirement years. For example, if you plan extensive travel, you may need the same or even greater than your pre-retirement income. Use the worksheet below to estimate your retirement expenses, adjusting for inflation.

To figure out more precisely how much you will need, however, consider which of your current expenses will be lower when you retire and which will be higher. For example, if you will no longer be commuting, your transportation costs should be lower. Other business expenses, such as clothing, meals and work-related

---

HOW FIT IS YOUR RETIREMENT FUTURE?

1. Annual Retirement Expenses

A. Current annual after-tax gross income, including salary, dividends and interest $ _____

B. Current annual savings, including regular savings, contributions to retirement plans, such as 401(k)s and IRAs $ _____

C. Current expenses—subtract B from A $ _____

D. Annual retirement expenses (in current dollars)—generally 75% of pre-retirement expenses, depending on your lifestyle—multiply C times .75 $ _____

E. Annual retirement expenses adjusted for 5% inflation, based on years until retirement—multiply D by estimated inflation factor* $ _____

2. Annual Retirement Income

F. Annual pension income $ _____

G. Annual Social Security benefit $ _____

H. Annual income from private savings and investments $ _____

I. Annual retirement income in current dollars—add F, G, and H $ _____

J. Annual retirement income adjusted for 5% inflation—multiply I by estimated inflation factor* $ _____

*Inflation factor: Number of years until retirement/percent—30 yrs./ 4.322%; 25yrs./3.388%; 20 yrs./2.653%; 15 yrs./2.079%; 10 yrs./1.629%; 5 yrs./1.276%.

Note: These figures are based on an estimated 5% inflation. Most financial planning guides (available at your local library or bookstore or online) include detailed retirement planning worksheets that show how to factor in higher or lower inflation rates as the economy changes. Or, ask your accountant or financial adviser about inflation factors.

insurance premiums, will decrease. On the other hand, you might spend more on health insurance and health care, travel or other leisure-time activities.

According to the U.S. Bureau of Labor Statistics, a typical retirement budget is:

Housing 33%
Food 28%
Health care...........................11%
Transportation 11%
Clothing...................................4%
Entertainment 3%
Other (gifts, personal
    expenses, education) 10%

NEVER TOO LATE

When should you start saving for retirement? Many people wait until they are in their 40s or 50s, after college tuitions have been paid. But financial planners will tell you that the sooner you start—ideally, in your 20s or 30s—the less you will have to save later.

Assuming an 8% investment return, a person who starts saving just $50 a month at age 25 will have $174,550 at 65. If the person waits until he or she is 35, the amount drops to $74,518.

Say you decide at age 45 to save $1,000 a year at an annual interest rate of 8%. At age 65, you will have $49,423. If you wait to start saving until you are 55, the figure drops to $15,645. If you start at 60, you would have $6,335 at age 65.

Bear in mind that only 40% to 60% of your retirement income may come from Social Security and pension benefits. The rest will have to come from savings, preferably in tax-exempt accounts, such as IRAs.

BENEFITS ESTIMATE

In calculating retirement income, you don't have to guess what you think you will receive in Social Security benefits. It's easy to get the facts.

A written statement of projected benefits based on pay level, years of work and retirement age is sent by the Social Security Administration (SSA) to every person 25 years or older, three months prior to their birthday. If for some reason you need your estimate sooner, or didn't receive one, just call the *Social Security Administration* (800-772-1213) and ask for your Earnings and Benefit Estimate Statement.

Check the figures carefully. If you think there is a mistake or an oversight—your employers haven't correctly reported all your earnings, for example, or the SSA hasn't credited your earnings to the right account—call the number above. You will need employment and earnings information to support your claim, including past W-2 forms, name

and address of employer(s), dates of employment and wages you received. But the effort is worth it. You don't want to lose benefits that you have earned.

The Social Security Administration's Web site at *www.ssa.gov* is loaded with information.

MOVE NOW, SAVE LATER

Moving to a less expensive part of the country is one of the best ways to get by on less during retirement. But make a move for sound reasons, not merely because it's somewhere you spent a few pleasant vacation weeks. If you aren't familiar with a community before you move—and don't know people who live there—you could regret your decision. Too many retired people sell their homes, then discover they don't like the new locale, but can't afford to move again. If you aren't completely sure about a move, try renting your current home for a year and rent where you think you might like to go. Then decide.

Another potential mistake: basing your move on where your children or relatives live. It's not unusual for a couple to move closer to a married child, only to have the child get transferred elsewhere. There's also the risk that a relationship with children

that's great from afar may not be so great when you live close by.

RELOCATE YOUR TAX BASE

Few people decide to relocate to a particular state solely because of tax reasons. But including taxes as a consideration can lead to substantial savings. Do your homework. While you may assume you will enjoy a better lifestyle in a new state that has a lower income tax rate—or none at all—there may be other taxes, such as higher sales or property taxes, that cancel out your gain. For example, Florida, which doesn't have an income tax, imposes an intangibles tax—a tax on stocks and other intangible assets.

Estate taxes can make a big difference, too. The best states to retire in are those that have what is known as a "pick-up" (or "soak-up") tax for estate tax purposes. (New York is one such state.) Pick-up tax credit runs from 0.8% of the federal taxable estate to 16%, which is the maximum amount of credit the federal government gives for state death taxes at this time. High-tax states go beyond the maximum credit. Find out from a reliable financial adviser if your state—or one that you are considering moving to—is a high-tax state.

Some states that impose only a pick-up tax on estates also have no income tax. They include Alaska, Florida, Nevada, Texas, Washington and Wyoming. Others exclude pension income for tax purposes. Among them: Alabama, Hawaii, Illinois, Massachusetts, Mississippi and Pennsylvania.

Twenty-five states and the District of Columbia exclude Social Security benefits, including Arizona, California, Georgia, Michigan, New Jersey, New York and South Carolina.

FIND THE TAX-FREE STATES

If you are planning to move to another state, check the various taxes in that state:

Income tax. Which incomes/assets are taxed? How are retirement plan distributions taxed? What is the rate? If there is no income tax, is there an intangibles tax? What is the rate of the intangibles tax?

Sales tax. What items does the state tax? What is the rate? Is there a city or county sales tax?

Estate tax. Which assets are subject to tax? What's the tax rate? Does the state have a marital deduction?

Gift tax. Does the state impose a gift tax? What's the rate? Is there a maximum exempt amount?

AVOID THE INCOME TRAP

Too many people invest entirely, or primarily, in fixed-income securities after they retire—figuring their expenses will go down. That was fine when people retired at 65 and died within 10 years. Now they retire at 60 or earlier and can live to 90-plus. The reality for those who have to live on retirement income for 20 or 30 years is that their expenses will go up. Thus, you should invest to produce a rising stream of income during retirement. Think in terms of total return, with your capital and your income continuing to build after you retire.

A WORKING RETIREMENT?

Many retirees decide to keep working after retirement, at least part-time. But those who want to work for financial reasons should be aware of the following drawbacks:

■ You can work and still collect Social Security benefits, but if you are under 65, for every $2 earned above a government-determined ceiling, you lose $1 in benefits. When you add in commuting costs, job-related expenses and payroll deductions, you may find that part-time work doesn't pay off. When you are 65 or older, however, you won't be assessed a reduction in benefits, no matter how much you earn.

■ If you continue working part-time for the same company, you may not be eligible to collect your pension. One way around this, if the company agrees, is to retire as an employee and return as a consultant or freelancer. Since you would be self-employed, your pension wouldn't be affected.

■ Although most employees can't legally be compelled to retire before 70, companies still set up retirement ages of 65 or less. You can work past that age, but you won't earn further pension credits. And you lose Social Security and pension benefits while you continue to work.

An attractive alternative to working part-time is to start your own business. Often, lawyers and accountants set up practices, working their own hours. Or you might consider turning a hobby into a business.

INCOME THAT NULLS SOCIAL SECURITY

If you work while collecting Social Security, you may face a reduction in benefits, depending on your age and your earnings. Here are types of income that do—and do not—count toward the earnings limits.

Do count: Wages or self-employment income, bonuses, commissions, fees, vacation pay, cash tips of $20 or more a month, severance pay. Also, some noncash compensation, such as meals or living quarters, can count under certain circumstances.

Do not count: Pension, investment and interest income; veterans' benefits, annuities, capital gains, gifts or inheritances, rental income (in most cases), income from trust funds, and jury duty pay.

PICK THE RIGHT PLANNER

At some point in your long-term financial decision making, you may find that you need professional help. There are thousands of financial planners out there eager to advise you. The problem is that there are no federal regulations, accreditation requirements or special licenses for financial planners.

How to choose? Unless you have highly recommended referrals from friends or family, look for planners who have passed degree programs or achieved special designations in the field—"CFP" after a planner's name, for example, means that he or she has achieved certification from the *Institute of Certified Financial Planners*. "RFP" means the person has met the academic requirements of the *International Association of Registered Financial Planners*. Other designations are CFA (Chartered Financial Analyst), ChFC (Chartered Financial Consultant) and PFS (Personal Financial Specialist).

Several national associations have publications to guide you in your search. These include "How to Choose a Financial Planner" from the *National Association of Personal Financial Advisors* (800-366-2732); "Selecting a Qualified Financial Planning Professional: Twelve Questions to Consider" from the *Financial Planning Association* (800-322-4237); and "Selecting a Financial Planner" from the *Council of Better Business Bureaus* (703-276-0100). *Web site: www.cbbb.org.*

Before selecting a financial planner in your area, it's always wise to check with your local Better Business Bureau and state Attorney General's office to find out if any complaints have been filed against the planner.

You can also contact the *National Association of Securities Dealers* (800-289-9999), which keeps records of investment advisers' work histories and information on any fraud or securities-related complaints. *Web site: www.nasdr.com.*

TAKING THE MYSTERY OUT OF PLANNERS' FEES

Before signing on with a financial planner, make sure you get a written estimate of the services he or she will provide—and at what price. Basically, there are three ways a planner might charge you for services:

Commission. Commission-based planners offer free financial advice, but receive a commission on the products you purchase, such as a mutual fund, annuity or insurance policy. The main advantage of this arrangement is the planner can handle all of your different types of investments (one-stop shopping). The disadvantage is that because the planner works on commission, he or she may have a vested interest in selling you certain products.

Fee. Some planners charge a flat fee for financial planning and advice on implementing their recommendations. It might be an annual fee, based on your income or assets, or an hourly fee, based on the time spent with you. The advantage of working with fee-based planners is that they have no financial interest in having you buy one product over another and thus may suggest investments a commission-based planner may not mention. The disadvantage is that you will be charged for the planner's advice, whether you follow it or not, and you will have to pay commissions on any investments, insurance, and other products you purchase.

Fee plus commission. In this arrangement, you pay a fee for an overall financial plan, plus a commission on investments you purchase. The advantage here is that generally both the fee and the commission are lower than those of fee-only or commission-only planners. The disadvantage is that the planner still earns most of his or her income from selling you products that you might find cheaper elsewhere.

In all cases, don't be reluctant to ask about fees and/or commissions. Above all, you have to trust your planner's advice. If you don't, you don't have the right planner for you.

---

i RETIREMENT RESOURCES

➤ *Social Security Administration,* 6401 Security Blvd., Baltimore, MD 21235. 800-772-1213. Offers numerous free booklets explaining benefits. "Understanding Social Security" is particularly useful. *Web site: www.ssa.gov.*

➤ *Federal Trade Commission,* 6th St. & Pennsylvania Ave. NW, Washington, DC 20580. 202-326-2222. Provides brochures on working with financial planners. *Web site: www.ftc.gov.*

➤ *Institute of Consumer Financial Education,* P.O. Box 34070, San Diego, CA 92163. 619-239-1401. Nonprofit group offers advice on financial planning; also publishes books and newsletters on related topics. *Web site: www.financial-education-icfe.org.*

➤ *Financial Planning Association,* 5775 Glenridge Dr. NE, Atlanta, GA 30328. 800-322-4237. Financial planners' organization provides referrals and a consumers guide. *Web site: www.fpanet.org.*

➤ *American Association of Retired Persons* (AARP), 601 E St. NW, Washington, DC 20049. 800-424-3410. Trade association offers wide range of publications on pre-retirement and retirement-related topics. *Web site: www.aarp.org.*

Pensions & Other Benefits

It pays to take full advantage of the present—and future—benefits your employer offers you. How sound is your pension plan? Do you need additional funds before you retire? What will your retirement income consist of?

PLAN BEFORE YOU LEAVE WORK

The target retirement date you set will have a big impact on planning strategies and the amount you must save each year. If you work beyond your planned retirement date, the extra income will simply make you better off. But if you are forced to retire early, you will be glad you planned for it. To avoid common retirement planning mistakes, make sure that you fully understand the financial impact when you leave full-time work.

Your Retirement Plan

- *How do benefits differ:* If you are terminated? Take early retirement? Leave at the normal retirement age? If you left the company today?
- *Is there a vesting schedule that requires you to stay with the company a set number of years in order to receive full benefits?*
- *Will you receive a fixed pension with a dollar value you can estimate now?* Or does the company have a profit-sharing plan under which its contribution to your account varies each year, making your final benefit an uncertain amount?
- *Are plan benefits adjusted in line with inflation?* Danger: If inflation continues at the 5% rate of recent years, a fixed pension will lose half its value in 14 years. You may need extra income.
- *How and when will you get paid?* Payouts may not occur until months after you retire and if a company has more than one plan, payouts may be made at different times. This can dramatically affect personal cash flow, so anticipate the plan's red tape.
Bottom line: Ask your employer for an annual benefits statement showing how much you would receive, when, and how, if you left the company now or at various points in the future. You might

find, for example, that if you retire at 55 instead of 65 that your pension benefits will be cut in half. Be sure to ask for these figures with and without salary increases.

Social Security

Most employees think of their pension benefits as separate from Social Security. But beware! Many companies have "integrated" plans under which the designated pension amount includes Social Security—the company's contribution toward your pension is reduced by the amount of Social Security you receive. Find out whether your company's plan uses this permitted disparity. The Tax Act of 1986 specifies that in most cases employers can't subtract more than 50% of your pension benefits, regardless of how much you receive from Social Security.

If you think you might retire early—before you are eligible to receive Social Security—explore your options. Some firms will increase early pension payments by the amount of the monthly Social Security that the retiree will ultimately receive. When Social Security payments start, pension payments are reduced accordingly. The result is an even flow of income that can facilitate early-retirement planning.

Life Insurance

If your company doesn't have a life insurance program that will continue past retirement and you will need coverage then, take

steps to secure it now. Some companies have group policies that allow departing employees to convert their term insurance into whole life coverage without going through a physical examination. If this benefit isn't offered, be aware that it may be more difficult to pass a required physical to get insurance.

Health Insurance

Ask if your company provides retirement health benefits, and what, specifically, are the plan's limits: doctor's fees, hospitalization, prescriptions, home care. You might not be able to use the doctor or hospital of your choice unless you pay out-of-pocket. If you will have to pay for your own coverage, consider it a cost of retirement, and start saving for it now.

Also, ask about nursing-home insurance and Medigap insurance for expenses Medicare doesn't cover. Don't make the mistake of thinking, "It won't happen to me."

DO-IT-YOURSELF PENSION CHECKUP

You can become your own pension watchdog by reviewing the financial information given to you by your employer's plan. Federal law requires larger company and union plans to provide an overview of the plan's finances each year—usually in the form of a one-page Summary Annual

Report (SAR) that is either handed out or mailed to all plan

⚠ EXPLORING PENSION HEALTH

More and more people are discovering—to their horror—that their pension plans are on shaky financial footing. Keep yourself informed. Read your pension plan's annual report carefully and make sure you know the answers to these fundamental questions (if in doubt, ask your company's pension plan administrator):

➤ What, exactly, is the pension fund invested in?

➤ Is the pension portfolio heavily loaded with the company's stocks?

➤ How sound is the company? Monitor quarterly reports and business news affecting the company.

➤ If the company offers a guaranteed-income contract portfolio, is it provided by a single insurer? If so, how solid is it?

➤ What are the ratings of insurance companies involved with the guaranteed income contract portfolio? Consider a B- (or lower) rating from A.M. Best, Moody's or Standard & Poor's as a warning sign.

members. The SAR tells you how much money is in the plan, whether plan investments have performed well or poorly, and how much the plan trustees have paid out in administrative costs. Large losses and excessive costs can be red flags signaling problem areas.

The SAR will tell you how to get a copy of the detailed financial statement the plan is required to file with the federal government—Form 5500. The form discloses the type of investments (i.e., stocks, bonds, real estate) the plan had made and how much money those investments have gained or lost.

To help employees analyze their form 5500s, the *U.S. Department of Labor's Pension Benefits Administration* publishes two free booklets: "Protect Your Pension—A Quick Reference Guide" and "What You Should Know About Your Pension Rights." Contact the *Department of Labor's* field office in your area.

BEST WAYS TO TAKE OUT FUNDS

Should you take your retirement money in the form of a lump-sum payment or in the form of annual pension or annuity payments? That decision could be the most important financial decision in your life—but it is difficult to get an objective opinion. People in

🚫 10 PENSION PLAN WARNING SIGNS

1. Your 401(k) or individual account statement is consistently late or comes at irregular intervals.

2. Your account balance does not appear to be accurate.

3. Your employer failed to transmit your contribution to the plan on a timely basis.

4. There is a significant drop in account balance that cannot be explained by normal market ups and downs.

5. Your 401(k) or individual account statement indicates that your contribution from your paycheck was not made.

6. Investments listed on your statement are not what you authorized.

7. Former employees are having trouble getting their benefits paid on time or in the correct amounts.

8. There are unusual transactions, such as a loan to the employer, a corporate officer, or one of the trustees.

9. There are frequent and unexplained changes in investment managers or consultants.

10. Your employer has recently experienced severe financial difficulty.

Source: U.S. Department of Labor, Pension and Welfare Benefits Administration.

the insurance business are likely to tell you to take your pension as an annuity, while people in the investment business will tell you to take a lump sum and roll it over into an investment account.

If you are willing to sacrifice some potential income for the assurance that you will receive steady payments, you should consider taking part of the money as a lump sum and part as an annuity. But if you retire at or before the normal retirement age, generally you should take the lump sum. Then when you are older,

you can invest in an annuity. Lump-sum distributions can be rolled over into an IRA.

If you take a lump-sum distribution and you were born before 1936, the IRS provides a tax break in the form of 10-year income averaging—it's treated as if it had been received over a period of years, thus avoiding top-bracket tax rates. Technical rules apply, so ask your tax adviser about making the right choices.

An important consideration: If you or your spouse go into a nursing home, your lump-sum distribution would have to be used to help pay nursing home costs. A lot of people in that situation wish they had chosen an annuity for part of their savings because nursing home care severely depleted their long-term savings. An annuity at least assures a continuing income.

SELF-EMPLOYED PLAN

Anyone with self-employment income from personal services, including sideline business income, consultant's fees, freelance income and director's fees, can have a qualified retirement plan. The main benefits are contributions to the plan are tax deductible, earnings on contributions are not taxed while in the plan, and taxes are deferred until retirement, when you are likely to be in a lower tax bracket.

There are two types of plans: *defined contribution* and *defined benefit*.

With a *defined contribution* plan, in the form of a profit-sharing plan or money-purchase plan, or both, your contributions are based on what you earn. The main consideration in deciding whether to participate in a defined contribution plan is your age. The most you can put away each year in a defined contribution plan is 25% of your net earnings, minus your

contribution, up to a maximum of $40,000 in 2002. This might be enough for someone who has many years to save before retiring, but not for those who are 50-plus and closer to retirement.

A *defined benefit* plan pays you a fixed monthly amount when you retire. With this plan, you can contribute a much larger percentage of your income, depending on what you want to withdraw each year after you retire—based on your age, income and number of years remaining before retirement. The older you are, the more you can contribute to the plan each year; thus, it's particularly well suited for someone who has 10 to 15 years to go before retirement. Because contributions are tax deductible, you can shelter large amounts of income during your peak working years. Potential drawbacks with a defined benefit plan are that you have to make a minimum contribution each year or face a 10% underfunding penalty. Also there is a limit to the amount you can withdraw each year after retirement (indexed annually for inflation).

STOCK UP WITH STOCK

If your company offers a program to purchase company stock at a reduced price or with an income-tax benefit attached,

you could come out way ahead in your holdings—assuming the company is financially sound. Two plans which offer employees the opportunity to buy company stock are Employee Stock Ownership Plans (ESOPs) and Employee Stock Purchase Plans (ESPPs).

Employee Stock Ownership

These plans allow you to invest in company stock up to an annual maximum amount. The money spent to buy the stock is not subject to income tax until the stock is distributed from the plan. Your tax savings enable you to buy more stock. For example, if the stock is $20 a share and you decide to invest $100 a month, you'd have five shares a month if you bought them on the market. Say you are in the 27% income tax bracket. Your tax savings on the amount of money used to buy the stock would enable you to buy two more shares a month. That means rather than owning 60 shares worth $1,200 at the end of the year, you would own 84 shares worth over $1,650—tax deferred!

Employee Stock Purchase

These plans allow you to buy company stock at a reduced price, up to certain maximum amounts, without being taxed on any gains until the stock is sold. Typically, companies with ESPPs allow employees to buy up to $10,000 in company stock at a discount of 15% from its market value. If you

BONUS: WORKING SPOUSE'S BENEFITS

There's a common misconception that a wife who has worked for many years outside the home loses out on Social Security because the most a couple can receive is the husband's benefit, plus 50% of that benefit for the wife. Not true. Working spouses are not viewed the same as stay-at-home spouses when it comes to Social Security benefits.

The 50% of a husband's benefit for a wife applies only if the wife never worked. However, if the husband and wife were both maximum earners under Social Security, she can receive maximum benefits on her own income record—independent of her husband's benefits.

For example, in 2002, the top benefit at age 65 was $1,660 a month. A working husband and working wife who were due the maximum benefits would receive $3,320. If the wife had never worked, her benefit would be 50% of the husband's benefit, or $830, for a total of $2,490.

Note: If your spouse didn't work, taking early retirement can affect the Social Security benefits your spouse receives. If you start taking benefits early—at age 62, for example—your spouse's percentage of your benefit will be reduced from 50% to 37.5%.

invest the full $10,000, that means a $1,500 annual gain! Because companies usually offer employees the option of making a cash purchase or having a percentage of their salary withheld, there is flexibility in how you make payments. Although many employees often flip the stock soon after they buy it, if you are in a high tax bracket, you should wait more than 12 months to sell to take advantage of a potentially lower capital gains rate.

EARLY 401(K) WITHDRAWAL

401(k) plans can have a special feature that allows money to be withdrawn in case of hardship. Although the funds are subject to income tax, plus a 10% early withdrawal penalty if you are under age 59½, it may be the best choice you have in a bind. To qualify as a hardship, a distribution must be:
- For an immediate and heavy financial need of the employee
- Sufficient to satisfy the need (plus penalties and taxes), but not more than that amount

A person withdrawing funds must first exhaust all means of borrowing from other retirement plans and make no contributions to the 401(k) plan for the following 12 months.

Expenditures that qualify as hardship include:
- Medical expenses for the employee and his or her dependents (if these expenses exceed 7.5% of your adjusted gross income, you won't have to pay an early withdrawal penalty)
- Down payment on the purchase of a principal residence for the employee
- Tuition payments for post-secondary education for the employee and his or her dependents
- Payments to keep the employee from being evicted from his or her principal residence
- Funeral costs for a member of the employee's family

401(K) BORROWING: LIMITS/LIABILITIES

You can borrow up to 50% of the amount in your 401(k) plan, but not more than $50,000. But you will have to pay interest on the loan—typically 1% or 2% over the prime rate—and you will have to repay the loan within five years, unless the money is used to purchase your principal residence. Often companies require that you repay the loan in regular quarterly payments or through payroll deductions, which reduces your take-home pay.

The longer you take to repay the loan, the higher your interest

costs over the life of the loan. And the interest is not tax deductible. In addition, you lose valuable tax-deferred compounding of the amount you took out. *Better:* If you own a home, get a $50,000 tax-deductible home equity loan instead.

TIPS FOR WHEN YOU TOP OUT

Investors in 401(k) plans who have reached their maximum contribution and who want to keep saving for retirement often wonder where they should invest next. Some ideas:
- *Reduce your debt.* Use your extra cash to eliminate or reduce any credit card debt. No other investment pays a guaranteed annual 18%—the average rate on a credit card. Then pay off other loans on which you pay interest.
- *Fund your IRA.* If you contribute $3,000 a year to an IRA, or $3,500 if you are 50 at the year-end, the money will compound tax free. Have your IRA withdraw funds electronically from your checking account.
- *Go for insurance.* If you own a variable or universal life insurance policy, consider contributing to the cash-value portion of the policy. But be sure your policy is structured so additional cash builds investments, not buys more insurance.

What You Should Know About IRAs

Individual retirement accounts (IRAs) are one of the best ways for Americans to save for retirement, but many people fail to make the best use of these tax-advantaged accounts. Here are some of the most common mistakes people make with their IRAs and how you can make the most of your investment.

IRAs: Better Now Than Ever

IRA tax-deduction rules have become so complicated that many people don't bother with IRAs anymore or assume that they can't participate because of their income level. This can be a big mistake! You may be missing out on valuable opportunities to invest in your future financial well-being.

With the current law more people than ever are eligible for deductible IRAs. First of all, the law increased the limits (see box). Also the deductibility of an individual's IRA contribution is no longer affected by a spouse's participation in a retirement plan—spouses qualify on their own—unless the couple has an adjusted gross income of more than $150,000.

A married couple can contribute up to $6,000 in IRA funds in 2002 ($7,000 if both spouses are at least 50), even if one spouse has little or no income.

If neither you nor your spouse participates in an employer's retirement plan, you can have a deductible IRA regardless of your income level—even if you gross $1 million!

Make Money on Tax Savings

If you qualify for an IRA deduction, sock away the tax savings the contributions provide and watch them multiply! In the 27% tax bracket, the tax on $3,000 is $810. Invest that $810 instead of spending it. Over 20 years with after-tax earnings of 5.5%, those additional investments will grow to nearly $30,000!

IRA Booster: More Relief for Your Dollar

Under current tax law, the adjusted gross income levels for full deduction of an IRA contribution will increase as follows for individuals participating in an employer's retirement plan:

Year	Joint Return	Single Return
2001	53,000	33,000
2002	54,000	34,000
2003	60,000	40,000
2004	65,000	45,000
2005	70,000	50,000
2006	75,000	50,000
2007	80,000	50,000

Best: Plan to invest your tax savings at the same time as you file your income tax. Let your tax preparer know that you intend to do this, so he or she can remind you.

Advantages of Roth IRAs

The Roth IRA presents tremendous opportunities to save with no future tax obligations.

Previously contributions made to nondeductible IRAs (with after-tax dollars) were treated as non-taxable return of capital upon withdrawal, *but* gains from the investment were treated as ordinary income for tax purposes.

With the Roth IRA, however, the contributed funds *and any accumulated earnings* can be withdrawn tax-free. Basic provisions of the Roth IRA include:

Eligibility

Nondeductible contributions of up to $3,000 ($6,000 per couple) can be made each year. The $3,000 limit is reduced if your adjusted gross income exceeds $150,000 ($95,000 for singles) and is eliminated if your adjusted gross income exceeds $160,000 ($110,000 for singles). The $3,000 limit is also reduced for amounts contributed to a deductible IRA (an individual's annual contribution for both can't exceed $3,000).

Unlike traditional IRAs, contributions are allowed after age $70\frac{1}{2}$

and distributions do not have to start at age 70½.

Withdrawals

You cannot withdraw funds until you have had the Roth IRA for five years. Withdrawals may be made after age 59½. Prior to that, withdrawals may be made if the owner dies, is disabled or uses the funds for a first-time home purchase—subject to a $10,000 lifetime limit—for the owner, a spouse, child or grandchild.

The main attraction of the Roth IRA is that in the long term, tax-free compounding of your investment can be far more valuable than a one-time tax deduction. Once funds are placed in a Roth IRA, you don't have to worry about future taxes.

WHY TO AVOID BANK IRAS

Bank IRA interest rates are historically one to three percentage points less than those of other market IRA vehicles available from brokers and mutual funds. In later years, when your IRA balance is substantial, that could mean tens of thousands of dollars in interest lost every year.

The banks' below-market IRA interest rates can be even more unfavorable, depending on how the bank calculates interest.

Ideally, you want interest from day-of-deposit to day-of-withdrawal,

compounded and paid daily. Under some plans, the bank also maintains the right to change the basis on which it pays interest, at its own discretion.

IRA TRANSFERS: SAVE BIG

If you decide to switch your IRA account from one institution to another, you have 60 days from the date you receive the proceeds—typically in the form of a check made payable to you— to place the funds in a new account without penalty. Plus, once you have transferred the assets (or "rolled over" your IRA), you cannot do it again for another 12 months.

To avoid potential penalties, it's wiser to arrange for the old trustee to send the IRA balance to the new trustee directly (and never get your hands on the money). You can do as many of these transfers as you wish within a year without being subject to tax.

Similarly, when you receive a distribution from a pension or profit-sharing plan and roll it over into an IRA, the plan trustee will withhold a hefty 20% from the distribution *unless you ask that payment be made directly to the trustee of the new IRA* (trustee-to-trustee transfer)—regardless of whether you had planned to

roll it over within 60 days. With more people receiving large distributions from their 401(k) plans because of corporate downsizings, this has become a major issue. If you're not sure which investment is best for your plan money or you haven't found another job yet, have the trustee roll the money into an IRA money market fund.

If you do not roll the money over into a tax-deferred account, you will owe income taxes on the entire amount in the year you receive it. Plus, if you haven't reached the age of 59½, you will owe a 10% penalty.

HIGH-COST IRA MISTAKES

■ *Taking distributions too early.* Many people start taking money out at age 59½ because that's the first time they can withdraw from an IRA without a 10% penalty. Unless your IRA is a major source of retirement income, there's no reason to start taking money out that soon. The longer you compound that money without paying current taxes on it, the better off you will be. During the next 11 years, you could double your money!

However, if you have no other available resources and need funds to help pay for higher education or a first-time home purchase for

yourself, your spouse, a child or a grandchild, you can withdraw funds prior to age 59½ without penalty. A first-time home buyer distribution is subject to a $10,000 lifetime limit.

■ *Failing to take distributions on time.* Some people who don't need the income from their IRAs forget to begin taking withdrawals by April 1 of the year they turn 70½, as required by law. Then, they have to pay a 50% excise tax on the amount they should have taken out. The minimum withdrawal is based on the amount in your IRA and your life expectancy, or the combined life expectancy of you and a beneficiary. To prevent excess tax deferrals on IRA money, the IRS deems the age of any beneficiary (other than your spouse) to be no more than 10 years younger than you.

SMART IRA MOVES

If your IRA is going to be the sole source of retirement income, you may be wise to invest conservatively and concentrate on preserving capital. Your account will be safe and future growth will be more predictable.

If you can afford to take a chance, use your IRA to invest in aggressive, long-term growth. Typically, IRA investments are

HOW TO TURN $2,000 A YEAR INTO SIX FIGURES

Tax free accumulations of IRA earnings can produce the following funds for retirement, assuming $2,000 invested annually, with interest compounded daily:

Year	6%	8%	10%
5	$ 11,670	$ 12,794	$ 13,633
10	27,398	31,879	36,109
15	48,642	60,349	73,164
20	77,318	102,820	134,252
25	116,275	166,176	234,962
30	168,275	260,688	400,993

IRA CAUTION

One of the biggest mistakes people make is failing to change IRA beneficiary designations when situations change (e.g., following divorce). Don't let your money go to the wrong person.

more extensive than your choices in a company pension plan.

PICK THE RIGHT IRA BENEFICIARY

Many otherwise well-informed married couples don't know the basics of how to handle an inherited IRA. You have several choices. Make the wrong one and the IRA dies with the surviving spouse. Make the right choice and the IRA can continue for decades, accumulating tax-deferred income.

Naming your spouse as your IRA beneficiary is generally the smartest move. If you name someone else, that person must begin withdrawals within five years of the date of your death. However, a spouse who inherits an IRA has two choices:

1. Take the inherited account as a beneficiary. When the spouse takes the inherited IRA as a beneficiary, distributions must continue at least as rapidly as under the method used before the IRA owner's death (assuming, as is usually the case, that the deceased spouse was over age 70½—and had already begun taking distributions). When the surviving spouse dies, amounts remaining in the account are distributed and subject to income tax.

2. Treat the inherited account as one's own and roll it over into a new account. When the spouse takes the inherited IRA as his or her own, distributions can be made over the combined life expectancies of the spouse and a newly named beneficiary.

Because the beneficiary may be much younger than the inher-

iting spouse—40 or 50 years younger in the case of a grandchild—a huge tax deferral can result, producing an extra 40 or 50 years of compound tax-deferred income in the account before it is fully distributed.

In the fairly common case where an inherited IRA contains a few hundred thousand dollars—which may represent a lifetime of retirement savings rolled over from a company pension plan—several decades of tax-deferred compound earnings can easily amount to a million dollars or more.

Another option altogether is to leave the IRA to charity and give other assets to your family. The charity doesn't pay income tax on the IRA, whereas family members do.

EARLY IRAs GET THE INTEREST

Too many people think that the main benefit of an IRA contribution is the deduction at tax time, so they wait until the last minute each year to make their contribution. The longer you wait, the more you stand to lose. If you make your contribution on January 1 of the tax year rather than just before the April 15 deadline in the following year, you gain 15½ months in which your tax-deferred funds

are compounding.

For example, a $2,000 IRA contribution saves $800 for a person in a 40% combined federal and state tax bracket. If the IRA earns 10%, $2,000 contributed a year before the deadline will earn $200, and over 30 years, this $200 will compound to $3,490—all of which is forfeited if you make your contribution at the last minute. Over time, the increase in your total retirement funds can be quite substantial!

SHOULD YOU CONSOLIDATE?

Taxpayers who have set up a number of IRAs over the years should consider consolidating them into one big IRA. *The advantages:* saving on trustees' fees—instead of paying separate administration fees for each account, you'll pay only one; simplified paperwork; and the accumulation of larger balances for investment—thus a higher rate of return.

The main disadvantage of consolidating IRA accounts is that you lose the flexibility you might otherwise have with smaller accounts if you have to make early withdrawals.

PENALTY-FREE IRA WITHDRAWAL

Unless you are disabled, if you begin withdrawing funds from your IRA account before age 59½, you'll be subject to an early withdrawal penalty of 10% of the amount of the distribution. On top of that, you must pay income tax on the distribution.

One way to avoid the 10% penalty (but not the income tax) is to stretch out distributions by taking them in the form of a lifetime annuity—that is, a series of substantially equal payments made at least once a year over your life expectancy or the joint life expectancy of you and your beneficiary. If you are age 55, for example, and your life expectancy is 20 years, you can withdraw around $1,000 a year from your $20,000 IRA without penalty. The annuity approach works especially well if your spouse is your beneficiary and is considerably younger than you are.

This approach also presents tax-planning opportunities. In one

IRS case, for example, a person took early annuity payments from an IRA and used them to make mortgage payments on a new house. The mortgage-interest deduction sheltered the annuity payments from income tax, while the undistributed funds that remained in the IRA continued to earn tax-deferred income that could be used to make future mortgage payments. In short, the person had found a tax-favored way to finance his new home. In a private ruling, the IRS held that the arrangement was proper.

IRA CASH-IN: THE RIGHT WAY

Once you reach age 70½, the law provides a choice of two methods for making required annual withdrawals from your IRA. Both methods are based on your account balance divided by your life expectancy to determine the amount that must be withdrawn. The two choices are:

1. Recalculation method: This method assumes that as you grow older, your life expectancy is extended; thus, life expectancy is recalculated every year. Because life expectancy under this method drops by less than one year each year, the time over which you can take the distributions is increased. That makes this method initially very appealing.

The downside is that within a year of your death, your estate must receive all the money from the account and pay income tax on it. If your spouse is the beneficiary, the IRA is taxable in the estate of the spouse one year after the spouse's death. In short, the IRA abruptly comes to an end and beneficiaries are forced to pay taxes on it. To avoid this, a surviving spouse may roll the account over into an IRA of his or her own to break the recalculation method.

2. Term-certain method: Under this method, IRA withdrawals are spread out over a fixed number of years, regardless of how long the account holder actually lives. If the account holder dies two years after payments begin, for example, his estate can continue to receive annual payments from the IRA account for the duration of the fixed term. The advantage here is that taxes are lower because only a small part of the account is subject to tax each year, and the IRA continues to earn tax-deferred income until the end of the term of years.

How to elect a method: Ask your IRA provider for an election form on which you can indicate whether you want the term-certain method or recalculation method. If you don't have an election form on file, you are likely to be placed, by default,

⚠️

IRA-KILLER PENSION PLANS

Participation in any of these retirement plans may void IRA deductions. See your accountant.

➤ Simplified Employee Pension (SEP) plan

➤ 401(k) plan

➤ 404(b) annuity

➤ Profit-sharing plan

➤ Defined benefit plan

➤ Employee stock option plan

➤ Government employee retirement plan

➤ Union retirement plan

into the recalculation method. Whichever method you choose, make sure it is in writing and clearly understood by your IRA provider. You may want to check with your financial adviser or accountant for specifics relevant to your situation.

Conquering College Costs

How well are your children provided for? They have food, shelter, clothing and many other amenities...but have you planned ahead for one of life's most expensive investments— their college education? Even if you have started saving, there are many ways to build your funds wisely and find financial aid to meet college costs.

TAX BREAKS FOR COLLEGE KIDS

Several provisions in the tax law are designed to help offset the high cost of college tuitions. These include tax credits and interest deductions on student loans. Be sure to take advantage of these tax breaks, if eligible:

Hope Credit

This provision provides a tax credit for qualified tuition and related expenses—tuition and fees, but not room and board or books—during the first two years of postsecondary education for your child, yourself or your spouse. The credit is 100% of the first $1,000 and 50% of the next $1,000 in expenses, for a maximum of $1,500 during a tax year (adjusted for inflation in 2002).

The Hope credit phases out for couples with an adjusted gross income of between $80,000 and $100,000 and for singles, between $40,000 and $50,000. The phase-out ranges will also be adjusted for inflation beginning in 2002.

Lifetime Learning Credit

Unlike the Hope credit, the Lifetime Learning credit is available for graduate-level education as well as undergraduate studies, and also applies to courses taken to acquire or improve job skills.

The maximum annual credit is $1,000 a year, rising to $2,000 in 2003 (it is not adjusted for inflation). The phase-out adjusted gross income range is the same as for the Hope credit (see above).

Coverdell Education Savings Accounts

Coverdell Education Savings Accounts (ESA) are solely for the purpose of paying future higher-education expenses. You can make contributions of up to $2,000 per year for each child up to the age of 18. (Contributions cannot be made if the beneficiary has reached age 18.)

There is no deduction for contributions you make to a Coverdell ESA, but the funds grow tax-deferred and can be withdrawn tax-free to pay for college. If you contribute $2,000 a year from the day your child is born at an 8% return, for example, you could have about $90,000 by the time he or she is ready to go to college at age 18.

The eligibility for contributions phases out for couples with an adjusted gross income of between $190,000 and $220,000 (between $95,000 and $110,000 for singles).

Education Loan Deductions

An annual deduction of up to $2,500 can be made for interest paid on higher education loans. The loan may be for tuition, fees and room and board for you, your spouse or any dependent attending a post-secondary educational institution. No deduction is allowed, how-ever, for individuals who are claimed as dependents on another taxpayer's return for the tax year. The deduction phase-out ranges—between $100,000 and $130,000 for couples, $50,000 and $65,000 for singles—will be adjusted for inflation beginning in 2003.

LOW-TAX COLLEGE FUND

The simplest and most commonly used method of saving for college education is to set up a savings or investment account in a child's name under the Uniform Gifts to Minors Act (UGMA). You can set up an UGMA account through a bank, broker or attorney. You act as the account custodian, thus controlling the investments. The income from the account is taxed to the child:

- *If the child is under age 14,* the "kiddie tax" applies: The first $750 of unearned income (interest, dividends and capital gains) is tax free in 2002, and the next $750 is taxed at the child's rate, normally 10%. Income over $1,500 is taxed at the parents' rate. *Bottom line:* It's beneficial to put money in the child's name, as long as it doesn't exceed $1,500. *Best:* You can minimize taxes by investing in tax-exempt bonds or appreciating stocks, and then cash them in for income-producing assets after the child reaches age 14.
- *If the child is age 14 or older,* the first $750 of unearned income is tax free, $6,000 is taxed at 10%, the next $27,950 is taxed at the child's 15% rate. The benefit of the 15% bracket is that it lowers the family's tax

bill overall. For example, if you are in the 27% tax bracket and have $10,000 in investment income, you would have $7,300 after taxes at your tax rate. If you put the $10,000 into the college fund of a child over 14, the fund could have over $8,900 after tax at the child's tax rate.

On the downside, UGMA accounts can have two major drawbacks:

1. Upon reaching the age of legal majority—18 in most states—the child receives full legal ownership of the funds. The child can use the funds in any way he or she chooses. A child who decides to spend the money on something other than education has the right to do so.

2. When a college financial aid office determines how much aid a student is qualified to receive, the first thing it looks at is the child's own wealth. If you've shifted a large amount of assets into a child's name, the amount of tuition aid the child receives may be dramatically reduced, a loss that may far outweigh taxes saved through the UGMA account.

WHERE ARE THE LOAN PROGRAMS?

If you need additional funds for your child's college education and you don't want to borrow against your assets (see

---

FOUR TUITION ASSETS YOU MIGHT OWN

Even if you have been careful to stash away funds for college tuition, you may find that expenses are higher than you expected or other financial obligations leave you strapped for cash. If you have to borrow to bridge funding gaps, consider:

Life insurance loan. You can borrow against the cash value of a life insurance policy. The interest rate is low—often between 6% and 8%, but it varies depending on your contract—and you can repay the loan in any increments that you choose, whenever you have the money to do so.

Home equity loan. You can take out a home equity loan through a bank, credit union, savings and loan organization or brokerage firm. Interest on loan amounts up to $100,000 is tax deductible.

401(k) loan. Many companies allow employees to borrow from their 401(k) accounts to pay for college tuition. The interest payments on your loan go back into your 401(k) account—rather than to a bank or other institution. However, there is no tax deduction on the interest you pay.

Company loan. Many companies offer college education loans to employees and their dependents at low interest rates. Ask if your firm makes such loans. If not, but you participate in a salary-reduction or profit-sharing plan, most companies will let you borrow against that money and arrange for repayment through payroll deductions.

---

box), your child can apply for a loan. In addition to loans offered by individual colleges (ask about specific programs) and state governments (call your state education department), two other sources are federal government loans and commercial loans. Some examples:

Government Loans

■ *Perkins loan.* The college or university administers this program, using federal funds. Needy students (as determined by the school) can get loans of up to $3,000 a year at a 5% interest rate. Graduate students can borrow up to $5,000 a year, with a total ceiling of $30,000 in loans for undergraduate and graduate study. The loans can be repaid over 10 years.

■ *Stafford loan.* This low-interest loan is available to all students, regardless of financial status. However, students who demonstrate need can obtain interest subsidies, while those from higher income families pay

higher interest rates—generally around 6.5%. Loan limits are adjusted annually for inflation. Total undergraduate loans cannot be more than $23,000. Graduate students can borrow $8,500 a year, with a total loan ceiling of $65,500 for all loan years. A student can apply for a Stafford loan at a bank or other financial institution.

■ *PLUS and SLS loans.* Parent Loan to Undergraduate Students (PLUS) and Supplemental Loan for Students (SLS) are as their names suggest: one is a loan made to parents and the other to students. The interest rate on both loans is based on the one-year U.S. Treasury bill rate plus 3.1%, and is capped at 10% for PLUS and 11% for SLS. Parents can borrow any amount, regardless of financial need, but the loan cannot exceed the student's cost of attending school, less other financial aid.

With the SLS program, students can borrow up to $4,000 for freshman and sophomore years and $5,000 for junior and senior years, not to exceed a total of $23,000. Graduate students can borrow up to $10,000 a year, not to exceed $73,000. Repayment of SLS loans can be deferred until a student leaves school, but interest will continue to accrue. The loans can be obtained through financial institutions.

For more information on federal government loan programs, call the *U.S. Department of Education's Federal Student Aid Program* at 800-433-3243.

Commercial Loans

- *TERI loan.* The Educational Resources Institute (TERI) loans are available through local banks. Amounts start at $2,000 and can go up to the amount of your child's education. The interest rate is the prime rate plus 1.5% to 2%, depending on the lender. Repayment of principal can be deferred while your child is in school, but must be repaid within 25 years. TERI also has a loan program for graduate students. For more information on TERI loans, call 800-255-8374.
- *EXCEL loan.* The Nellie Mae (formerly the New England Education Loan Marketing Association) EXCEL program offers loans from $2,000 to the full cost of education, less other financial aid. The interest rate on one-year renewable loans is the prime rate plus 3% to 4%. Payment on principal can be deferred while the student is in school. The loan can be repaid over 20 years. For more information, call 800-634-9308.

FINANCIAL AID

There are three types of college financial aid, according to Bruce Hammond, college counselor at Sandia Preparatory School in Albuquerque, New Mexico:

- *Merit-based.* Offered by individual schools. Look for local activity-specific or affiliation-specific programs; state programs listed by the Education Commission of the States: *www.ecs.org.*
- *Need-based.* Eligibility based on Free Application for Federal Student Aid (FAFSA) application filled out by parents. For information: *www.estudentloan.com.*
- *Merit-within-need.* To find out which colleges offer the biggest aid programs, try these Web sites: *www.fastweb.com, www.easi.ed.gov www.finaid.org.*

KNOW ABOUT COLLEGE GRANTS

Educational grants for college-bound children don't cost you anything, and they don't have to be repaid. But you have to look for them. There are literally thousands of grant sources, including state programs, private grants and grants from the colleges themselves. Many companies give grants to their employees' children. Locally, chambers of commerce, trade groups and service associations often have grant programs. Remember that grants aren't necessarily awarded on the basis of need. A child might receive a grant for academic achievement, athletic abilities, music skills, school activities or community work. Have your child ask the guidance counselor for a list of grants in your area.

In addition, there are two federal government grant programs—*Pell grants* and *Supplemental Educational Opportunity Grants (SEOGs).* Pell grants are generally given on the basis of need and range from $400 to $2,300 a year. Even if it is unlikely that your child might receive a Pell grant, he or she should apply for one if other loans or grants are being considered. Most financial aid programs won't consider applicants unless they have applied for a Pell grant.

Under the SEOG program, funds are distributed to college financial aid offices, which then distribute them to students. Grants range from $100 to $4,000 a year, based on a family's income. Students may receive both a Pell grant and SEOG.

INCREASE AID WITH PENSION

Most college financial aid formulas either do not count your retirement funds as available to pay tuition or include only a small portion of them. Thus, by

FREE COLLEGE CREDITS FOR LIFE SKILLS

Maybe you or your child don't have to pay for certain courses. College credit for life experience may be available to past, present and future students who show they have mastered course fundamentals through a job, hobby, volunteering or other activities. For more information, contact the *Council for Adult and Experiential Learning* at 312-499-2600 or online at *www.cael.org.*

Also, more than 2,800 colleges give course credits to anyone who passes a standardized test.

➤ Exams in many subjects, including military and corporate training. Web site: *www.excelsior.edu.*

saving money in an IRA, Simplified Employee Pension (SEP) plan, Savings Incentive Match Plan for Employers (SIMPLE) or 401(k) plan—instead of a taxable savings or investment account— you may increase the amount of college financial aid a child can receive.

In addition, you will have the benefit of a contribution tax deduction, if eligible, and tax deferral on earnings that compound within the retirement account.

BUILD *YOUR* SAVINGS

After investing the maximum allowed in retirement plans, keep any additional savings invested in your own name. Put the money in tax-favored investments, such as appreciating stocks, tax-exempt bonds or variable annuities. By keeping money in your own name, you retain full control over it and avoid reducing a child's eligibility for financial aid (if the assets were in his or her name).

Grandparents also should avoid making well-intentioned gifts to children that reduce their eligibility for financial aid. It's better to set aside funds to help a grandchild pay for college, but keep the money in your own name. When the child enrolls in school, make a direct payment to the school for the child's tuition. A special provision of the tax code exempts such payments from the gift tax. And a grandparent can make an additional $10,000 direct payment to the school free of gift tax to pay for room and board.

SMART HOUSING

Many families save a great deal on college expenses by having their college students rent apartments rather than live in dormitories, which are often cramped and expensive. Several students can share large apartments and split the cost of rent and meals. Meal plans at private colleges can run as high as $2,400 to $3,000 a year.

Or consider cutting the cost of college housing by buying a small house for your child and other students to live in. Your mortgage payments give you equity in an asset of value, while payments for a dorm or apartment would be lost forever. Rental income from other students may offset the cost of the property or even provide a profit. And by treating the property as an income-producing asset, you can deduct related expenses —insurance, maintenance and depreciation. You may also be able to deduct trips made to inspect the property, while visiting your child at the same time.

EARLY FILERS GET THE AID

If you are applying for financial aid for your college student, file your tax returns early. Aid is often dispensed on a first-come, first-served basis, and you will have to include a copy of your tax return with the aid forms. Financial aid applications at most colleges are due between January and March.

Also, if you think you are entitled to more financial aid than a college offers you, explain your case. One parent who appealed a college's decision on the basis of a $25,000 income shortfall and major medical expenses received an additional $4,000 in financial aid.

BEST BARGAINS IN COLLEGE CHOICE

Ivy League and other elite colleges are not always the most appropriate choice for top students, academically or financially. Most highly selective schools attract an abundance of academically superior applicants, and award financial aid based entirely upon financial need.

Many less selective colleges have programs designed to attract top students with lucrative merit-based scholarships. These schools often have honors-rated programs in specific academic fields in which good students can shine more than they would in elite schools. In addition to saving on college expenses, your son or daughter can take advantage of the opportunity to demonstrate academic competence for admission to a first-rate graduate or professional school.

The best bargains are public universities, particularly in your own state (out-of-state universities will be more expensive). Most offer a high-quality education at less than a quarter of the cost of a prestigious private school.

i

COLLEGE LOAN RESOURCES

➤ *U.S. Department of Education, Federal Student Aid Program,* 1050 Thomas Jefferson St. NW, Washington, DC 20202. 800-433-3243. Agency in charge of all federal aid programs; provides information and useful brochures on choosing colleges, preparing your child for college, financing college, and financial aid opportunities. Web site: *www.ed.gov.*

➤ *The College Board,* 45 Columbus Ave., New York, NY 10023. 800-416-5137. Offers numerous publications on financing college, plus a software program on sources of aid and how to apply for it. Web site: *www.collegeboard.com.*

➤ *National Association for College Admission Counseling,* 1631 Prince St., Alexandria, VA 22314. 800-822-6285. Publishes informative booklet on "Guide to the College Admission Process." Web site: *www.nacac.com.*

Insuring Your Future

Buying insurance can be a complicated and confusing process. You don't want to pay too much for coverage you might not need, but you don't want to leave yourself unprotected in case of an accident or illness. What you don't know about insurance can hurt you financially. Here are solutions to getting the best coverage for the least amount.

HOW MUCH LIFE INSURANCE?

How much life insurance should you buy? Some insurers recommend at least three times your annual income; others say five times your annual spending, plus taxes. There is no precise formula because every situation is different. The amount varies depending on your assets, liabilities and income requirements, as well as your age and number of dependents. If you and your spouse both work and you have one child who has graduated from college, you will need less coverage than if your spouse doesn't work and you have younger children.

Basically, you should have enough life insurance to pay for expenses following your death and to replace the income your family will lose as a result of your death.

- *Expenses as a result of death.* These include funeral expenses, unreimbursed medical bills, federal and state taxes, probate costs and attorney's fees.
- *Future expenses.* These include all expenses your family will incur—for children's education, food, clothing, housing (mortgage, utilities, maintenance), insurance premiums, taxes, transportation, loan payments, recreation and entertainment. Estimate how long each of these expenses will continue. Most of them, for example, may continue for the rest of your spouse's life. Others, like college education and mortgage payments, will end at a certain point in the future. Some insurers recommend that you add a lump sum equal to half a year's salary to anticipated expenses to cover the unexpected—a major family illness or other debts.
- *Future income.* When calculating income, include any benefits your survivors might be entitled to—Social Security, life insurance, pension, trusts—as well as investment income, such as dividends and interest, and your survivor's salary, if applicable. Remember you need only to replace your net income minus the benefits your family would receive in your absence. But don't forget the impact of inflation, which will render income that is calculated in today's dollars less valuable tomorrow. Compare sources of income with expenses. If there is a shortfall, or "gap," as is commonly the case, seek advice from a competent outside professional on how to close that gap.

BEST-CASE LIFE INSURANCE

First-to-die life insurance—which pays off on the first death of two covered persons—can increase the financial security of a married couple:

- When both spouses work, the insurance benefit compensates the surviving spouse for the loss of the income that the deceased spouse formerly earned.
- When both spouses have worked and earned pensions, first-to-die insurance lets each spouse choose the larger annual pension payout that can be taken over one life instead of a smaller payout that provides survivor benefits.
- When one spouse dies, the lost pension money will be made up by the insurance benefit.
- After retirement, first-to-die insurance protects against the risk that a costly illness of one spouse will consume a couple's savings and leave the surviving spouse poor.

LIFE INSURANCE TAX TRAPS

Proceeds from insurance on your life will be taxable in your estate if you die owning "incidents of ownership" in the policy, such as the right to borrow against it or change beneficiaries. Have some other family member own the policy or set up a life insurance trust to own it. You can then make tax-free cash gifts to the policy owner to help cover the premium cost using your annual gift-tax exclusion.

Caution: One drawback to an insurance trust is that it limits a spouse's authority over the proceeds—the payout to the spouse is subject to the trustee's discretion. Make the trustee "spouse-friendly" by naming someone who is sympathetic to the spouse's interests (e.g., your spouse's brother). And don't make distribution of income from the trust to your spouse mandatory. This will put money into your spouse's estate that might create additional estate taxes on the spouse's death.

INSURERS' PICTURES CAN LIE

Don't be misled by life insurance policy "illustrations" that project how a policy will perform many years in the future. Insurance companies tend to inflate their figures so they look good on paper. Make sure the illustration clearly indicates whether premiums may rise or death benefits may lapse early.

PAY PREMIUMS ANNUALLY

No matter what type of life insurance policy you own, premiums are always lower when you pay in one lump sum, rather than spreading out payments on a monthly or quarterly basis. If you can pay the single premium, you will save between 6% and 20%, depending on the interest rate your insurer charges for paying in installments.

Also look for numbers showing the death benefit and cash value in future years and the "guaranteed" worst-case scenario—assuming the lowest interest rate and highest costs possible for the policy. Compare different policies and what each is willing to guarantee contractually.

Two key questions to ask a prospective insurer:

1. For level term-life insurance policies, how long is the premium absolutely guaranteed? Is the premium rate fixed for a term of 5, 10, 15, or 20 years? Remember that your policy must be renewed at the end of every "term," with premiums increasing each time.

2. For permanent (cash-value) insurance policies, what is the minimum premium necessary to guarantee the full death benefit to age 100?

INSURANCE RIDERS YOU SHOULD LOSE

Nearly every life insurance policy offers riders—extras that push up the cost of owning the policy. You may have riders on your policy that you aren't aware of and don't really need. Call your agent for a list of riders on your policy and an explanation of each one. Then determine which you want to keep and which you want to eliminate.

One rider that might be elimi-

nated, for example, is waiver of premium for disability. If you already have disability coverage at work or bought a policy of your own, coverage through your life insurance policy is likely unnecessary. If you don't have disability coverage, you're still better off eliminating this rider and using the money to buy a higher quality plan. However, make sure that you qualify for a new disability policy before you cancel the rider.

DISABILITY TRAPS

Many insurance companies have recently redesigned their disability policies to limit the amount of benefits they'll pay if you can't return to your present job or don't choose to work at a job they deem comparable. Some insurers no longer offer policies that guarantee there will be no

increases in premiums. How to buy the best policy?

■ *Don't rely on an employer to provide all the disability insurance you need.* Most employers offer only short-term disability coverage, but you need coverage until your Social Security takes effect. Also, many employer-sponsored policies have provisions that reduce benefits if you are eligible to receive Social Security, worker's compensation or other state programs. Instead of buying a policy with a fixed benefit, buy one that guarantees a specific income when benefits are combined with Social Security—with the policy paying more if Social Security benefits are denied or reduced.

■ *Ask for a policy with "own occupation" coverage.* You can protect only about 50% of your former income with a general disability policy you buy on your own. Look for a policy that covers loss of income from your "own occupation." These policies pay benefits if you can't work at your specific occupation, even if you are capable of holding another lower paying job. Expect to pay 15% to 20%

extra for this protection, but it is well worth the extra cost; especially if you are a highly paid professional.

- *Avoid "loss of income" policies.* Touted as the successors to "own occupation" policies, these are supposed to provide benefits that bring you up to your old income level—but not necessarily so. The insurer may argue that you must return to any reasonable job for which you are suited and which pays you at least 50% of your former earnings. If you don't choose to return to work at "any reasonable occupation"—or can't find work in your area of expertise— you would get only 50% of your benefit.
- *Look for a noncancelable and guaranteed-renewable policy.* A noncancelable policy can't be canceled unless you die or fail to pay your premiums on time. It has fixed premiums throughout the life of the policy. A guaranteed-renewable policy cannot be canceled and the terms of the policy cannot be changed, even if you change occupations or your health history changes. However, the insurer can raise your premium if it does so for all policies in a certain class.
- *Compromise on the waiting period for collecting benefits.* Choose a policy with the longest waiting period you can afford between the time of injury and

the time when benefit payments begin. A 90-day wait rather than a 30-day wait may cut premiums significantly. If you have the resources to support yourself for 180 days—rather than 90 days—you can cut your premium by 20% to 25%.

Shop around for the best deals, but keep in mind that unlike other types of insurance policies, disability insurance companies are likely to sell you less coverage than you need.

THE MERITS OF MAJOR MEDICAL

Most hospitalization and surgical medical policies do not cover the entire cost of a hospital stay or surgery. Many plans, for example, only cover a semiprivate room up to $200 a day. To supplement these policies, get a major medical plan that "wraps around" your primary hospitalization and surgical coverage.

A major medical plan generally pays 100% of hospitalization charges up to a certain time limit, such as 120 days, and then 80% of your bills thereafter. Other types of major medical plans require you to pay a deductible and a percentage of the covered medical costs up to a certain "stop loss" limit, after which the insurer pays 100%. For example, you pay the initial

deductible, say $250, and then 20% (insurer pays 80%) of medical costs until you have paid a total of $2,000. After you have reached the "stop loss" limit, which is generally $2,000 to $5,000, depending on the plan, your insurer picks up 100% of the bills.

Most major medical plans have a lifetime or per-cause limit. The difference is important. If you have a $250,000 lifetime limit and have used up the $250,000 on treatments for a particular ailment, you cannot collect money for treatments if you have another serious ailment.

If you have a per-cause limitation of $250,000, the insurer will pay up to the limit for each separate ailment. After you use up $250,000 for heart disease, for example, the insurer will pay another $250,000 for cancer treatment. If you get any other disease, then you can get still another $250,000 for treatment. Most major medical policies, however, have a cap on the total amount you can receive. Check with your insurance company.

AVOID HMO "SQUIRM" TACTICS

Many Health Maintenance Organizations (HMOs) hold down expenses by holding back on medical services that might be important to you. Knowledge and assertiveness will help your case. Some suggestions for better care:

Know the Rules

Many HMOs have adopted policies that make it more difficult for patients to obtain care, such as requiring preauthorization for emergency services and approval for specialized therapies. Carefully read your membership booklet, your contract and any newsletters with benefit information so that you understand how to get around those obstacles.

If you are denied coverage for something, file a formal appeal. All HMOs have grievance procedures, though they don't always advertise the fact. Ask explicitly what the appeal procedure is and follow it. If you are still denied approval and the services you need are expensive, consider hiring an attorney who specializes in HMOs.

Know Your Doctor

Determine whether your primary care doctor will go to bat for you if the HMO takes a hard line, like denying an extra day in the hospital, a visit to a specialist or an expensive test. If you get the impression that your doctor is primarily interested in the financial well-being of the HMO and not as concerned about your health, ask to switch to another primary care doctor or consider switching plans.

Find out how your doctor is paid. Doctors who are paid set salaries by an HMO have no incentive to deny services or recommend ones that you don't need. However, many HMOs pay bonuses for saving on expensive services, while others pay doctors a fixed monthly fee per patient— a system known as "capitation." This means doctors have an incentive to see as many patients as possible in one day, which could cut down on time spent with patients. In addition, the cost of any extra services may come out of a doctor's capitation checks, thus encouraging the doctor to order as few as possible.

To find out how your doctor is paid, ask the benefits coordinator where you are employed or ask your doctor directly. If your doctor says that the HMO contract forbids him or her from revealing that, consider changing plans.

Know Your Ailment

Learn as much as possible about your medical condition so that you can ask informed questions and know whether the treatment your doctor and HMO recommend is the normal course—or just the most economical. Most library reference sections have medical encyclopedias, as well as periodical indexes to help you find articles on specific topics. Research about your condition may also involve seeking the

opinion of a doctor outside of your plan, even though you will have to pay. Some managed-care plans allow you—for a higher copayment—to consult a doctor of your choice. If you later need to appeal to your plan for a service that was denied, the second opinion could prove valuable.

IS YOUR HMO THERE IN AN EMERGENCY?

Before you join an HMO, make sure you understand its policies on emergency care:

Hospitals. For most HMOs, you will have to go to member hospitals. Find out the nearest hospital you should go to and how to get care if you are away from home. Most plans cover out-of-area emergency care for acute conditions; others require that the condition be life-threatening. If it is a major emergency while you are traveling, forget about the HMO. Seek care immediately and work out payment problems later.

Coverage. Find out how your HMO defines an emergency. If coverage depends on the diagnosis, you may be denied coverage for a false alarm, no matter how costly. If coverage depends on "severe symptoms," find out how they are defined.

Approval. Most HMOs require that you notify them within a certain period of time after receiving emergency care. You may also need advance approval for ongoing treatment. Make sure you understand the requirements for approval.

After-hours care. Find out which steps to take and which permissions are needed if you have to see a doctor after normal work hours or on holidays. HMOs usually have health-care professionals on call 24 hours a day, but some are better than others when responding to an emergency. Emphasize that your case requires immediate attention. For example, don't say you've been having chest pains for two weeks. Say you've had a sudden onset of pain or that it just got much worse.

CHECK NOW FOR FAMILY COVERAGE

Your older children's medical care may not be covered under your policy. Many insurance companies and HMOs stop covering dependents once they reach age 21, and HMOs may not cover medical expenses when students are away from home. Also, if your child is going to school part-time, he or she may not be covered. Generally, students must be enrolled full-time to be able to extend their parents' coverage to their college years.

Know your plan's requirements and limitations before your child goes away to school. Find out about buying insurance directly from the college. Some make coverage available to students at attractive group rates.

MEDICAL CLAIMS: GET YOUR DUE

When you file a medical claim, opportunities for errors and misunderstandings abound. Insurers are more likely to question, deny or reduce the amount you are claiming when mistakes occur. Here are five strategies for getting what is due you:

■ *1. Keep careful records.* Write down—and keep in a special file —all contacts with your health insurers, in case you need to refer to them at a later date. Keep notes about any telephone conversations—with whom you spoke, when you had the conversation, and what was said. With such data to substantiate a claim, you will have a stronger case if you decide to challenge an insurer's decision to reject or reduce that claim.

■ *2. Watch for clerical errors.* When a doctor's office gives you

an insurance form filled with codes, ask for the meaning of each code. Incorrect codes are a major reason insurers reject bills, which then become the patient's responsibility. Often, this is the result of a clerical error. If the insurer says that your treatment was not related to the diagnosis or was inappropriate, that could be a sign that the codes are wrong. Also watch for clerical errors in the way your insurance group or Social Security numbers are reported on your claim.

■ *3. Challenge in writing.* When challenging a claim, a letter carries more weight than a phone call because you can send copies to all parties involved to muster support. Many people are intimidated by having to write letters, but if you keep it simple and to the point, it shouldn't take much time. For example, a brief note stating, "With regard to my claim for Dr. Smith's services on June 20, I disagree with your denial for the following reasons..." is sufficient. Send copies to the doctor and to the hospital, if applicable, and keep a copy for yourself.

■ *4. Get your doctor's help.* An insurer may rule that your doctor's charges are more than the "usual, customary and reasonable" fees. It's in your doctor's best interest to explain why the charges are reasonable,

and he or she should be willing to write to your insurance company detailing the facts. Your doctor should also be able to provide the names of insurance companies that pay the full amount or an amount closer to his or her fee for the procedure —to show your insurer that the charge is not so out of line. In some cases, the procedure may be more complicated than the insurance company realizes. Ask your doctor to provide a more detailed explanation of treatment and services.

■ *5. Go to a higher authority.* If you're not satisfied with what a customer service representative tells you, ask to speak to a supervisor, customer relations vice president, medical director or the person in charge of the appeals process. If your medical insurance is provided by your workplace, complain to the benefits staff. Since they are responsible for choosing the health coverage and they deal with the insurance company directly, they have more clout with the company than an individual employee does. Finally, if you are still dissatisfied, contact your state insurance commission and tell the insurance company that you are doing so. Just threatening to contact the state insurance commission will likely trigger a review of your claim.

APPEALING A MEDICARE DECISION

When receiving Medicare treatments, keep a record of all doctor visits and procedures. This will help you determine if you are billed incorrectly and if you have to file an appeal for additional payment. Review every bill carefully. Medicare bills from hospitals and doctors often contain errors. If a Medicare claim is denied:

➤ Ask the carrier that handled the claim to review it. You must do so within six months of a denial.

➤ If you are not satisfied with the review and the amount in dispute involves at least $100, ask for a hearing before a carrier hearing officer.

➤ If you are still dissatisfied, and the amount in dispute is at least $500, you have 60 days to request a hearing before an administrative law judge.

ENSURE FULL COVERAGE

If you have assets of more than $100,000 or have personal or professional liabilities that make you vulnerable to lawsuits, "umbrella" liability insurance, which protects your assets in case of a large judgment against you, is an excellent investment. This addition to your homeowner's policy protects you against such damage suits as physical injury, libel, slander, mental anguish, sickness or disease and other

MAKE INSURANCE COMPANIES PAY UP!

Faced with the complexities of filing a medical claim or disputing a rejected or reduced claim, too many people simply give up, losing money owed them by an insurer. Don't throw in the towel! Help is at hand: In response to a growing demand for professional advice, a new type of service has emerged to help people file claims and battle insurance companies.

Known as claims assistance professionals, many of these advisers formerly worked for insurance companies as claims administrators. They charge anywhere from $25 to $90 an hour, and with their help, an estimated 50% of the claims that are challenged end up being paid by insurers.

To find a claims assistance professional near you, write to the *National Association of Claims Assistance Professionals*, 5329 S. Main St., Downers Grove, IL 60515. Include $1 to cover postage and handling.

causes. Damage awards these days often exceed $1 million, even when the incident was beyond the control of the person being sued. Your assets can be seized or your wages garnished to pay awards.

The cost for about $1 million of coverage is about $100 to $300 a year. You may be required to increase automobile and homeowner liability limits before an umbrella policy will be issued.

COVER PROPERTY FOR ALL RISKS

When assessing your homeowner's insurance policy, make sure you are adequately covered for potential property damage or loss. A "named-perils" insurance policy protects only against specific losses set forth in the contract, such as fire and theft. A better route is an "all-risks" policy that provides the broadest possible coverage for any loss you might suffer. You can never anticipate every possible cause of a loss —and it is precisely the "surprise" loss that is most likely to leave you in need of insurance.

Sources of loss or damage not covered in an all-risk policy are specifically named in the contract, such as floods or earthquakes. You will need separate insurance to cover those risks.

To offset the extra cost of an all-risk policy, increase deductibles to

the maximum you can afford— that is, don't pay your insurance company to cover losses that you can afford to pay.

KNOW WHAT YOU OWN

Once a year, videotape the contents of your entire house for insurance purposes. Do a walking tour, including a description of what you have in each room. Then store the tape in a safe-deposit box or in a location away from the house. If you make a major purchase during the year, you can add documentation of it at the end of the videotape. If you don't have videotaping equipment, you can rent it or hire someone to do the documentation for you.

■ *Option:* If you have a computer, a program such as *Quicken Deluxe* or *Home Inventory Builder* enables simple, fast recording of virtually every item in your home. Even serial numbers and original costs can be recorded.

REPAIRS: DON'T GET CHEATED

Before filing a home insurance claim, get a repair estimate from a contractor so that you will have a cost guideline before the adjuster arrives. If the insurance

company makes a much lower estimate, insist that repairs be made with materials that are the same as, or equivalent to, whatever existed before the damage.

If the damage is so severe that you must make immediate repairs, take photos first, then make only temporary repairs before the adjuster arrives.

AUTO COVERAGE TO BANK ON

It's easy to make mistakes when selecting the right insurance coverage for your car. Here are a few of the most common pitfalls.

■ *Not taking advantage of discounts.* Use all the discounts to which you are entitled. You could be spending hundreds of dollars more for insurance than you have to. You can receive about 20% off the cost of insuring two or more cars if you buy coverage from one insurance company. If you have a car alarm, you can shave the cost of theft coverage by about 20%. Air bags can mean large discounts for bodily injury coverage. *Caution:* Pay attention to the bottom line. Some companies with big discounts have high costs. Shop around for the best deals.

■ *Buying a car without considering insurance costs.* Too often, people who are in the market for a new car with several options to choose from fail to consider the cost of insurance before they buy. Some less glamorous models can be costly to insure if they're stolen frequently for parts. Expensive cars that have done well in crash tests and have safety features, such as antilock brakes and air bags, are often less expensive to insure for collision than cheaper cars without those features.

- *Buying too much or too little coverage.* The most important coverage is bodily injury liability, which pays for another person's medical care when you're found at fault in an accident. You need coverage of at least $100,000 per person and $300,000 for any single accident. *Where to cut back:* Most drivers have too much collision and comprehensive insurance. If your car is old—seven years or more—the cost of collision and comprehensive may not be worth it. A good rule of thumb is that when collision and comprehensive coverage cost more than 10% of the car's market value, drop it.

- *Setting your deductibles too low.* While low deductibles may be appealing, you pay a lot for protection that is often unnecessary, since you can afford to pay the amount yourself. Raising your deductibles from $100 to $250 can save about 15% on your collision and comprehensive coverage. Raising them to $500 can save about 25%. Raising them to $1,000 can save about 33%.

YOUTHFUL DRIVER SAVINGS TIPS

To save on a child's auto insurance, buy an older used car equipped with air bags. Four-door cars cost less to insure than two-door cars or sports models. Also, ask about good-student discounts, which can cut rates significantly for full-time students with high grade averages.

Important: Make sure your children understand the financial consequences of speeding and other unsafe driving habits. One ticket can lead to a hefty premium hike that lasts for several years.

POST-ACCIDENT CAUTIONS

If you have an automobile accident and your car has to be towed, have it taken to a repair shop, but do *not* authorize repairs on the spot. Call your insurer to have a claims adjuster assess the damage and to get a list of recommended repair shops before you decide where to have the repairs done. Comparison shop, however. Sometimes you can do better with a local repair shop than you can with those on your insurer's list.

Have your insurer send the check for the repairs directly to you—not to the shop—so you can check to make sure the repairs are satisfactory before you give the shop the money. Or have your insurer send an adjuster to inspect the car before a check for the repairs is issued.

INSURE THAT LAPTOP!

Because of their value and compactness, laptop computers have become desirable targets of theft. If you travel frequently with a laptop, make sure you have insurance for it in case it is stolen or damaged.

Your homeowner or business insurance policy may cover a laptop computer used at home or in the office, but not one that is used primarily when traveling. Ask your insurer if yours is covered while you are on the road and, if not, whether the coverage is available.

INSURANCE RESOURCES

➤ *National Insurance Consumer Helpline.* 800-942-4242. Provides consumer information and brochures on life, health, automobile, home and business insurance; also refers complaints to agencies.

➤ *National Association of Insurance Commissioners,* 444 N. Capitol St. NW, Suite 701, Washington, DC 20001. 202-624-7790. Oversees regulations to protect consumers. *Web site:* www.naic.org.

➤ *Consumer Federation of America,* 1424 16 St. NW, Suite 604, Washington, DC 20036. 202-387-6121. Advice on how to evaluate insurance policies. *Web site:* www.consumerfed.org.

➤ *Insurance Information Institute,* 110 William St., New York, NY 10038. 800-331-9146. Publishes booklets on property and casualty insurance and how to file claims. *Web site:* www.iii.org.

➤ *Centers for Medicare and Medicaid Services,* 7500 Security Blvd., Baltimore, MD 21244. 410-786-3000. In charge of Medicare and Medicaid insurance; provides free brochures as well as "Consumer's Guide to Long-Term Health Insurance." *Web site:* www.hcfa.gov.

How to Ax Your Taxes

No matter how often the tax code changes, it's always complicated. If you're in a high tax bracket, you need professional help with your returns and decisions in between. If you're in a low bracket, you could probably use some help, too. High or low, the actions you take make a difference in the taxes you pay. Here are some suggestions to help you lessen your taxes.

BUMP GAINS, LOWER DIVIDENDS

The long-term capital gains tax of 20% for those in the highest tax bracket (10% for those in the lowest bracket) means that it pays to explore investments where your returns will be largely in the form of capital gains instead of dividends, which are taxed at rates up to 39.6%. To take advantage of the rates, the law requires that you hold on to the assets for at least 12 months before selling them.

If you haven't done so already, it is well worth taking the time to review your portfolio to maximize capital gains benefits. You should decide which assets to hold in tax-deferred plans and which to hold outside such plans. You will also need to figure out how best to play the holding period to ensure long-term gains benefits. Some strategies:

- Explore small-cap growth stocks (companies with capitalization of $150 million or less). Your investment return will largely be in the form of capital gains instead of dividends. When you sell, the capital gains will be taxed at the low rate, assuming you have held them for 12 months.
- Shift assets from income-producing assets to appreciating assets.
- Have tax-favored retirement accounts hold income-producing assets and taxable accounts hold capital gains assets. *Reason:* Distributions from qualified retirement plans are taxed as ordinary income. The capital gains tax break will be wasted on long-term gains held in such plans.
- Choose growth-stock mutual funds that keep their taxable short-term capital gains to a minimum. Also look for funds that have a low turnover rate—those that tend to hold stocks for a longer period before selling. This will help ensure that distributions are long term.
- *Big bonus.* Invest for the long haul. In 2006, the top capital gains tax rate will go down from 20% to 18% (10% to 8% for those in the lowest bracket) for assets held for more than five years.

Special: If you are in the 15% tax bracket, you can use the 8% capital gain rate for assets you've held for more than five years.

BEST TIME FOR GAINS & LOSSES

Under the tax rules, it's important to plan when best to incur long- and short-term gains and losses. Consider:

- Long-term gains are favored over short-term gains, which are taxed at the higher ordinary income tax rates.
- Short-term losses are advantageous when used to offset short-term capital gains.
- Net capital losses of up to $3,000 are deductible against ordinary income. The balance can be carried forward to be deducted in future years, until used up.

While you may want to hold gain assets until they become long term, you may want to *sell loss* assets before they become long term. Since gains and losses are netted at year-end, you don't want short-term losses offsetting tax-favored long-term gains. Tally up your gains and losses as year-end approaches, then make some transactions to net out advantageously.

For example, if you have long-term gains and short-term losses, you may be able to take some short-term gains. The income tax you would normally pay on those gains will be offset by the losses. *The result:* You'll get a short-term gain tax-free and preserve the tax-favored status for your long-term gains.

Timing your gains and losses can be tricky. It's wise to seek professional help.

REITS GET HIGH RETURNS

Real estate investment trusts (REITs) offer a unique opportunity to bolster current income and take advantage of the capital gains tax reductions. On average, about 28% of the dividends paid by REITs (which by law must pay out 95% of their annual income) do not have to be included in ordinary income. Instead, they are considered to be return of capital, which for tax purposes, can be deducted each year from your original cost basis in buying REIT stock. When you eventually sell your shares in the REIT, your capital gain will be the amount that you have reduced your original cost basis by then.

PUT "KIDDIE TAX" TO WORK

Investment income received by a child younger than age 14 is taxed at the parents' tax rate beyond a total of $1,500—each child can receive $750 per year of tax free income, plus another $750 that is taxed at the child's own rate, usually 10%. Make this "Kiddie Tax" work for you.

For example, when funds are in a CD that pays 4% taxable interest, each child can have about $25,000 in savings to earn $1,000 of tax-favored interest. The Kiddie Tax can be avoided on additional savings held in the child's name by investing them in tax-exempt bonds or appreciating assets, such as growth stocks, shares in real estate partnerships or Series EE or I savings bonds.

Have the child hold the appreciating assets until after reaching age 14, then cash them in. The child will owe tax on them at his or her own low tax rate (generally 10%), instead of the 20% capital gains rate you would probably pay.

GIFT TO A LOWER BRACKET

You may be able to reduce capital gains by giving assets to a child age 14 or older or to low tax-bracket family members—and have them sell the investments and pay tax at their own lower rates.

For example, if you sell $10,000 worth of stock to pay for your child's college education, your capital gain probably will be taxed at the top 20% rate. But if you make a gift of the stock to the child and have him or her sell it, the gain may be taxed at 8% or 10%—saving taxes that can be used to pay college costs.

Each year, you can make tax-free gifts of up to $11,000 (in 2002) each to as many recipients as you wish. The limit is double when you make gifts jointly with your spouse.

NO TAX ON SALE OF HOME

Under the current tax laws, most homeowners will be able to avoid paying taxes completely when they sell their homes, regardless of their age. Previously, to avoid taxes, a homeowner had to buy a replacement home of at least equal value to the one sold within two years.

TAX FORECASTING MADE EASY

To determine the best time to realize income and claim tax deductions, you need to estimate your real tax rate for this year and future years.

For many taxpayers, that sounds like an impossibly complicated task. How can you estimate tax rates for future years? Where does one begin?

Best advice: Buy one of the several tax preparation programs available for personal computers. Input your numbers from last year's tax return. Then modify the numbers to reflect this year's tax situation. This will provide a good estimate of this year's tax liability.

Then use the program to estimate your likely tax bill for future years by adjusting the income and deduction numbers to reflect your expectations. Experiment with "what if" income and deduction amounts. You may be surprised at the size of the impact they have on the bottom line, and get a much more realistic picture of your real tax rate.

This exercise will show you the benefits that can be realized from multi-year tax planning.

Two of the more popular tax preparation software programs are:

Quicken TurboTax, from Intuit, Inc. Can be purchased in retail stores, by direct mail (800-446-8848), or online at *www.quicken.com*. Available in Macintosh and Windows versions.

Kiplinger TaxCut, from H&R Block Customer Service. Can be purchased in retail stores, by direct mail (800-235-4060), or online at *www.kiplinger.com/software/*. Available in Macintosh and Windows versions.

Now up to $500,000 of current and deferred profit is tax free for a couple filing jointly ($250,000 for singles). The only requirement is that the home has been your principal residence for two out of five years (so you can only use the exclusion once every two years).

However, taxpayers who relocate suddenly without having met the two-year waiting period can exclude an amount equal to the portion, or fraction, of two years that the house was their principal residence. For example, a move after one year would mean that one-half of the exclusion can be claimed.

$ BIGGER MEDICAL BREAKS FOR THE SELF-EMPLOYED

In 2001, self-employed tax-payers could only deduct 60% of the premiums they pay for health insurance for them-selves and their families. The deduction will rise to 100% by 2003.

Year	Deduction
2002	70%
2003 & thereafter	100%

MORE HOME OFFICE BREAKS

Home offices are deductible under more generous rules than in the past. A home office qualifies as the principal place of business if it is used exclusively and regularly by the taxpayer to conduct administrative or man-agement activities—and if there is no other fixed location where he or she conducts substantial administrative or management activities of the business.

In short, home office deductions are allowed for space essential to the running of a venture, even if it's just for doing administrative paperwork. Previously, to be eligi-ble for a deduction, a home office had to be the place where you regularly conducted your actual work, met clients or spent most of your business hours.

If you do not deduct home office expenses, you can still deduct phone calls, supplies, equipment and various other business expenses.

TAX-FREE FRINGES

Instead of a salary raise, which will likely trigger a rise in your taxes, ask your employer for tax-exempt fringe benefits or a reimbursable expense account instead. Tax-exempt fringe benefits are deductible by your employer. Plus, benefits that cost your employer less than a salary increase may be even more valu-able to you after taxes. Examples of tax-free benefits in 2002:

- Free parking worth up to $185 a month
- Transit passes and subsidies up to $100 a month
- Work-related education up to $5,250
- Child-care assistance up to $5,000 a year
- Group life insurance up to $50,000
- Employee discounts for com-pany products or services

Most employees incur unreim-bursed business expenses, such as subscriptions to business periodicals, dues for professional organizations, use of one's car for work, some business meals and dry-cleaning costs on business trips. Those are counted among miscellaneous expenses, which are deductible only to the extent that they exceed 2% of your adjusted gross income, which is unlikely. However, reimburse-ment for those expenses under an expense account plan is deductible for your employer, and you will not owe taxes on the payments. Both sides win.

MORE MEDICAL DEDUCTIONS

Unreimbursed medical ex-penses are deductible only to the extent they exceed 7.5% of your adjusted gross income. Special deductions often over-looked that can raise unreim-bursed medical expenses to that level include:

- The costs of qualified long-term care services
- Home improvements for med-ical reasons, to the extent that their cost exceeds any increased value to your home.
- Costs of trips for health reasons ($50 limit per night for lodging)
- A special diet prescribed by a doctor, to the extent it costs more than a regular diet
- Eyeglasses, contact lenses and contact-lens insurance
- Medical equipment, such as wheelchairs, braces, crutches and hearing aids

- Dental services, such as X rays, cleaning and tooth extraction
- Premiums for health-care insurance

TAX-FREE DEATH BENEFITS

If you face severe health prob-lems in the future, the tax laws allow you an exclusion for accel-erated death benefits. A person who is chronically or terminally ill can take life insurance benefits before dying—tax free. The tax-free amount is limited in some cases. And certain requirements must be met to receive the bene-fits. Check with your accountant for specifics.

BOND TAX TRAPS

Inflation-indexed U.S. bonds paying market-rate interest represent a new opportunity for investors and a tax trap for the unwary. *The trap:* The IRS con-siders an increase in such a bond's value to be taxable income.

For example: A $1,000 bond paying 4% earns $40 during the year. If inflation runs at 3%, the bond's value will be increased to $1,030 after one year. It will then pay 4% interest on this new value—$41.20—in the next year. Thus, the owner of the bond faces $70 of taxable income in one year, even though the bond pays only $40 in cash.

Strategy: If you buy such bonds, keep them in a tax-deferred retirement account, such as an IRA or 401(k).

DON'T TAX YOURSELF TWICE

Many people automatically reinvest their mutual fund dividends or capital gains in additional fund shares. But taxes are owed in the year the dividends are paid, even though you receive no cash from the fund. Unaware investors pay taxes twice: once when dividends are paid and again when they sell their shares.

To avoid double taxation, keep records so that you can add reinvested dividends and capital gains to your tax cost (basis) in your fund shares. Increasing the tax cost reduces your tax bill when you sell—you pay capital gains tax on the difference between the selling price and your tax cost of the shares.

TAX BRACKETS

Know your marginal tax rate *before* making investment decisions, says Lynn O'Shaughnessy, author of *The Unofficial Guide to Investing.* Your marginal tax rate is the percentage of federal tax you pay on the highest dollar of your earnings. It ranges from 10% to 38.6% in 2002. Tax brackets can change annually. *Examples:* A raise or bonus could push you into a higher tax bracket...a few weeks of disability could move you into a lower one.

Some investments make sense for people in specific brackets. *Example:* Municipal bonds may work for people in high brackets —but taxable bonds are better for people in low brackets.

MANAGE TAX LIABILITY

It's important to plan ahead for how you should shift your income and deductions for maximum tax benefits. *Possibilities:*
- Enter into a deferred compensation agreement with your employer to defer part of your income into a future year when you will be in a lower tax bracket.
- Postpone receipt of interest income into next year by buying Treasury bills that mature after year-end.
- Time the payment of discretionary deductible expenditures to occur before or after year-end. These might include charitable gifts, Schedule C business expenses, deductible medical expenses or miscellaneous expenses. *Note:* Expenses and charitable contributions incurred on major credit cards are deductible if incurred by year-end, even if charges aren't paid off until next year.
- Prepay state and local income tax payments that aren't due until next year by December 31, to get a deduction for them on this year's federal return. *For example:* State estimated payments due January 15 and any payment that will be due on your April 15 return.
- Postpone paying local taxes until after year-end to get a more valuable deduction next year if you expect to be in a higher tax bracket then.

PLAY PERCENTAGES TO AVOID UNDERPAYMENT PENALTY

If your adjusted gross income for a preceding tax year exceeds $150,000, the percentage of that preceding year's tax that you will need to pay to avoid an estimated tax underpayment penalty for the following years is:

Tax Year	% of Previous Year's Tax
2002	112%
2003 & thereafter	110%

- If you have self-employment income, you can time deductible expenditures for supplies, equipment, advertising and other business costs before or after year-end. You may defer income by not sending out invoices until late in the year, so payments won't be received until the following year.

WITHHOLDING SHORTFALL?

Avoid tax penalties by making sure you have paid enough through a combination of wage withholding and quarterly estimated tax payments to cover the tax due on the income you will receive during the year. However, if you experience an unanticipated windfall—from self-employment or other sources of income not subject to withholding—don't panic. You will not be penalized if your withholdings for the year amount to the lesser of:
- 90% of the current year's final tax liability, or
- 100% of the taxes you owed the previous tax year, or 112%, if your adjusted gross income was $150,000 in 2002.

If you have a salary income, the best way to make up a tax shortfall is to increase taxes withheld from your salary during the last weeks of the year. This is because withholdings are treated by the IRS as taking place at an even rate over the whole year. So by withholding more late in the year, you can retroactively erase a tax payment shortfall and avoid a penalty.

On the other hand, if you make up a tax shortfall with an extra

DEDUCT JOB SEARCH COSTS

The cost of looking for a new job in your current line of work is deductible as an employee business expense—even if your job search is unsuccessful.

Deductible
➤ Travel to job interviews
➤ Résumé preparation, mailing, and so on
➤ Fees paid for career counseling and placement services
➤ 50% of the cost of meals and entertainment incurred while seeking a new job
➤ Relevant telephone calls
➤ Cost of placing advertisements
➤ Cost of newspapers and magazines bought for their advertisements

estimated payment, you will still owe the penalty for the underpayment in the earlier quarter.

USE 401(K) TO DEFER INCOME

The government allows any source of income reported on a W-2 form to be put away in a 401(k) account, up to a maximum of $11,000 in 2002 ($12,000 if you reach age 50 by the end of the year). That means you can defer taxes on income from commissions, bonuses—even monetary compensation for unused vacation time—in addition to your regular paycheck. Check with your employer. Some plans limit contributions to base pay only.

ADJUST WAGE WITHHOLDING

Almost everybody's tax situation changes from year to year. Even if your salary doesn't change significantly, your tax bill is likely to. Your investment income may go up or down; you may lose old deductions you were able to claim in the past or the number of dependents you can claim may change.

Get a new W-4 form from your employer every year, and use the worksheet to determine the optimum amount of tax to be

withheld from your pay. This will maximize the amount of each paycheck without risking tax-underpayment penalties.

The number of withholding allowances you can claim is not limited to the number of your dependency exemptions. You can claim all the allowances you need to balance the tax withheld from your pay with your final tax bill for the year.

Don't claim fewer withholding allowances because you want a large tax refund. Granted, it's a form of forced savings. But you will have made an interest-free loan to the IRS when you could have been earning interest on the money yourself.

TAX REFILE: 3-YEAR GRACE

What if you discover a new tax-saving strategy or deduction you forgot to take after you have mailed in your return? Don't assume that once the IRS has your return, that's the end of it. You can file an amended return any time for three years after the original return was due. Call your local IRS office and ask for Form 1040X.

TAX RESOURCES

➤ *Internal Revenue Service,* 1111 Constitution Ave. NW, Washington, DC 20224. 800-829-1040; 800-TAX-FORM for forms and publications. Official source of information on tax returns; has recorded information on more than 140 "Tele-Tax" topics; also a Problem Resolution Program. Web site: *www.irs.gov.*

➤ *Research Institute of America,* 395 Hudson St., New York, NY 10595. 800-431-9025. Publishes numerous newsletters and books on tax topics, including up-to-date explanations of changes in the law; also offers information on state and local taxes. Web site: www.riahome.com.

➤ *CCH Inc.,* 4025 W. Peterson Ave., Chicago, IL 60646. 800-248-3248. Offers publications on federal and state tax topics, as well as tax courts' decisions affecting tax laws. Web site: www.cch.com.

➤ *Ernst & Young Tax Guide* (John Wiley & Sons Inc.). Annual publication that explains how to file your taxes and provides the forms you need. Available at bookstores and libraries, and online at *www.amazon.com.*

Home-Buying Tips & Selling Traps

Buying or selling a house is a complex process—financially and emotionally. In the anticipation of a successful home search or sale, it's not uncommon to overlook the finer points of getting the best deal.

HOW MUCH HOUSE CAN YOU AFFORD?

If you are in the market for a home, before you even begin looking, sit down and come up with a ballpark price range that you think you can afford. Without some idea of where you stand, you could waste a great deal of time looking at low-priced properties that don't meet your needs or ones in a higher range that you can't afford. Use the estimated price range worksheet (next page) or other similar worksheets you can get from mortgage lenders or real estate agents.

As you come closer to making an offer on a home, get yourself prequalified by a lender. Then you can show a seller that based on the lender's preliminary assessment of your finances, you can afford the home. Many sellers will not even respond to an offer until they are assured that a buyer is qualified to buy. Better yet—often the next step—get yourself preapproved, which means the lender is prepared to approve your mortgage application.

DO YOUR HOMEWORK

If a house has been on the market longer than the average time for other homes in the area, it could indicate major structural or neighborhood problems, or in many cases, the house is overpriced. Most real estate agents have access to a multiple-listing service database and can tell you how long a home has been listed and how it compares to other properties for sale—or sold—in the area.

Check the photographs of the home in the listing book and real estate publications. If the house was photographed in the winter and it's now summer, there are probably some problems you should know about.

TEST SELLER'S MOTIVATION

If you find a home you like, try to determine how eager the seller is to sell. It could help you swing a better deal. The person or couple selling the house may be facing a pressing need to sell, such as a job transfer, divorce or pending purchase of another home. In such situations, sellers are often eager to entertain an offer, even if it seems low, and negotiate a final selling price that is more favorable to you.

Ask your broker why the house is on the market. If you meet the sellers, ask them, too. If the sellers have already moved to a new location (house is empty), this could mean that they are supporting two mortgages and are anxious to sell.

INSPECT NOW OR PAY LATER

Buyers watching their pocketbooks carefully often wonder whether they really need to spend the money on a home inspection before closing a deal. Yes, you do! *Never buy a home that hasn't had a professional inspection,* no matter how well maintained it might seem. Even if you are buying from a friend or a highly reputable seller, it's better to be safe than sorry. There could be any number of defects that the seller isn't aware of and that you will have to pay to fix. The cost of an inspection is worth it relative to the purchase price of a home.

Make sure your offer includes a contingency clause for a home inspection that is satisfactory to you—or the deal is off and your deposit must be returned in full. If the home inspector discovers problems, you can negotiate with the seller for the cost of repairs.

TAKE ADVANTAGE OF SELF-SALE HOME DEALS

If a particular neighborhood is just over your financial limit, a home for sale by owner may be your ticket.

First step: Shop for your mortgage, meeting with your banker first, then others. Learn your mortgage limits so you can home shop with assurance that the money is available.

Drive around your ideal neighborhoods looking for home sales by owners. Call quickly. Many self-sellers engage a broker after only a month or two of trying to sell themselves.

BE SMART ABOUT YOUR MORTGAGE

The chart below shows the cost of principal plus interest on a loan (per $1,000 of principal) at standard fixed 15-year or 30-year mortgage rates. You can use it to estimate your price range.

Also use the chart to estimate monthly principal and interest payments. Find the appropriate factor for your projected loan and multiply it by the total mortgage amount divided by $1,000. For example, for a $200,000 mortgage at 7½% for 30 years, you'd multiply the factor 6.99 times 200 to get $1,398 in monthly payments.

Factors Per $1,000

Rate	15 Year	30 Year
6	8.44	6.00
6¼	8.57	6.16
6½	8.71	6.32
6¾	8.85	6.48
7	8.99	6.65
7¼	9.13	6.82
7½	9.27	6.99
7¾	9.41	7.16
8	9.56	7.34
8¼	9.70	7.51
8½	9.85	7.69
8¾	9.99	7.87
9	10.14	8.05
9¼	10.29	8.23
9½	10.44	8.41
9¾	10.59	8.59
10	10.75	8.77

IGNORE SELLER WARRANTIES

To attract buyers, a seller will often offer a home warranty—in which the seller guarantees the home's condition and payment for repairs for a specified time. The warranty is presented as a substitute for a professional home inspection, thus saving you the fees (usually $150 to $250) you would have to pay an inspector.

Beware: All warranties come with limitations, deductibles and exclusions. Such gaps in coverage can be large enough to make a warranty useless and the buyer ends up liable for most repairs. A warranty is not a substitute for a professional home inspection.

PLAN YOUR MORTGAGE TIMING

The growing variety of mortgage options available to home buyers is making it easier for buyers to customize loans to suit their needs. At the same time, the increasing choices cause confusion. Here are some mortgage options you should consider, based on how long you expect to stay in your home.

Short-Term Mortgage

The best mortgage for someone who is likely to be transferred—or trade up to a bigger home—in

HOW TO ESTIMATE THE PRICE YOU CAN AFFORD

How much house can you afford? Use this worksheet to calculate an approximate price range based on fixed 15-year or 30-year mortgage rates. The amount of your mortgage will vary, depending on the size of your down payment, the specific terms of your loan and other long-term monthly obligations.

A. Gross Annual Income $ _____
(Before Taxes)

B. Gross Monthly Income $ _____
Line A divided by 12.

C. Monthly Allowable Housing $ _____
Expense and Long-Term Obligations
Line B multiplied by .36 (36% of your gross monthly income is normally allocated for principal, interest, taxes, insurance and other long-term monthly obligations, such as installment debt, automobile loans, credit cards and child support)

D. Monthly Allowable Housing Expense $ _____
Whichever is less: (1) line C minus monthly long-term obligations or (2) line B multiplied by .28 (as a rule, monthly housing expenses should not exceed 28% of gross monthly income on line B)

E. Monthly Principal and Interest $ _____
Line D multiplied by .80 (80% of the monthly allowable housing expense is normally allocated to principal and interest payments, excluding taxes and insurance)

F. Estimated Mortgage Amount $ _____
Line E divided by the appropriate factor from the Interest Rate Chart (see box), multiplied by 1,000, and rounded to the nearest $100

G. Estimated Price Range $ _____
Line F divided by .80 or .90, depending on your down payment (20% or 10%)

three to five years is a 5/25 loan. For the first five years, you have a fixed rate that is about one percentage point lower than a 30-year fixed rate. After five years, there is a one-time adjustment to a rate that is about one percentage point above the prevailing 30-year fixed rate. The advantage of a 5/25 loan is that it gives you a lower starting rate, and unlike an adjustable-rate mortgage (ARM), which can change from year to year, the lower rate is set for five years.

If you think you will be moving after five years, but likely before 10 years, an alternative is a 7/23 loan. You pay a rate that is generally one-quarter point higher than a 5/25 loan, but you will lock it in for an extra two years.

Mid-Term Mortgage

The best mortgage for people who are fairly certain that 10 years from now they will be earning enough to "move up" in housing, but who aren't sure what will happen during the years in between, is a 10/1 loan. For the first 10 years, you have a fixed rate that is about one-quarter lower than a 30-year fixed rate. After 10 years, the loan converts into a one-year ARM, and you can refinance if rates have dropped or stay with the ARM. Even if rates are higher after 10 years, your earnings will likely be higher as well, enabling you to afford a higher rate.

Long-Term Mortgage

If you are buying a home to live in for at least 20 years, get a 15-year—rather than a 30-year-fixed-rate mortgage. By paying a few hundred dollars more per month, you could save more than $100,000 on finance charges over a 30-year period. However, if you are stretching to buy a home, get a 30-year mortgage. When your circumstances improve, consider prepaying it so you will discharge the debt in 15 or 20 years. But make sure that your mortgage doesn't have prepayment penalties.

DON'T FALL FOR BANK INSURANCE

Mortgage insurance from a lender may cost you more than buying Private Mortgage Insurance (PMI) on your own. PMI is required when the down payment on a house is less than 20% of its cost or when the loan-to-value ratio exceeds 80%. Many lenders now offer to sell PMI when making a loan and fold the PMI premiums into payments due on the loan.

The advantage of buying PMI on your own is that the coverage can usually be dropped once your home equity reaches 20%, either through mortgage payments or because your home's value has increased. If the PMI is from your lender and folded into your mort-

NEW HOME: KNOW YOUR REAL COSTS

Buyers are well aware of what it's going to cost them to close on a home. But many fail to look beyond that to anticipate expenses once they've finally moved in. Some "new" costs to consider:

Appliances. The stove that was left behind might be hopelessly outdated. In many cases, you will need a new refrigerator, unless you already own one that is adequate for your needs. The same is true for a washing machine and dryer.

Furniture/furnishings. If it's your first house, or you are moving to a larger house, you will likely need furniture to fill additional rooms. You may also need new curtains (and hardware to hang them), carpets, rugs, beds, bedding and linens.

Tools and equipment. If you don't own basic landscaping equipment and household tools that are in good condition, the cost of rakes, shovels, hoses, sprinklers, shears, fireplace accessories and other basic nuts-and-bolts needs can mount considerably. Not to mention lawn mowers, weed trimmers and leaf and snowblowers.

Landscaping, decks, fences. No matter how much work your seller might have done to get the property in "selling" shape, you'll want to put your own stamp on its appearance and add on to meet your needs—plant trees and shrubs or reseed the lawn (or buy sod). If you have children or pets, you might need to fence in the property. And what about that deck overlooking your new backyard that you intended to add the minute you moved in?

gage, you might not be able to cancel it—a potential cost of thousands of dollars.

NEGOTIATE THOSE MORTGAGE FEES

With increasing competition in the home mortgage market, lenders are more willing to negotiate fees. The most negotiable costs are: points, attorney's fees and documentation fees.

Call at least four lenders to ask about those costs. Use a chart to track the total amount of each loan. After the name of each lender, record: up-front fees (for credit check, appraisal and so forth), total interest cost for the first five years (average stay in a home), and all closing costs, including points.

The best deal will have the lowest total amount. However, you might be able to get an even better deal if one or more of the other lenders offers a lower fee or cost in a specific area, such as the attorney's fee. Don't hesitate to try to negotiate!

Warning: Beware of no-points mortgage offers. If a loan is at a higher interest rate than one with points, you might be better off paying the points. For example, a mortgage with no points and an 8% interest rate is not as good a deal as a mortgage with one point and a 7.75% interest rate.

To help you compare rates and fees, *HSH Associates* (800-873-2837) will send you, for a small fee, a Home Buyer's Mortgage Kit that lists the terms offered by lenders in your area.

SAY NO TO THESE LOANS

High loan-to-value mortgages can reduce your financial security. Some lenders are making loans for up to 25% more than homes are worth, primarily for debt consolidation or home improvement purposes. These loans have high interest rates and fees, and lenders often won't allow you to pay the loans off early.

Unless the value of your home skyrockets, you won't be able to sell it, since you won't have enough proceeds to pay off the loan. Also, you probably won't be able to refinance to take advantage of lower rates.

DON'T PAY FOR BIWEEKLY PLAN

Avoid biweekly mortgage plans that charge fees—sometimes $300 or more—as a one-time charge, plus an annual renewal fee. In these types of plans, you make half of your mortgage payment every two weeks to a mortgage-payment firm instead of to the lender. The firm then pays the lender at the end of the month.

Instead, it's best to pay down your mortgage principal by doing it yourself, at no additional cost. Simply send a prepayment of principal with your regular monthly mortgage check, clearly indicating that the second check should be applied to principal. Then watch your mortgage statement to be sure that the prepayments are credited correctly. Make sure, however, that your mortgage agreement doesn't have a prepayment penalty.

TAX BETWEEN THE CRACKS

Real estate taxes that are paid to the seller when buying a home are tax deductible. Your payment reimburses the seller for taxes already paid, and the amount should appear on your settlement sheet.

The annual statement from your lender showing taxes paid may not show this payment, so it is important to check the settlement sheet and include the reimbursement as part of your tax deduction. If you assumed your seller's mortgage, you should do the same for interest payments.

FINANCING A "FIXER-UPPER"

Buyers of houses that need rehabilitation can now get one long-term, market-rate loan—instead of separate loans for the home purchase and the repairs. The program, which falls under the *Department of Housing and Urban Development's Section 203(k)*, is designed to promote housing rehabilitation by enabling buyers who might not otherwise be able to afford a home to purchase and repair a "fixer-upper."

Under the 203(k) program, the home must need repairs that go beyond the cosmetic, with an estimated cost of at least $5,000. Improvements might include structural changes, additions, modernization of kitchens or

---

i BEST TIME TO REFINANCE

If mortgage rates have dropped since you took out your mortgage, you should definitely consider refinancing. Many people simply don't want to be bothered with going through the application process and paperwork. But not taking advantage of lower rates is like throwing your money away! You could save thousands of dollars over the long term.

The rule of thumb in the mortgage industry is that the new mortgage rate should be two percentage points lower than your existing mortgage to make refinancing economical. Use the worksheet below to calculate whether you should refinance and how long it will take to realize savings. Generally, if you start saving within two to three years, refinancing is worthwhile.

1. **Current Monthly Mortgage Payment** $ _____
   (principal and interest)

2. **Monthly Mortgage Payment** $ _____
   After Refinancing

3. **Monthly Savings** $ _____
   (subtract Line 2 from Line 1)

4. **Total Closing Costs and Fees** $ _____

5. **Months Needed to Break Even** $ _____
   (divide Line 4 by Line 3)

Be Aware of Broker's Motives

If you decide to enlist the services of a real estate agent, before you begin looking at homes make sure that you clearly understand your agent's role. There are three types of agency representation—seller's agent, buyer's agent, and disclosed dual agent.

Seller's agent. Although buyer brokerage is growing in popularity, most real estate agents work for people selling their homes. When a seller lists a property with a broker, the broker becomes the seller's agent. That agent, plus other brokers who represent her in showing the property, are obligated to act in the best interests of the seller in obtaining the best price and terms for the sale.

A seller's agent is required to share with the seller any information buyers reveal that could affect a transaction. However, the agent also has obligations to the buyers, which include honest and fair dealing and disclosure of all facts relative to the value or desirability of a property. In some parts of the country, seller's agents are more knowledgeable about properties on the market than buyer's brokers who are not familiar with an area, for example. Also, the agent's working relationships with the seller can be of advantage in the negotiating stages.

Buyer's agent. A buyer's agent represents the buyer and is obligated to put the buyer's interests first in negotiating the terms of a sale. Buyer's brokers typically share the standard commission (which costs you nothing) or they might charge an hourly fee or flat fee if they find you a home. If you decide to work with a buyer's agent, make sure you have a signed contract specifying how the agent will be paid.

Buyer's agents often use problems revealed in a seller's disclosure or perceived shortcomings in a property as bargaining chips in trying to lower the price. The potential downside here is that an agent could push negotiations to the point where a seller calls the deal off completely, particularly if the seller knows there are other, less picky buyers in the wings.

Dual agent/agency. A dual *agent* represents the buyer and seller on the same property with the informed, written consent of both parties. A dual *agency* is when both parties in a transaction are represented by different individuals within the same real estate agency. With the increasing number of buyers' brokers and agencies with multiple offices, you should decide if a dual agent or dual agency arrangement is acceptable to you.

other rooms and removal of health hazards, such as lead-based paint and asbestos.

Once the scope of the proposed rehabilitation work is determined, the buyer can apply for a mortgage —from a list of 203(k) lenders— based on the property's after-rehabilitation market value. The down payment is normally as low as 3% to 5%. The cost of acquiring the home is paid at closing. Rehabilitation funds are held in an escrow account, to be paid out after certain inspections are completed.

For more information on this subject, contact your local *Department of Housing and Urban Development (HUD)* office.

Buying from the Owner

Buying a house directly from the owner, without real estate agents involved, can substantially reduce the final price. Agents can charge 6% or more, and sellers are often willing to share a portion of the savings with the buyer.

Beware, however: People selling homes on their own tend to over-price and negotiating with them can be difficult because of their emotional attachments to the home. It's better to find a buyer's agent to represent you in such situations. Many sellers are willing to pay a buyer's agent 50% of the usual commission.

If you don't want to use a buyer's agent, make sure that you have a real estate lawyer draw up a purchase contract to protect you in a direct transaction.

Be patient if you are interested in a for-sale-by-owner (FSBO) home. Most self-sellers give up within 60 days and list their homes with agents, who generally set the asking price closer to market value.

Broker Benefits

For many home buyers, working with a real estate agent simplifies the house-hunting process and saves hours of time they might spend trying to find a home on their own. An agent can provide detailed information on all current listings and help you identify the appropriate properties for you. If you are not familiar with an area, the agent can answer questions you might have about schools, property taxes, transportation, medical facilities and other concerns. An agent will also provide advice and serve as an intermediary during negotiations over a sales contract.

If you choose to work with an agent, make sure you stay in control of the process. Be specific about what you want in a house and cut short any tour of a home that clearly isn't what you asked to see. Bear in mind that *you* are the customer. You have no obligation to a broker, unless you have signed an agreement (don't, unless it is for a limited time frame—-30 days maximum, with renewal options, if you are pleased).

If you are dissatisfied for any reason, find another broker who seems more competent and compatible. But don't just change brokers unless you have a good reason to. Brokers find out about buyers who shop around real estate offices in the same area and consider them a risky investment of their time. If you find a broker you like, stick with him or her. You will get better service.

IF YOU BUY A LEMON...

When serious defects show up in a home after buyers move in, they can sue for damages —and may be able to get out of the purchase contract altogether. Courts in several states have ruled that two situations that may void an entire sale are: (1) misrepresentation by the seller of an important aspect of the house and (2) the presence of multiple serious defects. In one case, for example, a builder assured the buyer that there would be no water problems. Soon after the closing, the house was completely flooded. The court ruled that the related damages to the home would be impossible to repair.

Buyers should not always assume that defects were known to the seller prior to the sale, however. If the seller was not aware of the problems, you may be able to negotiate directly with him, rather than pursuing legal action, which could turn out to be much more costly. Many problems can be solved for $1,000 or less, in which case it's common for buyers and sellers to split the cost of the repairs.

If you think that defects should have been detected during your home inspection prior to the sale, carefully reread the inspection report for disclaimers as to what was—and was not—included in the inspection. If it still seems the inspector should have noted the problem or problems, you can request that the company investigate and evaluate possible compensation. Some companies offer a one-year warranty that covers defects that were not detected during the inspection.

HOW BROKERS LIST HOMES

The most common listing agreement with a real estate agent to sell a home is *exclusive right to sell*. In this contractual arrangement, which normally lasts 90 days with an option to renew or cancel (at any time), the seller owes a commission to the listing

broker no matter who sells the home, even if the owner finds the buyer. Two other types of listing agreements let owners sell the property themselves with the opportunity to save on a commission:

- *Exclusive agency.* In this agreement, the listing broker gets his commission if any broker makes the sale. But the owners don't pay the commission if they sell the home themselves. Owners might choose this agreement if they know of several people who have expressed an interest in their property. But generally a listing broker will not be as motivated to spend time and money marketing this type of sale as he would with an exclusive right to sell contract because a commission is not guaranteed.
- *Open listing.* In an open listing (also known as a nonexclusive

or general listing), the seller is obligated to pay a commission to the first agent who produces a ready, willing and able buyer. If the owners sell the property without the aid of any broker, they are not obligated to pay any commission.

This "cooperating with brokers" (sometimes called "protecting brokers") arrangement is frequently offered by owners who are selling their homes themselves as a means of encouraging agents to bring their customers in, thus expanding the pool of potential buyers. While the terms of an open listing can vary, sellers often agree to pay the broker who sells the property half of the 5% to 6% going rate for a full commission—or 2½% to 3% of the selling price. Even at that, a seller would still end up saving $3,700 to $4,500 on the sale of a $150,000 home.

SELLING A HOME YOURSELF

Pros

Selling your house yourself can save you thousands of dollars. Agents typically charge 5% to 6% of the selling price. That means they will take $7,500 to $9,000 of your equity from the sale of a $150,000 home. Since you don't have to inflate your price by the amount of the commission, you could sell sooner than a comparable agent-listed property.

Remember, however, that *buyers don't care* whether an owner is paying a commission or not. If your home is priced at the same level as a comparable agent-listed property, buyers may not perceive the "deal" they expected in a "for-sale-by-owner" home and they may walk away.

Beyond saving money, the other main advantage of selling your home yourself is that you maintain control over the whole process. You decide where and when to advertise your property, when the property will be shown, when to hold open houses, and so forth. In short, you avoid the pressures attendant with listing your house with an agent, who would want to have a hand in marketing and scheduling decisions.

Also, many owners don't like the idea of "strangers" trooping through their homes with brokers

BEWARE REVERSE MORTGAGE SCAMS

Older home owners should be alert to potential scams when considering a reverse mortgage to get cash out of a home. With a reverse mortgage, a lender makes you a loan in the form of a credit line or monthly payments, with the loan paid off by the sale or refinancing of the home when you die.

Scam: Telemarketers call homeowners and offer to arrange loans for a fee of as much as 10% of the loan's value when, in fact, you don't have to pay such a fee if you deal with a lender directly. For information about reverse mortgages and help in finding a lender, call the *National Center for Home Equity Conversion*, 360 N. Robert, Suite 403, St. Paul, MN 55101; tel: 651-222-6775; or go online at *www.reverse.org*.

(owners are generally encouraged to be absent during showings). In selling yourself, you are in charge of how your home is shown and have the opportunity to size up potential buyers in person.

Make sure you have plans for where you will go if your home sells quickly. However, unless you can afford two mortgage payments, don't get involved in purchasing another property before your house is sold.

Cons

An important consideration in selling your home yourself is that you will not be able to reach as many potential buyers as you would if you listed with a real estate agent. Basically, your exposure will be limited to the markets in which you advertise, people who see your sign and word-of-mouth referrals.

With an agent, your home will be in a multiple-listing service, which

opens up the possibility that the network of brokers who see your listing will bring in potential buyers who would not have seen your ads—transferees from other parts of the country and buyers living in cities outside of your advertising range. Large agencies also have nationwide referral networks that can bring in customers from all parts of the country interested in buying in your area.

Another important consideration—too often overlooked by eager would-be self-sellers— is that while selling a home might seem like a simple undertaking, it requires a tremendous amount of time and hard work, if it is done right.

In short, if you plan on selling your home without an agent, don't underestimate the tasks— and pressures—that are involved in doing everything yourself.

IF YOUR HOUSE DOESN'T MOVE...

If your home has been on the market for a longer time than the average sale period for homes in your community, take a second look at several important factors that might be affecting a sale:

■ *Price.* Don't decide that your home is worth more than comparable homes on the market in your area because *you* think it is more appealing or in a better location. Buyers decide that. They will pay what *they* think your house is worth. Consider having a professional appraisal done. You will have another opinion of value, as well as something to show to buyers who might question your price.

■ *Marketing.* Review your marketing plan. Are you getting enough exposure through advertising? Are the ads written in a such a way that they attract calls from buyers? Are you having enough open houses? Perhaps it's time to make adjustments in your marketing to reach more potential buyers.

■ *Condition of your property.* Ask your broker for feedback from buyers about changes or repairs you could make to enhance your property's appeal. If you are showing your home yourself, don't shy away from asking people their honest opinions.

ADVICE FOR SELF-SELLERS: LEARN WHAT THE PROS KNOW

If you are thinking about selling your home yourself, make sure you are fully prepared for the process. Too many homeowners assume it's simply a matter of putting up a sign and running a few ads. Then they end up overwhelmed with the demands on their time and energy. Even if you feel confident that you can handle the tasks involved, get advice before you start: read books and articles on the subject and talk with people who have had experience selling their homes.

Some tasks to consider:

Preparing for a sale. Before you put up your "for sale" sign, you will want to: Do a comparative market analysis of your property or get a professional appraisal to help you determine your asking price; create a fact sheet or brochure with photos, floor plan and plot plan to hand out to potential buyers; write advertising copy; get offer forms and other contracts you may need; have a home inspection (optional, but preferable); and make necessary repairs to get your home and property in top condition.

Dealing with brokers and buyers. Once you have put up your sign and started advertising, be prepared to deal with telephone calls at all hours and unpredictable disruptions in your daily schedule. Real estate agents in your area will call to offer their listing services. Eager buyers who just spotted your ad will want to see your home immediately, with little or no notice. Without an agent to schedule and screen qualified buyers, it's up to you to cope with browsers, passers-by who just saw your sign and the simply curious who want to "see" your house. If you are committed to selling as soon as possible, you will want to be at home and ready to show it, even if that means sacrificing weekends or vacation trips.

Closing the sale. Once you find a promising buyer, negotiating the final sale yourself can be the hardest part, particularly if the buyer is intent on getting the best deal for the lowest possible price. What if the buyer asks you to throw in the refrigerator or other extras? Do you want to hire a lawyer at an hourly rate to deal with these issues? Even with a smoothly negotiated sale, expect to spend time working with lawyers, yours and the buyer's, drawing up the sales contract and handling closing details.

HOW TO QUALIFY A BUYER

Whether you decide to sell your home yourself or list it with a real estate agent, always make sure that *the buyer is financially qualified to purchase your home* before you get into serious negotiations. At the very least, you will want a "pre-qualification" letter from a mortgage lender, which states that after a preliminary review of the buyer's finances, the buyer should qualify for the mortgage amount needed to purchase your home.

A prequalification letter doesn't guarantee that the buyer will get the mortgage, however. Better yet, ask for a "preapproval" letter, which states that the institution has verified the buyer's financial information and has approved the application for the mortgage.

A prequalification letter is usually sufficient to start negotiating. But you will want to get a pre-approval letter before you get to the final stages.

GET YOUR OWN INSPECTION

If home inspections are worrisome for anxious buyers, they can be even more so for sellers, particularly if you are counting on a sale to purchase another home

or have taken a home off the market in anticipation of a sale. At that point, you can't afford unexpected surprises.

If there are serious defects, such as structural problems, a buyer might simply walk away from the deal. Or you may have to pay for the repairs and/or renegotiate the sale price. Less serious problems do not normally make a deal fall apart, unless there are a significant number of them, in which case a buyer might decide not to take the risk of purchasing a home that could have perhaps even more problems in the future.

To avoid such situations, have your home inspected before you put it on the market. For a cost of between $150 and $400, it will be well worth it to know beforehand what problems exist so you may be able to avoid unpleasant surprises later. This is particularly true if you bought your home 10 or 20 years ago and it may never have been inspected.

REAL ESTATE ON THE WEB

Most real estate agencies have their own Web sites where they advertise with their listings. Check those out if you are interested in a particular area or areas served by the agencies. You will be able to "view" homes on the market, as well as obtain information on

SEE YOUR HOME FROM THE BUYER'S VIEW

When selling your home, you can enhance your chance of a prompt sale, at a better price, by doing cleanup and repair work in advance. Ask your broker, neighbors and close friends for suggestions for improving your home's appearance. Put yourself in potential buyers' shoes. Even seemingly minor things that you have become accustomed to, such as squeaky doors, will detract from your home's appeal.

Here are some questions to ask yourself.

Outside: How is your curb appeal—the first impression buyers get when they drive up and walk around the property? Should you...

➤ Paint or power wash the exterior? Improve the appearance of decks, balconies, porches? Repair or repaint the trim?

➤ Repave or resurface the driveway? Clean up the front path and front steps (cracks, stains and moss are common flaws)?

➤ Repair/replace gutters and downspouts? Repair/replace shutters?

➤ Spruce up the landscaping: Reseed bare patches in the lawn? Trim shrubs? Prune trees? Edge and weed gardens?

➤ Clean up the yard: Put away toys and equipment? Remove brush, wood or leaf piles?

➤ Improve the appearance of the front door? Replace doorknobs and locks? Put up new house numbers?

Inside: Is your home clean, bright and appealing? Does it need sprucing up and straightening up? Should you...

➤ Replace old carpeting or linoleum (stains and scratches are definite no-nos)? Refinish hardwood floors? Replace worn area rugs?

➤ Repaint or repaper walls?

➤ Clean up/unclutter rooms, closets and storage areas to make them seem more spacious? Throw out musty magazines, books, broken tools? Get rid of worn furniture, unused clothing, long-forgotten toys?

➤ Wash the windows? Pull back curtains and blinds to lighten up rooms?

➤ Get rid of pet, smoking, cooking or other odors that buyers are sure to notice, but you may have become accustomed to (ask a friend for an honest assessment)? Have drapes, carpets, upholstery cleaned?

➤ Are all light fixtures, faucets, door hinges, locks, door bells and toilets in good condition and working order?

specific towns. You can also tap into the Web in general and surf "real estate" topics until you find what you want. Here are a few Web sites you will find useful to help you get started:

■ *www.homefair.com*—Homebuyer's Fair has "popular exhibits" and "main booths" that provide self-help tools and information on home buying and selling—saving money in the process.

■ *www.homescout.com*—Homescout enables you to search more than 600,000 property listings nationwide, plus tap into real estate articles of interest to buyers and sellers.

■ *www.homeseekers.com*—Homeseekers has information on homes for sale in specified market areas, plus tips on foreclosure properties, relocation issues and resort vacation opportunities.

■ *www.realtor.com*—National Association of Realtors helps you find an agent, a home (more than one million listings with customized search), mortgage information and other home selling/buying information, including a "mover's toolkit."

■ *www.nfsboa.com*—National For Sale By Owner Association (NFSBOA) features properties offered by members, in addition to articles and information on selling your home yourself, such as how to do your advertising/marketing program.

HOUSING RESOURCES

➤ *Department of Housing and Urban Development,* 451 7th St. SW, Washington, DC 20410. 202-708-1112. Regulatory agency in charge of housing and real estate issues; offers consumer-oriented publications and information on funding and purchasing a home. Web site: *www.hud.gov.*

➤ *Mortgage Bankers Association of America,* 1919 Pennsylvania Ave. NW, Washington, DC 20006. 202-557-2700. Trade group which offers a wide range of publications on all aspects of mortgages, from how to shop for a mortgage and what you can afford to settlement costs and tax considerations. Web site: *www.mbaa.org.*

➤ *Appraisal Institute,* 550 W. Van Buren St., Suite 1000, Chicago, IL 60607. 312-335-4100. Sets standards for real estate appraisals; provides references to qualified appraisers in your area. Web site: *www.appraisal institute.com.*

➤ *National Association of Realtors,* 430 N. Michigan Ave., Chicago, IL 60611. 800-874-6500. Trade group helps you find a real estate agent in your area; also offers informative publications with guidelines and advice on selling or buying a home. Web site: *www.nar.realtor.com.*

Estate Planning Know-How

You have worked hard to build up your assets. Now you want to make sure that your property will go to your heirs for their benefit and enjoyment—not to Uncle Sam or state coffers. Here are some key points for planning ahead.

PLAN NOW

When it comes to estate planning, too many people put off until tomorrow what they should do today. Some simply don't want to think about making plans for what will happen after their death, and assume that somehow their estates will take care of themselves. Others are intimidated by the planning process—working with lawyers, financial planners and insurance agents to draw up wills and other estate-planning documents.

The fact of the matter is that if you don't address the issue of where your estate goes after your death, someone else will do it for you. You have the choice of controlling how your estate is settled or leaving it up to a probate court, which might distribute your property in a manner that you would not approve of. Plus your estate might have to pay thousands of dollars in taxes that could have been avoided.

With careful estate planning, you can ensure that your spouse, children, grandchildren and others for whom you might want to provide will benefit from your hard-earned labors, according to your wishes. And in planning to minimize estate taxes, they will receive larger inheritances. You also gain peace of mind knowing that your affairs will be handled properly after you die.

In planning your estate, it's never too late, but the earlier the better. The only challenge is getting started. If your estate is large enough to face a tax liability or if you anticipate that trusts and other long-term planning considerations will be involved, you should seek professional advice from an estate planner. If your estate is less complicated or you want to get started on your own at first, there are several easy-to-use computer programs and do-it-yourself books on estate planning on the market (see box).

THE HELP YOU NEED TO PLAN WISELY

If you need help with your estate planning or want to get started on your own, you will want to check out a number of computer programs and how-to books that are available on the subject. Ask your local computer store or bookstore for advice on programs or books that will meet your needs. (Many software programs that deal with legal issues in general include estate-planning forms; some programs are designed simply to help you write a will or set up a trust.)

Some resources to consider:

Quicken Family Lawyer, The Learning Company at 800-395-0277. Software program provides legal documents customized for each state, including estate-planning worksheets and forms for wills and trusts, including information and instructions. Online at *www.learningco.com*.

Living Trustmaker, Nolo Press, 950 Parker St., Berkeley, CA 94710. 800-992-6656. Software program for setting up trusts to transfer property to heirs while avoiding probate and legal fees.

Willmaker, Nolo Press, 950 Parker St., Berkeley, CA 94710. 800-992-6656. Software program (CD ROM only) that helps you write your own will.

Plan Your Estate, by Denis Clifford and Cora Jordan, Nolo Press, 950 Parker St., Berkeley, CA 94710. 800-992-6656. Explains estate planning, wills, trusts, gift giving, and tax planning; includes sample documents and forms. Also visit Nolo's Web site at *www.nolo.com* for an array of estate-planning products.

The Complete Book of Trusts, by Martin Shenkman, John Wiley & Sons Inc., 605 Third Ave., New York, NY 10158. 212-850-6000. Explains numerous different types of trusts, including living, bypass, charitable and children's trusts.

MINIMIZE TAX EXPOSURE

The first step in planning your estate is to calculate the actual size of your estate and your potential tax liability. Using the "Calculating Your Estate's Taxable Value" worksheet (see next page), total your assets and subtract your liabilities to estimate your estate's taxable value. If you plan on using the services of a professional estate planner, he or she will ask you for these figures, so it's best to be prepared. If you already have an estate plan, but you haven't updated it recently, use the worksheet to get an idea of how your resources might have changed. If the figures are significant, make an appointment with your adviser to do an update.

As you calculate your assets, include only those held in your own name and 50% of those owned jointly with your spouse. If your spouse has holdings that might affect your estate plans, go one step further: Use a separate sheet to indicate the ownership of all of your assets and your spouse's assets—those in your name, those in your spouse's name and those that are jointly held. You can then look at the total figures and decide whether you should alter resources, establish trusts, or change ownership to avoid estate taxes.

Also, bear in mind when you consider your estimated estate's taxable value that in addition to debts and unpaid mortgages (liabilities), deductions also can be taken from your estate to cover funeral expenses and the estate's administrative expenses, such as executor's commissions, legal fees, accounting fees and court expenses.

KNOW YOUR ASSET VALUE

To estimate the size of your estate accurately, you may want to have certain assets

appraised, such as real estate holdings and collectibles (antiques, coins and stamps). They are taxable at their *current fair market value*, not what you paid for them originally. If you bought your home prior to the real estate boom of the 1980s, for example, the market value of your home alone may push your estate over the tax-exemption limit.

Also, don't overlook assets such as intellectual property (patents, copyrights, etc.) that are considered part of your estate. Proceeds from a life insurance policy are also included, even though they aren't subject to probate.

DOUBLE ESTATE DEDUCTIONS

Many married couples waste the opportunity to take full advantage of both of their individual estate tax exemptions—that is, doubling the amount that can be passed tax free—by leaving everything in the estate of the first spouse to die to the surviving spouse. This is particularly costly if it causes the surviving spouse's estate to exceed the individual estate-tax exemption. The unlimited marital deduction is only a tax deferral—assets left to a spouse become taxable when the spouse dies. However, if each spouse makes separate bequests, together they can pass

up to twice the individual deduction tax free.

If you want your estate to provide for you spouse's welfare, you can leave assets in a credit shelter trust (also called a bypass trust) that will pay its income to your spouse for life.

Upon the surviving spouse's death, the assets in the trust pass automatically to named beneficiaries, typically the couple's children. There is no estate tax on the assets in this trust when the surviving spouse dies.

TAX-PROOF YOUR INSURANCE

Life insurance payouts are considered part of a person's estate. Combined with other assets, these sums could subject an estate to high taxes. To protect your heirs, create an irrevocable life insurance trust to own the policy, thus removing insurance proceeds from your estate.

You can contribute to the trust to pay the premiums. Generally,

CALCULATING YOUR ESTATE'S TAXABLE VALUE

Subtract total liabilities from total assets to determine the amount of your estate that would be subject to federal estate taxes.

Assets

Bank accounts	$_____
Stocks & bonds	$_____
Mutual funds	$_____
Pension & profit sharing plans	$_____
IRA accounts	$_____
Real estate holdings	$_____
Life insurance benefits	$_____
Personal property	$_____
Other investments/assets	$_____
Total Assets	$_____

Liabilities

Charge account debt	$_____
Personal/investment loans	$_____
Home mortgage(s)	$_____
Home equity loans	$_____
Other debts/liabilities	$_____
Total Liabilities	$_____
Assets Minus Liabilities	$_____

these payments are counted among the tax-exempt gifts you can make to individuals each year.

While there are definite pros to setting up such a trust, there are also some cons you should consider: Once the trust is established, you cannot change its terms or the beneficiaries. You also lose control over the policy's assets. You can't borrow from or surrender the cash value.

DIVIDE ASSETS, CONQUER TAXES

Jointly owned assets pass automatically to the surviving owner and are not affected by the terms of the deceased's will. However, upon the survivor's death, the entire property will be subject to tax. If the survivor's taxable assets exceed the exemption level, estate taxes will have to be paid that might have been avoided with better planning.

Look at the value of your estate and your spouse's estate. If one of you were to die, would the value of jointly owned property in the survivor's estate cause the estate to exceed the tax exemption level? If so, make arrangements to ensure that sufficient assets are held in each spouse's name so that you each can take advantage of the individual estate tax exemption in both estates. For

example, if you have a joint brokerage account, ask the broker to divide the assets into two separate accounts—one for you and one for your spouse. The same can be done with bank accounts. Titles to real estate can also be changed to eliminate automatic survivorship rights.

Exception: If you and your spouse's combined assets are less than the individual estate-exemption amount, joint ownership can be an advantage in passing assets to the surviving spouse. Because they do not pass through the deceased's probate estate, there are no probate expenses and delays associated with passing assets by will.

LIVING TRUST— STILL A TAX

Don't make the mistake of assuming that a living trust will save estate taxes. A living trust is a written arrangement in which you place assets into a trust during your lifetime. When you die, the assets pass to your heirs directly, thus avoiding probate. However, the property is included in your estate for estate-tax purposes. Living trusts provide advantages such as savings on probate costs, but they do *not* provide any special estate-tax savings beyond those that can be created by a will.

WATCH OUT-OF-STATE TAXES

Even if your estate is smaller than the federal tax-exemption amount, your estate may still owe state taxes. If you own real estate in more than one state, for example, your estate may be subject to taxes in each state, and the properties may have to go through ancillary probate proceedings in those states. You can avoid those probate requirements by putting your out-of-state property into a revocable trust.

Some states impose an inheritance tax on those who receive property from an estate. Make sure that you understand the estate and/or inheritance taxes in your state. They may affect the way you decide to structure your estate plan.

SPEND NOW, AVOID TAX LATER

If your estate is large enough to be taxed, it may be wise to reduce your retirement plan balances while you live and leave other assets to heirs. *The reason:* You have to account for two taxes. Your retirement account is subject to estate tax. Distributions from it are *also* subject to income tax. Combined, these two taxes can

significantly reduce a retirement account's value. This could come as a rude awakening to people who think their retirement accounts are "tax-favored" and have most of their life savings in them.

EXEMPTIONS RISING— SOAR WITH THEM

Through 2006 the unified estate-tax exemption for individual tax payers will increase to $1 million (see below). Because this can have a significant impact on your estate planning, be sure to review your wills and trusts as the rates change.

You and your spouse should hold enough funds in separate accounts to take full advantage of the exemption. Remember, too, that as estate-tax exemptions increase, you can give away more in gifts during your lifetime without incurring a gift tax.

Year	Exemption
2002 & 2003	$700,000
2004	$850,000
2005	$950,000
2006	$1 million

FIVE "MUST HAVE" DOCUMENTS

1. **A will** that specifies how your estate will be divided and your family will be cared for. You and your spouse should have separate wills. Make sure to update them as circumstances change.

2. **A durable power of attorney** that authorizes a trusted person to make financial decisions on your behalf if you become disabled or incapacitated.

3. **A living will** giving details of whether you want life-sustaining medical treatment should you have a terminal condition and are unable to communicate your wishes.

4. **A durable health-care power of attorney** authorizes someone to make health-care decisions—not just for life-or-death matters—should you be unable to.

5. **A financial inventory** listing all important financial information, including account numbers and addresses, that your family may need in an emergency. Also list the names and addresses of your lawyer, accountant, financial adviser and other contacts or friends who might be of service.

COUNT WHAT YOU *WILL* HAVE

You will be ahead in your financial planning if you take the time to consider not only the size of your estate today, but its size in *future* years. You probably own assets that are rising in value, such as retirement accounts, real estate and investment accounts.

Even if you wouldn't owe an estate tax if you died today, you might become liable for it sooner than you realize. If you anticipate that the value of your estate might rise over the exemption limit, take steps *now* to plan to avert a future tax liability.

IN BUSINESS? GUARANTEE CASH

If you have closely held business interests, consider a buy-sell agreement that guarantees that your interests can be converted into cash following your death. The agreement, normally made in cooperation with your co-owner(s) or the business entity, can meet both your—and their—professional and personal interests. For example, your heirs may have no interest in the business and you would prefer to leave them cash. Your partners might be agreeable to such an arrangement because they are anxious to retain control.

KEEP HARMONY IN THE FAMILY

Even in the closest of families, arguments erupt over the distribution of parents' estates. Don't think, "It won't happen in my family." Plan ahead now to avoid possible conflicts that might arise. Decide how *you* would like *your* estate distributed and discuss it with family members so that they understand your reasoning.

Here are some sticky situations to consider:

One child is wealthier than the other. If you divide your estate evenly, your less fortunate son or daughter might not have enough money to send his or her children to college. But if you decide to give the poorer child more money, the wealthier child might complain that he or she is being penalized for doing financially better—has a higher paying job, for example—which is not his or her fault.

Sometimes a wealthier child will be content inheriting a particular family asset that he or she especially wants. Or he or she might be satisfied with a particular method of inheritance, such as a trust, to save income or estate taxes. Consider making gifts to your less wealthy grandchildren to help fund their college educations.

Who will get the house? Nasty disputes often erupt on issues of the ownership or sale of a house. A home is often an estate's largest value, but there is sentimental value as well.

Raise the issue with your children. Sometimes one child will want to own the house and buy out the siblings. But even if the others agree, there can be battles later on. Make sure there is an agreement among all siblings as to when the purchase will take place (how soon after your death) and what method will be used to determine the fair market value of the home. If reaching an agreement on the disposition of the house is impossible, the best way to avoid wrangles is to stipulate in your will that the property must be sold within a set period of time, and the proceeds divided among the children.

Who will get the heirlooms? Often, several heirs will want the same family heirlooms, antiques, furniture, or jewelry. These items have both emotional and financial value.

One common approach is to allow each child to make one choice (first choice by lot) and then rotate turns until everything at issue is distributed. Specify this process in your will. If you think there will still be arguments, stipulate that the disputed items will be sold after your death, with the proceeds divided among the children.

Index

Index

Index

Index

dairy products, 81
eggs, 81-82
fruit, veggie preparation, 75-77
leftovers, 82
meats, poultry, fish, 78-80
mess busters, 75
odors, 75
Knots, 85

L

Lamps, repairing, 56
Lead, 16-17
Leasing cars, 297-298
Leukemia, 189
See also Cancer
Lice, 28
Life insurance, 320-322
companies, 321
disability, 321
premiums, 321
riders, 321
trusts, 320-321
Lightning strike, 141
Listening skills, 221-222
Lists, 66-67
Lizards, 31
Loans, 274
See also College costs; Mortgages
Locks, 37
Luggage. *See* Packing
Lymphoma, 189
See also Cancer

M

Magnesium, 115
Massage, 124
Measurement, 71, 83
conversions, 85
formulas, 84

Meats, 78-80
cooking, 79
preparation of, 78-79
preventing spattering and, 79
seasoning, 79
Medical care
chiropractors, 122
complementary, 124-125
conventional, 121-122
doctor selection, 120-121
osteopaths, 122
traditional, 122-124
Traditional Chinese (Oriental) Medicine
(TCM), 123-124
Medical costs, 285-286
doctors' fees and, 285
free health care and, 285
health clubs and, 286
insurance and, 285-286
prescriptions and, 285
tax deductions and, 286
Medical insurance, 322-324
claims, 324
HMOs, 323-324
Medicare and, 324
Medicare, 324
Medicine(s)
antibiotics, 127
choosing, 126
food, drink interactions and, 128
food as, 131
herbal, 129-131
homeopathic, 132
laughter as, 132
lingo, 127
over-the-counter, 128
pharmaceutical drugs, 126-128
placebos, 132
Melatonin, 116, 175
Mental health, 154-159
anxiety, 154-156

depression, 157-159
fears, phobias, 155
hypochondria and, 156
panic disorders, 154-155
Mercury, 17
Mice, 28-29
Migraines. *See* Headaches
Mind-body connection, 98-101
friendships and, 101-103
habits, good and bad, 100-101
household organization, 99-100
stress, 103-106
visualization, 98
Moles, 30
Money management, 281-284
coupons and, 282-283
discounts and, 282
energy cost savings and, 284
phone quotes, 282
rebates, 282
sharing tools, time and, 281-282
supermarkets and, 282
telephone service savings, 284
Mortgages, 274, 333-334
biweekly, 335
fees, 334-335
refinancing, 335
reverse, 338
Mosquitoes, 30
Moths, 30
Motion detectors, 64
Muscle cramps, 202
Music therapy, 125
Mutual funds, 279-280
Myotherapy, 124

N

Natural disasters, 21-23
earthquakes, 22
family plans for, 21

floods, 22-23
hurricanes, tornadoes, 23
must-have list for, 22
pets and, 21
survival readiness, 21
thunderstorms, 23
Nutrition, 72-73
Nutritional supplements.
See Vitamins, minerals

O

Odors, 75
Oil, safety management, 11
Opossums, 31
Organization tips
clutter, 68-69
home office, 69-70
lists, 66-67
time management, 66, 68
Oscillococcinum, flu and, 166
Osteopaths, 122
Over-the-counter drugs, 128-129

P

Packing, 224
air travel and, 236
carry-on rules, 242
luggage protection, 243
tips, 243
Panic disorders, 154-155
Parenting. *See* Child rearing
PCs, shopping for, 299-301
brands and, 300
hard disk space and, 301
monitors and, 301
prices and, 299-300
printers and, 301
processors and, 301
See also Computers

Index

Index

IN CASE OF EMERGENCY

From:

The Bottom Line Book of
EVERYDAY SOLUTIONS

You may want to copy this page and leave it in your kitchen.

GAS

SAFETY PRECAUTIONS

Make sure you know where the main gas valve is situated and how to use it. In most cases, it is near the gas meter. If the main supply has to be turned off, remember to relight gas pilot light when supply is restored.

If gas smell is strong

1. Turn off the main gas valve.
2. Call the local utility immediately day or night.
3. Do not attempt to trace the leak with a naked flame.
4. Extinguish any naked flames in the area and switch off electric appliances.
5. Do not enter a room where the smell of gas is very strong: the build-up of gas many have reached an overpowering stage.
6. Carry anyone overcome by gas fumes into the open air and send for ambulance. Give the kiss of life.

Gas utility (telephone number).

If a gas smell is slight

Often, cause of escape will be obvious – for instance, a pilot light or stove burner which has gone out.

1. Turn off the pilot light or burner concerned.
2. Switch off and remove an electric appliance if used in same room as the escape.
3. Extinguish naked flames.
4. Open all windows and wiaht for the smell to go.
5. Relight pilots or burners.
6. If smell does not go, turn off gas supply at main valve.
7. Call local gas company immediately: a round-the-clock service is provided. Do not attempt repairs.

ELECTRICITY SHUTOFFS

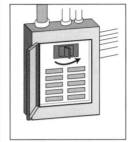 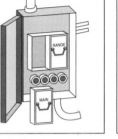 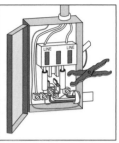

Shut off main power on a circuit breaker system by flipping the main switch.

Shut off main power on a fuse system by pulling the furse blocks.

Use a fuse puller to remove cartridge fuses on older systems.

HOW TO GIVE THE KISS OF LIFE

If the person has stopped breathing, give the kiss of life immediately. Continue – until there is normal breathing or until help arrives.

1. Place victim on his back. Clear any obstruction from the mouth.
2. Pull his head back and lift the chin up.
3. Pinch his nostrils together (except in the case of a child).
4. Cover the mouth with your own (in the case of a child cover the mouth and nostrils.)
5. Blow gently into mouth. Check that chest rises.
6. If it does not, pull head further back and blow again into the mouth.
7. Remove your mouth and wait until chest falls.
8. Repeat procedure every five seconds until the person breathes normally or medical help arrives.

Call 911 IMMEDIATELY

Doctor (telephone number).